MOZART'S PIANO CONCERTOS

MOZART'S PIANO CONCERTOS

C. M. GIRDLESTONE

CASSELL
LONDON

CASSELL & COMPANY LIMITED
35 Red Lion Square, London WC1R 4SG
and at Sydney, Auckland, Toronto, Johannesburg,
an affiliate of
Macmillan Publishing Co., Inc.,
New York

First edition October 1948
Second edition September 1958
Third edition March 1978

ISBN 0 304 30043 8

Printed in Great Britain by
Lowe & Brydone Printers Limited
Thetford, Norfolk

To
Dame Myra Hess

Contents

CONTENTS

Preface

I HAVE attempted in this book a study of Mozart's piano concertos. This important part of his work has never received the attention it deserves and, until within the last few years before the war, orchestras and executants had neglected most of his great concertos, whereas less personal compositions, such as his piano sonatas and trios, were known to everyone. The only studies of his piano concertos, at the time when this book was written, were those found in works dealing with him or with the genre as a whole, such as those of Abert or Engels,[1] or in articles like those of Fr. Blume.[2] No study had been devoted to them exclusively.

I have sought to observe the growth of Mozart's form and inspiration throughout his twenty-three piano concertos. From one period to the next, sometimes from one work to the next, I have sought to understand the unfolding of his art by using the piano concertos as landmarks in my journey. Their importance in the history of music is generally recognized; there remained to define their part in his work as a whole.

I have insisted perhaps a little more upon the growth of his inspiration than upon his technique. But as in the last resort the two are inseparable, both have their share in these pages. Moreover, as it is arbitrary to isolate this or that category of an artist's work from its context, I have related the concertos to the most representative of his other compositions.

My aim has been to follow the unfolding of his genius throughout his piano concertos and to give them their place in his work. It is not for me to judge with what success this aim has been attained; it is enough that there should be no doubt of the excellence of the aim itself.

In making an English translation of this book, the original of which appeared in French in 1940, I have shortened a few passages

---

[1] H. Engels: *Die Entwicklung des deutschen Klavierkonzerts von Mozart bis Liszt* (Leipzig, 1927).
H. Abert: *Mozart* (Leipzig, 1919–21).
[2] Fr. Blume: *Die formgeschichtliche Stellung der Klavierkonzerte Mozarts* (*Mozart Jahrbuch*, II, 1924).

and corrected a few mistakes in the examples. The chief change in
the text concerns the remarks on pp. 49–50 about the origin of the
sonata rondo.

C. M. G.

PART I

PART 1

1. Introduction

THE twenty-three concertos that Mozart wrote for his favourite instrument play, in the history of their genre, a part comparable to that played by Beethoven's nine masterpieces in the history of the symphony. Just as Beethoven's works established the form of the symphony for nearly a century, so Mozart's piano concertos, owing to their number and the great beauty of most of them, were at the source of the modern concerto and laid down the lines along which it was to develop for many years. The structure of most concertos of the last century is fundamentally the same as that of his own and even modern works show proof of his influence.

Mozart has enriched the concerto form with a larger number of masterpieces than any other of the great composers. In the work of most of them concertos have occupied but a small place, much smaller than that held by symphonies or quartets. With him, on the other hand, they are more numerous than any other kind of composition except symphonies, and he has left in all some forty for instruments or groups of instruments of all kinds. The partial neglect of the form by most of the masters has thrown his into greater prominence, especially those which he wrote for the piano.

Nevertheless, for the music-lover who is less concerned with the history of the form than with the personality of each work, with the thought that inspires it and the joy it gives, his twenty-three concertos are still more precious. They are an inexhaustible spring of delight. Their diversity corresponds to our most varied moods, from the state of quiet content in which all we ask of art is entertainment, exquisite rather than deep, the exuberance of animal spirits, the consciousness of physical and moral health, to melancholy, sorrow and even revolt and to an Olympian serenity breathing the air of the mountain tops. The comparative uniformity which we notice between them at first sight disappears with closer scrutiny. The feeling is never the same from one to the other; each one is characterized by a personality of its own and the variety of their inspiration shows itself ever greater as we travel more deeply into them.

Thanks to this variety, Mozart is one of the few composers who can become one's daily bread. Formal diversity matters little; what we demand is diversity of inspiration. Many composers have a more varied form than he and yet their work, when we steep ourselves in it, soon brings on a tedium which his greater works never cause and from which we suffer only when we persist in studying him in compositions where he did not express his full being.

It is this privilege of giving lasting satisfaction to mind and spirit, even more than their historical importance, that causes his concertos to rank among the masterpieces of their art. We shall therefore seek above all to discover the inner character of each one of them and the nature of the emotion which makes it what it is. Formal study cannot be neglected, however, for form is never separable from matter and formal analysis often reveals beauties of an emotional order. Formal studies exist already[1] but no one has attempted to show how rich and deep is the inspiration of these works. The tendency has been rather to underestimate their inspirational value, to consider them as "drawing-room music", and to put them below his symphonies and chamber music. We hope to show that they deserve a higher place and represent as worthily and as fully as these the personality of their creator.

Not only in the work of Mozart but in general, musical critics have been inclined to deny the concerto an exalted position and to regard it as an inferior genre, unworthy to stand beside the symphony. Such an attitude is seen in definitions like that of Ebenezer Prout in the first edition of Grove[2] and in pronouncements like that of Paul Dukas: "The concerto, compared with the symphony, is an inferior genre since its only object, generally speaking, is to show off the talent of an instrumentalist."[3]

Similar definitions are still current and depreciate the genre by accusing it of placing the executant's muscular agility and his vanity above artistic expression. They are just when they apply to the virtuoso concertos of certain soloist composers, but it is unfair to take the poorest representatives of a form as its models. Mozart, Beethoven, Schumann, Brahms, Franck never devoted their genius to satisfying the

---

[1] A. Schering: *Die Geschichte des Instrumentalkonzerts,* Leipzig, 1906; H. Engels: *Die Entwicklung des deutschen Klavierkonzerts von Mozart bis Liszt,* Leipzig, 1927; H. Abert: *Mozart,* Leipzig, 1919-21.

[2] "An Instrumental composition designed to show the skill of an executant."

[3] Quoted by J. G. Prodhomme: *La question du concerto,* in *Zschrft. der Internat. Musikgesellschaft,* 1904-6.

vanity of a virtuoso, to helping an "executant" to "show his skill". The numerical preponderance of bad concertos is alone responsible for these definitions; there lies the reason why the mass of the public, when it hears a concerto, whatever be its value, admires first of all the accomplishments of the soloist, and why the meaning of its applause is less "How beautiful this music is!" than "What a lot of notes this performer gets in!"

The essence of the concerto lies in the struggle between the orchestra on one hand, and the solo instrument, or group of instruments, on the other. The struggle is broken by truces during which orchestra and solo collaborate on friendly terms, and it ends with a reconciliation—but it is none the less a struggle. Sometimes the weapons are common to both sides—the main themes which return in solos and tuttis; sometimes each side has its own—themes reserved for the solo and others that belong to the orchestra. There are vicissitudes; the strife may remain indecisive, and solo and orchestra may toss the chief subjects from one to the other; the tutti may win a momentary victory and loudly proclaim its triumph, or the soloist may see his endeavours carry the day by dint of chords, scales and arpeggios, and spurn the vanquished orchestra with a series of scintillating trills. But, whatever the temporary issue, we know that in the long run neither side will win and that the final cadence will conclude peace and alliance between the former adversaries.

For this result to appear likely, the forces must be evenly balanced. The orchestra uses its polyphony, its mass, its colour; the soloist, his virtuosity. Semi-quavers and demi-semi-quavers are his only means of defence against the weight and colour of the band. Take away this defence and his instrument is just one among fifty; the orchestra crushes and absorbs it. Virtuosity is not a mere display of "skill"; it is a source of beauty and the very condition of survival for the solo instrument. The orchestra is not forbidden to exploit its colour and its mass; why forbid virtuosity to the soloist? The fact that certain composers of concertos have misused the weapon is irrelevant; the soloist must have recourse to it or succumb.

The danger of absorption by the band is a real one for the solo instrument, and it is often by reaction against it that so many mediocre concertos fall into the extreme of limiting themselves to being just series of runs, preceded, interrupted and followed by interventions of the tutti. This danger threatens especially concertos for string and wind instruments; those for the piano fear it much less, for the tone of the instrument stands out clearly against the orchestral background.

For this reason, the piano concerto is perhaps the ideal of the form. The battle between a single fiddle and the whole host of strings, woodwind and brass always appears unequal, but with the piano we know that the orchestra will find its match.

If, then, we consider the concerto as a struggle between two forces, one simple, the other complex, it ceases to be an "inferior genre" and becomes as worthy of study as the sonata, quartet or symphony. Now, of all the concertos that exist, those of Mozart form the largest group of masterpieces. That is one of their claims to a special study. There is another. Nowhere in all the composer's work is there a form wherein he has expressed himself so completely. His twenty-three piano concertos, extending from his eighteenth to his thirty-sixth year, reveal him at all ages; they are the most varied and most extensive witness to his artistic life. We find in them his joys and sorrows, his hopes and disappointments; we penetrate through them into the inner sanctuary where the harassed and overworked man found afresh the radiant life which never ceased to spring up within him. Not that his finest concertos are greater than the best of his other works; the four great symphonies, certain of his quartets and quintets and many other compositions are in every way their equals. In almost every one of the manifold genres within which he poured forth his treasures one finds one or two works which are among his finest, but none of these genres show so abundant a succession of masterpieces as his piano concertos. He wrote some fifty symphonies, but thirty-eight of these were composed before the age of twenty-one and only the last four of the remaining ten can be called great. He composed also some thirty quartets, but only the last thirteen date from his maturity; the others were all written before he was twenty-three and most of them much earlier. The eight quintets, too, do not form a homogeneous group. One is very early; the horn quintet and that for piano and wind belong to his twenty-eighth and twenty-ninth years; the next two were written at thirty-one; the clarinet quintet at thirty-three; and the two others right at the end of his life. It is the same with the rest, except the operas which space out fairly equally over the years of his maturity, and are the only group which might vie with the concertos in reflecting fully the personality of their creator. If only one part of his instrumental work had survived,[1] the one which would give us the completest picture of

---

[1] The idea is not far-fetched. It happened with Clementi whose piano works have alone survived, whereas his symphonies, overtures and concertos have almost all been lost.

him, the one whose survival would come nearest to consoling us for the loss of the rest, would be the group of the piano concertos.

Mozart's life is so short that it does not seem possible to give to his work the threefold division which, since Lenz, we recognize in that of Beethoven and which, according to Vincent d'Indy, can be found in the life of every creative mind. In his life of thirty-six years it seems impossible to distinguish the ages of initiation, of maturity, and of full self-possession which mark the "law of the three periods". Is it reasonable to suppose that Mozart could have reached before the age of forty the point which most artists reach only after fifty? Moreover, in a work which seems so uniform, how can one discover three "periods"? The opinion once prevalent that all his works are alike and show no sign of development would make it seem arbitrary to divide into three periods the music of a composer who, from one end of his short life to the other, always harped on the same theme.

And yet, despite appearances, a deeper knowledge of his music shows that one can apply the "three periods" law to him without losing oneself in hair-splitting distinctions. To deny its existence in his work is to go against the facts. The notion that he never changed is due to the fact that so many people still know little of his work beyond the piano sonatas, often "interpreted" by the pitiless hands of children, and these are the weakest and least personal part of his output. When one gets beyond them and comes to the quartets, quintets, concertos and symphonies, the impression vanishes and one recognizes in him a variety indicative of growth.

If, therefore, we divide his work into three periods, the first, that of initiation and formation, will cover the years of his youth, at Salzburg, in Paris, and during his travels, from 1762 to 1780. The second, his maturity, begins at twenty-five with *Idomeneo* and finishes with the three great symphonies and the last quartets, at the moment when the silence of 1789–90 marks the lowest point of discouragement and wretchedness. The third is when the artist, overstepping the limits which had bounded him hitherto, enters new lands and walks under new skies; it is the culmination of his existence. True, with Mozart one hardly dares to speak of culmination; his career was checked too early for him to reach one, and this third period, which corresponds to the works of his last year, is incomplete. It is but the beginning of a period of which the *Magic Flute* and the *Requiem* show how magnificent the harvest would have been. None the less, his last year is distinguished from his earlier periods. After the almost complete silence of 1789 and 1790 it is a new and sudden blossoming of masterpieces. His two "testaments", the *Magic Flute* and the *Requiem,* the one secular and humanitarian, the other Christian, bear indeed a stamp of finality. Their place is at the end of a life and they strike chords which Mozart had never touched so deeply till then. Other works of that year show this character to a lesser degree and justify our calling it his "third period".

For the composer's biography, two rather than three periods is the right division. The watershed is his departure for Vienna in 1781. Freed from the yoke of the Archbishop of Salzburg and from the guardianship of his father, against whom he rebelled, not only by leaving the Archbishop but also by marrying in the following year, Mozart asserted his independence as son and as servant, and his newly-won freedom was soon reflected in a greater originality in his music. The story of both his life and his work agrees in marking 1781 as the date of a deliverance, of a taking-off, and the turning-point of his career.

This taking-off happened at twenty-five. At an age when most artists begin to produce, Mozart reached his maturity. Although so young he stands almost alone in that his creative life up to this point is long enough to constitute a "period", and one which includes works of which several, notably some of the violin concertos, still survive in our concert halls and the mass of which is bulky enough to have provided material for the two large volumes of Wyzewa and Saint-Foix.[1] Schubert and Mendelssohn alone are comparable to him in this.

Nevertheless, despite this voluminous output, he was not an infant prodigy. The works of his youth contain neither a *Gretchen am Spinnrade* nor an *Erlkönig* nor a *Midsummer Night's Dream* overture. It is true that before he was twelve he had composed seven symphonies. But the symphony in 1760 was a slight thing, hardly more than "drawing-room music", and these symphonies are merely the play-things of a clever, imitative child, of quick sensibility, able to in-corporate in his work anything that strikes him in what he hears. Most of what he wrote before eighteen is not more valuable than the sonatinas which Beethoven, it is said, composed at twelve, and Beethoven has never been looked upon as a precocious composer. On the contrary, he is always contrasted, as one who ripened late and whose growth never stopped, with the precocious geniuses who

---

[1] *La jeunesse de Mozart* (1756-77), Paris, 1912. These volumes have been republished and with three later volumes constitute *Mozart: sa vie musicale et son œuvre,* by Saint-Foix (Paris, 1937-46).

gave all they had to give at twenty and produced nothing later. This contrast is partly valid when it is applied to Mendelssohn; it is less so of Schubert who produced real masterpieces at an early age but continued, nevertheless, to evolve all through his short life; it is quite invalid for Mozart who wrote nothing great before his journey to Paris at twenty-two, and who went on developing to the very end, to the *Magic Flute* and the *Requiem*.

Mozart wrote his first concerto in 1773 at the age of seventeen. At this time the period of youthful journeys was over and the young man, who had visited Vienna, France, Holland, England and Italy (the latter country thrice), was back in Salzburg. Until his final departure, in 1781, his only absence was to be his journey to Mannheim and Paris, during which he wrote no piano concertos. We can therefore look upon his six first, written between 1773 and 1780, as belonging to one period.

But they were composed at dates too widely separated for them to constitute a homogeneous group. The first is distinct from the five others and, indeed, from all those that follow it; the second, third and fourth, on the other hand, are alike and are his best examples of the *galant* concerto; the fifth and sixth, again, stand out from their neighbours and can be included with them in a chronological sense only. But in spite of these differences it is convenient to class these six Salzburg concertos together and we can thus distinguish four groups.

The first group comprises the works composed at Salzburg between 1773 and 1780.

The second is made up of the three concertos written at Vienna during the summer of 1782.

The third, by far the most important and interesting, includes the twelve masterpieces written in 1784, 1785 and 1786; and the fourth, an arbitrary group, will serve to bring into this classification the two last concertos, composed at nearly three years' interval in 1788 and 1791.

The concerto, therefore, covers all Mozart's active life fairly evenly from seventeen onwards, and preponderates and produces its finest fruits between the ages of twenty-eight and thirty.

The harpsichord concerto had existed for more than half a century when Mozart first attempted it. Of all the concerto forms it had been the last to appear. The concerto for solo violin was known before 1700 but it was only towards the first third of the 18th century that the harpsichord began to figure as a *concertante* instrument. It had tried at first to play, all alone, arrangements of concertos written for other instruments[1]; then it had attempted concertos written for itself but without orchestra and imitating alternations of tutti and solo, like Bach's Italian Concerto. Finally, it came to play in concertos with stringed instruments, and here, again, among the earliest examples we find works of Bach.

Hardly fifty years separate Bach's concertos from Mozart's. The growth of the form during this half-century takes place in three main "schools": those of Northern Germany, of Vienna, and of London, whose chief representatives are respectively Philip Emmanuel Bach, Wagenseil, and John Christian Bach. It is curious that two of these three should be sons of John Sebastian, and if one adds that another son of his, Wilhelm Friedmann, also cultivated the harpsichord concerto, it may be said that before Mozart the form was almost a fief of the Bach family. In any case, it is possible to outline its history and enumerate its principal features without leaving that family, and no composer earlier than Mozart produced such fine examples of it as John Sebastian and his three sons.

The North German school and those of Vienna and London consider the concerto from different angles. In the first, the roles of orchestra and solo are fairly equivalent; the two work and strive together on equal terms and one is not subordinated to the other. The Viennese concerto and John Christian's English concerto, on the other hand, assume the predominance of the solo, to whom the orchestra acts as an accompaniment and as a framework to enhance its dignity, just as a crowd of courtiers enhances the dignity of a monarch. The tutti is limited to announcing the solo's entry and, by playing the part of ritornellos in an operatic aria, to allowing the soloist a moment's rest and to avoiding monotony by affording contrast of tone.

Of these two conceptions, the first is indisputably the more fruitful whilst the second is the cause of the unfavourable criticisms of the concerto form to which we have alluded. The treatment implied by the Viennese conception is bound to be limited and to degenerate quickly into mere virtuosity. But the combination of orchestra and soloist, as instanced in the concertos of Philip Emmanuel Bach, affords developments as varied and as rich as those of a symphony. The second of these two forms was destined to triumph towards the

---

[1] Such as those of various Italian and German composers arranged by Bach.

end of the century at the time when the cembalo was giving way before the hammerklavier. But in its very triumph the Viennese concerto was transformed and found in Mozart one who was to unite the lightness, brilliance and melody of John Christian with the *concertante* style of his brother.

The period which precedes that of Mozart shows a great diversity in the concerto form. The three-movement plan is not yet predominant, neither is the tradition of the *rondo finale*, and the structure of each movement varies from composer to composer. Together with the form with three or four separate movements, which is beginning to assert itself, we find also works with two of the movements—and sometimes all of them—linked; we find, also, the more frivolous concerto in two movements whence the andante—too serious for the *galant* taste—has been banished. In his magnificent work in C minor[1] Philip Emmanuel has left a one-movement concerto, where the sonata form is combined with one in four movements, the exposition being followed by an andante and a minuet, after which the beginning returns in the subdominant as a recapitulation, all four sections being continuous. The original cadenza contains quotations from all three sections, rather in the manner of the ninth symphony. The works of Philip Emmanuel, a musician who ranks immediately after the greatest in his century, besides great formal variety contain many unsuspected treasures. The andante of a certain concerto in D is an ancestor of that of Beethoven's fourth; solo and orchestra converse in majestic phrases, each one keeping its theme and character; the orchestra, in E minor, speaking sorrow and tragedy; the harpsichord, in major keys, seeking to console with its bright, serene tones.[2] This formal variety in the concerto before Mozart is more a sign of fumbling and hesitation than of riches. Each composer is looking for his path, and the differences between one and the other come less from great personal originality than from the absence of a type capable of acting as a model. They are in the manner and not in the matter; they are the disorder of primitive and transitional periods. The age of Philip Emmanuel has, indeed, characters which belong to both kinds; it is at once primitive and transitional. It is a transition

---

[1] A. Wotquenne: *Carl Philip Emmanuel Bach: Thematisches Verzeichniss seiner Werke* (Breitkopf und Härtel, 1905); no. 43, IV; published in two pianos arrangement by Steingräber.

[2] Wotquenne no. 43, II; published by Steingräber.

between the polyphonic and harmonic periods of instrumental music, and as, at the same time, it turns out to have been a preparation for a great classical age, it also appears primitive. One finds scattered in it the elements that the age of Mozart and Beethoven were to organize and blend into a well-moulded whole; one sees it feeling its way and trying to grow in many directions before finding the right one.

Philip Emmanuel himself is not devoid of these hesitations. His work is one long search for novelty and the quest is not always successful. Too often one is conscious in him of a straining which takes us nowhere and leaves the spirit unsatisfied. His thought is too often but a roughcast which fails to shape and express itself. In his music one finds veins of gold that he has not known how to exploit, and whose existence he does not appear to have suspected; sometimes from his composition there arises a sense of incompleteness that saddens. This does not detract from the value of some very fine works in which he rises above the transitional character of his age.

Philip Emmanuel is the only great composer whose active life fills the middle of the century. His father, Handel, Rameau, all belong to the first half; Haydn and Mozart to the second; the work of Philip Emmanuel, comprised between 1733 (the date of his first concerto) and 1788 (that of his death) fills the interval between the two groups. He might have accomplished the task that fell to Mozart, consolidated the gains of the new music and built up an orderly construction with them—in a word, given it a classical character. His own genius rather than circumstances prevented him. His work is sometimes the outcome of intellectual vagrancy; he is too much on the look-out for what is new and unheard-of to cultivate what he has already acquired. It is as if novelty stood him in the stead of all other virtues, and he identified originality and beauty. His object is too negative—to rebel against his predecessors, against the contrapuntal school of which his father had been the last representative, to avoid all they had done, and to refuse to incorporate in his work anything of theirs instead of building upon them to raise his new structure. Hence, not only hesitation but also a certain dryness repels us at times and discourages us from going into him further. Yet a deeper knowledge of his music, especially of his concertos, shows how unjust it is to extend this condemnation to all he wrote, and a critical selection of his compositions would give him the place he deserves.

The talent of John Christian, John Sebastian Bach's youngest son, is much inferior to Philip Emmanuel's, but his concertos lead up to those of Mozart. He who used to say, "Philip Emmanuel lives to compose; I compose in order to live," confined himself within the limits imposed by a frivolous society. His public wanted music that amused it and dispelled tedium; it feared earnestness and depth, "the great commotions of the soul", and its taste banished from the galant style the minor mode that expressed these things. John Christian has left a few robust pieces like his C minor piano sonata, Op. 5, VI, but they are rare and one seldom or never finds their like among his concertos. His music is a succession of graceful and refined melodies; his allegros are amiable and playful; his andantes, tender, sometimes languishing and idyllic, reflect the pastoral dream that enchanted the society of 1780; his prestos are not devoid of vigour, but everything is cloaked with a mask of smiling impersonality which expresses superficially the society for which he was writing and does not give one a glimpse of the composer's own feeling. John Christian is a soulless Mozart, with the external qualities of grace and measure, but without the deeper beauties which have made Mozart live. And yet, with all his levity, he has a sense of shapeliness and construction more highly developed than that of Philip Emmanuel. Taste replaces genius with him; his ideas are trifling but they are elegantly presented; he has no gold mines but he makes the most of his tinsel. He arranges and orders his ideas with art, and the different parts of his movements are well balanced. John Christian's music is more plastic than his brother's; its lines more clearly defined, even though what they circumscribe be less significant; its gestures are more regular, even though they betray no strong emotion. It is effortless, and so is our grasp of it. A vigorous spirit may have been slumbering in him, and if he had reached old age he might have blossomed out as did Haydn in his later years. But he died in 1782, at forty-six, without having been more than a society musician.

Mozart's first concertos show his influence. John Christian is, perhaps, not the first to make the piano "sing" nor give the solo a theme of its own, but melodic passages and special solo themes recur so regularly in his concertos that they owe their origin partly to him, for an art form springs less from the man who first uses it than from him who uses it consistently and bequeathes it to the common inheritance. The formal changes he made in the piano concerto bring it to the point at which Mozart takes it up. Between his Op. 13 and the young Salzburger's first concertos, the differences are in the personality, not in the climate or the form.

2. General considerations on Mozart's piano concertos: Structure

WITH all their variety of form and content, Mozart's piano concertos keep throughout certain features which never change. They all have three movements: the first always begins with an orchestral prelude; the second is nearly always an andante; the third generally a rondo. It will therefore be convenient to study them briefly as a whole before turning to each one separately.

The first movement is in sonata form modified according to the concerto formula. This suffers no exception. The second is generally an andante or an andantino; only once[1] do we meet with an allegretto. Its form is often that of a sonata in two or three sections, with or without a *development*, but variations and rondos also occur. The finale is a rondo in two or three episodes; the only exceptions are the first concerto, where it is a *sonata*, and those in G and C minor which end with variations.

In the classical concerto, as in the symphony, the first allegro is the chief movement, the one which sets its mark upon the work, and on it one is tempted to found one's judgement of the concerto as a whole. It begins with a fairly long tutti, at the end of which the solo enters. This prelude, which serves as a first exposition and contains the movement's main subjects, finishes in the tonic. The solo's entry starts a new exposition, usually longer, which ends, as in a symphony, in the key of the dominant or the relative major. Apart from this double exposition, a concerto first movement follows sonata form; the *development* comes next, then the recapitulation.

Post-Beethovenian concertos generally bring in the soloist with the very first bars, and Mozart does this in K.271. Elsewhere, he lets the orchestra play alone in an introduction which lasts from thirty to sixty bars.

---

[1] In K.459.

One tends to imagine that the opening tutti of a classical concerto corresponds point by point with a sonata exposition, except that the second subject is given out in the tonic. This conception has the advantage of being clear and simple but it is true in only a few cases. To limit ourselves to Mozart, out of twenty-three piano concertos only thirteen conform to such a scheme; all the others show "irregularities". Sometimes the second subject is in the dominant[1]; sometimes it is absent[2]; sometimes the phrase which in the first tutti appeared to be the second subject does not reappear till the *development*[3] or the recapitulation,[4] whilst the true second subject appears first only in the solo. One cannot generalize further than to say that the opening tutti opens with the first subject and contains some of the ideas which are to return in the rest of the movement.

Let us follow it step by step.

It begins, we have said, with the first subject. Slow introductions are unknown in Mozart's concertos, as in the classical concerto in general.[5] His last concerto begins with a bar of accompaniment before the violins attack the first subject—a practice followed also in the G minor symphony.

Once given out, the first subject is sometimes repeated, either in part[6] or wholly.[7] Of variable length, it generally ends on the tonic and has a well-marked conclusion. In a few movements it loses itself in what follows and links up by developments with the second subject. The concertos of the great 1785-6 period show some examples of this, but in most, as in Mozart's work in general, the inspiration takes breath before going on. The clear articulation which this gives the work is not a personal quality; only, whereas with lesser composers it often makes the music disjointed and patchy, Mozart gives his successions of phrases an internal unity which is felt but cannot be analyzed, and binds together, with a single flow of emotion, themes whose outlines are very different. However changeful their shape and however clear-cut the separation between them, the continuity of the emotion is not broken; we grasp it intuitively when analysis reveals but a series of apparently independent subjects. On occasions, however, Mozart uses external devices of development comparable to those of Beethoven.

The first subject once completed, there begins the phrase or series

---

[1] K.413, 449.   [2] K.415, 459, 466.   [3] K.365, 503.   [4] K.450, 467, 482.
[5] There are two in Philip Emmanuel's concertos: Wotquenne's catalogue nos. 41 in E flat and 43, V in G.
[6] K.449.   [7] K.242, 271, 414, 456, 459, 466, 491.

of phrases leading to the next stage, which is generally the second subject. They form a continuous chain of subsidiary themes, nearly all destined to reappear at one moment or other of the movement and to assert the unity of it by reiterating passages already heard. They are the links that connect the different parts of the movement, the mortar of the building whose stones are the main subjects. Though only mortar, many of them have nearly as pronounced a personality as the main subjects themselves.   In the first tutti, they do not move far from the tonic and are generally content to lead to a dominant chord, whence the second subject, or its equivalent, brings us back at once to the tonic.   At the most, one of them risks staying for a while in the regions of the dominant[1], of the sub-dominant,[2] less often of the relative minor,[3] of the "double-dominant"[4] or the relative major.[5]   The presence of remote keys is uncommon; E flat bursting in suddenly in the tutti of the G major concerto, after the second subject, is unique.

We have just said how uncertain is the appearance of the second subject in the opening tutti.   In the great 1784-6 concertos it is often absent and is then replaced, either by a chain of subsidiary subjects[6] or by one whose importance gives it the appearance of being the true second subject but which we are later surprised not to find in the solo exposition[7]; in K.503, this "mock" second subject reappears in the *development* and takes it over completely.

The second part of the tutti joins on to the conclusion with a chain of subsidiary subjects—passing thoughts, devoid of independent existence but prolonging the idea, if not the form, of the main subjects.   Yet Mozart, like all his age, tends towards formal unity, towards the use of a single theme which permeates the whole movement, and twice, towards the end of his career as a concerto writer,[8] he repeats the first subject after the second and draws new developments from it before concluding his exposition.

There only remains to conclude the first tutti and prepare the solo's entry.   Here again there is as much diversity as with the second subject.   The conclusion of the tutti includes often a regular third subject, of greater consequence than the subsidiary ones, which may be utilized in the course of the movement and which comes back at the end.   When the character of the work does not forbid it, it is readily playful and more rhythmical than melodic.

The moment of the solo entry counts among the most impressive

---

[1] K.415, 453.   [2] K.246.   [3] K.449.   [4] K.449, 503.   [5] K.466.
[6] K.415, 459.   [7] K.450, 467, 482, 491, 503.   [8] K.467, 491.

in the movement. In the typical concerto, such as one imagines all classical concertos to be, the orchestra concludes and is silent at the end of the tutti; the solo then gives out the first subject. This is the "regular" form, as we find it in Beethoven's C minor concerto. But Mozart, much more "irregular" than is usually believed, follows the conventional practice in only fourteen of his piano concertos; the nine others, among which are nearly all his greatest, prepare an original entry for the solo and vary it from work to work. Sometimes orchestra and solo overlap, the piano beginning the first subject before the instruments have finished the conclusion;[1] sometimes the solo's impatience is betrayed by a trill before the orchestra has completed its phrase and it breaks forth into brilliant fireworks as soon as it can[2]; sometimes it asserts itself by giving out a new phrase, unknown to the orchestra, which will remain its exclusive property[3]; sometimes the orchestra itself repeats the first subject and the solo accompanies it[4]; and sometimes orchestra and solo share the new phrase which will bring back the first subject at the beginning of the second exposition.[5] So many different ways, so many unforgettable instants; Mozart's solo entries, when he leaves the beaten track, are among the loveliest moments in his music.[6]

The soloist's appearance, however original, ends always by leading back to the first subject, generally given out by the orchestra.[7] The second exposition is in its structure much more like the exposition of a symphony than the first, but the effect it produces on the listener is quite different from that of a true exposition. It gives one more the impression of a development. Some of the chief ideas are already known; they have been heard in the tutti, and the second exposition seldom reproduces them without change. The true *development* itself is so short compared with the rest of the movement, especially in Mozart, that one hardly thinks of isolating it from what precedes. The result is that, for him who listens without worrying about forms or formulae, the real development begins with the solo entry, and instead of dividing a concerto first movement into four parts as do

---

[1] K.413. [2] K.271, 450. [3] K.415, 466, 482, 491. [4] K.467. [5] K.503.

[6] We are thinking also of the shadowy and suggestive entry of the solo in the A major violin concerto, surely one of the most beautiful, and the first appearance of the solo violin and viola, hovering "above the tumult", in the *Sinfonia Concertante*.

[7] But in K.271, orchestra and solo give it out together, and in K.450 the solo, not content with a particularly long and brilliant introduction, attacks the theme alone without tolerating any intervention from the tutti.

the textbooks, it would be more sensible to keep a threefold division,
as for the sonata and the symphony: tutti exposition, *development*
(including the solo exposition and the *development* in the textbook
sense), and recapitulation.

The second exposition[1] is therefore really the beginning of the
development. Some themes, it is true, which we have not yet heard
will appear in it; the solo's own subject, for instance, and sometimes
the second subject; but the greater part of them are already familiar.
The first subject we know; the concluding subject, heard at the end
of the tutti, comes back at the end of the second exposition in
about half the concertos, and several subsidiary themes are common
to both expositions. Most of the thematic material has been presented by the tutti and comes back, not to be "expounded" any
longer, but "developed", in this first solo.

The second section of the allegro, the longest and most interesting,
comprises two landmarks which, however diverse the concertos,
are found in all of them. They are the appearance of the second
subject and the return of the tutti which concludes this part and
leads to the so-called *development* section.[2] These two stages are
constant; it is the intervening part that changes from work to work.

The piano's appearance settles the character of the composition.
The opening tutti might have announced a symphony, but with the
soloist's entry, however brilliant the orchestral part, the interest
shifts and the orchestra henceforward takes second place. In vain
does it start the first subject; the soloist nearly always takes it away[3]
and forges ahead alone, or almost alone, through scales and arpeggios.
From these bravura passages, occasionally interrupted by the band,
there arise by degrees melodic ideas, subsidiary subjects already
heard or new ones. Sometimes an echo of the concluding subject
returns to link up the second exposition with the first; sometimes,
too, the solo's special subject follows immediately on the first one.
But generally, once the first outburst of the solo has calmed down,
the orchestra intervenes with more authority, recalling fragments
of ritornelli, repeating and altering the last phrases of the solo, starting

---

[1] Or first Solo.

[2] Or second solo.

[3] K.415 is an exception; after the exposition of the first subject by the
tutti, beneath a solo trill, the piano follows completely new paths and leaves
the first subject to one side.

new passages. Finally the agitation dies down altogether and from out of the confusion arises an independent subject, either the second strain of the opening tutti, or, more often, a new idea that the soloist gives out alone and that the orchestra will not seek to take from him. It is the solo subject which may just possibly deceive us and pass as the main second subject, especially as it often appears in the dominant.

To John Christian Bach has been attributed the notion of giving the solo instrument a theme which belongs to it alone. If he did not invent the device, he is probably the first to make a constant use of it. Mozart took it from him, but he gave the theme a more personal character and made it more prominent. With him, it really characterizes the solo instrument: instead of being, as with John Christian, a little ephemeral tune, it generally possesses an individual outline which distinguishes it from the two other main subjects and enhances the piano part by entrusting it with the expression of something all its own. One thinks of the witty, syncopated theme of the concerto in G, of the *minor* ones of K.467 and 482, and of the spacious subject of K.503.

The second subject marks a halt in the struggle between solo and tutti. The *galant* concerto, which had reduced the orchestra to being mere accompaniment, bestowed on the piano exclusively the privilege of announcing it, and the tutti did not raise its head whilst the solo pursued its triumphal progress towards the dominant trill which closes this part of the movement. Mozart, too, had begun that way. But Mozart, it cannot be repeated too often, started from the narrow conception of the *galant* concerto and raised the genre little by little to the level of those reputed "serious" by associating the tuttis with the fate of the work and giving them a symphonic character. If his first attempts conform still to the *galant* formula, the concertos of his maturity free themselves altogether from it. Its lazy ways soon cease to satisfy him and already in his second concerto he gives the orchestra a part in the exposition of the second subject. In his Viennese period nearly all his concertos do likewise. Of the nine where the tutti is left out at this point, six are earlier than 1783. On the other hand, when later he still gives the piano the duty of announcing the subject, the orchestra, in every case but one, takes it up again to the answering or the accompaniment of the solo instrument. In some of the 1784-6 concertos, we hear the subject actually given out first by the orchestra, and taken up by the solo only when the tutti has done with it. This happens in the

flashing concerto in D, K.451,[1] among others, in the C minor, and
in the last, in B flat. The equality between orchestra and solo which
is at the base of the symphonic conception of the concerto, the
"emancipation of the orchestra" once attributed to Beethoven, is
already an accomplished fact with Mozart.

The end of the solo exposition which heaves in sight once the
second subject is passed varies from one concerto to the next.[2] After
the second subject a solo passage—or a succession of them—of rising
strength and strain culminates in a triumphal affirmation of the
dominant or relative major and in the customary trill; after which
the piano rests, for a few moments, upon its laurels.

Thereupon the tutti enters with long-pent-up vigour. In about
half the concertos, it brings back the concluding subject. Others
tighten even more firmly the bonds of the movement and assert its
unity still further by bringing back, not only the conclusion but also
the first subject,[3] a survival of an earlier age when each part of the
movement began with it. When neither concluding nor first subject
is heard, the orchestra recalls a few subsidiary themes. It does not
always enjoy a clear field, for the piano sometimes intervenes early
and hastens on the second solo.

The section from here to the recapitulation bears the name of
development by analogy with that of the symphony and sonata. In
reality, five concertos only[4] offer *developments* containing material
taken from the body of the exposition, and of these K.503 and 595
alone really develop this material. The work for two pianos, K.365,
after a new passage, recalls a theme of the first tutti (the mock second
subject); in the D minor, this section begins with the tragic lament
which the piano had uttered on its first appearance; then, during the
grand, stormy solo which follows, the orchestra punctuates the strong
beats with a triplet motif taken from the first subject, and that is all
that it owes to the rest of the work. K.503 builds its whole *develop-*
ment on its mock second subject, a march theme which the opening
tutti had given out, and develops it in a masterly way, but it builds
it upon this theme alone and the many other ideas already expressed

---

[1] "Soldierly", is Tovey's epithet for it.

[2] The C minor concerto musters three distinct main subjects; the second
and third correspond to the ordinary second subject and both are in the
relative major. In the recapitulation they reappear in the tonic in inverse
order.

[3] K.467, 491.

[4] K.271, 365, 466, 503, 595.

are left aside. K.595 confines itself to the first subject, which it varies and breaks up and treats contrapuntally under a running piano commentary. In the other concertos, the development is rather a fantasia, an improvisation, than a logical working out, and only the fact that it sometimes begins by playing with the last phrase of the exposition connects it with the rest of the concerto.

The relation between solo and tutti has made the repetition of material in the exposition specially impressive and characteristic, and the recapitulation and coda will make it still more so; and therefore the *development* needs to be more simple and more contrasted than it would be in a symphony or sonata, apart from the enormous difficulties of balancing solo against tutti in a *development* on ordinary lines. Accordingly, we find that in the finest classical concertos there is hardly an exception to the rule that the *development* is either based on the least weighty of the themes of the exposition, or on one that the solo had omitted (a most brilliant device of Mozart's), or it transforms the themes almost beyond recognition, or it has much episodic matter.[1]

It must, moreover, be owned that in Mozart as a whole the *development* ill deserves its name. True, there are works where he conceives it as do Philip Emmanuel Bach, Haydn and Beethoven. In addition to the concertos mentioned, nine out of ten of the "great" quartets, the four great quintets, the piano allegro in F (K.533), the string trio in E flat (K.563), and the four last symphonies afford examples of *developments* worthy of the name. But these are only some twenty instances against more than sixty sonata form movements of his Viennese period which show nothing of the sort.

Most often, Mozart looks upon the *development* as a transition. It is a return towards the tonic, the first subject and the recapitulation, rather than an autonomous section of the movement. In many cases it would be fair to say that the Mozartian sonata form is made up of two symmetrical parts, one of which repeats the other, joined by a transition passage or bridge. The first movement of the E flat serenade (K.375), for wind instruments, shows an extreme case of this. The *development* is limited to a few chords and a fragment of theme borrowed from the exposition which brings in at once the first subject and the reprise. In certain andantes, the device is pushed even further and the middle section drops out completely. The movement is then composed of two similar halves of which the second repeats the first with a few alterations of detail. In fact, Mozart's first movements belong to the tradition of the *da capo*

---

[1] D. Tovey, from an unpublished programme note.

aria rather than to that of really ternary movements like those of
Philip Emmanuel and Haydn.

But though the *development* be brief, it often holds the finest
bars of the work. The darkest hours come before dawn and Mozart's
inspiration reaches its highest peak of sombre power in the bars just
before the reprise. They are the critical moment, the climax of the
movement; they reveal the maximum of intensity reached by the
flow that carries it on. The most joyous and most serene allegros
wear at this moment a melancholy or even tragic air; chromaticisms
and *sforzandos* come piling up and the tempest appears to reach its
highest point, despair seems to be complete, when suddenly the veil
is torn aside and the radiant dawn of the first subject announces the
recapitulation. One could quote numberless examples: the first
movement of the violin sonata in E flat (K.380) where piano and violin
chords follow on each other like thunder on lightning and make one
think of Beethoven's Op. 111; the string trio, with its pathetic *minor*
scales; and the quintet in C, one of Mozart's most majestic *developments*, where, after the sinister rising scales of the third subject and
the poignant cries of the second, transposed into the minor, the cloud
is riven and the great peaceful line of the opening theme appears on
the landscape. One remembers also the reprise in the clarinet
quintet: the arpeggios of the clarinet, crossed by the ascending and
descending strings, hurrying ever more restlessly, ever more feverishly,
sinking ever deeper into the minor; then, when the agitation reaches
its highest point, suddenly holding their peace before the suave presence of the returning main theme. In the concertos themselves, those
in D minor, C minor, A (K.488) and C (K.503; rondo) speak here in
threatening tones which grip the soul like the forebodings of disaster.

The reprise with Mozart is therefore often a deliverance; it is
never, as with Beethoven, a transfiguration. After the increased
passion, accompanied by sorrow and anguish, of the end of the
development, the return of the tonic and of the first subject relieves
one like an arrival in port after a stormy passage. The reappearance
of the first theme is a return to the fold, which closes a painful exploring
of unknown lands; on seeing it one knows oneself to be on a friendly
shore. With Beethoven it is not quite the same. The theme is
unchanged but its presentation is often different. What a triumph
in his violin concerto for the first subject, so retiring, so shy at first,
with its almost inaudible drum taps, when the recapitulation brings it
back *fortissimo* and the drums have become brass!

Such apotheoses are unknown in Mozart. And in his minor key

works the reprise is neither apotheosis nor even deliverance, but just relapse. The *development* of the G minor quintet and symphony sought to cast off the load of anguish which oppressed the work; weary, vanquished by the struggle, they fall back, and with the implacable return of the first subject the movement resigns itself to its fate and follows despairing the road along which it is driven.

One cannot reproach the concertos, as one can some of Mozart's works, with not varying their recapitulations. In his lesser pieces more particularly, the last section sometimes repeats almost note for note the first; it avoids merely passing into the dominant and it finishes, as it began, in the tonic.[1] That was no doubt an advantage when the sonata was a new and unfamiliar form. To-day, we notice only too easily the monotony of the procedure. No group of Mozart's works is more free from it than his concertos. Even the most bloodless, the most *galant*, vary the re-exposition, either by omitting themes already heard, or by introducing themes heard in the opening tutti, but not since, or by changing the order in which these themes appear and making solos and tuttis alternate. The concerto as a genre is much less a prey to the monotony of recapitulations than the sonata and the symphony; the variety is much easier to obtain; and if one allows that the object of literal repetition is to make it simpler for the audience to understand the new form, there is less risk of such variety confusing the listener here than elsewhere.

In a general way, Mozart cuts down very much the bravura passages in this part of the movement and here the 19th century concerto writers have followed him. The work hastens towards its climax and tolerates with difficulty what is not essential. Collaboration, too, becomes closer between solo and tutti. The solo, after the strain of the *development*, is somewhat exhausted and shows itself more accommodating towards its adversary, leaving it nearly always the first subject and only speaking again when this is complete. The most exquisite combinations of piano and orchestra are met with here, as in the E flat (K.482) where piano and first violins converse in phrases that interplay as if they were canons. And finally, we meet again the various themes which have played an outstanding part in the movement. The true and the mock second subjects jostle and link up, affirming their kinship;[2] the more characteristic of the subsidiary themes appear also, throwing light upon each other and

---

[1] Here again Mozart's sonata form is akin to the *da capo* aria.

[2] K.450, 482, 503.

acquiring their full significance. Mozart loves especially to keep back for this moment some subsidiary motif which had been given out in the opening tutti and not heard since.[1] In fact, this third solo is the meeting place of the sometimes very diverse elements that had made up the two expositions, and it is delightful to speculate concerning the manner in which this meeting will be managed. At length the movement reaches the awaited pause where begins the cadenza which Mozart never omits in his piano concertos. The conclusion is sometimes perfunctory, as in the D major (K.537), sometimes the ending of the opening tutti is repeated, as in the D minor where the voice of the orchestra, pathetic and sombre, resounds long after the solo has been silent; sometimes, too, a new conclusion follows the last trill of the cadenza, as in K.467. This, the most interesting, is also the rarest kind of ending.

Here should come the coda. Less numerous and less extensive than Beethoven's, fine codas are not uncommon in Mozart, especially in works in a minor key. The opening allegros of the three great G minors, quartet, quintet and symphony, sum up in their codas, with passionate conciseness, the main thought of the movement; the C minor sonata likewise. The quartets in D minor, B flat and F, the E flat quintet, also crown their first movements with codas which epitomize all that has gone before; the C major quintet, before repeating the conclusion which had already served in the exposition, inserts a development full of mystery. The quintet in D begins over again the slow introduction which had opened the work, then interrupts it and, returning to a few bars of the allegro, ends abruptly on this joyful note. The sonata form finales of several quartets reach also great heights in their codas. The queen of all these perorations is, of course, that of the *Jupiter* symphony, incorrectly called Fugue, where the first subject returns inverted, the three chief themes reappear and are given out simultaneously, with a skill and a vigour equal to those in the well-known passage of the *Meistersinger* overture but with that lightness and grace which only Mozart can ally with strength and intensity.

Mozart never enriched his concertos with such great perorations. The coda of the first movement of the C minor is the only example one can compare with the G minor quintet and symphony. The piano's re-entry right at the very end, very rare with him, closes this movement of storms and darkness and deepens still further the

---

[1] K.246, 413, 414, 415, 449, 450, 453, 595.

mysterious twilight which envelops it. In general, the endings of his concerto allegros contain nothing that has not already been heard and do not transform elements already familiar. They are not the equals of the much more original endings of the rondos.

We so seldom hear to-day works of the *galant* age other than those of Mozart and Haydn that it is difficult for us to admire with what perfection Mozart has embodied his thought in the form imposed by the æsthetic conventions of the time. To understand a great creative genius, one should be familiar with the average work of his period and thus be able to compare him with his inferiors, recognize the points of contact between them and measure the distance that separates them. Only thus can one eliminate what is of the time and reach to what is personal in a work.

It is for lack of knowing Mozart's lesser contemporaries that even an enlightened public credits him with features which are in no wise his own. The articulated form, the sections marked off by noisy cadences, the transitions so simple and swift as to appear rudimentary, all these belong to the *galant* style; Mozart should be neither praised nor blamed for them. What belongs to him is the craft with which he used these forms that were everyone's to express his thought without the one suffering by contact with the other.

He took over and made use of the current forms: sonata, variations, rondos, with such ease that if he had had to invent his own forms he would hardly have been able to find any better suited to his thought.

The forms of the classical sonata are the Mozartian ones *par excellence*; he seldom uses others in his first movements. With him, they take on their full significance and answer, not only to a structural need, but to the claims of the feeling which quickens the work. The adaptation of the personal matter to the classical form is absolute, to such an extent that one is never conscious in his best work, as one is with lesser composers of the time, that certain themes come back at certain points, that such a development takes place at such a place, not because the composer felt the need for it but because his plan, laid down beforehand, required it of him.

Even in Mozart's lesser works, the slow movement remains generally above the level of a purely formal excellence. Never more than here does he show to what extent his self-expression complies with the form which the conventions of the age offer him. Seldom, under the clothing of the movement, does one feel the skeleton which supports it; seldom does one's attention settle more on the form than on the feeling. (We speak, of course, of the ordinary musical person, not of the critic whose habits lead him to look for the structure before all else in a work.)   It may happen to us, in some of his weaker allegros and rondos, to be aware of the symmetry and regularity of a passage and to be more impressed with these features than with the thought; this seldom happens in an andante; inspiration and technique, lyricism and construction blend with such unity that nothing takes away our attention from the beauty of the music itself.

The concertos would not deserve in his work the highly representative place they occupy were not their andantes the equals of the best of those in his quartets and symphonies.   No group of movements in his work surpasses them in variety.   It is difficult to class movements according to their content and the result of such a classification risks being somewhat arbitrary; content escapes definition and it is only approximately that one can describe the general character of a movement.   One feels well enough that some are gay, some sad, but the epithets that one can bestow thus are soon exhausted and when one has called a piece "joyful, melancholy, brilliant, amiable, vigorous, majestic, delicate", one is at the end of the list; to go any further is to fall into fancifulness.

And yet we feel that certain movements are akin to each other, that there are "families of movements" just as there are "families of minds".   They are akin in the work of the same composer; they are also akin from one composer to another.   This kinship of movements is really but one aspect of the kinship between the composers themselves.   Just as between father and son, brother and sister, we recognize a family likeness difficult to define, so between works and composers we notice affinities which defy a precise analysis but are nevertheless indisputable.

The kinship which we notice between works of different composers is even more recognizable between works of the same man. Thus it is that Mozart's andantes, despite their richness and their diversity, can with a few exceptions be brought under four or five heads which we may label, for convenience, the *galant* andante, the "dream", the "meditation"; the "singing" andante or romance; the "tragic" or "dramatic" andante.

No one will be taken in by this classification to the extent of thinking it absolute, but it can help us to grasp more easily as a whole these slow movements into which Mozart has poured such precious music.   Every classification is, by its very nature, approximate and arbitrary, especially when it deals with something as indefinable as the content of music. Let no one accuse us of seeking to break the most poetic of musicians upon a Procrustean bed! We only propose this division as a method which will lead us in the long run to a truer and finer understanding. Approximate and loose though it be, it is still too rigid to embrace all Mozart, and some of his best known andantes are impossible to fit into one or other of its categories.

With these strictures, and provided one interprets freely the terms we use as labels, we think that most of his movements justify this division.

The *galant* slow movements are those which belong least to their author. The taste of the time is more obvious in them than the personality of Mozart. Several of them might be signed John Christian Bach and, were it not for external evidence, one would have difficulty in fixing their authorship. They possess a certain sensual, languorous or idyllic charm which does not survive frequent hearing. They were the delight of an audience which would bear with a little emotion on condition it was neither strong nor personal and did not demand any prolonged concentration. Only at distant points does some deep beauty reveal the master's soul. This kind of andante is naturally found most often during his Salzburg period when he subordinated his originality to the requirements of his public with the greatest severity for himself and the greatest indulgence for his listeners. This was due, not only to his youth (he was but twenty-five when he left the town for good) but to his official position at the archbishop's court which obliged him to conform to his patron's tastes.

The *galant* part of his work is not much known and that is natural. Were it not for the nine lives of his sonatas which owe their longevity less to the beauty of a few of them than to their didactic qualities, nothing of it would be familiar to-day to the ordinary public. To find a *galant* andante known to everyone, it is to them one has to turn: to those, for instance, of the violin sonatas in C (K.296) and B flat (K.378). The famous and verbose *Haffner Serenade*, K.250, which dates from his twenty-first year and appears sometimes on our concert programmes, affords one of the best specimens of a *galant* slow movement: the andante in A, not undignified, with moments of spriteliness and even wit, but without much personality.

The period par excellence of these movements is the Salzburg one but they occur all through his life. The very year of the great symphonies saw the composition, during the summer when they were written, of two sonatinas, for piano in C (K.545) and violin in F (K.547). Their andantinos are pure *galant* toys, the last he was to

produce. But at this stage he could no longer be only *galant* and
even in these trifles the presence of the composer of the *Jupiter* is
felt.

Long before this, the *galant* andante had undergone a transformation. The true *galant* slow movement was tender but lacked flame.
Little by little, Mozart introduced into it his own personality. The
first signs of this change are seen early. Already several years before
he left for Paris, certain andantes and adagios had thrown off their
pink and blue silk ribbons and were quite personal.[1] They were
exceptional at the time, but as his life at Salzburg drew to its end
personal accents became louder and more frequent, and we are thus
led gradually towards the type of andante which, during his Viennese
period, replaces almost entirely the movement of his youth. The
andantino of the flute and harp concerto is a witness of this transformation. The work dates from 1778, the year he spent in Paris,
that is, the decisive period in his career and his artistic growth. Its
general appearance is that of a *galant* piece, with a slightly dreamy
tenderness, a beribboned softness; but certain features are thoroughly
Mozartian. It marks the passage from the impersonal idyll to the
more individual *romance* of his maturer years.

It is the *romance* which corresponds to the *galant* andante in his
work after 1780. He used neither the term nor the form before he
went to Paris and the form does not appear regularly till his break
with the archbishop had ensured his artistic freedom. He first gives
the name to a slow movement in 1781, in his B flat serenade for
wind instruments (K.361), and from this moment *romances* are more
and more frequent and *galant* andantes fewer and fewer. The last
piano concerto, the E flat quintet, both have *romances*;[2] at the end
of his life's work, he finds in it his favourite type.

It is a far cry from the *galant* slow movement of his adolescence
to the *romance* of his greatest period. And yet the descent is clear.
The *romance* of his second horn concerto, the andantino of the E flat
piano concerto (K.449) are still quite close to the *galant* style, and the
personal accent is as yet not very pronounced. But soon, to the
colourless sweetness of the fashionable *romance* there is added a more
pungent feeling, tones of passing sadness, and the sweetness itself
becomes more quivering; we feel in it that "passionate tranquillity"

---

[1] We are thinking especially of the C minor andantes of the E flat symphony (K.184), and the quartet in C (K.157).

[2] The title is not used in these movements but they are none the less clearly
romances.

which is one of his most personal traits. At the time of his master-pieces, from 1784 to his death, all his *romances* disclose now and again these depths of melancholy which his exuberant joy sometimes covers up but never fills. The *romance* of the C minor concerto is so calm outwardly, with the broad and peaceful lines of its refrain, but how pleading are the strains of its episodes! The refrain of the *romance* in the *Coronation* concerto (K.537) is serene, too; but, once it is complete, the orchestra adds a phrase of heart-rending yearning. The *romance* of the last concerto is one long farewell, poignant yet resigned; and once at least a *romance* whose peace seemed unshakable breaks forth in its middle portion into tragic cries: we refer to that of the D minor concerto.

The transition from his slender *galant* andantes to the *romances* of his last years leads us from the imitative labour of his childhood to the awakening of his personality and the full blossoming of the end of his life. But it must not be thought that the term *galant* applies to everything Mozart wrote before the urge of his genius made him throw off the yoke of contemporary conventions. There is another group of slow movements which goes back to his years of childhood and into which he cast all the riches which the domination of an im-personal taste kept out of his sonata movements and rondos. It is that of his "dream" andantes. This title is but a label and we do not defend it on condition a better one is found. The name "noc-turne" would perhaps express the limpidity, as penetrating as moon-light, of certain andantes and adagios, but the word is linked to Chopin and might suggest between these movements and the Roman-tic composer a kinship which occurs but seldom.

The "dream" belongs to Mozart's childhood and the early part of his maturity. After giving of its best in the fine andante of K.467 it disappears. It is, therefore, mainly a youthful form and if the best example dates from 1785, the most numerous and most characteristic belong to Salzburg. The "dream" andantes of the violin concertos, of the G major especially, express best the ideal that Mozart sought to render in it, for that of K.467 mingles with the dreaming certain dramatic strains that carry us away from it and bring the movement nearer the *romance* and the "tragic" andante.

The true "dream" does not imply any strong emotion; it does not exclude passion, but the exquisite fancy of a fresh and rich nature is its chief character· True, the "dreams" of Mozart's early years in Vienna are deeper and richer than those of the Salzburg concertos, but fancy predominates over melancholy and when melancholy speaks it is not with a tragic voice. They are inspired by a spirit of fairyland, too far removed from reality to know sorrow. Their form is often that of a long, winding melody which cannot be broken up into phrases and follows on almost uninterruptedly from one end to the other, and Mozart's rhythms are found here at their freest.

Just as the *galant* andante gave way before the *romance*, so the "dream", by growing deeper and richer, loses a little of its fancy and unreality and becomes the "meditation" of riper years. The transition is even more gradual than with the *galant* slow movement. Some andantes, like those of the quartet in C or the *Prague* symphony could be classed in either group and already that of the concerto for three pianos, with the quivering motion of its *development*, announces a more concentrated vision than that of a mere "dream". The truth is that the two groups are closely related and if some works belong clearly to one or the other, like the adagio of the G major violin concerto, which is a "dream", or that of the D major quintet, which is a "meditation", many others mingle too intimately "dreaming" with "meditation" and "recollection" for one to label them without hesitation. It is better to recognize the mixed character of such movements, which nearly all date from Mozart's first years in Vienna, whereas the "dreams", pure and simple, come from his Salzburg time and the "meditations" from the years later than 1782 and especially 1785.

The "meditative" second movement, which is more often an adagio than an andante, is ordinarily less purely melodic than the "dream" and the writing is richer and given to polyphony. It is in his string quintets, that genre so peculiarly his, where few have followed him and none have excelled him, that we find his biggest and most searching adagios—the largest, too, both in dimensions and inspiration. The magnificent polyphonic adagio of the G minor quintet and the still more complex adagio of the quintet in D, the more vocal one of the quintet in C, with its hymn-like line, that of the quartet in D (K.499) contain what is most exalted in his thought, the firmest product of his craft, and it is to them, and to the andante of the concerto K.503, that we would refer those who are surprised that we dare place the amiable Salzburger on the same plane as Bach and Beethoven.

The four groups of andantes whose chief characters we have just been sketching correspond to fairly precise periods in his life: the *galant* one and the "dream" to his childhood and adolescence; the *romance* and "meditation" to his maturity. There is a fifth group the works of which spread out irregularly over most of his life: that of the "tragic" or "dramatic" andantes.

Mozart's slow movements in minor keys are distinctive enough to be set apart from the rest of his work. We have called them indifferently "tragic" or "dramatic" and both names distinguish them from his other slow movements. It may seem useless to speak of "drama" to distinguish one composition of his from another, since his whole work is habitually looked upon as dramatic. But this quality is most apparent in his allegros. His andantes show it much less. He has to be impelled by a keen and sorrowful inspiration to give them a dramatic character. Their themes appear, then, to be sung by ideal voices and to await words. All his minor key andantes are in this sense dramatic, whether they adopt the form of the variation, the sonata or the rondo. There are not many of them; a dozen between 1777 and his death, but nearly all are among his finest slow movements. Like his contemporaries, he uses the minor mode little, but when he does it is always to compose a masterpiece. His *minor* works occupy, amongst his finest works, a place quite out of proportion to their number, some twelve or so during his Viennese period, and yet these twelve contain a good part of the compositions that have made him live. And so with his andantes, when one thinks of the greatest, there come first to mind the D minor variations of the violin sonata in F (K.377), the G minor andante of that in E flat (K.380), the G minor variations and the F sharp minor *Siciliana* of the concertos in B flat (K.450) and A (K.488) and the C minor andantino of the *Sinfonia Concertante* (K.364) and C minor andante of the concerto in E flat (K.482).

His finest minor key andantes begin with that of the concerto K.271, in 1777, and finish with the prelude and fugue for string quartet (1788)[1] and the adagio of the first organ fantasia in 1790, but already several years before 1788 they become rare and the last work in sonata form where one is found is the A major concerto (K.488) which belongs to the early spring of 1786. The sadness is so transfigured in them that they leave no feeling of depression or disheartenment, but rather comfort and strengthen us as much as his most exuberant allegros. The beauty first glimpsed, then reached, through tears, is of such brightness that the listener is spell-bound and forgets the bitterness, forgets the suffering whence the movement sprang. These sorrows, which are nevertheless a young man's

---

[1] The fugue, intended originally for two pianos, had been composed in 1783.

sorrows, since Mozart was only thirty when he ceased composing "tragic" andantes, are rich and beautiful with all the strength of his throbbing, vital nature.

The piano concertos offer some of the best examples of these five kinds of slow movements. Mozart has left no more typical instances of *galant* andantes than the second movements of K.413 and 415. The *romance* produces some of its finest examples in the concertos in D minor, C minor and B flat, K.595. The "dream" of his twenty summers, which sweetens the hard brightness of many of his drawing-room works, is met with in the first concerto, in those for three and for two pianos, and in two of the "great" period, K.451 and 467. The "meditation" which succeeds the "dream" is found four times: in 1782, with K.414, one of its earliest appearances; in 1784, with the hymn-like variations of K.450 and the more tormented andante of K.453; and a last time with the superb andante in F, of K.503, one of the most spacious that he ever wrote.

Hitherto, we have seen that the piano concertos represent as well as any other group the chief tendencies of his genius. But when we come to his "tragic" andantes, we find they are almost the only ones at the period of his maturity, to reflect this side of it. It is remarkable that from his first year in Vienna onward, from the time when his genius takes possession of itself, minor key andantes are rare in his chamber music and vanish completely from his symphonies. Apart from the moving adagio for piano in B minor, an isolated piece, in 1788, and the adagio (introduction and conclusion) of the first organ fantasia, in 1790, and some other movements of lesser importance[1] the only ones are those of his piano concertos. At earlier periods, minor key andantes had been commoner, but even then the best were those of K.271 and of the *Sinfonia Concertante*. And after 1781, the year of his finest violin sonatas, two of which contain splendid minor slow movements (K.377 and 380), the expression of the shade of tragic emotion which needs a slow *tempo* for its embodiment is reserved throughout the greatest period of his creative life for the piano concertos. There must we seek the dark and saddened Mozart of the slow movements. What corresponds in his andantes to the

---

[1] Preludes for string quartet: K.546 in C minor, and for string trio: K.E. 404a, in F, G and D minor; a rather insignificant adagio in C minor, K.617, the first movement of the quintet for harmonica, flute, hautboy, viola and 'cello (1791).

allegros of the C minor serenade, of the G minor quintet and symphony is found in his concertos and there only.

It is tempting to look in Mozart's andantes for a relation between the nature of the emotion and the form used. If one could say, for instance, that "meditations" always adopt sonata form, how satisfying it would be for a systematic mind! Waste of effort! Such a relation does not exist, at least in the andantes. One can, it is true, discover something like it in certain allegros; some of them, inspired by the same emotion, show likenesses of form; thus, the *developments* of passionate *allegros assai* in minor keys tend to be more concise than others:[1] but in his slow movements such a parallel between form and matter is impossible to establish. The "singing" movements called *romances* are often rondos, but that is a merely outward likeness due obviously to the fact that the rondo is the most vocal of forms and that the *romance*, as its name implies, recalls an actual song. We must therefore resign ourselves to keeping separate matter and manner.

Mozart never seeks those contrasts of key between movements of which Philip Emmanuel and Haydn are fond and which have become almost obligatory since Beethoven. His second movements are generally in the sub-dominant. The quartet in G has its andante in C, the *Jupiter* symphony, in C, has its andante in F. Exceptions are negligible. When they exist, the sub-dominant has more than three accidentals and Mozart does not like heavy key-signatures. Four sharps or flats are rare with him; five one never finds save for an instant in the *minores* of a few variations or of minuets in B or E flat. Rather than write four accidentals in the signature, he prefers to give up the sub-dominant and have recourse to the dominant; he does it here and there in his E flat works, among them two of the four piano concertos written in that key, K.365 and 449. At other times he uses the relative minor (*Sinfonia Concertante*); more seldom, the relative minor of the dominant (quartet in F, K.158; violin sonata in E flat, K.380). Those works whose key is minor generally pass into the relative major in their slow movements.[2] Finally, once or twice, perhaps as an archaism, he retains the same key in all the movements. But these exceptions do not affect more than a third of his andantes.

---

[1] See the C minor sonata, the violin sonata in G, K.379 (second movement) and the G minor quintet.

[2] The D minor concerto is an exception; its *romance* is in B flat, the sub-dominant of the relative major.

The structure, on the other hand, is varied. For his first movements, he uses almost exclusively sonata form, occasionally replaced by variations in his Parisian works.[1] But for his andantes he has at his disposal several models, especially the variation which fits all movements, the rondo, another universal form, and the sonata whose ample and majestic outlines suit perfectly the meditative phrases of an andante or an adagio. This latter is sometimes in two sections, the *development* being absent, sometimes in three. Finally, several andantes follow no fixed scheme.

He did not use these moulds indifferently at all periods. He turned to the *sonata* in two sections after 1787. The *sonata* in three was common at the beginning and end of his life, rarer between 1783 and 1789. The rondo, which is found from time to time in the works of his youth, such as the early D minor quartet, K.173, did not become common till 1783.

The piano concertos prefer the three section *sonata*; out of twenty-three, eight make use of it, all of them belonging to the later half. The two section *sonata* is nearly as popular; five concertos at different periods use it. Two andantes in variation form belong to 1784 and two others of irregular plan, in 1784 and 1785, are modifications, one of the rondo, the other of the *sonata*.

The three section *sonata* appears in the first concerto and vanishes in 1786 after the A major, K.488; it covers therefore almost all Mozart's career as a concerto writer and it may be considered as the typical andante of his concertos. It goes with broad and ample themes which unfold slowly and melt one into the other. The sonata form is less clearly articulated than in the allegro; its divisions are less sharply distinguished; the elements of its structure less recognizable. Its texture recalls rather those masses of cement in which the Romans buried bricks and rubble and which form a compact and inseparable whole. It is, one might say, more monolithic than in the allegro. This is one feature. The aspect of the second section is another. This part is hardly ever a real development, recalling themes from the earlier part. Most of the time it is but a transition destined to lead us back to the beginning and sometimes its reduced dimensions make us hesitate to consider it as a separate section.

When the andante of a concerto is a three section *sonata*, the

---

[1] Sonata in A, K.331; quartet in A for flute and strings, K.298, a work in a French form, though composed in Vienna in 1787 (cf. Saint-Foix, op. cit., IV, 307).

movement nearly always begins with a tutti introduction, which contains the first member of the phrase. That of K.488, the structure of which is rather different from the others, is the only one to begin directly with the solo. Sometimes this introduction is of the briefest and only sketches the beginning of what will become the solo[1]; sometimes, and more often, the two themes are given out, as in the tutti of an allegro.[2] As for the phrase which will conclude the movement, it appears sometimes thrice.[3] In K.414 it also accounts for the *development*. Elsewhere it is content with two appearances, at the end of the tutti and of the movement[4] or at the end of the first solo and of the movement[5]; or it may appear at the end of the movement only.[6]

The two section *sonata* is a less familiar form. Mozart is the only great classic who has made much use of it; Haydn and Beethoven attached great importance to the *development* and one can understand that a form whence that section was absent did not attract them. But Mozart, as we know, lingered little over his *developments* and he uses the binary form without scruple. Towards the middle of his career it is one of his favourite moulds; after 1788 he comes back to the ternary *sonata* and henceforward his only binary movement will be the larghetto of his B flat quartet, K.589. The highest point of the binary *sonata* is reached in the three magnificent andantes of the C major concerto, K.503, and the quintets in C and in G minor.

The rondo andante is, with the ternary *sonata*, the andante par excellence in his concertos. It is found, we have said, at all periods, but it becomes common only after 1783 and even then Mozart keeps it chiefly for the smaller genres, sonata, trio, *Musical Joke*. It appears once, it is true, in a quartet[7] and one other time in a symphony,[8] in a modified form somewhat different from the rondo of the sonatas; the last quintet also uses it. With these few exceptions, the concertos are the only works where Mozart appears to treat it as a serious form.

The first rondo andante in a concerto dates from 1784; it is that of the D major, K.451. Three other great concertos use it, the D minor, E flat, K.482 and C minor. The concerto in D, K.537, and the last, in B flat, also make use of it, and towards the end it becomes his favourite movement in the genre.

The rondo andantes in his concertos have not the uniformity of

---

[1] K.415. [2] K.175, 242, 246, 271, 365, 414, 453. [3] K.242, 365. [4] K.175, 415. [5] K.242, 365. [6] K.488. [7] D minor, K.421. [8] E flat, K.543.

structure of the sonatas. That of the D minor is distinguished by
the G minor prestissimo which interrupts it, a quick interlude in a
slow movement which is most uncommon in his work.[1] That of
the E flat, K.482, is quite unique in its varied refrain, which make it
a cross between rondo and variation. It is moreover characterized
by the couplets being reserved for the orchestra whilst the soloist
confines himself to varying the refrain; the coda unites both. Those
of the D major, K.451, and the C minor are more regular: a refrain,
given out at first by the solo, then by the tutti, two couplets and a
coda. The two last concertos recall the romance of the D minor,
without the prestissimo: refrain in the solo and the tutti, first couplet,
refrain and coda, new couplets, and return of all the first part including the coda (ABAC D ABAC). It is an application to the andante
of the masterly form of the sonata rondo which Mozart developed and
used so often in his finales.

Variations, a form of which the *galant* age was madly fond, are
always uncommon in his serious work. He considers them as an
amusement without significance and the great number of those he
wrote for the piano, though often charming, are not among those
pieces into which he put the whole of himself. Yet, now and again,
he uses this form in more important compositions. Those of the
violin sonata in F, K.377, a transformation of those in the divertimento, K.334, and forerunners of the finale of the second D minor
quartet, K.421, are among his most passionate movements; those of
the quartet in A lead to a grandiose coda, and the serenity of his last
months expressed itself in the variations of the second organ fantasia,
K.608.

The two concertos which have slow variations are both in B flat
and both date from 1784. Those of the first, K.450, are valuable
especially for their theme; those of the other, K.456, are akin through
their key, G minor, to great works; their richer and more tortured
inspiration drove Mozart to elaborate the form, and the interplay of
piano and orchestra, the transformations of theme and especially the
coda are of the first order.

Two concertos use free forms for their slow movements. The
andantino of K.449 is a kind of three-part *sonata* with the air of a
rondo; it could almost be looked upon as a series of variations.
The majestic concerto in C, K.467, has an andante whose "nocturne"

---

[1] There is another example in the *romance* of the B flat serenade,
K.361.

feeling proclaims the coming of Chopin. Five or six themes can be distinguished in it, but the order of their return and that of their keys do not correspond to any fixed plan and this magical andante proves that the "formalist" Mozart was as much a master of fantasy, when he wished, as the dreamiest of Romantics.

Into all these movements, so varied by their plan and their feeling, Mozart put the best of his soul. The qualities which make his best andantes and adagios precious to us are all found in these concertos to the same degree as in his works belonging to the genres deemed "serious": quartet, quintet, symphony.

It is seldom that the finale of a work is the equal of the andante and the opening allegro. How often are we obliged to own that the last movements of works whose first ones had pleased us have left us dissatisfied! This does not apply to one single age; it is common to all, and to all composers from the 17th century to our own days. There are, of course, exceptions; many works have in their last movement their best part; but, generally speaking, it remains true that a composer, for one reason or another, does not reach in his finales the height of his andantes and allegros.

How can we explain this? There are doubtless several reasons and they vary according to the period. At the time of Mozart and Beethoven the inferiority of the finale was deliberate. A *galant* public must have listened with difficulty to music whose character was unremittingly serious[1]; it felt more than we do the need for contrast, and two serious movements on end were no doubt enough. After an allegro and an andante, it needed relaxation, and this was provided by the light and skipping finale; it would not have tolerated a third serious movement. For the same reason Haydn inserted scherzo minuets in his quartets and symphonies and caused thus two serious pieces to be followed by two lighter ones. When Mozart started placing his minuets between his allegros and his andantes (as in several of his quartets and quintets), the alternation of the frivolous and the severe was assured.

The frankly superficial character of the finale is therefore intentional with *galant* composers. Haydn sometimes and Mozart often, nevertheless, reacted against it; but Beethoven, except in his minor key finales, generally kept up the tradition of the light-hearted rondo

---

[1] Possibly because its concerts were longer than ours.

and passed it on to the Romantic generations. Schubert, Schumann, Mendelssohn, even Brahms think fairly often of the finale as a relaxation rather than as a crowning of the whole, and the ideal of the "entertainment" finale is still alive to-day.

Out of some hundred finales in Mozart's "great" period, about forty rise above the merely recreative tone of the ordinary rondo and a score are in no wise inferior to the opening allegros. Such are those of the four last symphonies, of the quartet in A and the concertos in D minor, C minor and C major, K.503. In his greatest works he casts away the ideal of the happy ending and crowns them with finales of a serious and sometimes overcast mood. In a score of others the happy ending survives, but the emotion is deepened and attains grandeur, as in the quintets of 1787 and 1791, the quartets in C and G, and the concertos in G, K.453, and A, K.488. The proportion of last movements that place themselves definitely on lower ground and aim only at amusing and relaxing through a round of merry, skipping tunes hardly exceeds one half of the works of these fourteen years and one should remember that most of them belong to that part of his output that he composed for his fashionable *clientèle*, such as the trios and piano sonatas. Most of these are rondos; he keeps rather the sonata form and variations for his "serious" finales.

The frivolous conception of the concerto that prevailed in the *galant* age and with which Mozart himself had started, survives till the end in the use of the rondo. He transforms it, however, to such an extent that one has to be warned in order to recognize it. It is clearly his favourite form. Out of a hundred and eleven finales in his "great" period, seventy-six are rondos, eighteen sonatas and seventeen variations or minuets. The mere numbers show his preference. But it is proved also, and more decisively, by the care which he brought to the elaboration of the form and the infinite art with which he varied it from work to work. If, for his inspiration at its loftiest, one has to turn to his andantes, it is in his rondos that he shows himself at his greatest as master of form.

It is a far cry from the simple little rondos of the early 18th century to the sonata rondos of the quartets, quintets and concertos of Mozart's last years. It is a far cry, even, from the rondos that John Christian wrote for his London public and with which he ended at little cost sonatas, quartets and concertos, to the last rondos of his disciple. From the year of his childhood when his musical personality began to shine through, Mozart was never content with the dryness of the rondos which John Christian and all his contemporaries were turning out in tens and hundreds.

The Mozartian sonata rondo is not a development of the simple rondeau form used by Couperin. The rondeaux of Couperin do not go beyond a straightforward succession of couplets, or episodes, separated by returns of the refrain. Each couplet is independent and there is no repetition of earlier ones; the only organic link in the movement is the refrain, which usually comes back unaltered. The number of couplets is not fixed. This kind of movement occurs all through the century; some of Mozart's finales[1] show it in a form hardly more complex than that of Couperin.

The origin of the sonata rondo must be sought in the dances *"en rondeau"* of the French operatic composers. These differ from the simple rondeau in that there is generally only one couplet and seldom more than two. When a pair of such dances is combined we are well on the way to the sonata rondo. Many of Rameau's dances point in this direction. Let us, for example, examine the rigaudons and tambourins that close the first Entrée in *Les Indes Galantes* (1735). Each of these dances has the same plan. The first is a rondeau in G major with a single couplet that leads to the key of the dominant. The second follows the same course but is in the minor; after it, the first dance is repeated. The likeness in plan between such a pair of dances and a sonata rondo is easily seen.

A   G major.
B   Leading to D major.
A   G major.

C   G minor.
D   Leading to B flat. (This part closes in B flat in the tambourin, returns to G minor in the rigaudon.)
C   G minor.

ABA as before.

Often the second dance is in binary form (C D); even so, the analogy with the sonata rondo is close. The first dance corresponds to the refrain, exposition couplet and first return of the refrain; the second dance, to its *development* couplet; and the *da capo* to the further returns of the refrain and the recapitulation.

The main difference in the later form lies in the absence of hard

---

[1] E.g., those of his serenades in B flat and E flat, K.361 and 375.

and fast lines marking off refrain and couplets. But even these are not always pronounced in the earlier rondeau. Couperin seeks more than once to unify his rondeaux by the use of themes or motifs that recur throughout the movement and Rameau carried this practice further, as in the E minor tambourin for harpsichord, *Les Cyclopes*, *La Follette* and *La Villageoise*. In this latter, the first couplet opens with the same phrase as the refrain and, after the second episode, which has a semi-quaver bass accompaniment, the same figure is carried into the refrain.[1] *Les Cyclopes* carries us very near indeed to the Mozartian rondo, as the following analysis will show.

Refrain:	A	(a)	4 bars.
		(b)	47 bars; a number of strains, with reminders of (a). All in D minor.
1st Couplet	B		33 bars. D minor (13 bars); modulating (6 bars); F major (14 bars).
Refrain:	A	(a)	4 bars.
		(c)	8 bars; a new transition. All in D minor.
2nd Couplet:	C		27 bars. D minor (7 bars); A minor (20 bars).
Refrain:	A	(a)	4 bars. } Unchanged.
		(b)	48 bars. }

The long and complex refrain, the second part of which contains many reminiscences of the opening bars, would be comparable to an exposition if it did not remain in the same key; but it is quite like the rich, many-themed refrain of a Mozart or Beethoven sonata rondo. Only the first four bars are repeated between the first and second couplets and the return of the whole fifty odd bars of (a) and (b) gives one the impression of a recapitulation. In fact, were it not that these bars do not modulate to the relative major on their first appearance, *Les Cyclopes* might be considered as an early example of the sonata rondo. It is in any case one of the closest anticipations of that form.

The Mozartian rondo is, then, but an elaboration of the French combination of two dances "en rondeau" with a return of the first part.

---

[1] The same device occurs in the second half of the rondo of K.449.

We find it fully formed in the second piano concerto, a perfect example of that sonata rondo which he was to use in most of his piano concertos and which in all his work he adopts more often than any other form, for his finales, from 1778 to his death.

This movement repeats, like the dances "en rondeau", the whole of the first part after the second, and is thus nearly as closely unified as a true *sonata*. It turns all its last section into a recapitulation and for that reason we have proposed calling it a *sonata rondo*, to distinguish it from less organic rondos. One might say that it is a *sonata* where each section is separated from the other two by the same subject, the refrain, and where the exposition, instead of finishing in the dominant, returns to the tonic.

There are few "regular" sonata rondos in Mozart for, in this form which was so much his own, he has confined himself less than elsewhere to a fixed plan. That of K.451, in D, is one of the few which conform in every way to the type and it will be convenient to analyze it.

After the exposition of the refrain which consists here of two strains and does not depart from the tonic, there begins the first couplet or exposition. Two themes can be distinguished: the first extends over some forty bars, in D; the second is in the key of the dominant. It is a first section of a *sonata* up to the point where it modulates and returns at the same time to the tonic and the refrain. This latter is repeated unchanged, and the movement enters on its second couplet which, after giving out a third theme, in the minor, develops the refrain subject and the second subject of the first couplet. This section corresponds to the *development* of the *sonata*. Finally, the refrain is once more repeated; the whole of the first couplet returns with modifications of detail and without departing from the tonic. The refrain is heard once more; it brings in the cadenza, after which the movement, which is in 2-4, closes with a fairly long coda in 3-8. We have therefore the following outline:

Refrain: A ⎫ D major.
        B ⎭

1st or Exposition Couplet: C D major.
                               D A major.

Refrain: A ⎫ D major.
        B ⎭

2nd or *Development* Couplet: E   B minor.
                               A and D: "developed",   modulating.

Refrain: A ⎫
          B ⎬ D major.

3rd or Recapitulation Couplet: C ⎫
                                D ⎬ D major.

Refrain (shortened): A D major.

Cadenza.

Coda: Continuation of the Refrain with change of time-signature.

This sonata rondo is perfectly regular and, what is more, comes close to the true *sonata* in that its second couplet is a real *development*, a feature which it shares only with the finales of the E flat string quintet and the concertos in B flat, K.450, and C, K.467. All Mozart's other sonata rondos show some kind of irregularity, sometimes small, sometimes pronounced, sufficient to give them as a whole a variety which appears the greater the more one considers them. Sometimes the refrain returns bereft of some of the themes which made it up on its first appearance; certain rondos, even, appear to be reduced to two couplets by omitting it altogether between the *development* and the re-exposition.[1] Sometimes the first couplet, instead of starting in the tonic to end in the dominant, sets out from the latter and unfolds in different keys more or less remote from the tonic. And sometimes, finally, the third couplet leaves out a part of the exposition or else brings in new subjects or yet again recalls phrases from the second couplet or the refrain; the possibilities are endless.

After the last couplet the refrain is often shortened; once it is even absent.[2] It is generally followed by a coda, long or short, and more or less new according to the composer's fancy.

Some rondos, moreover, cannot be reduced to any definite form, even when one allows for "irregularities". The finale of the *Kleine Nachtmusik* of the piano sonata in B flat, K.570, of the B flat quartet, K.589, are built on plans of their own, and this is true of some of the concertos.

After the slow measures of the andante, the piano springs forth joyously to meet the theme of the finale. The solo expounds it and claims it before the orchestra is able to put in a note; the strings just keep up a murmur of repeated chords, a misty and approving back-

---

[1] K.413, 414, 456, 459, 488; sonata for two pianos, K.448; E flat piano quartet, K.493; string trio, K.563; K.478.

[2] Piano trio in C, K.548.

ground against which the luminous outline of the refrain stands out radiantly. The tutti is seldom the first to take up the finale; it never does so with passionate themes; when the character of the movement is quiet and pensive or when the form is that of theme and variations the solo consents sometimes to leave the first place to the instruments.[1] In general, this first appearance is short; in K.271 it is unusually indiscreet in its length, some fifty bars long, but this is exceptional. The theme once outlined, the orchestra repeats it and adds several subsidiary motifs. This opening tutti is sometimes followed by a regular conclusion and leads to a full close on the tonic,[2] after which the piano opens the exposition couplet. For these concerto refrains are no longer the agreeable ditties of galant rondos but true developments with several distinct subjects[3] and a concluding codetta.

In the couplets, the foremost part belongs generally to the piano without the orchestra ever withdrawing completely. The traditional virtuosity of the rondo—traditional especially since the 19th century with its Hummels, Moscheles and Chopins—is as absent from Mozart's rondos as from his first movements. Pure virtuosity is almost unknown to him; the brilliant runs with which he embellishes his themes and thanks to which he develops them and links them up one with the other are always expressive and it is impossible to make the cuts in them which one can make with advantage in those of Dussek, Hummel, Cramer, Field, Steibelt, Kozeluch and other pianist-composers of the *galant* age. The exposition couplet unfolds, passing from tonic to dominant, allowing itself only seldom to drift into distant keys and hardly ever to change its *tempo*.[4] However, it readily inserts between the first and second subject a minor episode corresponding to the solo subject in the first movement which is also often in the minor. At the end of the couplet, the task of bringing back the refrain falls usually to the solo and the orchestra repeats it afterwards.

The middle couplet affords as much unexpectedness as the *development* of the first movement. It is the essential part of the rondo, the one for the sake of which, in certain cases, one listens to the rest.

---

[1] K.382, 386, 413, 414, 449, 453, 491, 503.

[2] K.488.

[3] Two or three; K.482 has four.

[4] K.415 inserts in this first couplet a short and moving adagio in the tonic minor.

In K.450, piano and wind enter upon a refined and witty conversation anent the refrain, sporting with it until it comes back for good. K.415 recalls and develops here the three motifs which make up its refrain; K.246 uses a theme of the first couplet as a bridge to return to the refrain and K. 271, one of the most eccentric, before proceeding to the minuet with variations which fills two thirds of this section, recalls in the minor the first strain of its refrain.

But most of the concertos, faithful in this to the tradition of the dance "*en rondeau*", bring new elements to the building of this second couplet and (another French trait) put it in the minor. These new elements are less definite themes than passages and runs, melodic as all Mozart's passages are, but not forming clear-cut tunes. They give this couplet the character of an extemporization and one recognizes once again that Mozart, sometimes so formal, is also a master of fantasy.

It is impossible to sum up the characters of these middle couplets. When Mozart has surprises up his sleeve, it is here that he springs them on us; it is here that, in the middle of a 2-4 presto, he unfolds a sinuous minuet which he varies up to four times[1]; it is here, in a 6-8 gallop, that he stops and recollects himself in an andantino in three time, like a huntsman who in the heat of his fiery course suddenly finds himself before a broad, poetic landscape and pulls up to contemplate it lovingly.[2] It is here, finally, that the tragedy, which is never as near as when he appears most carefree and most over-brimming with mirth, breaks forth and covers a whole section of the rondo with a dark minor hue. We are thinking particularly of the magnificent finale of K.503; its second couplet, an apotheosis of the modest *minore* of the French rondo, is one of the most stirring utterances of the great dramatist.

But little by little, dusky storm-clouds, minuets and andantinos, free fantasies, all scatter and vanish, and the familiar outline of the refrain brings us back to well-known lands. This return of the refrain, perhaps a little too well-known, is the weak point in the rondo and Mozart, in five concertos,[3] has strengthened the movement by omitting it and passing straight on to the recapitulation. At other times, it comes back so much curtailed that it is hardly recognizable,[4] or else in a key other than the tonic, as in the last concerto, K.595, where it is stopped before it can be finished and vanishes before the impatience of the recapitulation.

---

[1] K.271. [2] K.482. [3] K.413, 414, 456, 459, 488.

[4] Piano quartet in G minor, K. 478; clarinet concerto.

The third couplet, in which the piano plays a smaller part than in the first, is also very diverse from work to work. Most concertos shorten it by leaving out themes that had been heard in the first couplet, and realizing that it can easily become tedious, hurry it on towards the conclusion. The only reproach one can address to the splendid C major concerto, K.503, is precisely that this third section of its rondo is too long and too like the first; a slight weariness is the result.

The first movements seldom culminated in codas; the composer reserved them for the finale. The coda of K.450, through a repeated triplet motif in the bass, leads to a *strepitando* statement of the key of B flat and the reckless gallop of the rondo winds up in an increasingly frenzied stamping before the goal. That of K.595 is more peaceful; it carries on the motion of the finale without intensifying it and keeps the note of good-humoured but slightly saddened sweetness which belongs to the whole work. Some of them violate the rule that a concerto should end with a sound of noisy triumph and fade away to *pianissimo*. Two of the violin concertos had finished thus. That of the C major piano concerto, K.415, seizes a little piece of the refrain which had already played a certain part, and this fragment, tossed between piano and orchestra and multiplied *ad infinitum*, sails through the whole coda like a flight of fairies in a darkening wood; everything dies out little by little till it alone survives as a mere shimmer and ends by losing itself in its turn in the dusk.[1]

The external form of the Mozartian concerto is, in its main lines, roughly the same from one work to the other. The succession: *sonata* allegro, *sonata* andante, rondo or variations finale, is seldom broken. But when one goes beneath the surface the variety is boundless. We have enumerated some of the changes of detail that the passage from one concerto to the next holds in store for us; our enumeration has seemed long to us and we were sometimes afraid of bewildering the reader; yet it covers but a small part of the transformations which rondo and *sonata* undergo. We shall not regret this bewilderment if it helps to correct the very false idea one has of Mozart's sameness, but we will stop and leave to the examination of each concerto the task of revealing other aspects of his infinite multiformity.

---

[1] To be complete, one should add that two concerto rondos, K.415 and 449, are quite irregular and follow no definite plan, and that K.357 is a two couplets rondo, a form which, like the two section *sonata*, leaves out the *development*.

3. General considerations on Mozart's piano concertos: Relations between piano and orchestra

IN the sorry midden of dead and buried concertos of the last century, there lie many which reduced the orchestra to being a mere backcloth against which stood out the lightning excursions, the "quips and cranks and wanton wiles", of the piano. In the 18th century one was still too close to the traditions of the *concerto grosso* for such a deformation to become the rule, but the school of John Christian Bach, at any rate, did not entertain a much more exalted idea of the orchestra's function. The disfavour into which polyphonic writing had fallen was accompanied by a general impoverishment of the style, betrayed in the concerto by an overweening preponderance of solo over tutti.

Mozart was one of the first to reconcile the fullness of the polyphonists with the new style. After a period during which he was only the pupil of John Christian he regained little by little the point from which the concerto had started, and placed solo and tutti face to face, not as monarch and courtiers, but as equally matched adversaries or collaborators. In a general way, his first nine concertos keep to the practice of John Christian whilst from the tenth onwards orchestra and piano fight with equal weapons, and the study of their relations, which is the subject of the present chapter, is full of interest.

One often reads that Beethoven was the first to "emancipate the orchestra" in the concerto. This has been contradicted more than once.[1] The study of each of Mozart's concertos will show again, we hope, that the older musician had already emancipated it. But he was not the first to do so since, without going back to John Sebastian, the orchestra is already as emancipated as it can be in some concertos of Philip Emmanuel. For the present, we shall limit ourselves to summing up the problems which Mozart, like all composers of

---

[1] E.g. by D. Tovey, *Essays in musical analysis*, III, 26.

concertos, had to face, and to sketching the general lines along which he solved them.

When an instrument breaks away from the mass of the orchestra and asserts its independence, either temporarily or, as in the concerto, for a whole work, it can take up several attitudes towards the others. In bad concertos, it sticks to one, the simplest and laziest: it attracts all notice to itself, drives into the shade the instruments which are playing at the same time and compels them to be content with accompanying. The polyphonic style of the earliest concerto composers had lent itself perfectly to diverse combinations of solo and tutti but the abandonment of polyphony led to a relative abandonment of these combinations and the orchestra took to subordinating itself to the solo.

Mozart's merit was that he reacted against this without, nevertheless, returning to polyphonic writing, and obtained thus once again the collaboration of solo and orchestra by using, not counterpoint, save occasionally, but the new symphonic style.

With him, as with all composers who have taken the concerto seriously, the relations of solo and tutti, of tutti and solo, are of three kinds. The tutti can submit to the solo and accompany it. The solo in its turn can submit to the whole or a part of the orchestra and accompany it. Both, finally, can be of equal importance and combine or converse without one lording it over the other or claiming a larger share than the other of the public's attention. It will be easier to study in detail the forms these relations take in Mozart when we come to each concerto in turn; we can, however, outline their general character here and now.

The natural state of a concerto, so to speak, is for the tutti to be subordinate to the solo. However much the orchestra "emancipates itself", the bars where the solo is to the fore are bound to be the most numerous. It is thus with Mozart as with John Sebastian and Philip Emmanuel Bach, as with Beethoven or Schumann or Liszt. In this respect Mozart's concertos are in no way remarkable. The role of the orchestra, even in his finest works, is often that of an accompanist. It accompanies, generally, by using the customary devices: sustained notes, repeated figures, rhythmical contrasts, arpeggios in contrary motion to that of the solo, chords containing the harmonies implied in the runs, rhythmical motifs opposed to *cantabile* themes: such are the commonest of the many shapes assumed by the orchestral accompaniment. None of these is peculiar to Mozart and there is no need to dwell on them. We will merely point out the presence, in half a dozen of his concertos of the "great" period, of thematic accompaniment, that is to say, of one which uses as its motif one of the main themes of the movement or a part of this theme. This device goes back to John Sebastian Bach who uses it often and to his sons Wilhelm Friedmann and Philip Emmanuel. Philip Emmanuel, especially, makes more of it than his father; in his magnificent D minor concerto,[1] he fills out a good part of the first movement with the opening subject, repeated and varied *ad infinitum* under the decorations of the piano.

Mozart has made less use of it. One can nevertheless quote several memorable examples in the concertos in D minor and A, K.488. Few moments are more exquisite than that when, in the finale of K.488, a passage of imitation is transformed by the simple action of the piano ceasing abruptly to answer and going off on its own, whilst the woodwind continue their calls which suddenly turn into a thematic accompaniment (ex. 1). The bars in the *development* of the D minor where, under the fiery piano arpeggios raining down on to the bass, there rumble in the depths the ominous triplets of the first subject, are of a kind which sum up a whole work in one lightning vision (ex. 245). Thematic accompaniments, used less dramatically, are found also in the concertos in C, K.467, C minor and D, K.537. In some cases, the accompaniment is not far from being as important as the solo itself. One can trace a regular evolution from the use of a theme as an accompanying motif to its complete development, with piano accompaniment, as in the allegro of the last concerto, an evolution whose stages are marked by the finale of K.415 and the first movements of K.467, 491 and 503.

---

[1] Wotquenne no. 23. After several others, may we put in a word for this neglected musician? Some forty of his fifty-three piano concertos have never been printed, even in his lifetime. Out of a hundred and fifty cembalo sonatas, only a hundred have been printed, several for the first time in our own day. There should be a critical edition of his best work, based on a complete examination of all that is known, which would omit the second-rate compositions and keep only the very numerous masterpieces. There should be, above all, instrumentalists willing to take advantage of what is already published, of the admirable piano concertos edited by Riemann at Steingräber's, especially those in D minor and C minor, great works in all respects and admirable for pianists who have only a chamber orchestra at their disposal. The study of these concertos cannot be recommended too warmly to all pianists who are not deaf to the art of the 18th century.

Ex. 3 (suite)

The tutti's accompaniment, without borrowing any definite theme, may owe a certain originality to its outline or to its orchestration. More numerous than examples of thematic accompaniment are those where the subordinate parts, without asserting themselves as much as the solo, free themselves completely from conventional forms and develop independently, almost outlining melodies. No need to quote passages; they abound in the concertos of 1785 and 1786. This setting free of the accompanying parts is common also in Philip Emmanuel; one finds it in the first movement of his D minor concerto, W.23. What could not be found before the growth of orchestration at the end of the century was the colour due to the diversity of timbres which characterizes Mozart's accompaniments. One thinks especially of the woodwind chords that sustain the fiery triplets of the piano in the andante of the D minor (G minor interlude; ex. 243), of the chords climbing and descending in contrary motion to the piano scales in the *development* of the allegro of the E flat, K.482, of the agitated jumps of the bassoon and of the flute and hautboy scales passing like an Ariadne's thread through the labyrinth of solo arpeggios, in the first movement of the G major (ex. 155).

The tables are sometimes turned and the situation becomes even more interesting. One has a malicious pleasure in seeing how submissive the once conquering instrument has become and how the orchestra wins back the rights lost on the entry of the solo. But one has also another pleasure, a more artistic one, in seeing the solo reduced to accompanying the tutti, because of the increase of colour thus produced. Condemn the piano to accompanying the orchestra and you take from it momentarily its personality; you oblige it to lose itself in the mass of instruments and you enrich thus the palette of tone colours.

Mozart saw this early. In his first concerto he sometimes gave the piano a back place. Those that followed it till 1782 were devoid of interesting relations between solo and orchestra, but after this date he renewed the practice and varied it cleverly.

The simplest way to subordinate the piano is to give it a commonplace accompaniment formula, such as an Alberti bass, broken chords in triplets, or ascending and descending arpeggios. There are instances of this in most of the concertos of the "great" period (1784–6). Mozart has a fondness for clarinet solos accompanied by the piano which will be shared by Beethoven and Schumann.

Piano accompaniment becomes more original when it avoids the beaten tracks. It is already more enterprising when it doubles the

melody given out by the orchestra. It seldom does this literally; it
prefers to play round it, embroidering it, repeating it in broken
octaves, treating it as a theme to be varied, but without moving far
from it, as in the two fine pedal passages in the finale of the G major
and the andante of the C major, K.503. The piano part, more brilliant in the first (ex. 173), differs less from that of the orchestra whose
chords it is content to reproduce without breaking them. Broader
and nobler in the C major, it consists in triplets spaced over two
octaves, rising and falling like a swell as the harmonies descend
majestically, one step at a time, to the unison which brings back the
main subject.

Without being subordinated one to the other, solo and orchestra
may collaborate.

We speak of collaboration, when the two adversaries play together
and both appeal with equal force to the attention of the listener. They
can do it in several ways.

In the repetition of a passage already heard in the opening tutti,
the piano can take hold of a part previously granted to an instrument
of the orchestra, and replace the instrument. Generally, it is a first
violin part that is thus appropriated. Mozart has made it do this in
his concertos K.449 and 450, after which the device is met with only
occasionally and for a few bars. This substitution of the solo for
an orchestral instrument causes a somewhat amusing surprise but it
is an effect that soon wears off.

A more fruitful device is that of descants, or counter-subjects.
Here, the theme is given out by the orchestra and the piano traces
above it an independent line. These counter-themes are very diverse.
Generally, they are melodic—a new melody being given above one
already known; but when, exceptionally, they fall to the orchestra,
they usually consist in scales. From K.451 onward after the solo's
first appearance, Mozart likes to take up again unchanged fairly long
passages from the opening section, adding to them a solo part which
unfolds freely above or amidst the voices of the orchestra. This free
counterpoint, this new personality mingling with the familiar ones
of the tutti, has the effect of suddenly broadening and moving back
the horizon of the work. From K.451 to 503, Mozart acts thus in
almost all his first movements, but never with more genius than at
the beginning and end of the series, in the D major concerto of
1784, K.451, and that in C, K.503, the *Jupiter* of the concertos,
of 1786.

The andantes, too, offer good examples of this practice. One of

the most felicitous is at the solo entry in the poignant slow movement of the E flat, K.271; the orchestra opens with a grave, rhythmical
subject, not very melodic; the piano enters and the orchestra gives
out its theme again, whilst the piano superposes a quite different one,
lyric and *cantabile*, which ends after a few bars of collaboration by
assuming supremacy and reducing the orchestral subject to silence.
It is a beginning in an archaic style that recalls the andantes of older
concertos (exs. 17 and 19). Another example occurs in the D major,
K.451; it is a regular descant; one tune is placed above another and
each one keeps its independence (ex. 2). Other instances come mostly
from the conclusions of andantes; the orchestra is speaking, but from
time to time the piano puts in a word, almost like an echo, and without
interrupting the orchestral song. The concertos in G, A (K.488), C
minor, C (K.503) and B flat (K.595), all have andantes which end
thus. Two of them afford also examples in their finales, K.453 and
488; in the first, the passage is repeated, solo and tutti wittily exchanging their parts; in the second, the solo which has just given out a
pert tune catches up a fragment of it and sports with it while the
orchestra repeats the theme itself (ex. 319).

There are also some examples of imitative counterpoint. That
in three parts, between flute, bassoon and piano, in the G major
concerto; that, also *a tre*, in the finale of the F, K.459, between piano,
violin and 'cello; that *a quattro* between the two hands of the piano,
the hautboy and the bassoon in the andante of this same work, belong
to 1784, the contrapuntal period in Mozart's life. Let us note also
the exquisite moment just after the reprise in the allegro of the E flat,
K.482, where, over the Alberti bass of the second fiddles and the piano
chords, first fiddles and right hand mingle and imitate in lines of free
counterpoint, flowing and gracefully canonic.

Twice, in the first movement of the concerto in D, K.451, and the
finale of the D minor, we find another form of free counterpoint.
The material is here, in each case, one of the themes of the movement,
cut in two and shared between piano and woodwind, one half to
each. The finale of the D minor prolongs for some time this lively
situation and a little episode derives from it. This device does not
occur again and it seems to have been the result of a passing fancy of
the composer's, for we find it in the minuet of the A major quartet,
written a month earlier than this concerto.

Mozart, whose growth, contrary to what has so often been said,
never came to a stop, and who was developing strongly at the time
of his death, foresaw a still more fruitful use of the solo to which this

last practice could lead. The piano has dared to add itself to an already familiar orchestral passage; it will go further; it will mingle its embroideries and bedizenments with episodes entrusted exclusively to the orchestra. In the middle part of the allegros of K.488, 503 and 595, the tutti returns to familiar subjects,[1] repeats them, varies them, plays with them, develops them, in short, then brings them back gradually to the recapitulation, whilst the piano spreads itself in arpeggios, scales, *fioriture* of all sorts, independently of the work of the other instruments. The most remarkable of these three *developments* is that of the last concerto, a work which, despite its modest size, reveals unfamiliar and interesting aspects of its composer. It is a *development* which Hermann Abert calls Beethovenian, but which it is not at all helpful to label thus, for no comparable example exists in Beethoven's concertos and this one is a very authentic possession of Mozart's.

À distinction must be made between collaboration and dialogue. It is not an idle one. In collaboration, piano and orchestra combine simultaneously; in dialogue, they do it alternately. It has seemed clearest to us to keep the two separate, especially as the second occurs much more often than the first.

The varieties of dialogue are more numerous and more diverse than those of collaboration. The orchestral link, the echo, the answer, phrases that alternate between solo and tutti, imitation: all these devices are found in most of the concertos after 1780.

The most frequent and most commonplace form of dialogue is the orchestral link. It is a little phrase or fragment of phrase interposed between two solos, which both separates and links them, and fulfils, most often, a purely formal function. It is a punctuation mark, warning us that one passage is over and another about to begin. The dialogue principle exists in it in only a rudimentary state; it is the "Yes, madam," the "No, sir" of the super. But it happens now and again that these apparently inoffensive little phrases acquire a psychological import and an emotional as well as a formal value. They then become short, incisive commentaries on the piano's doings and their effect is often that of a witty and mocking interruption. At such moments, they are not far from being echoes, and it is

---

[1] In K.488, the theme had been given out for the first time at the beginning of the *development*.

indeed towards the echo, a device of which Mozart is very fond, that the link tends. In its simplest form, the echoing instrument repeats unchanged the end of the previous phrase. It matters little whether it be a member of the orchestra which echoes the solo or vice versa; in point of fact, the first is the more frequent. Most often, the echo answers by transposing the phrase, sometimes a third lower, more often a second, a fourth or a sixth higher; more seldom it modifies the fragment, but without transposing it. It is naturally the wind rather than the strings that make echo.

Pretty examples of echoes are fairly abundant in all the concertos. We will quote three. One of the simplest and most poetic is in the G major where the piano reproduces the last three notes of the theme without changing them or altering their value (ex. 3). Another is drawn from the finale of the C major, K.415; here, the echo is entrusted to the hautboy and the bassoon which repeat the same notes but augment them (ex. 4). The andantino of the E flat, K.271, uses the echo with more dramatic effect in the moving dialogue between piano and first violins towards the end of the movement. Here, the echo is in the form of a canon, but the academic character of the form does not detract from the emotional power of the passage (ex. 5).

In these three examples as well as in some ten more, the echo repeats the fragment without change. On other occasions, more numerous, it differs from it and gives the impression of an echo without really being one. Thus, in the first movement of the concerto for two pianos, it has the brevity of the echo and keeps fairly close to the outline of the phrase which it answers; the hautboy plaint, in spirit if not literally, is an echo of the second piano's sinuous line (ex. 23). The very varied accompaniment in the andante of the C major, K.467, fulfils at times the function of the echo (ex. 270) and repeats in a simplified shape the piano's more ornate lamentations. But usually the relation of this half-echo with what precedes it is that of an answer with a question, and it completes it or comments on it, rather than repeats it. Such is the case in the biting or pensive calls made by the woodwind in the first subjects of the G and B flat concertos, K.453 and 595, and in the little flutterings of the flute in the middle of the second subject in K.451 (ex. 6). Sometimes the answer goes as far as completing the meaning of the phrase; it then takes on frequently the form of piano arpeggios that finish off the orchestral theme. Finally, it may end by constituting a true phrase of its own, subordinate but distinct, as in the first movement of the E flat, K.449

(ex. 7) and the andante of the G major (ex. 8), but that is an uncommon use of the answer.

In all these forms of dialogue the game is unequal; the echo, answer, link are bound to be less important than the themes which precede and follow them. The dialogue is better distributed when the adversaries share a phrase of which each one takes a member. The phrase is usually given out only once; less often it is repeated twice or thrice, either unchanged or transposed. On two occasions, it is not only repeated but also developed, and in the finale of K.415 this development, shared between piano and tutti, provides an episode of exceptional beauty.

The different members of what appears at first to make up a single phrase may turn out to be so distinct and so well characterized that it is fairer to consider them as so many separate phrases, some belonging to the orchestra, others to the solo. This is a form of dialogue by alternate phrases, a less common form with Mozart than the preceding.

The phrases here are generally short and nearly always go in pairs; the coda of the finale in the E flat concerto, K.449, offers an example of phrases alternating in groups of three. Sometimes, they are alike and make up a symmetrical whole; sometimes, the solo is a scale or arpeggio passage. In several cases, nevertheless, all of them to be found in *developments*,[1] it is regular sections, and not just phrases, that alternate and answer each other. By alternating, the phrases can be modified, but here diversity is too great for one to generalize.

Finally, it is sometimes the same phrase which is repeated from one instrument to the other, unchanged or modified. Examples of this device which lends itself less to elaboration than the former, are not numerous. There is a masterly instance of it in the concerto in C, K.467 (*development* couplet of the finale, ex. 272).

To be complete one should add that imitation, of which we have already spoken, instead of being simultaneous, alternates sometimes between one part and the other and assumes the aspect of a canon; it then becomes "dialogue" rather than "collaboration". The finale of the G major shows an example of this; that of the D minor has a more remarkable one, where piano, flute and hautboy send back from one to the other the different fragments of a phrase taken from the preceding couplet.

It is hardly necessary to add that the distinctions we have made, not only between sundry forms of dialogue but also between dialogue and collaboration, between collaboration and accompaniment, are not rigid and exist only for the needs of clarity. Many passages can be classed in more than one of these divisions; we have adopted them only to show more easily what diversity of genius exists, in these concertos, in the relations between orchestra and solo.

The concerto's problem is to combine solo and orchestra without, on the one hand, the orchestra being treated as a simple accompanist, or, on the other, the solo losing its personality by blending too intimately with the mass of instruments. Balance of the two forces, struggle without triumph, collaboration without blending: such is the ideal of every concerto worthy of the name.

This intercourse between solo and orchestra, the modalities of which we have been studying in Mozart, is the soul of the concerto.

---

[1] First movements of K.466, 488 and 491, and finale of K.450.

Melodic ideas, modulations, development, poetic value: all this is common to it with other genres; what characterizes it is the struggle between two adversaries of equal strength. Progress for a concerto consists therefore in rendering more and more complex the relations between solo and tutti, in bringing the protagonists closer and closer together without ever uniting them or crushing one to the advantage of the other. This progress, of course, remains subordinated to the value of the content. It is clear that a concerto where this essential element is present but whose thought is mediocre will be less precious than one where the orchestral part is only an accompaniment, but where the thought is interesting.

When one goes through Mozart's twenty-three piano concertos in chronological order, one finds a progress in complexity and intimacy of relation between piano and orchestra. But this progress is not constant. It includes halts and even sometimes retrogression. Moreover, it does not correspond precisely to the no less unmistakable progress in significance and depth. To say that complexity of intercourse goes hand in hand with a heightening of musical significance would satisfy a tidy mind but it would be only partly true.

'Let us go quickly over the concertos considered from this double standpoint. The passages which are interesting for solo and tutti interplay are infrequent in the first nine (1773-82). Before 1784, Mozart does not tackle the fundamental problem which he resolves later on. But, though no work of these years is really *concertante*, two of them, the first in D, K.175, and the fifth in E flat, K.271, rise above the gentle heights of *galant* music and answer to an inner experience. Here, thought is ahead of technique.

From the tenth concerto to the twenty-first, K.449 to 503, there is, on the other hand, a marked though irregular growth. The first one of the great Viennese series, K.449, in E flat, a work of moderate size, has a finale which is rich in complex relations between solo and orchestra, whereas K.450, in B flat, of more ambitious dimensions and more brilliant virtuosity, tends to return to the level of the *galant* concertos and loses the ground gained with K.449. The distance is caught up with K.451, in D; the work is even more flashing than K.450 and its psychological import is greater; at the same time, the protagonists interplay elaborately. The gain is kept up with the G major, K.453; the thought is more intimate and more personal; the relations are as close in the first two movements as in K.451, and much more in the finale, which was rather poor in the D major. These early 1784 concertos form a group and the G major marks a stage in Mozart's progress. With it, musical import and richness of interplay reach similar points in their development.

The next four concertos also form a group, but merely a chronological one. They belong to the musical season of the winter of 1784–5 and spread out from September to March. In character they are not homogeneous; the first two go with those of 1784; the other two are akin to those that follow.

K.456, in B flat, is more intimate in character than K.450, 451 or even 453. Its lyrical tone makes it almost a chamber concerto. But this intimacy does not exclude depth and it turns to tragedy in the andante variations. It is less varied than the G major but quite as poetic. Technique, on the other hand, loses a little ground in it; piano and tutti intercourse is less sustained and the orchestra is ready to stand down before the solo instrument. But with K.459, in F, the complexity of the relations between the two again progresses; the interplay is, indeed, more continuous here than it will ever be again. The piano often plays a subordinate part; the orchestra, especially in the grand *fugati* of the finale, has a part of great richness, and one has at times the impression that one is listening to an orchestral concerto with piano accompaniment. On the other hand, the inspiration is on a lower plane than in the three preceding concertos; the first and third movements express a mainly physical vigour and high spirits; and it is the only concerto not to have a slow movement; a 6-8 allegretto takes its place. Mozart has not reached here the balance of the G major, which united richness of interplay and depth of feeling.

The immense psychological progress accomplished by the celebrated D minor, K.466, a work of a very different climate from the first fifteen concertos, does not restore equality. But here, the complexity of combination is sacrificed; carried away towards the new world of emotion he has discovered, Mozart has ceased for the time being to take interest in it. The examples of interplay that survive, however, are more original than in earlier concertos. The emotional value of K.467, in C, the antithesis of the D minor, is no less, and technique begins to catch up again. Moreover, in these two masterpieces the combinations of piano and orchestra, which had been hitherto of mainly formal interest, acquire dramatic value.[1]

The four concertos of the winter of 1785–6 are also masterpieces. In inspiration they are all on the same level as K.466 and 467, but

---

[1] This was already so in the andante of K.271 and, still more, in that of K.453.

their personalities are most diverse. The E flat is as graceful and majestic as a queen; the A, "innig" and prone to sadness; the C minor, elegiac and, at moments, tragic; and the C major, Olympian. The technical advance is kept up. The moments of interplay are not numerous in the E flat but they are the most beautiful in the work; the coda of the andante shows at its highest point the art with which Mozart can express the dramatic nature of his genius in a symphonic form. The A major, among the concertos of this year, corresponds to the B flat, K.456, among those of 1784; its feeling is nevertheless deeper and its interplay of piano and tutti as exquisite as in K.482. Finally, the last two of this series of twelve regain the balance broken since the G major; here, on the plane of the greatest masterpieces, there reigns absolute equality and unity between the interplay of the protagonists and the spiritual value of the music. The C minor and C major, K.491 and 503, are on all accounts the highest peaks in Mozart's concertos.

With them finishes the development we are sketching. Eighteen months later, Mozart wrote the concerto in D, the so-called *Coronation*, K.537, but, despite its size, the work is poor in both respects. As for the B flat, K.595, of 1791, it might perhaps have opened a new period if death had not cut off the young composer eleven months later; in this last work for piano and orchestra, the same problems are again tackled, and solved in partly new ways, whilst the emotion is as earnest as in the great concertos of 1785 and 1786.

PART II

PART II

1. The Salzburg Concertos: K.175 in D; 238 in B flat; 242 in F (for three pianos); 246 in C; 271 in E flat; 365 in E flat (for two pianos)

IT is always with a certain reverence that one approaches the work of art which, not itself a masterpiece, is at the head of a series of masterpieces. Beethoven's first quartet, Wagner's first opera, Shakespeare's earliest tragedy may or may not have little value in themselves; their position at the entrance of a road along which stand great works is enough to make them venerable in our eyes. It is with a feeling of reverence, likewise, that we undertake the study of Mozart's earliest concertos. They are slight in comparison with those that follow; they are nevertheless their elders and, if only for that reason, they are entitled to our respect.

But it happens that Mozart's earliest concertos, and especially the first one of all, have no need of their seniority to interest us. They have a charm of their own and he who is willing to linger by their limpid waters and gaze at their beauties with an affectionate and searching eye will be well enough rewarded by the joys of the task, without needing to be heartened by the distant view of the grander concertos that are to come.

One cannot deny, however, that modern hearers need a certain good will—we would almost say, a certain training—to enjoy gems of so small a magnitude. Successive schools of music for the last century and a half have so well blunted our sensibility by the growing complexity of their productions that we easily pass these merits by without heeding them. And this is true, indeed, of all Mozart, if not of all older music. Mozart seems to-day to be the most discreet of the great masters.[1] He never forces his entry into our midst. He

---

[1] We say to-day, because the epithets of "Stormer and caresser" (*Stürmer und Schmeichler*), which were applied to him in his life-time, prove that some of his contemporaries held a different opinion.

comes without noise or show. If we will have him, well and good;
if we ignore him, he will not thump the table, he will not raise his
voice. He is reserve itself. His intimate meaning escapes us most
easily. He allows us to penetrate him less readily than Beethoven
and one remembers how Schumann saw in his G minor symphony
only "that hovering Hellenic Grace" (*diese schwebende griechische
Grazie*), perceiving, that is, in that work of passion, merely qualities
of form. One almost regrets his exquisite plastic loveliness when
one hears him reduced to the level of just a graceful composer,
a pure stylist, and when so many ignore the life that pulsates in
his music.

The fact is that the delight given us by his perfect form is such
that we are tempted not to ask anything more of him. The casket
is so fair that we are content to look on it without opening it. We
recognize in him an admirable goldsmith; we overlook the thinker
(in the sense in which this word can be applied to a composer).
We even sometimes reproach him with lacking a soul; his music
comes from his head; it is superficial; the words of the reproach vary
with the critic but in all cases the complaint is that he wants warmth
and emotion.

When one hears such statements, one's first idea is that, of all
his works, the speaker knows only the too well-known sonatas.
Now, whilst one renders full homage to the delicate taste and feeling
of these torments of one's childhood and whilst granting readily
that some half-dozen of them will bear comparison with his best
compositions, it must be admitted that their average level is below
that of all his other works except his trios and his lieder. Abert has
very judiciously divided his output into three parts: what he wrote
for his public; what he wrote partly for his public and partly for
himself; what he wrote wholly for himself. Five-sixths of the sonatas
belong to the first category; they show his most impersonal side. His
reputation has suffered from his music being best known by its
weakest part; it is as if one judged Shakespeare on *Titus Andronicus*
and *Timon of Athens* and started from these plays to express a comprehensive judgement on him.

Yet even in his greatest works Mozart is never emphatic. He
never dwells on his thought, and the swift and shimmering succession
of emotions through his music runs the risk of slipping by without
imprinting itself on his listeners' minds. On knowing him, one
catches his least beauties as they fly past, enjoying them, but ears
too exclusively accustomed to the Romantics perceive in him little

that deserves to attract notice and inspire admiration. For that reason we say that he is one of the hardest composers to understand.

In 1773, young Wolfgang is back in Salzburg. For the third and last time he has left Italy, having composed there, for the stage of Bologna, *Lucio Silla*, the last opera he is to write for an Italian audience. He is crossing the threshold of adolescence and entering his eighteenth year and the passions which, in the operas of his childhood, *Mitridate*, *La Finta Semplice*, *Ascanio in Alba*, he so often depicted imitatively and from hearsay, as it were, now graze his youthful soul. Precocious in musical intelligence, in every other respect he has remained a child and he awakens to the life of the passions no sooner than less abnormally gifted men do. At seventeen, the composer of quartets, symphonies and operas is still little more than a boy, over whom passes for the first time a breath of Romanticism.

The awakening of his sensibility causes individual strains of hitherto unknown intensity to resound in his works. It is after his last stay in Italy that he begins to be himself. Before that journey, one could point out indications and promises of personality; from then on, one finds whole works that belong entirely to him. In a sense, he was to remain imitative for a long time to come; but the imitation was henceforward to be different and take the form of assimilation instead of copy. Before 1772, his work has a documentary interest; the quartets of this year[1] are his first compositions to enjoy a life of their own and to deserve survival in virtue of their beauty. It is significant of the importance of the piano concerto in his life that his first attempt in this genre should date from this very period.

The fine, youthful ardour of these works of 1772 and early 1773 dies down in the routine-laden atmosphere of Salzburg, with the return to the small town after the stay in the greater world outside, a depressing experience which everyone knows and from which we suffer more or less according to the strength of our ambitions and aspirations, according also to the ease with which we accept the domination of our surroundings. We cannot be certain that Mozart experienced, on his return to Salzburg, the impression of collapse which seizes us when drab reality succeeds the enthusiasm of illusions; but it is likely that he felt already what he was to feel in 1778, on another return home.

---

[1] K.155 to 160, and perhaps Köchel-Einstein *Anhang*, nos. 210-213.

Salzburg, with its circumscribed life, dominated, musically, by the narrow taste of Archbishop Colloredo, was a prison for him. He put up with it as best he could since he had to, but already at seventeen his genius, perhaps unwittingly, was compressed in it, and the five years that separate his return from Italy from his departure for Paris are characterized by an impoverishment in the quality of his music.

If there is a tradition more popular than any other and slower to die, it is that of a dapper, powdered, beribboned and bewigged Mozart, the darling of the court and drawing-rooms of Vienna and expressing in his music nothing more than the superficial elegance and frivolity of 18th-century aristocratic life. This is the Mozart of minuets and contredanses, charming, no doubt, but bloodless, empty, incapable of serious thought and feeling. Mozart's work, it is said—and one adds: Haydn's, for Haydn has suffered the same injustice—breathes the scent of the salons and boudoirs of the Ancien Régime . . . and little else.

It is needless to say that such a tradition could arise only at a period as prejudiced against "Classical" art as the first half of the 19th century. Appearing at the time when the gigantic shadow of Beethoven was throwing darkness over what had gone before, it maintained itself largely because of the public's knowledge of his sonatas and relative ignorance of his masterpieces.

The period concerning which this traditional opinion, happily fast dying out, is least unjust is that which extends from his return in 1773 to his departure for Mannheim and Paris in 1777. During these four years, Mozart is no more than the musical purveyor of pleasures to His Grace the Prince-Archbishop of Salzburg. Succumbing to the debilitating air of his town, he endeavours to refine his style, but, save in a few adagios, under the graceful exterior he utters only commonplace thoughts.

Before yielding, however, to the lethargy of these four years, he knew an instant of wonderful creativeness. In March, 1773, he came back to Salzburg. He left again four months later and his summer was spent in Vienna, his final return taking place in the early days of October. Now, although the romanticism of his stay in Italy had quickly worn off in contact with Salzburg, the two months in Vienna brought new fuel to his energy and stimulated it with new influences. If the six quartets he composed there in August and September[1] no longer shine with the same flame as those he had written in Italy,

---

[1] K.168 to 173.

they bear witness to a serious conception of the genre and to an elaboration which would make them worthy of their predecessors, were it not that a certain awkwardness and the newness of the style sometimes hinder the inspiration. The curiosity and desire to explore and break new ground which mark them were to resist for some time the influence of Salzburg; they survive in the first piano concerto and traces of them persist in the bassoon concerto written in July of the following year.

Mozart's first concerto for a solo instrument and orchestra[1] dates from December of this year and is written for the harpsichord.[2] The young musician's interest in the genre goes back a long way. Not only is his first concerto composed for a keyboard instrument but the first evidence we have of the little man's musical activities concern a harpsichord concerto which he was writing in 1760, with manifold blots of ink, at the age of four. An old friend of the family, the trumpeter Schachtner, records the following dialogue:

> *Papa:* What are you doing?
> *Wolfgang:* A harpsichord concerto; the first part is nearly done.
> *Papa:* Let me see.
> *Wolfgang:* It isn't done yet.
> *Papa:* Let me see; it must be something wonderful!

Schachtner goes on:

> His father took it and showed me a scribble of notes, most of it written over blots which had been rubbed out. Little Wolfgang, out of ignorance, had dipped his pen to the bottom of the inkwell; the result was a blot, but he at once took his decision, passed the back of his hand over it, smeared it over, and started merrily writing again. We laughed at first at what seemed to be just nonsense, but the father then gave heed to the important part, the notes and composition, and he remained for a long time motionless with his attention fixed on the sheet. Finally he let fall some tears—tears of admiration and joy. "See, Herr Schachtner," he said, "how correct and regular everything is; only it isn't playable; it's so terribly hard that no one could perform it." "That's just why it's a concerto," interrupted little Wolfgang; "one must practise it until one succeeds, you see; it should go like this." And he set about playing, but he could only just manage to show us what he was driving at. He had already the grasp of the concerto form.

We no longer possess this springtide sketch of the genre wherein his genius was to bear its finest fruit but there remain several

---

[1] The *concertone* in C for two violins, K.191, is a divertimento rather than a true concerto.

[2] The manuscript, now lost, bore the title: *Concerto per il Clavicembalo.*

adaptations as concertos of sonatas by sundry contemporary harpsichord writers; first, three by John Christian Bach;[1] then, later, movements drawn from works of Schobert, Eckardt, Raupach, Philip Emmanuel Bach and Honauer[2] grouped so as to form concertos, with tuttis inserted in the usual places. These arrangements passed for a long time as original works; MM. de Wyzewa and de Saint-Foix and Dr. Alfred Einstein have restored them to their real authors. They were no doubt exercises undertaken under his father's supervision.

CONCERTO No. 1 IN D MAJOR FOR HARPSICHORD AND ORCHESTRA (K.175) December, 1773[3]
    Allegro: C
    Andante ma un poco adagio: 3-4 (in G)
    Allegro: ¢
Orchestra: Strings; two hautboys, two horns, two trumpets, two drums.

This little concerto is full of a vitality that we shall not find again for some years in Mozart's work. It is a final personal outburst before the slumber of the years of *galant* music. Its character is marked enough to distinguish it from all other works of his; that is saying a lot and would not be true of its immediate successors. Its originality would still suffice to earn it a public performance and makes it capable of delighting the pianist who plays it in the intimacy of his home. It is enlivening rather than joyful, very physical, robust and muscular, rather knockabout, without any of the melancholy which pierces through the music of Mozart's Vienna years. No hidden depths, none of the shady and enigmatic nooks which, in later works, charm us and set us dreaming. Its frankness and openness,[4] its athletic vigour, win at once our sympathy; we love this busy and spritely little being as one loves a jovial and easy-going companion; it reveals a side of its creator that we do not often see and we are grateful to it for doing so. It is the counterpart of the Beotian Mozart, the Hanswurst of his letters.

Its brio does not prevent it from taking itself very seriously. The orchestra it opposes to the harpsichord is an ambitious one; no other

---

[1] K.107. [2] K.37, 39, 40, 41.

[3] No. 5 in the *Gesamtausgabe*.

[4] "Aperto" is an indication that Mozart has written at the beginning of several pre-Viennese works, for instance, the flute concerto in D, K.314, the manner of which recalls, with more delicacy, that of this concerto.

concerto of Mozart's before 1782 uses one as large and so many instruments do not become habitual till 1784. As in the classical symphony,[1] the whole nature of the work is indicated by the first theme (ex. 9), a long, wiry, sparkling phrase, given out in three periods and continuing into a little development filled with the same spirit, bounding and skipping in turn. The movement it introduces is, likewise, rather unmelodic; even the second subject is mainly rhythmic and the harpsichord's Alberti basses emphasize the character of a bustling little person, greatly concerned about nothing in particular, which is that of the whole allegro.

The interest lies mainly in the rhythms. Not many works of Mozart, even in his "great" period, have such varied ones. The first

subject affords three, and its codetta introduces a fourth. The second subject in *galant* works is frequently in contrast with the first; a rhythmical and pompous theme is followed by one singing and tender. But here, the difference is not strongly marked. After the harmless tumult of the opening, the pace slackens a little, and nearly two piano bars of tremolo octaves allow us to take breath. The next subject is calmer and more tuneful than its predecessor, but it is not the *cantabile* that John Christian would have given us here and it shows as original a set of rhythms as the first.

It soon lets itself go into *forte*, with amusing alternations of *piano*, and closes the tutti introduction with a last display of fireworks, whose rhythmical outline is still more personal. It quite cuts across the four-beat rhythm of the movement.

The piano in nowise protests against the example of agitation which the tutti has set and, in its turn, reviews the themes we have just heard, with their dazzling richness of rhythm, expanding them a little but without adding anything new. The orchestra does not let it speak with as much docility as in the next few concertos; it cuts in from time to time to resume leadership, notably towards the end of the exposition when a dominant trill lets us think the harpsichord is tired and about to be silent. It is amusing to see the solo interrupt

---

[1] Except, of course, when a slow introduction precedes them; this, on the contrary, generally contrasts with what follows.

at once, repeating the very phrase the tutti had begun, then be interrupted itself, and finally regain mastery until it has finished its job and rests awhile to let the band conclude the exposition.

The tumult dies down somewhat in the *development* and the harpsichord starts a theme in the minor, the only sentimental passage in the movement; it ceases quickly, however, and the semi-quavers revive the bustle.

The andante belongs to those we called "dreams". It is as individual as the first movement and Mozart's personality, which will be somewhat overlaid by that of his age in the succeeding concertos, still stands out with vigour. It is a *sonata* in three sections whose *development* is but a short transition with an accompaniment characterized by an enchanting murmur of violins and violas. It opens and finishes on a note of languor, but between-whiles the range of feeling is fairly wide; a spritely phrase with dotted quaver rhythm, in particular, contrasts with the softness of the opening and closing themes. The movement is a first expression of the mood which is to inspire the andante of the A major concerto, K.414. Throughout a composer's work, we meet with diverse embodiments of the same thought, reappearances of the same theme transformed, and expressions of the same mood.

The finale is one of the most original in all his concertos. Not the most beautiful, not the deepest, but one of the most original, if only for its form, a *sonata* shot with polyphony, a first sketch of the finales of the G major quartet, the F major concerto, K.459, and the *Jupiter* symphony.[1] Its character is that of the opening allegro: bustle, incessant and aimless restlessness, the frisking of a little dog glad to be taken out for a walk. Its themes are more melodic than those of the first movement, and more numerous; in the thirty-nine bars of the first tutti alone there are four; the first one, a canon; the second, a syncopated figure that recalls one in the finale of the G major quartet; the third, tuneful and light, which resembles another subject in the same movement; and the fourth, a rhythmical concluding theme, given out by violas and basses in unison beneath the repeated semi-quavers of the fiddles.

Polyphony, which had been present at the opening, returns with the harpsichord entry. The canon starts over again and the solo adds a pleasing line of ornament which, from one hand to the other,

---

[1] Sonata form finales occur also, according to Engels, in concertos of J. F. Lang (1724-?94) and Al. Förster (1748-1823).

varies the theme of the strings. Whimsically, the game stops all of a sudden and a dialogue passage follows, the tutti appearing to want to begin the canon again, the harpsichord interrupting with arpeggios and introducing a fresh subject. The tutti's two other subjects follow; the solo forges ahead with a bravura passage and the orchestra winds up the exposition with the rhythmical concluding theme.

The *development* is the least interesting section. At first, the solo dominates it completely; then, after a few new exploits, it makes way for the orchestra which brings back the canonic subject, and the recapitulation opens, almost unchanged. The most remarkable part of the ending is the passage which leads to the cadenza; generally, this is a pompous succession of chords; here, it is a canon opening in four parts, one last contrapuntal sally which stops as soon as everyone is present. The cadenza follows, then the rhythmical subject already heard at the end of the two expositions.[1]

The vigorous tone, abundance of ideas and touches of counterpoint of this movement are found also in the finale of the contemporary string quintet in B flat, K.174.

Mozart kept long a warm spot in his heart for this little work. During his travels in 1777 and 1778, he played it in an *Akademie* which his friends the Cannabichs gave at Mannheim; he wrote to his father: "This concerto is much liked." He took it up again in Vienna in 1782 and 1783 and composed a new finale for it, a series of insipid variations which are a very poor substitute for the beautiful original *sonata*.[2] Provided with this unfortunate last movement, it was played at an *Akademie* in March, 1783, and Mozart, in a letter to his father, called it "the favourite concerto".[3]

CONCERTO NO. 2 IN B FLAT MAJOR (K.238)
January, 1776.[4]
    Allegro aperto: C
    (Andante un poco adagio): 3-4 (in E flat)
    Rondeau: Allegro C
Orchestra: Strings; two hautboys (two flutes in the andante), two horns.

---

[1] When Mozart returned to this concerto in Vienna in 1782, he wrote a cadenza for each of the first two movements (K.624, I, II; facsimile publication by Mandyczewski). The andante cadenza is particularly attractive.

[2] K.382.

[3] It was with this new finale that it was published by Boyer in Paris in 1784; the original finale was published only much later.

[4] No. 6 in the *Gesamtausgabe*.

CONCERTO No. 3 IN F MAJOR FOR THREE PIANOS (K.242)
February, 1776[1]
> Allegro: C
> Adagio: C (in B flat)
> Rondeau: Tempo di minuetto: 3-4
Orchestra: Strings; two hautboys, two horns

CONCERTO No. 4 IN C MAJOR (K.246)
April, 1776[2]
> Allegro aperto: C
> Andante: 2-4 (F major)
> Rondeau: Tempo di minuetto: 3-4
Orchestra: Strings, two hautboys, two horns

The three concertos that follow form a homogeneous group. They were written in the space of three months; two years separate them from the first concerto and nine months from the fifth. They represent a "manner" of Mozart's, the *galant* manner of his twentieth year, and if, for that reason, they no longer have for us much intrinsic value, they are still of biographical interest.

The years 1774 and 1775 had gone by without any great event in his life. At the close of 1774, Munich had ordered an *opera buffa* and father and son had stayed in that town early in the new year to supervise the rehearsals. The opera, *La Finta Giardiniera*, had come on in February; it met at first with some success but did not last for more than three performances and all hopes of a settlement at the court of the Elector vanished.

It is during the four years between his return from Italy in 1773 and his departure for Mannheim and Paris in 1777 that Mozart bowed most resolutely to the ideal of the age and made his most determined efforts to assimilate the style of *galanterie* and submit his own expression to the taste of his aristocratic public. He repressed the fire of his Italian works; he refined the native rudeness of his style, which was still apparent in the abrupt rhythms of his D major concerto; he silenced emotions the utterance of which would have surprised or shocked his hearers, and he confined himself to expressing feelings politely commonplace in a form graceful and smooth. The works of this period are as numerous as usual; they comprise the Munich opera, a pastoral drama, *Il Ré Pastore*, masses, motets, litanies, serenades

---

[1] No. 7 in the *Gesamtausgabe*.
[2] No. 8 in the *Gesamtausgabe*.

and divertimenti, only three symphonies,[1] and finally two well-known groups: the early piano sonatas and the five violin concertos.

The sonatas represent this period at its lowest; there is nothing more mediocre in his whole output, in spite of a few good movements like the andante of the F major, K.280, and it is really a pity that such uncharacteristic works should be so well-known. The violin concertos are better, at least those that are usually played, in G, D and A, but they are far from reaching the level of the great piano ones and it is for non-musical reasons that they are more often performed than these. They fully deserve their survival, however, and on the whole they are the best things that Mozart produced before his journey to Paris.

The violin concertos date from his twentieth year; he was turned twenty when he composed the three concertos we are about to consider. By this time his change of style is complete; no greater contrast can be imagined than that between them and the concerto in D. The fine unity of this work has gone; sentiment has replaced emotion; the themes are separated (or connected), not by significant workings-out but by amiable virtuosity passages; the recurrent motifs that give a movement its unity are lacking. The recapitulations are even less varied than in the first concerto; one single rhythm, established at the opening, is kept up to the end, and it is a commonplace one; the little galant *rondo*, which had been ousted by the grand contrapuntal finale of K.175, reappears for good and banishes in its turn the last traces of polyphony. These three concertos make us realize better the bold originality of the first,

> wherein were expressed the fairest dreams of his youth, a joyful assault on life, mingled with a graceful tenderness verging on melancholy.[2]

The transition is fairly well marked in the bassoon concerto of 1774. The tone is already that of *galanterie*; virtuosity has spread; the rhythm is smooth; the *rondo alla menuetto* has taken possession of the finale; but certain witty rejoinders between solo and tutti in the *development* of the first movement recall the living whirlwind of 1773 of which they are a last eddy.

It is therefore with some disappointment that we come to these concertos. Yet they are not without charm. The balance is perfect

---

[1] Abert thinks that the excessively "modern" character of one of them, K.183, in G minor, had displeased the archbishop.

[2] Abert, op. cit., I, 393.

between form and matter. The substance is commonplace but the style is neat and, except in the finale of the F major, one does not meet with those empty passages so common in the sonatas. Without standing out as clearly as the first, each one has its own *nuance*; the B flat, more tender, the F, more playful, the C, more dapper. They deserve that we should linger by them for a few moments.

No. 2 in B flat. For depth, there is nothing to choose between these three little works, but in none of the three is the deportment quite the same. This one is the most distinguished of them. More than any other work of Mozart it represents the ideal of the 18th-century gentleman. It is a thing of good taste; the feelings to which it gives utterance could be expressed in the most fastidious drawing-room. At the same time, it is witty and bright and keeps a certain individuality. What is lacking is strong and concentrated emotion, but that was lacking in the very milieu for which it was written. It touches on many subjects and goes deeply into none. This is the ideal of *galant* music; it is the ideal of Mozart's own music during these years and particularly of these concertos, but it is attained in a peculiarly felicitous manner in this one.

The first subject is smooth, amiable and harmless (ex. 10); it has none of the rhythmical audacities of K.175; it replaces them by the alternatives of *piano* and *forte* beloved of all *galant* music and much beloved of Mozart who, later on, made serious use of them, treating them no longer as mere condiments but as a means of expressing deeper feelings. The phrase, like so many of his, unfolds in three sections. A passage in rising thirds follows it and reaches the dominant close which marks the halt before the second subject. This latter, quite Mozartian, is the only distinctive part of the tutti. It is a soft rustle of syncopations, *piano*, like echoing sighs, from first to second violins over held notes of violas and 'cellos. A more commonplace phrase succeeds it, again shifting from loud to soft, then the concluding subject, a mere figure. The solo takes up the first subject, passes to the dominant and inserts a theme of its own, the solo subject which John Christian had been the first to use systematically. All this is graceful and melodic. The strings give out the second subject, but *forte*; the piano takes it from them before they have finished and after two bars strings and solo conclude it in a very charming working-out passage, almost the only one in the concerto, where the rhythms criss-cross with gentle shimmering (ex. 11). This is linked up with the *development* by means of a rising passage which, in the opening tutti, had followed the first subject and of another passage which had separated the second subject from the conclusion; the loose construction allows the composer to assemble, undo and reassemble at will the different elements with which, like a puzzle, he builds up his work. This rearranging of themes and passages is destined later to gain in significance as the cohesion and unity of the whole asserts itself.

Save, perhaps, for the exquisite murmur of the second subject, nothing up to now could not have been signed John Christian. The *development* gives us a glimpse of the true Mozart. In a general way, however important a work of his may be, however commonplace, Mozart keeps back a few personal strains or modulations for his *developments*, especially for just before the reprise. This is so in a number of the *galant* pieces he wrote for the little Salzburg court; it is so here. The piano begins with a harmless phrase in F, twin sister of the solo subject. Then comes a rush in the strings and, suddenly, a little thunder-clap, and we are plunged into C minor by a falling arpeggio on a diminished seventh.[1] The strings are silent; only the acid tone of the hautboy accompanies the momentarily unbridled piano. An agitated and sorrowful tune in D minor breaks forth, crumbling away by degrees in solo runs and modulating to end up in G minor, whence the tutti has no difficulty in driving away the clouds and bringing us back to B flat. The piano, once more at peace, in a bravura passage behind which the composer's true face is again hidden, leads back the first subject whose well-bred, aristocratic good temper makes us forget the passing storm, and the recapitulation unfolds without change.

No more *élan*, no more fire, no more dominating emotion, consequently no more vigorous unity; the work is not disjointed but it holds together mainly by formal means. The little concerto in D, despite its childishness, we felt to be necessary; it answered to a mood of its creator. Not so the B flat, nor the two following concertos. They are well-regulated successions of agreeable sentiments whose order might be different without the work losing anything thereby. The D major concerto was as single, as undissociable, as the G minor symphony of 1773; it is this unbreakable oneness which for the time being goes out of the young Mozart's compositions and which he recaptures fully only after regaining his freedom in Vienna.

From the first concerto's andante to this one, too, it is a far cry.

---

[1] The principle of a *minor* passage after the first part of a movement is, of course, traditional.

The form is that of the *sonata* in two sections, the second of which
repeats the first with a few changes of detail. The orchestra starts
the first phrase and the piano enters at the eighth bar. The character
is that of the first movement—an impersonal sweetness expelled one
instant by the agitation of the second subject in C minor. Here,
too, it is the middle part—the reprise, since there is no *development*
—whose yearning and languor are most truly Mozartian (ex. 12).

The rondo is the most homogeneous movement. It is constantly spritely and gay, with a discreetly plebeian tone not unpleasing to the declining Ancien Régime. In his violin concertos of the preceding year, Mozart had used for his finales the *rondeau* of the contemporary French violin composers. Very different from Rameau's dances *en rondeau*, this form was nearer to the ordinary rondo with its indefinite number of episodes and its inorganic nature. The main difference lay in that it allowed episodes of varying rhythms and beats, whereas the older rondo, or rondeau, usually kept the same *tempo* from one end to the other.[1] Mozart now gives up this heterogeneous model never to return to it. His taste for organic construction leads him to adopt the form of the French dance *en rondeau*,[2] whence he develops the *sonata rondo*, the Mozartian rondo par excellence, one of the richest forms of the classical period. It has been repeated over and over again that the invention of this form is due to Beethoven. This is an injustice to Mozart, and all the more grievous because, in the matter of form, he innovated little, and this rondo is his only important contribution to the growth of structure. Beethoven used it, certainly; but he did not modify it and he left it as he received it from Mozart.

The Mozartian rondo is simple but organic: refrain, first couplet, generally in the dominant or relative major, first return of the refrain, second couplet, moving further away from the tonic, second return of the refrain, followed by a repetition of the first couplet and a last return of the refrain. Originally, the lines of refrain and couplets were clear cut. John Christian[3] began to break down their stiffness and, in his concertos, he mixed pianistic passages with the themes and thus softened the hardness of the outlines. But he would pass, abruptly, from couplet to refrain with a double bar followed by a *da capo*, and the segmentation of his couplets was still very marked. Moreover, at least in his concertos, he does not repeat the first couplet after the second return of the refrain. Mozart does, and he also effects transitions between the different parts, so that the plan is no longer so rigid and the unity is greater. The main lines are not yet submerged in the whole as they will be in his Viennese rondos and the

---

[1] Compare for instance the rondo of Bach's E major violin concerto and the finales of Mozart's concertos in G, D and A.

[2] Cf. pp. 49-50.

[3] He used it, not only in his concertos, but in his chamber music and in at least one of his symphonies, op. 18, II, in B flat.

return of the subjects is still regular and predictable, but there is a distinct advance on the simple little rondos of John Christian.

Following French practice, in this concerto Mozart puts his second couplet in a minor key; this is a first likeness to the *development* of sonata form which, at the *galant* period, often opens in the relative minor.[1] The other couplets are, the first in the tonic and dominant, the third, which repeats the first minus one of its four subjects, in the tonic only. This third couplet is a true recapitulation and when, in later works, the second couplet, instead of introducing a new theme, "works out" material already heard, the transformation of the French rondeau into the sonata rondo will be complete.

The themes themselves in this rondo are more interesting than in the allegro and andante. Their popular gait makes the movement more racy. The piano preponderates as it does in the rest of the work; the taste for collaboration with the orchestra, save in a very few bars, has passed with the first concerto and will not return till 1784.

Mozart played this concerto at Munich in 1777 and also, with the two following, at Stein's in Augsburg and Cannabich's in Mannheim the same year. He tried later, apparently without success, to have all three engraved in Paris.

No. 3 in F major for three pianos. The B flat concerto had been composed for himself; the next two were written for others. A sister of Archbishop Colloredo, Countess Lodron, whose husband held a position in his brother-in-law's court, and her two daughters, Louise and Josepha, who were perhaps pupils of Mozart, played the piano —the mother and elder one with ability, if the evidence of the music is to be trusted—and it is for them that he wrote, in February of the same year, a concerto for three pianos.

It is certainly the least interesting of the whole series. The idea of three pianos in one concerto makes us think at once of Bach and the rich contrapuntal effects he drew from this combination. It seems inconceivable to us that one should write for three pianos without utilizing counterpoint, and the ingenuous homophony of this concerto upsets us.

It is obviously unfair to insist on this. The ideal of 1776 was not that of Bach, and Mozart is not responsible for the absence of polyphony in his work, although later, and even in his concertos, he was to give it a generous share. But, once we have granted this, the work is none the less weak. The ideas are commonplace; they have

---

[1] In the *da capo* aria, too, the second part is often in the relative minor.

not even the impersonal charm of the last concerto. No working out; harmonies almost always commonplace and hackneyed; and the advantage he takes of the interplay of three soloists is limited to echoes, a few answers, runs divided between them and relations of theme and accompaniment. The orchestra's part in all this is of the smallest; it is almost completely silent for the greater part of the work.

The first movement has the same plan as in the last concerto; the solo subject appears twice, each time in C major. A new theme, also in C, opens the *development*; it goes quickly into C minor and leads to a sequence of arpeggios alternating between first and second-pianos and recalling the sequences of virtuosity motifs which make up the middle sections in the concertos of John Christian, Haydn, Schobert, Schröter and other contemporaries. It is the only instance of this wearisome device in Mozart's piano concertos; it had occurred the year before in the violin concerto in D, K.218, and he used it later in a violin sonata in D, K.306, composed in 1777.

The rondo has the form of the Mozartian rondo, but its *tempo* is that of a minuet, its themes are colourless, and it has nothing of the wit and vigour of the B flat. In all three movements the third piano part is so reduced that Mozart was able to arrange the work for two pianos without losing anything important. No doubt Josepha was less expert than her mother and sister.

The strictures we have just made do not apply to the adagio. Here indeed the true soul of Mozart is revealed. Generally speaking (we have already mentioned this point), whatever the scope of the rest, his slow movements proceed nearly always from a personal inspiration. His own ideal is fused here with that of his public and inspires movements that are among the purest and most poetic of his youth. One of the most recognizable signs of his genius is the oft-proclaimed superiority of his andantes, for they are the movements that suffer mediocrity least gladly and come off worst at the hands of second-rate composers. It is moderately easy to polish off a dashing scherzo, but only the greatest succeed in their slow movements.

The adagio of this concerto is a *sonata* in three sections, like that of the first one, but here the *development* is more than a mere transition; it is broad and has its own importance. The usual orchestral prelude gives out the two subjects; the pianos enter with the first, then modulate to F. The second piano gives out the *cantabile* solo subject, accompanied by its own left hand and the right hand of the first piano. After a few bars, they exchange sides. This winding theme leads without interruption into the true second subject.

This latter consists in a very simple, almost sketchy theme, syncopated, with a rather peculiar wavy accompaniment which attracts as much notice as the theme itself. It is the first cast of a subject which will return in the F major andante of the great concerto in C, K.503. We have already noted the frequence with which families of themes and even of movements recur in Mozart, and their transformations often bear witness to an interesting growth.

The seven bars of the *development* and the two bars of the cadenza that are derived from it are the finest in the work. Above another rather sketchy subject, one of the pianos outlines in staccato demisemi-quavers the most exquisite accompaniment one can imagine. It is one of Mozart's most captivating examples of impressionism. Leaving aside clear-cut and limpid contours, he seeks for a few bars blurred lines, misty effects, which contrast with the clarity of the rest (ex. 13). Here too we think of a passage in a later work: of the

Ex. 13

Ex. 13—*contd.*

development in the allegro of the quartet in D, K.499. Half-way
through, the hautboys enter and cast their biting tone over the rustlings
of the pianos. It all ends rather abruptly and resolves into the first
subject.

Mozart has left cadenzas for the first two movements. The one
for the adagio makes at once for the lovely passage in the *development*
and goes over it for two bars before unwinding into commonplace
fioriture.

No. 4 in C major. The third and last concerto of this group,
written for a Countess Lützow, is a trifle more interesting (ex. 14).
It has recovered something of the spirit of the D major (that kind of
golden age to which one is constantly looking back at this stage of
Mozart's life, when *galanterie* seems to have conquered him!), combined with the grace of the B flat, but it still remains somewhat impersonal. Like the two others, it inserts a solo subject between the

first and second ones, and the *development* is in the minor; a new
theme appears in it but has not the sincere note of anguish of the one
which had blossomed forth at this point in the B flat.   The beginning
of the andante is very Mozartian in its yearning, but soon the piano

Ex. 14

Ex. 15a

Piano

K.246.
(a)

Ex. 15b

Piano

K.415.
(b)

Ex. 15c

Piano

K.503.
(c)

Ex. 16

Tutti

loses itself in inexpressive meanderings. The finale is again a minuet, rather wittier than that of the three pianos concerto, but this is not saying much.

This concerto would not detain us long were it not for its solo subject. It is the earliest version of a theme which appears twice more in the piano concertos and both times in C major works (ex. 15, a). It is simple and might be by any composer round about 1785. Six years later, the same position, key and association of ideas recall it to Mozart's mind, but enriched (ex. 15, b). Finally, it reappears for the last time four years later, having attained its full stature, both simplified and deepened (ex. 15, c). The origin of this beautiful tune is in the C major Salzburg concerto of 1776, and this is our concerto's main title to remembrance.[1]

Mozart played this concerto at Munich in 1777; he taught it to a pupil at Mannheim where Abbot Vogler played it in January, 1778. He referred to it in a letter to his father of April 10th, 1782, asking to have it sent him in Vienna, which shows that he still took an interest in it at that date.

CONCERTO NO. 5 IN E FLAT (K.271)
January, 1777[2]
    Allegro: C
    Andantino: 3-4 (C minor)
    Rondeau: Presto: ϕ; Menuetto: Cantabile: 3-4; Presto: ϕ
    Orchestra: Strings; two hautboys, two horns.

One has to listen very attentively to these three last concertos to find in each one a distinctive personality under the selfsame court livery which they all wear, whereas from the very first bar of the fifth a sharply marked character proclaims itself. Proud and self-assured,—it curries no favours either by smiling benevolence or by playful amiability; it is just itself and it cares little whether the public

---

[1] Mandyczewski has published in facsimile a manuscript of part of K.246, now in the Mozarteum, which shows how Mozart understood the soloist's part during the tuttis. He did not remain silent as he would to-day, but took his place as a *ripieno* with the other instruments, filling out the bass, unless there was a second piano to fulfil this function. The manuscript shows that the filling out was quite impersonal. The performance of these concertos with large orchestras has rendered this *ripieno* function of the solo part unnecessary.

[2] No. 9 in the *Gesamtausgabe*.

greet it well or ill.   The arrogance of its entry is to be somewhat softened later on, but its independent attitude reappears and keeps it clear of the golden chains of *galanterie*.   The contrast is as great as between the first concerto and those of 1776.

Only nine months separate this work from its predecessor and these nine months, though well filled, did not see the composition of anything important.   Church sonatas, masses, divertimenti and "table music", serenades, arias—nothing of all this affords much interest; nothing of it has survived except the Haffner serenade which figures occasionally on our programmes, one of the few rather medi-ocre works of Mozart's youth which still keep afloat—one wonders why—when so many of his masterpieces are submerged.

Nothing in all this series would lead one to foresee any change. Yet under the apparently stagnant surface of these years new depar-tures were preparing.   Only some external circumstance was needed to set the young musician free from the bonds imposed on him by convention and to enable the hidden workings, of which this con-certo was to be the result, to come to light.   Such a circumstance occurred in January, 1777.   There passed through Salzburg a French pianist of a certain fame, Mlle. Jeunehomme, and Mozart was asked for a concerto.   The presence of the foreign virtuosa aroused all his fire; anxious to appear at his best before a more interesting executant than the Countess Lodron and her daughters, he brought to con-sciousness the labour which, unbeknown to him, had been going on within.

In the 1776 concertos the importance of the public taste was supreme; it determined the tone of the work.   Now it is the com-poser who matters; the audience takes second place.   He is much more concerned with "expressing himself" than with timidly nursing his listeners; this alone explains the differences between this concerto and its foregoers.   Let us enumerate some of them.

The very personal opening is unique in all Mozart.   The themes of the first two movements are characteristic and the middle of the allegro is no longer an episode but a true thematic development. Orchestral and solo interplay is at times very close.   The whole andantino bears witness to this independence.   It rises far above the slow movements of the earlier concertos and personal expression makes no concession in it to the taste of the day.   And even the finale, although it is the most conventional movement of the three, betrays the same originality by the extreme freedom of its con-struction, its high spirits and the absence of all inexpressive virtuosity.

I. The allegro opens with one of those square-cut unison themes, founded upon the common chord, which occur so often in E flat works of this period. The orchestra starts it but, to our surprise, the solo, instead of waiting patiently for the end of the usual tutti, enters as a usurper and finishes it. The orchestra starts again; the same square-cut, unison, *forte* theme is repeated; the same interruption from the piano finishes it once more. With a change of tactics, the orchestra re-enters, *pianissimo*, with a fresh motif and the piano, apparently put out, keeps silent till the usual hour for its entry (ex. 16).

This appearance of the piano before the customary time is on the whole a rather facile trick which the composer uses to compel attention and Mozart, who always disliked any obvious and forceful device, never returned to it. Beethoven made use of it twice, with a different object; since his time, the solo entry at, or near, the beginning of a concerto has become the rule.

Once the piano has been put in its place the strings continue in a gentler tone. A *cantabile* passage leads to another square-cut motif, which takes us to the second subject through little phrases in which loud and soft alternate sharply. The second subject is a pleasant sinuous theme, entrusted to the first fiddles, which unfolds in two fragments, separated by a horn and woodwind call; in its latter part the second fiddles add a graceful counterpoint. It is followed by a rhythmical passage; then, after a sudden rest, the violins whisper very softly a little hesitant motif which is broken into a moment later by the general fanfare that closes the tutti and ends, according to rule, on a full-close. This time we expect a regular piano entry with the first subject. Fresh surprise! The violins open a rustling theme based on the three notes of the chord, and it is over this, with a dominant trill, that the solo makes its bow. Then, once the strings are silent, it goes on with a new strain whose tone recalls that of several we have just heard. Only then does the first subject come back, shared once again between the orchestra in unison and the piano.

To the accompaniment of discreet held notes on the hautboys, the solo instrument forges ahead and develops the first part of the subject (ex. 16, a) like a serious-minded symphonist. It has modulated to the dominant before it remembers that it is playing a concerto and lets off a few fireworks which bring back a ritornello already heard in the tutti, then the second subject. The piano attacks it alone; the strings add their strength in the fourth bar. The graceful counterpoint which belonged just now to the second violins passes to the first and when the subject is over these repeat it to the piano's accompaniment. The solo resumes command a few moments later and the sinuosities of the theme turn little by little into passage work which leads to the usual trill and close.

Yet we have not reached the end of the exposition. The figure of the close had concluded the first tutti and it is followed by the same rest as formerly. But now, it is the piano which enters with the hesitating phrase whispered just now by the fiddles, and when the orchestra seeks to crush it with the fanfare that had heralded the first solo entry it answers back with the very theme, *piano*, with which the strings had silenced it a minute earlier! A manifest robbery, accomplished with perfect wit and ease! The orchestra, once again taken aback, can at first do no more than accompany the victor rather piteously. But suddenly it changes its mind and, taking advantage of the piano's arrival on the tonic, trumpets forth in unison the opening subject. The piano hits back; the orchestra starts afresh; the piano likewise, an octave higher. Its victory is assured and, just as it did after its second entry, it sets about working out a fragment of the subject. The exposition is over.

All this part is more compact and more concise than in the earlier concertos. The first virtuosity passage is short and no theme is reserved for the solo. On the contrary, the piano takes a mischievous delight in sneaking all its subjects from the enemy and using them for its own ends.

The *development* is quite as thrifty. It is entirely thematic, a rare thing in Mozart's concertos. We meet in it no subject we do not already know. The first theme provides most of it; orchestra and solo throw back its two halves from one to the other and, having become friends again, play ball with its dislocated limbs. When they weary of their sport, they wend their way towards the reprise with a chromatic scale begun by the piano and finished by the orchestra.

The recapitulation is not without a few changes. As soon as it has replied to the orchestra, the piano launches forth with a new development of the first subject, modulating from E flat to F minor and G minor and returning to the tonic in descending semi-tones. After which it follows more calmly in the track of the exposition. In the cadenza it asserts itself and carries further with a fiery flight the rising line of the orchestra which had led up to it and which makes us think of the G minor quintet.[1] The cadenza is like the other solo

---

[1] It is a characteristically Mozartian motif; we meet it in the most unexpected places; flute and strings quartet in D, K.285, allegro; E flat symphony, K.543, finale.

developments; no pure virtuosity, but thematic passages based on two subjects, one of which, square-cut, had been heard in the opening tutti and had appeared for an instant at the beginning of the *development*. It is not the superfluous adornment which most cadenzas are, even when they are the composer's own, but just one last working out, entrusted to the solo and forming part of the movement. It is therefore wrong to substitute another one.

The fanfare which had concluded the first tutti closes the cadenza. Have we at last exhausted this little work's bag of tricks? By no means. After the close the fiddles take up again the hesitating theme which occurred before the solo entry. The piano reappears on the scene with the trill with which it had entered originally, and we begin to wonder whether a double bar has not announced a repetition of the movement when the orchestra breaks off and the solo bursts out into a display of rockets, of clearly conclusive character, which from arpeggio to arpeggio, the piano incessantly asserting itself, lead us to the final chord.

II. This hopeful and energetic allegro is succeeded by a very different piece. It is in C minor, the first minor movement we have met in the concertos. For Mozart, as for all his contemporaries, the minor is an exceptional mode. Reserved for the utterance of more individual emotions, it reflects well-characterized and, on the whole, uncommon moods. Even the least interesting composers generally find something touching to say when they turn to it.

We have already spoken of the "tragic" andantes to which this one belongs. This family is well represented in the concertos. Among the movements we have thus grouped together, several of those in C minor are closely related. From 1766 to 1791, and particularly between 1772 and 1784, Mozart composed some twelve andantes or adagios in this key. Three of them are somewhat similar to our concerto; they are those of a C major quartet, K.157, and E flat symphony, K.184, and of the *Sinfonia Concertante*, K.364. Differing in their rhythms, they all begin with themes whose feature is a swing

from tonic to dominant and a little motif of three notes

a sigh or a sob, the presence of which reveals the same mood.[1]

---

[1] It is interesting to observe that these elements are all present in the pathetic C minor andante of an overture of C. F. Abel, op. 7, III, which Mozart had copied out at the age of nine or ten and which passed for a long time as one of his symphonies under the Köchel, no. 18.

Ex. 17

K.271

Ex. 18

K.364

Ex. 19

It is to the fine andante of the *Sinfonia Concertante* that ours is most closely akin. The same mood has sought utterance in both movements, or rather—since the same mood never recurs completely —two moods as similar as can be. Not only are the themes almost identical but the time signature is the same (ex. 17). Both give vent to that despairing sorrow of the very young, a sorrow that feeds on itself and refuses to admit the least ray of hope. In the *Sinfonia*, it is more concentrated, without any bright moments; in the concerto, it is more outward and its themes more dramatic; and there are

some almost peaceful periods; the andantino of the concerto has
still something child-like which the other has lost.

At first hearing, what we notice is the recitative-like nature of
this movement. Mozart has adopted in it the opera seria style to the
extent of stopping some of his phrases on the dominant and concluding
them with a full close of the whole orchestra. As Wyzewa and Saint-
Foix have remarked, one could almost mistake it for a tragic recitative
from some opera of Gluck's and transferred from the voice to the
first violins or piano. The strings start, with muted violins, and ni
so tranquil a manner that the contrast with what has gone before is
most striking. The phrase we have just quoted continues for some
time; the wind come in to strengthen the fundamental with held notes
or to double the strings, and when the theme stops on a G of the first
violins the whole band enters, *forte* and in unison, for the full close
(ex. 18).

The piano raises its voice and climbs slowly to the octave. Hardly
has it reached it when the strings resume their *melopoeia* to which
the solo adds a singing counterpoint, a bird of mourning hovering
over the funeral train. Little by little, the *melopoeia* weakens and
dies away and we are left with the piano's song which mingles with
the recitative (ex. 19). When it is over, the orchestra returns in
strength; a quick modulation and we find ourselves suddenly under
the serene skies of E flat!

The change is abrupt and characteristic of Mozart. It may well
surprise some people. Accustomed as we are to the broad developments of 19th-century symphonists, we tolerate less easily these sharp
about-turns carried out almost without warning and justified, it
seems, only by the rule which demands at a given moment a passage
from minor to major. Yet they are never without emotional significance in Mozart and do not take place just to satisfy a law of form. It
is true that we notice them in the places where they are usual in sonata
form, but we meet them at many other moments where no rule
requires them. They correspond to a fundamental need of his nature.
His mercurial temperament, as unstable as an April day, shifts incessantly from one pole to the other; in the midst of the most boisterous
laughter a sad thought will come like a cloud to darken his daylight,
just as through bitter tears there appear sometimes the sudden rays of
a smile. We are not astonished to find this feature of child psychology
in a work written at twenty-one by a youth who was in no way
precocious and was still as near to childhood as to man's estate.

The part that follows is in E flat. It is a long solo, broken once by the orchestra with a phrase from the first recitative transposed into the major and culminating, like it, in a full close, still in E flat, not without a hint of a *minor* modulation.

A noisy codetta, with syncopated accompaniment, concludes the exposition. The piano enters with the theme of the codetta, according to a custom always dear to Mozart, especially in his concertos, and repeats it with ornaments. The orchestra joins in; both give out the theme a third time and there follows a short *development*, similar to that of a first movement and quite thematic. But it is not much more than a transition and, quickly, two bars of dreamy and shimmering sadness, based on a descending scale of a minor seventh, fall back, discouraged, into the opening *melopoeia*. Their disillusioned grace reminds us of Ernest Hello's definition of Romanticism as "the musical acceptance of organized despair".

All that follows is a repetition of the first part, transposed into the minor. After giving out the first subject, the orchestra modulates as it did just now into E flat and the piano tries to follow it, but after a few bars it yields to weariness and returns to C minor.

What exactly is the transformation that comes over a passage like this when it is transposed from major to minor? Play the part of this andantino between bars 33 and 53 and then pass at once to the corresponding part of the recapitulation (bars 92 to 113). What is the difference? Nothing is changed and yet everything seems different. The outlines, the landscape, the rises and falls are the same; the voices too, and they speak at the same times. But the eye that gazes on this landscape is changed; what it saw in joy it sees again through tears, and details which it overlooked just now appear to it laden with a message of sorrow. It is the same view, with suffering added.

After a moving dialogue between piano and first violins (bars 110–15) the codetta with the syncopated accompaniment leads to the cadenza, a true development like that of the allegro and an integral part of the work. There is first of all a descent enriched by the successive entries of the parts and leading to a pause on a chord of the diminished seventh. Then a fragment of the *melopoeia* gradually emerges which the composer, a few moments later, banishes impatiently, uttering a succession of passionate accents which rise again to the high E flat where he had started. Finally, exhausted, the music falls back on the trill which announces the orchestra's return. The voice of the piano has almost died away; yet, as the orchestra fails to enter, it drags on dejectedly a little longer with a few shreds of a strain, until the violins, now unmuted, and all the other instruments, take up the end of the *melopoeia* at the very place where the cadenza had intruded on it. Then the piano regains courage and leads the *melopoeia* to its conclusion; the orchestra rounds off with a full close and the curtain falls upon this fragment of a nameless tragedy.

III. The brio of the first movement revives with even greater impudence in the rondo. The piano has recovered its strength and it chatters joyfully for close on forty bars before the orchestra appears. The dialogue is more marked than in the other movements and piano and tutti answer each other back with vivacity and good humour. Refrain and couplets, themes and passages run into one another with singlemindedness and there are really no "subjects". The form is that of the Mozartian rondo until the return of the passage which acts as refrain.[1] But then, instead of going on at the same breakneck pace, piano and orchestra start modulating from E flat to F minor, then to G minor and C minor, with a foreboding of some momentous change. A passage based on the beginning of the refrain completes the transition and after a pause on the usual chord of the diminished seventh, rhythm and *tempo* change and the piano opens, *cantabile*, a minuet which makes up the second episode! It is a theme and four variations, in which the piano plays sometimes alone, sometimes with the strings' pizzicati; a coda follows composed of piano arpeggios sustained by tutti chords. The whole leads up to a cadenza—of virtuosity, this time—and we return to the refrain. It is an episode of highly charming fancy. In all the series, for freedom of form, no other finale surpasses this movement, and only one, that of the 1784 E flat, K.449, equals it.[2]

It would be an exaggeration to pretend that Mozart has attained in this delightful work the level of his great compositions of 1784–86. Maturity is wanting here, and even the andantino, however moving, expresses a more youthful, more external sorrow than the "tragic" andantes of the Vienna years. But it is the earliest of his piano concertos which survives to-day on its own merits and, in the history of the young composer's growth, it is an important landmark. We have insisted upon its originality, its independence, even its arrogance, towards its public. It is the first time that Mozart allows himself such freedom, and he will not take it every day. In 1777,

---

[1] This passage announces Monostatos' air in the *Magic Flute*.

[2] Mandyczewski has published in facsimile two *intratas* that Mozart wrote for this finale.

he feels sure of himself, but a short while hence he will be leaving for
Mannheim, then for Paris;[1] he will have a fresh public to win, other
tastes to conciliate, and once again he will submit to external requirements. Then, upon his return to Salzburg, he will try once more to
please those of whom he had sought in vain to be rid; finally, at
Vienna, he will be in the same situation as in France and for some
time he will bow to the taste of his new patrons. Only seven or
eight years later, towards 1784, will he recover for good the audacity
which the French pianist's visit had given him the opportunity of
displaying.

CONCERTO NO. 6 IN E FLAT FOR TWO PIANOS (K.365)
1779 or 1780[2]
    Allegro: C
    Andante: 3-4 (in B flat)
    Rondeaux: Allegro: 2-4
Orchestra: Strings; two hautboys, two horns, two bassoons.

Between the sixth concerto and its predecessor there elapsed an
interval of eighteen months or two years, an interval filled with
important events since Mozart's last journey abroad took place during
this time.

A few months after the composition of the fifth concerto, he left
to seek fortune away from Salzburg, fortified by the presence of his
mother and the counsels of his father. The departure was sad;
the young sister Nannerl was particularly afflicted and wept, says
Leopold, all day long; her tears dried up only in the evening, at the
hour of piquet. Mozart and his mother stopped one month in
Bavaria: at Munich, where he vainly solicited a post, and at Augsburg,
where he made the acquaintance of his cousins and, in particular, of
his girl cousin, the celebrated Bäsle, with whom he was to keep up
a correspondence the lively tone of which has caused certain commentators to raise their eyebrows. From Augsburg they went to
Mannheim where they spent the winter and where the favourable
welcome given them by the Elector Charles Theodore raised a few
hopes. There, Mozart composed some works for flute, some piano
and some violin sonatas, and found his first love, Aloisia Weber, whose
sister Constance he was later to marry. Mannheim not producing

---

[1] On the way, at Munich, he played this concerto on October 10th.
[2] No. 10 in the *Gesamtausgabe*.

anything, mother and son wended their way to Paris, where Wolfgang stayed through the spring and summer of 1778. Three months after their arrival Frau Mozart died and her son was harboured by the Grimm d'Epinay *ménage*. His letters inform us of the desperate attempts he made to win a footing in Paris, all the more frantic for his knowledge that their failure would spell a return to his abhorred native town. He won a certain fame; he found pupils in the nobility, among others the daughter of the Duc de Guines, for whom he wrote the concerto for flute and harp (the father played the flute, the daughter the harp and, moreover, "composed" under the bored guidance of Mozart); the *Concerts Spirituels* gave a symphony he had composed for the occasion in the "Parisian taste"[1] and a *Sinfonia Concertante* for four wind instruments[2]; Noverre, ballet master at the Opera, entrusted him with the music for a ballet which was cut out at the last moment, mislaid, and rediscovered by Victor Wilder in 1874.[3] The narration of these events is accompanied in his letters by recriminations against the country and its inhabitants and expressions of patriotism as interesting for the historian of German national feeling as they are unpleasing to French ears.[4]

The result of all these endeavours was that Grimm advised him to pack up and get home. He left empty-handed but the wiser for his experience of the world, on September 26th, 1778. He passed through Mannheim where friends kept him for another two months, and Munich, where he found Aloisia, now unfaithful, and returned to the fold on January 15th or 16th, 1779.

These eighteen months are of no great interest for the student of his concertos, but for himself they are most important. The artist in him gained from them, by seeing at its source in Mannheim the new instrumental style of which only traces had reached him hitherto, and by entering into contact in Paris with an operatic art other than that of Italy. The influence of these new musical experiences was to be lasting. Moreover, as a man he gained much. During his stays in Bavaria, the Palatinate, France, he learnt to face life alone and to drink deep of disappointments, both amorous and professional.

---

[1] K. 297 in D, called the *Paris*.

[2] Köchel-Einstein 297 b, in E flat; or perhaps another work now lost.

[3] *Les Petits Riens*.

[4] E.g.: "My whole body seems to be on fire and I tremble from head to foot with eagerness to teach the French more thoroughly to know, appreciate and fear the Germans" (letter to his father, July 31st, 1778; tr. E. Anderson, II, 872).

It was in the course of these eighteen months that he emerged for good from childhood. The difference between movements as similar as the andantino of the 1777 concerto and the andante of the *Sinfonia Concertante* of 1780 consists in that the former is the work of an adolescent, the latter the work of a man. There lay the most important result of the journey.

Mozart, therefore, returned to Salzburg to lie down again under the yoke of the archbishop. For the tourist who attends Mozart festivals in his native town, his music, "all grace and smiles", cannot have a more pleasing setting. The position of the city, its perched castle, its baroque churches, its vegetation, its belt of mountains seem to harmonize intimately with the works to which he listens and he feels that Mozart's genius could not have been born and nurtured anywhere but in such a paradise. Without denying the possibility of discovering a superficial relation between Salzburg's charm and the great musician who was born there (of a Bavarian father), it is well to remember that no town in the world was better hated by Mozart than the one where he saw the light of day and where, apart from his travels, he spent the first twenty-five years of his existence. It is to Munich or Mannheim or Prague—to Prague especially, which alone fêted him as he deserved—rather than to Salzburg that he would come back to-day to attend a festival of his works.

His return to Salzburg in January, 1779, was full of painful contrasts. Not that his duties as *Kapellmeister* to Archbishop Colloredo were onerous, but, dazzled and inebriated by his view of a world outside, despite his disappointments in it, he was returning perforce to bury himself, without a future, in a narrow-minded town where no one, except perhaps his father, sympathized with his ambitions or understood to what heights his genius could soar. Here he now saw himself fated to live and die, the servant of a master for whom an artist was an official less important than his chamberlain, art an agreeable but unessential pastime, and from whose taste in music his own was moving further and further. How he must have chafed, and with what despair he must have seen again the baroque domes of the city, as he remembered the vain attempts he had made to free himself!

It is from the spirit in which he speaks of Salzburg in his letters from Munich, Mannheim and Paris that we picture his state of mind, for his correspondence with his father naturally ceased with his homecoming. His only consolation was his music. Even so, it had to please listeners whose ideal was rapidly ceasing to be his. The difference between what he could compose and what he had to compose can be measured in the two masses, K.317 and 337, which he wrote at this period, and the *Kyrie* in D minor, K.341, so darkly splendid, which he wrote at Munich a few months later, away from the constraint imposed by his Grace's taste.

This does not mean that everything he wrote during this last stay (January, 1779, to November, 1780) shows constraint. A certain number of fine works dating from these years are the authentic children of his untrammelled genius and among them is the concerto for two pianos. It is a work of joy which he could not have conceived and fashioned otherwise even if he had neglected completely the reigning taste.

We do not know its precise date. We only know that it was written at Salzburg between January 15th or 16th, 1779, the date of his return, and November 4th or 5th, 1780, the date of his departure for Munich. Neither do we know the circumstances in which it was composed but its well-developed virtuosity makes it likely that he intended to play it with his sister. The agreement between the two pianos is so perfect, their collaboration so single-hearted, that one would like to think it was so.

Ex. 20

Ex. 21

Ex. 22

Ex. 23

The tone of the work is one of dignity, worthy of expression in the presence of sovereigns. The impulsive themes of the fifth concerto have no counterparts here save in the rondo where a more "unbuttoned" gaiety, as Beethoven would have said, is always allowable; the composer's personality asserts itself more discreetly and the purely physical go of its predecessor is absent from the first movement. But if it is less full of fun, it is more graceful and of fairer countenance. The less ambitious flight is made up for by a breadth and ampleness in its themes and proportions which was lacking in the restless concerto of 1777. We return to the ideal of the B flat concerto of 1776 with an added ripeness and gravity in the personality. Even to-day, its charm is deeper and it can be taken more seriously than the earlier work.

I.   It opens with one of Mozart's most grandiose subjects—a

unison theme based on the common chord, like almost all his E flat
first subjects; only, whereas many of them are square and rhythmical,
as in K.271, this one is ample and flowing like a wave borne upon a
ground swell. It starts on the tonic, falls at once by an octave, rises
then along the degrees of the common chord, falls still lower and
stops on the dominant. At this point it becomes harmonized and,
from *forte* to *piano*, it climbs little by little in a wavy line and, after
breaking, draws back gracefully upon the tonic (ex. 20).

The whole orchestra now enters and we continue in a more jovial
strain, frolicking with themes in semi-quavers and repeated notes, very
different from the opening. We modulate to C minor, A flat and
F minor, return to E flat, and land finally on a dominant seventh
chord and a pause. Then, under the repeated notes of the fiddles,
pianissimo, and emphasized by a horn call, we hear violas and 'cellos
whisper a rhythmical motif. It is at first just perceptible, like the
tramping of a distant army. The strings repeat it, *crescendo*, and the
hautboys reinforce them. It comes nearer, asserts itself; we take it to
be the second subject. Finally, it invades the whole band and leads
triumphantly to the conclusion (bars 30–42).

The two pianos enter gaily with a unison trill, an indication of
their mutual relations throughout the work. They repeat the grand
first subject whose opening phrase in their hands appears somewhat
flounced and frilled, whereas the second strain keeps its austere outline. The first piano gives it out; the second gives another reading
of it an octave lower. The nature of their collaboration is clear
from the outset. There will be no more counterpoint than there was
in the work for three pianos; the soloists will repeat, echo, and
accompany each other, but never work equally; each one in turn will
be the master. From this conception, admittedly less fruitful than
that of Bach, Mozart draws all its possible consequences.

After a short solo founded on the first subject, the tutti re-enters
with the figure which had just concluded the introduction. This is
a device borrowed from aria form which Mozart has used in three
other piano concertos.[1] It gives us the feeling that the past is definitely
closed and that the work is turning its prow towards new shores.
The concerto derives a certain impetus from it and sets off again more
merrily than ever.

Freed from the past, the two pianos seek joyous adventures with
a bold theme which skips a tenth at its second note, returns to its

---

[1] K.238, 414, 537.

starting-point, and, once both soloists have given it out, divides
between them in charming ripples, breaking and coming together
until a second melody appears (bars 84–95). This is the second half
of the solo subject and is in B flat. It is entrusted to the second piano,
whilst the ripples continue to flow in the first and accompany the
engaging melody (ex. 21). One bar of tutti (all this time the orchestra
has kept silence or has confined itself to held notes) and the first piano
dives into the true second subject, which is not at all the one we had
spotted in the introduction but a sister theme to ex. 21. It, too,
splits up into two strains; the first belongs to the first piano alone and
comes limpingly forward with a ♫𝄾♫𝄾 rhythm in the right
hand and a 𝄾♫♫𝄾♫♫ rhythm in the left; the other is given to the
second under a trill of the first, and when it is over the first piano
advances again and adds a third strain as a coda (bars 104–20). Few
of Mozart's concertos are so rich in themes; they succeed each other
unceasingly from the solo entry and relieve us of the need for any
bravura passages. The second piano re-enters; the two answer each
other, playing shuttlecock with the arpeggios, and again scales and
trills ripple down, sparkling from one to the other, dazzling with
life, and hint at motifs which melt into runs without ever ceasing
to be expressive. At length, with chromatic scales in thirds, they
swoop down upon the dominant trill which closes the exposition.

The orchestra plays but a sorry part. It has no themes of its own
and now that the coast is momentarily clear all it can do is to rake up
old memories and go back to the codetta which had followed the
"tramping army" subject in the introduction. This is an unlucky
stroke for it calls up at once other memories in the soloists. Hardly
six bars have elapsed since the end of the exposition when the first
piano returns with a theme from the first tutti transposed into G
minor. The other piano follows and the game begins again. We
expect a working-out of this theme like that in K.271, but Mozart
is far too prodigal of his riches to dally with developments. Six
bars later, the first piano enters C minor and the second gives out a
new subject. This one comes before us threateningly, "in shining
armour", with a *tremolando* in the upper register, like a drum roll,
and a menacing semi-quaver triplet in the bass (ex. 22; bars 160–69).
But it is only a cardboard warrior and does not disturb the fun;
we refuse to take it seriously; it passes into the good-humoured key
of B flat and disappears as suddenly as it came. In its place another
theme is outlined—the ninth and last!—as graceful as the foregoing

and so laden with yearning that it cannot express itself completely
on the pianos and appeals to the hautboys at what is perhaps the
most enchanting moment in the whole movement.[1] In three
thoroughly Mozartian bars the woodwind echoes the solo instruments, prolonging and completing the theme (ex. 23). The spirit
of this delightful subject persists in a few quiet scales which pass antiphonally from one piano to the other and once again we are in well-
known climes when the soloists halt on a dominant seventh chord. A
murmur of the violins and we hear afar the "tramping army" subject
which had not returned since the first tutti. The pianos take it up
and it soon invades the whole band. The *development* has reached
its close and through beautiful piano *melismas* we glide back to our
starting-point.

We have said that Mozart never varied his recapitulations as much
as in his piano concertos. The five first hardly confirmed this statement for their recapitulations reproduced largely their first sections.
It is no longer so here. The majestic opening subject reappears and
for an instant an air of gravity passes over the face of the work.
From grave it becomes sombre as one of the pianos takes up the first
fragment of theme in the minor and the other continues, still in the
minor, with the second fragment. An almost oppressive atmosphere
suddenly reigns over the hitherto serene and light-hearted movement
and is rather increased than dispelled when there comes to the fore a
little figure of fluttering seconds dear to Mozart and always indicative
of heightened stress (ex. 24; bars 212–23). From the first piano
this figure passes to the second, in the middle and then in the upper
register, then more feebly in the bass, after which it vanishes suddenly
and the dark shadows with it.

This excursion into the minor immediately after the reprise is
uncommon in Mozart.[2] It appears to have been characteristic of
the Viennese school and to go back to Wagenseil who liked to repeat
his themes in the minor, not only at the reprise but at other times. It
may be from Schobert that Mozart adopted it, for it is frequent with
him[3] and his influence on the young Salzburger was still alive in 1779.

---

[1] It is with this theme that the solo violin and viola enter in the first movement of the *Sinfonia Concertante*.

[2] The symphony in C, K.338, contemporary with this concerto, and the
Mannheim sonata in C, K.309, offer examples of it.

[3] It is found in his sonatas Op. V, 1 (1st and 3rd movements), Op. VI, 1;
Op. VII, 1 (1st and 3rd movements); Op. XVII, 1 (do.); and in his concerto
in C, Op. XV.

Mozart admired his music and during his stay in the French capital had taught his sonatas to pupils. The fine A minor sonata, K.310, composed most probably in Paris, contains in its andante an almost literal quotation from Schobert's Op. XVII, 1.[1] Mozart, who assimilated so many and such diverse influences, took from them only what suited his nature, and if this sudden appearance of the minor is a widespread device at this time, it corresponds nevertheless to his unstable temperament which passed without transition from laughter to tears and bordered on sadness at its merriest moments. The angel of sorrow was always watching within, ready to unveil its face.

The rest of the movement recovers the zest which had reigned until the reprise. Only the second of the solo subjects appears here. The true second subject is given out entire and is followed by a felicitous recall of the second fragment of the opening subject, modified in its conclusion and made less grave by a sparkling codetta which scatters itself in wavelets. A bravura passage, the only one in the movement, concludes the pianos' performance; a bridge leads to the cadenza,[2] after which the tutti winds up as it had done in the introduction.

II. The sharp opposition between the allegro and andantino of K.271 does not occur here. On the contrary, the andante, in B flat, sings in more meditative tones of the same happy thoughts and affectionate joy as the first movement. The dark strains that had interrupted, for an instant, the flow of happiness reappear here as fleeting expressions of melancholy. The *development* theme in C minor that feigned ferocity also has its counterpart. The character of the themes is similar, their abundance also; Mozart is as prodigal as ever of his store and there is no thematic working out.

The movement opens with a phrase in broken rhythm—a sigh that dies into a threefold echo. The thought is expressed in fragments but the held note of the hautboys which hovers aloft gives it unity. The pianos enter almost at once with the same motif; the

---

[1] Bars 13-16 after the double bar in the andante of Mozart's sonata in A minor are almost identical with bars 17-21 after the double bar in the andante of Schobert's sonata. The Schobert movement is one of those which Mozart had arranged as a concerto in 1767 at the age of eleven.

[2] There exist in the archives of St. Peter's church in Salzburg cadenzas for the first and third movements, partly autograph, partly in Leopold's hand. They were published by Mandyczewski in 1921, in a facsimile edition. Both are a little perfunctory. That for the allegro makes use of exs. 20, 22 and 23; that for the rondo deals with the refrain and is largely composed of imitative passages between the two pianos. See App. I.

"sighs" devolve on the second, the held note, in the shape of a trill, on the first. The second continues alone with a wavy chromatic theme full of melancholy. The feeling becomes intense when the first piano intervenes to follow the second a third below. But it soon vanishes into arabesques and the soloists attack a vigorous subject to reach a bar of chords of the seventh which they strike together. The mood changes; the pianos are silent and, under more *tenuti* on the hautboys, the strings whisper a figure of trills and repeated notes. The pianos return at the end of two bars but the orchestra, for once, does not withdraw and there follows one of the few dialogues in the concerto. The hautboy *tenuti* turn into a theme which the pianos accompany with broken chords. The passage is repeated with a change of accompaniment; a short intervention of the whole orchestra, with a motif destined to play a more important part at the end of the movement (ex. 25), concludes the first part.

As in the allegro the middle section is a succession of subjects which appear and vanish off-handedly with no thought of development. First come two bars of introduction, in B flat, given to the first piano, and two more, for the second, which repeat them in E flat. Then, abruptly, a new subject is announced in C minor. It would fain be tragic but hardly succeeds, for the first piano takes it up in B flat and it then falls into line with the general tone of the movement. A dialogue is carried on between the soloists and soon a winding figure, more and more split up, brings back the theme in broken rhythm of the beginning. The recapitulation unrolls without important changes until the arrival of the motif (ex. 25) that had closed the first section. When the tutti has finished it, the first piano takes it up, accompanied by the second, in four bars full of charm, to which the orchestra, with a true Mozartian gesture, adds a discreet codetta.

III. The part played by the orchestra, almost inexistent in the first two movements, is more extensive in the rondo. There are also a few thematic developments. A certain kinship can be recognized between the subjects. Passages such as the first and second returns of the refrain, and the beginning of the third couplet, are founded on figures which the pianos work out in various ways, or upon the refrain-theme. In form, therefore, this is the most interesting movement of the three, and while it has recourse to development devices it is as tuneful as the first.

The orchestra opens it. The refrain is a two-step theme which may be based on a French ariette. It has a certain likeness to the refrain of the finale in a divertimento in E flat, K.252, of 1776, and was used again by Mozart with a different rhythm in the last movement of the *Hunt* quartet (ex. 26). It is full of life and, with its silent first beats, not devoid of piquancy.

The tutti takes charge and does not let in the soloists till the refrain is over. The pianos must therefore find something new and the first one springs forward with a subject akin to it but different in rhythm and detail of outline. The second, at first silent, then joins in to

Ex. 28

repeat, an octave lower, what the first has just said.   Certain members
of the orchestra add their voices and, after the first fragment of the
theme, we hear a witty echo from the hautboys (bars 64 and 68).
Then all the band returns to the attack with the last bars of the refrain.
The pianos seize hold of it forthwith, in unison, and set out for adventure, one armed with its repeated semi-quavers, the other astride its
triplets, and for a while there is a desperate struggle between the trot
of the first and the gallop of the second (bars 87–98).   The galloping
triplets win and form a well-characterized melodic accompaniment,
whilst a stiff, rhythmic theme appears in the second piano (bar 99).
Then the tables are turned and the orchestra adds the richest and
most original accompaniment it has devised hitherto, filling out the
harmonies and progressing with contrary motion to that of the
pianos (ex. 27; bars 113–27).   The hour of the return is at hand and
we meet, for the first time in the concertos, an example of that art
of the reprise which is one of Mozart's charms.   The first piano
sketches a fragment of melody whose spirit recalls the refrain but which
is not derived from it; starting as it does a semi-tone below the tonic,
it might be the conclusion of some theme already heard.   The second
piano repeats it; the first echoes its last notes; the second likewise.
Then, with two almost ridiculously simple elements—a scale fragment
of five notes and the two thirds of the chord of B flat,[1] Mozart spirits
us away into fairyland and we are still marvelling at what has happened
when the refrain theme is once again merrily sent upon its way (ex.
28; bars 142–70).

The second couplet conforms to the tradition of the French rondo
by opening in the relative minor.   The new subject unfolds in the
same order as before: subject given out by the second piano and
accompanied (in broken octaves) by the first; then reversal of the
parts and entry of the strings, which accompany the soloists with a
rhythm of their own.   A few arpeggios lace themselves from one
piano to the other and the orchestra answers with a fragment which
also recalls the refrain; we modulate from G minor to F minor, E
flat, G minor and C minor.   The first part of the subject returns
(bar 255) and the band accompanies the second piano, whilst the first
supports it with its broken octaves.   Then, once more, Mozart
prepares us a magical reprise.   The C minor theme completed, the

---

[1] A similar but simpler passage, a forerunner of this one, occurs in the
finale of the Mannheim sonata in C, K.309, after the last return of the refrain,
forty-three bars from the end.

Ex. 29

first piano gives out alone a motif in G minor, which also looks as if
it was broken off from something we had already heard; it is characterized by the "fluttering seconds" figure so beloved of Mozart (bar
270).[1] The second piano repeats it, whilst the first adds a counterpoint of trills. Motif and counterpoint pass from one to the other

---

[1] It resembles a passage in Papageno's part in the *Magic Flute*:
"*O wär'ich eine Maus, wie sollt'ich mich verstecken,*
Wär'ich so klein wie Schnecken so kröch ich inm Haus!"
(Finale of Act I.)

and modulate to G major, whence other chromatic modulations, founded upon two notes of the scale, bring back with masterly economy the key of E flat and the refrain.   In his later concertos, Mozart will write grander rondos, but in his whole work one will not find many passages of greater expressive power than these two reprises, so simple in the means they use (ex. 29; bars 270-96).

The whole refrain is given out by the second piano and repeated by the tutti; it leads suddenly to a pause and concludes briefly in A flat.   Although we are in the recapitulation couplet, Mozart has not yet reached the end of his inventiveness.   Instead of the theme with which the soloists had made their entrance the first time, it is the refrain itself that the first piano picks up, and some thematic working-out follows—a rising sequence founded on the first four bars of the refrain, each piano taking on at the point where the other leaves off. We pass thus from A flat to B flat minor, C minor and F minor; then, we descend on a derivative figure and reach B flat, in which key the tutti enters with another bit of the refrain.   After this escapade, we return to the beaten paths of rondos and the main theme of the first couplet reappears with a slightly different ornamentation and accompaniment.   It concludes on the tonic, and a short tutti bridge, based on the refrain which decidedly dominates this rondo even more than refrains usually do, leads to the cadenza.[1]   The rather long conclusion that follows belongs almost wholly to the soloists; it is a last appearance of the refrain; the orchestra adds only the customary affirmation of the common chord.[2]

These last two concertos are like enough for a comparison to be justified.   Both are more closely akin to each other than to those that come before and after; both belong to the years immediately before Mozart settled in Vienna and during which his genius was beginning to be enriched by contact with a wider world than Salzburg.

Of the first movements of both, it is true to say that each one represents a mood.   One cannot say as much of the 1776 concertos. But, though both be personal, their personalities are different.   The fifth is self-assertive and aggressive; it overrides the *galant* conventions.

---

[1] See note 2, p. 111 and App. I.

[2] In a performance at Vienna with Frl. Aurnhammer, Mozart added two clarinets, two trumpets and two kettledrums in the first and last movements.

One finds only faintly in it the ideal of "society music" reflected by most concertos of the time. It is the expression of a young, inexperienced, unsubtle, rather dogmatic spirit; originality rather than depth is, quite naturally, its principal feature, and its exuberance is not without stiffness. It is athletic, not sentimental; it is an "extrovert" and recalls in this respect the little D major concerto, K.175.

The sixth concerto, on the other hand, though quite as personal, is more tactful. Before his journey to the Palatinate and France, Mozart could put himself at his public's level, but then his work lost proportionately in personality; sometimes, he would assert himself, but then he removed himself from his public and risked offending it. On his return, however, he showed that he possessed already to a high degree that art of satisfying his own aspirations and placating his public which is still to-day one of the reasons for his popularity. To put oneself within reach of one's audience without demeaning oneself: that is what he learnt in 1777-8; that is what he felt strong enough to do in the concerto for two pianos. Its first movement is not less personal than that of K.271, but it emphasizes most that aspect of the composer's personality which is closest to the collective personality of the Salzburg public. Mozart's own personality is richer and riper than it was two years earlier; it has lived more; it sees life less simply.

In the slow movements, the relation between the two works is different. The C minor andantino of K.271 is not only personal but deep; it expresses an intimate sorrow. It is not its personal character which separates it from the allegro; it is that, below the plane on which we are all alike, below that deeper plane on which we differ, it penetrates to a region where the personality of each of us finds again the common foundations of the human soul, where the artist, although he sings of his own sorrow, becomes also the voice of all. This andantino still keeps, nevertheless, the simpleness and immaturity of the first movement; this is what distinguishes it from the andante of the *Sinfonia Concertante* to which in other respects it lies so near.

The andante of the concerto for two pianos remains on a middle plane; its personality is an everyday one. A few bars promised to light up deeper zones; they were but fleeting.

In the rondos, the relationship is appreciably the same as in the first allegros. That of K.271 contains parts, such as the pretty minuet, which are chiefly rococo; that of K.365 sings from end to end the soul of its maker. The latter work is therefore the more homogeneous; whereas K.271 passes from a personal movement, full of

exuberant joy, to one deeply sorrowful, ending upon a rondo where
the taste of the day is more obvious than the spirit of Mozart, the
other keeps throughout its three movements that note of con-
ciliation between audience and composer which it struck at the start.

We have arrived at the end of the group of the first six concertos.
A group, strictly speaking, they are not, save for one whom the
abundance of material compels to classify. They do not form a
group as do the concertos of 1782, and 1784 and 1785-6. Three years
part the first from the second, and three years during adolescence is a
long time. More than a year separates the fourth from the fifth,
and between fifth and sixth comes the great journey. It is only from
time to time that Mozart thinks of the genre; after 1773, a few symphonies (the last before Paris), serenades and divertimenti especially,
occupy him; then, in 1775, his five violin concertos. Passing occasions call forth in 1776 the composition of three more piano concertos and the visit of Mlle. Jeunehomme produces in 1777 the E
flat. Betweenwhiles, serenades and divertimenti continue to pile
up. At Mannheim and Paris, nothing brings him back to the genre;[1]
the concertos he writes are for other instruments and are ordered
from him by amateurs or by the Concerts Spirituels.

There is, then, no succession in the composition of these works
and it is natural that they should show no connected growth. It is
indeed the first of them that shows most clearly the dramatic conception which is Mozart's great contribution to the form. This
conception vanishes altogether with the 1776 concertos which, with
all their charm, are pure concertos "für Kenner und Liebhaber," where
the orchestra serves only to introduce the solo and fill in the gaps
left by its silences. The dramatic conception is more visible in the
two first movements of K.271, but less than K.175; as for K.365,
though it be no stranger to the idea of the dialogue, it is a dialogue
between soloists, not between solo and tutti, that it gives us. If
Mozart, after leaving Salzburg, had written no more piano concertos,
we might have said that he had half grasped several conceptions of
the genre without developing any one of them.

Two years separate Mozart's return to Salzburg from his final
departure in October, 1780. These two years are too important in

---

[1] But at Mannheim he sketched the beginning of a *Sinfonia Concertante*
for piano and violin, in D, Köchel-Einstein 315 f.

the history of his work, if not of his life, for us to skip them once we have completed the study of the sixth concerto. They are more decisive even than his year at Mannheim and Paris for it was during them that the fruits of his journey, and especially the enrichment of his personality which was its principal result, appear in his compositions.

They are important, above all, for the growth of his musical thought. For that of his style the works written in the Palatinate and in France are more significant, but the *Stilwandlung* of 1777–8 was over by the time he got home; it is the renewal of his inspiration that is shown by his last period in Salzburg and his first months in Vienna.

The half-dozen symphonic works of 1779–81 speak of something new; there are in them strains as yet unheard. We discover, clearly constituted for the first time, some of the fundamental elements of his musical personality as we know it at the period of his maturity. These works are the symphony in C, K.338, the serenade and divertimento in D, K.320 and 334, the woodwind serenades in B flat, E flat and C minor, K.361, 375 and 388, and the *Sinfonia Concertante*, K.364; to these one should add the *Kyrie* in D minor, K.341. The period of his prime begins with them. All of them exceed, both in scale and power of thought, what he had written hitherto, and they are worthy to rank with the best compositions of his Viennese period. There is a world of difference between his most ambitious works written before 1779 and the symphony in C, the *Sinfonia Concertante* and the E flat serenade. Only a single movement, from time to time, like the andante of the violin concerto in G and the andantino of the piano concerto in E flat, K.271, had reached at one bound the heights whither, after 1778, he will arrive almost every time he seeks to write "for himself". They are beautiful, no doubt, but in their promise rather than in their fulfilment; the others attain what the earlier compositions had only half seen. Before 1779, Mozart wrote interesting works; only after then did he produce works of genius.

We would go even further and say that in the orchestral sphere we must wait till the 1784 concertos to find works as fine as the best of the period we are considering. After he settled in Vienna, one recognizes uncertainty, almost timidity, in his symphonic writing; his genius opens out in his chamber music and in his C minor mass, but the three concertos of 1782 and the 1783 symphony (the *Linz*) are less daring than the concertos, symphony and serenades of 1779 to 1781.

Two elements, particularly, in his later Salzburg works, show us by their presence that his musical personality is approaching maturity —two fundamental elements, traces of which can be discerned earlier but which henceforward were always to be present. One is the breadth and majesty that we are wont to call Olympian; the other, the sorrowful restlessness, reaching at times to tragedy, which Heuss many years ago called *"daimonisch"*—a word that has since become a stock part of Mozartian terminology. The alternation of these two moods—of vigorous joy, majesty, sweetness and sorrow is characteristic of Mozart; it is present throughout his work after 1782, and it is in several passages of the works we are considering that, for the first time, with a somewhat primitive brutality, it asserts itself.

The beginning of K.365 is a good example of the Olympian tone; the opening subject is one of Mozart's longest and fullest themes. But beyond this majestic portico the dignity unbends and gives way to graces and smiles. The majesty is more sustained in the C major symphony, a work which begins with a well-known Italian overture motif (ex. 30) common with him and always the expression of a solemn mood. But it is in the allegro of the *Sinfonia Concertante* and the E flat serenade that this feature is most impressively illustrated. Both movements begin with common chords, at first sustained, then repeated with a dotted crotchet rhythm. This too is a favourite form of opening, especially in E flat works; we find it again, condensed and more wiry, in the E flat piano concerto of 1785, K.482. It occurs often with John Christian Bach and the other *galant* composers and appears in the initial chords of the *Emperor* concerto.

In the E flat serenade, solemnity alternates with other feelings; the tutti of the *Sinfonia Concertante*, on the other hand, retains its majesty up to the entry of the soloists. Indeed, there are few works where Mozart keeps up so long an Olympian strain; we have to wait till the concertos of 1785 and 1786 to find an introduction where nobility and serenity of thought are so constantly sustained. This solemn beginning is not just a façade; the whole movement has the same character, though from time to time its serenity is coloured with pathos. The same nobility inspires the slow introduction of the B flat serenade, but the rest of its allegro is playful rather than solemn.

At the other extreme is the anguish which we sometimes perceive, like a sinister undercurrent, in his most joyful works. It is not a new feature but hitherto it had appeared only intermittently. From

1778 onward it comes to stay, and it is in certain movements of these three years that we see it asserting itself for good.

Sometimes it alternates with other emotions, falling into the middle of a quiet passage like a bolt from the blue. In the first movement of the *Sinfonia Concertante* the soloists have hardly come in when they give out a disturbing theme under which the orchestra outlines a plaint-like accompaniment. The mood persists and the anguish heightens till suddenly it disappears as abruptly as it had arisen, with one of those charming emotional about-turns so typical of Mozart.

The intrusion of the threatening *daimon*, the sudden rent that discloses the depths, is still more marked in the E flat serenade. The first movement begins like the *Sinfonia Concertante* with majestic chords, but majesty gives way at once to sweetness; the chords break up and a sensual, caressing theme succeeds, with shimmering clashes of seconds that enhance the woodwind colour. The music progresses for some time in a calm and playful mood, not devoid of vigour, when, abruptly, the second subject dies down in a fluttering of trills. From the ensuing silence arises the desolate voice of the hautboy in a tragic soliloquy. This lament ceases as suddenly as it started (ex. 31). It is heard again, as unexpectedly, in the short *development*, but loses itself in the return of the majestic chords that opened the movement, and does not reappear in the recapitulation. In its place a melody full of hope unfolds on the horn and ends, somewhat ironically, with the same cadence as the lament. The appearance of a new subject in this section, an effective touch, is found again in the C minor serenade and nowhere else in Mozart.

Sometimes it is in short passages like minuet trios that the anguish is poured out and it is perhaps in such places that we meet with the bitterest harmonies in all his work. The D minor trio of the first minuet in the divertimento in D, K.334 (ex. 32), and the B flat minor trio of the second minuet in the B flat serenade concentrate into their sixteen or twenty bars a cruel poignancy. In their stark desolation they make one think of much later periods, of the *Masonic Funeral Music* and the *Magic Flute*.

And sometimes a whole movement is a prey to this tragic mood. We have already spoken of Mozart's *minor* movements and we shall have occasion to return to them. There are four in the last Salzburg works, counting the magnificent fragment, the D minor *Kyrie*. All four have in common a feature of style frequent in Mozart's *minor* andantes: the alternation of tonic and dominant in the first bar of the theme. It is a common feature in the music of the time; one finds it in the Abel symphony already mentioned. The association between a certain mood and a melodic line or an accompaniment figure is very close in Mozart. The likeness in form between the beginning of the andantes of the E flat piano concerto, K.271, the serenade in D, K.320, and the *Sinfonia Concertante* is particularly marked, and so is the kinship of inspiration between the three. They are three phases of the same work in which the thought grows deeper and richer from one to the other. The final shape is in the andante of the *Sinfonia Concertante*, one of Mozart's most moving pieces. The D minor *Kyrie* recalls it, both by its general character and by certain melodic figures. One feels that both movements have arisen, not only on the same plane of consciousness but also at the same hour of the composer's life. The *Kyrie* leaves earlier religious works as far behind it as the *Sinfonia Concertante* and the symphony in C leave the earlier symphonies and concertos. A mass written on its scale would have had the proportions of the C minor and the *Requiem*.

The D minor variations of the divertimento, K. 334, have the same tragic character but with more violence. They, too, are poignant in their starkness, and they too are the first state of a thought which, more fully clothed, more ingratiating, reappears twice, each time more complete: in the andante of the F major violin sonata, K.377, and the finale of the D minor quartet, K.421.

Themes that betoken agitation are therefore common in Mozart's music of this period, and in all his output there are few movements where the alternation between serenity and anguish is as pronounced as in the allegros of the *Sinfonia Concertante* and the E flat serenade. May we not recognize in this the reflection of the young musician's increasing dissatisfaction with the stifling atmosphere of Salzburg? His attempts to escape from the little town and settle elsewhere had failed: he appeared more and more inevitably doomed to the archbishop's service and, as his wings grew, he felt the oppression of the narrow humdrum and the inept company of the Brunettis and Ceccarellis to be more and more unbearable. The anguish called forth by the cleavage between ideal and reality, which lasted into the first months of his stay in Vienna,[1] inspires the sorrowful andante of the *Sinfonia Concertante* and the acid trios of the minuets. This same anguish, enriching his experience with fresh sufferings, made him throw himself body and soul into the subject of *Idomeneo*, where the themes of departure and deliverance are so important; it caused him to show there, not only a more developed technique than in *Lucio Silla* and *Mitridate*, but a feeling for tragedy absent in his earlier operas. *Idomeneo*, the first of his dramatic masterpieces, the occasion of his final departure from Salzburg, closes worthily two years of works full of majesty and restlessness; there, in the overture, in certain arias of Ilia and Electra, in the temple scene, the magnificent farewell quartet and the choruses, we meet in the highest degree the Olympian and the tragic, the serene and the tortured inspiration which characterizes the symphonic works of Mozart's last months in his native town.

---

[1] The E flat and C minor serenades were composed in that city in 1781 and 1782.

2. *The Concertos of 1782: K.413 in F; 414 in A; 415 in C*

I am seething with rage! And you, my dearest and most beloved father, are doubtless in the same condition. My patience has been so long tried that at last it has given out. I am no longer so unfortunate as to be in Salzburg service. To-day is a happy day for me. . . . Please be cheerful, for my good luck is just beginning and I trust that my good luck will be yours also.[1]

THUS wrote Mozart to his father on May 9th, 1781. From this date he was free—free to shape his destiny or think he was shaping it, free to taste the flattery of capitals, free to end in destitution and a pauper's grave.

His letters relate the circumstances that preceded and followed his break with the archbishop. They show only one side of the picture and for a long time no other was apparent. Of recent years, however, the attempt has been made to prove that all the wrongs were not to be ascribed to the prince of the Church. For some time, Mozart had been airing desires for greater independence and been making attempts, displeasing to his master, to set himself free from the obligations of his position. The prelate had granted him, un-willingly, it appears, six weeks absence to allow him to compose and produce his opera *Idomeneo* which the Munich court had ordered for the Carnival of 1781. The six weeks had become four months without the archbishop taking action. But he was determined to hold him henceforward and keep him within the bounds of duty. He summoned Mozart to Vienna, where he was paying his court to the Emperor. The musician would have welcomed a stay in the capital; unfortunately, the archbishop laid down a condition which took away much of its charm. He made him put up in his own house and treated him as a member of the archiepiscopal suite. Mozart found himself confounded with the lackeys, eating with

---

[1] *The letters of Mozart and his family*, tr. by E. Anderson, III, 1081-3.

the two valets, that is, the body and soul attendants of His Worship, the contrôleur, Herr Zetti, the confectioner, the two cooks, Ceccarelli, Brunetti. . . . The two valets sit at the top of the table, but at least I have the honour of being placed above the cooks.[1]

This was not exceptional treatment; the manners of the day allowed of the incorporation of musicians in the domestic staff. But it is easy to realize that his free life at Munich made such an existence unbearable. In point of fact, the archbishop was not treating him otherwise than his peers treated the musicians in their service, except that his payment was more niggardly; but Mozart aspired to be free; advances had been made to him from several quarters and he was convinced he could win both better earnings and more honour by remaining in Vienna. One day in particular, when he had to play without a fee at a concert in the archbishop's house, he was obliged to refuse an invitation from Countess Thun, whose house the Emperor was to visit that very evening. He was "almost heart-broken" over it. The crisis came when the archbishop, without leaving him as much as one day to get ready, ordered him to set out for Salzburg and, in an interview which Mozart has described, punctu-ated his behest with insults. It was as a result of this scene that the young man left his service and wrote to his father a long letter whence are taken the words quoted at the beginning of this chapter.

This revolt has some historic significance. In the person of Mozart, music cast off the golden fetters of official patronage; his gesture on May 9th, 1781, makes the date the 1789 of musicians. It was he and not Beethoven who caused a "revolutionary wind" to blow in the world of composers; it was this twenty-five-year-old, in whom we are so often prone to see the type *par excellence* of the court musician, who first put the dignity of his art above an assured position and, in order to "live his own life", broke with the tradition honoured by Bach, Haydn, and so many others, seeking to be at the service of none but his genius.

A child of the Revolution without knowing it, the young genius was never really happy till he had wrenched himself free, to his father's intense horror, of the feudalism that oppressed him.[2]

It is on May 9th, 1781, that the Viennese period of his life begins. It was to last ten years and seven months and from it dates most of

---

[1] Id., III, 1060.

[2] Warde Fowler: *Stray notes on Mozart and his music.*

the work we know to-day, except the piano sonatas. The first three of these years, those of his setting up in Vienna and of his marriage, are a somewhat confused time for his art. Full of activity, he is still feeling his way, and many genres interest him. We hear in them a few reminders of the past: the serenades in E flat and C minor, representatives of a form which he was to give up almost entirely. To his new life belong his chamber music, to which he returns after nine years, his C minor mass and sundry fugal compositions, and his first German opera, *Die Entführung aus dem Serail*. To them go his affections; in them we must seek the expression of his soul. The symphony and concerto afford only by-products of his work. It is nevertheless as a soloist that he intends conquering the Viennese public; he calls the piano his "speciality" and adds, "Truly, this is the land of the piano!" but his concertos are less significant, during these three years, than his works for piano solo or two pianos: fantasias, fugues, suite and sonatas.

His first year at Vienna was rather unproductive. The most notable works were four violin sonatas, K.376 and 377 in F, 379 in G, and 380 in E flat, three of which are among his finest; the three wind serenades, of which the B flat had perhaps been composed at Munich, and the two pianos sonata, K.448. Of the B flat and E flat serenades we have already spoken; they are associated with his Salzburg life not only by their genre but by their inspiration, which is close to other works of his last days in that town. But the third, the C minor, which dates from the middle of 1782, opens new paths. It is true that this work, which lacks completely the spirit of a serenade, is related to the two others. It has the changeable temper of the E flat, its abrupt passages from night to day, its rhythmical themes based on the common chord. But despite this it differs from all that had gone before since the E minor violin sonata of 1778. The *galant* frippery has been entirely cast off; the composer's soul lies bare. It is the first of a series which will include the great *minor* works of 1783 to 1788.

RONDO (VARIATIONS) IN D (K.382)
March, 1782[1]

    Allegretto grazioso: 2-4

Orchestra: Strings; flute, two hautboys, two horns, two trumpets, two kettledrums.

---

[1] No. 28 in the *Gesamtausgabe*.

At about the same moment as the composition of this stormy serenade, we meet the first work for piano and orchestra written since Mozart's departure from Salzburg. He had played again at Vienna his 1773 concerto and it had met with success. But the finale in sonata form must have sounded old-fashioned and, to rejuvenate the work, he replaced it with a "rondeau varié", in other terms, a series of variations, which seem to us to-day very paltry beside the original finale.

These variations and the C minor serenade are contemporary also with the superb fantasia and fugue in C, concerning which he tells his sister that he transcribed the fugue while he was meditating the prelude, thus emulating the White Knight who, it will be remembered, invented a new pudding while he was consuming the meat-course. The almost simultaneous appearance of three such different works, two of which are compositions of genius and the third mediocre and frivolous, shows clearly how possible it was for him, as indeed for all the older masters up to and including Beethoven and Schubert, to work on several planes at once, according as he laboured "for himself", for a "select public" or for the "general public". Nevertheless, the distressing banality of these variations for piano and orchestra which, when played as they are meant to be as a finale to the first concerto must make a woeful contrast with the sturdy personality of the two other movements, cannot be explained away by the public they aimed at pleasing. After all, the four Parisian sonatas, K. 330-3, too, had been composed for a similar public and, without reaching the level of the fantasia and fugue, they are far worthier than the variations and bear clearly their author's imprint. The same is true of the two pianos sonata of 1781.

The lack of personality in them should no doubt be considered as the result of the uncertainty in which Mozart stood concerning the likes and dislikes of the capital where he had just arrived and where he was anxious to carve out a place for himself. He felt it necessary at first to travel warily and not to scare his audience with too original works. Let him conquer it first and give it stronger meat later on! The important thing was to live, and to achieve recognition by the Viennese public one had to be ready to sacrifice a little boldness. These variations were made to be performed before an audience unfamiliar and incalculable. The fact of substituting a new movement for the splendid finale shows a submissiveness to prevailing taste which vanishes later.

We must not think that Mozart was distressed by this enforced

docility.   His taste appears to have coincided with that of his hearers.
He was pleased with his rondo.

"I beg you to guard it like a jewel. . . ." he writes to his father and
sister.

"I composed it *specially* for myself—and no one else but my dear
sister must play it."[1]

The movement is seldom played to-day although it has been
recorded, and there is no reason why it should be.   It has nothing
to please modern ears and adds nothing to Mozart's glory.   It is
made up of a theme, seven variations and a short coda.   The theme,
in 2-4 time, is undistinguished; it moves almost entirely within the
compass of five tones and trills mark the weak beats in ten out of its
sixteen bars.   The first six variations are entrusted exclusively to
the piano; at distant intervals, the tutti comes in with the first half of
the theme.   The variations themselves are of the most impersonal
galant type; the first, melodic; the second, in triplets; the third, a
repetition of the theme in the right hand with triplet quavers in the
left; the fourth, the least commonplace, is in the minor with octave
passages for the right hand; the fifth is a trill for one hand and a
repetition of the theme for the other; the sixth, the usual irritating
adagio variation.   The seventh and last, opened by the orchestra,
is in 3-8 time, according to a common and not very felicitous practice;
the piano works away with semi-quavers, the two hands in contrary
motion.   It is followed by the cadenza; then the coda returns to the
tempo primo and to the theme which, shortened, winds up the
movement.

Something of this submissiveness to public taste persists in the
three concertos of this same year.   They form, nevertheless, a genial
little group and Mozart characterizes them with acuteness when he
writes to his father on December 28th, 1782, that they

are a happy medium between what is too easy and too difficult; they are
very brilliant, pleasing to the ear, and natural, without being vapid.
There are passages here and there from which connoisseurs alone can
derive satisfaction; but these passages are written in such a way that the
less learned cannot fail to be pleased, though without knowing why.[2]

Nothing is truer than this appreciation.   "A happy medium

---

[1] March 23rd, 1782.

[2] Id., III, 1242.

between too easy and too difficult": the technique, indeed, remains moderately easy, and the passage work is simple. "Brilliant, pleasing to the ear": we would hesitate perhaps to grant the first epithet to those in F and A, but one must bear in mind the resources of the pianos of Mozart's day. "Natural, without being vapid": strong emotion is indeed absent, but, with the exceptions mentioned in the next paragraph, the music never dissolves into formulæ. As for the "satisfaction" offered to connoisseurs, analysis reveals many exquisite features in the structure that rejoice the delicate and those who do not always require their beauties to be on a large scale.

In these few words, Mozart has himself summed up the characters common to all three. The only point to add is the relative importance of the rondo in two of them. In no later concerto save K.449 does the significance of the rondo so nearly equal that of the first movement. The andantes, on the other hand, are less interesting; two of them are as insignificant as a Mozart slow movement can be.

CONCERTO No. 7 IN F (K.413)
   Summer or autumn of 1782[1]
      Allegro: 3-4
      Larghetto: C (in B flat)
      Tempo di menuetto: 3-4
   Orchestra: Strings, two hautboys, two horns. (Two bassoons were
      added later in the larghetto.)

Set between the last Salzburg concertos on one hand and the great works of 1784 to 1786 on the other, the first piano concerto that Mozart composed in Vienna appears a very timid thing. If we do not take care to consider it with the myopic sympathy we recommended for his first attempts, it will seem commonplace and impersonal. More than one fervent Mozartian has been deceived in it and the writer of these lines owns that he has not always done it justice. Its timidity is perhaps only modesty. It is anxious to remain close to the average feelings of its public; it does not wish to provoke emotions other than those which it is permissible to express in polite

---

[1] No. 11 in the *Gesamtausgabe*. The first of these three concertos was ready to appear by the end of December (letter of Mozart to his father of December 28th, 1782). All three were published by Artaria in the first half of 1783. It is possible that the A major was composed first as their order in the series is K.414, 413, 415.

society; its ideal, in a word, is that of a gentleman in a drawing-room.   Like K.238, 242 and 246, it is a product of the Ancien Régime, one of the few works of Mozart's prime which can be so styled. Everything in it is measured and well-ordered.   Was it not of music such as this, *mutatis mutandis*, that Abbé Goussault was thinking when, at the end of the preceding century, he wrote:

> Music has so close a correspondence to the manners of a gentleman that 'tis no wonder if it please him and he like it.   The agreement of voice and instrument which flatters agreeably and charms his ear, is a constant image of what happens in his life; everything there is in accord, no one thing gives the lie to another, and it can be said that his words, his thoughts, his designs and his deeds are the diverse parts of another music which all men hear and which pleases and edifies all.
>
> On the other side, 'tis no wonder if libertines often savour not this innocent pleasure.   'Twould seem to reproach them for having neither measure nor refinement in their way of life; it fits not with their humour, therefore, to be enamoured of a pleasure which would continually accuse them, and they look for others more suitable to their inclinations and their profligacy.[1]

So much for the libertines; let them seek to go no further! Mozart's seventh concerto would be no country for them to traverse!

But this apparent return to the ideal of a John Christian is not a renunciation of his personality.   If the heart of the work represents the collective soul of his hearers rather than his own, originality is not lacking in the form.   There are delicacies and ingenious traits peculiar to it and it is they which, although noticeable only upon analysis, make the public who listens without studying the score be pleased "without knowing why".   One of its most original features is the manner in which the smoothest phrases can be broken up into fragments which return separately, at distant points one from the other, and act as links between the various sections of the movement. Mozart has never carried further than in the rondo of this concerto his practice of "link themes".   Here, these themes are not only independent ideas; they are the *disjecta membra*, so to speak, of main themes joining together different parts of the whole and unifying it by the discreetly used means of repetition.   This is one of its most interesting characteristics.

It is not the only one.   The themes themselves, though none of them is among those rare melodies of which Mozart had at other

---

[1] *Réflexions sur les défauts ordinaires des hommes et sur leurs bonnes qualités*, 1692.

times the secret, are not commonplace, and their dancing grace,
slightly mischievous, is truly his.   One cannot realize it better than
by playing one after the other the first movements of K.238 and of
this one.   What the earlier work stood for at twenty, this one represents at twenty-six; the ideal is the same but differently realized; and

the difference shows us the full growth of Mozart's mind since the
days when he played at Countess Lodron's at Salzburg.

I. The allegro is one of his few concerto first movements that
is in three-time. (The others are those of K.459 and 491.) It begins
with a rhythmical theme of four bars, followed by a contrasted melodic
one, of seven; the whole forms the first subject (ex. 34). Then
come two secondary motifs, both rhymical and very alike; the second,
the longer of the two, leads to a dominant chord. All this is quite
normal. But then, instead of starting off again in the tonic, according
to custom, Mozart introduces his second subject in C major and does
not return to F for eight bars, an "irregularity" which recurs in K.449.
This second subject bears a first-cousinly likeness to ex. 34; it, too,
alternates between rhythm and melody (ex. 35). The strings give
it out; then, once it has returned to orthodox ways—that is, to the
tonic—the wind joins them. A codetta rounds it off, a passing
thought which does not reappear; then two more motifs, consisting
mainly of scales, and we reach the conclusion. We expect the customary *ff*, with an operatic close, to finish the tutti and announce noisily
that the orchestra is abdicating before the solo. Here comes a fresh
surprise. The *forte* dies down to *piano* and we hear a third subject,
cousin to the other two. Its mildness is encouraging and its
example leads to imitation; the piano, encouraged and imitative,
falls shyly into line behind it, without treading on its heels, and
before it has finished comes upon the stage with yet another
cousin (ex. 36). We have already referred to the originality of
Mozart's solo entries; here is surely one of the most graceful and
most personal.

The second exposition follows the same general lines as those of
the 1776 concertos. After the introductory phrase whose *incipit*
we have quoted, the orchestra gives out the rhythmical half of the
first subject and the piano repeats the melodic part and follows it up
with a short virtuosity passage, very simple, consisting in rising
arpeggios and falling broken scales, and modulating from F to C.
It attacks next the solo subject which gives us the impression of
having been heard before; it resembles less the main subjects than the
subsidiary ones. Another virtuosity passage, no longer than the first,
satisfies for the nonce the piano's ambitions and the orchestra ushers
in the second subject. It gives it out in its entirety and at the point
where, in the tutti, the wind had joined in, the piano resumes and
substitutes an ending of its own. A third passage, as simple as the

foregoing, and a little hesitating chromatic figure lead to the usual trill.

In all this section none of the numerous secondary themes of the tutti has appeared. The orchestra enters now with the last of these and as soon as it is given out the piano opens the *development* with a new subject, the ninth or tenth! This one is different. It is in the minor—C minor—and tries to behave accordingly. It has a would-be passionate air about it which convinces neither us nor the tutti, and the orchestra answers it mockingly. It starts again, this time in G minor, hoping that a change of key may impress us more. As no one interrupts, it grows bolder, modulates to D minor and turns into a charming bravura passage, based on arpeggios, with guileless crossed-hands effects. This passage, the most vigorous in the movement, is longer than the earlier ones, but at length the piano grows weary and, as changeable as a child, and almost without our knowing it, passes from major to minor, from allegro to adagio, and after a few sighs gives way a moment to the tutti which brings in the subject, ex. 36, of the original solo entry.

Only a few changes of detail mark the recapitulation. But, on the very brink of the cadenza, Mozart remembers the abundance of themes he had scattered over the first tutti and quickly sets about rescuing them from oblivion. He places two between the solo's trill and the cadenza and another one after it,[1] and at last we reach, *ff*, the common chord of F. We are getting ready to clap when he pretends to start all over again. *Piano*, the strings murmur ex. 36, but it is only a joke, and just as we await the solo entry, three chords, *forte*, end the game.

II. The larghetto which follows this pleasing allegro is one of the most ordinary movements Mozart wrote during his Viennese years. Almost its only rival in this respect is the andante of the C major concerto of the same year. It is a movement in binary form where the first subject is given out by the tutti and repeated by the piano. Its rhythm of six-beat phrases overlaps agreeably the four-beat rhythm of the bars, but that is its only originality. The whole

---

[1] A very fine cadenza, beginning with an energetic pedal more redolent of the concerto K.459 than of this one, preserved in the archives of St. Peter's in Salzburg, was published in facsimile by Mandyczewski in 1921; we give it in Appendix II, and recommend it earnestly to pianists. The MS. is in Leopold's handwriting.

movement unfolds without any change of tone, with melodic developments of a banal sweetness in the right hand and an unflagging Alberti
bass in the left.   A more personal note is sounded in the lovely
strain which acts as a lead back to the first subject (ex. 37).   One
recognizes in it something of that refined and sensuous dreaminess
peculiar to Mozart, but this passage, which returns just before the
cadenza,[1] is the only one where the composer removes his mask.

III. The rondo has all the qualities of the first movement and
more; it is not only the finest part of the concerto but also one of
Mozart's pleasantest finales in its melodic development and one of the
most original in its form.   We find in it the same breaking-up of
themes as in the allegro and yet the flow of melody is continuous and
nothing less stiffly articulated could be imagined.   The theme of the
refrain looks as if it had been conceived as a whole and yet it allows
itself to be split up with the best grace in the world and its pieces,
once separate, take on with goodwill the parts allotted to them.
When the refrain itself comes back, it is not content with identity;
at each return there is a change, either in the melodic order or in the
harmonization.

The tutti starts and gives out the refrain, a minuet theme of thirty-
two bars which breaks up into phrases of four bars each.   This regularity pertains to the dance character of the movement and is kept up,
on the whole, to the end.   It is the only time that the refrain is presented entire; at each of its two other returns it is shortened and modified, either by having a different bass or by the addition of a new
motif.   With its indolent treble and its very active bass, it recalls the
rondo of the violin sonata in E flat, K.302, and is one of Mozart's
most lovable refrain themes (ex. 38).

The solo enters with a new motif which is not much more than
a variation of the refrain; there is indeed between the different ideas
of this movement the same cousinship as between those of the first.
This motif, repeated in an octave passage, does not reappear.   It is
followed by a short orchestral interruption, a first instance of the
fragmentation already mentioned.   The fragment with which the
tutti intervenes is drawn from the second half of the refrain (ex. 39).
The piano takes it up again and launches forth into a bravura figure
destined to enjoy much working-out in the second couplet.   The

---

[1] A charming cadenza in Leopold's handwriting, based on this phrase,
has been published by Mandyczewski.   See note on p. 133, and Appendix II.

tutti prepares the return of the refrain by borrowing from it another
fragment of its second half (ex. 40) which the piano repeats and
varies.   Then, with a miniature horn fanfare (still on the piano), the
first part of the refrain returns to view.

One regrets sometimes that 18th-century composers, especially
those of that part of the century which saw the triumph of the rondo,
did not more often vary their refrains, and this regret is called forth
by certain works of Mozart himself.   There is no cause for it here,
and at the first return the piano repeats the refrain with a fine triplet
bass, a generous variant of the original falling scale (ex. 41).   The
second part of the refrain is not repeated; in its stead there appears
a new "fragment" which will henceforward take the place of ex.
40, which vanishes for good.   The last four bars of the refrain conclude and the second couplet opens with the new strain we have just
heard, given out again by the piano.

This second couplet is also the last, for Mozart gives up in this
concerto and the next the sonata rondo form in three sections in favour
of the binary rondo.   This latter, from its very structure, tends to
be less homogeneous than the ternary one, but here it is not so, and
the close kinship of nearly all the themes and the constant return of
fragments of the refrain make it a well-blended whole in which only
a close analysis can discover "sections".   At a hearing, in spite of the
apparent symmetry of the phrases, they melt one into the other without any of the usual clear-cut divisions of many contemporary rondos.

In principle, this second couplet repeats the first, but there are a
good many differences.   The figure with which the first began is
replaced by the new refrain fragment.   The virtuosity figure sets
off now in F minor and for a few moments the placid minuet catches
fire, modulates rapidly through minor keys and dies down in the horn
fanfare already heard, which once again announces the refrain's
return.   With the fragment ex. 39, it is the only element that comes
back unchanged.

On the third and last appearance of the refrain, it has a coda-like
breadth.   Here, the variation consists in attributing the theme to
the strings, whilst the piano accompanies with a spacious scale which
drops and rises over a compass of three octaves.   The latest comer of
the fragments leads into one last short bravura passage, after which
the main theme returns with a descant, a sort of diminution of the
original bass, first in the lower register, then in the treble (ex. 48).
A new figure, also related to the earlier ones, serves as coda; the
solo adds to it a counterpoint of scales in the right hand and after one

last *forte* the concerto dies down to *piano*, a conclusion as original as the plan of the rondo, fitting for the mild temper of the whole work.

CONCERTO NO. 8 IN A MAJOR (K.414)
Summer or autumn, 1782[1]
    Allegro: C
    Andante: 3-4 (in D)
    Allegretto: 2-4
Orchestra: Strings; two hautboys, two horns.

I. The general character of this concerto is the same as the last; the two works are close relatives. Both live and breathe in the same temperate climate and avoid not only what might shock but even what might merely astonish their public. Both are perfectly urbane.

But the likeness goes no further. Formally, the A major is less interesting than its predecessor. Its thought, on the other hand, is more personal. Its first four bars not only are true Mozart; they are also the Mozart which we at once hail as unique, whereas the Mozart of K.413 was merely he who said, better than anyone else, what was on everyone's lips. Then, in the tenth bar, the simple held note in the woodwind (one bar late) on the return of the theme raises the work at once to a poetic plane.

The first subject has the graceful and melancholy nonchalance, the melting sweetness, which belong to many an A major composition of the master, which reappear with greater breadth in the concerto of 1786 and rise to serenity (not without remembering their sorrowful starting-point) in the clarinet quintet of 1789 (ex. 43).

It is the sentiment whose development we are tracing here; the form has a different history. The theme belongs to a type fairly common in Mozart. One of its first appearances is in the adagio which opens the finale of the *Haffner* serenade (1776), where its meaning is not the same as here. It reappears in the *Prussian* D major quartet of 1789, where it is closer in significance to our concerto. This dissociation of the outline of a theme from its meaning is curious; the number of outlines is perforce limited but the power of expression is infinite.

Warlike strains in the wind, to which a scale fragment answers in the first violins, are now heard thrice; then the violins bring us

---

[1] No. 12 in the *Gesamtausgabe*. See note on p. 129.

back, *piano*, to the starting-point and the subject begins again.   A new string figure, with a rhythmical opening, resolves itself into a retarded scale succeeded abruptly by the usual noisy close on the dominant.   The repetition of several of the most important phrases and the tendency of the melodic line to progress by conjunct degrees or at least by small intervals, characterize the whole allegro; through them are expressed the slow-beating emotion and the melancholy and languishing sweetness with which it is so deeply marked.   This passage does not reappear; its place later on will be taken by the solo subject.

The noisy close with its very conventional outline is irritatingly, or humorously, contrasting.   We know of no other work of Mozart's prime where so marked a contrast occurs between the substance of the thought and the conventional lines that bound it.   In the preceding concerto, which resembles this one in the likeness between all its themes, such operatic closes were absent, and greater unity was the result.   Here, it is as if each theme was anxious to keep its independence and remain in its own home.   For this purpose, they raise between them these barriers, so stereotyped in design, which come and interrupt, some may think intempestively, the flow of feeling.

The second subject has a march rhythm like many subjects in Mozart's Vienna concertos.   It is one of the earliest examples of them.   But it is an unexhilarating march, still touched by the wilting nonchalance of the beginning and inclining us to dream rather than to step out.   It calls up a cohort of ghostly marionettes crossing a two-dimensional landscape.   The tune takes great care to avoid the tonic and to repeat the sharpened passing note, and its main stress falls against the beat (ex. 44).   The design is cleverly divided between unison violins and violas.   Its outline blurs into a beautiful passage which prolongs it: a bass pedal on which there rises in tiers a scale climbing one tone every bar, marked by short runs, where first and second violins overtake each other in turn.   Thanks to the clashing seconds that result, the dream atmosphere of the march is retained till the momentary *ff* of a full close (ex. 45).   A third subject, similar to the preceding, comes forward, and the tutti ends with a short scale passage, repeated, and a close on the tonic.   All this introduction does not leave the key of A major.

We have already said that, if the inspiration is more personal here than in the concerto in F, the form is more commonplace.   There is no original solo entry; the piano simply takes up the first subject and expounds it twice, the first time without accompaniment, the second with held notes in the strings.   The tutti then comes in with the figure of the close just heard and the piano, catching at one of its motifs, derives from it the solo subject, similar in character to the others. After a bravura passage, as simple as those of the last concerto, we reach the key of E major and the tutti opens the march; the solo snatches it away at the end of four bars and, adding a semiquaver accompaniment, instils some activity into it. The orchestra relapses into silence, or almost, and comes out of it only at the end of the exposition to applaud what the piano has been saying with the familiar cadential figure.

The movement remains rather prim throughout the *development* in spite of the usually greater freedom of this part. At first comes a new theme, entrusted to the piano alone and having also a march rhythm. Like so many others in this concerto it is given out twice. We are still in E major. A breath of vigour inspires the solo; after four bars of arpeggios we are in F sharp minor and piano and violins engage in a short conversation in which the answers overlap in an almost dramatic manner. The vigour rises to passion; orchestra and piano stride quickly over the regions of the tonic and relative minors, landing finally, with strong emotion, on a succession of trills and a pause. This is the most exciting passage in the movement and the most interesting for the interplay of piano and strings. The left hand and bass strings double; the harmonies are provided by the violins and violas and right hand arpeggios of the piano an octave higher.

Mozart's reprises are most various and often masterly; this one is simple and even perfunctory. After a pause a cadenza is indicated, a falling scale of three octaves; then a silent bar, and the strings take up the first subject. The idea of filling the hole, as it were, between the end of the *development* and the beginning of the recapitulation with a cadenza comes back three years later when he composes another piano concerto in A: an instance of the fact that not only the feeling but the technical imagination follow similar paths in identical keys. This kinship of thought and form between works in the same key is particularly clear in him; a journey through his music is constantly reminding us of it.

Yet, if kinship exists between keys, it also exists between works of the same period, and this passage recalls also a resemblance of this kind. It is only in the concerto in A that Mozart has used the reprise with a mere cadenza, but the feeling which this device expresses— the emotional about-turn which consists in passing sharply from one mood to another very different one—is found again, at the same point, in each of the 1782 concertos. Here, the cadenza expresses it; in K.413,

a modulation and change of *tempo*; in K.415, a modulation, change
of rhythm and short cadenza—three different ways of translating the
same experience.

The recapitulation does not repeat the first part unchanged. It
condenses the passages that follow the solo subject and second subject;
in the last, Mozart repeats a figure from the exposition but wittily
inverts it, retaining the same harmonization. The third subject,
given out by the strings, taken up by the piano, follows this passage,
and the last runs, most of them a mere assertion of the chord of A,
prolong it. Only then does the dreamy pedal return (ex. 45); more
hurried now, it leads to the cadenza. The collection of cadenzas
contains two for this movement;[1] the shorter one of the two, based
on the third subject, is by far the more attractive. Then, with a
certain flippancy, a codetta ends the movement.

II. The andante is far from having the insignificance of those of
the other two concertos of this year. It begins with a solemn theme,
almost religious, exceptionally fully harmonized.[2] To hurry it as
is sometimes done is to rob it of its meaning and full value should
be given to the bass (ex. 46). It is given out by the strings and
followed by a second theme whose outline recalls the first subject of
the allegro; the repeated notes of the accompaniment give it a lighter
step than the first. Then, in the briefest glimpse, we see lands full
of poetry through a half-opened door that closes again immediately,
leaving us full of wonder and desire (ex. 47).

The piano repeats the first theme, then, before passing to the
second, inserts a fresh one reserved for it and which does not return.
The second subject appears in A; its melodic line is ornate and it leads
to the trill which closes the first solo.

---

[1] The manuscript of the cadenzas for this concerto (K.624, 7-14) has on
the back sketches for the other A major concerto, K.488, of 1786; this may
help to date them. It is curious that Mozart should have taken up this little
A major work again, no doubt for teaching, at the moment when he was
thinking of the greater work in the same key.

[2] This theme is taken from the first bars of the second movement (andante
grazioso, 3-4, in D) of an overture of John Christian Bach, composed in 1763
for a revival of Galuppi's *La Calamità dei Cuori* (Saint-Foix, III, 323; C. S.
Terry, *John Christian Bach*, 272). John Christian had died on January 1st,
1782, and the presence of this theme, surmises Saint-Foix (V.319), may well
be an act of homage to the deceased composer whom Mozart always loved
and whose death day he called "a sad day for the world of music". See
p. 388, note 1.

Ex. 45

Ex. 46

Ex. 47

Ex. 48

Ex. 49

Ex. 50

Again the door is half-opened and our eyes light upon the mysterious region seen just now.   But this time after the two bars, instead of closing, it opens wider and we launch forth into fairyland.   The piano enters it boldly with its very first chord.   We pass from major to minor—a transition seldom without special meaning in Mozart —and suddenly the mystery deepens.   The rustling thirds of the fiddles and violas end one phrase; those of the piano open another.   Already in the major they were crepuscular, but the twilight was that of a beautiful day going to rest; in the minor, it is threatening and bodes of ill to come.   The strings die away to *pp*; the solo re-enters *mf*;[1] there is not only a change of light but also an uprush of energy, a greater strain and a motion towards the unknown.   What does the future hold for us? the piano seems to ask.

It travels on, forsaken by the orchestra, with the air of a solitary rebel.   It repeats the figure an octave higher and adds a stormy commentary, then quietens down somewhat upon the chord of E minor (ex. 48).   The orchestra, conquered, devoid of initiative, can only murmur its theme afresh, *piano*, but still in the minor.   The solo sets off again in an angry climb, punctuated by accents against the beat, and stops in B minor.   Again, the orchestra raises its voice and, still submissive, repeats the same lesson (ex. 49).   A third time the piano returns, but, more at ease, it brings back the major now, though only for an instant, and first the horns, then the hautboys sustain and accompany its steps.   Without leaving the figure, but with a fresh significance at each repetition, it leads it through a threefold assertion to the point where the strings take it up again, in A minor, whilst the piano confines itself to announcing with a trill the end of the exploration (ex. 50).

Mozart is fond of linking up the *development* to the exposition by opening it with the last motif of the latter, especially in concerto first movements where the absence of a double bar makes the device easier than in a symphony or quartet.[2]   But he does it seldom in andantes and yet more seldom does he build the whole *development* upon this motif.   This time, not only does he begin by taking up the theme which had just died down but, held by its beauty, he is unable to tear himself from it.   However, even with new material, he could not have created anything more unlike what had gone before.

---

[1] The *piano* marked in the solo arrangement published by Breitkopf is not in the *Gesamtausgabe*, but is clearly needed by the feeling of the passage.

[2] K.482, 537.

The recapitulation leaves out the solo subject and repeats the others without change. Of the two cadenzas in the collection K.624, the longer is based on the second subject; the other, on the third; this latter is by far the more attractive.

III. If the andante of this concerto is much superior to those of the F and C major, its rondo is less interesting than theirs. Its refrain is a 2-4 theme whose tripping step and decided air contrast with the melting sweetness of the first movement and the solemnity of the second. The rondo keeps this character throughout; there is nevertheless more contrast between its themes than in the minuet-finale of K. 413.

This rondo is also in two parts, the second of which, with a few modifications, repeats the first. The tutti alone gives out the refrain which is composed of three motifs, the second of which is in unison (ex. 51, a, b, c). The first couplet begins with a new theme; then the strings recall the unison motif (b) and the piano takes it up with contrapuntal treatment. The first violins then accost a fresh subject which the piano completes and the two converse for a few bars. The motif (b) reappears in the piano with a triplet accompaniment. The rest of the couplet is concerned with it, repeating it with different harmonization and passing it from piano to orchestra and back again.

Piano, then tutti, repeat the first part of the refrain; the tutti broaches (b) but before finishing it modulates epigrammatically from A to D. The solo opens the second couplet with a new subject; violins and violas converse upon it for a few bars, then the piano concludes. After a moment of energy, passing through B minor and E, we rediscover, in A, a subject of the first couplet. The working-out of (b), transposed from E to A, is taken up again without change and an interesting section of eleven bars—the most interesting in the whole rondo for its orchestration: a contrapuntal development of (b) on a tonic pedal of horns and second fiddles—leads to the cadenza. The *ad libitum* part of the cadenza ends with the subject that had opened the first couplet, but after six bars the piano tires of it; the tutti seeks to complete it but also gives it up; the piano makes one last effort, then, accompanied by the strings, adds a few bars of *cadenza obbligata* and ends up on a dominant seventh chord instead of the usual trill. The movement infringes the conventions still further by giving the last return of the refrain, just after the cadenza, to piano and allowing the orchestra to join in only six bars from the end, with ex. 51 (c).

Apart from the lead to the cadenza, the most interesting moments in this rondo are the rare ones when piano and orchestra interplay. Thus, in the development of (b) which we have mentioned, the violins give out the motif, whilst the piano accompanies with chords on the strong beats, a combination which does not occur elsewhere in Mozart (ex. 52).

RONDO IN A (K.386)
October 19th, 1782
    Allegretto: 2-4
Orchestra: Strings, two hautboys, two horns.

Another source of interest in this rondo lies in its likeness to a second rondo in A for piano and orchestra, entered by Köchel under the number 386. The score of this was not published in Mozart's time and the manuscript, not quite finished, but still almost intact in the last century, seems to have been disleaved at the casual hands of auctioneers.[1]

The date inscribed on the manuscript and noted by André: October 19th, 1782, leads one to think that it was conceived as finale for this concerto. It has the same tone of melancholy nonchalance as the first movement of K.414; possibly Mozart considered that a certain monotony might arise from the likeness of the two movements. He may then have substituted the present finale, whose lively and dapper step is very different from the allegro. It certainly belongs to the same period and may be studied here.

It opens with a tutti of unusual length. Most of Mozart's concerto rondos let the solo give out the subject; some of them, however, make it wait till after a short tutti exposition; but in no other is this exposition as extensive as here. It includes the three sections of the refrain, of which only the first will return each time (ex. 53). The second one is rather insignificant and only eight bars long; the third, fuller, consists in a unison passage, *piano*, then *forte*, and leads to four bars of coda.

Thereupon the piano enters with the first strain, slightly modified.

----

[1] It belonged at one time to Sterndale Bennett. Two leaves have been retrieved of late and from these, as well as from a piano arrangement published by Cipriani Potter for Novello's in the 'forties of the last century, Alfred Einstein has reconstructed the whole movement (Universal, 1936).

It leads with three transition bars to the first couplet which opens in
E with a favourite Mozartian theme.[1]   The solo then opens out into
passages of measured and graceful virtuosity where hand crossings
play a part, but comes quickly back to the *cantabile* with a tune which
constitutes the movement's second subject (ex. 54).   It is a close
relation to the second subject of K.415 (ex. 15 b).   A very short
virtuosity passage follows it and ends on an interrupted cadence,
after which the tutti concludes the section.   This is the only moment
in the rondo, with its repetition later on, where the regular and rather
languid rhythm is broken by something harsher.   A lovely dialoguing
passage brings back the refrain (ex. 55).

This latter returns first in the solo, then in the orchestra, which
adds the octave figure and modulates to F sharp minor, the key in
which the second couplet is laid.   It opens with demi-semi-quaver
arpeggios on the common chord, which the tutti crosses with an
accompaniment in contrary motion, partly indicated in Potter's
arrangement.   But the virtuosity soon ends and from the threats of
storm there arises ex. 54, transposed into the minor with an alteration in the bass which makes these bars the most original passage in
the movement (ex. 56).   The melody starts again, modulating by
falling degrees to D major, where it halts a moment, to pass next
into A minor, E, and thence back to the tonic key and the
refrain.

The rest of the movement is made up of the refrain, repeated completely by the tutti and followed by a very short piano passage which
leads to the interrupted cadence of the first couplet, after which the
beginning of the refrain is given out for the last time; the piano
adds bars of runs and the rondo ends in a typical manner with a
couple of sharp rejoinders from tutti to piano.

The very moderate virtuosity of this movement and its technical
simplicity are its chief external characteristics.   In form it resembles
the two-couplet rondos of K.413 and 414.   It modulates less than
the last and its rhythm is more uniform.   If Mozart really wrote
it for the concerto in A, there is no cause to regret that he replaced
it by the present rondo, which is better.   But it is a pleasant little
piece and its reconstruction by Alfred Einstein is a work of piety for
which all Mozartians are grateful.

---

[1] Based on the third, fourth and fifth degrees of the scale.   See the first
movements of the C major concertos K.246, 415 and 503; also the beginning
of the *development* in the first movement of the D major quartet, K.575.

CONCERTO No. 9 IN C (K.415)
Summer or autumn, 1782[1]
  Allegro: C
  Andante: 3-4 (in F)
  Allegro: 6-8; Adagio: 2-4
Orchestra: Strings, two hautboys, two bassoons, two horns, two trumpets, two kettledrums.

The first two concertos of this year had kept within moderate limits of thought, technique and orchestration. If the appreciation expressed by Mozart which we quoted earlier is true for them, the epithet "brilliant" is more suitable for the third and its orchestral part, at least, is proof of a real emancipation. After the prudence of his beginnings, Mozart grows bolder; he indulges his taste for counterpoint and rich instrumentation. The orchestra is the biggest he has used till now. Unhappily, the piano part still remains timid and the counterpoint ceases when the solo comes on the scenes. The result is an unequal and heterogeneous work where great beauties remain unknown because they lie side by side with weaknesses and banalities. After the piano entry, the work loses itself in conventional virtuosity, smiling and sparkling but empty, and we are reminded of those ambitious churches which the Middle Ages had left unfinished, where behind a magnificent Flamboyant façade lies a mean nave, hastily put up with insufficient funds in later times. Yet, just as there may exist inside a few pillars from the grander epoch, so the tuttis bring back something of the opening splendour. But each time the piano speaks, endless scales and arpeggios drive away the counterpoint and finish off the work poorly, just as the patched-up supports and plaster ceiling of a debased period complete the Flamboyant fragment.

We have said enough to show that the work, although not perfect, is far from being uninteresting. It is interesting, first of all, in that it shows the influence of the polyphonic masters upon Mozart. This influence dates from this very year 1782 and this concerto is the first of the genre where one notices it. Engrossing while it lasted, like all those Mozart underwent, it inspired a certain number of fine works. Two of the best known of these are the first of the six quartets dedicated to Haydn, in G, in the finale of which *fugato* alternates with homophony, and the first movement of the *Haffner* symphony, K.385. There are also some attempts in out-of-date forms where

---

[1] No. 13 in the *Gesamtausgabe*.

Mozart's personality has left its imprint: the superb fantasia and fugue in C, K.394, and the fugue in the suite in the style of Handel, K.399, movements full of fire which are in nowise exercises "in imitation of . . ."; a prelude and fugue in A for violin and piano, K.402, unfortunately incomplete,[1] and especially a four-part fugue in C minor, of great beauty but almost as enigmatic as Beethoven's Great Fugue. It is generally known (if indeed it can be said to be known!) in the version for two pianos, but it is more intelligible in the arrangement which Mozart made of it for string quartet; it is illuminated by the harrowing adagio, K.546, which he added to it as a prelude. The crown of these polyphonic works is the choral part of the C minor mass, that masterpiece of sacred music which, after more than a century of neglect, is at last coming into its own. The *Qui tollis*, *Cum sancto spiritu* and *Hosanna* (to quote only the contrapuntal numbers) are summits which lose nothing of their greatness when they are heard in the neighbourhood of Bach's finest choruses.[2] Counterpoint is here as vital a means of expression as harmony and nothing is more unfair than to see in it a pseudo-archæological curiosity. It has that limpid, singing quality which is the charm of Mozartian polyphony and which is found at its highest in the finale of the *Jupiter* symphony.

The first movement of this concerto is interesting also in that it is another example of that Olympian strain that we saw appear in his musical personality towards 1780. The mood to which it corresponds finds several times expression in the key of C major; the concerto, K.503, the quintet and the *Jupiter* symphony are notable instance, of it. Sometimes, Olympian serenity is allied to physical energys and it is so here.

I.   The work begins, with a mildness belied by the rest of the movement, on a march rhythm: ♩ ♫♩♩. We have already met this rhythm; henceforward, it will be frequent. It is typical of concertos and Mozart is merely complying with custom in adopting it.[3]

---

[1] The fugue was finished by Sechter. A great many sketches of fugues, for one or two pianos, string trio and quartet, given in the second appendix of the original Köchel, are also proofs of his infatuation at this period with polyphonic composition.

[2] The best pages written on it are in Saint-Foix's third volume and in Henri Gheon's *Promenades avec Mozart*.

[3] This theme, in its outline but not in its rhythm, is a variation of the first bars of the mass in C major, K.337.

The first violins give out this subject alone. For one moment it might be taken for a fugal entry. But when the theme (ex. 57), at the end of two bars, starts again two degrees higher up, the second violins repeat it at its original pitch, doubling the firsts a third below. The fugue is nothing but a canon! Then violas and basses take the place of the seconds while the firsts continue with a counter-subject in broken rhythm in which the other strings, giving up the march, end by joining.

The whole orchestra, hautboys, bassoons, horns, trumpets, drums and strings, thereupon bursts forth *ff* with a fresh subject. Proud and mighty, it climbs with a dignity not devoid of liveliness the eight degrees of the scale; then the basses pick up a new fragment and the violas pursue them in a canon at the octave while the violins emphasize the weak beats with chords: the whole leads to a full close.

The emotional strain has gone on heightening rapidly since the entry of the full orchestra. One would expect the full close to call a halt. But Mozart, instead of stopping and setting off afresh with a new theme, holds on the G, the fundamental of the last chord, with the basses, bassoons and horns, and this note, falling suddenly from *forte* to *piano*, becomes a pedal on which for twelve bars there is built up a dashing contrapuntal development in three parts. It is the most authentically polyphonic part of the whole work. Over this pedal the violas trace a moving figure, whilst the fiddles converse in phrases which resemble each other without being identical and link together in a single discourse (ex. 58). At the end of eight bars, the strain is relaxed; the pedal loses its power through repetition; the counterpoint fades away and in the first violins we hear a new theme— the fourth—of an archaic and Handelian cast.[1] All this passage is highly poetic and intensely vigorous; it is the image of a young god and the idea it gives us of the work is one of splendour. But, alas, it is deceptive! None of its first part—eight bars out of twelve —will come back; the polyphony is not much more than make-believe; it bears little relation to what follows the solo entry.

From the beginning of the pedal, the mark is *piano*. We return to the broad daylight of *forte* with a variant of the first subject which, like it, comes forward with mock fugal gestures and, like it also, breaks its promises. After a brief return to *piano*, the concluding subject brings back the full orchestra, *forte*. All of a piece, it is

---

[1] Beethoven works it hard in his overture *Zur Weihe des Hauses*, itself an archaistic piece.

nevertheless destined later on to break up, like the themes of K.413;
the first part, spacious, based on the scale, does not return till after
the cadenza; the next, formed by the favourite Italian overture motif
(ex. 59), and the third, a mere formula, conclude also both exposition
and recapitulation.

Let us cast a glance back at this unorthodox tutti. It is an experi-
ment, and interesting like all that is new. But can it be called
successful? It has fifty-nine bars. Now, of these, twenty-three—
that is, two-fifths of the whole—will not be heard again, and they
comprise some of the finest and most vigorous stuff in the tutti.
Out of the thirty-six that return at one time or other, only nine will
be utilized by the piano; as for the remainder, seventeen will not be
heard till the end of the movement, either before or after the cadenza.
There remain the first seven (the march), the last eight (the second
and third fragments of the concluding subject) and four towards
the middle (the Handelian figure); these are the only ones that we
shall meet several times in the body of the allegro. What conclusion
can we draw from this?

First, that few elements are common to tutti and solo; orchestra
and piano have each their own themes. This, for a *galant* concerto,
is exceptional; we know that the custom is to let both give out
most of the subjects, only one or two of them being reserved either
for the solo or for the orchestra. One might be tempted to consider
Mozart in this respect as a forerunner and this concerto as an ancestor
of modern works where each instrument has its motifs, never borrows
its neighbour's or lends him its own. We think that it should rather
be looked upon as an archaism, a return to the practice of the preceding
epoch. In the works of the older concertists, harpsichord and
orchestra tend jealously to keep their own themes and nothing, or
almost nothing, in the melodic material is common. This is still
sometimes the case with Philip Emmanuel Bach, and in the best of
Schobert's six concertos, op. 12 in E flat, written only fifteen years
earlier than this one, all that the solo keeps of the first subject is the
chaconne-like bass. When we remember that nearly everything in
the introduction of our concerto has an archaic aspect, it seems clear
that Mozart owes this feature to the studies he had been making of
the Bach and Handel period.

Only, in his age, the structure of the concerto allegro is no longer
the rondo-concerto of an earlier time, in which the main theme came
back like a refrain in the tutti between each solo. Mozart's concerto
is the sonata-concerto and the sharing of subjects is a condition

implied in its very formula.   The result is an upsetting of the balance, a heterogeneous character which strengthens the impression we had already and prevents us from classing the movement, in spite of its beauties, among his successful works.

The piano enters with seven bars of new material, of no great originality and rather colourless after what has gone before.   Then the strings repeat the first subject as we had it at the beginning; in the middle of the fourth bar, that is, just before the violas' and basses' entry, the piano adds a trill to the counterpoint, then continues alone and finishes its phrase.   From this time on to the end of the exposition the orchestra's part is confined to accompanying, or to interposing very short, commonplace figures, mere links between one solo phrase and the next.

There is no solo subject or rather the second subject is itself entirely reserved for the solo. The bravura passage which separates the orchestra's silence (at the end of the first subject) from the second subject is most ordinary; it consists mainly in a one-bar figure repeated seven times on different degrees of the scale of G major.   As for the second subject, it belongs to the family of those we find in two other C major concertos, K.246 and 503, and in the rondo K.386. These four subjects are at bottom merely transformations of the same idea, whose fullest realization is reached in the great K.503 of 1786.   (Exs. 15 and 54.)   The piano expounds it twice; the second time, the soloist should vary it; it is meaningless to play it again exactly as it is written. Then another virtuosity passage brings something more original; the Handelian theme from the introduction, given out first in the right hand, in double counterpoint with a semi-quaver running figure. The usual trill which one expects to close the exposition does not check the piano's volubility; it pursues uninterruptedly with the second fragment of the conclusion (ex. 59) and only after a new display of high spirits and a series of scales does it come to the end of its race.

The tutti's intervention, generally important at this stage, is short. It consists in a reassertion of the first subject in unison in violas, basses and bassoons, under the repeated notes of the fiddles, followed by the third fragment of the concluding theme.

The *development* is, after the opening tutti, the most interesting part of the movement. The piano starts off with a vigorous and contrasted theme, in minims and semi-breves followed by semi-quavers, treated in imitation, and for four bars we plunge again into the polyphonic atmosphere of the beginning (ex. 60). Two bars of tutti take us from G to C (the whole movement modulates extremely little; we hardly leave the tonic or its dominant), and the vigorous figure is repeated. It lands us in E minor and here the orchestra tries timidly to join in. But of all its riches at the beginning the poor thing has preserved only the first subject, and it keeps on going over it as if it was reciting a lesson. Moreover, only the first fiddles know it; the other strings and the hautboys just sustain and accompany them. For six bars the first member of the subject passes from key to key, rising from A minor to C, from C to E minor. But the piano does not remain aloof. To each repetition of the theme it adds a graceful counterpoint (ex. 61), a figure formed of a falling scale and a held note, and itself of polyphonic origin. This is one of the loveliest moments in the concerto and the only one in the movement where there is interplay between piano and orchestra. At last, at the end of the sixth bar, the piano gets rid of its feeble antagonist and forges joyously ahead, borne on a characterless arpeggio figure which it repeats half a dozen times in different keys, and comes quickly back to C major. Naïve, and not highly original!

But now, after this effervescing of carefree virtuosity, a change of one note (from E to E flat) carries us suddenly into the minor. Mozart pulls up abruptly, almost tragically, and drops in a broken scale to the tenor regions, where he lingers a while with his favourite and touching figure of fluttering seconds, before coming back, via a cadenza, to the first subject. He is like a child at play whose brow is suddenly overcast and who cuts short its game, assumes for an instant a serious look, then throws it off and returns to its former occupation.

To the end of the solo, the exposition is followed except for insignificant changes and without, of course, leaving the key of C major. Few of Mozart's concertos reproduce the first section so slavishly. After the last trill, the orchestra comes in with the "proud and mighty" subject which had followed the first theme in the opening tutti. It ends again with the little canon between basses and violas, then we stop on the dominant chord for the cadenza. Mozart has left a most vigorous cadenza for this movement. It sets off with fiery flight in the canon that has just stopped, each hand playing in octaves. Then comes a recall of the second subject and finally the Handelian theme, treated as in the solo part. To conclude, the orchestra gives out the whole of the final subject and the allegro finishes, note for note, like the first tutti.

II. The andante is a ternary movement: A—B—A—Coda. We

have already alluded to its complete insignificance. It has not even momentary glimmers of personality, like that of K.413; its commonplaceness is constant from end to end. It is, moreover, afflicted with repetition mania; thus, the uninteresting first subject is heard six times in all! Mozart had at first thought of a movement in C minor, four and a half bars of which he wrote and then crossed out; the mood this movement would have expressed is no doubt that of the C minor interlude in the finale.

III.   The rondo is the best movement.   By its construction and the ingenious use it makes of its material, it ranks among Mozart's most original finales.   During his first years in Vienna, he amused himself with composing rondos that follow no fixed model, where the refrain comes back unexpectedly and mingles with the episodes.   This one and the finale of K.449 are the most whimsical of them.   To its agreeably irregular structure, it adds changes of movement, twice interposing an adagio in the minor, 2-4, whereas the rest is a 6-8 allegro.

Its character is different from that of the first allegro (as far as one can speak of a general character in that heterogeneous movement); the Olympian sereneness, the "young god" vigour of the finest bars in the opening do not appear.   The unexpectedness of the form reflects that of the thought; its spriteliness, vivacity, whimsicality and ingenuousness, and its constant Mozartian changes of temper, make it one of the master's most lovable, if not his deepest, pieces.

The piano opens the game with a 6-8 motif (ex. 62).   Though reminiscent of a jig, its rhythm is not really that of any set dance form. It makes one think of a solo performed by a rustic who has an elf among his forebears and who adds to the yokeldom of his confrères a light, mischievous touch inherited from his distant ancestors.   It appears simple and, at first, inoffensive, but it has plenty of tricks up its sleeve.   Let us call it A.

The tutti repeats it and adds a second motif, less characterized, which we will call B, after which a codetta with a syncopated rhythm, of the same stock as A but more roguish, leads us to a dominant seventh close (ex. 63).   We start again with a third motif (ex. 64), C, which also ends with a codetta based on A (ex. 65), and only after this long introduction which ends on the common chord of G does the piano speak again.

This opening corresponds by its position to the refrain of a rondo, but by its content it is more like the first tutti of an allegro.   It is composed of five elements which we have rather arbitrarily distinguished one from another; such riches is not the rule in a mere refrain.   Moreover, except for the adagio which follows it and which is a parenthesis, all the movement is built upon the material of this beginning.   No new tune appears in the rest.   It is more than one

can say even of many allegro tuttis, including especially the one we have just been studying; these are often content to present us with a selection of the main themes. Here, the whole cast files past us. One hesitates, therefore, to call such an introduction a refrain; but, whatever name we give it, it is truly one of Mozart's most felicitous finale openings.

Very different is the plaint exhaled by the piano on its return. We had stopped on the chord of G; we start again in C minor. Since the E flat concerto of 1777 we had not heard so desolate a lament. For some fifteen bars there unfolds one of those "tragic" andantes like those of that concerto and of the *Sinfonia Concertante*, like that which will be heard a few years hence in the great E flat concerto of 1785 (ex. 66). All this interlude has a recitative-like tone; it is a lonely voice, singing of suffering, which rises in the midst of the communal joy. The orchestra, startled by the intrusion of this unknown being, is at first almost silenced; then, at the conclusion of the first strain, violins, hautboys and bassoons echo it (ex. 4). They repeat the same fragment a bar later and finally, when the close is reached, the whole orchestra joins in perfect accord with the piano and corroborates its declaration. And once again we stop on the chord of G, as before the beginning of the interlude. The return to the same point emphasizes the parenthetic nature of these fifteen bars, a mere insertion which one could skip without the logic of the movement suffering thereby.

A pause, which should not be curtailed, and theme A comes back, first in the piano, then in the tutti, exactly as if nothing had happened. But what follows is different. We compared the first part of this rondo, up to the adagio, to a first movement introduction; that which now opens is like a *development*. It unfolds entirely in the key of the dominant and bases itself only on B and C and one of the two codettas of the refrain. When the tutti has done with A, the piano goes on with B and, supported by the strings which supply the intermediate parts, enters on a bravura passage (ex. 67). But virtuosity finds little place in this movement and after ten bars it ceases and the syncopated codetta ex. 63 leads us back to C, given out first by the tutti then, an octave higher, by the piano. Another solo passage, rather longer, and again there appears the syncopated rhythm, but inverted (ex. 68). A cadenza prolongs it[1] and the return of A marks the end of the second part of the rondo.

---

[1] K. 624, 17; printed also in the piano part in the *Breitkopf* edition.

In the sonata-rondo form, which Mozart has used in half his concertos, the third couplet is a recapitulation. But this movement has nothing regular about it. And the third part which opens here is certainly not a recapitulation. Indeed, it is rather a continuation of the *development*. Now it is that the innocent motif A opens its bag of tricks. Hitherto, it has quietly kept its place, appearing when it was needed, in the piano or the orchestra, with as reserved a mien as its elfin boorishness allowed. Henceforward, it unmasks itself and all this is changed. Hardly has the tutti stopped on the chord of C major when, without any preparation, and *ff*, it attacks that of E minor and passes, after three confirmatory bars, to *piano* and the key of A minor. And then open the most bewitching pages of the concerto.

For a moment which one would wish to be longer, strings and piano engage in a fairies' game with two bits of this theme (cf. ex. 62): the first bar and the "fluttering seconds" which end each half. The movements of the players lead them through the keys of A minor, D minor, C, A minor and G. The fragments play the part of accompaniment, while the solo's right hand performs arpeggio and scale passages, unless one considers these as accompaniment and the thematic fragments as the chief thing, which is quite defensible.

To begin with, the first fragment comes forward in the fiddles, playing in thirds, then in the violas and 'cellos; next, the "fluttering seconds" travel quivering from top to bottom of the orchestra (ex. 69), and this time violins on one hand, violas and 'cellos on the other, play in sixths and thirds. Like a rustle of wings, the game is carried on to a fresh return of the first fragment. Then the piano overcomes its reserve and lets itself be drawn into the sport; the infectious seconds invade it and appear in its right hand. The theme crumbles away more and more; reduced to its first three notes, it alternates with the fragment (ii). It sways between C minor and G, flitting from fiddles to piano, from piano to fiddles. The horns support it, the other instruments are silent. One feels that the end of the exquisite entertainment and the return to business are at hand. The first codetta of the refrain, again inverted, and theme C bring us back to familiar ground. But this rondo does not desert so easily the paths of fancy; theme C itself sets about modulating and passes into C minor when the strings take it up. The wandering lasts only a moment, however; we get back to the tonic and a bravura passage already heard, concluded by the refrain's second codetta. And the past seems to be deleted and the movement to start all over again when this codetta, as of yore, stops on the chord of G and the "tragic" andante raises its lamentation. We were far from it and the reappearance of this mournful ghost is weird in the highest degree.

> At the hour of greatest joy, a kind of bottomless gulf opens suddenly, then closes up,

says Joseph Baruzi with deep understanding of the master and, if one

Ex. 68

Ex. 69

had to say what distinguishes Mozart from his peers more than aught else, "opening a gulf", precisely, between them and him, one would reply: the bringing together in his work of two infinities. . . .

The adagio unfolds with very little change and vanishes as suddenly as the first time. And then begins the coda, as wonderful as all that precedes it. After a last hearing of theme A, regular and complete, the piano, which had been expounding it, instead of stopping to allow the orchestra to repeat it, as had happened hitherto, pushes on at once with fragment (ii) and keeps it going in both hands, in unison, whilst violins and wind whisper a variant of fragment (i) and add a new conclusion. Then the parts are reversed. The quivering goes over to the violins and violas and fragment (i) falls to the piano, where the parts are doubled; this device, which strengthens the tone and becomes regular in the 19th century, is uncommon in Mozart. Little by little, the rustle of wings of fragment (ii) spreads, from fiddles to violas, from violas to 'cellos and basses, at the same time as *piano* drops to *pianissimo*. To the very end, the solo keeps up its version of theme A; it adds two final bars, and shimmer of strings, piano chords and woodwind *tenuti* die away in a concluding *pp*, like the hum of the countryside at the end of a beautiful day.

We have already pointed out the characters which are common to these three concertos: their moderate technical difficulty, the "average" level of their emotion, the peculiarity that all three pass from *development* to recapitulation by means of a cadenza, or a change of *tempo*. Moreover, in two of them, K.413 and 415, the preponderance of rondo over andante helps to distinguish the group from the concertos that precede and follow it.

What can these concertos mean for us to-day? No more than the first six can they hope for great popularity; they will never be the possession of more than a small number of hearers and performers. Moreover, the inequalities of the C major risk causing its undeniable beauties to go unnoticed.[1] But those in F and A (as well as K.271) deserve a place in the repertory of amateur societies whom the technical difficulties of more famous works discourage. Both are perfectly homogeneous pieces, graceful without pettiness, genial without banality; moreover, the A major awakens deeper feelings by the smiling wistfulness of its allegro and the gravity of its andante. We earnestly recommend amateur orchestras and soloists to revive these lovely things, for it is in the intimacy of a small group rather than on large platforms that this art, still so close to chamber music, most fully exerts its charm.

Let us now put back the group we have been considering in the work of its composer as a whole, whence, for the purposes of study, we isolated it.

Compared with the earlier examples of its genre, can we say that it registers a development? Its ideal is still the *galant* ideal which

---

[1] It is precisely the existence of these beauties that make a recording of this concerto desirable, since it deserves better than the complete burial it suffers at present.

inspired the Salzburg concertos; the languor of the second, the Olympian carriage of a few bars in the third are its chief expressions of personality. But personal strains had also been heard in the Salzburg works; there is nothing new in this. As regards form, we have noted the freedom of the rondos in the F and C major. But the finales of the two E flats also showed freedom and that of the two pianos concerto had, moreover, organic unity. Such unity, it is true, is even greater in the 1782 works; there is some progress here, but of a secondary kind.

On the whole, we must own that Mozart, at the end of this year, is no nearer the great concertos of his maturity than he was on leaving Salzburg. These three works are not distinguishable in any essential from those that went before them. The orchestra is not "emancipated", save for a few bars here and there; the wind instruments, far from being the soloists they will become later, are not even the strings' equals. In vain does Mozart increase his band for the C major; it remains in essence a string orchestra and the wind has merely *ad libitum* parts.[1] If Mozart had written no more concertos after his ninth, he would have left charming pages to which we could still listen with pleasure, but he would not have been the "father" of the modern concerto.

And if we compare this group with the principal works of the same year, its importance does not appear any greater. We have said that the concerto, as well as the symphony, in 1781, 1782 and 1783, interests him much less and draws much less upon his deepest forces than chamber music, opera and polyphonic writing. The two great wind serenades in E flat and C minor belong to the first eighteen months of his life in Vienna and three of the four violin sonatas he wrote in 1781 are among his grandest. Already in the summer of 1781 he was working at *Die Entführung* and the idea of composing operas, which was never far from him, continued to absorb his attention till 1783, since the unfinished *Oca del Cairo* and *Sposo deluso* date from that year. The C minor mass must have been begun about the time he was composing the three concertos.

And finally, it is in 1782 that, after eight years of neglect, he takes up again string-quartet writing. Here, in the G major quartet, the first of the six dedicated to Haydn, far more than in the piano concerto, must we seek the complete Mozart of this period. There had been works as sincere and moving before it, but none as full. The C minor

---

[1] He says so himself in a letter to his father of April 26th, 1783.

serenade, deeply personal as it was, had uttered but two opposing, complementary sentiments; sorrow and serenity. But in the quartet it is impossible to isolate one single dominating emotion; its affective life is as rich as that of the soul itself and the various facets of his sensibility are lighted up in turn. The emotional quality of this work is particularly hard to sum up. It may be that the minuet does not mark any progress, in this respect, over the magnificent minuet in canon of the serenade, but the three other movements are all richer and fuller than their predecessors; through the whole work there flows the sap of a vigorous spring.

His chamber music, then, is ahead of his orchestral work. The gain had been marked since the last year at Salzburg and the B flat serenade. The significance of the *Haffner* and *Linz* symphonies and of the 1782 concertos is slight beside that of the C minor serenade, this quartet and the D minor which comes a few months later. Only in 1786 and, especially, in 1788 will the symphony catch up; the concerto will do so sooner, in 1784 and 1785, in those twelve great works to the threshold of which our study has at length brought us.

PART III

1. The Tenth Concerto: K.449 in E flat

CONCERTO NO. 10 IN E FLAT (K.449)[1]
February 9th, 1784
  Allegro vivace: 3-4
  Andantino: 2-4 (in B flat)
  Allegro ma non troppo: ¢
Orchestra: Strings, two hautboys and two horns *ad libitum*.

MOZART had married early in August, 1782, the summer in which he composed the concertos we have just been considering. His wife was Constance von Weber, the daughter of a music copyist and stage prompter, who had died several years earlier. She lived with her mother and three sisters.[2] They had once dwelt in Mannheim and Mozart had made their acquaintance when he stayed in that city; he had then fallen deeply in love with one of the sisters, Aloisia, and she is often mentioned in his letters to his father. On his return from Paris, he passed through Munich, whither the Webers had moved, but Aloisia had forgotten him and he felt the blow keenly. When he met the family again in Vienna she was married and he then noticed Constance, of whom no mention had been made three years earlier. He married her after a long struggle with his father, who, possessed of sounder judgement than his son in practical matters, was much averse to the union. Outwardly, he ended by yielding, but he was never reconciled to the idea of seeing Wolfgang married to "a Weber" and he was not wrong. Constance was not a bad soul, but to be a helpmeet to Mozart she should have had two qualities she lacked: enough vision to appreciate her husband's genius, enough practical common sense to compensate for the almost total absence of it in him. Without deep understanding, without practical qualities, she was a burden rather than a help. They remained united, nevertheless, during the eight and a half years of their

---

[1] No. 14 in the *Gesamtausgabe*.

[2] She was the first cousin of Carl Maria von Weber who was some fifteen years younger.

married life, and if there were domestic quarrels they were not serious.

These first years in Vienna were happy. Mozart won a certain success, modest perhaps compared with that of more fashionable *artistes*, but enough to make him comfortably off. Lessons came in abundance; *Akademien* or concerts, where he played as soloist, performing his works or those of others, succeeded one another with some frequency.

> Altogether I have so much to do that often I do not know whether I am on my head or my heels. I spend the whole forenoon giving lessons until two o'clock, when we have lunch. After this meal I must give my poor stomach an hour for digestion. The evening is therefore the only time I have for composing and of that I can never be sure, as I am often asked to perform at concerts.[1]

Thus does he describe a typical day in a letter to his father of December 28th, 1782. His letters are expressive of happiness; he relates complacently the success with which he has played a concerto—his or another's, he does not say—in an *Akademie* given by his sister-in-law Frau Lange.

> The theatre was very full and I was received again by the Viennese public so cordially that I really ought to feel delighted. I had already left the platform but the audience would not stop clapping and so I had to repeat the rondo; upon which there was a regular torrent of applause. It is a good advertisement for my concert which I am giving on Sunday, March 23rd. I added my symphony which I composed for the Concert Spirituel. My sister-in-law sang the aria *Non so d'onde viene*. Gluck had a box beside the Langes, in which my wife was sitting. He was loud in his praises of the symphony and the aria and invited us all four to lunch with him next Sunday.[2]

In the same letter, dated March 12th, 1783, he announces that he is himself to give an *Akademie* on the 29th of the month and the next letter, written on the evening of the concert, speaks of its success and, what interests us more, enumerates the items played; it shows that the patience and musical appetites of a hundred and fifty years ago were more extensive and capacious than ours.

> I need not tell you very much about the success of my concert, for no doubt you have already heard of it. Suffice it to say that the theatre could not have been more crowded and that every box was full. But what pleased me most of all was that His Majesty the Emperor was present and,

[1] Trans. E. Anderson, III, 1242.
[2] Id., III, 1254-5.

goodness, how delighted he was and how he applauded me! It is his custom to send the money to the box-office before going to the theatre; otherwise I should have been fully justified in counting on a larger sum, for really his delight was beyond all bounds. He sent twenty-five ducats. Our programme was as follows:

(1) The new *Haffner* symphony (K.385).

(2) Madame Lange sang the aria "*Se il padre perdei*" from my Munich opera (*Idomeneo*) accompanied by four instruments.

(3) I played the third of my subscription concertos (K.415).

(4) Adamberger sang the scena which I composed for Countess Baumgarten (K.369).

(5) The short *concertante Symphonie* from my last *Finalmusik* (K.320).

(6) I played my concerto in D major (K.175), which is such a favourite here, and of which I sent you the rondo with variations (K.382).

(7) Mlle Teiber sang the scena "*Parto, m' affretto*" out of my last Milan opera (*Lucio Silla*).

(8) I played alone a short fugue (because the Emperor was present) and then variations on an air from an opera called *Die Philosopheen*, which were encored. So I played variations on the air "*Unser dummer Pöbel meint*" from Gluck's *Pilgrimme von Mekka* (K.398 and 455).

(9) Madame Lange sang my new rondo (K.416).

(10) The last movement of the first symphony (K.385).[1]

The success of *Die Entführung aus dem Serail*, of which we hear frequent and satisfied echoes in his letters, kindled his desire to write other operas, and more than once he alludes to some libretto or other, German or Italian, which had attracted his notice. In 1783 he undertook another Turkish opera, but in Italian this time, on a libretto of Abbate Varesco, the Salzburg chaplain who had put together *Idomeneo*; this work, *L'Oca del Cairo*, was given up after the first act had been completed. Either from ill-will or from incapacity, the librettist did not comply with the composer's requirements. The same year, he began another Italian opera, *Lo Sposo deluso*, but abandoned it even more quickly. Only three years later did he meet the ideal partner, the Abbate Lorenzo da Ponte, from his collaboration with whom arose his greatest *opere buffe*, *Le Nozze di Figaro*, *Don Giovanni* and *Così fan tutte*.

His letters home follow at the rate on an average of three a month. As they have all been kept for the period we have reached, they provide us with fairly copious information on his life. From the beginning of the year, they had been announcing his visit and that of his

---

[1] Id., III, 1256-7.

wife to Salzburg, a visit which was delayed, now by the fear that the Archbishop might keep him there, now by his wife's pregnancy and the impossibility for her (according to Mozart) to be delivered in Salzburg, now merely by "the weather and circumstances". This reconciliation visit finally took place in the summer and the young couple, accompanied by the little Raymund Leopold, born in June, stayed three months with Leopold and Nannerl. This was Wolfgang's last visit to his native city, that city which absence never made dear to him.

> I have no desire whatever to see Salzburg or the Archbishop. . . . It would never enter my head voluntarily to make a journey thither, were it not that you and my sister lived there.[1]

External civilities were observed but cordiality does not seem to have been established between Constance and her new family, and Mozart returned to Vienna disappointed. On his way back he stopped a few days at Linz, where he gave a concert of his works. A symphony was apparently indispensable; as there was no time to send for parts from Vienna, he composed one in four days, that in C. K.425, known as the Linz, the first he had written since he had settled in the capital.

The concertos K.413, 414 and 415 were composed, it is thought, during the summer of 1782. Between that moment and February, 1784, no piano concerto came from him. The most significant works of these fifteen or sixteen months belong to choral, dramatic and chamber music. He had vowed to have a new mass performed in Salzburg if he succeeded in leading Constance thither as his wife. This vow won for us the great C minor mass. If God held to the letter of the vow, He may have reproached His votary with defaulting, for the mass is unfinished; but it is probable that the exceeding loveliness of what was written has made up in His eyes for two thirds of the *Creed* and all the *Agnus Dei*, which are missing; the work, unfinished though it be, is worth all Mozart's completed masses together, and much more! During the second half of the year, the young man worked at *L'Oca del Cairo* and his letters are full of remarks and complaints on the progress of the work and the difficulties arising from his collaboration with Varesco. His only orchestral composition was the Linz symphony which still keeps a place in the repertory but had neither the power nor the variety of the C major symphony of 1779, and of the four great works of 1786 and 1788. Finally, he

---

[1] Id., III, 1276.

continued at leisure the series of quartets he had begun and by the
end of the year had added two more to that in G—those in D minor
and E flat.   The D minor was written out, we are told, during the
night which preceded his child's birth; he went from his table to his
wife's bedside, and back to his table, without this constant shifting
interrupting the continuity of the music.   It is probable that he was
not composing but merely writing out the music which had already
been worked out in his brain.   A prodigious memory enabled him
to do without written notes; he could rig up his constructions and
modify their details in his mind, as less talented beings draw up their
plans and make their erasures on paper.[1]

Such is the list of the important works of the year.   There is
another group to which no masterpiece belongs but of which we
must say a few words, for it touches closely the piano concertos.   It
is that of the concertos for horn.

These four works are the only concertos he wrote for an instrument other than the piano after leaving Salzburg, with the exception
of the E flat work for violin[2] and the clarinet concerto.   Some of
them owe their existence to his friendship with Ignaz Leutgeb, an
old Salzburg acquaintance settled in Vienna.   Leutgeb, who had been
a horn player at Salzburg, had set up in the capital where he supported
the cult of music with the earnings of trade, and had a little cheese
shop in the suburbs—"the size of a snail's shell", said Leopold[3]—
prosecuting the while the practice of the horn.   He seems to have
been a good soul, with an excellent temper, patient and simple.
He allowed himself to serve as a butt for Mozart's Beotian humour,
the exuberant overflow of which was poured out on him.   For him
were written at least two concertos and a quintet for horn and strings,
works themselves conceived as playthings, and the conditions Mozart
laid down for their composition show that he did not take them
seriously.   Thus, at one time he compelled Leutgeb to pick up on
his hands and knees a number of orchestral parts he had thrown on
the floor.   Another time, the virtuoso cheesemonger had to remain
kneeling behind the stove whilst Mozart began a concerto.   The
musician perpetuated on the scores the pitiless fun he made of him;
the dedication of the second concerto, K.417, runs:

---

[1] We have been told that a contemporary composer, Frédéric d'Erlanger,
worked in the same manner.

[2] Saint-Foix thinks that this work was written in 1786.

[3] Letter to Wolfgang of December 1st, 1777.

Wolfgang Amadeus Mozart took pity on Leutgeb, donkey, ox and fool, at Vienna, March 27th, 1783.

The fourth is written with red, black, blue and green ink; one page is adorned with a drawing showing the horn player in action; one movement is headed allegro in the orchestra and adagio in the solo; another is annotated with a whole humorous commentary upon the performer's execution:

> A lei Signor Asino—Animo—presto—sú via—da bravo—Coraggio—e finisci già—bestia . . . ajuto—respira un poco!—avanti,—avanti! questo poi va al meglio . . . ah! trillo di pecore—finisci—grazie al ciel! basta, basta!

One would expect works conceived in such a mood to belong to the class of "musical jokes", an agreeable specimen of which Mozart composed a few years later. Not at all. Without boasting either the scope or the variety of his piano concertos, they are authentic Mozart pieces, the shavings of his workshop, the small change of his genius, and all four can be listened to with pleasure. As all four by their structure and style are analogous to the more ambitious concertos that precede and follow them, we shall not be straying from our path if we cast a rapid glance at them.

The allegro of the first was dated by André 1782, but its finale was not completed till 1787.[1] The second bears the burlesque dedication and the date we have quoted (March, 1783); the third is not dated and Saint-Foix suggests that it is later than the others; the fourth dates from 1786. The first is in D and has only two movements; the three others are in E flat and have the habitual three movements. The allegros of all four are in that concerto-sonata form which Mozart never gave up; the andantes or larghettos are *romances* with one or two couplets; the finales are rondos, also in two or three couplets. The orchestra consists of strings with either hautboys or clarinets; in addition, the first and third have bassoons, the second and fourth have horns.

Generally speaking, the first movements, which are the most interesting, reproduce on a miniature scale the design of the piano concertos. The main formal dissimilarities come from the difference in the problems to be solved by the composer in the two sorts of concerto. From its very nature, the horn is less independent than the piano; it cannot play alone and its power of expression is limited. It will therefore be less the orchestra's adversary than its collaborator and will from time to time fall back into the bosom of the tutti.

---

[1] It is not by any means certain that the two movements belong together; their orchestration is not identical.

Like all solo instruments other than piano, harp and organ, it is *primus inter pares* and not one of a different order. The tutti's share will be therefore much more important than in the piano concerto and the places where the solo takes an inner part and subordinates itself to the other instruments more numerous. Moreover, as its means of virtuosity are limited (for the valve horn had not yet been invented), the development passages will fall mainly to the strings. And as, for the same reason, the easiest manner for the horn to play as a soloist is to sing, the melodic richness of the works will be relatively much greater than in the piano concertos. The composer scatters treasures of melody throughout these trifles with a profusion which seems to us to border on waste, and *cantabile* subjects, compared with developments and bravura passages, are even more important than in Mozart's other works.

In the three concertos in E flat, riper and more daring works than the first, Mozart's ingenuity, the field of which is restricted by the nature of his solo instrument, bears mainly on the setting forth of the various tunes. He has taken a delight in dividing and reuniting them, in upsetting their order, in the three sections of the first movement, so that the terms, second subject, mock second subject, solo subject, have no meaning, and even the first subjects are not always the same in tuttis and solos. In this respect, the formal study of these concertos is fascinating and offers, so to speak, microscopic examples of the master's infinitely fruitful imagination and of the care he lavished on even the humblest tasks when his heart was involved. There is nothing like it in the great piano concertos; this aspect of his genius can be studied only here.

The first, K.412 in D, is a trial work. Its structure is not different from that of the piano concertos; it has only three main subjects, one of which, as in K.365, is a mock second subject, and its rather hesitant *development* does not stray far from the first subject. The horn part is more timid than in the other concertos. Mozart had no doubt underestimated the good Leutgeb's capacities. As if to inspire him with confidence, he gives the first violins an important, almost a *concertante* part, so that the work is not far from being a *Sinfonia Concertante* for violins and horn.

The second, K.417, is the most broadly-planned of the four. The spacious tunes, their number and their expressive power strike one at first hearing and the work deserves to be performed more often in our concert halls.[1] It is all melody; the linking figures and codettas

---

[1] As its andante is weak, in performance the beautiful *romance* of the fourth, K.495, could be substituted.

are almost entirely absent. The game of disintegrating and changing round subjects is carried here to its highest point.

The third, K.447, is less attractive at first sight and treats the soloist less bountifully, but it is the most interesting for the orchestra,

Ex. 70

Ex. 71

Ex. 72

whose part is considerable. The tutti repeats each time the second half of the first subject after the solo, and each time, too, it gives out the second subject. But it is in the *development* that it breaks loose. This section, short as it is, is one of the most remarkable symphonic passages in all Mozart. It starts with a new tune, given out by the solo in D flat, which stops abruptly after ten bars. The horn then sounds a G flat which it holds for two bars. At first it is alone; then the strings begin again, but in D major, and the G flat, which was the subdominant, pivoting upon itself in a daring enharmonic modulation, becomes F sharp, the third of the new key. There follow eight profoundly Mozartish bars (ex. 70) of weird modulations. The horn is reduced to holding semibreves while the orchestra, repeating a restless motif, rises from D major to D minor, E flat minor, G major, C minor and back again to G major, where it stops, engages in a conversation with the horn, and whence it passes to G minor and finally to E flat for the reprise. This is one of the earliest examples in Mozart of those *fantasia developments* which characterize the great concertos of 1784 to 1786.[1]

The fourth and last concerto, K.495, displays no such audacity. By the time it was written, Mozart had composed nearly all his greatest piano works and was no doubt growing tired of the concerto game. It is as fruitful in tunes as the others but is on an even smaller scale. Its most remarkable features are its *development* subject, a well-known theme in Bach and Beethoven[2] (ex. 71) and its concluding subject, the accompaniment of which affords a masterly instance of the poetic manner in which Mozart can use the "fluttering seconds" figure (ex. 72).[3]

The andantes are less interesting. The best is the *romance* of K.495 which makes use, with a slight difference of rhythm, of the same theme as the andante of the exactly contemporary sonata for piano duet in F, K.497. The *romance* of K.447, in A flat, is a rondo, the frequent returns of whose refrain—five in all, one-half of the movement!—and the insignificance of whose episodes relate it to the rondos of Philip Emmanuel Bach; with that in D, K.485, for piano, it is the only one of the kind in Mozart. Its theme reappears in an episode of the finale.

The four finales are much alike. They differ less than the first movements from their counterparts in the piano concertos. The most lively is that of K.412 which was completed in 1787. The orchestra

---

[1] The manuscript of this concerto bears none of the jokes for Leutgeb's edification which adorn the others, and Saint-Foix surmises that it may have been written for a professional horn player.

[2] St. John Passion, B minor aria for alto, no. 31; 'cello sonata in A, op. 69, middle of first movement; A flat piano sonata, op. 110, in the *arioso* which breaks in upon the fugue.

[3] A whole study could be carried out on the use he makes of this figure; it appears often in his work and nearly always with an unmistakably passionate meaning.

is treated with a sure and experienced hand. We meet again the little "seconds" figure of the K.415 finale (ex. 62, II and 69) ; it appears likewise towards the end of the movement and ends by taking possession of the whole orchestra (73 a and b). Of all these horn works, it is this rondo, through its coda, which resembles most the group of piano concertos which we were studying in the last chapter.

On February 9th, 1784, Mozart completed his tenth piano concerto.[1] Between this date and December 4th, 1786, that is, in two years and ten months, a dozen concertos for his instrument were to flow from the fruitful store of his genius. The date is important; henceforward Mozart, who had been hitherto a composer amongst whose works were counted a few concertos, as many for string and wind instruments as for piano, becomes a piano concerto writer *par excellence*. The genre predominates absolutely in his compositions for the next three years. The nine earlier concertos were but preliminaries; it is in February, 1784, that the story of his piano concertos really begins. The importance of the genre in his work is due to its importance during these three years. The twelve masterpieces which extend between these dates constitute the true canon of the concerto.

It is enough just to glance at the list of his compositions during these thirty-four months to recognize this predominance. If we neglect the lesser forms—arias, variations, dances, lieder, cantatas— and confine ourselves to the operas and works in sonata form, we find from twenty-five to thirty items. The operas are the curtain-raiser, *Der Schauspieldirektor*, and *Le Nozze di Figaro*. The *sonatas* comprise ten trios, quartets and quintets,[2] five sonatas and fantasias, one horn concerto and one symphonic movement, the *Masonic Funeral Music*. By extending the period for two days we bring into it a symphony, the *Prague*, composed at the same time as the last concerto of the series. The preponderance of the piano concerto is obvious. Only chamber music can rival it, and even there, works with a piano part number six out of ten. Every winter, throughout this period,

---

[1] It is the first entry in the catalogue of his works which he kept from that date till his death.

[2] One quintet, three trios, two quartets with piano, four string quartets.

concertos succeed each other at the rate of almost one a month, in February, March and April, 1784 (two, even, in March!), in September and December, 1784, and February and March, 1785, in December, 1785, and February and March, 1786; the last one arrives all alone in December of the same year.

We crave forgiveness for these dates and figures; they enable us to see at a glance the numerical importance of concertos in the master's activity at the period on whose threshold we stand. The musical importance of each one of them is no less. Neither among the foregoing concertos, nor among the earlier symphonies or *sonatas* are there works into which Mozart's thought and soul entered so deeply and which he undertook in so serious a mood. The only exceptions to this generalization are to be found in *Idomeneo*, the *Sinfonia Concertante* for violin and viola and the first quartets dedicated to Haydn, and of these the quartets antedate by only a few months the concertos we are about to study.

The reason for this preponderance is clear; it is Mozart's success as a pianist. From 1784 to 1786, he is a fashionable virtuoso, perhaps not the most fashionable, but certainly one of those who received abundantly of the public's inconstant favours. At that time the virtuoso-composer had not yet become the almost extinct species he is to-day, when we wonder at, even more than we admire, a Dohnanyi or a Rachmaninov playing his own music, and Wolfgang's success as pianist called for a more abundant output of works. It was natural that the quality as well as the number of such works should gain by his rise to fame.

What differences are there between these Viennese concertos of 1784–6 and the nine compositions of Salzburg and Vienna which cover the twelve preceding years? They can be summed up in the words: elaboration of form and deepening of thought.

It is not so much that the movements are longer and the themes more numerous, though this is true in most cases. It is especially that the structure is more complex and more daring; that the relations between solo and orchestra, which hitherto had been almost rudimentary, become closer and more diverse; that the orchestration grows richer and draws on more resources. Most of them are more richly scored than the first nine and, apart from actual number of instruments, Mozart gets much more out of his orchestra.

The emotional scope of these twelve concertos surpasses indisputably that of the earlier ones. Not only each one has its own personality, but the personality is vaster and richer and the elaboration of form is but the manifestation of this growth.   Whereas in five out of the six Salzburg concertos and in those of 1782 Mozart, for fear of scaring his public, has held back the more essential part of himself, henceforward he gives himself whole-heartedly to his work and throws himself into it completely, so thoroughly in fact that he ends by getting ahead of his audience and, after barely three years. finds himself forsaken by it. The dramatic and individual character of his themes is emphasized;   the passages which reveal an inner life return more often and no compositions, whatever they be, are more authentically, more exclusively, more fully his own than these twelve concertos. Had he been a more conscious creator he could have said, like Jean Cartan:

> I have won for music new parts of myself which had hitherto stood apart from my work.   Now they are coming in and taking part of their own accord without the slightest effort.

The result of this expanded form and deepened thought and feeling is seen in movements more ambitious, more charged with meaning than anything he had written hitherto for piano and orchestra and even, with the few exceptions already mentioned, for any combination whatsoever.

In his well-known book, *Beethoven et ses trois styles*, Lenz said that the study of Mozart's music showed that the artist, but not the man, had changed with time, that the latter had remained the same from beginning to end of his career, whereas with Beethoven the man as much as the artist had developed.   This view is most unfair to Mozart. If one takes into account the fact that he lived twenty years less than Beethoven, one must admit that the importance of the "man's" development, with all that this word implies of inward and elemental forces, was no less great in him than in the later musician.   He died at the age when Beethoven had written his three first symphonies and his op. 18 quartets, when he was, that is, at the beginning of his "second manner".   Now, if it is a far cry from Beethoven's first compositions to the *Eroica*, it is quite as far from the *galant* baubles that Mozart was writing in 1775 and 1776 (and we forbear from going back further, though at that time thirteen years of composing reached away behind him!) to the *Magic Flute* and the *Requiem*.

Ex. 73a

Ex. 73b

Ex. 74

Ex. 75

As Mozart took care to tell his father,[1] the first of the four concertos written for the Lent[2] of 1784 requires but a small band: strings, hautboys and horns—in which the wind parts are *ad libitum*. It is best, however, to retain these latter; not only does their colour relieve the greyish hues of the strings, but also here and there they add important elements to the score.[3]

I.   The first movement is, in the series of the twenty-three concertos, one of the few in three-time. The others are those of the F major, K.413, and the C minor, K.491, and its closest relationship is with the latter. The instability which this time-signature connotes and which one expects in a *minor* work is surprising in the usually serene key of E flat. But it is unmistakable. The whole movement is born of an unstable, restless mood, sometimes petulant and irascible, uncommon in Mozart, and this makes the concerto something exceptional in his work, something which, by its climate if not by its form, reminds one of Philip Emmanuel Bach.

The first four bars betray this mood (ex. 74); the key is affirmed by the first, doubted by the second (are we in the relative minor?) and gainsaid by the third and fourth (we are in the dominant). Such an entry, neither major nor minor, neither tonic nor dominant, is unique in Mozart; its closest analogy in classical music is with the opening of Schubert's G major quartet.

The four remaining bars of the first subject bring back the tonic

---

[1] Letters of May 15th and 16th, 1784.   This concerto and that in G were written for Babette Ployer, one of his pupils, the daughter of the archbishop's agent in Vienna and niece of the Abt Max Stadler.   It was for her that he set the composition exercises preserved in the National Library in Vienna.   Her autograph album, which came into the Mozarteum collection some years ago, contains a .funeral march by him, signed "*Del Sigr. Maestro Contrapunto*" (Köchel-Einstein, no. 453 a).

[2] See note at beginning of next chapter.

[3] This is so in the first tutti, bars 51-2, for the little hautboy phrases echoed by the violins; in the andantino, bars 41-4, 70-3 and 118-22; and in the finale, bars 213-18, 238-42 and 262-6, where the hautboy and hord *tenuti* add not only to the *timbre* but also the harmony of the whole.

key and this is confirmed by the codetta of seven bars. But then comes a fresh surprise! Plunging and rearing there rushes up in unison a fiery little theme which stampedes into C minor and adds ferocity to instability (ex. 75). Against the incessant agitation of the second violins and violas, it renews itself on different degrees of the scale, then, just touching on E flat major, bivouacks an instant in B flat and camps in F where the frenzy of its semi-quavers is somewhat quietened. But F major is only a stage; it is as dominant of B flat and not for its own sake that it is sought out and our motif does not tarry in it. We return to B flat, in which key the second subject unfolds. This theme, harmonized in sixths and thirds, full of yearning and still glowing with ill-quenched fire, is broken up by a commentary of dotted quavers and finishes as it began, on the chord of B flat (ex. 7).

The appearance of the second subject in the dominant instead of the tonic is exceptional in an opening tutti.[1] Already Mozart's concerto in F, K.413, had allowed itself this violation of the rules but only for a moment, and the subject, born outside the fold of the tonic, had quickly entered it. Here, the excursion into the dominant dates from before birth and only after expounding the whole of it does the movement resume the high road of E flat. Besides, what was just a formal and non-significant irregularity in K.413 is here yet another symptom of the feverish mobility and restlessness which have reigned since the beginning and which, though a little quietened after the solo entry, persist to the end.

The charming link theme which leads us, on a B flat pedal and through rustling harmonies where seconds preponderate, towards the conclusion, is one of those passing thoughts which Mozart sometimes sprinkles so bountifully in his concertos. We have already noted in three of them characteristic and interesting subjects playing their part in opening tuttis and then returning no more.[2] We shall find another in K.459. As the composer progresses towards compression and unity, this waste ceases.

At length, the concluding subject affirms with the four times repeated common chord the key of E flat, so neglected hitherto, which had risked becoming a mere man of straw, lending its title to a work full of wandering modulations. The subject is rhythmic and manly and contrasts with the sometimes passionate, sometimes tender

---

[1] It occurs in two of John Christian's concertos, op. XII, 5 and 6, in G and E flat, but both times the subject concludes in the tonic. In Beethoven's C minor concerto, the second subject is given out wholly in the relative major.

[2] K.365, 413 and 415.

but always uncertain strains heard hitherto.   The conclusion is rather long and ends with a trilling figure which will be important in the *development*.

Let us glance back over this tutti.   Its instability struck us at first sight; the restless subjects and the frequent modulations are the clearest mark of this mood.   Almost one half is spent outside the main key: in the relative minor, the dominant and the "ultra-dominant". But there is more to it.   Even in the E flat parts accidentals are abundant enough to undermine the feeling of the key.   Now an A natural threatens us with a sally into B flat (bar 3); now a D flat hints at an escape into A flat (bars 65-6); now a B natural carries us past the dusky fringes of C minor (bar 71).   Thus, at no time, till the final codetta of four bars closes the tutti, are we safe from the quicksands of modulation or the threat of them, and this is the expression of a most exceptional state in our composer.

The great majority of his other tuttis keep within the tonic or, if they modulate, do so only for a few bars and generally into closely related keys.   (The E flat major swooping suddenly into the G major of K.453 is unique.)   Generally, these tuttis modulate little or not at all, with three exceptions, two of which we know, this work and K.413; the third is the great C major concerto of 1786, K.503.

Sir Donald Tovey has often insisted on the importance of Mozart's concertos and, in particular, of the relations between their opening tutti and the rest of the allegro.

> The most important aspect of classical concerto-form is . . . the relation between the opening orchestral ritornello, with its procession of themes, to the solo exposition which works out these and other themes in sonata-form.   No two ritornellos of Mozart repeat each other in all points of this relation, and in every concerto there is some unique feature which is no minute detail, but a matter affecting large areas.[1]

Here, the unique feature is the modulation which covers such a large part of the introduction, and especially the giving out of the second subject in the dominant.   Should one consider this departure from the rule to be happy innovation?   Is there not rather in it the danger that a tutti thus treated may, as Tovey says, resemble a symphonic exposition so closely that the arrival of the solo will be merely an unjustified surprise?   The beginning of Beethoven's C minor concerto is not free from this peril, but there, between the subjects, there is change of mode as well as of key.   Moreover, the size of the

---

[1] *Essays in Musical Analysis*, III, 42.

movement gives it almost the dimensions of a symphonic exposition.
Not so here. It is true that the keys are somewhat diverse at the
start, but the brevity and speed of the work are such that we do not
linger in any of them, not even in B flat; the concluding theme comes
back to the tonic and dwells on it long enough for the subordination
of all the others to appear indisputable.   On the whole, these secondary
keys do not open up independent paths that stray far from the main
road; they are rather loops or short cuts which run near it and culminate in the end at the same point.

The piano's entry exerts a calming influence. From now on,
nerves are less on edge and there is not so much restlessness. It is as
if the piano had the advantage of experience and years over the
orchestra. It has in any case more muscle; its entry is the most
vigorous and most direct in all Mozart. Not only is there no introduction but also the first subject, which in the orchestra was merely
wiry, has brawn added to it by the piano which fills it out with all the
notes in the scale and clothes its spareness in sinuous outlines (ex. 76).

Typical of this change of mood is the non-appearance of ex. 75.
In its place we have a short but interesting development of the first
subject with collaboration between solo and strings. After twelve
bars of solo, the notice of the strings is attracted to a little element
of three rising notes (bar 7 of ex. 76, marked ⌐⌐) which plays a
discreet but important part in the first subject. They seize hold of
it and repeat it murmuringly whilst the piano carries down into the
bass the figure which ends this same subject (bar 11, marked [   ]).
The solo continues with a scale motif, related to the subject just given
out, though not derived from it, and the strings go on whispering
their now falling three-note theme.[1] Then, after eight bars, the
adversaries exchange weapons; first violins and violas take the scale
and the piano the three-note motif which it decorates with an arpeggio
line.   Having calmed the orchestra's fever with this game of battle-
dore and shuttlecock, it attacks almost alone the solo subject. It
begins in C minor in a questioning strain, repeats the question in B
flat and finds the answer in F with the figure which, in the opening
tutti, had concluded ex. 75 and introduced the second subject (ex. 7).
This latter has nothing new to say and it says it, as before, in B flat,
dividing itself between piano (harmonized part) and first violins
(answer in dotted quavers). For the pedal point in the introduction

---

[1] The harmonization of this passage is characterized by Mozart's mannerism
of the flattened leading note.

Ex. 76

Ex. 77

Ex. 78a

Ex. 78b

Ex. 79

the piano substitutes a few bravura bars, the first and almost the only ones in this concerto, which is one of the least virtuosi; and the whole orchestra concludes in B flat with the rhythmical and manly subject already noted.

The second half of this subject includes an element of repeated quavers in the treble and a chain of trills in the bass (ex. 77), trinkets with which orchestra and piano amuse themselves during the *development*.[1] The piano repeats at first the end of the exposition,

[1] Mozart is fond of building the first parts of his *developments* on elements drawn from the concluding subject of the exposition; cf. K.482 and 537.

modulating; upon its return to B flat strings and hautboys again give out
the trill, in unison; the piano interrupts them with an arpeggio figure;
the orchestra starts afresh, this time in C minor, the piano does
likewise; and this innocent manœuvring is reiterated, with modulations, three times.   Combination now succeeds alternation; the
piano gives out the trill and the strings the quaver figure, passing
through sundry keys to end the game in A flat (ex. 78).   All this
passage is in a thoroughly Mozartish delicate vein of humour.

What follows is different.   As in the last concerto so here, just
before the reprise, a cloud passes over the face of the work.   The
change of mood is much less abrupt than in K.415; it is less joy yielding
to sadness than playfulness giving way before earnestness.   The
change is marked in the disappearance of the trill figure and the slowing
down of the strings, whose quavers turn into crotchets.   The new
passage, a short one, carries on the interplay; it is based on arpeggios,
quavers in the piano, crotchets in the strings, balancing and crossing
each other gravely, yet reminding one of a game of ball (ex. 79).
The earnestness deepens as the orchestra passes to held notes, then
contents itself with punctuating the strong beats with quavers, and
finally, is silent.   In the piano, the emotional stress that so often precedes Mozart's reprises heightens, yet without reaching the uncertainty of the opening; then, just as it is on the point of turning to
anguish, it breaks on a dominant close and four bars of simple and
profoundly quiet music bring us back to the beginning of the story
(ex. 80).   Are we not reminded here of the three sister bars, quieter
and profounder still, which close a moment of much more emphatic
restlessness, in the corresponding part of the great E flat symphony
of 1788?   Thus, from masterpiece to masterpiece, moving thoughts
foreshadow and recall one another like memories and premonitions
throughout a life.

The orchestra comes in with the first subject; the piano takes it
up at the ninth bar and engages with it the same conversation as before,
with a few slight alterations, and passing through the key of B flat
minor.   The solo subject begins in F minor and closes in B flat,
whence the codetta carries us back to E flat and the second subject.
The recapitulation follows the same track as the exposition but the
bravura passage is twice as long.

Drawing to its close the movement remembers its stormy origins
and lets loose the fierce little ex. 75.   Its innings is brief and after ten
bars it is cut short by the pause for the cadenza.   But its message is
taken up again at once by this latter, which starts with the same figure

of dotted crotchets and arpeggios. Written no doubt for Babette Ployer (since Mozart extemporized his own), it is more curt than most; it reflects admirably the spirit of the concerto. The only other theme brought in is precisely (with ex. 86) the most vigorous of all: the upstanding concluding subject. And the allegro ends with the nineteen bars which had concluded the first tutti, repeated unchanged.

II. The andantino[1] has none of the agitation and vigour of the first movement. It is a *cantilena* in two strains, guileless and calm, neither deep nor complex. Its chief interest, although it still uses only the strings with woodwind *ad libitum*, lies in its scoring.

It consists in two alternating themes, preceded by a tutti introduction which contains only the first of them. After the piano entry, each theme is given out thrice and the movement breaks up therefore into a short introduction and three stanzas.

Introduction:	A	(1st half only)			
			Orchestra	22 bars	B flat
1st stanza:	A	(whole)	Piano	18 bars	,,
	B		Piano, accompanied	11 bars	F
2nd stanza:	A	(whole)	Orchestra, then piano, accompanied	18 bars	A flat
	B		Piano, accompanied	10 bars	E flat
3rd stanza:	A	(whole)	Orchestra, then piano, accompanied	18 bars	B flat
	B		Orchestra accompanied by the piano; then alternating tutti and solo	21 bars	,,
Coda:			Orchestra and solo	6 bars	,,

Exs. 81–3 give the *incipits* of the main themes.

The most interesting details are the following:

The flowing accompaniment of ex. 83 which returns in the third stanza beneath the piano *canto*.

The string answers in A, stanzas 1 and 2; on them is based the charming little coda.

The Alberti bass accompaniment of B; it is carried out by the

---

[1] Mozart asks his father, in his letter of May 9th, 1784, to note that in none of the four concertos (nos. 10 to 14) is there an adagio.

Ex. 84

Ex. 85

Ex. 86

violas the first two times; the third time, the piano uses it to accompany the violins and hautboys.

The first two stanzas are alike; the second confines itself to repeating the first in the new key of A flat (the "double-subdominant"). The third is more of a variation; the theme B is treated with great felicity (ex. 84).

The presence of four-note chords should be noted in this movement; Mozart seldom uses such dynamic effects and when he does he means them. The pianist should therefore play them with full strength, here and at the beginning of the solo in the allegro and, generally, wherever he meets them in Mozart.

III. The gait of the finale is neither that of a gallop, nor of a race, nor even of a dance, but just of a swinging walk, swift and regular, and the virtue of its refrain, with its sketchy outline and its "sillabato" diction, as the Italians would say, rests in its rhythm rather than in its melody. It is one of Mozart's few rondo refrains which are not tuneful and the movement obeys no strong emotional impulse. But the grace of the ornamentation with which piano and fiddles clothe the bareness of its outline; the way in which the movement keeps up its pace, hardly ever taking breath; the wonderful fruitfulness with which it renews itself unceasingly, even though it is for ever coming back to the same point; its mixture of rondo and variation; all make this finale one of the most lovable in all Mozart and, as regards its form, the most fascinating in all his concertos.

It is usually possible to divide Mozart's rondos into two, three or four sections, separated by returns of the refrain. The stanzas are easily recognized and the mind is not obliged, for the needs of analysis, to see divisions and sections where the composer himself has not placed any. But this one is different. From the moment the piano is first heard, in the thirty-second bar, it is almost a *moto perpetuo*, without even a quaver rest and almost without a full close. The greater part of its progress, carried out at a brisk pace but never breathless, is founded upon a single theme, taken up, adorned, varied, developed, with a bewitching diversity, seconded from time to time by another, less well characterized, subject, whose part is inconspicuous. Here it is, as we see it at the outset (ex. 85). The orchestra expounds it and follows it up at once with the other subject (ex. 86), concluded by a codetta in E flat.

The piano repeats the beginning of the refrain, embroidering it; then, half-way through, guided by the first fiddles that outline the theme, throws itself into a variation (ex. 87), which leads to a full close in E flat. Here one might see the start of the first couplet if one wanted to divide this strongly unified finale into the usual sections.

Picking up a figure of the variation (marked: I in ex. 87), through a short contrapuntal passage provided by another figure of the same example the solo reaches the second subject of the refrain which it gives out, somewhat modified, in the dominant. But this is not what interests it. It leaves it a few bars later and, after a *fantasia* passage where crossed hands play a part[1] and strings collaborate in echoes, the violins bring back ex. 85. Whilst the strings banter with a little three-part canon entry, the piano joins them with a fresh variation of the theme, derived from ex. 87, I. Then it monopolizes the game: the strings are again reduced to accompanying whilst it plays with contrapuntal runs, of which that in the right hand has grown out of the same figure I (ex. 88). But there is more than that in the run, and we recognize with some astonishment a theme destined to reappear six years later in the clarinet quintet.[2] The counterpoint soon ceases and the solo forges ahead with a volubility that makes us think of the irrepressible and garrulous finale of K.271. Then the rhythm slackens an instant; minims mingle with the quavers; finally, we set off again with a new rhythm ♪♫𝄾♪♫𝄾♪♫ and in this disguise the refrain reappears, with its skeleton outline still sketched out by the violins (ex. 89). All the strings take it up, and now they too decorate it and borrow figure I from the piano.

The refrain closes abruptly and, without any mention of ex. 87, the piano, roughly, lets loose a new subject. (Note again here the thick chord, to be sounded with due strength.) It is in C minor, a kind of hasty homage which the rondo pays to its ancestral form where the second stanza is in the minor. It is but a gesture; Mozart is far too good-tempered and too much at peace with the world to penetrate into the profundities of the minor mode and after four bars, neither more nor less, he again comes back to sunny keys. Without pulling up, the piano pursues its course which, thanks to triplets, becomes a gallop, breaking ground with new themes. But the main subject is on the watch; the movement belongs to it and never escapes it for long. In the midst of the triplets, here it is, first in C minor, then, quickly changing its mind, in A flat and, eventually, in sundry major keys. The piano, recalled to order, adorns it with a scion of figure I, with which the triplets intermingle. Still irresistible, neither breathless nor dishevelled, piano and strings pursue their exploration through what one might almost call the rondo's second couplet until a passage already heard (the crossed hands and echoing strings) summon all

---

[1] Crossed hands are not common in Mozart's concertos and their presence here is a likeness with the finale of the little E flat concerto, K.271. There is, moreover, a certain kinship of climate between the two movements; this one is a more sober reincarnation of the other.

[2] And also a phrase from the *Magic Flute*, in the second trio of the third act: "*Soll ich dich, Teurer,*" at the words: "*Der Götter Wille mag geschehen*".

together. And then, without loss of speed, the mood becomes dreamier and we dive under the sparkling surface of the waters. With a spaciousness seldom surpassed by him, Mozart makes ready for the return of the refrain. It has, in fact, so often shouted: Wolf, wolf! in season and out of season, that our credulity is exhausted and has to be restored. A sudden return would leave us unconvinced. It must therefore proceed with some ceremony and, in an extended transition, make us believe once again in the necessity of its appearance.

This transition takes up nineteen bars—two more than the main part of the refrain. It consists in a B flat pedal point held at first by the strings, then by the wind whilst the strings murmur in unison Mozart's beloved "fluttering seconds" figure. The piano part is exceptionally rich, almost constantly in three-part harmony, and the Mediterranean softness of the sixths tempers the feverishness of the broken chords (ex. 90).

The return of the refrain does not spell rest for the piano. As before, the violins outline the skeleton and the solo clothes it, this time in broken octaves, thus prolonging into the refrain the rhythm of the end of the couplet—one of the many devices[1] thanks to which the unity of this rondo is so perfect.

The impetus of the movement is nevertheless beginning to wear out. There is indeed a third couplet but it is quite perfunctory; it confines itself to recalling the *minore* of the second (but in the major), and passes straight on to a passage from the first, to stop on the dominant seventh chord which introduces the cadenza. Its vitality is not extinguished, however, and in the middle of this passage it slows down and, dreaming, soars away into the distant realms of D flat where it muses a while before returning to earth. In so hard-working a finale, this is even more unexpected than the pedal point we heard just now (ex. 91).

After the cadenza, the conclusion is in 6-8 time, a common practice of the period which Mozart has followed more than once.[2] Here, it is hardly felicitous. The threefold rhythm appears lopsided and halting after the spritely gait of the rest. The refrain returns one last time and after we have heard it so often, upright with the crotchets, flowing with the quavers, but always assured, it seems enervated in its new shape. Yet it is not at the end of its tricks and its

---

[1] Not invented by Mozart, of course; there is an expressive instance of it in Rameau's *La Villageoise*.

[2] In K.382, 459, 491; K.451 ends in 3-8 time.

last bars, based on a three-note figure which announces the main theme of the E flat string quintet, hold a delightful surprise in store (ex. 92).

Despite all the affection we feel for the first movement of this concerto, we tend to think that the main interest of the work lies in its finale, a judgement we should not express concerning any other concerto except K.365, 415, 459 and perhaps 450. It is indeed a masterpiece, the equal of the superb finales of the F major in that same year, of the D minor and A major in the following ones. Its distinctive quality is its oneness, by which it differs from the ordinary Mozartian last movement. When, score in hand, one notes each return of the first subject, in its entirety and in the tonic, it is possible to pick out the four expositions of the refrain and the three couplets of the Mozartian rondo; but on hearing it one's impression is that the refrain never leaves the stage and that the whole piece is built up on its variations and their derivatives. And this is so. Our short analysis will have given an idea of the many shapes in which it unceasingly presents and re-presents itself; a study of the score or of the piano arrangement can alone reveal all its exquisite detail. To this unity in multiformity must be added the unity of rhythm, broken just enough to prevent monotony, and the breadth and gradualness of the linking passages which spare us the clear-cut divisions occurring between the sections in some rondos. Especially noteworthy are discreet devices like that, already mentioned, which consists in introducing the new rhythm with which the refrain is to return some little time before its actual reappearance, so that this reappearance seems to be the unbroken sequence of what has gone before. Also the distinctions between solos and tuttis are less hard and fast than usual and the collaboration between piano and orchestra is almost continuous. Such formal unity, we repeat, is unmatched in Mozart's concertos and, in his other work, one has to reach the last rondos of his chamber music, those of the B flat *Prussian* quartet, K.589, and of the E flat string quintet, K.614, to find parallels to it.

Despite its small dimensions and the exiguousness of its orchestra, this composition is therefore most individual. It opens worthily the era of the greater concertos. Yet it is not closely related to any of these. In reality, it is isolated in Mozart's work; its first and last movements fall in with no group of his compositions and do not bear clearly the mark of any period in his life. Mozartian they certainly are, but not in the narrow sense in which this word is sometimes used; they do not clearly recall anything else in him; their originality was long taken for queerness and they have been treated as one usually treats originals and eccentrics: they have been left to themselves. Performances are however now more frequent and the work has been recorded; a wider public has thus been introduced to the rather rough beauties of the first movement, the wavy lines of the andantino and the passion for unity of the finale. It is now more fully realized that if its size may cause it to be classed as a minor work, in its deep sincerity, in the strength and concentrated nature of its feeling, it belongs truly to the race of the twelve masterpieces at the beginning of which it stands in date.

The three 1784 concertos written for himself achieve with marvellous art this balance between personal and social ideals. The Salzburg concertos and the first of the 1782 group insisted most on the latter; the 1785 and 1786 works will dwell more and more on the former; those of 1784 succeed with incredible skill in mirroring the soul of their creator while yet giving utterance to that of their public. So classical an achievement could be obtained only during the very brief moment when a perfect concord of feeling and thought, a perfect community of culture and civilization existed between the deeper nature of the musician and the collective soul of his listeners. The rather rapid growth of Mozart's personality in the years that follow dissolves this unity and carries him away from the Viennese public's elegant but restricted conception of beauty.

I. If one reached this concerto after having run through the ten preceding ones and without knowing those that follow, one would be surprised in its very first bars by its originality. Not by its originality of theme or rhythm or harmony, nor by any uncertainty of key, as in K.449, but by its orchestration. Nothing like it had occurred hitherto in any of Mozart's concertos (ex. 93). Anyone who heard the beginning of this movement without knowing it was a concerto might fancy he was listening to a woodwind serenade or divertimento.

Then, when he heard the elegantly balanced answer of the strings (ex. 94), he might think it was a *concertante* serenade for strings and woodwind. And the continuation of this opening, with its repeated alternations between the two groups, would confirm his impression, until the complete blending of both in the *forte* of the fourteenth bar enlightened him as to the symphonic nature of the work.

Such an introduction is indeed quite new in Mozart. And its charm is equal to its novelty. There is no stiffness in the antiphonal treatment of the two groups and the repeats are not literal. See how the notes with which the wind concludes are minims the first time and the second time have the value of a minim and a crotchet, and how the strings, which the first time began after the third beat, start the second time after the first. And admire how delicately the blending in the fourteenth bar is prepared. After the sharp opposition of the beginning, the distinction between wind parts and string parts becomes gradually less clear cut (ex. 95), and, in the three bars before the *forte*, wind and strings, whilst keeping their individuality, play together (ex. 96).

Considered thematically, these thirteen bars exhibit equally delicate

details. The second strain, instead of being brutally contrasted with
the first, resembles it in that the interval of a second predominates
in its outline; the wind call in bars 8–10 (ex. 95) is derived from this
same strain, the first notes of which it reproduces, and when in the
eleventh bar wind and strings unite without blending, each sketch the
same figure, one lot ascending, in quavers, the other descending, in
semi-quavers (ex. 96).

A proud and stalwart passage follows this discreet beginning,
according to a formula common in the *galant* style which returns
more than once in Mozart's concertos, and we stop on a loud close
in F major. This concerto is a well-bred gentleman; it does not
wander off into the eccentric paths of K.449 and keeps to the key of
B flat prescribed by the code of musical good manners. It is therefore
without change of key that a new subject comes forward, an occasion
for wind and strings again to disclose their separatist tendencies
(ex. 97). So skeletal a silhouette predestines it to variation; it demands such treatment as imperiously as the rondo theme of K.449;
and as soon as it has been given out, the woodwind reiterate it whilst
the violins trace above it a decoration strangely recalling the outline of
ex. 87, I, in K.449. We say, strangely, because these two concertos
are in truth, of the whole series, the two between which one would
least expect to find a likeness, and this is indeed the only one.[1]

The rest of the tutti is taken up with a rising passage on a pedal
of repeated quavers, or *Trommelbass*, straight from Italian opera, and
with the concluding subject which comes perhaps from the well-
known French song:

> *Il a passé par ici,*
> *Le furet du bois joli.*

In giving out this latter, wind and strings divide at first, then come
together, as in the opening theme (ex. 98).

Their last notes coincide with the first of the piano. The solo does
not tackle the first subject straight away. In Mozart's concertos, solos
which start at once with the first subject are about equal in number to
those which prefix a few introductory bars. In 1784, however, he
prefers the simpler method and this concerto is the only one in the
year where the piano makes its bow with a passage of its own. It is a
cadenza obbligata of some ten bars, accompanied by the strings,
leading us to a trill on the tonic.

----

[1] It also recalls the clarinet quintet; cf. p. 188.

The piano entry drives the orchestra into the background. With his return to the *galant* ideal Mozart appears also to have returned to the virtuoso conception of the concerto where the orchestra is neither collaborator nor adversary but just accompanist. After their assertive introduction, strings and wind keep their peace or at the most interject a few modest comments, a few punctuation marks. The piano monopolizes almost entirely the subject which had been so gracefully distributed between fiddles, hautboys and bassoons; only the little figure (a) of ex. 95 remains to the wind. The solo subject follows at once (ex. 99); it begins in G minor, a key unsympathetic to the mood of the movement, quickly escapes from it and modulates into F. After a rather long bravura passage, consisting in broken scales and octaves, the piano expounds the true second subject (ex. 100),[1] which had not yet been heard. We are still in the exposition which, in the classical concerto, is in two parts; the first and second do not always utilize completely identical material; it is enough if most of what is presented in one or other of them reappears somewhere in the course of the movement.

In the virtuosity passage that follows, the strings intervene shyly, seeking, maybe, to collaborate on equal terms, but only succeeding, so purely rhythmic is their contribution, in stiffening slightly the line of pianistic ripples (ex. 101). The piano does not even notice their presence and continues along its royal road, once they are silent, with undiminished splendour.

The trill on the chord of F at length sets the orchestra free or rather transfers the piano's vitality to it for an instant, and it enters in full force with the "stalwart" theme of the first tutti. This time it does not lead to a close but loses itself in the concluding subject, scored as before. The piano, as if remembering the trick which had come off so well in the last concerto, picks up its last notes, puts semi-quavers in the place of quavers, and sails off afresh with a joyousness undimmed by the key of F minor. Right hand, then left, then right again run over the keyboard in passages derived from the conclusion. For the nonce, the orchestra is silent and one hand accompanies the other, but, in the greater part of what follows till the reprise, both hands play in tenths or octaves and the instruments complete the harmonies, sometimes following, sometimes opposing the piano line with sketchy figures. All take part; woodwind echo strings, strings echo woodwind; groups divide up, bassoons against hautboys, 'cello and basses

---

[1] It is almost the same as that of the E flat quintet for piano and woodwind (first movement), composed one month later.

against fiddles and violas (ex. 102)! The song of joy which grows out of this lofty game, although it is confined to the piano and violins, is a kind of idealized horn fanfare. But everything has an end and beneath the trill, in which the piano at last finds peace, whispering violins call up the shadow of the first subject. Little by little its chromatic outline is defined and illumined; the piano's decisive tone gives it precision and, ere the solo instrument reaches the end of its run, hautboys and bassoons are giving it out as at the opening of the movement.

The *development* which is just over is, as is befitting, the part of the movement where fancy plays most freely. In true *developments*, the composer is expected to build up elements already "exposed" in the first section and to make a new whole out of familiar themes. Such *developments* are the rule in the greater part of the chamber music and symphonies of Mozart's Viennese period, but exceptional in his concertos. Instead, we find those which have been called *fantasia developments*, the type which before Mozart is found in the sonatas of Schobert[1] and in at least one sonata of John Christian Bach,[2] actually one of those that Mozart, as a child, had arranged as a harpsichord concerto. In this kind of development, says Abert,

> what matters is the continuous flow of harmony which drives the same ideas, with few changes, through the most diverse keys. No goal is sought; the motion is itself the essential; the figures carried on it, first of all based on simple chords, then, in the later works, thematic, serve only to strengthen the harmonic structure; there is no question of a development in the strict sense. Around this harmonic erection, built mainly on progressions in the bass, the solo, here at the climax of its virtuosity, weaves a rich design of figures and passages, romantic adventures, bold flights towards an unknown, always hidden goal; only at the beginning and end, as often in Schobert, smaller phrases arise, melodic and harmonic, like bridgeheads.[3]

It is in his concertos, we have said, that Mozart varied his recapitulations most. Yet the ten concertos we have studied hitherto have only partly borne us out. The work which showed greatest freedom in its recapitulation was the concerto for two pianos. Even K.449, in other respects more emancipated than its predecessors, had been content to repeat the main outlines with a few changes of detail. The concerto we are studying is the first to break sharply with this unenterprising practice and open new paths in its last section.

---

[1] Op. II, 1; IV, 1; XIV, 3, 5.

[2] Op. V, 4, in E flat.

[3] Op. cit., p. 207

It does it from the very reprise. The chromatic subject, ex. 93, formerly monopolized by the piano, is now shared between it and the wind, the piano appropriating the part taken earlier by the strings. In the first exposition, the "stalwart" passage succeeded the first subject; in the second, the solo gave out almost at once its special subject. Now, the recapitulation has to recall the main features of the first two parts. How is Mozart to manage this? He recalls, to begin with, the "stalwart" passage which unfolds for several bars. But this is a mistake; the passage has been heard twice already; that should suffice. The movement changes its mind, stops on a broken cadence with a brusquerie unwonted in so courteous a work, and calls on the solo subject. This latter, however, does not return in person but is represented by a variation, in C minor. The bravura passage which followed it in the exposition, the second subject (in B flat) and the runs that concluded it, ex. 101, are brought back with no changes save those of key and of a few details in the figuration.

Before the piano has finished its last run, the violins broach one of the two members of the cast of themes that have not yet been heard again: the mock second subject so gracefully shared and commented upon by them and by the woodwind in the first tutti, ex. 97. They start it beneath a trill into which the whole life of the piano is concentrated for the time being. The woodwind repeat their earlier part and it is now the piano's turn to decorate the theme with a variation. After this interlude, it comes back to the passage which concluded the exposition, reproduces it with slight changes and leads to its final trill. There is still one theme to return, the *Trommelbass* passage after ex. 97 in the opening tutti. Here it is, first of all *pp*, then raising its voice and heralding the solo cadenza. The cadenza which Mozart wrote for a pupil, K.624, 19, reviews the concluding subject, ex. 98, the solo's last passage and the mock subject; it is commendably brief. The piano does not speak again and the end belongs to the orchestra which repeats unchanged the last bars of the introduction. Only, when we think we have reached the end of our course, a prank, already played at a similar moment in K.271 and 413, calls back the motif which the violins had used to accompany the solo entry and the allegro ends up, so to speak, like a whiting at dinner, with its tail in its mouth.

This recapitulation is therefore far from being a facsimile of the first solo, with the tonic key instead of the dominant. Nevertheless, it is rather by reshuffling its materials than by transforming any of

them that it renews itself. We have described elsewhere[1] the means
Mozart uses to carry out this reshuffling, here and in his other concertos. In this work, he calls up two themes from the introduction
which had been missed out in the second exposition; the passage
which followed the first subject in the opening tutti comes next time
at the end of the solo, before the conclusion, and, in the recapitulation,
retrieves its place in the wake of the first subject; the solo subject is
repeated in the shape of a variation; and finally, twice over, the piano
replaces the strings in a dialogue with the woodwind.

II. Associations which are foreign to the mind of the artist but
present in our own are sometimes in danger of making us see in his
inspiration elements which are absent from it. The influence of
19th-century Church music may incline many a modern listener to
find a religious inspiration in the andante of this concerto. The
theme has the bearing of a hymn (ex. 104). Yet it is doubtful whether
its pious character is more than accidental. It is unlikely that Mozart
intended a religious piece here; neither the fashionable public for
whom the concerto was written, nor the composer, proud and careful
of his popularity, who was playing it, would have thought this the
place for such an emotion. But this will not hinder some concert-
goers from finding its theme devotional and recognizing in it "Sunday
echoes in weekday hours".

This movement, of which Mozart is careful to tell his father[2] that
it is an andante and not an adagio, has the form of a theme with two
variations and a short coda. Even if we banish the epithet "devotional" we cannot deny that its tone is solemn, yet at the same time
simple and almost naïve. It is Mozart at his best,[3] peaceful with
the peace of passionate natures, deeper and richer than the negative
tranquillity of merely placid souls. It is the counterpart in Mozartian
language of the theme of the Kreutzer sonata variations. The movement has also in common with the andante of the celebrated sonata
that almost all its interest consists in the theme and that the variations
themselves please us mainly because they allow us to hear more than
once a well-loved tune.

The variations are double, that is to say, each half is given out

---

[1] Part I, Chap. 2.

[2] Letter of June 9th, 1784.

[3] Several bars of this theme were radically rewritten after a part of the
movement had been composed (cf. Köchel-Einstein, p. 570).

twice. The theme and each variation comprise therefore four parts. The interest resides, we have said, in the loveliness of the theme; the variations themselves are decorative and embellish it rather than transform or throw changing light upon it, and their greatest charm is in their orchestration.

Each half of the theme is given out by the strings and repeated, with slight decorations, by the piano. The first variation also belongs to the piano and strings. These latter repeat the first half with slight changes in the harmony, and above them the piano weaves a beautiful design of demi-semi-quaver arpeggios (ex. 105). Then the instruments are silent and the right hand goes over the theme again, richly harmonized with chords,[1] whilst the bass embroiders a design similar to that of the right hand in ex. 105. The second half of the theme is treated likewise.

The piano starts on the second variation alone. It is a slightly modified repetition of ex. 104, except that the rhythm is syncopated; in the fourth bar, the strings take hold of it and treat the theme a little more freely and the right hand superimposes a flowing figure of embroidery in demi-semi-quavers. The woodwind, which had hitherto kept out of the picture, take up the tune in their turn; the piano reproduces it in arpeggio sextuplets and the string pizzicati punctuate it with a variation in semi-quavers; this is the fullest passage in the movement (ex. 106). The second half follows the same plan, but the sextuplets are replaced by double semi-quavers. The end of this variation is prolonged by a few bars where the piano chords repeat those of the wind one bar late. The coda, as simple and moving as the theme, is treated antiphonally by the solo and the whole orchestra, after which the melody, escorted by hautboys and horns, dies out in the upper register of the piano (ex. 107).

III. The finale is a rondo in 6-8, a time which is used by Mozart in three out of his four piano concertos in B flat, but elsewhere much less commonly than 2-4.[2] Its refrain, given out by the piano and repeated by the tutti, which adds a long ritornello, is one of his most pleasing rondo themes (ex. 108), both fiery and graceful, and perfectly illustrative of the union of these two qualities which characterize Mozart's genius. With what power and ease it sails down from the fifth degree of the scale to the second while appearing to be rising ever higher, creating its illusion thanks to the fact that the ear is more struck by the three degrees climbed by three consecutive notes (bars 1, 3, 5) than by the leap downwards of a sixth (bars 2, 4, 6)! The

---

[1] We have already said that it is important to give Mozart's comparatively infrequent chords their full weight.

[2] About two-thirds of his finales after his return from Paris in 1778 are in 2-4 time and most of the others in 6-8. 6-8 is unusual in first movements, where he prefers C, or, less often, ¢.

very outline of the tune, apart from its rhythm, calls up a galloping horse, and the three repeated notes at the beginning of each fragment (a similarity with the finales of K.456 and 482) is like a horn call.

The rondo it draws after it and which at times, so to speak, it carries upwards on its wings, is a sonata rondo, one of the few in Mozart which are quite regular. We have spoken at length of this form elsewhere.[1]

Among Mozart's numerous rondos of his Viennese period which adopt it only a dozen are "regular" in that they use in the second couplet elements already presented in the first. The majority bring in at this point completely new material. But nearly all treat the third couplet as a recapitulation. A few leave out the refrain between the second and third couplets; the rondo then assumes the appearance of a binary movement, especially when the *development* section is abridged. All these varieties are found among the piano concertos.

The exposition couplet in this rondo begins after the ritornello with a subject in the piano, closely related to the refrain itself in outline and rhythm. Having given it out twice, the piano passes on; it is a fugitive thought that does not return. It is followed by a solo passage where the strings accompany the piano and which, after a short tutti intervention, leads to what may be termed the second subject. This is really a whole section, in elaborating which first the piano and strings take part, then the flute,[2] and lastly the hautboys. It consists in the spinning out of a six-note figure which winds upward from the low B of the fiddles to the high C of the flute. In the piano, the figure is wreathed round with arpeggios in a particularly tricky crossing of hands which proves fatal when one is sight-reading the work (ex. 109). The end of its climb settles us into the key of F, sheltered from further modulations, and a third theme, *cantabile*, unfolds in the solo, then in the flute with a piano arpeggio accompaniment; the orchestra, and particularly the woodwind, emboldened perhaps by its importance in the andante, no longer confines itself to an intermittent part, as in the first allegro (ex. 110).

After a pause for which Mozart has left an *intrata*,[3] the piano gives out the refrain, accompanied as at the outset by the strings and the held notes of the bassoons. The orchestra takes it up vigorously

---

[1] Cf. pp. 49 *seq.*

[2] Present for the first time in these concertos, save for the andante of K.238 and the variations K.382.

[3] K.624, no. 21.

Ex. 110

Ex. III

Ex. 112

Ex. 113

Ex. 119

and engages in a dialogue in imitation, a kind of irregular canon, between basses and trebles.   After a close on the chord of D minor, we await the traditional *minor* episode when another modulation flings us wittily into the air and catches us again in E flat (ex. 111).

The *development* couplet which opens now is the most interesting of the three.   Like many first-movement *developments* in Mozart, it begins with a new theme, made up of a rhythmic first part and a singing second part, a close relative of ex. 109; it belongs to the piano, supported now and again by the fiddles.   The very last bars of the passage, which finishes on E flat, are solo, but ere the piano is silent the hautboys, very softly and still in E flat, begin recalling the refrain motif in a slightly varied form and there opens the most ingenious and enchanting section, not only of the rondo, but of the whole concerto.

For some forty bars, until the end of the *development*, everyone —flute, violins, violas, 'cellos and basses, but especially piano and hautboys—together or in turn, expound wholly or in part the refrain theme which seems truly to carry the movement into the air like a winged steed.

The hautboys opens the game by giving out twice, in E flat, the first four bars of the theme, but starting one degree higher up the second time and modifying the last descending interval which becomes a seventh instead of a sixth.   The piano continues, beginning one degree higher still, turning the last interval into a fifth, and leaving us in F minor where the sport is resumed two degrees lower down with the hautboy the first two times and the piano the third.   We are now in G minor (ex. 112).   (The quotation shows the first ascent of three degrees and the beginning of the second.)   Having climbed up, we must now come down, but it would be unadventurous to do so in the same manner and by the same steps.   So the hautboys remain silent and now all the strings in unison, doubled by the piano bass, undertake the operation, whilst the piano's right hand accompanies them with a new element, a swiftly flowing motif.   Not content with varying the scoring, Mozart modifies also the melodic line and the third time, instead of giving out (a) entire, he represents it by a kind of abridgment (ex. 113), which allows him to come down four degrees instead of three.   We are now on D, one degree lower than when we started.   The next bars pursue the same "working-out" of (a) but entrust it to the piano's right hand, whilst the florid accompaniment passes to the left.   The hautboys and flute sustain; the strings are silent.

As a sign that the entertainment is over and that we are going on to other things, Mozart interposes here a flowing passage where the strings have the theme and the right hand doubles them, *arpeggiando* the two highest parts; this passage interrupts the constant modulating and asserts for a moment the key of D minor.

But here comes again a reminder of the refrain.

Ex. 114

says the piano, and the hautboy follows suit. Then, with a mischievous alteration of one degree, the piano says (ex. 115) , but this time the hautboy also allows itself an alteration (ex. 116) The piano now says (ex. 117) . A third thief joins in and the flute echoes; and for the last three bars of the *development* the three instruments carry on a witty chirping with ex. 117. The flute has not finished its last (ex. 118) when the piano starts on the refrain, this time for good and in the tonic key.

This *development* has consisted in three things:

The repetition, on different degrees, with modulations and slight modifications, of the first bars of the theme;

The addition to it of an accompaniment whose outline recalls that of the theme itself;

The repetition on different parts of the scale, but without either modulation or modification, of a fragment of the "developed" figure.

It is clear that the last of these is what is most like a Beethovenian "working-out"; it is also the one which is least frequent in Mozart, except in a few works like the E flat quintet. The Mozartian "working-out" is most often a mingling of variation, modulation and instrumental dialoguing and the lesson taught by this passage is borne out by the study of his symphonies and chamber music.

There is no need to dwell on the rest of the movement. After the repetition of ex. 108 by the orchestra, the piano omits the solo subject which had opened the exposition and passes on at once to the solo that preceded the second subject (ex. 109). This latter follows, in B flat, and after one last bravura passage, the tutti prepare for the cadenza with a part of their first ritornello. The cadenza written by

Mozart[1] is a fragment of the *development*. It begins with the theme in the right hand and the florid accompaniment in the left. After recalling the subject with which the *development* had opened it introduces ex. 108 in the bass, again travels down three consecutive degrees, and this time the right hand accompanies it with a passage where arpeggios alternate with scale fragments. Then the arpeggios infect the bass; ex. 108 vanishes and the customary flourishes lead us promptly to the final trill. The refrain is heard one last time, followed now by its second half that we had not met since the beginning; and the work gives itself up with rapture to the *strepitoso arcistrepitoso, strepitosissimo*, with which, according to Da Ponte, every opera buffa finale should conclude, and few passages in Mozart's concertos show more indisputably the kinship between their genre and opera. The *strepitoso* is cleverly managed and Mozart keeps his full force in reserve. The whole ascent of ten bars in *pp,* and only when the movement has but four more bars to run does he let loose all his artillery. The passage is an amplifying of the common chord; a B flat pedal in the strings, emphasized by a violin gruppetto on the strong beats and a bass uprush of three notes before every other bar; arpeggios in the piano; fanfare on the horns, then on the flute and hautboys, and finally on the bassoons. Once everyone has fallen in, the orchestra throws itself into its last *ff*. There are more significant codas in Mozart's concertos; there are noisier ones, or ones that are noisier for a longer time; none is conceived on a larger scale and in none are the physical effects more astutely prepared (ex. 119).[2]

In opening this chapter, we said that this concerto was very different from the one composed a month earlier. This latter was unstable and, at times, stormy; the one we have just been studying is sunny and serene. K.449 had a passionate and introspective nature, at least in its first movement; K.450 is a fair, unreflective athlete, troubled by no problems. Not a cloud crosses its brow; not a bar in any of its three movements betrays sadness or doubt.

The difference is quite as noticeable in the relations between piano and orchestra in the opening allegros. K.449's orchestra was small but it behaved towards the piano like an equal. K.450 marks a step backward in this respect. Its first movement reverts to the stage of the Salzburg and 1782 concertos; the orchestra is silent when the piano

---

[1] K.624, no. 22.

[2] Eight bars in this part of the movement were added afterwards and are written on the back of the MS. (Cf. Köchel-Einstein, p. 570.)

speaks, or raises but a humble voice to accompany; gone are the collaboration and dialoguing which had enriched the earlier concerto.
No more symphonic passages between orchestra and solo; no more
sharing of themes; not only the solo subject but even the second subject
never fall to the tutti.   It is true that the andante and especially the
finale, with its splendid second couplet, regain some of the ground
lost; on the whole, nevertheless, K.449 is in advance of its successor,
not only in the depth of its emotional life but also in its symphonic
development.

It is as if the composer (and this is quite understandable) had not
been able to keep up his progress all along the line.   For progress
there is, but not here.   Not in the dealings of piano with orchestra
but in the orchestral parts themselves, in the relations between the
various groups of instruments, is there a step forward.   It consists
above all in the independence of the wind.   In this respect, the leap
forward, from the earlier works to this one, is truly gigantic.   In
none of his earlier symphonies or concertos[1] had the wind separated
themselves to such an extent from the strings nor been entrusted with
parts so original and so expressive of their nature.   It is not only that
they enjoy the right of expounding the chief themes as fully as the
strings.   They have indeed this right, but they have also themes of
their own.   The chromatic opening of the first subject, for instance,
is given out by them in the first place, by the piano in the second, and
again, in the recapitulation, by the wind.   It is true that violins and
violas murmur the rising scale that leads to its return, but that is an
announcement of the subject and not the subject itself; when it comes
back, it is reserved to the hautboys and bassoons.   The same is true
of the first, *arpeggiato* part of the conclusion, ex. 98.   In the *development*, where the accompaniment is most interesting, the wind group
stands out against the strings and formulates alternately with it the
figure that sustains the piano triplets and semi-quavers, ex. 102.   In
the slow movement its part is less striking and in the second variation,
it is only when piano and strings have each given out the theme, that
it sings it in its turn.   But in the finale, one of its members, the flute,
risen late to eminence, represents the whole orchestra in the third
subject, ex. 110, and we have seen with what expressive originality

---

[1] We must underline *symphonies* and *concertos*, for his chamber music
comprised already several works for woodwind, culminating in the magnificent serenades in B flat, E flat and C minor.   And in *Idomeneo* the wind had
been treated with as much freedom as in this concerto and had shown itself
in all respects the equal of the strings.

the hautboys behave in the *development*. In a word, though this concerto be poor in interplay between solo and tutti (and even that is true only of the first movement), in the importance given to the wind it opens a path along which are to travel most of its successors, several of which have been called: wind concertos with piano obbligato.

The piano part is harder than in K.449, by all the distance that separated Babette Ployer's talent from Mozart's. More difficult, and also more "modern". The use of thirds is fairly frequent in the first movement and owes perhaps something to the technical progress made by Clementi since 1772, but the harmonizing in thirds of the first subject, in the solo part, has quite the appearance of an imitation by the piano of a woodwind effect. There is another orchestral effect, already well-established at this period, in the right hand of a bravura passage which appears twice (bars 119–21 and 264–5).

We discuss later on the character of the key of B flat in Mozart's work; it is enough to say now that K.450 is far from being as isolated in his productions as its predecessor was. Among other compositions in the same key, the fine violin sonata of the same year, K.454, and the celebrated quartet called (but not by Mozart) *The Hunt*, K.458, also of 1784, sound the same hymn of joy under the same sunlit sky; an equally dazzling light fills them, and their first and last movements, at any rate, are equally free from even passing cloud. The kinship is emotional, not formal; their themes are not alike and their construction is as different as their genres; but the identity of the inspiration is unmistakable, and the B flat trio of 1786, K.502, belongs to the same race. Such kinship, on the other hand, is much less close between this concerto and that in B flat of the end of the year, K.456.

But if there be kinship between works in the same key, there is also kinship between works of the same period. The description: "fair athlete", fits the next concerto as well as this one. There is in it the same assurance, pride, lack of hesitancy and disquiet; it shows an almost identical aspect of the fashionable young virtuoso; and this holds good also of the F major concerto of the end of the year. K.450 is as representative of a period in its author's life as K.449 was unique, and it will be followed by works which form with it one single family full of life and joy.

3. The Twelfth Concerto: K.451 in D

CONCERTO No. 12 IN D (K.451)[1]
Finished March 22nd, 1784
  Allegro assai: C
  (Andante): ¢ (in G)
  Allegro di molto: 2-4
Orchestra: Strings, flute, two hautboys, two bassoons, two horns, two trumpets, two kettledrums.

HARDLY had Mozart completed his B flat concerto—perhaps even he had not quite completed it—when, in this miraculous winter of 1784, he started on another, the third in one month and a half! He finished it on March 22nd, one week after the last! By the letter to his sister where he tells how he had composed his C major fantasia while writing out the fugue we know that he could keep going several works at the same time, and he may well have been meditating the concerto in D before he had finished writing out the B flat. On the other hand, the fact, attested by a letter to his father of October 31st, 1783, that he composed his *Linz* symphony in four days, makes the composition of the present work in one week appear quite likely. The dates of some of his works, vouched for by his catalogue, as well as revelations like that about the *Linz* symphony, prove that he could compose at high speed. If one finds it difficult to believe what one reads about this, one should remember the feat performed by Paul Hindemith in January, 1936. He was to have played a viola concerto in London. The death of the king happened a few days before the concert and obliged the organizers to change the programme at the last moment. Hindemith thereupon offered to shut himself up for four hours and write on the spot a funeral piece to the memory of the deceased sovereign. The offer was accepted and the work performed. It was a composition which lasted some twenty minutes and had the scope of the first movement of a symphony. This contemporary example makes more credible the feats that anecdotalists tell us of Mozart.

---

[1] *Gesamtausgabe*, no. 16.

One feels here that at any rate the first movement was composed at one stroke. The pride and the joy of knowing oneself to be at the height of one's powers which inspired the last concerto quicken also this one; but these sentiments are raised now to the intensity of passion. And, with this growth in the degree and breadth of emotion, the form becomes richer. The first movement is the most powerful and most complex that Mozart has written hitherto, and one of the most powerful and complex in all his orchestral work. The only criticism that can be made of it is that it throws the two others somewhat into the shade. It is no longer in the finale that orchestra and solo collaborate most but in the first allegro, which contains the most splendid instances in all Mozart of interplay between the protagonists. It is a masterpiece of that brilliant art, sincere in spite of its display, radiating satisfaction, confidence and power, which was Mozart's in 1784. Among the six concertos of the year which express the ideal of the fashionable young virtuoso, it holds the place held by the great C major concerto, K.503, in the six that are to follow.

I. The allegro is not only the movement in which we grasp for the first time, in all its breadth, the symphonic conception of the concerto which Mozart had reached, but one of those where we grasp it best. Here is probably one of those works which fulfil so wholly the ideal of the genre that people have seen in them, as Spohr did, "symphonies with piano" rather than concertos for piano and orchestra—a false interpretation of the Mozartian concerto but one which has the advantage of reminding us of the supreme importance of the orchestra, the "emancipation" of which others, equally falsely, have attributed to Beethoven.

The orchestra is bigger than in K.450. Mozart retains the flute which had appeared in the rondo of this latter and adds trumpets and kettledrums. This is the largest band he has used hitherto in his concertos though all these instruments had already appeared in some work or other, the flute in the andante of K.238 and the rondo of K.450, the trumpets and drums in K.175, 382 and 415.

The movement opens to the same march rhythm as K.415, a rhythm we meet again in the three concertos that follow. But whereas in these works the march tune is first given out *pp*, by the first fiddles or woodwind only, here it starts *forte* and with the whole orchestra, dropping, however, to *piano* in the second bar. The first subject is a scale of D major which in the course of ten bars rises two octaves. Its line is indicated by the flute and first violins; bassoons

Ex. 121

Ex. 122

Ex. 123

and basses sound a tonic pedal with repeated quavers, and every two bars the *piano* is broken by a *forte* where hautboys, horns, trumpets and drums reinforce the rest of the orchestra. Moreover, each of these *fortes* marks a halt in the rhythm, so that this first octave gives the impression of a majestic stairway climbed with vigorous strides (ex. 121). After the first octave the pace quickens at the same time as a *crescendo* leads to *forte*, and the phrase ends on the tonic, two octaves higher than it began.

This first phrase is succeeded by a second, *ff*, consisting also in D major scales, but descending ones, with dotted quaver rhythm, and divided in imitation between the upper parts and the violas and basses (ex. 122). It leads to the dominant chord which is followed by an upper pedal, in semi-quavers, given to the second fiddles. A subsidiary theme is given out by the hautboys, horns and trumpets, and we fall back to *piano*, but, as at the opening, the other instruments burst in every other bar with explosive *fortes* (ex. 123). The *forte* ends by staying for good and with it the fragment (a) (in ex. 123) with which first violins and flute had interrupted the wind's *piano*; on it is built the dominant close which concludes this first section.

These twenty-five bars form in reality one single strain and they give the whole movement its character. The quivering power, scarcely subdued, bursting forth in *fortes* which are dynamic and not just *galant* "surprises", the pedals whose action is both to hold back the passion and intensify it, and the importance of scales in the melodic outline, are present all through this allegro.

The principle of contrast reigns in it but this principle, so dear to *galant* composers, is no longer a mere game. Mozart's genius gives it the significance of a struggle between two aspects of his own nature. Passion and gentleness strive here for mastery as, indeed, they do throughout the movement. Gentleness demands a calm and well-ordered bearing; it imposes the scale figure and the *piano* in the first and third sections of this passage. But it cannot restrain the impetuous rush of passion which breaks through constantly in the *fortes* that interrupt these sections and triumphs in the dotted quaver part and in the close. We are, of course, in a classical period and the struggle is stylized; the rhythm is regular and the outbursts of passion occur at equal intervals; the twofold nature is none the less evident. But, as the adversaries are after all but two aspects of the same soul, it has to be shown that, though foes, they are brothers; the underlying unity has to be expressed. This unity is safeguarded by the pedals, the lower one of which ties down the rising scale by its feet, as it were,

Ex. 124

Ex. 125

Ex. 126

Ex. 127   Ex. 128

Ex. 129

Ex. 130

Ex. 131

Ex. 132

and prevents it from losing touch with earth. The study of the rest of the movement in which *fortes* and *piano* alternate sharply, where subjects built on scales or common chord arpeggios predominate, where pedals are frequent, will show that this interpretation holds good, not only for the first twenty-five bars but also for what follows.

A less significant movement would stop after the close before starting off again with the second subject. But the concern for unity in duality which characterizes this allegro forbids such a procedure.

After the close, instead of the expected halt, the bass continues uninterruptedly with a fresh dominant pedal, a link with the preceding
passage, and over it flutters the fascinating transition section, nine
bars long, which leads to the second subject.[1] Its rhythm recalls the
fragment (a) (ex. 123) of the close. Here, passion is quiet and the
charming dialogue between violins, flute and hautboy unfolds with
idyllic gentleness (ex. 124). There is not in all Mozart a more enchanting instance of the expressive power with which he combines
wind and strings.

This last fragment is also built upon the scale of D. The second
subject is composed of the arpeggio of the common chord, divided
into two parts, the first of which belongs to the hautboys and horns,
the second to the violins and flute. Like nearly all Mozart's concerto
second subjects, it appears only to make its bow and then withdraws
without entering into the history of the work. Still *piano*, there
opens a modulating passage with a syncopated rhythm, dark and
mysterious, different from what has gone before (ex. 125). Just
before the end, we suddenly rise to *forte* (ex. 126).

One of those surprises which Mozart loves to keep back for the
end of his developments separates us from the conclusion. We
expect the *forte* to end upon a full close. Not at all; it leads to an
interrupted cadence. At once we drop to *piano* and the tutti appears
about to finish with a commonplace little phrase which Mozart has
used hundreds of times (ex. 127). Then the interrupted cadence is
taken up again, with a truly Mozartian change of harmony, and after
it the commonplace phrase once more, and only then, but without any
break, does the other little phrase, hardly less commonplace, which is
to serve as a conclusion, link on to it. Like the second subject, it
consists in a fragment of the common chord and its kinship with its
predecessors is recognizable in that it rests on a pedal, gaining thereby
more dignity and poise than its levity would otherwise allow it to
enjoy.[2] A conventional but assertive figure of four bars completes
the introduction.

This first tutti is to an eminent degree the *argument* of what is to
follow. This is of course true of all opening tuttis, but in varying
degree. That of K.415 was hardly an *argument* at all, incorporating
as it did only a small part of what was to enter into the substance of

---

[1] In the first concerto, also in D, the second subject had been likewise
ushered in by a dominant pedal.

[2] It recalls a concluding strain in the finale of the G minor quartet, K.478.

the movement and comprising a development which did not reappear. That of K.450 left out almost all the material of the first solo, including the second subject; K.482 will do likewise. Here, on the contrary, we have almost all the elements with which the rest of the movement is built up. The only absent ones are the unimportant solo subject (ex. 129) and the *fantasia* part of the *development*. Even the bravura passages, which at first sight seem so important in this concerto, derive from this tutti. The movement, then, is highly organized and unified —the most organic first allegro we have hitherto met. To find a movement comparable to it among the concertos already dealt with, we should have to look among the rondos, and even so we should hardly find one before K.449. These concertos of the beginning of 1784 register in truth the first great step forward that Mozart has made for a long time towards organization and unity.

The piano tackles the first subject with the abruptness of K.449. It tackles it alone and the orchestra lays down its weapons while the solo scales the two octaves. Compelled to compensate with brilliance of display for the relative weakness of its tone, it decorates the line of scales with embroidery.[1] No mark of any kind is indicated, but it is clear that it, too, alternates between *forte* and *piano*, and the noisy outbursts are rendered here by minim chords in the right hand and upward drives in the left. These nine bars of unaccompanied solo are exceptional in this concerto where close and continuous collaboration between piano and orchestra is the order of the day.

The tutti returns with the descending dotted quaver scale, ex. 122, given to the strings alone, and the piano accompanies it with a decoration of rising scales and arpeggios in semi-quavers, now in the bass, now in the treble (ex. 128). A solo passage, doubled by the strings, on a dominant pedal, leads to the key of F sharp minor and the solo subject (ex. 129), which is repeated one degree lower, in E, and ends in a short, pretty passage of interplay, where wind and strings toss backwards and forwards a little trilling motif, as if they were alone in the world, appearing quite to ignore the solo who seeks vainly to attract their notice by emphasizing each wind repartee with a run (ex. 130). All this episode is new.

We meet the opening tutti again with the exposition of the second subject, rescored. In the preparation passage, the upper pedal is now

---

[1] This opening is interesting as a piano rendering of an orchestral passage. It is Mozart transcribing Mozart; the equivalent of Bach transcribing Vivaldi and Liszt or Busoni transcribing Bach.

given to the right hand of the piano and the figure to the strings and flute; the fragment (a) seesaws between flute and piano. The fluttering figure is, if possible, even lovelier than in the introduction, for the piano's presence enriches the landscape with an additional hue. The whisperings of this figure so loved of Mozart and which he never uses without clear intent, circle now between flute, hautboy and piano; the former have the figure itself and the piano the echo (in the recapitulation it will be the other way round).

The second subject is given out by the flute, doubled at first by the first hautboy, then by the first violins; the solo—an indication of the band's uppish attitude towards it in this concerto—takes hold of it only when it is repeated and even then does not enjoy it alone, for the first violins continue to double it an octave lower. One would expect here a bravura passage; instead, falling suddenly into the minor with true Mozartish sensibility, the piano engages a short conversation with the wind; then follow three bars of *arpeggiato* chords (a resounding but brief return for its former subjection), a fragment of a downward scale in the wind, with piano *gruppetti*, and the strings' re-entry with ex. 125 which they reproduce without changing anything but the key, and which closes, still in A, with the *forte* of ex. 126. During these fifteen bars, the piano is not silent, but its part is merely that of a commentator, if not of an accompanist. After two bars of silence, it comes in and strengthens the lower parts with an Alberti bass in the left hand; then, growing bolder, it decorates with arpeggios the violin line; finally, in the *forte*, diatonic and chromatic scales, in one hand after the other, dart through the barrage of repeated notes and join up the top and bottom of the octaves which limit the leaps of the strings (ex. 131). Only then can it launch forth in a song of triumphant bravura, and even so it is still kept in sight by the held notes of the wind and the staccato of the strings which follow it until the expected arrival of the trill announces the end of the exposition.

As if to mark the oneness of the movement, the orchestra re-enters at this point with neither a new subject nor ex. 128, but with the downward scale figure in dotted quavers, ex. 122. It links up with the last bars of ex. 126, as one had heard it in the beginning, and joins on to the interrupted cadence and the little commonplace phrase, ex. 127. The interrupted cadence is repeated, as in the first tutti, then, instead of the little phrase, it resumes where it had stopped, one third higher, and finally, once again, yet another third higher. We are far from A major; far, too, from what has gone before, and thus, with silken tread, the *development* steals upon us (ex. 132).

Passion united with strength, complete self-assurance raised to the pitch of pride have reigned hitherto; more mysterious strains came to disturb them only momentarily in the modulating and syncopated subject, ex. 125. And now, in a twinkling, the boundaries set up by this superb certainty have vanished, and we awaken on unknown seas. When we realize it, we are already far from land. What has been needed to delete one world and call up another one so different? Four bars of modulation, the piano re-entry, a break in the rhythm, which cause the same figure, thrice repeated, to end by corresponding to a different personality.

In an instant, the interrupted cadence motif has led us to new shores. It is the piano which launches us upon the waters with an arpeggio of the diminished seventh chord of the super-tonic, one of the most suggestive of chords. When figure (b) returns, we are in E minor. It is just a port of call. The voyage starts afresh and, passing through the same modulations, the piano arpeggios land us in B minor (ex. 133).

The flight towards infinity of these sixteen bars is the greatest moment in this fine allegro. We have met nothing like it hitherto in these concertos. Formally, it is a *fantasia development*,[1] the immediate forebears of which are in Schobert and John Christian Bach. But the distance between them and it is immeasurable. There is even a great distance between it and the *fantasia development* of K.450. And yet, outwardly, the two are similar. Here as well as there, the second solo begins with the repetition by the piano of the last orchestral phrase, but what was just a bit of mischief in K.449 and 450 is now full of meaning. Here as well as there, the piano passages were a *fantasia*, but whereas in K. 450 we never lost our foothold, here, suddenly, we are possessed by a sense of depth and Mozart takes off into the unknown. If we look back, we must not stop at immediate predecessors ; to breathe the same air, we have to go as far as John Sebastian's D minor concerto and the great pedal point of its first movement. And, for even closer kinship, we must turn to the next concerto and to Beethoven—to his work in C minor and still more his violin concerto, with the "voyage on uncharted seas" at the beginning of its *development*.

Arriving in B minor, the *fantasia* continues, but a more square-cut rhythm marks a return to familiar regions and emotions. Through the rising arpeggios and the falling scale fragments there is outlined a misty theme, implied in the piano's right hand and traced by the

---

[1] Cf. p. 200.

Ex. 133

Ex. 134

Ex. 135

Ex. 136

fiddles. The dreamy mood of the opening of the *development* gives way to a passion which grows and reaches its climax, as so often happens, on the eve of the reprise.[1] As the moment draws nigh, the piano predominates and the accompaniment thins away, as though the satellites of the solo instrument felt it seemly to let it traverse alone the valley of tears that separates it from the triumphal return. At the moment of greatest tension, a succession of chords of the seventh on the super-tonic comes crashing down on to a pedal (ex. 134). Anchored for an instant on the chord of A major, the spirit of the work, which its twofold nature and its wealth of passion have shaken but not overwhelmed, gathers itself together in a unison ascent, made easier by stages, and, once victory is assured, the orchestra, which had forsaken it in the hour of its greatest distress, returns, but *piano*, with its tail between its legs, to beg a share in its glory.

The adventure of these thirty-four bars of *development* is magnificent, but how brief! Hardly one tenth of the whole movement! The shortness of his *developments* is the most constant formal feature in all Mozart, from his childhood's earliest compositions to those of his last year. And, in a general way, his most original, his most significant are precisely his shortest.

The recapitulation unites again piano and orchestra. At the beginning of the movement, the orchestra had been master of the first subject; in the second exposition, the piano; now, both combine. The march rhythm of the first bar and the soft scales belong to the orchestra; the forceful outbursts are punctuated by piano runs (ex. 135). The secondary subject, ex. 128, is treated as in the first solo, except that the piano adornments now take the shape of arpeggios in triplets. The solo subject does not reappear and ex. 128 leads straight on to ex. 123. The pretty figure with "fluttering seconds" which prepares the way for the second subject returns with no change save one of scoring (ex. 6) and of key. The same is true of the second subject, the syncopated passage, ex 125, and the *forte* which follows it, ex. 126, and we reach again the interrupted cadence and the little commonplace phrase along which we had formerly slipped into the unknown. Now, its business is to conclude and, instead of unexpected modulations, Mozart inserts here the final bravura passage, the sole one, in fact, only ten bars long and entirely organic, since it is but the assertion of the tonic key without which no classical symphonic movement is complete.

The dotted quaver figure, ex. 122, which had concluded the first

---

[1] Cf. p. 32.

solo, returns now and the codetta of ex. 123 leads to the cadenza.   The
one which Mozart has left[1] consists almost entirely of quotations
from the main themes and a passage of crossing of hands, all the more
remarkable because that species of virtuosity is absent from the concerto.   In the hitherto excessively uncommon event of a pianist
playing this work in public, we recommend the use of this cadenza,
tuneful and full of go and, most important, moderate in length.

The movement concludes with ex. 128 and its conventional
codetta.

This allegro, far superior to the andante and rondo, is one of the
peaks of Mozart's concertos.   Its most obvious character is its architectural strength and beauty.   It is monumental in the highest degree,
but less by its dimensions than by its robustness.   We have already
insisted upon the oneness of its first tutti.   This quality persists
throughout the rest of the movement which is derived from its opening
tutti more completely even than in other concertos.   One has the
impression that Mozart the orchestral composer felt in its creation
even more delight than Mozart the pianist, so thoroughly orchestral
is it.   This is so true—and the same holds good of many of his other
concertos—that a satisfactory performance of the work depends even
more on the orchestra than on the pianist.   A performance where the
band is excellent and the pianist passable will be nearer to the ideal
than one where the contrary obtains.   In theory, orchestra and piano
are equally responsible, but in practice the orchestra influences most
the nature of the performance.

Reading these lines, anyone who had never heard this concerto
would think that the piano plays but a subordinate part in it.   This is
not so.   Although its part, according to Mozart himself, is easier
than in the preceding one,[2] it is still brilliant.   Mozart combines here,
with a skill he has equalled only in K.503, the lustre of the band with
the splendour of the piano.   He satisfies the claims of both, so that
neither seems sacrificed to the other.   How does he manage this?
The best answer to this question will be a brief study of the relations
of piano and orchestra.   This question is at heart the central problem
of the concerto and we hope to be forgiven if, within a narrower
horizon, we go over ground already covered.[3]

---

[1] In the *Breitkopf* collection, K.624, it figures by mistake under the *Coronation*
concerto, K.537 (no. 32).

[2] Letter to his father of May 26th, 1784.

[3] Cf. I, 3.

One of two things must happen: either the piano plays alone or it must play with the orchestra. The passages of complete solo, so long in the last concerto, are uncommon and short here. The longest is the exposition of the first subject, which is interesting in that Mozart, instead of giving the theme unaltered to the piano, as he often does, or of dividing it between piano and orchestra, modifies it so that he makes the piano as far as possible the equivalent of the orchestra. In the four bars of chords that follow the second subject and where the piano plays alone, he seeks to contrast sonorities; chording being uncommon in his piano writing, his intention is unmistakable.

One sees therefore that the piano's independence is almost nil. It is significant of the importance Mozart gives to his orchestra that even the solo subject is accompanied by a held note on the hautboys, representing the other instruments, that the orchestra leads off in the second subject and that, when the piano takes up, it is doubled by the fiddles. There are only two bravura passages: those that assert the keys of the dominant at the close of the exposition and of the tonic at the end of the allegro, and here, though supported by the wind, the piano is temporarily master; but its virtuosity remains within the framework of the movement and never spreads itself in irrelevance.

All this does not amount to much. Most of the time the piano builds on the foundations of the first tutti. Thus, to ex. 122 it adds first its semi-quaver scales, ex. 128, then its arpeggio triplets; it adorns slightly the second subject by breaking up minims into quavers; it strengthens the bass of ex. 125 and sets off ex. 126 with its scales, and, at the reprise, other scales, spurting upwards like rockets, punctuate the orchestral *fortes*. In every case, its part is superimposed on that of the orchestra and is not indispensable to it.

But it is just as much based upon the opening tutti when it inserts itself into the orchestral score and takes over the part of one of the instruments. It does so in the complex of passages and figures which makes up the second subject. It gives itself the upper pedal which had at first fallen to the violins, takes from them fragment (a) and excludes them from the dialogue with the wind in the "fluttering seconds" passage, ex. 6.

Finally, in the few sections which do not derive from the opening tutti, its part sometimes consists in decorating the orchestral framework (bars 110-12, after the solo subject), sometimes is that of an interlocutor (bars 186-200, at the beginning of the *development*); now and again it combines so closely with the orchestra that there is no longer subordination of one to the other and its mass blends with

that of the strings and wind in one symphonic whole, as in the part
of the *development* which begins in B minor where piano and violins,
beneath the held notes of the flute and hautboy, give us a glimpse of
a new tune (bars 200 and foll.).

We see, therefore, that the unity of the work depends as much on
the extremely close collaboration of solo with band as on the various
devices we have been analyzing. Is it necessary to add that this unity
is far from being merely formal? Mozart lavishes so much care on
his work's architecture precisely because the thought which inspires
it is itself of architectural stature, a thought powerful and serene which
can express itself only in a well-builded whole. There is here no
opposition between matter and manner; if he attends to one, he does
not neglect the other; the thought is as important as the frame; the
inspiration, less tormented though quite as passionate as in K.449,
deeper and more original than in K.450, is worthy of the splendid
form in which it is embodied.

We have already characterized this thought. There are two aspects
of thought in a work of art: the revealing of the creator's deeper
nature, to which every work of value, whether the artist will it or not,
contributes something, and the expression of the mood reigning in
him at the moment the work was created. K.451 makes manifest, like
so many other compositions, this interplay, this blending of strength
and tenderness, of passion and quiet, of sun and shadow, which—as
far as it is possible to shut up a spirit in the nutshell of a formula—
is the central principle of Mozart's soul. But it manifests them at a
moment of happiness, in the joy brought by success and the recognition of his talent as composer and executant. Transpose this manifestation into a moment of conflict and trial and you will have the
concertos in D minor and C minor. There, we have struggle; here,
merely possibility of struggle. The difference is between one who is
capable of fighting and one immersed in the fight, between happy and
triumphant passion and a suffering passion at grips with disharmony.

The deeply personal stamp of this work is therefore indisputable.
And yet it falls into a long line which comprises not only other compositions of Mozart but also those of many other musicians: that
of the operatic aria. This is obviously true of all *galant* concertos
which owe to the aria a great many of the differences which separate
them from the concerto of the previous age. But whereas this kinship
is only formal and hardly recognizable in concertos like K.449 or
the D minor, it is here both deeper and more general. D major is
with Mozart the key *par excellence* of virtuosity blended with pride

and power. It is that of the passionate and haughty aria where a possibility of tragedy exists but which is not itself tragic. To realize this, the reader should turn to one of the grandest of these serious and passionate, but not tragic, D major arias: that of the king in *Idomeneo*: "*Fuor del mar ho un mar in seno.*" Mozart has often used the key of D major for works where virtuosity was to shine, but it is in this aria that he comes nearest to the spirit of our concerto and in it one grasps best the kinship between the two genres. The main formal differences are, naturally, the subordination of the orchestra to the voice in the aria, and the much greater breadth of themes and bridge passages in the concerto. In this latter respect, in fact, K.451 is remarkable. It has a sweep and a grandeur which are found again, in Mozart, only in a few other concertos and the string quintet in C, and of which even the quartets and symphonies know nothing. Remember the breadth of ex. 124, the link between first and second subject. In such a movement, one feels the accuracy of the judgement which says that if Mozart did what everyone else was doing, he did it very much better. And if, in the past, it points to the *Idomeneo* aria, in the future it shows the way towards the *Prague* symphony, also in D, also a work of power and passion without tragedy; also a work where, as Saint-Foix says justly, "there blend elements of drama and joy"; where, in "brusque and almost lashing rhythms . . . one divines the presence of more struggle and forceful impetus than real happiness"[1] —an appreciation which suits admirably the movement we have just been analyzing.

II.   In the andante the trumpets, one hautboy, and one bassoon are silent. A yearning, sensuous melody opens the movement, entwining itself round the fiddles like a creeper, then drawing the flute and bassoon into its coils. How far we have come from the vigorous allegro! And yet the pedal which holds down the creeper by the roots warns us that this languishing and seductive figure is of the same lineage as the resounding themes whose echoes have just died away. Its chromaticisms, too, are close to the first movement, and its dusky charm has already been felt in the syncopated motif, ex. 125. Its weariness, full of longing, is all Mozart's own; yet it would be difficult to find another page in him where it is expressed with such Chopin-like intensity! One does not know at what to wonder most: its formal likeness with the allegro, in the pedal and chromaticisms, or

---

[1] *Les symphonies de Mozart*, p. 139.

the absolute contrast which its enervated state affords with the power of the opening movement (ex. 136). As the whole theme is repeated and both halves contain the sinuous figure, this is heard four times, and each time the scoring throws a different light on it. First, *piano*, in the strings, with bass and horn pedal; then, *forte*, in the fiddles, hautboy and flute, with the same; a third time in the solo, unaccompanied, *piano*, and lastly in the woodwind, with a piano trill. The symphonist, master of orchestration and lover of woodwind, which the virtuoso composer has become, here displays with zest all the resources of his imagination.

The movement—an andante and not an adagio, as Mozart is careful to remind us[1]—is a rondo in two couplets. The first one is in D and consists in a succession of short, breathless phrases, given out by the piano, to which the beloved woodwind answers with a kind of echo (ex. 137). The "concerto with woodwind obbligato" character grows still more pronounced and we next have a long phrase, as sinuous and nostalgic as the refrain, which passes without a break from hautboys and bassoons to piano. The pedal, of course, is not absent; it is even doubled, in basses and flute, and its fixity redeems the instability and waviness of the middle parts. Thus, throughout the whole movement, Mozart makes up for the indecisiveness of his melodies with the firmness of his pedal points (ex. 138).

The sinuous figure winds through the strings with a piano descant; then through the piano itself, in half a dozen more bars where the supple lines intertwine and come asunder in turn with affectionate ease and heady charm—six bars which are a masterly instance of solo and orchestral collaboration (ex. 2). And so, rising and falling, then lifting up in one last effort and led from above by the airy sighs of the woodwind, the tune subsides on the tonic of D whence flute, hautboy and bassoons bring it back in two bars to the key of G. And how indeed, save by means of a pedal point, grounded in the basses and reinforced, then decorated, by a piano trill (ex. 139)? The refrain is repeated unchanged by the solo, then by the tutti, and the piano opens abruptly the second couplet on the chord of E minor.

This one is composed of two distinct parts. The first has the same character as what went before, with its plaintive accent, its panting phrases, its woodwind echoes and wavy lines; the strings are completely silent. Then, a rise of the woodwind on the chord of E minor,

---

[1] Letter to his father of June 9th, 1784.

a flattering of the leading note, a trill on B and suddenly the landscape changes: we are in the white light of C major.

The next section shows a very bare picture in the score. Here are its first three bars (ex. 140). The uninformed executant (and how many are informed, even among the great soloists?) who plays what he sees written and nothing more, is shocked by the insignificance of the passage. "Mozart is sometimes very empty," he says, and without going any further closes the volume and seeks out in the works of Liszt or Tchaikovsky the concerto he will play at his next "appearance". He is wrong. Far from being empty, Mozart leaves him here a fine opportunity of showing off his talent as extemporizer within the confines of a skeleton melody. The few notes, whose leanness on the staves disgusts our virtuoso, are but a canvas upon which the pianist is to build his own part, keeping, however, the outline sketched by the composer.

> In the same way as the singer (says Sigmund Lebert in his edition of the concertos published in 1880 by Cotta) performed his aria on the stage or in the concert-room, so the solo player on the pianoforte gave his *cantilena*, only with richer ornamentation, as he had to compensate for the poverty of tone with a greater quantity of notes. . . . Have we not heard in our younger days reliable men, who had themselves heard Mozart play, speak of the richness of improvised ornamentation and modulation, with which he embellished his performance? At that period ornamentation was an important element in pianoforte playing, so that a composer who did not want it had to mark specially: *senza ornamenti*.

This fashion survived the 18th century and in the Romantic period degenerated into an abuse; already the variants with which Hummel overlaid his master's concertos in his edition published by Litolff are no longer in Mozart's style. It is none the less true that some passages in the andantes of Mozart's concertos are but sketches and require completion, either by the soloist's own talent or rather, alas! by the science of the editor. Such was already the case with the *cantilena* of the first couplet. Here, the completion is indispensable.

To excuse the modern pianist who thinks he sees Mozart's complete and final idea in the score, it must be said that the composer's very sister asked for explanations about these bars, for in Wolfgang's letter to his father of June 9th, 1784, he wrote: "Tell her from me that, in the andante of the D major concerto, in the solo in C in question, yes, most certainly, something is missing. . . . I will send it her as soon as possible, with the cadenzas."

The additional bars sent to Nannerl escaped the notice of editors

Ex. 142

Ex. 143

Ex. 144

for a hundred and fifty years and only came to light when Alfred Einstein published his revised Köchel in 1936. They figure in it as no. 626a, M. on page 824. Saint-Foix identified them as belonging to this movement and Einstein confirmed the identification in 1941[1] (ex. 141).

The task of completing *cantabiles* was, therefore, not always left to the executant, even in Mozart's time. What Mozart did for his sister the modern editor must do for the pianist of to-day. Lebert, with Cotta, and Reinecke,[2] with Brietkopf, realized this, and one cannot urge too often pianists who play these concertos in public to follow their indications in passages like this—that is to say, wherever a theme in long notes demands more singing power from the instrument than it can give.

In the last part of this solo, the ascending echoes of the woodwind which we have already heard twice (ex. 137) answer the piano and a pedal point in the basses and horns warns us of the coming reprise. But here two bars are not enough to lead us back to the refrain and the tonic key. The breadth of the transition is worthy of the movement. Upon the pedal of D (as dominant of G minor), a variant of ex. 136 wreathes itself in imitations in the strings, and for a short instant counterpoint, much to its surprise, finds itself enlisted to sing nostalgia and desire; then everything is lost in the great pedal, whilst from the heavenly regions flutes, hautboys and bassoons sail down to join the cohort of strings, the first two in a straight line, but breaking step, the bassoons in graceful and expressive windings (ex. 142).[3]

At its last appearance the refrain belongs to the piano, then to the orchestra as a whole, with the difference that the wind vary its final bars. The coda is fairly long; it is made up of the same wavy and languishing phrases as the rest, given out by the piano, repeated by the wind with solo accompaniment (merely sketched). The strings enter only right at the end and even then their part is subsidiary. Till its last bar, this andante keeps its character of a dialogue between piano and wind; till its last bar, the soft rhythms and lines rest upon, and are supported by, the firm ground of a pedal point (ex. 143).

This movement has not the grandness of the former; its world is

---

[1] *Music Review*, vol. 2 (1941), p. 242.

[2] Reinecke not always, and notably in this concerto.

[3] Here too the piano part is but a sketch. Clearly the D of the right hand, held for five beats, then repeated as a minim an octave higher, is meaningless. These two bars must be filled out with scales, simple or ornate, and trills.

narrower and its thought affects a smaller part of us. But it is sincere and original; longing and nostalgia are feelings that have often inspired Mozart's music, but seldom as intensely and as continuously as in this andante, where there is scarcely anything else. It is one of the most moving as well as one of the last examples of his "dream andantes".

Rondo form is often used by Mozart in slow movements, but generally with the *romance* variety: ABA—C—ABA—Coda. Here, the plan is simpler: A—B—A—C—A—Coda. There are eight or ten examples of this plan in his work, nearly all of which date from the year of this concerto and the two following ones. They are to be found in trios and sonatas, in a serenade and in a horn concerto; there are no others in the piano concertos.

III. It is usual to consider Mozart as a pure songster whose works are a succession of enchanting and expressive melodies. He is contrasted (in this, as in so many other ways) with Beethoven, who is thought to have possessed to a lesser degree the gift of melody, but to a far higher one that of organization. Whereas Mozart was content with opening the flood-gates to his torrent of tunes, Beethoven, with apparently unpromising themes, built up vast architectural ensembles.

Very incomplete concerning Beethoven, such a judgement is quite untrue of Mozart. There are, of course, many melodies in his music and many expressive ones, but they are far from making up the substance of his chief works and in many movements they are insignificant. Such is the case in the finale of this concerto. Analysis can discover in it three or four themes, undistinguished melodically and more remarkable for their rhythm than for their outline, and it is with them, and with pianistic passages which derive more or less directly from them, that the whole movement is built up. There is no trace of those successions of tunes of which we hear.

This rondo has not the melodic interest of the two other movements, neither has it the triumphant power of the first or the sensuous charm of the second. But it has the broad build and spaciousness of the allegro, something of which had reappeared in the transitions of the andante. Despite its insignificant themes, it is one of the most monumental examples of that sonata rondo which was Mozart's main contribution to the growth of musical form.

We have spoken at length of the sonata rondo in an earlier chapter.[1]

---

[1] J, 2.

Let us say here, once again, that, deriving from the French dances *en rondeau*, it is treated with such breadth by Mozart, especially in his concertos, that he is practically its creator. And yet, one may still read in modern works that Mozart's rondo has the form: A B A C A, that is to say, a two-couplet rondo, and that Beethoven enlarged this form and made it more organic by adding a third couplet repeating the first, in the manner of a recapitulation, and thus produced a masterly cross between the sonata and the rondo. The number of Mozart's sonata rondos is so great and many are movements of such scope and conclude such important works that assertions like this are both inexcusable and deplorable. Of course, Beethoven left large-scale sonata rondos, like that of the Waldstein sonata, but they differ from Mozart's in their greater size and not in their more organic structure or stricter unity.

We have given elsewhere[1] a schematic analysis of this finale. The refrain (ex. 144) is given out by strings and flute and the piano enters only after the tutti has begun the first couplet. Such an entry after the beginning is original; the solo's usual behaviour is to make its appearance çoincide with the opening of the couplet. The new subject, like those of the refrain, has in common with several themes of the first movement the fact that it is built on the common chord. The couplet's second subject, in A, is limited to four degrees of the scale; it hesitates coyly on its first note, then rushes forward at full speed to the end of its miniature course. It recalls the rondo refrain in the flute quartet in D and shows once again what close kinship of manner and matter unites Mozart's works in the same key (ex. 145).

The refrain is repeated at first by the piano, which varies its second part, then, unchanged, by the orchestra; thereupon a *minor* subject, given out by the solo, opens the second couplet.

Hitherto the tutti's share has been less extensive than in the opening allegro. It is true that it gave out the second subject before the piano, but it has been content mostly to support the solo in its swift progress and accompany it with slight figures. In this second couplet which corresponds to the *development* of the sonata, its relations with the solo are more like what they were in the first movement.

The couplet begins with a theme in B minor. The piano gives it out twice, then no more is said about it. Now comes the most interesting moment. Still in B minor, the strings recall ex. 145 and the

---

[1] Pp. 51, 52.

Ex. 145

Ex. 146

Ex. 147

piano does at once likewise. This theme does not appeal to the protagonists either. They end by finding what they are seeking in the
refrain subject and start a game with it. But first the pitch has to be
settled. B minor being too much in the shade they enter G major

and the flute repeats in it the first four bars of the refrain. But, with
an abruptness which calls up for an instant the opening of the finale of
the ninth symphony transposed on to the comic plane, the piano dis-
agrees and, in two arpeggio bars, carries the business into E minor.
Again, the flute is cut short by the piano and the bassoon repeats the
same bars in C major. The new pitch pleases everyone and the game
can continue. Now reduced to its first four bars, our subject finds
itself tossed from hautboy to flute, from flute to hautboy, rebounding
like a ball from the jaunty sarcasm of the one to the canting suavity of
the other. The players do not remain stationary but each time work
a little higher up the field—that is, the scale—ending up where they
were a minute ago, in E minor. The strings are but onlookers,
following the players by the side of the pitch, but the piano accompanies them with a brilliant commentary of arpeggios of, alternately,
the common chord and the dominant ninth, and so voluble that it
silences them for a moment (ex. 146).

And now we have to get home. Each one does its best. Hautboys, flute, piano, fiddles, each time draw a little nearer the goal,
which is finally reached by the fiddles at their second attempt; whereupon strings and piano repeat together the complete text of the refrain
(ex. 147).

All this passage is worthy of the rondo *development* in the previous
concerto and of the finest bars of solo and tutti collaboration in the
two other movements of this one.

The third couplet, the recapitulation, repeats the first without
important change. The cadenza, which begins like the first solo,
consists in a passage of broken chords with crossings of hands and an
imitative development of ex. 145; it is brief and shapely. The refrain's
last appearance and the rather long coda are in 3-8, and this beat, even
weaker and more skipping than the 6-8 of K.449, is kept up to the
end. The coda brings in the second subject again and the rondo
concludes with a unison strain of the whole orchestra based on the
common chord.

Prolonged contact with this concerto has convinced us of its greatness. The first allegro is one of the most imposing movements, not
only in the concertos but in the whole symphonic work of Mozart.
It shows in him the great architect who can erect spacious, well-knit
wholes, inspired by one lofty idea. Earlier in this century, almost all
the concertos of the father of the modern concerto were unknown.
The years between the wars saw a good many of them issue forth
from the *Gesamtausgabe* and recover life in the orchestra, and by now

some dozen have been recorded. K.451 is not one of these. Will its turn ever come? The example of several others, which some years ago we had never expected to hear and performances of which are now almost common,[1] allow us to hope so. Mozart is far more played to-day than thirty years ago but revival of his work has been irregular and not wholly in relation with the importance of the compositions resurrected. Some of his childhood serenades and divertimenti might well be allowed to relapse into the shade without loss for either his reputation or our pleasure; some half-dozen first-rate pieces, amongst them the most monumental he has left,[2] still await a discovery which, let us hope, is at hand.

---

[1] E.g. K.449.]

[2] The quintet and concerto in C major, K.515 and 503, both of which have, however, been recorded; and this work. The London Theatre Concerts performed K.451 in November, 1937, and Dame Myra Hess has played it more than once during the war.

4. *The Thirteenth Concerto: K.453 in G*

CONCERTO NO. 13 IN G (K.453)[1]
Finished April 12th, 1784
    Allegro: C
    Andante: 3-4 (in C)
    Allegretto: Presto: ¢—2-4
Orchestra: Strings; flute, two hautboys, two horns, two bassoons.

A MONGST the friends and patrons whose names recur in Wolfgang's letters to Leopold was a family called Ployer, hailing from
Salzburg. The father was the archbishop's agent in Vienna; the
daughter, Babette, an accomplished pianist, was one of the young
composer's pupils.[2] He had written for her the concerto in E flat,
K.449; for her also he wrote the concerto in G.

In this wonderful Lent of 1784, for the concerts of which he had
already produced three masterpieces one after the other, his fruitfulness was not yet exhausted. Other years will know a more abundant
flowering; 1784 is the one in which he composed the greatest number
of first-rate works. Between February and May and between
September and December in this year, six concertos, two sonatas, a
quartet and a quintet followed close one upon the other—all of them
authentic masterpieces.

The twelfth concerto was finished on March 22nd. Mozart then
turned to a quintet for piano and wind instruments. This work,[3]
whose inspiration is close to that of many other of his E flat compositions, has also the self-assurance and grace of the concerto in B flat,
K.450; it is a piece of "society music", written "half for his public,
half for himself", and in a composite style related to the concertos its
contemporaries in its piano part and, in its wind writing, to the great
serenades of earlier years. As a whole, it has a *concertante* character;
the protagonists come to the fore each one in turn and pass their
themes from one to the other with a generosity that reminds us more of
the divertimento for string trio, K.563, than of the severer style of the
quartets. The presence of a theme from K.450 in its first movement
and, in the rondo, of an *obbligata* cadenza in which everyone

---

[1] *Gesamtausgabe*, no. 17.   [2] See p. 178, note 1.
[3] K.452.

takes part shows how near the work is to the concertos; at this
moment, Mozart is so much the "fashionable virtuoso" and is so
full of his public that, even when he composes chamber music, he
still thinks in terms of his favourite genre.   The same influence will
also be visible in the andante of the C major sonata, in the autumn.
The composer was well pleased with his quintet.

> For my part, I consider it the best thing I have written as yet in all my
> life (he wrote to his father on April 10th).   It has met with extraordinary
> success.

The quintet finished, he began at once another concerto.   It is
characteristic of his generous nature that two out of the four concertos
written this season should have been composed for others.   In spite
of their difference in personality from those he wrote for himself,
they are certainly not inferior.   Into the works composed for his
young pupil, Mozart poured as much of himself as into those which
were written to show off his own gifts.

The concerto in G is as much a masterpiece as those in B flat, D
and F, but the great differences between them and it bear witness to
the diversity and richness of his genius.   Expansiveness, joyous and
confident splendour reign here no longer; the inspiration is more
intimate and more subtle.   It is impossible to sum it up in a word,
as can be done, at a pinch, with the concertos in D and F; with its
mixture of the sad and the happy, the feeling that animates it is more
indeterminate and also comes closer to that of everyday existence.
Not every day do we feel "proud", like the concerto in D, or
"festive", like that in F; but the more complex strands of the work in
G enter into most moments of our life.   It is one of Mozart's most
ethereal concertos, with a pastoral strain—pastoral like the fields on the
Delectable Mountains—and it takes us close to the most ethereal of
Beethoven's concertos and the loveliest of his violin sonatas, both of
them in G (ops. 58 and 96).[1]   We welcome it, not at those times when
one single thought absorbs and masters us, but at those much more

---

[1] One wonders whether Beethoven's choice of G major for the expression
of this inspiration is not due to this concerto, where the same inspiration is
unmistakably present.   We would go further and see in Beethoven's work a
spiritual offspring of Mozart's.   The filiation between his C minor concerto
and Mozart's is a commonplace of musical criticism; only the neglect of K.453
has prevented musicians from noticing its kinship with Beethoven's Op. 58.
Prof. Sidney Newman has pointed out to me the likeness between bars 65-8
of Mozart's work and bars 60-2 of Beethoven's (first movements).   In both
cases the strains belong to the conclusion of the opening tutti.   Beethoven's
is a variation of Mozart's.

frequent moments when our mood is an ever-changing compound of diverse elements, equal in force, which come forward, rise, fall back, without any variation in the emotional pitch of the whole.

I. Here, again the first movement opens with a march rhythm, but how different from the massive strength of K.451 ! It is no longer the army itself but merely its shadow of which we catch a glimpse in the fifteen bars of the first subject. The body of the troops, represented by the first violins, are but ghosts; ghosts, too, the "drums" of the second violins and violas; ghosts again, but rather more substantial, the fifes of the flute and hautboys which finish off each fragment of the theme, according to an exquisite formula of Mozart's.[1] The subject grows ever so slightly livelier and more emphatic, repeats its last notes and finally draws in and closes on the tonic (ex. 148).

The favourite *galant* formula of a mysterious opening followed by a *fortissimo* then appears complete. The whole orchestra outlines a linking figure (ex. 149) with a codetta of scales, and we await the customary noisy dominant close. But Mozart is as much concerned here with formal unity as he was in the last concerto and the rigid, impersonal barriers of Italian opera style no longer satisfy him. Instead of a close, the orchestra repeats the codetta in a slightly different version, and the woodwind, omitting the semi-quaver scales, add an arpeggio theme (ex. 150), destined to provide later on a pleasing interplay between solo and orchestra (ex. 158). After pretending to stop on a cadence, this new theme follows on by throwing a bridge across to the second subject.

This latter comes forward, breathless and limping. Is it to be minor or major? It does not know at first; then it plumps for major. Reserved for the strings, it hesitates, like much of this movement, between laughter and tears. The wind take it up and the strings echo them (ex. 151). It is a reincarnation of ex. 148 and one of the most interesting instances of that kinship between various themes of the same work which, in Mozart as in Haydn, in Clementi and, later, in Beethoven, tends to replace the more rudimentary and less organic principle of contrast. Bars like these sum up the essence of Mozart's genius and, more clearly than any explanations, express its charm and reveal its secret. They are the best answer to the question: What did Mozart create that no one else created?

---

[1] The same woodwind flutterings, this time with mocking intent, occur at the end of Guglielmo's aria:"*Non siate ritrosi*",also in G, in the first act of *Cosi fan tutte.*

What follows is also very Mozartish.   From G major we dive into E flat, with an abruptness worthy of K.449.   This sudden change and the explosive *forte* after the first bar reveal a subterranean force ever ready to burst forth from under a polite and graceful exterior (ex. 152). The clamour dies down quickly and then at once begins a tonic pedal, over which for an instant the strings brood meditatively (ex. 153 a).   The pedal starts again an octave lower, the violins return to their meditation and a counterpoint of the woodwind in unison discloses for a flash a vision of immensity (ex. 153 b).   In the limits of a few bars Mozart, without grandiloquence, with simplest harmonic means, brings us to the edge of space and lets us see the heavens open; an instant later, a bright, sociable theme capped by a conventional figure concludes the tutti.

One cannot insist too much on the lack of uniformity in the concertos of his "great" period.   Far from falling into line, one after the other, in the same formation, nearly all progress along different paths.   Thus, K.450 gives out in its opening tutti only a part of the movement's materials, and in the solo after it the piano expounds almost entirely new subjects and passages, whilst the orchestra keeps silent.   K.451, on the other hand, pours forth straight away nearly the whole contents of the allegro, and the solo, without omitting anything but also hardly adding anything, does but embroider what is given, in continuous collaboration with the orchestra.   This concerto, finally, combines both methods.   As in K.451, the solo exposition repeats the greater part of the tutti whilst instruments and piano collaborate unceasingly, but it is like K.450 in that it introduces significant new passages.

The piano prefixes a rising scale to the first subject: the simplest form of the solo introduction.   It gives out the subject, decorating it and lengthening it slightly; the wind answer as they did just now. The strings start ex. 149 and the solo superimposes a decoration which extends into a bravura passage.   Its own subject, in D, is more important than in the last concerto.   Long and winding, it remains on the whole within the limits of five degrees and returns continually to its starting-point like a *moto perpetuo*.   It is repeated and its latter half spreads out into a dialogue with the woodwind (ex. 154).

Over this happy landscape there suddenly passes a cloud; the figure (a) of ex. 154 opens out and, tossed from flute to hautboys, wanders through minor keys whilst the bassoon adds a counterpoint and the piano accompanies it with downward arpeggios.   It is a charming Mozartian development where the free and aimless motion of the harmony matters more than the melodic line (ex. 155).   Its

Ex. 148

Ex. 149

Ex. 150

Ex. 151

Ex. 152

Ex. 153 (a)

Ex. 154

Ex. 155

ethereal, unemphatic melancholy, so "pre-Romantic", is as fugitive as the other moods that pass over the face of this concerto, a mezzo-tint work demanding delicate sensibility and subtle understanding rather than technical skill. It survives an instant in the hesitations of the second subject (ex. 151), then fades away in the self-assured conclusion. The second subject itself is given out twice, first by the

piano alone, then by the wind an octave higher; the strings accompany
them as in the first tutti and the piano takes over the echo (ex. 3).

The progress of the inspiration is now broken and virtuosity
speaks alone.   A mild virtuosity, indeed; the work is for a pupil and
Mozart keeps for himself the "difficult" concertos.   But its intrusion
is none the less noticeable.   The end of the exposition is one of the
recognized places where it is given free rein and often it arises without
effort from the substance of the music.   K.451 showed admirably
how a bravura passage could continue and develop what went before,
not only without interrupting it but even making it clearer.   Here,
these few pianistic bars are an insertion foreign to the spirit of the
movement which does not require virtuosity.   Its delicate nature,
full of shades, is expressed in gentleness and hesitation; the interplay
of solo and tutti in passages like ex. 151 and 155 render it perfectly.
Displays of skill are contrary to it and the arrival of these broken
scales, a petty ornamentation in which the concerto sacrifices to
convention, intrudes into the flow of its thought.

The transition theme ex. 149, abridged, links up with the closing
figure and we met again the Mozart of *fantasia developments*.[1]   The
expected cadence remains hanging in the air on a sub-dominant
chord, the strings whisper a little mock-innocent motif; then, without
preparation (we are in D major), strike the chord of F.   The piano
enters again and suddenly we are sailing in mid-sky, far from all
landmarks.   For some twenty bars, the solo rises and falls in arpeggios
of three octaves, whilst flute, hautboys and bassoons follow it in turn
like shadows.   Through the most diverse keys, constantly modulating,
like a wandering spirit, now here, now there, its beautiful restless soul
pursues its course.   Neither motif nor outline: it is pure motion, itself
its own aim, its own *raison d'être*.   It seems to say: "I climb up into
heaven, I go down to hell, I take the wings of the morning and remain
in the uttermost parts of the sea."

The most formal of musicians is here the freest.   His music has
indeed fixed points by which it passes, but between them it soars
upward with a fancy no Romantic has surpassed (ex. 156).

In the course of the cruise, we put in at B major and the mass of
the orchestra, delegating its powers to horns and hautboys, rests
while the piano performs a run in two parts through which there
shimmers a melody, a passage recalling the episode in the same place
in K.451, to the *development* of which concerto this one is closely

---

[1] See p. 200.

akin.   A modulation of genius, one of the most striking in all Mozart
(ex. 157), brings in the piano once more, in C minor.   Thereupon the
solo starts a game with a little five-note motif, in which the strings
play a discreet part.

We have said elsewhere[1] that Mozart seeks constantly to vary the
recapitulations of his concertos.   This one combines elements from
the first tutti and the first solo and also brings in new material.   A
transitional figure, ex. 150, which had served to introduce the second
subject, behaves now as if it were a main theme and appears three
times in the course of the recapitulation under different shapes.   It
introduces the second subject, as it is entitled to do; but it seems to
be quite as indispensable to the solo subject, which it also heralds; and
finally, in the last bars, when we stop on the tonic, it returns and insists
on having the last word so that we shall remember the movement
by it.   These are not mere repetitions.   The second of these appearances is a fresh development, a dialogue in canon between flute, bassoon and piano (ex. 158).

In other respects, this third solo differs from the first mainly in the
greater length of its orchestral passages.   But, just as the piano finishes
its trill, a surprise awaits us.   Instead of closing on the tonic, it stops
on the chord of E flat and the orchestra repeats the "dive" of the
first tutti, ex. 152, which leads to a 6-4 chord and the cadenza.[2]   The
movement concludes with two of its most characteristic themes, the
mysterious pedal of ex. 153, followed by the original concluding
subject, and ex. 150, promoted to the rank of a main theme and clearly
determined to leave us the final impression of the movement.

II.   Andante, and not Adagio, says Mozart.[3]   In most of the earlier
concertos dissimilarity rather than relationship existed between the
first two movements; moreover, in the three concertos of this winter,
K.449, 450 and 451, the inspiration was slighter in the andantes, and
they contrasted with the allegros in feeling and importance.   But
here the andante is, in these respects, the allegro's equal—perhaps its
superior.   Far from contrasting with it, this second movement carries
on its thought, emphasizing it and bringing out its essential elements.

---

[1] P. 23.

[2] Neither of the cadenzas written by Mozart for this movement is interesting.   We recommend soloists to extemporize their own, remaining within
the limits of Mozart's own and, above all, ending up *piano* to link up with
the soft orchestral entry.

[3] Letter to his father of June 9th, 1784.

The mingling of serenity and sadness is more marked; the lights are higher, the shadows deeper. The neighbourhood of smiles and tears, in the music as in life, is closer, and their common origin in the depths of the composer's soul more visible.

The theme with which it opens is one of the most expressive, the most pictorial even, in all Mozart. Through its position at the head of the movement, its different returns, its transformation at the end, it presides over the whole andante. Yet it is not what a refrain is to a rondo for we are not led back to it; it is the theme itself that comes forward from time to time to remind us of its presence (ex. 159). Is it a lament? is it a meditation? A question it certainly is, and incomplete; a lonely voice rising in a desert and, later, when it is given to the flute, a forsaken faun in the light of a sun-bathed, empty "afternoon". It sums up the movement like an inscription carved over a portal and repeated at intervals inside the building. It is one of the few themes in Mozart which seem to need the help of literature to be complete, and to call for words.[1]

What follows expands rather than answers the query. It is a long, unbroken effusion, beginning with the voice of the hautboy, like a solitary reedpipe in the depths of marshes; then the flute joins it and finally the bassoon, and the three engage in a conversation whence the strings are excluded. The two upper parts intermingle and interlace with ease and suppleness. They commune in apparent calm; only the sharpened *appoggiatura* in the rising line of the bassoon and hautboy introduces a slight quiver. But calm in Mozart is often deceptive or fugitive. Passion lies deep with him, and even in moments as idyllic as this one we feel that it is at hand (ex. 160).

The strings interrupt this meditation with a call supported by the horns; the woodwind maintain their attitude and answer back with sinuous, caressing strains. The game begins afresh and the wind look as if they would have the last word. Suddenly the sky clouds over-the idyll becomes a lament and passion rises from the depths to over; whelm everything. The violins breathe out a plaint in C minor in which bassoon, hautboy and flute join in—not just a sigh of melancholy, but a lament rising from the bottom of the heart. As in the first movement (ex. 153), the depths close at once and order is restored (ex. 161).

And now the piano puts the question. It does so without changing

---

[1] Perhaps those of the fine aria: *Bella mia fiamma, addio!* K.528, of 1787, the 3-4 part of which shows kinship with our andante and where the pathetic ending of ex. 159 is set to the words: "*Resta, o cara!*"

Ex. 160

the text.   But how different is the commentary it adds!   After the
pause it plunges into G minor and then rears up in wrath (ex. 162).
The exceptional violence of the emotion is proved by the presence of
a chord, to which the executant should give its full weight.   But this
violence, like all emotion in this movement, is but passing; it dies down
quickly and loses itself in the all-pervading tranquillity of ex. 160.[1]
The piano pursues with (a), alone, and reaches the chord of G major.
Once more the clouds pile up; ex. 161 comes into sight with a new
casting of parts (ex. 163), and the solo adds an ornate coda, in triplets,
which weakens its pathos and intensity.   The piano once more silent,
we expect a new theme; instead, the flute puts again the same question,
ex. 159, supported only by the hautboys and bassoons.   Thus orches-
trated, the strain reminds us more than ever of an *Après-midi d'un
faune* in 18th-century idiom.

What answer will the piano give this time?   It finds it far away,
in a work dating from six years earlier, the "Paris" sonata in C, K.333.
It is the theme (F minor in the sonata, D minor here) which opens the
interlude in the middle of the andante (ex. 164).   It proclaims itself
with concentrated vigour, but this new spurt of energy has no morrow
and crumbles away in sinuous, broken phrases.   Its continuation
consists in short questions in the woodwind to which the piano replies
in phrases with free rhythms as thickly decorated with chromaticisms
as the calls of the woodwind are bare.   Modulations into distant
keys heighten the sense of anguish.   The whole passage is in reality
a single theme, divided between piano and orchestra (ex. 8), where the
thought wanders fancy-free.   Whenever the motion appears to
slacken, flute and hautboys spur it on afresh.   We halt finally in
C sharp minor and the strings, whose part in all this passage has been
almost nil, busy themselves with carrying us back as fast as possible
to the tonic.

To the question, put for the fourth time, the piano answers with a
variant of ex. 162.   Then the opening tutti is repeated with the addition of the piano in ex. 160 and, after the usual trill, we stop for the
cadenza on a 6-4 chord, led up to softly by the woodwind.   This is
the last time Mozart inserts a cadenza in an andante.   He has left
two; the better one is a short meditation, pungent in its conciseness,
upon the first notes of ex. 163.

The closing bars are among the finest in the movement.   For the

---

[1] The leaps of a twelfth towards the end of the solo are but a sketch which
the pianist must fill out himself; it is nonsense to play these two bars as they
are written; cf. pp. 229 and 232.

fifth time we hear the opening strain, sung by the flute and the haut-boy, but it is no longer a question (ex. 165). It has at last found its answer and this is no other (we might have guessed it, so natural does it now seem!) than the sombre strain of the conclusion ex. 161. In it the question dies away, trusting and peaceful (ex. 166).

This andante, on which analysis takes little hold, is the most closely knit we have met hitherto. Within its four divisions, marked off by the returns of the questioning theme, the thought is continuous and the substance intimately unified; the beginning of each division (exs. 162, 164) is characterized, but its sharp outline becomes blurred in what grows out of it and the only other independent theme is ex. 161. The inspiration flows unbroken, like a river, under changing skies, now clear, now overcast, but always full of colour. The wood-wind preponderance gives the whole movement bright and melancholy hues and a flavour of reeds and rushes that vanishes in the piano arrangement. Except for the opening bars, a few forte bars a little after ex. 160, some collaboration in ex. 161 and the end of the develop-ment, the strings are kept down to accompanying, either supporting the woodwind with a rocking figure (bars 6 to 11, 42 to 46, 102 to 104), or punctuating the angry strains of the piano (ex. 162). Once again we are listening to a concerto with obbligati wind parts!

No concerto andante of Mozart's had reached hitherto such full-ness. There had been pathetic ones, even tragic ones;[1] none had pene-trated into the soul with such breadth and depth. What is admirable is not only the quality of the inspiration but its variety.

Here (says Abert in his fine study of the concertos) here is the point where the fire of his genius has freed the traditional type most completely from the dross of fashion and period. All trace of the *galant*, such as we find it in John Christian and, much less, in Philip Emmanuel, is weeded out of these movements. True; in many of them Mozart still holds to the older conception, which presented here an idyll or an elegy, but the working out is personal and all conventionality is gone. On the other hand, there passes through most of these movements, as in the andantes of his piano music which are related to them, a strain of meditation and dreaming, which, together with an irresistible charm of sonority and melody, leads straight to a well-characterized type within Mozart's work.[2]

III. In spite of his unpractical nature, Mozart had certain orderly habits. Thus, he kept a thematic list of his compositions where he noted

---

[1] The *Sinfonia Concertante* for violin and viola, K.364.

[2] Abert: *Mozart*, II, 209.

down the day on which they were finished, from February, 1784, to a short time before his death, and for one whole year he kept his daily accounts in a notebook which contains also English exercises and translations of letters into English. So it happened that, on May 27th, 1784, he entered in it: "*Vogel Stahrl*"[1] 34 kr., and opposite:

adding: "*Das war schön!*"

The notes attempted by the starling are the beginning of the finale of this concerto. It was its song, no doubt, that endeared the bird to Mozart and made him buy it. When it died, he gave it a grave in his garden with an inscription in verse. This concerto is therefore placed, as it were, under the patronage of those feathered folk of whom Mozart was so fond.

For the first time since his trial work, eleven years ago, Mozart gives up the rondo form in a piano concerto finale. Instead, he writes a theme and five variations, followed by a long coda. The theme has the tone of a German folksong and reminds us of Papageno's first air (ex. 167). It has repeats; the first variation also; the others are double variations.

The first variation belongs almost entirely to the solo.

The second is shared between solo and tutti; the theme is given out by the wind to a brilliant triplet accompaniment in the right hand; then by the piano's right hand, doubled by the fiddles, while the left hand performs a similar accompaniment. The interest bears on the accompaniment and the scoring for the theme itself is unvaried.

The third is a true variation. The expositions are given to the wind which present the theme in a new form, now separately, now together. The strings are silent or accompany with repeated notes. The piano performs a slightly different version of it with an Alberti bass in the left hand and a rhythmic accompaniment figure in the violins. The second half contains a charming passage in free imitation for the woodwind (ex. 168).

The fourth is in the minor. Even in his most insignificant *airs variés*, Mozart always gives us something of himself when he comes to the *minore*, and this variation is the most interesting of the five. The orchestral part is remarkable for the bareness and archaic character of its melody and the even more archaic character of the writing, in three and four parts, and of the scoring. Wind and strings are not separated and the former double the violins. The effect is strikingly

---

[1] Starling.

Ex. 169

Ex. 170

Ex. 171

Ex. 172

Ex. 173

austere (ex. 169). The syncopations occur again in the piano, whose melodic line is a little more ornate; Mozart also makes use of contrast between the registers.

All impressions of sadness or inwardness are banished by the vigorous variation that follows, with downward rushes of five notes in the wind and piano trill in the first half, and rising semi-quaver scales in the orchestra in the second. The solo is quieter in the second half and instead of concluding it breaks off abruptly, whereupon strings and piano join in an original transitional passage where the solo instrument overlays the syncopated downward progress of the strings[1] with fragmentary chromatic scales in octaves (ex. 170). A long pause announces the sixth variation or coda.

This is pompously preceded by a double bar and headed: Presto: finale, an allusion to opera buffa. And, true enough, this coda, unique in Mozart's instrumental work, has quite the style of comedy. Its length is about one third of the movement. Mozart rejuvenates his theme by retrieving it after starting far away from it, by recalling it several times, always incomplete or varied, and by inserting between these recalls a development on a figure derived from it. The beginning of the presto, with its mock mystery, its horn calls, its quick, dry oppositions between wind and strings, between short fragmentary figures, and its sudden *forte*, plunges us straight into opera buffa. It is repeated with the addition of the piano and reaches a state of great excitement. After a noisy close and a pause, it falls again to *piano* and starts "developing" a figure derived from the theme. This is the most interesting part. To the semibreves of the strings, flute and hautboys oppose this figure, and the piano links up the two with the fireworks of its scales (ex. 171).[2] This performance is gone through thrice. Piano and wind combine, still discussing the same motif, and ascend the scale over a tonic pedal of basses and horns (ex. 173). The growing excitement breaks out in a *forte*, then loses itself in a chain of spluttering gruppetti in the piano which ends by retrieving the theme, one half of which it gives out, accompanied by the strings. The wind do likewise; a loud and long close brings us back to our starting-point (ex. 171) and the game begins once more with some reshuffling in the teams. Then piano, hautboys and bassoons imitate one another with another fragment (ex. 170) and,

---

[1] Compare with the duet "*La mia Dorabella*", also in G, in *Cosi fan tutte* (bars 41–9).

[2] Compare with Despina's and Don Alfonso's "*Secondate! per effetto di bontate*", in the finale of the first act of *Cosi fan tutte*.

after a dazzling succession of closes and alternating *fortes* and *pianos*, the whole orchestra stops to allow one last return of the theme. But the patience of the players is exhausted; the woodwind mockingly prevent the piano from getting beyond its fourth bar, and the concerto finishes abruptly, in the highest of spirits, after hacking up beyond all hope of repair the unfortunate theme, the last shreds of which, as the curtain falls, woodwind and piano are merrily throwing to and fro.

Certain formal likenesses connect this concerto with that in D composed a few weeks earlier. The long themes, the spacious transitions and, especially in the allegro, the general breadth of plan, which reaches its highest point in the development, are features common to both. But this one is less architectural; it does not move forward, like the other, in great, evenly balanced masses; the sections are not opposed, but derive one from the other and are related instead of being contrasted, especially in the andante which is a veritable stream, full of changing hues of emotion rather than themes. And the movements, too, are nearer to each other than in K.451. We have noted the kinship between allegro and andante. Their relationship with the finale is at first sight less evident; yet the opening of the variation theme is similar in form, if not in feeling, to the first subject of the allegro. And in the presto, we find something of the breadth of the two other movements: large-scale workings-out, themes inseparable from their developments and, between the returns of the opera buffa cadences, an uninterrupted flow of thought.

As in the last concerto the orchestra's part is important and there is frequent interplay. Conventional accompaniment figures are rare; the woodwind answer the solo or converse with it, or add characteristic accompaniments (ex. 156); the orchestra repeats passages from the first tutti and the piano adds a fresh part (ex. 166) or replaces one of the instruments (ex. 163). There are many fine passages where the piano combines intimately with the body of instruments, especially in the first movement (exs. 154, 155, 158) and variations; in the final presto, piano and orchestra play together symphonically for many bars (exs. 170, 171, 172). This concerto ranks with those in D, K.451, and C, K.503, in the forefront of the whole series for the interest in the relations of solo and orchestra.

The first two movements, we said, are more alike than in earlier concertos. They both have the same quiet temper, the same delicate sensibility, the same moderation. Both proceed by allusions rather than direct statements: allusions to passion (ex. 152), depth of feeling (ex. 153), mirth (end of the solo subject), power (ex. 149), melancholy (ex. 156); only the flight of fancy ex. 156 is completely realized, and for this reason the *development*, although it is non-thematic and contains nothing but fresh material, is not a digression but the moment in which the movement attains its full significance. The andante, it is true, has deeper shades, but on the whole moderation, too, reigns in it; it passes close to idyll, elegy, tragedy; but none of these succeeds in mastering it. And if, at times, it recalls Debussy, the delicate and restrained playfulness of the first movement, the reserve with which it hints at greater things without insisting, brings to mind the art of Watteau and the comedy of Marivaux.

Mozart has left a certain number of works in G major but only three or four times has he chosen the key for important ones.[1] It is therefore hard to say that it shows definite characteristics with him and Lüthy[2] is right in pointing out that keys with few accidentals, such as G and F, are those in which the emotion is least clearly characterized.

Though our concerto does not belong to a family of works in the same key, two of its movements come from the same source as parts of other works in G major. The andante is a close relative, both in its sentiment and in its themes, now dark and meditative, now ornate, of the andante of the quartet, K.387—another 3-4 movement in C whose themes also alternate between austerity and ornamentation. And is not the "moderate" tone of the allegro, half-sunshine, half-shadow, that of those two lovely rondos in G major—in the first duet for violin and viola, K.423, and the first quartet for piano and strings, K.478—two works approximately contemporary with our concerto?[3] In these three movements we find a clear utterance of one same mood.

---

[1] Violin concerto, K.216; string quartet, K.387; this concerto; and a violin sonata, K.379, which one hesitates to include, for its most characteristic movement, the allegro, is in G minor.

[2] *Mozart und die Tonartencharakteristik,* Strasbourg, 1931. He notes also that joy, which Mozart expressed by G major in his youth, finds its outlet rather in D and A in his maturer years.

[3] 1783 and 1785.

5. The Fourteenth Concerto: K.456 in B flat

CONCERTO No. 14 IN B FLAT (K.456)[1]
Finished September 30th, 1784
  Allegro vivace: C
  Andante un poco sostenuto: 2-4 (in G minor)
  Allegro vivace: 6-8
Orchestra: Strings; flute, two hautboys, two horns, two bassoons.

We now have here the famous Strinasacchi from Mantua, a very good violinist. She has a great deal of taste and feeling in her playing. I am this moment composing a sonata which we are going to play together on Thursday at her concert in the theatre.[2]

THE "famous" Mantuan is known to-day, if at all, only by the sonata which Mozart composed for her and the "extraordinary" story concerning it, one of the more trustworthy of the many tales of the kind related about him.

As usual, Mozart had made up the whole work in his head, but had negligently put off transcribing it to the last moment. As time was pressing, he contented himself with writing down the violin part and played his own from memory, to the astonishment of the Emperor who followed the performance from his box with opera glasses and saw on the piano, instead of a score, a sheet with merely the violin part and a few scanty indications.

Like the quintet K.452, the sonata[3] betrays in its style the proximity of the concertos. Each part is *concertante* in turn, and as the work was written for a violinist the fiddle part is the equal of the piano. There is no longer any trace here of the piano sonata with violin accompaniment, a type to which some of Mozart's other sonatas still belong. Its inspiration is close to that of the B flat concerto, K.450; it reflects the same self-assurance and the same joyous sense of power and success; but in the magnificent andante, the starting-point of

---

[1] *Gesamtausgabe*, no. 18.
[2] Letter to his father, April 24th, 1784; E. Anderson's translation, III, 1304.
[3] K.454; no. 15 in Peters' edition.

which is the same as the concerto's, the inspiration is much deeper. His genius may have been stimulated by the charm and talent of the twenty-year old virtuosa, for Leopold Mozart who heard her at Salzburg a year later declared that "no one can play adagios with more feeling than she; she puts her whole heart and soul into the melody she is rendering and her tone is as beautiful as it is strong".

This sonata is the last of the masterpieces composed by Mozart since the beginning of February.   Six great works in three months! Such wonders are so well known in his case and his biographers have thrown such light on his periods of intense production that we readily imagine him to have spent all his short life working at the same rate. As a matter of fact, these prodigious periods are exceptional; not more than four can be counted in the eleven years of his life in Vienna. This one, and the summer of 1788 when he composed his three last symphonies in six weeks, are the most extraordinary.   Usually, his activity was far more normal and sometimes he would write nothing for months at a time.   The Mozart who wrote untiringly and poured forth without rest or effort his treasures of melody is just a myth.

Between the end of April and September, 1784, composing stopped almost completely.   The concert season was over; the nobility and gentry had scattered; if Mozart composed at all, it was for himself and nothing went down on paper.   He does not seem to have left Vienna, even for his sister's wedding in August; he wrote to promise her a visit the following spring, a promise he was never to fulfil.   At this point the letters to his father which are one of our main sources of information concerning his life come to an end. The correspondence between parent and son did not stop, but, with one exception, no letters after this date have been preserved.   It has been supposed that those destroyed contained allusions to Freemasonry, into which Mozart had been initiated a short time earlier and to which Leopold himself was soon to belong.

After a rather grave illness, which was probably responsible for his not attending his sister's wedding, work was resumed in September with a new piano concerto.   For whom this work, at a time when concerts had not yet started again?   On February the 14th of the following year, Leopold Mozart was staying with Wolfgang and wrote to his daughter: "Sunday" (the 12th) "your brother played a magnificent concerto which he had written for Paradis in Paris" (*nach Paris*).[1]

---

[1] "*Dein Bruder spielte ein herrliches Konzert, das er für die Paradis nach Paris gemacht hatte.*"

Maria Theresia Paradis was a blind pianist and a friend of the Mozarts who had formerly stayed in Salzburg and was planning a tour in Paris.[1] It has generally been assumed that the reference in this letter is to the concerto in B flat, K.456. The "magnificent concerto" cannot be any of the previous ones, for Mozart speaks of all of these several times in his letters and never says that they were written for anyone but Babette Ployer or himself. On the other hand, the D minor is mentioned separately by Leopold in the same letter; there remain the F major, K.459, of December, 1784, and this one. But the F major has the self-assured, proudly joyous and rather external character of those in B flat and D, K.450 and 451, which we know to have been written for himself, whereas the more intimate feeling of K.456, its less showy piano part, connect it with those in E flat and G, K.449 and 453, both of them composed for someone else.

There are, however, objections to accepting it as the concerto mentioned by Leopold, and these apply equally to K.459.

Maria Theresia's stay in Paris had taken place in the first half of the year. She played fourteen times there between April 1st and June 10th. The programmes of her concerts given by the *Journal de Paris* contain works by Kozeluch, Gervais and Haydn, but say nothing of any by Mozart.

The word *nach* is ambiguous. If it means: For Maria Theresia Paradis to take with her *nach Paris,*—Leopold's remark can be explained only if we suppose that Wolfgang had promised a concerto for her tour and that K.456 was a belated carrying out of this promise, nearly four months after she had left France, or that she had planned a second visit which never came off, and for which Wolfgang wrote this concerto.[2]

If the *nach* can be understood as meaning: After her stay in Paris— the remark is intelligible. Maria Theresia Paradis, having returned to Austria, had asked him for a concerto, which he completed in September. But there are difficulties in the way of accepting *nach* in this sense. The identity of the *herrliches Konzert* must therefore remain doubtful.[3]

I. The orchestra is as large as in the G major but the scope of the

---

[1] Haydn composed his concerto in G for her.

[2] Perhaps for the *Concerts Spirituels* in Advent.

[3] Cf. H. Ullrich: *Marie-Therese Paradis and Mozart* (Music and Letters, October, 1946).

Ex. 175

Ex. 176

Ex. 180

Ex. 177

Ex. 178

Ex. 179

work is smaller, its aim less ambitious. Very Mozartish, this concerto is nevertheless far from containing all Mozart. In the E flat, K.449, the musician had displayed the variety and instability of his moods; in the B flat, his joy in success; in the D major, his pride and strength; and his joy in covering much ground in little space in the G major. Here, he draws in and exhibits but a small part of his riches.

The tutti which opens the allegro contains nearly all the important elements of the movement; the only one absent is the piano's special theme. Its personality breathes mildness. No abrupt modulations, like the dive into E flat in the concerto in G; a mainly smooth rhythm, where one recognizes the march of the three last concertos, firm but supple, without roughness or haste, and a readiness to slacken and pass from crotchets and quavers to minims and semibreves (ex. 179). Instead of the vigorous repeated notes of K.451 and 453, the gentle undulations of broken thirds, fourths or fifths preponderate in the accompaniment and give the movement its velvety softness.

The themes themselves have this soft, reticent character. They all show a strong family likeness.[1] Three of them contain the same figure (ex. 175 a). Four give prominence to repeated notes and in three cases the note repeated is the tonic. They tend to return to the tonic and rest on it. The figure of the falling and rising scale (ex. 175 b) is common to two of them; all avoid wide intervals and move usually in conjunct, or at least proximate, degrees. Quiet, rather lyrical, their outlines are not clear-cut. There is in them neither drama nor eloquence, and they are melodically undistinguished.

And yet this tutti is not monotonous. Twice over, without ceasing to be mild, it introduces variety; once at the opening of the second subject; once before the concluding theme. In both passages, the rhythm slows down and the emotion concentrates into chords. The first is perhaps the finest moment in the allegro; a silence marks it off from what precedes; uncanny progressions lead it into B flat minor, and at the end, when one expects to hear the second subject enter in the minor, it rediscovers the major with arresting simplicity (ex. 177). The subject itself (ex. 178) would pass unnoticed but for what went before it; admirably enhanced by this preparation, by the great circuit which Mozart makes to bring it in, its innocence is almost dramatic. By seeking afar what he had at hand, Mozart makes us

---

[1] The first subject occurs in a concerto of John Christian Bach, op. 13, IV (bars 5-6 of the first movement); it had already been used by Mozart in the andante of his violin sonata in B flat, K. 378.

believe that he sets great store by it.   Seldom does he set off his themes
by delaying them so long; seldom does he appear to consider them so
important.

On the brink of his conclusion he uses a device which had succeeded
in the G major (ex. 153 a and b).   Over a *cantus* given out by the
strings he superimposes when repeating it a woodwind descant (ex.
179).

In its dynamic marks, the movement shows a favourite *galant* practice, frequent in these concertos: the *piano* exposition of the first
subject, followed without transition by a *forte* passage;[1] the second
subject and its long preparation given out softly; and a concluding
forte.

As in the three last concertos, the scoring gives as much weight to
wind as to strings: one wonders even whether the wind is not favoured.
The two groups are opposed, mass against mass, in the first subject,
as in K.450, and they mingle in the *forte* transition theme (ex. 176)
which follows.   The fine modulating preparation of the second subject combines both, but leaves each one its individuality; questions
and answers succeed quickly but the parts remain distinct.   The second
subject itself belongs to the wind and at first the strings accompany
them with repeated thirds; in the codetta the wind play alone.   There
is the same opposition of groups in the concluding subject (ex. 180).
Simpler than its immediate predecessors in key progression, rhythm
and melody, this concerto is their equal in orchestration.

The solo exposition follows the same paths as the tutti.   It neglects
none of the contents of the latter and adds two fresh passages: the
first, before the second subject—the solo theme; the other, before
the conclusion.   Its innovations are therefore insertions; in other
respects it goes over, almost bar by bar, the opening tutti, modulating
to the dominant at the beginning of the solo subject and decorating
and enriching the orchestration with the piano part.   The chief
interest lies in this intervention of the solo.   Thus, piano and wind
fill in the silence which, in ex. 175, marked off the different parts of
the theme; in the repeat of the transitional subject, ex. 176, the right
hand accompanies the hautboys and flute with a figure of repeated
broken octaves which plays an important part in the andante.   The
wind descant, ex. 179, is replaced by a piano flourish, and hautboy,
flute and bassoon merely double the strings.   As in the tutti, the

---

[1] With variations of detail, we meet it in more than half of Mozart's Vienna
concertos: K.414, 415, 450, 453, 456, 459, 466, 467, 488, 491, 537.

Ex. 181a (a)

Ex. 181b (b)

Ex. 182

Ex. 183

moment of greatest loveliness is the announcement of the second subject; when the rest is forgotten, one remembers still the way in which the piano filigrees play round the austere lines of the orchestra and soften their harshness with their wavering contours and shimmering chromaticisms (ex. 181 a and b; cf. with ex. 177).

The solo subject has the same character as the others; we find in it the repeated notes, the falling and rising scale and the accompaniment of undulating thirds and fourths. On the whole, the piano part is much less brilliant than in the concertos which we know to have been written for Mozart himself. The writing recalls that of the G major, but chords are more frequent, both in the piano transposition of the orchestral theme, ex. 179, and in the solo passages, repeated at a few bars interval, which follow it (ex. 182). This is a somewhat uncommon feature in Mozart, whose style, in this respect, lags behind that of some of his contemporaries.

As in the two previous concertos, the orchestra is well occupied; the strings, discreet but indispensable, take part even in the solo theme. The second subject is given out by the wind and the piano takes it up as it is repeated. Seldom does the solo have a completely free hand; even in the great virtuosity passage at the end, the wind add an accompaniment figure of an individual nature.

The *development* is neither a *fantasia* nor a thematic working-out but a mixture of the two. The beginning and end comprise new elements, *cantabile* passages given to the piano.[1] But the middle is a series of repetitions in the orchestra of ex. 180, the martial, square-cut rhythm of which carries scale passages in the piano; scales and figure progress in fourths through various keys, from D minor to B flat. The presence of this figure gives the *development* a certain thematic character, whilst the incessant modulation and the nature of the solo part assimilate it to the *fantasias* of the previous concertos. But it is far from soaring like them; it is the least attractive part of the movement and one of the least interesting *developments* in Mozart's greater concertos.

The reprise takes place with the mildness that characterizes the whole movement. There is no rise in the emotional pitch at the end of the *development*; just a short obligatory piano cadenza, accompanied, and *in tempo*; then, three bars of transition in the woodwind, in long notes, rising from soft to loud, bring back the first subject, on whose arrival everything drops again to *piano*.

The recapitulation has few surprises for us. Sometimes, after omitting in the solo exposition themes given out in the first tutti, Mozart retrieves them in the last section. Here, he has not allowed

---

[1] The first of these constitutes a new subject. The introduction of a new subject at the beginning of the *development*, the invention of which practice Torrefranca attributes to Sammartini, is fairly frequent in Mozart's chamber music (cf. K.458, 478, 575), but rare in his concertos (cf. K.414).

himself the chance of doing so and the recapitulation reproduces in its main lines the solo exposition, keeping, of course, to the key of B flat. The main changes are in the decoration which the piano adds to the first subject. Even the bravura passages are faithfully repeated; nevertheless, at the last moment, as if such literalness had ended by annoying him, Mozart introduces in midmost solo two astonishing bars of woodwind, highly personal in their chromaticisms (ex. 183: they follow what corresponds, in the recapitulation, to ex. 182), the only true "surprise" in this, the best behaved and most conventional first movement in all Mozart's Vienna concertos.[1] Right at the end of the solo the return of ex. 180, accompanied by piano scales, is a felicitous recall of the beginning of the *development*. The more pleasing of the two cadenzas written by the composer for this concerto, the first, contains a noteworthy chord passage based on ex. 179, which itself returns in the last tutti, with its flute descant.

Every work of art worthy of the name creates a world of its own. It induces in those who approach it a particular mood, perhaps not identical with that in which the artist found himself when he conceived and carried it out, and liable to vary from observer to observer, but the existence of which is undeniable. Our awareness of this mood, different with each work, constitutes what we may call its *world*.

The differences between such *worlds* are infinite; no two great works induce the same mood. Nevertheless, generally speaking, the world into which a work leads us belongs to one of two sorts, according as it is contained in time or is outside it. This is independent of its medium. A work belonging to an art whose formal exigencies require duration, like poetry or music, may nevertheless be outside time; whilst a picture may, in the sense we intend, imply its presence. For it is not by its form that art participates in time; it is by the conditions obtaining in the mind of the artist at the moment he conceives his creation.

There are *crisis* works, whose whole existence arises from an experience in time, having, like a drama, beginning, middle and end. Their world, when one enters it, has but a limited duration; they have a conflict to resolve, a course to run; this task once completed, their world vanishes. Everything in it is movement and becoming; instinctively, we identify ourselves with these works and call them *dramatic*. This is independent of the medium; although it occurs more seldom in painting, sculpture, architecture, than in literature and

---

[1] Cf. a comparable outburst at a similar point in the allegro of K.537.

music, there too the work may have the qualities of a drama and imply the existence of a precise and supremely important moment. Such an element is recognizable, for instance, in sculpture like the tympanum of Autun cathedral, in the painting of Van Gogh, in many a Flamboyant or Baroque piece of architecture.

Other works, on the contrary, belong to a universe in which time has no part. They are born outside it, outside a precise moment in their author's life, and their world is unchanging. It is the same in all its parts. It seems to have existed from all eternity; we go into it in our turn, we experience its domination, we bathe in its atmosphere; but we do not identify ourselves with it, as we did the drama of the *crisis* works; it will go on living when we leave it. All forms of art can call forth this world, as well as the other, but none as fully as music and architecture. We *enter* a motet of Byrd or Palestrina, or a fugue of Bach, as we enter Westminster Abbey, and we leave it similarly. You can go into the cathedral by any door you please; you can begin many fugues (not all, of course, for some fugues are dramatic) at different points; no doubt the composer intended them to be played from beginning to end, but you can nevertheless begin at one or other entry without the work becoming thereby nonsensical. Its world, like the cathedral's, is accessible through several doors. And when we leave the cathedral, we know that its world will persist, that we can enter it again as often as we like, that we shall find it again every time we cross its threshold. The world of the fugue and motet, likewise, which predates our hearing of the music, will endure, unchanged, when the notes have ceased sounding. We enter and leave it at will.

What a difference with *crisis* works! These bear witness to a moment in the artist's life; they have an historic or at least a biographical significance; like a drama, they unfold in a time sequence and any disarrangement in it makes them unintelligible. Their episodes follow each other as inevitably as those of the conflict whence they spring; you cannot make your way in where you choose; you must go through the door and there is only one. Their world lasts only as long as the recital of the conflict; once this is over, it scatters and will not live again till you choose yourself to live through the drama once more.

The world of the movement we have just quitted does not belong to this category. In it, everything is description, not drama; environment, not crisis; being, not becoming; rest, not action; stability, not change. No experience, bounded in time, unfolding like a drama— even like a happy drama—stands behind this still music, one of the few

completely still allegros that Mozart has left us. Its world is without
boundaries or frontiers; we enter it where we will, by the gate of our
choosing; the obligation to follow the movement in the order of the
notes is a purely formal one. The only reason that prevents us from
stopping at the end of the exposition or beginning at the *development*,
or from repeating this or that section, is that we should upset the order
of key sequence: a valid reason, no doubt, but a formal one, not
affecting in any way the meaning of the work. It would be much less
serious to change the order of the different sections and the tonic-
dominant-tonic sequence than to intervert two of the variations in
the andante that follows it, although all of them, save one, are in the
same key, for it is a dramatic movement and its episodes succeed each
other in an order prescribed, not by rules, but the law of its own
emotion. The allegro, on the other hand, is comparable to the cathedral whose world has neither beginning nor end in time, or to a landscape with quiet outlines and indefinite horizons, which we can
approach from all sides, where we can sojourn as long as we like.

We would not dare to say this of the other concertos of this year.
K.449 is to a high degree the experience of a moment; K.451 is a
work of passion, expressive, it is true, of happiness and triumph, but
passionate notwithstanding. And if the word passion appears too
violent for K.450 and 453, there too, nevertheless, the first movements
are narratives and not descriptions. It would not be hard to show, by
means of a purely formal analysis, to what extent this dramatic element
is lacking in K.456; that its themes, with their soft outlines, are hardly
distinguishable one from the other and mingle their personalities; and
especially that Mozart, by laying almost all his cards on the table at
the first stroke and repeating in his first solo all the elements of the
tutti, deprives himself of the possibility of causing us surprises, without
which there can be no dramatic interest. But that is touching merely
outward signs; the static, non-dramatic quality of the movement
resides in the thought which inspires it.

Therefore let us not reproach it with its absence of surprises and
contrasts and its lack of variation in emotional pitch. Let us wander
without effort in these peaceful vales; let us yield without reserve to
their pervasive influence; they cannot exert it if we persist in seeking
to receive from them strong impressions which they do not desire to
impart.

II. The andante consists in variations, an uncommon form in the
important works of Mozart, who generally treats the *air varié* as a trifle.

It is the first concerto andante in a minor key since the *Sinfonia Concertante*, K.364, and, in the piano concertos, since the E flat, K.271, of 1777. There seems to be some relation in Mozart's andantes between the variation form and sadness, for most of those which adopt it, in important works of his maturity, express a feeling of melancholy.[1]

There is no need to say that a movement in G minor forms a complete contrast with the allegro. Mozart is not, of course, the only musician to put side by side the reverse and obverse of the medal, mildness and passion; but the opposition between two moods is particularly sharp in him, not only from one movement to another but also between different sections of the same movement. The transitions, which sometimes take the shape of conflicts, by which a Beethoven or a Franck passes from darkness to light are very rare with him; he prefers to turn the picture round suddenly and show one face after the other.[2]

The variation, we said, is a form he uses seldom in his serious work. But it happens that in 1784 and 1785 he has recourse to it several times: in three of his concertos and in his string quartet in A.[3] These four movements, with the finales of the serenade and concerto in C minor and the andantino of the divertimento for string trio, K.563, are the most interesting examples he has left of this form.

When he introduces variations into an unimportant work, he expends his ingenuity, like other *galant* composers, on decorating the melodic line of the air varied. He brings in a few superficial changes of rhythm, but the harmonies remain much the same from one variation to the next. Music-lovers of the end of the 18th century, who made a Gargantuan consumption of *airs variés*, liked to hear their favourite theme as often as possible, and the composer's task was to present it to them with just enough variety to avoid monotony.

Such is, on the whole, the goal in the variations of the B flat concerto, K.450, where the changes bear mainly on the accompaniment.[4] But the three other examples of the year aim higher. Those of the G major concerto, nos. 4 and 5, bring forward new versions of the

---

[1] The D minor variations of the divertimento in D, K.334; those, in D minor also and akin to them, of the violin sonata in F, K.377; the C minor andante of the piano concerto in E flat, K.482, whose form is a cross between variations and rondo.

[2] See the discussion of this point in IV, 1, pp. 327–9.

[3] Without counting an *air varié*, K.455.

[4] Including under this term the piano ornamentation.

theme, and in the presto decompose it and reconstitute it again. The coda of the variations of the A major quartet goes further and launches out into a grandiose development, surpassing in scope all the rest of the movement.

The andante of our concerto is worthy of the neighbourhood of these two movements. Formally, it is less ambitious than they, but it surpasses them in strength and depth of feeling. It consists in a theme and five variations followed by a coda which corresponds in length to a sixth one. The theme, in which the rhythm ♩♩♩ predominates, is divided into two parts; the first has eight bars grouped two by two; the second breaks the symmetry with a codetta which prolongs it to thirteen.[1] The first variation has repeats, like the theme; the second, third and fourth are double; that is, the repeats are themselves varied, so that the subject is varied in reality twice within each variation; the fifth is single and flows into the coda.

Except in the *major* variation, the harmonic basis remains the same; the most important alterations are in the third, which is also the most daring in rhythmic and melodic changes. The outline of the theme remains intact in those variations (nos. 2 and 5) where the *cantus* belongs to the tutti and the decorations to the piano; in the third, where piano and tutti are contrasted, and the fourth, where it is so much altered that it is practically a new subject, it undergoes notable changes. The original rhythm is altered only in the third variation.

Except, again, in the *major* variation, the changes consist in breakings up and diminutions of the melody by the piano (nos. 1 and 3); in decorations of the theme with demi-semi-quavers (nos. 2 and 5); in differences of scoring; and in a renewal of the melody and especially of the rhythm (no. 3, the only *minor* variation where the orchestra is entrusted with the task of varying).

The piano never expounds the theme in its original state. In the first variation it decorates it with sobriety. In the repeats of no. 3 it does likewise, but here its alterations are less purely decorative and affect also the significance. In the *major* variation it is content with repeating, with very little ornamentation, the theme in the new form in which the wind have just given it out. The decoration it adds in the second and fifth variations consists in arpeggios and scale fragments in one case and in repeated broken octaves in the other; these latter give it a certain impressionistic character; the style is rather different

---

[1] Except in the *major* variation, where the second part is eight bars long like the first.

from Mozart's usual piano writing, where misty effects are uncommon. In the coda, a dialogue arises between the solo and the orchestra and decoration gives way to the mere repetition of thematic fragments.

We said that the order of these variations revealed a dramatic inspiration. They are indeed the story of an emotional experience full of anguish, of that dramatic anguish which will fill the G minor quintet and which, in this same concerto, reappears most unexpectedly for an instant in the finale. The theme, which resembles a French *ariette* rather than a German or Italian song, expresses despair carried almost to a point of physical suffering, but without agitation, without a hint of rebellion. We are at a later stage than that of revolt, at the last moments of a tragedy. It is an expression of that complete hopelessness, that utter disillusion, accepted without attitudes or eloquence and all the more poignant, which 18th-century music renders with an intensity seldom equalled by the passionate and feverish cries of Romanticism (ex. 184).[1]

The piano repeats this lament with ever so slight a touch of dreaming or meditation; by diminishing the note values it holds the movement back and likens it to recitative; it is as if it recoiled upon its own emotion and took delight in it (var. 1; ex. 185). The wind give it out again in its primitive shape (var. 2); then, in the repeat, strings and piano combine. The theme is expounded by the first violins, still unchanged, and the piano surrounds it with expressive embroidery where arpeggios predominate (ex. 186). The second half is treated likewise. The stress increases slightly; the nature of the feeling remains unaltered.

The orchestra then breaks out in a *sforzando*, after which everything drops again to *piano* except the violas and basses which rush to the attack with scales of demi-semi-quavers (ex. 187). They end by carrying the other strings with them and giving them a series of jerks (a) to which correspond repeated chords in the wind. The piano resists this fury and returns, dreamier than ever, to the mood of the first variation (ex. 188). The impatience and irritation of the orchestra at the sight of such disdainful aloofness hardly leave it time to finish and when it reaches its conclusion the raging scales again surge upwards. This time they infect all instruments and follow each other with dramatic imitations. After two bars of truce, the vigorous figure (a) resounds throughout the orchestra and we finish with a return of the scales. This time, the piano reply betrays a little more

---

[1] The example gives only the upper parts.

Ex. 188

Ex. 189

Ex. 190

agitation, but on the whole it maintains its own position against the orchestra and the opposition between them makes this variation the most stirring in the andante.

After this outburst of wrath, the only one in the movement, mildness prevails again. In the exquisite *major* variation, the theme, transformed, is given to the hautboys, and the flute answers with a free canon at the octave (ex. 189). The piano repeats it in a new form. Is it peace, and has the vanishing of the hopeless mood suddenly opened the heavens to us? The return to G minor proves that it was but a respite of calm, a night of happy dreams amid successive days of suffering.

The violins take up the theme for the last time and the piano's commentary transforms it. The embroidery line in the bass and the repeated broken octaves in the right hand add a restrained quivering, all the more impressive for its being *piano* (ex. 190). There is no repeat and in the second half the subject is divided between strings and wind and the accompaniment confines itself mostly to the quivering treble octaves. The motion does not stop this time with the end of the theme but, with light *sforzandos* against the beat in the hautboys and basses, and rising passion, climbs to a dominant close, the climax, after which the coda, calmer but not less despairing, unfolds itself. Like warriors recalling the episodes in the struggle on the evening of a battle, woodwind and piano converse upon the first notes of the theme, against the ever-darkening background of strings, and the movement dies down with the violins humming in feverish throbs (ex. 191).

III. The finale is in 6–8 time, like those of Mozart's two other Vienna concertos in B flat. This is the only feature which its refrain has in common with theirs. It is, on the other hand, strangely like the theme of the andante (ex. 192). But the likeness is one of those which strike the eye and not the ear. It would be wrong to think it intentional. It is not meaningless, however; it arises because Mozart, in composing this concerto, and in spite of the difference between its

movements, was haunted by the figure and themes

with repeated notes, prominent in all three. His choice of themes betrays this perhaps unconscious obsession.[1]

It is a sonata rondo like most of the finales in his Vienna concertos, but its plan differs greatly from those of the sonata rondos we have studied hitherto. The piano starts it but gives out only a small part of the refrain (ex. 192). The orchestra repeats it and in the course of some fifty bars pours out a flow of melody which appears to form one single idea but which later on breaks up and provides four or five motifs, destined to come back separately and to act as links between the main sections. This structural device is peculiar to his rondos

---

[1] A Kozeluch trio in G minor, "op. 24 or 27" (sic), affords a curious coincidence with exs. 184 and 192 and, more curiously still, recalls for the ear as well as for the eye these two themes which, when we hear them, do not recall each other (ex. 193)! The melody recalls the andante and the rhythm the rondo. The refrain of the rondo is also met with in an unfinished string quintet in E flat, reproduced by Jahn and Abert (App. II; Einstein-Köchel, no. 613 a).

and we noticed it in the first and third movements of K.413.[1]   We quote three of these motifs (exs. 194, 195, 196).

This long prelude, which corresponds to a first-movement tutti, since nearly all its elements are made use of in the course of the rondo, finishes up in the tonic.   The first couplet or episode which starts at this moment has the form of a sonata exposition.   The first subject (ex. 197) is given out by the piano and followed by a fairly long solo into which its first notes intrude from time to time to remind us of our starting-point.   The orchestra has little to say; at distant intervals, a bar of woodwind links up the different solo strains.   We modulate quickly through E flat, C minor and G minor, and land in F.

The second subject then displays its lopsided mass; it advances with the nimble haste of a cripple, one of whose crutches has been stolen, and who pursues the thief brandishing the other.[2]   The wood-wind mock it (ex. 198) and, when it changes places and gives itself to the hautboy and bassoon, the piano jeers at it too.   After another solo in which the orchestra is a little less reticent, a fragment of the refrain is heard, ex. 195; the woodwind give it out, then, while they repeat it, the piano answers with a variant of ex. 194 (ex. 199).   After a third fragment, ex. 196, we halt in B flat upon a dominant seventh chord, whence an extempore solo cadenza brings us back to the refrain.

If the *development* of the allegro disappointed us after the *fantasia developments* of the previous concertos, what comes now may console us.   After the repetition of the refrain, the orchestra rapidly rids itself of the bonds that tied it to the B flat-F alternation and to the mild and festive world of the first couplet; it traverses with rising audacity and passion the keys of E flat and C minor and, without changing its figure—a fragment of the refrain—proclaims the key of B minor, whose dusky reign spreads over the middle section of the rondo.

A silence; then the piano confirms the proclamation.   And now, each one with a different rhythm with impressive singleness of notes and purpose, bassoon, violins and solo emphasize the new key.   The flute and the hautboy alone have held notes; the violins crackle furi-ously; the bassoon moves in great strides against the stormy sky across which zigzag the piano arpeggios (ex. 200).[1]   All this, however

---

[1] Cf. pp. 130 and 134.

[2] Cf. the refrain of the rondo in the G minor quintet, K.516.

[4] The bassoon and violin parts are not accompaniments and should be played prominently to equal the strength of the piano; the nature of the passage is not expressed if the piano arpeggios preponderate like a solo.

Ex. 199

Ex. 200

Ex. 201

dramatic, is but preparation; the stage is set, the world called up; the voice has now to speak.

Bassoon, hautboy and flute are silent; the strings start an accompaniment of repeated chords and against this restless background the piano gives out a tragic recitative (ex. 201). It has a familiar sound and is laden with associations, even for us who know but by hearsay the music tragedies of the 18th century; even we are reminded of at least one masterpiece of the century, the contralto aria in the St. John Passion, and the years which have elapsed since then have enriched it with Beethoven's 'cello sonata in A and his op. 110.[1]

The voice ceases and the storm, momentarily arrested, resumes its angry course. It travels through the skies of minor keys, from B to E, to D and B flat, proclaiming each time the furious assertions of ex. 200 which the message of the recitative has exasperated instead of appeased. Then the intensity drops to *piano*, the storm moves off; minor turns into major; while the recall of a passage which had preceded ex. 198 in the first couplet announces the disappearance of one world and the return to another.

This episode, only some thirty bars long, is the most stirring part of the rondo and perhaps of the whole concerto. With its harmless opening, this movement puts side by side in rash propinquity the mild, durationless world of the allegro and the world of conflict of the variations. No example could light up more clearly the distinction we made between the two. Bold though it be, it is not without precedent, for it falls into the tradition of the *minor* couplets of French rondos whose unrecognizable prodigy-offspring it is.

In a regular sonata rondo we should now hear the refrain once more. But the tornado we have come through carries us beyond that stage and the appearance of ex. 192, carefree and skipping, would jar painfully on our quivering nerves. So the movement passes straight away to the third couplet with ex. 197, whose more reserved merriment does not offend us with an indecent contrast.

The sonata rondo in which the second return of the refrain is missing and the second couplet joins on without a break to the recapitulation appears some ten times in Mozart, thrice in his piano concertos.[2]

---

[1] Middle of the first movement; *arioso dolente*. Mozart was to remember it two years later in another work as remote from tragedy as this one, the fourth horn concerto, K.495.

[2] K. 456, 459 and 488. Among other instances of this form are the rondos of the sonata for two pianos, the quintet for piano and wind instruments, the two quartets for piano and strings and the divertimento for string trio.

The omission of the refrain is not always as dramatically significant as it is here.   In some of them, the second couplet itself is much reduced and the form comes near to that of the rondo in two couplets, where the second repeats the first and the last traces of the *development* are a few bars of modulation, after the first return of the refrain.[1]

The third couplet or recapitulation follows the lines of the first, except that it does not modulate to F.   The few differences are in the figuring of the piano runs and in a witty insertion of three bars at the end of the last solo, where hautboy and bassoon forestall the tutti entry by punctuating the piano passages with the first bars of the refrain.   Ex. 194 leads to the pause for which Mozart has left a short cadenza which incorporates bits of the refrain, of exs. 198 and 201 and of a run from the last solo.   The final return of the refrain is divided between orchestra and piano which relieve each other with gusto every two or three bars.   The exs. 199 and 196 conclude the movement.

This concerto has a twin most unlike it, the fiery piano sonata in C minor, completed four days later.   Several times in his life Mozart wrote two important works in quick succession and in most cases there was between them a contrast of inspiration as complete as between the first and second movements of this concerto or between the concerto as a whole and this sonata.   The concertos in D minor and C, K.466 and 467, in 1785, the quintets in C and G minor in 1787, the symphonies in G minor and C in 1788 are illustrious examples of this coupling of two opposites.[2]   The quick succession of two such different works is but another manifestation of his tendency to pass without transition from one aspect of reality to another, to show abruptly the other side of the medal.   Obviously, the variations and the dramatic episode in the rondo of the concerto could form a link with the sonata; but, in spite of the likeness between all Mozart's *minor* compositions, it is a far cry from the melodious and dramatic sorrow of the first to the burning passion of the second, whose allegro

---

[1] As in the quintets in C and G minor and the *Coronation* concerto, K.537.

[2] Here are some others: the quartets in D minor and E flat (June-July, 1783); the concertos in A and C minor (March, 1786); and, without emotional contrast, the quartets in A and C (January, 1785); the concerto in C, K.503, and the *Pragne* symphony (December 4th and 6th, 1786); the quartets in B flat and F (May-June, 1790).

flies up as straight as a tongue of flame and whose expressive power is concentrated more in rhythm than in melody.

Five weeks after the concerto Mozart entered in the list of his compositions another B flat work, the quartet known as the *Hunt.* Here, we are nearer the world of K.456. Compared with the three previous quartets of the "Haydn" series, it appears somewhat superficial. Has the habit of the platform led Mozart to produce a more fashionable work? In any case, it belongs truly enough to the lineage of the concertos and the Strinasacchi sonata. In the andante, we hear an echo of the anguish which inspired the variations of K.456; on the other hand, the sunny counterpoint in the finale announces the concerto in F.

6. *The Fifteenth Concerto: K.459 in F*

CONCERTO NO. 15 IN F (K.459)[1]
Finished December 11th, 1784
    Allegro: ¢
    Allegretto: 6-8 (in C)
    Allegro assai: 2-4
Orchestra: Strings; flute, two hautboys, two horns, two bassoons.

THE works of the autumn of 1784 succeeded each other at less prodigious speed than those of the winter and spring. From October to January they spread out at the rate of one a month: the C minor sonata on October 4th, the B flat quartet on November 9th, this concerto on December 11th, the quartet in A on January 10th. And, with one exception, this was the rate at which they were to appear throughout the following twelvemonth.

The new concerto is of the same race as its five predecessors. Composed almost certainly for Mozart himself,[2] its inspiration is near to that of the B flat and D major, K.450 and 451. It sings the same confidence and happiness, the same triumph of the composer and executant, master of his talent and his public. It sings them in the highest degree and never more in his work shall we hear so wholehearted a joy so ingenuously expressed. Not a cloud comes to darken, even for an instant, the brilliant sky of the allegro and rondo, and the appearance of the minor in the allegretto, however pathetic, is but passing and exerts no influence over the rest of the movement.

I. If the emotion of the work puts it close to the other concertos of the year, its first movement contains nevertheless a number of elements peculiar to it which distinguish it as clearly from the works that precede it as from those that follow.

What Mozart aims at is clear.

On one hand he wants a movement with numerous and well-marked themes. The first tutti is a succession of somewhat *cantabile*

---

[1] *Gesamtausgabe*, no. 19.
[2] See p. 259.

subjects whose strains are all of much the same length. It is one of his most varied and most loosely knit first tuttis. Moreover, after the first subject, nothing preponderates; the other themes are all of equal importance and none of them turns out to be the second subject, not even a mock second subject (as in K.450 and some concertos of the years to come). From this multiplicity of themes arises the divergence between the tutti and the solo exposition. Only one half of the former and one third of the latter comprise elements common to both.

On the other hand he wants this rather rhapsodical diversity of the opening to be compensated by the predominance of the first subject throughout the rest of the movement. It predominates through its rhythm, almost always present, even in the solo passages, and through its melody, reminders of which are frequent. The presence of one same accompaniment figure in the piano part is also an element of unity, and the absence of exceptional modulations is perhaps due to this same concern for singleness.

Finally he wants a movement which returns to the ideal of K.451 and where the orchestra shall be as important as the solo. In no other concerto are the bars where the orchestra predominates and where the solo confines itself to accompanying or decorating its part so numerous. And, as in four earlier concertos of this year, the wind have parts as personal as those of the strings.

Throughout the movement, whether the orchestra or the piano be to the fore, square-cut phrases of two or four bars preponderate; in the uniformity of its rhythm, this concerto is unique.

All this converges towards one object: the expression of a single feeling which infuses the whole movement, to an even higher degree than in the last concerto.

Let us look more closely at some of these points.

There is no need to indicate in more detail the multiplicity of themes in the opening tutti. Six can be counted after the first subject. The first of them is a bird of passage which does not return; the next two figure fairly prominently in the solo exposition and recapitulation; the other three in the recapitulation only. They have distinct personalities: all those that make their first appearance in the solo exposition, on the other hand, derive from the first subject. It is as if Mozart, once the end of the tutti reached, had been frightened at his wastefulness and felt he must economize.

Let us make the acquaintance of this first subject and follow it through the movement. Here it is, as it comes forward at the beginning, *piano*, given out by the typically Mozartian combination of

Ex. 202

Ex. 203

Ex. 204

Ex. 205

Ex. 206

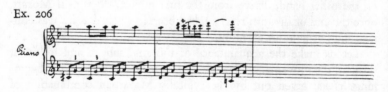

Ex. 207

Ex. 208

Ex. 209

Ex. 210

violins and flute (ex. 202). We recognize the march rhythm with
which the three last concertos had also begun. It is repeated, *forte*,
in the wind doubled by the violins—a fresh example of the *galant*
formula of a soft opening followed by a *forte*. Its strophic **character**

and its division into four-bar sections are obvious. Its second part is
similar (ex. 203). We meet it again at the beginning of the solo
exposition, first in the piano only, then in the hautboys and bassoons,
accompanied by the solo (ex. 204).[1] After the short and rather insignificant solo subject, with which the movement concerns itself no
further, the wind, instead of letting the piano perform its bravura
passage without interruption, recall in imitation the opening notes of
the theme (ex. 205) and it is to its rhythm, with its triplet accompaniment which now becomes an integral part of the subject, and partly
with its very notes, that the piano throws itself into its first solo (ex.
206). But at the end of nine bars, the flute and then the bassoon
return with the fragment (a) of ex. 202 which ends by being
not only the title but also the matter and the signature of the
movement, and the piano meekly resumes its accompaniment
triplets (ex. 207).

The second subject's entry dethrones the dotted rhythm and the
triplets for an instant, but not the two and four-bar phrases; as soon as
tutti and piano have given it out, however, march rhythm in the
orchestra and triplets in the piano begin again and after a few bars of
virtuosity lead up once more to ex. 202, the last three bars of which
are repeated by the wind in C minor, whilst the piano supports them
with its untiring triplets.   The end of the solo contains at first elements
from the first tutti, but as soon as the usual trill sounds the end of the
exposition, the whole band starts a fine working-out with (a).   Beginning *forte* and in the treble, it sweeps grandly down to the bass, whence,
after two bars of minims and semibreves, it climbs back to the treble
and modulates to A minor, the key in which the piano re-enters for
the *development* (ex. 209).

The middle part has the free and easy ways of a *fantasia development* but even here the dotted rhythm does not slumber and, in the
wind parts, it punctuates the piano's two-bar phrases and ends by
spreading to the right hand.   The triplets, of course, are not
inactive, and except for the explosive chord, struck twice over,[2]
which opens the section, they do not cease for a single beat in one
hand or the other.   And when the solo stops on the dominant
chord of D minor, it is still to the rhythm of (a) that, with one of

---

[1] In performance, the wind should stand out and the impression should
not be given that the piano triplets are the chief thing.

[2] Cf. p. 300 for the likeness between this passage and the andante of the
D minor concerto.

those short cuts customary in Mozart at such points, we reach the recapitulation—we cannot say, return to the first subject, for we have never left it (ex. 208).

Its mastery is almost undisputed throughout the recapitulation. The second subject is episodic, as it was earlier—a mere interlude, like so many second subjects in these concertos, whose presence does not affect in any way, it seems, the course of the movement. After it, the same dotted rhythm calls, the same triplet passages and the same echoes of (a) continue.

It is still to the tune of the first subject that the orchestra announces the cadenza. This, one of the finest that Mozart has left, strides up the keyboard in triplet arpeggios and starts off for a brief adventure on the stilts of (a) before condescending to the neglected second subject, and closes with a return to the triplets.

But in the conclusion—a tardy revenge by all that is neither march rhythm nor triplets!—the movement discards them completely. The orchestra repeats unchanged the last twenty bars of the tutti that had not been heard since the solo entry and the movement finishes without alluding again to the obsessive ex. 202.

Such concern with one rhythm, one theme, one accompaniment figure, is unparalleled in these concertos and is the chief originality of this movement. But this feature which is peculiar to it is not more attractive than another which it shares with its predecessor in D, to wit, the equality of orchestra and solo and the practice on the piano's part of repeating orchestral passages, accompanying or decorating them the while. These passages, less continuous than in the D major, are four in number. The first occurs in the second half of the first subject (ex. 203); the left hand displaces the violas and basses and the right hand adds a decorative counterpoint (ex. 209). The second is in a passage in minims of the first tutti to which the piano contributes a brilliant arpeggio decoration (ex. 210). In the other two the novelty consists in the substitution of piano for violins in the repeat of a strings and wind dialogue in the first tutti, and of a passage from the end of the exposition where the seconds accompanied the enunciation of the first subject by the wind (ex. 211; towards the end of the last solo).

This concerto is no more dramatic than the last. It has no story to tell and no action to reproduce; it is content with radiating a mood of youthful happiness, irresistibly cordial. The symmetrical cut of its phrases and the springing step of its accompaniments make it a kind of dance; despite its rhythm, its texture is too light and too diaphanous for it to be a march.   It is a relaxation and a game, every movement of which is carried out to a ballet step.

For some people, says Tovey, all Mozart's concertos are alike . . . just as, for some, all Chinamen appear alike.   But a superficial acquaintance with the works of 1784 at any rate is enough to make us capable of distinguishing them.   At second sight, one cannot confuse the restlessness of the E flat, the confidence and grace of the first B flat, K.450, like a girl who is pretty and knows it, the "soldierly" pride of the D major, the mixture of tears and smiles, the "middle course" of that in G, the mildness of the second B flat, K.456, and finally the carefree but self-assured joy of this one.   So many works, so many different moods, so many worlds!

In form, and confining ourselves to first movements, the differences are as great.   Let us review quickly the main points of comparison between this concerto and its predecessors.

It is like the first B flat in the placing of its themes and the absence of the second subject from the opening tutti.   It is like the D major in that it repeats passages already given out by the orchestra and adds to them, or inserts in them, a piano part, and in that it treats the orchestra as the solo's equal.   It resembles both, and also the second B flat, in the absence of modulations in the opening tutti and, generally, throughout the movement.   Finally, it is like all the others except the E flat (where the wind parts are optional) in the importance it gives to flute, hautboys and bassoons.

It is unlike all, except the first B flat, in that its first tutti is an introduction rather than an *argument* of what follows and in that the solo exposition, instead of going over its traces, departs from them.   And its lack of modulations distinguishes it from the G major and especially the E flat, the most modulating of all the concertos.

It is unique, finally, in that its first tutti, amongst its many motifs, contains neither second subject nor mock second subject, in that it departs so little from the rhythm and melody of the first subject, and in the uniform design of its phrases, where two and four-bar divisions predominate.

This comparative analysis confirms the impression we had already, that it is closest to the two concertos which, like it, were written for Mozart himself—the B flat, K.450, and the D—and farthest from the three composed for others—the E flat, G and B flat, K.456.[1]

.   .   .   .   .

---

[1] With the reservations made on p. 259.

II.   The second movement is a 6-8 allegretto which has somewhat the nature of a Brahms intermezzo.   The absence of a slow movement is characteristic of this work, whose joyous high spirits are so foreign to meditation.   An andante or an adagio, after such a first movement,

Ex. 216

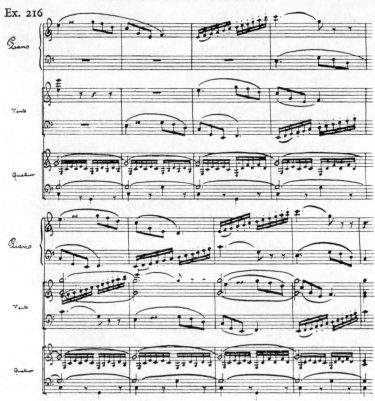

would be a contrast, and Mozart, returning to the ideal of homo-geneity which had inspired the G major, avoids contrasts.[1]

---

[1] It may be that Mozart had thought at first of a movement in a more usual *tempo*. Among the concerto fragments in the Mozarteum there is the beginning of an andante in C, Köchel-Einstein 466 a, the scoring of which suits this concerto perfectly, despite the third edition of Köchel which says by mistake "trumpets" instead of "bassoons" and which, basing itself on this erroneous datum, connects the movement with the concerto in D minor. However, key and scoring fit equally well the concerto in G. The spirit of the thirty-seven bars of the fragment (twenty-five of tutti, eight of solo, four of tutti, followed by a sketchily indicated fresh solo entry) is akin to the andante of K.453 of which it might be a first sketch, inferior to the final realization; this may be an argument for connecting it with this work. One might say quite as well, however, that Mozart, having begun it for the concerto in F, found that it merely repeated less felicitously what had already been said in the G major and decided thereupon to compose a completely fresh move-ment; whence the present allegretto. The only clear conclusion is that it was probably destined for one of the two concertos.

To the light-heartedness and serenity of the allegro this allegretto adds an easy grace, capricious and, at times, melancholy. In a more moderate *tempo*, it is quite the counterpart of the first movement. It has the binary form common to several of Mozart's andantes and adagios.[1] Preceded by a tutti, it consists in two identical halves, each of which is made up of a main subject, given out first of all in the tutti, of a plaintive theme, in G minor the first time, C minor the second, and of a little conclusion. The movement ends with a coda built on the first subject. It is therefore a *sonata* without a *development*, a form which must have been all the more acceptable to Mozart that the *development* is always the shortest section of the three with him.

The tutti is more than an introduction; it is almost an independent section prefixed to the movement. After the first subject (ex. 212), fiddles and hautboys bring in a sinuous, climbing figure with a taste for modulation, which tarries a moment in F minor and foreshadows the sombre-hued second subject before disappearing for good and all. The modulations by which it returns to C major recall the transition to the second subject in the first movement of K. 456 (cf. ex. 177).

The piano expounds the first subject in its turn and adds a gruppetto which gives it an unexpected likeness with a theme of Brahms's sextet in G (ex. 213).[2] It is about to repeat, but at the second bar flute and hautboy stop it by echoing the same motif a sixth above; the solo answers back, a third below; hautboy and bassoon reply yet a third lower, which lands us in D minor, whence a modulating piano passage leads to a close on the dominant of G major.

Here, a "regular" movement would bring in its second subject. But our concerto is much too original to be regular; moreover, this movement shares with the other two a liking for single subjects. Instead of presenting us with a new one, it entrusts the flute with re-expounding the opening of the first theme (ex. 212) in its upper register, and the first violins accompany it with an Alberti bass figure destined to become almost as prominent as the famous triplets in the allegro. Flute and bassoon start a canon on the first subject; the piano

---

[1] Piano concerto in C, K.503; quintets in C and G minor; string quartets in G, B flat (*Hunt*), and C and B flat (K.589); piano quartet in G minor; and others.

[2] This sextet contains another figure common to Brahms and Mozart, the

of its first movement, an important element in the andante of the *Prague* symphony, K.504.

takes it from them almost at once and the violins continue with their seesaw figure. This passage returns, much extended, in the second half.

The piano pursues with a new codetta and ends up in G major. Thereupon the second hautboy and second bassoon sound repeatedly the chord of G major which it has just struck. Then, after one bar, they flatten the third and at the same time the first hautboy, then the flute, put forth a moving lament, far removed from everything we have heard hitherto in this concerto, except for the few F minor bars in the prelude.[1] The piano repeats it, embellishing it slightly (ex. 214). The wind give out the second half, just a downward scale, full of hesitation with its halts of three beats at each stage. This time, the strings take it up with a slight reshuffling of the parts, and the piano unfolds at the same time a winding variation (ex. 215).

This sorrow, so simple and straightforward in its expression, is quickly allayed and the major mode comes back as suddenly as it had departed. Two short fragments, which afford piano and wind a game of ball, conclude the exposition and a solo transition brings back the tonic key and the first subject.

The second half reproduces the first with a few changes of figuring in the piano part, until it reaches the passages which modulated to G. This time we do not leave C major. The first subject returns as formerly, inclined to consider itself as a canon. Piano, hautboy and bassoon ask for nothing better and the game starts again on a broader basis. A rising scale tacked on to the subject for the occasion is a particularly useful participant, and its straight path makes a graceful contrast with the windings of the rest (ex. 216).[2]

The second subject steps forward in C minor and is followed by the same fragments and codetta as in the exposition. They bring back the first subject, upon which the coda is founded. The conclusion of the first tutti is repeated, a reminder by piano and orchestra of the theme's first bars. The coda itself is a four-bar pedal on which upward scales are built; the piano comes in last. A short series of gruppetti is like one last regret for the first subject; then the scales begin again and the movement, borne aloft on the wings of the flute, loses itself sky-high (ex. 217).

---

[1] It recalls a theme of the finale of the F major piano sonata, K.332 (bars 50 and foll.).

[2] There is at this point some likeness with the andante in C of the string quartet in G, K.387.

By its *tempo*, this movement is unique in Mozart's concertos. But it has more than originality in its favour. It is one of his pieces where apparent simplicity is most closely allied to subtlety. What delights us in it are the curves and counter-curves of its melodic lines, the presence of a certain contrast to which the allegro had made us grow unaccustomed, and diversity of rhythm. Gone, the phrases of two and four bars; here, the themes and their fragments, often quite short, are of very various lengths. The graceful irregularity, the charming wilfulness of its first and main subject (ex. 212) are qualities that belong to the whole allegretto, and, though it does not embody an experience of any poignancy or depth, it calls up a world of harmonious and changing shapes, where sadness speaks but to make us enjoy the better the serene air in which we move.

III. However original the allegro and allegretto, however infectious the spirits of the first and harmonious the motion of the second, the strongest part of this concerto is the finale. There lies its centre of gravity; when we think of the work, it is what represents it in our memory.

A formal analysis, of the kind which boils down the most complex works to the state of

> Theme A—1st subject—23 bars.
> Theme B—2nd subject—15 bars, etc.

might present this finale as a sonata rondo with omission of the refrain after the second couplet, similar in design to those of K.456 and 466, and within the narrow field of truth assigned to it, such an analysis would not be wrong. But a glance thrown on the score presents a different and more essential picture. The first page and several of those that follow have a neat, regular appearance; notes of equal value, rests, pauses, line the leaves from top to bottom, one correctly above the other in vertical construction. Twice, however, this symmetry is broken by the intrusion of a different texture, where lines, long and short, straight and winding, wander in all directions, but rather from side to side than from top to bottom: a polyphonic texture.

The juxtaposition of homophony and counterpoint is the fundamental character of the movement—that, and not its irregular sonata rondo plan. We have here one of those pieces where exist "essentially academic elements and light, even popular or bantering tunes",[1] the best known instance of which in Mozart is the finale of the quartet in

Ex. 217

Ex. 218a

Ex. 218b

Ex. 219

G, but to which belongs also in the last resort the finale of the *Jupiter*. Saint-Foix reminds us that "the predominant use of *fugato* in a symphony finale has precedents"[1] and that examples can be found in Austrian composers, some of whom like Dittersdorf and Michael Haydn were elder contemporaries of Mozart. (We are not speaking of the finale in fugue form, such as Joseph Haydn had written in some of his op. 20 quartets and Mozart in those he composed at Vienna in 1773, but of the alternation of the two styles.) To the three movements just mentioned should be added the finale of the E flat string quintet, his last instrumental work,[2] where twice over a five-part *fugato* comes to give zest to the adventures of a most un-solemn 2-4 tune.

The presence of limpid homophony and strict counterpoint within the framework of the same movement, a manifestation of the principle of contrast in unity, gives this finale a rich, strong organism. We shall see that there is not really juxtaposition, even in the masterly manner of the quartet in G, but union, and that the matter of the harmonic part occurs in the *fugatos*. It is largely with the same motifs that the movement passes from homophony to counterpoint and comes back to homophony. The sharing of themes is not as complete as in the finales of the *Jupiter* and the quintet; in this respect, the concerto stands half-way between the quartet in G and them.

Although analysis reveals a certain number of themes, at bottom there are only two subjects: one, rhythmical, belonging in the first place to the harmonic parts; the other, melodic, belonging to the *fugatos*. The first one is the refrain. Each of its two halves is given out in turn by piano and orchestra (ex. 218 a and b). (The fragment marked (i) and the alternations in the parts at the beginning of (b) play an important part later on.)

Once that is done, instead of the orchestra continuing with the usual ritornello, the basses strike up at once a fugal entry on a new motif (ex. 219). There follows the exposition of a four-part fugue, in close counterpoint, with the answer treading on the heels of the subject two bars behind it, followed by a miniature *stretto* which reduces the distance between them to one bar; then polyphony gives way to harmony. The race continues with frenzy; violins and violas break out in *tremolandos*; and, after opening the gates of D minor, B flat and G minor and shutting them immediately, it stops clamorously on the

---

[1] G. de Saint-Foix: *Les symphonies de Mozart*, p. 233.

[2] With the partial exception of the clarinet concerto, a good deal of which is an any case earlier.

chord of the dominant.   The horns sound a C, the beginning of a
long pedal, and, *piano*, the fragment (i) of the refrain is whispered by
the basses, gains the upper regions, starts twice, extends to the whole
orchestra, and finally breaks forth, *ff* and alternating, in wind and
basses, whilst violins and violas return joyously to their *tremolandos*.
With vicissitudes of *piano* and *forte*, the fragment (i) or its rhythm and
the *tremolandos* lead us by degrees towards a full close, after which,
upon a tonic pedal in the basses, the concluding theme, entirely homo-
phonous, scampers up and down; it is one of the most unblushing
borrowings the concerto makes from opera buffa, a regular comic
finale, chattering, busy about nothing, quite brainless (ex. 220), but
scored and eked out with irresistible wit.

This tutti is so long—almost one fifth of the movement—and so
important, that only its loyalty to the key of F prevents us from
forgetting we have a concerto, for a symphony would have modulated
by now.   The piano's entry gives us the feeling of a lost child found
again; it appears a little lustreless after this scintillating introduction.
The solo comes forward in the company of a rather undistinguished
theme which remains inconclusive and loses itself in the virtuosity
that follows it (ex. 221).   That follows it, or rather that would follow
it if only the irrepressible woodwind allowed.   For, hardly does the
piano return to the tonic than they disturb the peace with drum taps of
(i).   The piano tries to start off again, and again they interrupt it;
this happens several times until the unescapable victory of the piano
silences them.   Even so, once its rockets have carried us into the key
of the dominant, the rhythm of (i) begins again, this time in the strings,
beneath a solo trill; its infectiousness conquers the piano and only
when everyone, solo, strings and wind, has surrendered to it is it
possible to get rid of the obsession; whereupon the piano forges ahead,
sole master, in a passage of descending scales.

The second subject is launched by the strings and quickly taken up
by the wind (ex. 222); the piano repeats it, decorates it and at once
forgets it to surrender to virtuosity.   But the orchestra has a better
memory.   Whilst the solo runs up and down in scales, wind and
strings answer each other with the fragment (ii) of ex. 222 (ex. 223);
then arises in the bass the polyphonic figure (cf. ex. 219), lengthened
and broadened, whose appearance marks the first union between the
two elements in this rondo (ex. 224).   And in it, as in the bravura
runs of the right hand, there triumphs the figure of the descending
scale, so prominent in this movement.

After a pause on a dominant seventh and a cadenza, the piano

Ex. 220

Ex. 221   Ex. 222

Ex. 223

Ex. 224

Ex. 225

Ex. 226

Ex. 227

Ex. 228

resumes the refrain. It gives out each half alone, then decorates it
while the orchestra repeats it. Whereupon, with the same suddenness
as the basses just now, first fiddles, flute and hautboy dive into a
fugato. The subject is the same (ex. 219), but this time it is underlined by a counter-subject, the little rhythmic figure (i) from the refrain
(ex. 225). The counterpoint is as closely knit as at first but richer, for
a certain independence in the second hautboy and second bassoon
raises at times the number of parts to six. Moreover, the entry is
not in F major but in the dusky key of D minor, and this, as well as
the presence of the counter-subject, gives the passage extreme vigour.
The whole power of action of this concerto is condensed into these
thirty-five bars. Their swing is irresistible; they are no longer a
regular fugal exposition, calling its parts on parade in turn in the same
key; they are a series of inroads, at varying intervals and in diverse
keys: D minor, A minor, G minor, C minor and, in the last place, B
flat major, of ex. 225, which its transposition into the minor has made
ferocious, and of its counter-subject with its feverish rhythm. When,
in comparative silence, violas and first bassoon make a last entry in
B flat, the atmosphere clears without the flight losing any of its strength;
at this moment, the mark drops to *piano* and the solo instrument adds
its part to the orchestra.

But at the same time it breaks up the game; it will not subordinate
itself to the contrapuntal discipline and insists on playing as a soloist.
The fiery flight continues none the less; in double phrases, where
tumbling arpeggios in the right hand answer sinuous, climbing octaves
in the bass, we rise one degree at a time, whilst the ♩♩ ♪𝄾♩♩ ♪𝄾
of the strings are there to protest against this expropriation and to
keep alive the threat of the expropriated (ex. 226). Nevertheless, the
piano's return to D minor and the substitution of the polyphonic
subject for these drum taps brings the enemies closer, all the more as
the piano, giving up its arpeggios-versus-octaves, consents to follow
the line of the subject, embellishing it with a sweeping gesture (ex.
227). Little by little, its fierceness is tamed, the landscape becomes
familiar, and without a shock, almost without noticing it, we are back
at the piano trill, accompanied by (i) of the first couplet. The
recapitulation is at work and already half over; the lightning course of
dramatic counterpoint has swept the rondo out of its boundaries and
made it skip the first subject, ex. 221, and land at the beginning of the
solo passage before ex. 222.

After this, the third couplet reproduces fairly accurately the first, keeping of course to the tonic. We recognize the second subject, ex. 222, and the return in the bass of the polyphonic figure, quieter, and in F major; then, to prepare the *strepitoso* which is to usher in the cadenza, Mozart introduces a superb passage on a tonic pedal, the grandest moment, after the *fugatos*, in the rondo. Its elements are a two-bar figure in the piano, rising degree by degree, a syncopated motion in the strings, a divided figure, derived from (i), shared between hautboys and bassoons, and a strengthening of the pedal in the treble by the flute (ex. 228). The mighty wave swells, breaks, and its crest crumbles into falling arpeggios, still urged on by the alternating ♩♩ ♪ᵧ of the orchestra. The piano is silent and a short preparatory passage brings in the cadenza (K. 624, no. 30). It is worthy of the rest. Ex. 224 opens it, but instead of keeping within the two octaves of the original, with a magnificent sweep it drops three and a half and climbs up again a part of them; then, starting high up, the right hand travels down four and a half octaves and reascends in broken sevenths. Then it is the turn of the other subject, figure (i); only its rhythm survives, and there arises out of it a quivering passage based on an upper tonic pedal, which is more like the preparation than the conclusion of a cadenza; with its cluckings in every other bar, it reminds one of a cackling hen, one of those imitations of nature beloved of French harpsichord composers. The cadenza ends on a trill in the right hand and a recall of (i) in the left hand, a reminder of a passage in the first and third couplets.

The conclusion of the rondo consists in a last return of the refrain with a triplet accompaniment which makes it limp comically—the equivalent of the change to 6-8 which sometimes closes 2-4 rondos[1]— and in a much lengthened version of the opera buffa motif, ex. 220, the chatterings of which make this end sound like a council of magpies.

In this very fine rondo, with a conjuror's skill, Mozart, from a subject with dry outlines and a skimpy rhythm, has drawn a broadly wrought movement, with powerful curves, ample, generous contours, a great variety of rhythm and a single, well-sustained inspiration. The allegro was contained, on the whole, in the first bars of the solo; the main elements of the movement were there, a dotted march rhythm and a triplet accompaniment. But no one, on hearing the refrain of the finale, would divine the splendour that is to follow.

---

[1] Cf. K.449, 451, 491.

And yet, the bustling three-quaver rhythm which characterizes it belongs to almost the whole movement; the first *fugato* is the only important section whence it is absent, and the subject itself, whole or in part, provides not only the refrain but also a fugal counter-subject and accompaniment figures.

The fieriness of its motion sweeps the virtuosity along with it. There is not a single bar of idle passage work. Not once do we mark time while the piano performs its flourishes; scales, arpeggios, broken octaves advance, always making for a goal; everything moves forward and one never goes round in circles as one does sometimes in concertos, even Mozart's. We are borne along by a hurricane of undeniable strength.

This strength is not that of passion and the movement's heat is not the heat of the soul. Big and strong though it be, this rondo is not a deep movement. The heat it radiates springs from the speed of its progress, from the distances it covers at one go from top to bottom of the keyboard, the incessant clashes between the fragments of the refrain, the speed of the counterpoint, too, and its closely knit texture. Though it does not avoid *fortissimos*, it is not through noise that it seeks to make our blood tingle but through the use of a rhythm productive of a sure and immediate response—that muscular rhythm of three strokes followed by a rest, one of the most Dionysiac. It is the piling up and the simultaneous attack of all these siege batteries that makes the second *fugato* so breathless and so apparently dramatic a moment—this, and not the presentation of any inner conflict. For in no movement of this concerto is there conflict. Though at times its goal seems to coincide with that of music that is truly passionate, though its effect on us appears to be the same, its starting-point is far from that of passion. It is but acting, and we recognized on our way formal details taken from comedy; it mimics anger and ferocity, and successfully, but this is only a game and it leaves no disturbance or bitterness in its wake.

This is a game, we say; and such a judgement is indeed true of the whole work, even of the touching minor theme in the allegretto, an imitation and not the expression of a melancholy mood. But it is so near in its *tempo* and its form to its stormy successor that we wonder whether the game is not being played "on a volcano". This apparently passionate movement of the rondo Mozart was to rediscover two months later, strangely similar, but under the sway of true passion.

For the concerto in F, so springlike and so carefree, coincides more than once with that in D minor. The choice of the key is itself a sign of kinship and one should perhaps not be surprised if here and there a melodic line or a harmonic progression in the first recalls the second, for the space of a flash, to the listener who knows both of them. But it is impossible to think of a merely fortuitous encounter when one hears the *development* of the first movement open with the same chord and the same piano passage as the fiery presto which interrupts the andante of the D minor. The only notable difference between the two passages is that of the key: A minor in one, G minor in the other (ex. 229; allegro of K.459). It is just a moment of physical excitement, one may say, in the concerto in F, and a traditional minor modulation at the beginning of the second solo; but to one who knows the D minor, these few bars appear pregnant with foreboding. They are the warning of the storm, the loosing of which will be recounted two months later.

And over the finale, too, the work that is to come casts at times its shadow. There is nothing remarkable, no doubt, in that the *tempo*, 2-4, is the same in both rondos. But a premonitory spirit of the D minor passes undeniably over the second *fugato*; these thirty-five bars would not be out of place in its finale; one feels it instinctively and a closer glance shows us that a subject in the D minor, ex. 247, is but the inversion of the *fugato* theme, ex. 225. In spite of the absolutely contrary characters of the two works, somewhere in the depths of Mozart's soul they draw from a common spring and beneath their contrasts a kinship unites them. We have linked up the concerto in F with the "fashionable virtuoso" concertos of 1784 and it does indeed wear their livery and walk with their gait; yet one wonders at times whether it has not something in common with its austere successor?

This fifteenth concerto is the third and last of those Mozart wrote in F. The first was the trifling concerto for three pianos, where the composer's personality counted for little; the second, the graceful, shy work of 1782 which had tried before all to be acceptable to the Viennese public to which it was introducing its author. The third alone is representative.

The key of F, in Mozart, like that of G, is one of those whose character is least distinctive. The composer does not often have recourse to it for important works. Only four other compositions in F are comparable to this concerto: a violin sonata, K.377; a piano duet sonata, K.397; a piano (two hands) sonata without a finale,

K.533[1] and his last string quartet, K.590. One might add to this list the first fantasia for mechanical organ, K.594, consisting in an F major allegro between two F minor adagios. It is not enough for one to speak of a "family" of F major works. In this key such important compositions are exceptional, for F major is the key of trifles —divertimentos, light sonatas and sonatinas, *Musical Jokes*.[2]

It is nevertheless possible to single out likenesses between our concerto and each of these works. With the duet sonata and the fantasia, there is indeed no formal similarity, but both unfold with the same vigour and spirit. The frequent triplets in the accompaniment and the important counterpoint in the allegro of K.533 connect it with the first and third movements of the concerto, and in the quartet we recognize, not only (in the finale) the spirits and the vigour and also the use of counterpoint, but also (in the allegro) a similar theme.[3]

The only one of these movements which shows a true analogy in form and inspiration with our concerto is the allegro of the violin sonata. There, as in the first movement of the concerto, triplets preponderate; starting as the simple accompaniment of a bare, wiry theme, they end by clothing its nakedness as ivy adorns and blurs the outlines of a leafless tree. There too, in the main subject, we meet again the motif of the downward scale and the silhouette of ex. 219. The allegro of the sonata, like that of the concerto, has really only one subject whose rhythm and melodic line, fostered by the accompanying triplets, pervade the whole movement. In it, also, a certain detachment with, in addition, a touch of austerity and dryness foreign to the concerto, is expressed with a lively, muscular rhythm, and both movements keep constantly on the go. That of the sonata is a true *moto perpetuo* and recalls the finale as well as the allegro of the concerto. The sonata is the elder by three years; its allegro is, as it were, a first version of the concerto's and has something of the stiffness and severity of first versions; three years later, when the same inspiration

---

[1] It has always been published (except in the *Gesamtausgabe*) with the rondo, K.494, as finale, a movement which it is best to omit for it is unworthy of the other two and has no connexion with them. A counsel of laziness may have urged Mozart to allow them to be published together, if perchance he be responsible for it.

[2] This is not so with the most interesting and strongly characterized group of the F major andantes, in 3-4 or 6-8 time, of works in C major; it comprises a dozen movements, some of which are among the finest in Mozart; by its beat and its inspiration, the *Recordare* of the *Requiem* also belongs to it.

[3] Solo subject in the allegro of the concerto; second subject in the quartet.

revisits Mozart, it puts on more flesh, rounds itself off, and adds good temper and freedom from care to its original liveliness and strength.

The few warning signs of the concerto in D minor we fancied we found in this concerto would not justify our skipping two important compositions of the beginning of 1785 as we passed from one work to the next. They are the quartets in A and C, the last born of the six dedicated to Haydn.

After the effervescence of 1784, the quiet and inward nature of the quartet in A indicates a withdrawal into himself on the part of the young master. It is planned on a broad scale; in his chamber music, its dimensions are equalled only by the quintets in C and G minor. Its *developments* are true workings-out and not *fantasias*; its finale is a climax and not a relaxation. Its andante, a theme and variations, ends with a fine coda which, instead of winding up the movement, rises above it, meditating on what goes before and interpreting it in a detached spirit worthy of the epilogues of Beethoven. The writing is closer than in the other quartets and the bravura passages for the first violin, turning up regularly towards the end of the exposition and recapitulation as in a concerto, are absent.

The winding, chromatic themes of the allegro and the finale correspond to a state of calm after suffering, almost of resignation, of which we caught a glimpse in the concerto and rondo K.414 and 386, and which will be henceforward the character of his works in A. This after-taste of suffering is somewhat saddening but, after the works of the previous year, what an answer this quartet gives to those who maintain that Mozart has only one string to his lyre!

The inspiration of the quartet in C is less original. A certain vivacity appears to connect it with the compositions of 1784, but it belongs rather to the same family as the C major concerto which follows it two months later. It is the earliest and least imposing of the series of works in C which includes the two concertos, K.467 and 503, the quintet and the *Jupiter* symphony. Next to the over-celebrated introduction, its most notable features are the threatening shadows that return several times in the first movement and in the trio of the minuet.

These quartets open a fresh page. The period of the "fashionable virtuoso" is closed; let us attempt to sum it up. Surface qualities of brilliance, attractiveness, colour, sparkle, proud bearing, predominate over intimacy and inwardness of feeling. This does not prevent these works, in contrast to his former *galant* compositions, from being highly personal; only, they reveal Mozart's personality at a moment when it does not draw in upon itself, when it expresses itself, on the contrary, most fully by spreading its gifts lavishly on all sides. This "revelation" reaches its highest point in the *Hunt* quartet and the concerto in F, works which speak of joy and strength.

Side by side with this, however, the deeper life goes on. We catch a glimpse of it in the andantes of some concertos, of the sonata and quartet in B flat; but the veil is completely torn aside only in the C minor sonata.

Two strains of thought thus run through the works of these ten months—one, brilliant and external; the other, intimate, sometimes restless, subordinate to the first, but ready to reveal itself unmistakably. One speaks to the actual public; the other turns away from it, or dreams of an ideal one.

PART IV

1. *The Sixteenth Concerto: K.466 in D minor*

CONCERTO NO. 16 IN D MINOR (K.466)[1]
Finished February 10th, 1785
    Allegro: C
    Romanza: ¢ (in B flat)
    Rondo (Allegro assai): ¢
Orchestra: Strings; flute, two hautboys, two bassoons, two horns, two
    trumpets, two kettledrums.

WHEN, in our childhood, we asked to have the same stories told us again and again till we knew every detail of them by heart, no familiarity could ever dull the poignancy of certain moments and their power to stir us. As they drew nearer, our hearts beat faster; we held our breath and wished we might stay the march of time, so as to derive thereby a more prolonged savour from the expectations of their coming.

In as well-known a story as that of Mozart's music, the coming of the D minor concerto is such a moment. Just as we approached with emotion the awaited episode in the childish story, so, when we turn the corner of 1784 and come into sight of this concerto, our excitement rises. Despite the grand spectacle of the year that is just past, our emotion increases, the story becomes more stirring and more full of colour, and there enters into it a sense of adventure and heroism, hitherto unexperienced.

For the birth of the D minor is one of the great stages in its author's musical journey and, at the time he reaches it, the work is one of his newest, one of those that confound most thoroughly those people who still imagine that Mozart was all his life content with following beaten paths. It refutes those who have it that his celebrated "beauty of style", his "perfect form" are but the deftness of the craftsman repeating day after day the same gestures, of the runner who, by dint of always following the same course, knows every inch of it, never stumbles and can find blindfolded the shortest way from one point to the next.

---

[1] *Gesamtausgabe*, no. 20.

At the end of the last chapter, we said that two currents of thought flowed through his works in 1784: one, sparkling and shallow, the other, deeper and more intimate. This second current triumphs over the former in the concertos of 1785 and 1786, not by cutting it out but by absorbing it. How could we characterize it more precisely? We found easily enough the appropriate epithets for the group of the 1784 concertos; these latter had a marked family likeness; but it is much harder to describe in one word the great concertos of which the D minor is the eldest. When we say: intimacy, depth, introspection, we exhaust the words equally applicable to all of them. For in addition to the general difference there is another difference between the concertos of 1785-6 and those of the previous year. Not only was the thought of the latter less inward, but each one of them was less unlike the others. Here, however, between the six of the next two years, diversity is far wider. From the D minor to the C major, the E flat, the A, the distances covered are much greater than between the 1784 concertos. Generally speaking, then, the thought grows deeper and the works have more sharply defined personalities. It was still possible to speak of a series in connexion with the previous concertos; it is not so with these.

Such considerations make us place these works at the summit of Mozart's concertos. One cannot make a selection, even a small one, of what is most valuable and most characteristic in his production, of what is most living and most his own, without bringing in every concerto of these two years. With as much right as his three great symphonies, his finest quartets and quintets, his best operas, his C minor and *Requiem* masses, the concerto in D minor and the five that follow it may claim to represent him at his highest point of creative power.

On February 10th, 1785, wrote Leopold Mozart to his daughter, there was performed in the Mehlgrube an "excellent piano concerto by Wolfgang . . . When we arrived, the copyist was still copying it out and your brother had not yet had time to play the rondo because he had to revise the copies".[1] The concerto in question is the D minor.

Whatever differences we may have noticed between one concerto and another, never was the contrast as brutal as between the F major work and this one which was separated from it by only two months.

---

[1] Letter of February 14th, 1785.

We leap at one bound from one world to another totally different. There is no longer any trace of those march or dance rhythms, those opera buffa closes, those good-humouredly symmetrical strains which made up the framework of the F major concerto; had we to discover, in the year that is just past, a counterpart to the new work, it is in the D major that we should find the obsession, insistence, straining, the pursuit of a single idea, which strike us in the opening bars as strongly as the unconcern of the previous concerto had done. But the kinship would remain distant and the D minor contains too much that is foreign to the D major for us to bring them together.

I. It is generally imagined that the opening tuttis of classical concertos are all alike in their general lines, all fulfil exactly the same functions with regard to the rest of the movement and show only minor differences from one to the other. To give out the main themes and outline the main paths along which the rest of the allegro is to pass: such would appear to be the task of all first tuttis.

This simplifies the matter too much. Far from all of them being alike, in Mozart alone two types can be clearly distinguished. The first one—the type which the usual description of a tutti suits best —gives out the chief themes on which the movement is built, in the order in which they are to return later. It is the summary, the *argument* of what one is about to hear. The concerto in D, K.451, is a perfect example of this kind; those of the E flat, G and B flat, K.449, 453 and 456, are also *arguments*, but rather less complete.

In the second type, on the other hand, the tutti is a mere introduction. It gives out the first subject, then busies itself mainly with secondary elements which either do not reappear or prove to be subordinated to other subjects not included in it. The beginning of the concerto in C, K.415, is an extreme example of the introduction tutti; those of the concertos in B flat and F, K.450 and 459, belong to the same category but stand less aloof from what follows. This second type is less organic and ushers in a movement of looser form; the *argument* tutti precedes a more unified movement.

The fine tutti which opens the D minor concerto is an *argument*. It lets us hear all the themes of the movement save the solo introduction and the second part of the second subject. Not only does what follows not add anything essential; the very character of the whole movement is expressed in the first fifteen bars. This, the most personal concerto we have met hitherto, proclaims its originality in the first subject itself. None of the singing themes here, with well-marked rhythms and clean articulations, with which *galant* concertos habitu-ally begin, including most of Mozart's, but one same note throbbing against the beat, whilst, under its monotonous pulsation, a menacing bass emphasizes each bar with an uprush of three little notes—a formula usually expressive of passion and threatening. Repeated notes, piano, with a syncopated rhythm, and the formula of the rising triplet: with these two elements common to all the music of the time is built up this opening, one of the most personal and the most powerful in Mozart.

Out of this misty background a melodic outline arises and is at once swallowed up; after a further bar of repeated notes the figure begins again one degree higher (ex. 230; bars 1 to 5). Then, cutting out the melodic motif, with heightening stress, thrusting home ever more swiftly and more truly, whilst the woodwind from horns to flute one after another add their colour to that of the strings, and still *piano*, the phrase rises, degree by degree, to the octave, where the strain is relaxed somewhat and whence we climb down again to the starting-point (bars 5 to 15).[1]

The *fortissimo* then breaks loose.

On analysis, one recognizes the old *galant* formula of the soft beginning followed by the sudden *forte* which opens so many of Mozart's concertos, but renewed with genius. For here, instead of driving ahead with a fresh subject,[2] the movement retraces its steps.[3] The syncopated murmur breaks out into a *tremolando* of semi-quavers; the rumbling triplets turn into flashes of lightning and rend the instru-mental web, springing from bass to treble with gathering speed;[4] woodwind and horns plunge into the midst of the tumult, through which one perceives, punctuating each first beat, the metallic note of the trumpets, like armour glinting through the depths of a forest. The working out unfolds with alternating violence and pathos, with-out ever abating its intensity, and concludes with a five-bar close on the dominant, another conventional gesture into which Mozart infuses life by making it expressive of passion (bars 16 to 32).

---

[1] As this concerto is so well known we give fewer quotations of it than of the others and we confine ourselves as a rule to referring the reader to the bar numbers.

[2] Cf. K.414, 415, 450, 453, 537.

[3] The concertos, K.456, 459, 467 and 491 also repeat the first bars forte after a soft opening.

[4] The kinship of these bars with those that open the Queen of Night's second aria in the *Magic Flute* will be recognized.

Ex. 229

Ex. 230

Ex. 231   Ex. 232

Ex. 233   Ex. 234

Ex. 235   Ex. 236

Ex. 237

Ex. 238

The second subject, in the relative major, is shared by flute and hautboys, supported by bassoons and fiddles; it opens with a series of questions and answers, in contrasted rhythms (ex. 231; bars 33 to 34), rising each time by one degree, then breaks into a chain of short sighs which the fiddles send backwards and forwards beneath the held notes of the hautboys (ex. 232; bars 39 to 40); these bring us back into D minor.

Again passion proclaims itself. The powerful, agitated passage that follows (bars 44 to 71) is based on a rising figure of great strength (ex. 233; bars 44 to 45) and on a wailing one (ex. 234; bars 49 to 50), against which beat falling arpeggios (ex. 235; bars 48 to 49). The general line is that of rise and fall which characterized the first bars of the allegro; the forces rush to the attack, withdraw and start afresh, with alternating *fortes* and *pianos*. The music surges with the frenzy of a soul driven on by irresistible passion. Then, suddenly, on a suspended cadence, the rhythm breaks off, the mark falls to *piano* and a few sighs in the violins conclude the fiery passage and announce the closing subject.

This speaks of peace—a peace of desolation, almost of despair. Flexuous and caressing, its rhythm is freer than usual with Mozart; it unfolds in three fragments with one same movement of rise and fall, over a most graceful and expressive counterpoint (ex. 236; bars 71 to 74).

For many who write on Mozart, there appears to be no greater compliment than the word "Beethovenian". When a critic is at a loss for terms to express his admiration for a passage he declares it "worthy" or, more often, "*almost* worthy of Beethoven". Even Abert scatters his pages with, "fast Beethovensche" which would lead one to believe that the Bonn master is the sole paragon and that perfection can be attained only inasmuch as one resembles him.

This doubtful compliment, which sees in our composer an inferior variety of Beethoven, is seldom deserved. If "fast Beethovensche" pages abound in Haydn and Clementi, they are rare in Mozart. Many pages, likewise, of the young Beethoven recall Clementi and Haydn; very few recall Mozart and these are precisely the least Beethovenian ones. At distant intervals, a detail in one may make us think of the other, and we have ourselves occasionally used the word "Beethovenian" when speaking of Mozart. But they are only passing moments. Here, nevertheless, we have a whole movement over which there passes unmistakably a breath that heralds Beethoven.[1]

---

[1] At a time when Beethoven's glory eclipsed Mozart's, this concerto was the only one of its composer's which was commonly performed.

What is like Beethoven and is uncommon in Mozart is the persist-
ence of the strife and passion.   Usually, with him, a passionate outburst is followed by relaxation and a softened, sentimental answer,
the alternation of passion and sentiment, of tension and relaxation, is
typical and frequent;[1] it is thus, and not in a continuous flow, that the
feeling progresses in his passionate movements.   With Beethoven,
on the contrary, the struggle is carried on relentlessly; no rest, no intrusion of another mood comes to interrupt it; no appeasement comes to
break the effort until it has achieved victory.

Now, we find precisely this in the D minor concerto.   The easing
off in the fifteenth bar was a return to the beginning rather than a
break or a slackening in the strain; the silence which parted the fiery
close from the second subject was dramatic and brought no relief.
And from bar 44 (ex. 233) to bar 68, the urge is constant and the
passion advances, not in a series of forward and backward movements,
but in an unbroken flood of increasing power, in a way unparalleled
in Mozart outside this concerto but representative of Beethoven.   The
only truly Mozartian feature is the sudden drop in the sixty-ninth
bar and the despairing gentleness of the conclusion (ex. 236).   Relent-
less struggle, a piling and speeding up instead of alternation in the
progress of the passion make this allegro a work of Mozart's which
may rightly be termed Beethovenian.[2]

One awaits the solo entry with some anxiety.   What does it hold
in store?   So dramatic a work cannot belie its promises to the point
of returning to its start and repeating the beginning of the tutti as if
nothing had happened since, as if its world was as serene and timeless
as that of K.456.   How will it incorporate the new element into the
substance of the drama?   In what shape will it bring back the first
subject?   Our expectation is great.

We are not disappointed.   With the corresponding passages in
the C minor and C major, K.503, the piano's first words constitute
the most moving solo entry in all Mozart's concertos.   The piano's
appearance gives us the feeling, not of an instrument added to many
others, but of a personality substituting itself for the anonymous
orchestral mass; it fills us with the same awe as a human voice rising

---

[1] Openings of K.457 (i), 550 (iv), 388 (i), etc.

[2] Even the piano writing has two features uncommon in Mozart and typical
of Beethoven: much use of the lowest registers and wide spacing.   In our
opinion, despite the absence of formal likenesses, there is kinship between
this allegro and the first movement of Beethoven's D minor sonata, op. 31, II.

suddenly from a body of instruments. Taking up the thread of the discourse where the tutti had broken off, the piano gives out a theme similar in feeling to the last but even freer and more wandering. Though written out in bars it has a recitative character which the performance should retain; to play it too strictly is to empty it of its soul. Three times it climbs and falls back, with increasing languor; it rises one last time, breaks up completely and streams away in semi-quavers to a woodwind accompaniment (bars 77 to 78, and 88; ex. 237).[1]

Its impetus once exhausted, the strings take up again the throbbing of the first bars and the piano almost at once adds the excitement of its semi-quavers. It quickly leaves behind the rumblings of the orchestra and, shortening the exposition, reaches with one leap the cadence preceding the second subject (bars 91 to 114) and this subject itself (ex. 231).

Making use of a favourite device, Mozart now casts his parts differently, giving the piano what had formerly belonged to the flute. A short passage introduces the key of the relative major and leads to a fresh subject distinguished from the rest of the movement by its singing and almost blithe nature (ex. 238). Expounded by the piano with a witty addition of the strings, it is repeated by the wind whilst the piano decorates it with a scale (bars 127 to 143).

In the key of F major the air clears but the movement loses none of its vigour. The thirty solo bars which follow let loose a torrent of passion and energy, and the tension is no less than before, even though the struggle and anguish are less apparent. The piano speaks almost alone. With the scales, arpeggios and broken octaves which are the usual elements of its speech, it mingles memories of its fiery ascent, ex. 233. Twice its course leads to the trill of F major; twice it starts afresh, with increased impetus, as if carried away despite itself beyond all appointed bounds. The section is longer than the usual bravura passages which close first solos, but never savours of padding; there is no vain display of skill; the piano, in its turn and to the best of its ability, carries on the work started by the orchestra.

After so long a silence the force with which the tutti enters again appears even greater than usual. It repeats and transposes into F the

---

[1] There is a great likeness of mood between this movement and Philip Emmanuel Bach's magnificent D minor concerto (Wotquenne, no. 17; unpublished) which also opens with a stormy tutti, even more raging than this one, followed by a cembalo entry in a quiet, elegiac tone, with a new rhythm.

passage which, in the first tutti, preceded the vigorous close,[1] then, leaving out the close itself, skips to ex. 236, a subject which Mozart considers particularly important, for he seldom gives out his concluding themes at the end of a first solo (bars 174–93).

A glance back over this exposition justifies our calling the first tutti an *argument*. The piano has expanded its message; it has made the intention clearer; but, apart from the first strain and the singing theme in F major, it has brought nothing new. As for the orchestra, each time it had to speak alone, it just repeated its first words; moreover, its part was smaller than in the previous concertos; as if it felt that after its first tutti it had nothing further to say, it drew aside and let the piano go over in its own way the paths already opened.

The dramatic temper of the work was obvious at the start, but hitherto there has been the announcement of a drama rather than a drama itself. Now we penetrate into the heart of the conflict.

To the concluding subject there joins on quite naturally the solo recitative, ex. 237. This return to the beginning of the exposition is a feint.[2] The times, indeed, are changed. The solo will no longer speak alone and in the short struggle about to open the parts will be shared out equally between piano and orchestra. The latter will have the threatening subject, ex. 230; the former, the strain with which it made its bow, ex. 237, and virtuosity.

Twice does the piano raise its wandering song, first in F major, the key where the tutti had stopped, then in G minor, and each time with changes which alter its meaning. Twice do the instruments answer it with the rumbling theme from the opening, as if they were seeking to lead it towards a fuller utterance (bars 192–220).

The second time, they land in E flat and in this optimistic key the piano re-enters with a third variation of its theme. But the triumph of this subject is short-lived. Hardly is it finished when the piano sweeps down into the bass and forsakes it completely. Three times

---

[1] Mozart remembered this entry (bars 175–8) in Fiordiligi's aria in the first act of *Cosi fan tutti*; the words of the passage are an expression of constancy in a tone of indignation:

"E potria la morte sola
Far che cangi affetto il cor."

The key is the same in both passages and the notes almost identical.

[2] The plan of starting the *development* with the solo introduction of the exposition and of omitting this introduction in the recapitulation occurs again in Mozart only in his other minor concerto, K.491; it is used by Beethoven in his violin concerto.

over (subjects in three strains or repeating themselves three times are among Mozart's most authentic signatures) the solo scales the keyboard in arpeggios of the common chord and comes tumbling down it in diminished sevenths, rising from E flat to F minor, from F minor to G minor, while in the sky rent with lightning the full body of strings re-echo the wild triplets of the first subject (ex. 239)—a most dramatic reduction of it to its simplest shape.[1] The piano forges ahead, with hands widely spaced; then, in one last torrent of fire, the flood streams from top to bottom and gathers in the bass (bars 247–50), whence, with momentarily weakened but still unbroken spirit (the sudden *forte* of the last bar before the reprise bears witness to this), regains the starting-point of the movement by the shortest road and with the simplest means (ex. 240).

The second subject, ex. 231, appears unchanged[2] but the singing theme, ex. 238, is now given out in D minor, a key we shall leave no more. The long solo that follows it (bars 318–55) corresponds in the main to that of the exposition; we meet again the threefold trill and ex. 233, but the change of mode is enough to infuse it with a very different spirit and the figuring of the runs is also new. All this part has a vigorous, striving quality which persists with growing intensity till the end, but not the angry nature of the development; it is indeed the issue of the movement, but an issue of despair; the fight continues, but we know now there can be no triumph. The ray of hope in the singing theme, ex. 238, has died out with the theme's return in the minor, and it is to win exhaustion, not victory, that the struggle goes on. These thirty bars and those of the *development* are amongst the finest instances of expressive virtuosity that the music of the genre affords; Mozart attains perfect formal beauty thanks to the very might of his passion.[3]

Mozart has left no cadenzas for this concerto which he composed, as well as those that follow, for himself and which he no doubt never taught to pupils. But there is one by the young Beethoven

---

[1] Cf. the *più allegro* of the C minor fantasia, K.375. It is tempting to play all this with a shattering *fortissimo*. But Mozart, contrary to what our taste would expect, has marked bars 232–52 *piano*, at least in the tutti.

[2] This is the only example in Mozart of a second subject appearing all three times in the same key.

[3] "The most permanently satisfying art is that which arrives at formal beauty as a consequence of intense preoccupation with something else, as impassioned speech tends to be metrical, rather than by deliberate organization" (*Times Lit. Supp.*, article on Raphael, January 27th, 1927).

Ex. 239

Ex. 240

Ex. 241

Ex. 242

Ex. 243

which is a shrewd commentary on the movement and which, both
Beethovenian and Mozartian in character, corroborates with unexpected emphasis what we said just now on the nature of the work.
One would like to hear it more often and one regrets that in the
recording by His Master's Voice the soloist should have inserted instead of it a cadenza full of commonplace virtuosity which, far from
throwing light upon the movement or summing it up, is just an
intrusion.

The end has not the perfunctory brevity of certain conclusions of
first allegros, where one feels that after the executant's display all
has been said. Some thirty bars long, it repeats more tersely the fiery
passage (bars 44–71) which, in the initial tutti, followed the second
subject; relieved of the repetitions which had emphasized its energy,
its wiry vigour is admirably suited to an epilogue. It is followed by
the concluding subject, ex. 236, whose languidness, after this last
spurt, sounds even more desolate. It has already closed two sections;
it cannot suffice to close the whole movement, so, in a short coda,
under the weary, drooping lines of the upper parts, Mozart calls up
in the bass one last echo of the "menacing" triplets which thus run
through the movement from end to end.[1]

Thought is so closely united to form in this allegro that there is
little to add about the latter. The concentrated and passionate inspiration imposes on the movement a strict unity. The first tutti contains
only important elements and it contains nearly all of them. The
development links up with the tradition of thematic *developments*,
not after the fashion of movements which play with secondary figures[2]
or bring in new motifs, but like those that are concerned with only
primary elements.[3] It is a summary, expressing the soul of the work at
its purest, not by freeing it from the shackles of form like certain
fantasia developments, but by confining itself to the use of significant
material.

In the recapitulation, Mozart is confronted with the problem which
confronts all concertos whose opening tuttis are *arguments*: how to
make it more than the repetition of the first solo. Here, the com-
pulsory return to the minor is itself a transforming feature; moreover,

---

[1] Note in these last bars the Mozartian "fluttering seconds" figure. Its
presence gives this ending a certain likeness with a movement whose inspiration is close to that of this concerto: the adagio for piano in B minor, K.540.

[2] K.449, 537.

[3] K.271, 491, 503, 595.

the great bravura passage at the end is remodelled and the coda adds novelty to the conclusion.

The roles of solo and tutti are well differentiated. On the whole, alternation or opposition preponderates over collaboration. The message of the movement is imparted first of all by the tutti, then repeated in its own tongue by the solo. The *development*, after a passage of contrasts, affords a few bars of interplay, then the solo again acts alone. In the last part, the solo predominates till the cadenza, and the eloquent conclusion falls to the orchestra. Save for the *development*, the only moments of interplay are in the second and third subjects, exs. 231 and 238, and especially the fine passages where the piano joins the orchestra to sustain or stimulate it in the main subject (bars 95–104, 261–7). And indeed, does not opposition rather than collaboration become the expression of a conflict?

II. In Mozart's works in minor keys, some contrast between allegro and andante is almost *de rigueur*.[1] Here, the contrast is complete. If anything in music depicts the moment when after a storm the sun shows its face and drives away the last shreds of cloud, the theme which opens this concerto's second movement does it. Nothing more fragrant and more springlike exists in all Mozart. There still abides in the air a slight humidity left by the storm and the face of the sky, though calm once more, is glimpsed through a hanging veil of moisture. Everything has taken on a brighter hue; everything revives after the tempest (ex. 241).

The movement which it ushers in has no *tempo* mark but is clearly andante. It is headed: *Romanza*, a term which does not connote any precise form and is given to any slow movement, rondo or variations, the character of whose chief theme recalls the "romance" of vocal music. This one is a spacious rondo. Like all concerto romances, it begins with the solo, and this gives it a personal and lyrical character, as if the composer himself was before us and was baring his heart. A summary will show its plan clearly.

Refrain: Main subject—tonic—piano, then tutti (1–16).
            Subsidiary subject, followed by the second half of the
                main subject—piano, then tutti (17–36).
            Codetta—tutti (36–9).

---

[1] The adagio non troppo of the G minor quintet is an exception.

1st couplet: Tonic, then dominant; return to tonic—piano, with
tutti accompaniment (40–63).

Codetta of the refrain and transition—piano (63–7).

Refrain: In a shortened form—piano, then tutti (68–83).

2nd couplet: Piano, with important wind accompaniment.

1st subject—double bar and repeat (84–91)—relative
minor.

2nd subject, with return to the 1st (92–107)—tonic,
then relative minor.

Long transition (108–18)—return to the tonic.

Refrain: Main subject—piano (119–26).

Subsidiary subject, as above (127–41).

Codetta (142–6).

Coda: Tutti, then piano, with accompaniment (146–62).

The key is B flat, the sub-dominant of the relative major of D
minor.

In the refrain and first couplet the strings do more work than the
wind; the latter intervene only in order to double the strings in the
fortes. Moreover, when the orchestra plays with the piano, it is
confined to accompanying. In the main theme of the refrain (ex. 241)
we recognize Mozart's "fluttering seconds" and, in the codetta which
closes the refrain and first couplet, the threefold division of a phrase
which is so characteristic of his rhythmical scheme.[1]

The opening of the second couplet affords an astoundingly brutal
contrast with what precedes it. Hitherto, nothing had belied the
smiles of the limpid, ingenuous song with which the romance had
begun. The rest of the refrain and the first couplet had led us through
a sunny and well-watered countryside and we had at length come
back to the refrain. The first half of it is over and has ended, *piano*,
in B flat, when suddenly a *fortissimo* breaks out in strings and solo, on
the chord of G minor; the andante turns into a presto[2] and the solo
sets off with breathless triplets in search of Heaven knows what wild
fancy. Full of anguish and fury, it pursues its quest in treble and bass,
with frequent crossings of the hands, whilst the wind, roused brusquely
from their torpor, follow it and trace out in quavers or crotchets the

---

[1] The solo in the first couplet, especially in bars 48–55, is but an outline;
the pianist must fill it out. (We suggest one of many ways of doing so:
ex. 242.) He must also fill in the chords of the bass in bars 56–67.

[2] No *tempo* mark; the proof of the change is in the note value.

melodic lines implied in its semi-quavers (ex. 243). How deceptive was the peace of the romance and how superficial! Calm in Mozart is neither deep nor lasting. We are plunged again without warning into the mood of the allegro's most feverish moments.[1]

After the double bar, the scoring is more subtle. Now the bassoon doubles the piano treble, now the hautboy doubles its bass, while the other wind sustain. Then, the episode goes back to its beginning (bar 100) and we finish as we had started, on the chord of G minor (bar 108).

A transition of great breadth links up this section with the refrain. Its task is to bring the movement back to its former state of mildness. The piano shows itself at first disinclined to be peaceful; it still pushes on with dishevelled triplets, then travels rapidly from top to bottom of the keyboard, both hands in unison, whilst strings and wind mark the beats; but at length it loses its impetus in a succession of grand bars where the wind and it move up and down in contrary motion from one end of the register to the other, the wind in quavers, the piano in semi-quavers, then in triplet quavers, finally in simple quavers—a transition whose masterly rhythm reminds us of a horseman reining in his steed from gallop to trot, from trot to walk, bridling it without hurting it and without the slightest jerk in its progress (ex. 244).

The piano writing has the same Beethovenian features as in the first movement. The G minor episode covers all registers of the keyboard. In the fine pedal point which constitutes the coda, the hands are well spaced and, as happens sometimes with Beethoven, the intermediate parts are given to the tutti (ex. 245). On the other hand, the Mozartian device of decorating a tutti passage by the piano on its second appearance is used only once (bars 142-5; repeat of bars 32-5).

The presence of the tempestuous episode in the middle of a peaceful romance makes this movement unique. The episode itself is but an extension of the *minore* of French rondos and there is another example in Mozart of a rondo romance broken by a *minor* allegro,[2] but so violent a contrast within a slow movement is unparalleled in his work.

· · · · ·

---

[1] We have already pointed out (p. 300) the likeness between the beginning of this episode and that of the *development* in the allegro of K.459. Leopold wrote to Nannerl that this part was "astonishingly difficult". He added (letter of January 14th, 1786) that it should be played "as swiftly as the possibility of bringing out the tune clearly allows".

[2] In the B flat serenade for wind instruments, K.361.

Ex. 244

Ex. 245

Ex. 246

Ex. 247

Ex. 248

Ex. 249

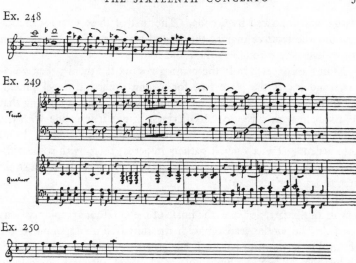

Ex. 250

Ex. 251

III. The finale is one of his few minor key rondos.[1] It is sometimes quoted as a noteworthy example of an irregular rondo. Irregular rondos are indeed not uncommon with him, but this finale is not one of them. It is a sonata rondo very similar in plan to that of the last concerto, where the second couplet—a true *development*—joins on directly to the third without a return of the refrain or of the first subject. Its chief formal distinction is its long coda in the major which follows the last appearance of the refrain.

This is shown by analysis. A general glance, however, gives rather the impression, as in the F major concerto, of a movement in two sections, each of them opening with an important orchestral

[1] The others are those of the piano sonatas in A minor and C minor and of the violin sonata in E minor. An earlier sketch of this rondo, thirty-seven bars long, is published in the André edition of Mozart's works. Cf. Köchel-Einstein, no. 466.

passage, and followed by a coda. The first of these sections modulates into the relative major; the second traverses several keys, then returns half-way through to the tonic.

As in the concerto in F, the piano gives out the theme, then withdraws and leaves the place free for a long orchestral development. The theme is one of the finest refrains in Mozart. It has nothing that we associate with a rondo. Its fieriness brings it into line with the mood of the first movement[1] but its passion is more external and more ardent. Twice over it gathers impetus; then, with some difficulty, breaking away in the treble from the tonic, it starts its last strain three times over (ex. 246).

Thereupon opens a magnificent passage. There is nothing more fiery in all Mozart, not even the finale of the G minor symphony (bars 14–63). The violins lead off with the initial climbing strain of the refrain, but in the fifth bar an E flat proclaims that the music intends modulating. Then, violins, violas and basses throw from one to the other the first fragment of the theme; we pass through, without stopping, the key of the relative major and we land on a dominant close where the quaver motion settles in for good. Without a break (bar 31), second fiddles, then firsts, strike and hold in quavers a dominant pedal which throbs and quivers against the background of woodwind and horns. From this mass a rising movement carries us degree by degree to the tonic where the pedal starts afresh, this time in the basses. One thinks of a swarm of bees whence now one, now another, emerges and re-enters it instantly. The game begins again in the opposite direction, then a theme in long notes, with wide leaps, is heard in the first violins. Finally, a short codetta, just a descending scale, closes the whole thing sharply in the tonic. A part of these riches will not return or will return so altered and in so fugitive a guise that one hardly recognizes it.

The piano begins the first couplet with a subject in a panting rhythm (ex. 247), already used in the *Domine Deus* of the C minor mass. It is a shortened version of ex. 237. It vanishes immediately before an aggressive return of the refrain to which is linked a run which modulates into the relative major (bars 74–92). But the hour for the major mode has not yet struck. The piano discovers another subject (ex. 248), in F minor this time (bars 93–8), dry and incisive, unaccompanied like the preceding one. The wind repeat it, *piano*,

---

[1] It recalls also a rondo for harpsichord in C minor of Philip Emmanuel Bach, Wotquenne 59, no. 4.

and the solo decorates it (bars 99-102). A few bars of virtuosity lead us into F major (103-11), and then, suddenly seized with a fit of loquacity, the piano launches out into a succession of lengthy runs in which the vitality of the fine flight in the earlier bars is scattered and lost (bars 112-39). We end by stopping—for the second time—on the expected trill and the wind give out a fresh theme.

This one is as different from the rest as was ex. 238 from the other themes in the allegro ; in its way, one of Mozart's most typical and most exquisite tunes. It has nothing any longer of what we have experienced hitherto: fire, strife, impetus (ex. 249). The piano takes it up without a change and adds a short passage which closes the first episode. Then it unceremoniously turns its back upon the theme and in three bounds reaches a pause; after which it gives out the refrain.

As in the concerto in F, the second couplet begins with an orchestral passage, based on the first notes of the refrain and transitional in character; it soon stops on the dominant chord of A minor. We enter then the *development* of the sonata rondo, entirely thematic and divided between tutti and piano. Its opening bars recall those of the first couplet: the main subject, ex. 247, is expounded by the piano and followed by an angry reminder of the refrain. Then, starting in the piano and spreading contagiously to the flute and bassoon, the first two bars of the refrain travel in haste through the most various keys, stopping at last in G minor, whilst the piano ravels their course with a figure in broken thirds which climbs up and down with a rhythm independent of theirs (bars 211-29).

And now comes the turn of ex. 247, hitherto so much kept in the background. The piano sounds it in G minor, then, with the flute and hautboy, proceeds to dismember it (bars 241-6), after which appears a rather insignificant fragment (ex. 250), close relation of the seventh and ninth bars of the last subject. This fragment is quickly followed by another, an echo of the bar 240, and the same trio, supported by the bassoon, play about with them for some time, driving them through sundry keys and registers, through which themes and instruments pass like roulette balls through the coloured strips of the croupier's circle. A chance stroke having made them pass into D minor, the game is up, and the piano hastens to make the return to the tonic key definitive (bars 247-71).

Here, a regular rondo would allow us to hear the refrain. But we have met it so often that Mozart leaves it out, as well as ex. 247, which we have just quitted, and begins the third couplet or recapitulation with ex. 248 in D minor, a key from which we shall stir no more

till the cadenza.   In its main lines this couplet reproduces the end of
the first one, but the passage which follows ex. 248 is much shortened.
Ex. 249, transposed into D minor, now shows us its once sunny landscape under cloudy skies; its spritely gait contrasts ironically with the
sadness of the minor mode.   A vigorous set of runs leads to the final
trill.   This is a signal for the orchestra, which rediscovers its initial
fire after this long interval and lets loose the "long notes" theme, with
wide spacings, which had concluded the first tutti (bars 339–46).   It
is but a transition and, like other fiery themes in these concertos,[1]
announces the cadenza.[2]

From now onward we enter new paths; everything is transformed
and the rondo becomes as original as it was at the outset.   The cadenza
concludes without orchestral intervention.   The pianist follows it
up with the refrain, but in the seventh bar breaks off and casts it from
him with a few angry chords (bars 247–54).   One bar of silence,[3]
then the horns sound their bass A, a pedal upon which the basses outline
an accompanying figure.   The hautboys give out the "happy" theme,
ex. 249, in D major, and the piano follows suit.   The whole band
bursts forth with a *ff*, the quaver movement of which (bars 371–6
and 383–8) recalls a passage in the first tutti (bars 33–51); the piano
hits back with flourishes (bars 377–82, 389–94).   Then, the mark
having again dropped to *piano*, over an Alberti bass of the solo's the
woodwind repeat a modified, more winged version of ex. 249, and
the brass round it off with a fanfare (ex. 251).   No louder, the fanfare
re-echoes from brass to woodwind, the piano opposes it with scale
thrusts, and after a further pedal of seven bars, still soft, the strings
rush upward, *ff*, in a joyful scale; and two sudden chords end the
movement.

Such is this rondo of very mixed merits.

Through its general build and its thematic unity (two main themes,
exs. 246 and 249; two subsidiary, exs. 247 and 248), it is a near relative
of the rondo in the last concerto.   But it differs radically from it by
its feeling and in some respects is inferior to its predecessor.

In works of the *galant* period in minor keys, custom allowed the
composer to end his first and last movements on a bright note by
passing into the major just where, in the exposition, he had entered

---

[1] For instance, in the allegro of K.449.

[2] Beethoven's cadenza for this movement is less successful than that for
the allegro.

[3] It must be given its full value.

the key of the relative major. Haydn often acts thus,[1] especially in his finales; Beethoven also.[2] Mozart, however, seldom takes advantage of this facility, and never in his first movements. Twice, a finale of his is entirely in the major,[3] and twice, too, a finale steps into the major in its last bars.[4]

The incentive to such a modulation into the major is emotional rather than formal. It is indeed possible to conclude in several ways a work which begins with a conflict like that which inspired the first movement of this concerto and which is at the origin of many minor key works of the *galant* period—a period, let us remember, when the minor mode is an exception and corresponds to well characterized moods.

The conflict can be brought to an end by triumph, as in Beethoven's C minor symphony and post-Beethovenian works like Brahms's first symphony or that of César Franck.

It may "triumph over sorrow by distraction" (Saint-Foix). As if the composer had hitherto described suffering rather than felt it, he turns his back on it abruptly and sings of a contrary mood. Haydn often appears to do this; Beethoven himself did it at least once, in his F minor quartet, where the intrusion of a coda in the major after a rondo full of anguish is puzzling. The major conclusion of the variations in the C minor serenade is perhaps a parallel instance in Mozart, and his G minor quartet for piano and strings avoids in its finale any allusion to the uneasiness of the allegro; everything has been said on the score of sorrow and the time has come to speak of other matters.[5]

---

[1] C minor symphony; several sonatas and quartets.

[2] Fifth and ninth symphonies; F minor quartet, etc.

[3] G minor quartet; G minor quintet.

[4] C minor serenade and this concerto. In the B minor adagio for piano the change to the major takes place in the last two bars.

[5] The finale of the G minor quintet is one of Mozart's movements about which opinions differ most. Some find it admirable; others condemn it absolutely as trivial and unworthy of the other three, "an unworthy finishing of an unfinishable work" (Dunhill).

It is hard to share such extreme opinions. It does not occupy among Mozart's finales the place of honour which the allegro occupies among his first movements, but neither does it deserve the hard things said of it. Some may prefer a pessimistic conclusion; Mozart himself has left enough such for us to take him seriously when, for once, he concludes a pathetic work on a joyful note. The movement is not a sham ending and it is clearly related to what goes before. There is no more "distraction" than in the concerto.

Continued on p. 328

We have just quoted what Saint-Foix says of Mozart. We ourselves prefer to say that the composer usually has recourse to defeat
or resignation after a work inspired by suffering. Of the chief minor
compositions of his maturity, more than two thirds close on a note
of sorrow or passion or, at most, find peace, formal rather than
emotional, in a major modulation in the last bar.[1] In these examples,
the finale either confirms the feeling of the beginning, with additional
passion,[2] or else comes back to such feeling with weary resignation.[3]

The case is at first sight less clear in the D minor concerto. Is
there just an about-turn here, a purely formal juxtaposition of a major
ending to a work in the minor? Or is there struggle and triumph?
Is the serenity of the end attained by "distraction" or by conquering?

Continued from p. 327

It is true that none of the first three movements announced so soaring a flight;
at the end of the adagio ma non troppo the mood was as sorrow-laden as at
the beginning of the allegro. But the adagio bars which prefaced the finale
prepared us for a change. In the very first, the rhythm spoke of motion
towards something new. Nothing is less static than this introduction, despite
its slowness. The atmosphere is dark but we do not abide in it. We feel
we are passing through a thick wood, or are living the cold, dark hours that
come before dawn. Towards the thirtieth bar we begin to glimpse the light,
when the first violin replaces the falling lament with a questioning and almost
hopeful rising figure. The branches thin out, the spaces of sky grow broader;
and with the refrain of the rondo, to which not only the outline of its theme
but also the rhythm of its accompaniment seem to give wings, we emerge
into open country and rise up into the air. The transition is quick and in
some ten bars we pass from deepest depression to perfect serenity, but a transition there unmistakably is. Mozart knows that neither struggle nor flight
are the only escape from suffering; it sometimes suffices to let time go by, to
pass through sorrow as we pass through a wood and reach the happy meadows
that stretch beyond it.

> "Souffre un moment encor; tout n'est que changement.
> L'axe tourne, mon coeur; souffre encore un moment" (Chénier).

Granted, withal, that the movement is on the long side; but that is not generally
the object of the criticisms made of it.

One might add that its kinship with the allegro is attested by the likeness
of certain themes in the two movements (bars 30 of the allegro and 66-8 of
the finale, for instance).

A sheet of sketches sold in 1928 shows that Mozart had originally thought
of a finale in the minor. Its refrain, in 6-8, with the same rhythm as the present
one, was a forerunner, in its melody, of the opening bars of the G minor
symphony.

[1] D minor quartet, K.421, finale; adagio in B minor, K.540.

[2] C minor sonata; G minor symphony.

[3] C minor concerto; first organ fantasia in F minor, K.594.

One's first impulse is to answer: by "distraction". The passage from minor to major is sudden; there is no transition. If the cadenza came immediately before ex. 250 the task of preparing the change might have fallen to the soloist, but this is impossible, for the few bars of the refrain which follow the cadenza oblige him to end in D minor. The appearance of ex. 249 in the major gives therefore the impression of a change of front like those in the C minor serenade, Beethoven's F minor quartet or many a work of Haydn.

But might not the change have been prepared by earlier moments? Have we not heard signs of struggle? Was not the great first tutti (bars 14–63) the result of a conflict even more savage than that which inspired the first movement? Surely; and if such a state of stress had been kept up throughout the rondo, we should not have been tempted to speak of "distraction". But there was no growth in the conflict. On the other hand, the spirit of strife had exhausted itself in bravura runs (bars 111–39). The return of the energetic refrain might have revived it, but the rather finicky interludes combined by piano and orchestra on ex. 247 and on the refrain itself carry us away from it again. The exs. 246, 247 and 248 wore a passionate air, but there was nothing inevitable or dramatic in the order of their appearance.

This was not the case, however, with the contrast between their group and the major subject, ex. 249. Between these there was not only difference but opposition; the first time, the contrast was really dramatic. It was less so when, in the recapitulation, ex. 249 reappeared in D minor, but became dramatic again in the coda. The use here of the only element which is opposed to the general spirit of the movement cannot be due to chance or to a purely formal need of ending the work in the major; one is compelled to see dramatic meaning in it, to look upon it as a climax, a victory of serenity over the tumultuous anxiety of earlier moments. With the significant emergence of the "happy" theme, cutting the refrain short after the cadenza, it is impossible to think of mere "escape"; there is conflict and triumph here, and though the progress of the battle is traced less continuously and less consistently than in Beethoven, this feature, unique in a Mozart finale, should nevertheless be added to the list of Beethovenian traits already noticed in this concerto.

There is no need to repeat how unique a place this work occupies in Mozart's concertos. It is further from the "entertainment" ideal than any of the earlier ones, even the most personal. It is an account of a poignant experience, a "crisis work" if ever there was one, and any performance which neglects this fact will be bad.   Nowhere are just graceful playing, "perfect phrasing" and an optimistic interpretation more unseasonable than here; soloist and conductor must agree to see in Mozart something more than "a charming blend of Susanna and Cherubino"[1] and to give full value to the stormy accents in the work.[2]

Through its depth and significance, the D minor concerto registers a great step forward.   Its form, in its first and third movements, is less original; we saw that the latter followed the same lines as the finale of the concerto in F.   In interplay between the protagonists, it loses the ground gained by several works of 1784: those in E flat, D, G and F afforded more numerous and more varied instances of collaboration.   Besides, the passages in the rondo where piano and orchestra combine are the least convincing in the movement and stand aside from its emotional progress.   It is in the concertos of 1786 that Mozart regains the ground lost here.

The D minor concerto is an isolated piece, not only in Mozart's concertos[3] but in all his work.   Its key has been little used by him. Besides this concerto, the two string quartets, K.173 and 421, are his only instrumental compositions in it.   He had recourse to it from time to time for slow movements: the andantino of the serenade in D, K.320, the variations of the divertimento in D, K.334, and of the violin sonata in F, K.377, the adagio of the hautboy quartet and the first part of the little piano fantasia, K.397.   The meaning which the choice of this key gives to all these works is made clear by the family of choral and dramatic compositions in D minor: the interludes and choruses of *King Thamos*;[4] the fine *Kyrie* of 1780, K.341; Electra's first aria and the chorus "Corriamo, fuggiamo", in *Idomeneo*; the *Domine Deus* of the C minor mass and, especially, the banquet scene in *Don Giovanni*, and the *Requiem*.   D minor is associated in Mozart with a dusky, foreboding, inward, unlyrical emotion, a passion of struggle rather than of laments and cries, expressive of threatening fate.

---

[1] Ernest Newman.

[2] "There are dark spiritual depths in the first movement of this concerto that merely dainty orchestral and piano playing is incompetent to reveal" (Ernest Newman).

[3] Amongst his unfinished works are six bars of a piano movement in D minor, perhaps intended for K.537 (Köchel-Einstein 537 b).

[4] Dating from 1774, but extraordinarily close to our concerto at times.

It speaks of danger, physical and moral: the danger of the storm which annihilates the wicked Pheres in *King Thamos*, that with which Electra threatens Idamante and Ilia, that of the monster from whom flee the terror-stricken throng of Cretans, that of the Last Judgement (*Requiem*) and of damnation (*Don Giovanni*). This inspiration, half felt in some parts of both quartets in D minor, so completely expressed in the *Kyrie*, *Don Giovanni* and the *Requiem*, is rendered fully, in all Mozart's instrumental work, only by this concerto.

2. The Seventeenth Concerto: K.467 in C

CONCERTO No. 17 IN C (K.467)[1]
Finished March 9th, 1785
  (Allegro maestoso): C
  Andante: C (in F)
  Allegro vivace assai: 2-4
Orchestra: Strings; flute, two hautboys, two bassoons, two horns, two
   trumpets, two kettledrums.

THIS concerto followed the last at four weeks interval. Between the two there is absolute contrast. On one hand, passion, conflict, storm of the spirit; on the other, calm and majesty. We have already noted[2] how, more than once, Mozart produces, one after the other, two first-rate works of highly contrasted inspiration: the autumn before, with the concerto in B flat, K.456, and the sonata in C minor; in 1786, with the concertos in A and C minor; and again in 1787 and 1788 with the quintets and symphonies in G minor and C. We said that it was but one manifestation of his very mobile nature, ready to leap without transition from one aspect of reality to another, from one mood to its opposite. Sometimes the sorrowful work precedes the joyful one; sometimes the contrary. In February and March, 1785, the order is optimistic: the song of peace comes after the tempest; the luminous C major exorcizes the sombre and *daimonisch* D minor. Nevertheless, the concerto in C is not a blithe work; it is powerful and motionless rather than joyful, and in its immobility we recognize, albeit frozen, the billows of the D minor.

I. The first movement is headed *maestoso*,[3] a mark which should be observed and not replaced in practice by *brillante*, as is done by some musicians who consider they know what Mozart wanted better than Mozart himself. But the first subject, as we hear it in the first eleven bars, belies this indication. It is a march like so many first

---

[1] *Gesamtausgabe*, no. 21.

[2] See p. 278.

[3] Not, it is true, in the autograph, but in all editions.

subjects in concertos of the period,[1] but a tiptoed march, in stocking feet, and even when woodwind, brass and drums interrupt the strings, it does not rise above *piano* (ex. 252). It is almost a comedy motif and we should not be surprised to see Leporello emerge from it.

But this impression is soon rectified. Conforming to the plan of the quiet beginning followed by a *forte*,[2] Mozart repeats the theme with all the resources of his orchestra, modulates at once with unusual freedom and, passing quickly through A minor and C minor, settles a while in G major on a tonic pedal. We are baulked of our expectation of meeting a new subject in this key and return to the tonic, whose domination has been strengthened rather than undermined by this excursion into the dominant. The work shows at its very outset a grip and an intensity worthy of the D minor.

The expected new theme is not the second subject; it is a rather more than fugitive idea, one of those we have called mock second subjects, and it plays no part in the body of the movement; we shall not hear it again till the end. It is shared out among the woodwind and the colour of its scoring enriches it with associations. Its horn and trumpet call makes it almost a Romantic, whilst the bareness of the answer, drawn and quartered between hautboys and flutes in their upper register and violas and basses, awakens the memory of the trial by fire and water in the *Magic Flute* (bars 28–35; ex. 253).

After giving out these two themes, it would seem that the tutti had but to conclude and admit the solo. But this concerto does not act like its predecessors. Instead of a closing figure, the march, ex. 252, begins again, first in imitations in the strings, *piano*, then, when all the orchestra has joined in, *forte*, and the music launches forth into a working-out whose progress, led with a steady step and insistent in its regularity, reminds us of the straining and pitiless vigour of the D minor (bars 36–63). There is no modulating; everything comes down, in the last resort, to rises and falls of one octave, repeated several times, without haste, now with the whole orchestra, now antiphonally, with strings and woodwind (ex. 254). Such calm perseverance is irresistible; its strength is in its mass, not in its fire or speed;[3] the music looks neither right nor left; its progress is due to singleness

---

[1] Cf. K.414, 415, 450, 451, 453, 456, 459, 537.

[2] See pp. 262, 283, 310.

[3] On condition, once again, that the movement is taken at a moderate speed and even heavily, *maestoso*, and not *brillante*. Played swiftly and lightly, this passage becomes a kind of breathless race that keeps on coming back to its starting-point, which is nonsense.

of will. No passage demonstrates better than this both the kinship and the contrast which unite and separate the twin concertos; in one, vehemence and wrath; in the other, self-assurance; in both, a will firm and inexorable.

The *piano* of all the last part of this section has but heightened its calm implacability. We suddenly return to *forte* with the third appearance of the march which, cut down to its first bar and repeated by the whole band, acts as concluding subject[1] (bars 64–8).

The orchestra lands on its full close with such finality that the solo dares not tread the stage without being invited. Three times over, a member of the woodwind family beckons it on, in three phrases which are the clearest revelation of Mozart's dramatic genius expressing itself in a symphonic idiom. Though the style owes nothing to that of opera, they are like three graceful maidens holding out their hands to the bewildered and fearful piano, three Ladies introducing Tamino into a new world. Admire their expressive gradation and the way in which chromaticisms give the third an almost suppliant tone (ex. 255; bars 68–74).

The solo's first bars show the effect of this shyness and the piano makes its bow with a delicate coloratura which certainly has nothing of the tutti's massive self-confidence. Strings and wind continue to beckon it on and support it; finally it plucks up courage on a pause where the soloist should improvise a short cadenza (bars 74-9).

The strings start the march and the piano adorns it with a trill, but in the fifth bar the solo takes it from them and advances alone. The last part of the theme, however, with transparent scoring, is shared as in the tutti between strings and wind, whilst the piano superimposes a decorative counterpoint (bars 80–91).

Instead of the development of bars 12–26, the piano sets out alone with an undulating theme in three strains (ex. 256; bars 91–4), recalling that with which the solo had entered in the last concerto, ex. 237. Like this latter, it is almost a recitative and should be played accordingly. This caressing tune, so different from what we have heard hitherto, quickens and melts into a virtuosity passage which modulates to G major. Two tutti bars assert the new key and the piano gives out the solo subject, which has no connexion with what has gone before; its half aggressive, half elegiac air brings back the world of the D minor and at the same time announces the panting tones with

---

[1] The return of the first subject in the conclusion is a device of the North German school, often used by Haydn in his quartets and already favoured by Mozart in 1773.

which the G minor symphony opens (ex. 257; bars 109-21). But
violence and sorrow are both out of season; Mozart casts them quickly
aside and in their place installs the sunny carelessness of the second
subject (ex. 258), crossroads where meet the paths of piano and
orchestra which seldom come near each other elsewhere in this concerto (bars 128-42).

The reader will remember that at the beginning of the solo, the
piano had avoided sounding the first notes of the march theme, ex.
252, and later on had sought to distinguish itself from the tutti. It
overcomes nevertheless for an instant its loathing to repeat what the
orchestra has said, and, following the latter's example in the first tutti,
it outlines imitatively the first fragment. But it quickly gives it up,
for the strings recognize the passage and catch on to the imitation,
and it hovers above them for a moment, motionless, with fluttering
broken octaves (bars 143-7). This concerto, however, is not one of
those which go over the lines of the first tutti with the docile collaboration of the solo. This recall of the first exposition was but transitory
and the strings' imitation, undertaken beneath the piano's presiding
octaves, grows into a splendid passage of pure virtuosity, the amplest
and most powerful we have met hitherto.[1] The march goes on
haunting us with the ghost of its first notes which it moves from
register to register, with a progression from subdominant to sub-
dominant which we meet again later on in the movement. The piano
comes down from its lofty immobility, and, with both hands, throws
itself into the thickest scrub of arpeggios and broken octaves that
Mozart has ever set up before his executants. It is a rich and splendid
passage, revelling unreservedly in beauty of tone. Virtuosity is here
at its own service, or rather, the work's strong vitality demands
virtuosity in order to be manifest; it overflows in this passage work as
the passion and bitterness of the D minor had done in the fierce diminished seventh arpeggios (ex. 259; bars 148-61). The intensity
reaches its climax in four heavy chords to which the pianist should give
their full measure of weight (bar 162); then, taking breath in a few
quiet bars, the movement regains its impetus on a trill whence it starts
off afresh as from a springboard (bars 163-8). And again a series of
arpeggios alternates with scales, rushing to the onslaught like troops
of Titans placing their ladders against the ramparts of Olympus.
The waves of sound break more and more generously, with periods
of an amplitude hitherto unattained in Mozart (bars 169-93).

---

[1] We exclude those of the D minor, for one cannot call them pure virtuosity.

The balance of the work demands a development of equal breadth for the tutti; so, instead of the usual short transition at the end of the first solo, we hear a prolonged and triumphal affirmation of the march,[1] where the dominant, G major, gives way before a modulation into E flat (bars 198–203), and a restatement of the second part of the great scale passage which had concluded the first tutti, ex. 254 (bars 52–63; here, 205–15). But we have travelled beyond this stage and the time is not yet ripe for returning to it. The expected cadence is dodged, the magnificent self-reliance of the music fades away; we modulate into B minor, and with a stroke of the wand Mozart throws open one of those windows on infinity through which the eye pierces all the more keenly for the opening being so unexpected (bars 215–21). We halt upon a note of wondering and, as before the first piano entry in the D minor, we sense without defining it a new presence.

The *development* opens with a tune which unfolds in groups of three and four sections. Not only does its temper carry us back to the last concerto, but the violin answer (ex. 260) is almost a quotation of the piano left hand part in ex. 237 (bars 222–30). The woodwind restate it with a variation, and the piano adds embroideries; the whole thing is one of those variations, uncommon in Mozart, which keep nothing but the harmonic basis of the theme (ex. 261; bars 231–7). Departing from this subject, so attractive nevertheless, piano and woodwind open fiery speech over a little figure (ex. 262 a), on whose back we travel through new keys. The progression is methodical, from subdominant to subdominant, but the feeling, more and more intense, ends by rising to a state of passion as the phrases are shortened from four to two bars (bars 249–52). A quieter passage begins when E flat is reached and after a long chromatic climb (bars 259–64) the motion breaks into a rapid glissade, with a fleeting sign of weariness; then, hoisting itself up for one last effort, drops degree by degree, decrescendo, on a dominant pedal, to the tonic (bars 265–74). This reprise, like the rest of the movement, is of unwonted breadth; in this respect it is surpassed only by that of the other great concerto in C, K.503, the harmony of whose reprise is similar.

The recapitulation opens, like the movement itself, on a soft note. Again, a long tutti development succeeds an extensive solo. The first nineteen bars repeat those of the beginning; then we modulate suddenly into F major, a vagary all the more unexpected in that Mozart seldom modulates after his middle section (bars 293–5). The fiddles

---

[1] This return of the first subject after the first solo is perhaps an archaism.

again go through their imitation; then the piano reappears. Profiting by the imitation in which it joins, it emits a brief lament, a distant memory, perhaps, in inspiration, of the G minor subject, ex. 257, but in form a development of the ever-present march (bars 297–305).

Save that it is in the tonic, the second appearance of the second subject differs from the first only in details of orchestration. Identical, also, is the great bravura passage that follows it, as far as the chords (bar 161); in their place, four transitional bars lead to the mock second subject, ex. 258, which answers the roll call here as a delegate from the opening tutti (bars 351–4). Its former emaciation is somewhat disguised beneath a richer scoring; then the piano restates it and, without more ado, enters upon its last virtuosity passage, the elements of which are those of the solo at the end of the exposition. There are a few superficial changes and a few additions, notably a fine rising passage in broken sixths, over a dominant pedal, doubled by the woodwind, of a fullness of tone recalling the passage in the same position in the F major concerto, K.459 (bars 375–7).

The rest of the allegro belongs to the march. It opens the way for the cadenza and, after the recall of bars 44–5 of the first tutti, provides the çoda, nearly as original as that of the D minor. We are led to expect a noisy and triumphant exit; instead, the movement dies away in quiet with the same furtive step as it had opened (ex. 263).

Many are the observations prompted by this movement, but we will confine ourselves to three of them. They concern the distribution of the material, the unity of the orchestral part and the richness and novelty of the piano writing.

In the D minor, the important thing was the drama in which piano and orchestra collaborated equally. Here, the game consists in each one saying what it has to say independently of the other, but without contradiction or opposition, for the message is the same for both and there is agreement of thought, although the words are different. In other terms, piano and orchestra seldom give out the same themes; the elements that fall to each are usually distinct. The mock second subject belongs mainly to the orchestra; only at its second and last appearance does the piano take an interest in it, and then not till the orchestra has dealt with it, and it is abandoned immediately. The true second subject, as transitory as many others in these concertos, belongs rather to the piano, although the orchestra restates it. The long solos owe absolutely nothing to the material given out by the tutti. And even the first subject, whose presence haunts the movement so tenaciously, is avoided by the piano most of the time; at the beginning of

the first solo, only the second half is expounded, the less characteristic
one; it is true that the piano feels bound to resume the imitative use
which the violins had made of it (bars 143-4, 297-8, 328-9), but it at
once takes refuge in virtuosity and with haughty indifference lets the
theme serve as an accompaniment figure in the hands of the tutti.
This dividing of the material into two lots, one for orchestra and one
for solo, is not peculiar to this concerto; in most of the others there
exist themes reserved for one or other of the protagonists; but in no
other does Mozart carry so far the separation between the two.[1]

Despite the presence of a more brilliant solo part than in any
earlier concerto, the orchestra is not sacrificed. The first tutti and the
three other great interludes, veritable symphonic developments thanks
to which Mozart balances the respective influences of the opponents,
are full of sustained power; their flow is continuous; nothing hold,
up their progress; scarcely a theme raises its head above the flood
and breaks the magnificent, smooth line of their advance; no closes
cut up their unity. These tuttis are permeated and dominated by
the presence of the first subject or at least of its first four notes, which
haunts them as the rhythm ♩♩♫♩♩ haunted the F major concerto.
It is always there, ready to slip on to the stage as soon as the other elements relax their watchfulness. Thrice over it takes possession in the
first tutti; the mock second subject drives it away for one moment, but
it reappears under cover of counterpoint; the great working out of bars
44-63, ex. 254, keeps it away a little longer, but it returns to close the
discussion, provisionally at first, at the end of the tutti, then for good
and all, when the allegro, alike in this to the D minor, ends with the
very motif with which it had begun (ex. 263).

What shall we say of the solo part? Passage work preponderates
in it, for the tunes, however personal they may be, are but bridges
over which one crosses to more important things. Despite their
length—two fifths of the movement—these passages are always sustained by the breath of grandeur and power which fills the whole work,
whose heroic soul they express in their own way. They never degenerate into loquacity as in a few bars of the G major or the rondo of the
D minor. One constant harmonic device, the subdominant progression, and the great number of runs based on scales, give them
cohesion and discipline. The writing shows several traits new in
Mozart and the simultaneous use of the two hands is more persistent
than in any earlier work including the D minor. The breadth and

[1] Not even in K.415.

richness of the piano part harks back to the ambitious prelude of the C major concerto of 1782; the piano has at last caught up with the tutti; Mozart has succeeded in making it as capable a vehicle of his thought as the orchestra.

All this combines to make it a single-minded work, majestic and strong, which the D minor concerto, alone among earlier compositions, could have led us to expect. These two concertos proceed unquestionably from the depths of the same soul, though the depths be different. The D minor was as forceful, but more violent, less broad, less smooth in rhythm. This one is Olympian, the first work in a family which includes the great C major works of the next three years and the first where this side of Mozart's many-sided genius is fully displayed.[1]

II. The world of the andante is that of the "dream" andantes,[2] a family which comprises some of Mozart's most beautiful slow movements in earlier years[3] and in the long succession of which it is the last; but its form is unique.

It is a piano cantilena preceded by a tutti prelude and sumptuously sustained and adorned by the murmur of the strings and the multi-coloured raiment of the wind. The tune winds from key to key, smooth and closely blended; it passes through various moods, some dreamy, some full of anguish, some serene, but the themes hardly stand out; it is a river, moving slowly but unceasingly, and only from time to time does an eddy in the current announce a fresh subject.

Yet it is not a fantasia. There is direction and progress in its emotion and its form. The stream advances, turns back, passes on again, and though its structure be free, it is never loose. Even though the ear does not at first distinguish themes, it picks out strains already heard, places already traversed, and the succession of these places and strains, as well as of the keys, satisfies our imagination and is also justified by our analytical faculty.

The movement unfolds in three periods (bars 1–23, 24–72, 73–104),

---

[1] We recognized an "Olympian" inspiration for the first time in Mozart in the *Sinfonia Concertante*, K.364. At first, the key of E flat expressed in his work the mood we have described thus; in 1780, C major is still the key of festal and joyous overtures; it is only in 1785 that, without losing this character, it becomes the key of those works that scale the mountain of the Gods.

[2] Cf. pp. 36, 39, 40.

[3] Those of the violin concerto in G, of the symphony in C, K.338, and of the string quartet in E flat, K.428.

in each of which we hear identical material. The first is that of the orchestral prelude, where this material, at first sight indissolubly welded, is given out alone almost without modulation; in the second, which opens with the solo entry, the elements come in the same order but their succession is broken by the intrusion of a new theme and another is added to them, whilst modulations are numerous; the third continues to modulate but goes over again the tracks of the first one and ends with a coda.

The key sequence in this andante is even more original. For clarity's sake let us say that the piece belongs to the large group of binary movements, where the sequence can be simplified to:

Tonic—dominant; various keys—tonic.

Through the labyrinth of keys, in fact, it is towards the dominant that we wend our way as soon as we leave F major, in the thirty-sixth bar. It is true that, when we reach it, we stay there for only four bars, but by utilizing the fragment, which had concluded the opening tutti (ex. 267) and which we therefore associate with stability, to establish the key, and by following up this fragment with one of the few full closes in the movement (bars 54-5), Mozart gives it a relief and a highlight which the other keys, through which his dreamy bark carries us, do not enjoy.

The end of the second period resumes the modulating progress and the next stage is reached with the return of the first subject in A flat (relative major of the tonic minor; bar 73), whence, after a few more turnings, we regain the key of F from which one half of the movement separated us.

To make these remarks more intelligible, we give a diagram of the movement with the *incipits* of the chief elements.

1	Ex. 264 F	7 bars
2	Ex. 265 F	3 bars
3	Ex. 266 F *minor*	6 bars
4	Ex. 267 F *major*	4 bars

1st period (tutti)

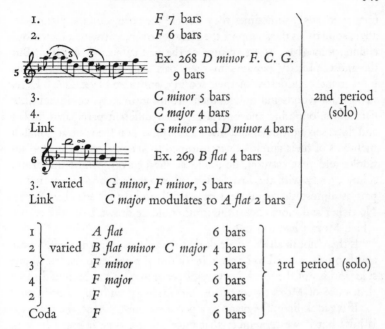

1.	F 7 bars	
2.	F 6 bars	
	Ex. 268 *D minor* F. C. G. 9 bars	
3.	*C minor* 5 bars	2nd period
4.	*C major* 4 bars	(solo)
Link	*G minor* and *D minor* 4 bars	
	Ex. 269 *B flat* 4 bars	
3. varied	*G minor, F minor,* 5 bars	
Link	*C major* modulates to *A flat* 2 bars	

1		*A flat*	6 bars	
2	varied	*B flat minor C major*	4 bars	
3		*F minor*	5 bars	3rd period (solo)
4		*F major*	6 bars	
2		*F*	5 bars	
Coda		*F*	6 bars	

But its structure is not the only feature worthy of admiration in this andante and, at any rate on a first hearing, it is not what we notice most. The colour and mass of the various instrumental tones move us more deeply. The scoring, increasingly rich in Mozart's concertos during the last year, reaches here a high level. We have no longer a piece with *obbligati* woodwind; all the instruments[1] collaborate in the work of beauty. The colour is made rarer by the mutes and by the fact that each time the highly characteristic accompaniment figure ♪♪♪ sustains the piano, pizzicati replace bows. On the whole, the business of the strings is to provide mass; to them fall the repeated triplets which throb persistently all through the dream and maintain a threatening state of uneasiness. After the prelude, they sing only when doubling the piano (in ex. 267), or when joining forces with the wind (in ex. 266; cf. also ex. 270).

To the colour of the strings enhanced by mutes and pizzicati is added, with profitable discretion, that of the woodwind. Longish rests between their interventions give to each one an impression of novelty. Sometimes the instruments reinforce *sforzandos* with held

---

[1] Except the trumpets and kettledrums, which are silent.

notes (ex. 265); sometimes they double the strings or the piano (ex. 267); sometimes they support the piano or overlay it with a melodious counterpoint (bars 75–81; return of the first subject in A flat). But the most masterly passages in their part and indeed in the whole movement, considered for their scoring, are those of ex. 266. Here, strings and woodwind mingle their groups intimately, confound their harmonies, opposing and interlacing their different parts (first fiddles and flute, second fiddles and first hautboy), or, on the contrary, match members of their families unaccustomed to keeping company (second fiddles and first bassoon, doubling at the octave), whilst the piano, siding openly with the first fiddles, adorns their line so freely that its part is almost the equivalent of a third group (ex. 270, bars 82–7). No richer and more enchanting tints could be drawn from the palette which Mozart had to hand.

Is there not in all this the risk that the solo instrument itself, whose apotheosis is deemed to be the *raison d'être* of a concerto, be left to one side, and is not the work by way of becoming, as has been said more than once of Mozart's concertos, a symphony with *piano principale*?

If we look upon the piano as a percussion instrument, the reproach is just; but if we remember that once upon a time it knew how to sing and was proud of doing so, we shall find that it remains despite everything at the front of the stage. After the prelude it is never silent for more than two bars and its silences are few. Only, except when it uses its left hand to relieve from time to time the strings' triplets, it is confined to singing. No chords, no mass effects; the most massive of Mozart's allegros is followed by the most cantabile of andantes.[1] No opposition, either, to the orchestra, as in the first movement. Never, it is true, does it descend from its position as soloist; yet it often collaborates closely with the other instruments. But there is no interplay; the close knit and continuous nature of the movement does not allow of this. It combines with the others as *primus inter pares*, as a solo singer with other singers. Sometimes, it hears itself supported by the wind and, whenever the unquiet theme, ex. 267, returns, it seconds the first violins without surrendering its independence. And all the time it never stops singing; one feels that its chief contribution here is its tone colour, the pale, delicate colour of the 1780 piano, whose beauty Mozart never set forth more felicitously than in this nocturne.

---

[1] The concerto in D, K.451, shows with less contrast the same opposition between its first two movements.

We say, nocturne, and in truth the *rapprochement* with Chopin can hardly be avoided. The hazy atmosphere of the mutes, the quivering calm of the ceaseless triplets, the slow, sustained song of the piano—more than all this, the veiled and sorrowfully passionate soul which this music expresses with such immediacy, do we not find them in the work of Chopin and especially in those nocturnes of which this "dream" of Mozart's reminds us? This andante, so placid at first hearing, betrays on further acquaintance an agitated mood. Its perpetual instability, to which its constant modulating and its unsatisfied quest for new places bears witness; its morbid disquiet, thinly concealed now and again under an appearance of calm, breaking forth with heartrending pathos in the chromaticisms and the discreet yet pungent hues of ex. 270, are unquestionably fundamental elements of Mozart's nature, but they are elements which he shares with Chopin, and indeed they come fully to light as they do here, much less often with him than with the Romantic composer.[1]

III. These two movements are summits of Mozart's work, witnesses of creative planes as far removed one from the other as those of one same individual can be. After the lovingly analytical study we have made of them, we do not feel inclined to go deeply into the finale. Not that it is unworthy of Mozart, even of the thirty-year old Mozart; but we have just left two movements which he never surpassed, whereas there are a dozen finales in his concertos more interesting and attractive than this one. . . . Yet we are pledged to study each movement of all his greater concertos and we must not shirk the task. Let us then give this one its due.

This finale is a sonata rondo of strict form, as strict as that of K.451. The theme of the refrain, a rough awakening after the glories of the andante, plunges us cruelly in midmost opera buffa and the rest of the movement does not belie it. The finale of the F major concerto, K.459, also began with a skipping subject in 2-4, very similar in character; but the rondo rose later to heights unsuggested by the refrain. Here, there is no such surprise in store; there is not a bar whose nature is not announced by the beginning (ex. 271). The first couplet, starting in C and modulating to G, has first, second and third subjects. It contains much less virtuosity than the allegro but its vitality is also less and it expresses and exhausts itself in less time. The *development*

---

[1] With this andante, the Chopin-like Mozart is best seen in the A minor rondo for piano, K.511, and the slow movement, in F sharp minor, of the concerto in A major, K.488.

couplet is based entirely upon the first notes of the refrain; as in the rondo of K.451, it is the most interesting part of the movement. Piano and woodwind banter wittily over their fragment and play ball with it; the passage recalls a similar one in the rondo of K.450

(ex. 272). When the game is over, the refrain returns complete. The third couplet is the recapitulation and repeats the first with minor changes and without modulating to the dominant. It leads to the cadenza and the last return of the refrain forms the coda.

If the material is commonplace, the realization is nevertheless good Mozart and after less grand first and second movements one would admire this rondo unreservedly. The scoring is sparkling; wind and strings engage in lively rivalry (ex. 273); the accompaniment is often original (bars 128-40, 207-12, 379-92), and exchanges between piano and tutti are more frequent than in the allegro (bars 162-9, 413-18, where the piano decorates the woodwind exposition of the third subject with fragmentary arpeggios or scales; bars 314-20, where the piano gives out the refrain and plays in tenths to a fiddle accompaniment; bars 371-5, where it adorns with scales the woodwind exposition of the second subject; and all the last section, where it sustains and enlivens the refrain, given out by the strings, with a brilliant Alberti bass and scales darting like rockets through the last strains of the theme). The development is more interesting than that of K.451, though not the equal of K.450; it recalls both of them and is an excellent example of a Mozartian thematic working-out.

If this chapter stops a little short, it is because this concerto does likewise. After such an opening it was hard to conclude; the C major concerto of 1786, whose allegro is still more majestic, does not hold its head up so well in its rondo. The C major quintet is luckier; but it is only with the *Jupiter* symphony that Mozart hits on the ideal finale with which to rival an Olympian first movement.

3. The Eighteenth Concerto: K.482 in E flat

CONCERTO NO. 18 IN E FLAT (K.482)[1]
Finished December 16th, 1785
Allegro: C
Andante: 3-8 (in C minor)
Rondo: Allegro: Andantino cantabile: Allegro: 6-8
Orchestra: Strings; flute, two clarinets,[2] two bassoons, two horns, two trumpets, two kettledrums.

THERE are experiences in our life that come to us but once. They seem to arise out of nothingness; no warning allows us to suspect their visit; once over, there is no rediscovering them; they may persist a while as fading memories but no circumstance can revive them; they have vanished as wholly as the minute which brought them.

Other experiences, less haughty, condescend to return. A given state of mind will have become familiar to us from being frequently with us; it is no doubt never identical from one visit to the next; different shades qualify it at each appearance; but in its essence it is the same. The experience comes back, ever richer, ever fuller, affecting ever greater stretches of our being. We end by recognizing its accompanying and determining circumstances; we succeed in foreseeing each of its returns, hoped for or dreaded; it may even come to us so often that it ends by being an almost constant companion.

To these two kinds of experience correspond two kinds of works of art. One kind is unique in the artist's creative history; it is the commoner, no doubt, especially with those who strive after originality before all else and seek to achieve the new at every throw. The other kind, on the contrary, falls into families whose every member is the incarnation of the same type, where the same general lines are drawn again in one individual after another. The work of the older masters, whether writers, musicians or painters, afforded many more

---

[1] *Gesamtausgabe*, no. 22.

[2] Clarinets instead of hautboys; it is their first appearance in these concertos.

instances of these creations in series, extending through the lives of their authors like garlands whose flowers are, at a distance, indistinguishable one from the other.   Not only have they the family air that is common to all born of one father; modern works, too, have that; but they have sprung from the same creative plane, from moods so similar that they are but a succession of returns of one same fundamental experience.

These general remarks apply to the work of Mozart.   Within the thirteen months from February, 1784, to March, 1785, in compositions like the concertos in E flat, G and D minor there crystallized experiences that either were unique or, if they ever came again to him, left no further trace in his work.   No other piece can be likened to them; they have, indeed, the Mozartian family air common to all; but in that family they are isolated.   This was not so with the concertos in B flat, D and F, to which we had no difficulty in finding parallels. This is not so, either, with the E flat concerto with which, on December 16th, Mozart opened the 1785–6 season of winter concerts.

In this work a long succession of attempts, expressing with various degrees of intensity and conviction the same state of mind, comes to fruition.   From the earliest days of his life as a composer, there is heard an ideal song which the child, and then the youth, tries to reproduce; we hear it in the symphonies of his childhood journeys, in those of his seventeenth year and, by snatches, elsewhere.   He has rendered it once for all in its perfection in his eighteenth concerto.

More than a dozen times already its inspiration had taken shape in different compositions.   The oldest was his first symphony, written at the age of nine, K.16; the most recent, the E flat quartet of 1783, K.428; between them spread out the two piano concertos, K.271 and 365, the *Sinfonia Concertante*, K. 364, the E flat serenade, K.375, and several other more unassuming pieces.[1]   Some began very similarly to our concerto;[2] others, or the same ones, went into C minor for their andante[3] as it does; in others, again, the kinship is less clearly defined but recognizable nevertheless.

Of this chain of works the eighteenth concerto is the culmination. In it we have the clearest proof that Mozart, as it has been said, did what

---

[1] Symphonies in E flat, K.132, 1772, and K.184, 1773; violin sonata, K.302, 1777 or 1778; concerto for wind instruments, Köchel-Einstein 297 b, 1778 (if it is authentic).

[2] K.16, 132; Köchel-Einstein 297b.

[3] K.16, 184, 271, 364; string quartet in E flat, K.171, 1773.

everyone else was doing, but did it better.   This is partly true of every great artist, since none, however powerful his individuality, ever withdraws completely from his environment.   No doubt, there are in Mozart precursory strains that hark beyond their period, but on the whole his work is the crowning of the closing 18th century, and nowhere better than in this concerto can we see with what art he realized the century's ideal, whilst yet casting aside the shackles of fashion.   If, then, this work sings of an experience that others had sung of, this is partly the result of personal circumstances; it is also because the experience was one of those with which the century itself, more or less consciously, was acquainted.   After the unflinchingly personal compositions of the beginning of the year, Mozart returns to an ideal more accessible to his public and common to him and them; after two works so individual as to be almost anti-social, here is once again a sociable concerto, a well-bred person, full of savoir-vivre, ingratiating, in contact with its environment.

The autumn and winter of 1784 to 1785 had witnessed, together with fashionable and spritely works like the concerto in F, considerable deepening and enrichment in that life of the soul of which Mozart's music is the expression and the fruit.   The C minor sonata, the quartets in A and C and the concertos in D minor and C are the chief products of this change.   The process had continued during the spring and summer as we see in the well-known C minor piano fantasia, so perfect a commentary on the sonata of the preceding autumn with which it is always published, and in a strange work, also in C minor, which is revived from time to time as a curiosity, but in reality lights up a fundamental plane of Mozart's nature: the *Masonic Funeral Music* (*Maurerische Trauermusik*).

This work is the only instrumental composition of his with a programme.   As its title indicates, it is a lament for the death of two brethren of the lodge to which Mozart belonged, the Duke George-Augustus of Mecklemburg-Strelitz and Prince Franz Esterhazy of Galantha, the grand-master.   But it is more than a farewell song to two departed friends.   It is a meditation upon death, quiet though sorrowful, and nearer in spirit to the *Magic Flute* than to the *Requiem*. A feeling of other-worldliness pervades it and the music passes effortlessly and without break from this life to that which the musician sees beyond the grave.   There is no tragedy and no violence; the beginning and end are expressive of the sadness caused by separation, but the middle portion, into which is woven a psalm tune, contemplates death serenely, without defiance or fear, as a friend in whom the composer sees no mystery.

One single letter has survived the destruction of those Mozart wrote to his father after his initiation as a mason, and though it was written two years later, on April 4th, 1787, it is relevant to this symphonic poem.

> I have made a habit of being prepared in all affairs of life for the worst. As death, when we come to consider it closely, is the true goal of our existence, I have formed during the last few years such close relations with this best and truest friend of mankind, that his image is not only no longer terrifying to me but is indeed very soothing and consoling! And I thank my God for graciously granting me the opportunity (you know what I mean)[1] of learning that death is the key which unlocks the door to our true happiness. I never lie down at night without reflecting that—young as I am—I may not live to see another day. Yet no one of all my acquaintances could say that in company I am morose or disgruntled. For this blessing I daily thank my Creator and wish with all my heart that each one of my fellow creatures could enjoy it.[2]

The intense inner life of which these works are the fruit was active throughout the summer. Written soon after the *Funeral Music*, the first movement of the G minor piano quartet still reflects at times the emotional storms of the past months. A little later, there escapes from his letters the first of those cries of distress which were so soon to succeed each other with harrowing regularity. We hear it in a letter to Hoffmeister, the publisher of this quartet, when Mozart asks him, "just for a moment", to lend him "a little money, for", he says, "I have the greatest need of it just at present." This letter is dated November 20th.

Four weeks later, he enters the E flat concerto in the list of his works.

After nearly one year of highly personal music, Mozart seems now to make an effort to recapture the public he sees slipping from him. Purely galant works reappear among his compositions. Since 1783, there had been no such "drawing-room piece", for instance, as the violin sonata in E flat, K.481, contemporary with our concerto. The allegro is one of his most lifeless sonata movements and the andante lives only through the echoes from the lovely andante of the G minor quartet that sound in it at times. Henceforward, "society" works,

---

[1] This has generally been taken to refer to freemasonry.

[2] E. Anderson's translation, III, 1351.

absent since the concerto in F, K.413, will be frequent and go on appearing till the end of 1788. Galant works before 1783 had been written with some delight and the gap between them and the more serious ones was less wide than now; the distance between the little concerto in F of 1782 and the B flat concerto, K.450, of 1784, is less great than that which separates this sonata and the concerto finished four days later. It is hard to realize that two such works should be contemporary, just as it is hard to understand how Mozart, whilst working at his great symphonies in 1788, could produce such trifles as the trios in E, C and G and the "easy" sonatinas in C and F. Such condescension towards an ideal he had transcended and to which he submitted now, it seems, without joy, can be explained only by the need he felt for recapturing his public. This need may account also, at least in part, for the more sociable and accessible character of the E flat concerto itself and for Mozart's return in it to an inspiration on which he had already often drawn.

I.   Of all his concertos, this one is the queenliest. Combining grace and majesty, the music unfolds like a sovereign in progress, the queen of the twenty-three. The work is of ancient lineage and utters what many earlier works have uttered, but it speaks with the language of an adult of thirty, whereas they had stammered with the tongues of children and youths. Thoughts once short-winded are here spread out with breadth and developed with rich orchestration and easy counterpoint. This is as true of the first movement as of the touching C minor andante, also the last of a noble ancestry.

The first six bars of the allegro conform to the same pattern as the openings of earlier E flat works: a vigorous and rhythmical attack and a light answer, quiet and tuneful.[1] It is in the childish symphony K.16, of 1765, that this kind of opening resembles most nearly what it has become in our concerto (ex. 274). On returning to it twenty years later, Mozart shortens the second part, thus improving the balance, but keeps the held notes with their syncopated progression, and sets against their stability a diaphanous dance entrusted the first time to the bassoon and the second to the violins, which fulfils the same function as the repeated crotchets of the bass in the symphony (ex. 275). A development based on a figure given out at first by the flute and repeated by the clarinets and bassoons links on to this first

---

[1] Its formula is a commonplace in *galant* music. It occurs in particular in an E flat symphony of Abel which passed for a long time as a work of Mozart's (no. 18 in Köchel), op. 7, III.

subject, whilst the violins mingle with them a winding counter-
subject derived from it (ex. 276). This, too, is repeated and a vigorous
passage follows whose most striking feature is the fragment ex. 277.
It leads to a close and a few solemn woodwind chords over a pedal
in the horns open the way for a new theme. The tune thus heralded
is a close relation to one in the overture of *Figaro* and reminds us that
Mozart had begun that opera about the time he was finishing the
concerto (ex. 278). In spite of appearances, it is but the mock second
subject; the true one is held back for the solo exposition. A loud and
energetic passage on a rising bass leads to the conclusion, the last bars
of which are a diminution of its theme and seem to sum up the last
part of the tutti (ex. 279).

Ex. 276

Ex. 277

Ex. 278

Ex. 279

Ex. 280

Ex. 281

Ex. 282

Ex. 283

Ex. 284

Ex. 285   Ex. 286

Ex. 287   Ex. 288

Ex. 289

With this prelude we return to the world of the 1784 concertos. The vital drive, the strong phrases of the two last works are absent; there are no more ample workings out; no more of that thematic unity which conveyed so much power to the C major nor of that concentrated thought and form which, abandoned for a while, is resumed a few months later with the C minor and leads up to the string quintets. In their place we have a succession of subjects, different from each other if not actually contrasted, with restatement instead of condensation. We pass through a variety of interludes; some graceful and tender, some mischievous, some energetic, but all seeking to be acceptable to their patrons. And over all, ensuring unity in spite of these formal differences, the same blend of grace and majesty, the same confidence; the queen not only anxious to please but sure of doing so.

This tutti is the *argument* of the movement in that, except for the second subject, it contains all the chief elements. The solo exposition, nevertheless, repeats only the beginning and end of it (bars 1-12, 58-76); between them, it inserts a new section provided by the piano. It opens with a solo prelude of seventeen bars, whose tunefulness, grace and strength answer faithfully to the nature of the tutti, and when the orchestra re-enters with ex. 275 the piano collaborates in giving out the subject by decorating it (ex. 280).[1] Instead of the working out of ex. 276 there unfolds a passage which modulates to the dominant. Two bars of orchestra introduce the solo subject, a fierce explosion in B flat minor, with massive chords underlined by the stealthy creeping strings (ex. 281). Its angry mood takes some time to subside and the virtuosity passage which follows it, with flute and bassoon taking it in turns to escort the piano, does not shake off the mourning garb of the minor mode till we near the second subject.

This latter bulks larger than in the last concertos. Not only is it in perfect agreement with the general sense of the movement but it is long and leisurely. The piano expounds it, repeating its first half; then, instead of passing it over to the orchestra, it restates it and the instruments' only share is a touching counter-subject in the woodwind, where flute and clarinets, hovering above the joyful restlessness of the piano, move down as if to meet it (ex. 282).

The solo into which it opens is one of those we have called loquacious. Bearable at first, this loquacity becomes tedious when Mozart repeats the chatter unchanged except for an interversion of the hands.

---

[1] The quotation combines both presentations of the theme.

It is true that he had done likewise in the C major concerto, but there virtuosity, much less obvious than here, had in its favour a passion and a vigour which constrained us; one felt that without it and without the precise shape it was taking, the experience could not be translated. Here there is nothing so inevitable.   These runs might be replaced by many others without altering the character of the concerto, and we protest when Mozart, by repeating the same passages twice over, attaches undeserved importance to them. Happily, only a dozen bars are affected and the beauty of the whole is not lessened thereby.

Here we join again the opening tutti. The exposition links on to the development by repeating its last eighteen bars in B flat.   Then the piano, like a kitten who has just spied a bit of thread and decides to play with it, seizes hold of the last notes of ex. 279, modulates into B flat minor and, thanks to them, exchanging the while a few short remarks with the orchestra, enters upon the long bravura passage which constitutes the *development*.

No theme guides its exploration. This concerto returns to the tradition of the *fantasia developments* of the previous year and carries through sundry keys a number of running figures which appear to repeat themselves but actually are always changing shape.   Sometimes the woodwind, sometimes the strings accompany the piano on its voyage, but neither comes to the fore.   Minor keys predominate and the excursion takes place under a threatening sky which has forgotten the sunny opening and announces the twilight of the andante.   These are grand and powerful bars, devoid of the capricious charm of the *developments* in the D and G major concertos. The movement puts into port for an instant in A flat with a tune very like ex. 282 and we work back to the reprise with a bridge passage entrusted to the woodwind and brass: a pedal in the horn and second bassoons with a syncopated counterpoint in the rest, and piano scales; there reappear the clashing seconds of the first subject which characterize this allegro and make it sound at times like a wind serenade (ex. 283).[1]

We saw that only the beginning and end were common to both expositions. The recapitulation has therefore to pick up the material from the first which the second had omitted, and to interest the solo in it.   This is done admirably in what is certainly the finest portion of the movement.   It goes again over the whole first tutti, with important changes in scoring and the addition, for most of the time, of the

---

[1] The reader will have noticed them also in the quotation from K.16, ex. 274.

piano. From the solo exposition it recalls the first half of the second subject, but it leaves out the solo subject, ex. 281, and the passage that followed it; the "loquacious" bravura passage is replaced by a new one, half as short. It is, on the whole, a repetition of the first exposition with the piano part added and the inclusion of only half the second subject.

Never hitherto had Mozart varied his recapitulation with such art. The piano, especially, is determined to make all things new. It decorates the violin answers in exs. 275 and 280 with sparkling two-handed scales. It is in the development of ex. 276 that it shows its genius best. Let the reader turn to the miniature score and take stock of the substitutions Mozart has carried out here, first of all introducing the solo in place of the wind, then reinstating the wind while the piano enriches the score with a new part. The bewitching mock, second subject, roguish and sentimental, tarries longer with us this time and everyone becomes busy with it. The piano gives it out, joined and doubled in the third bar by the flute and clarinet; fiddles and clarinet repeat it, and piano and flute unite in the rippling counter-point which belonged the first time to the clarinet and bassoon (cf. with ex. 278). This tune is now the fashionable one and the true second subject comes meekly behind, all the spritelier for being shorn of its second half. Save for four additional closing bars, the conclusion is unaltered. There is no coda: another difference with the last two concertos and a point of likeness with those of the previous year.

The piano has unlearnt the lessons of the D minor and C major concertos. Its writing is once again linear and mass effects are confined to the chords of ex. 281. Nearly everything is done in scales. The two hands seldom play both together and when they do it is in octaves. There is nothing like the two-handed passages of the D minor nor the muscular arpeggios in contrary motion of the C major. We have returned to the writing of K. 450 and the piano style is another feature that takes us back at one bound, beyond February and March, to the works of the past year.

II. The andante opens with one of Mozart's themes which speak most to the imagination and kindle our sense of the picturesque. It is a mournful, trailing tune, whose heavy sadness is emphasized by the use of mutes. The strings, with their veiled and muffled tone, unfold a long lament, irregular and tortuous, that moves almost entirely within the compass of an octave (ex. 284). It comes and goes upon

itself and calls up the picture of a blind man groping his way towards
the light; at times he draws near to it and thinks he has reached it;
he holds out his hands towards it, but he is alone and no one comes to
help him; at length, worn out by his sobs he lets his arms drop, gives
up his quest and sinks down in despair.

The tune, reserved to the strings, belongs mainly to the first violins
confined to their lower register, but the accompanying seconds mingle
with them at times (ex. 285).   A momentary halt on E flat lightens
it, but it falls quickly back into the minor, wavering between F, G
and C, and expires in C minor.   The very Mozartish lengthening of
its last strain by two bars more pathetic than the rest is peculiarly
moving (ex. 286).

The form of the movement cannot be guessed from these thirty
bars.   Theme and variations, rondo, sonata: all are possible.   The
piano entry appears to settle the question.   The solo takes up the tune,
unaccompanied, and varies it.   The instrument's incisive tone illum-
inates it; no longer do we hear a muttered lament nor glimpse a
fumbling, penumbral searcher; it becomes a supplication formulated
as clearly as a recitative (ex. 287).   Its vitality is suddenly increased;
the prayer of ex. 286 pulsates in its new garb (ex. 288); the apparently
purely formal change expresses in reality a change of feeling.   The
strings mark the last bars of each half by underlining the theme beneath
the solo ornamentation.

Till now the drama has been enacted between the muted strings and
the piano; with the wind entry and a fresh subject in E flat the colour
and atmosphere change.   So!   The movement is to be a rondo and
this is the first episode.   This subject is a caressing tune with clear,
gentle outlines, unfolding in two strains of eight and twelve bars,
each one followed by the same four-bar phrase or codetta (ex. 289).
The first part modulates into the dominant, the second returns to the
tonic; this is the plan of numberless airs and refrains of the time.   Its
galant symmetry contrasts with the almost extemporizing irregularity
of the first stanza.   It is natural that not only its scoring but also its
harmonization (accompaniment in thirds, repeated notes on the
horns, first clarinet and first bassoon doubling in octaves, Alberti bass
in the second clarinet, echoing from clarinet to flute) should recall the
woodwind serenades, especially the andante of the C minor with
which it has in common both key and beat.

It is a digression which does not affect the climate of the movement
and the piano comes in again at once with a second variation of the
subject where the tune is restated almost unchanged over an extremely

agitated bass in demi-semi-quavers (ex. 290). After the first bars of each half the strings also sustain the theme and the piano then allows itself to vary it.

The second episode is in C major and consists in a dialogue between flute and first bassoon, their sharp tones standing out from the dark mass of the still muted strings. The instruments state and counter-state, question and answer, after the fashion of the first fiddle and first viola in the andante of the C major quintet. The symmetry of the first episode has gone; the melody evolves with ease and breadth, rising and falling like a garland swaying in the breeze in front of a misty forest (ex. 291).

This episode is followed by a third variation of the main theme which draws upon all forces. It treats the subject more freely. It disintegrates the smooth, sinuous form and crumbles it up into short exclamations where the tutti attack *forte* and the piano answers softly. Strings and wind double, or one group gives out the tune, and the other a counter-subject. Then both groups resume expounding the theme and the piano adorns it. All this takes place successively and nothing lasts for long; the flow is irregular and jerky. In the second half, the wind counter-subject (ex. 292) comes to the fore and is responsible for modifying and lengthening the part that precedes the "beseeching" motif, ex. 286. This latter is twice repeated in two forms. Despite this apparent confusion clarity prevails; the three groups—strings, wind and piano—mingle, oppose, double and decorate each other, without losing their individualities; each one contributes its facet to the sparkle of the whole. Through the agitation a trilling figure leads like Ariadne's thread, now in the strings, with a descant in the wind, now in the piano, over the unison strings; finally, it rises chain-like towards the tonic whilst the line of the strings writhes beneath it like a wounded snake (ex. 293); then everything relapses into the sorrow of the "beseeching" motif.

At the end of this variation the strings open a slow drumming of repeated chords and we feel that the supreme moment is at hand. The coda which begins here is indeed one of the most magical passages in all Mozart. The passion rises to tragic intensity. Upon the throbbing strings there is laid a desolate theme of the clarinets and bassoons (ex. 294). Its outline is familiar[1] but it seems, as we hear it, strikingly original and it lifts up like a voice emerging from the unknown. The very soul of the movement, bereft of all adornment,

---

[1] See ex. 71; p. 173.

stands before us in its nakedness.   As it rises towards its highest point
the flute comes and rounds off slightly the asperity of the other instruments.   Then the piano repeats it.   The theme hovers above the
bassoon's staccato and the crossing curves of violins and violas and
comes to land, to our surprise, on the chord of C major and, for a
second, we expect an optimistic conclusion.   One bar later the minor
mode is re-installed.   The closing phrase unfolds wearily; all feeling
of tragedy has gone and saddened resignation alone remains (ex. 295).
It is divided between piano and woodwind and finds rest at length in
a chromatic rise of the solo which the tutti complete by repeating
thrice its last notes.

This andante is certainly the centre of gravity of the concerto and
the movement by which we remember it.   Its beauty was recognized at once and at its first performance it was encored.   It is the
last scion of a race of Mozartian slow movements in C Minor, belonging to works in E flat,[1] several of which, like it, are in three time,
3-8 or 6-8.   The most significant are those of the string quartet K.157,
of the symphony K.184, the piano concerto K.271 and the *Sinfonia
Concertante*, K.364—this latter a very great piece which, like our
andante, rises an instant to tragedy, whereas the others sing rather of
melancholy or hopelessness, and represents Mozart's art at its highest.
Two vocal works in C minor shed light on the meaning of this
andante.   One is the fine *Kyrie* of the *Missa solemnis*, so-called: in
C minor, K.426; it confirms our interpretation of the "beseeching"
nature of certain bars; the other is an aria of the oratorio *Davidde
penitente*, written for the Lent of 1785.[2]   In 3-8 like the slow
movement of this concerto, its beginning recalls closely that of
the latter, and it happens that the words, "Fra le oscure ombre"
("Through the deep shadows that surround us") justify the simile
of the blind man which these bars had, before we knew the
aria, suggested to us.

In form, this andante is unique in Mozart.   Its plan is not unlike
one often used by Haydn, a blending of rondo and variation,[3] but
none of the many instances of Haydn's that we know resembles it
exactly and its form is as original as its feeling.

---

[1] Or in C major: quartet, K.157; symphony, K.96.

[2] Mozart used the completed numbers of his C minor mass for this oratorio,
but added two new arias, of which this is one.

[3] The Salomon symphonies, nos. 2 in D, 6 in D, 11 in D and 12 in
G; etc.

In spite of its partly episodic structure, the flow of its emotion is unbroken. It progresses towards increasingly clear definition. Confused and uncertain at first, it begins already to know itself in the first variation; the E flat episode defines it by its contrary, by showing what it is not. The second variation with its greater vigour is the result, and a heightened consciousness of what it is. A further manifestation of its opposite, the C major episode, is followed by an outburst of wrath; then, in the "tragic" song of the coda, ex. 294, it possesses itself and is fully revealed. After which, exhausted, having uttered itself wholly, the emotion dies away in the slower snd slower steps of the last bars.

"Mozart's work is the opposite of his life. The life was all suffering and the work, almost all of it, breathed nothing but happiness." When writing this, Camille Bellaigue did but repeat what was usually said half a century ago. It is at the end of a movement like this andante that one is most astounded when one unearths this judgement of a period which knew not Mozart. Is it possible to see "happiness", or indeed anything but deep suffering, rising from variation to variation to the stress of the coda, in this song where sorrow, tragedy and collapse follow each other with, it is true, two serene but ever so ephemeral interludes? We have learnt better. Mozart who, truly enough, could sing of happiness when he wished, though never as full-heartedly as Beethoven, is a great poet of sorrow, a fact which could not be perceived by a century for whom sorrow did not express itself without shouting, for whom the violence with which an emotion proclaimed itself was the measure of its depth and intensity.

III.   The refrain of the rondo is a stiffer version of that of the B flat concerto, K.450, but it is more of a dance than a gallop (ex. 296). The piano gives out the first part and the tutti repeat it. The second half (ex. 297) belongs exclusively to the piano and a longish transition, braced by woodwind and horn calls, brings back the first part. This is the usual ABA design of rondo refrains. A very long ritornello follows it, the chief elements of which are an alternating motif, given out by clarinet and bassoon (ex. 298), and an active figure (ex. 299), quivering with the bassoon, chirping with the flute, which plays a part later on.

The piano's entry in the second couplet is more arresting than usual. It is preceded by nearly three bars where the silence is broken only by chords in the strings, lightly repeated, and when it occurs

Ex. 301

Ex. 302

Ex. 303

Ex. 304

the piano does not start with a well-marked theme[1] but with a faltering figure, a reminiscence of ex. 298 (ex. 300), all the clearer for being followed, as the piano grows bolder, by ex. 299, on the vaultings of which the solo instrument sets sail for its first cruise. The solo, long but varied, and sustained by strings and wind in turn, evolves into the second subject whose seesaw rhythm is well suited to 6-8 time. Given out at first by the piano, it is repeated by the clarinet and bassoon, accompanied by the piano bass (ex. 301). Near the end of a second solo occurs one of the most perilous sketchy passages in these concertos—perilous in that it is even more absurd than usual to play it as it is written (ex. 302).[2] Is it in order to hear the pianist pick circumspectly, with one finger, first at the top, then at the bottom of the treble of his keyboard that the instruments hold their peace or lower their voices to an impersonal murmur? Obviously not. We have here a kind of cadenza *in tempo*, an extemporization in which only the starting-point in each bar is given but which can take no other form than that of arpeggios and scales.

---

[1] As in all other concerto rondos except those of K.271 and 449—both, let it be noticed, in E flat.

[2] Reinecke draws attention to these bars in his little work: *Zur Wiederbelebigung der Mozart'schen Klavierkonzerte*, but in his Breitkopf edition he leaves them as they are, although in similar places elsewhere he suggests completions on an extra stave. In the only recording of this work the soloist unfortunately makes the usual mistake of playing the bare minims.

According to custom, only the first part of the refrain, ex. 296, is resumed after this couplet and the orchestra modulates swiftly through various minor keys to A flat major, where a pause on a dominant seventh chord leaves us an instant in suspense, awaiting the second episode.

What ensues is one of the most curious examples of the way in which Mozart's musical ideas are associated with keys. Consciously or not, our rondo behaves at this point like that of his first E flat concerto, K.271, eight and a half years earlier[1] and as no other rondo had behaved since. Instead of a *development* there unrolls a spacious minuet in A flat. The likeness, it is true, goes no further; the minuet of the Salzburg concerto was followed by five variations; this one is made up of two symmetrical halves, each one given out by the wind and the piano doubled by strings, and of a coda where the piano's staccato and the violins' pizzicato are reminiscent of the arpeggios of demi-semi-quavers in the last variation of the minuet of K.271 (exs. 303 and 304). In the repeats, Mozart uses only the right hand of the piano, doubling the first fiddles; his intention is clearly to treat the piano as an orchestral instrument and to mingle its tone with the others on a single line, as if it were a flute; this effect is destroyed if chords are added in the left hand as is sometimes done. It is an effect of the linear tone of the instrument and not of its mass which he intends.[2]

The episode culminates on a pause where the soloist should insert a short cadenza to bring back the refrain.

The third couplet corresponds to the recapitulation. The return of the refrain in the tutti brings back ex. 299 in the bassoon, then in the flute, as before, and the piano receives it from the lips of the latter. The solo is shortened; the second subject returns in the tonic and the cadenza follows it closely.

The refrain comes back complete after the piano's reappearance and is followed by a coda where exs. 298 and 299 are the main elements; a witty dialogue takes place between bassoon, clarinet and piano anent the second of these. There then sounds a flourish which appears to conclude the movement.

Here occurs perhaps the most original, certainly the most mis-

---

[1] And where, too, the slow movement was in C minor.

[2] Eric Blom points out the close likeness between this episode and the theme of the round, "Nel tuo, nel mio bicchiero", in the finale of the second act of *Cosi fan tutte*. The theme of the round is a variation of the concerto$_5$.

chievous, incident in this lively rondo. With the humour of a small boy hiding behind a chair to say Boo! to his elders as they go by, Mozart lets his flourish die away; as at the beginning of the solo, which these bars reproduce, the strings repeat softly the triad and the wind sustain; this appears to be the closing chord of the movement. This goes on for three bars. Then comes the surprise. Quietly, almost wheedlingly, the piano puts forward a little phrase recalling ex. 300. After thinking we were at the end, we fancy (if we enter into the spirit of the game) we are back at the beginning.[1] The little phrase unfolds in three bits, roguish and wily; then the flourish is repeated and the movement winds up with speed and noise.

The very Mozartish form of humour seen here is one we come across in his correspondence. The following lines from a letter to his father of January 22nd, 1783, is an instance of it. "Last week, I gave a dance in my apartment. . . . We started at six in the evening and finished at seven. What? only one hour? No, no! . . . seven in the morning. . . ." In both instances, there is a transparent misunderstanding, an innocent trick; the same spirit is at work in both concerto and letter. Seldom can one find so exact a parallel between the music and the words of a composer and seldom can the same mental feature be so clearly recognized in both orders of expression. The sentiment behind letter and coda is identical.

E flat is one of the keys that Mozart, like many composers of the 1700–1800 period, has used most often. Counting from his majority, there are more than twenty sonata-form works in it, as well as nearly as many andantes and adagios of works in B flat, G minor and C minor. Not all these compositions are important; not all stand out clearly enough for us to say that the key always has with him the same character. The technical limitations of the horn, for instance, led him to use it in three of the concertos and the quintet he wrote for his friend Leutgeb and the same cause was responsible for the choice of E flat in a wind serenade, K.375, and in the quintet for wind and piano, K.452. But there remain some fifteen E flat works which make up a spiritual family and thanks to them we can determine the features which seem to accompany the key in his allegros and finales. (The andantes form a group of their own and their nature depends

---

[1] A like device is used at the end of the first movement of K.413, but less humorously.

mainly on their relation with the rest of the work to which they belong.)

Among them there is a far from negligible work which one cannot bring into any category: the highly personal concerto of February, 1784, K.449. If we leave it to one side, we shall see that, generally speaking, E flat is, for Mozart as for all the *galant* period, the key of grace and happiness. A carefree joy, usually with elegance and light-ness, sometimes with energy, but without depth: this is what we find most often, sometimes unmixed, as in trifles, sometimes linked with other qualities in his more serious compositions.[1] In some works with piano, like the concerto K.365, this one and the piano quartet K.493, this joy is expressed with majesty: the work we have been studying is the best embodiment of this conception. At one period of his life Mozart chose this key to render an emotion we have called "heroic" or "Olympian"; in this he was following a convention to which Beethoven also conformed sumptuously in his third symphony and his E flat concerto. It can be noted in parts of the two pianos concerto and the serenade K.375; it is in the powerful allegros of the violin sonata K.380 and the *Sinfonia Concertante* that Mozart has expressed most fully this lofty sentiment in the key of E flat.[2] Already, at the same date (1779), it is found in a symphony in C major and later he always expresses it in this latter key.[3]

There remains a rather different sentiment of which E flat is the vehicle late in his life. It is a kind of refined and rarefied state of the light joy which characterizes this key in most *galant* composers. The term "blithesomeness" suits it better than "joy"—a disembodied blithesomeness, a play of happy spirits, or, as Adolphe Boschot puts it in speaking of one of the works we mean, "une allégresse francis-caine". This other-worldly feeling is in touch in some cases with the musician's Masonic experience. We meet it in 1788 with the symphony K.543 and the divertimento for string trio, K.563, still mixed with joy and marked in the symphony by a certain heroic tone which reminds us of the *Sinfonia Concertante*. It reaches its most rarefied state in the string quintet of his last year; the music still sings of play, but it is the play of Botticelli's Graces, not that of an

---

[1] Saint-Foix calls E flat in Mozart "at once gentle, sensuous and energetic" (op. cit., III, 179).

[2] Cf. pp. 120 and ff.

[3] Cf. p. 341.

aristocratic Viennese ballroom.[1]   And finally, in parts of the overture and finale of the *Magic Flute* it is frankly allied with an awareness of unearthly things.   The use of E flat, not only for important parts of this opera but also for two other Masonic works, the cantatas *Dir, Seele des Weltalls* and *Die Maurerfreude*, helps us to characterize still more precisely the nature of this quasi-mystical inspiration which the key serves to embody in the last years of Mozart's life.

---

[1] Cf. pp. 491 ff.

4. The Nineteenth Concerto: K.488 in A

Concerto No. 19 in A major (K.488)[1]
Finished March 2nd, 1786
    Allegro: C
    Adagio: 6-8 (in F sharp minor)
    Allegro assai: ₵
Orchestra: Strings; flute, two clarinets, two horns, two bassoons.

THE family of Mozart's works in A major is both smaller and more select than that of his E flat compositions. These latter, besides cultured personalities, comprised some rather ordinary members—undistinguished menials, wearing the livery of the key, good enough, and no more, to line up for the passage of personages of mark like the eighteenth concerto, the symphony or the string quintet; young men with urbane faces, shaven and inexpressive, in whom good manners made up for an absence of individual feeling and intellect, whose society was not unpleasant, but whose lustreless chatter allowed us to interchange them without gain or loss.

The works in A major, on the other hand, fewer in number, are all creatures of quality. Their fully formed personalities, with sharp outlines, characteristic gestures and feelings which are not interchangeable, forbid anyone of them being confused with its kinsmen. They compose a race of individualists, as well bred as those in E flat but provided with an ego of which they are aware and which they carefully cultivate. Belonging to a small family, they have been able to grow up more freely, have enjoyed more elbow room, whereas in the house of the E flats, where the inmates were legion, air and space were lacking, overcrowding prevailed, and only the sturdiest off-spring profited fully from life.

After his return from Paris, the event from which his maturity may be dated, Mozart composed only six whole works in A

---

[1] *Gesamtausgabe*, no 23. The autograph and earliest edition have Adagio and Allegro assai; all subsequent editions have Andante and Presto.

major.[1] Two of them are piano concertos; three are chamber works—a violin sonata, K.526, a quartet, K.464, and the clarinet quintet, K.581 —and the last is a clarinet concerto, K. 622. All are works of the first order.

Of these six works, the best beloved, with the clarinet quintet, is this concerto—the best beloved and, with the D minor, the most played of his twenty-three piano concertos. It enhances the technical skill of the executant less than most; it is the least virtuoso of the lot; but its loveliness is such that it attracts the notice of all pianists anxious to measure their talents with the master.

I. We recognize certain general features in it which we meet in other A major works, yet it stands quite apart from them and, like all the 1785-6 concertos, is one of its creator's most personal productions. Its first movement is simple in structure and engaging in disposition. It is remarkably homogeneous and all its themes have a similar character, perceived in its very first bars (ex. 305). Under the transparent disguise of a cheerful exterior, the heart of the work is sad and its mood hovers between smiles and tears.

> His luminous genius has so often sung the beauty of life and so often replied to his daily trials with songs of love and hope, that one does not discover at once the sadness which is veiled behind his geniality; in his soul and his music, even the shadows are shot through with light and the reflection of the sky makes them diaphanous.[2]

Of this intimate blending of joy and care, the flattened leading note of the second chord is an early witness; the discreet chromaticisms of the eighth bar and the second subject (ex. 306), the falterings between major and minor in the passage which follows this latter (bars 46-52) are others; and the light in the movement is one of a March day—the month in which it was composed—when a pale sun shines unconvincingly through fleeting showers. It is a commonplace to say that Mozart unites features of German and Italian music, and we may recognize here a Mediterranean brightness tempered and moistened by Northern sensibility. Very pre-Romantic, but *à la Rousseau*

---

[1] We say whole, because of an unfinished quartet whose first allegro is almost complete, Köchel-Einstein no. 464 a (170 bars), a prelude and fugue (or sonata) for piano and violin, where the prelude (the only part in A major) is finished but half the fugue (in A minor) is missing, K.402, and the rondo for piano and orchestra, K.386.

[2] Adolphe Boschot: *Chez les musiciens* (2me série, p. 19).

rather than after the wise of the *Sturm und Drang*, it is at the same time one of Mozart's most authentic movements.

Its scoring, like its size, is on a humbler scale than in the works of the previous year. Trumpets and drums are lacking. The first subject, ex. 305, given out *piano* by the strings, then repeated by the woodwind in a shorter form, links on to a *forte* passage for all[1] which in turn leads to a dominant close.

The second subject, ex. 306, is more tearful than the first; its sadness is more marked; its pathetic and rather wilting tenderness is a trifle morbid. Again, exposition by the strings, restatement by the woodwind, doubled by the first violins. There follow the passage already mentioned that alternates between major and minor (bars 46–52) and a threefold call tossed from woodwind to violins and back; then, *forte*, but without any rise in the emotion, without a *strepitoso* close, we reach the common chord which precedes the concluding subject. This latter, only four bars long, returns to *piano*; only the last chords are *forte*.

In the three great concertos of the previous year and in those that follow this one in 1786, the piano enters with a prelude of its own which is sometimes important enough to be recalled later on.[2] Here, with almost studied simplicity, it comes forward with the first subject, restated literally at first, then discreetly decorated and sustained by a very light string accompaniment. How far we are from the pompous, dramatic or mysterious entries of the other concertos of this period! The tutti come in with the strain which had followed the first subject (bars 18–22): an ancient device, simple and conventional, universally used in the aria, that form whence the *galant* concerto is partly derived. After a few bars the solo takes the words from the orchestra's mouth as the voice would in the aria. Here, in most concertos, the piano strikes out along new paths, brings in its own subject, launches out into bravura. But to-day it is content to follow the lines traced by the orchestra, with very moderate virtuosity, and, lengthening by only a few bars the transitional passage, just enough to modulate without haste to E major, it gives out the second subject, ex. 306. When the instruments have restated it with occasional collaboration on the piano's part, it resumes control of affairs and, dialoguing with wind and strings, repeats almost unchanged the major-minor passage of bars 46–52, tarries an instant to play with the fiddles,

---

[1] Note once again the *piano* to *forte* opening.

[2] K.466 and 491.

and, after a very short solo, different from the end of the tutti but hardly any longer, stops on the usual trill which concludes the exposition.

We have met with several argument tuttis whose function was to give out the chief elements of the movement in the order in which they were to reappear, amplified, in the solo exposition.[1]   But never, not even in the D major, K.451, have we found one where the solo exposition followed so exactly, so timidly the lines laid down by the tutti.   What it adds is insignificant; whereas in most of Mozart's concertos the relation in length between tutti and first solo is two to three, here they are of almost equal size.[2]   The piano confines itself to decorating most discreetly the orchestra's speech—an unheard-of fearfulness in a companion work of those in C and E flat.   It

---

[1] See K.451, 456, 466, 449.

[2] The solo is four bars longer.   The concertos which diverge most widely from this 2–3 ratio are, with this one, the very heterodox K.449, where the tutti is even longer than the solo exposition (eighty-eight bars to eighty), K.413 (fifty-five bars to a hundred and eight) and K.467 (sixty-eight to a hundred and twenty-five).

may be explained, perhaps—if, however, there can be any explanation outside the critic's mind!—by Mozart's wish to vary the relations of the protagonists from one concerto to the next.

The band comes in with the beginning of the passage which had followed the first subject, but at once sounds a D natural which threatens to bring back the tonic key, an unprecedented act of daring at the end of an exposition. The work changes its mind after three bars; then, quickening slightly with a few upward scales in the violins, suddenly breaks off. A rest; then the strings give out, softly, a new theme (ex. 307). New it is in its outline, but its spirit is that of the rest of the movement. Recollected and meditative, perhaps, it appears to dream of all that has happened, and its start on the third of the scale,[1] its irregular rhythm and its counterpoint in contrary motion give us the impression that it continues a discourse begun elsewhere instead of being itself a beginning. The piano, still imitative, repeats it, but this time in the form of a free variation[2] which nevertheless retains the counterpoint (bars 149–56). This kind of pianistic writing, new in the concertos, recurs in the finale of the next work. On this theme is built the *development*, an admirable example of piano and orchestral intercourse, where the instruments compete on equal terms without either obliterating or duplicating each other.

The variation having ended in E major, clarinets and bassoons recall in E minor the first two bars of ex. 307. The piano interrupts them with some irritation and substitutes a passage based on a wriggling figure in which fiddles and violas sustain (bars 156–60). The woodwind, reinforced by the flute, return to the beginning of ex. 307, but in C major; the piano again counters them crossly and a third time the woodwind go back to their theme; the key is now A minor. Quietened and won over, the piano answers in F major; interpellations give way to brotherly intercourse and there ensues a passage new in character in Mozart's concertos but of which two later works offer examples.[3] Clarinet and flute engage in a dialogue in free canon at the fourth upon ex. 307 whilst the solo's right hand bewreathes their two lines and binds them loosely one to the other with a decoration of broken scales (ex. 308). Thrice the clarinet starts its contrapuntal walk, dropping each time by one degree without

---

[1] And, especially, the chord of the sub-dominant ninth in its second note.

[2] The *development* of K.467 also began with a new theme followed by a variation of it in the piano.

[3] K.503 and 595.

leaving the region of A minor, and thrice the flute follows it; a fourth time, the walk is at once interrupted and all stop on the dominant of the key with an almost sinister sense of foreboding.[1] The idyll turns to drama. Suddenly from the depths surges up the *daimon* of Mozart. Wind and piano relapse into frightened silence and over throbbing basses the first violins sing a fragment of the theme, all the more questioning and threatening for being inverted, whilst second violins and violas complete the harmonies of a dominant ninth, one of Mozart's red-letter-day chords, reserved for moments of intense yet restrained emotion. Piano and wind answer the strings, maintaining the chord; the piano's broken chromatic scale adds the presence of a hunted suppliant to the mass of the instruments, which have suddenly become impassive (ex. 309). We know of no more poignant instance of the lightning appearances of Mozart's *daimon* in the midst of his least dramatic works.

The strength of such moments is a function of their brevity. Having half-opened the jaws of Tartarus, he shuts them immediately and scatters the piled-up emotion in a piano cadenza. This cadenza, accompanied by held notes in the tutti, brings back the first subject in a dozen bars and introduces the recapitulation. We know how close is the relationship in Mozart between keys and formal features. Once before he had led us to the reprise on the back of a cadenza, also in a concerto in A.[2]

After this *development*, at once one of his most individual in thought and one of his most firmly constructed, the concerto returns to regular ways. For this allegro, ironically, so original both in the simplicity of its first solo and the details of its *development*, is the only one of the series which obeys the "rules" of the classical concerto as textbooks state them! Alone in Mozart, it abides by the laws which make the concerto an adaptation of the symphony and sonata and which were laid down after the event when 19th-century Aristotles drew up statutes for a genre which had never had any and which, at that time, was declining.

Docile, then, to the teaching of posterity, Mozart repeats his exposition unaltered, managing to keep his second subject in the tonic and changing a few details in the scoring and the sharing of parts

---

[1] In all this passage (bars 169-78), it is most important to hear the flute and clarinet, beside which the piano part is but decoration, and subordinate to them. The wind should play out *forte* and the soloist should not rise above *mp*.

[2] K.414.

between piano and tutti. We thus come quite uneventfully in sight of the last trill, when, only a few bars off it, the solo, seized with a belated desire for emancipation, wends its way towards the rising violin scales which had preceded ex. 307. The reason is that the theme on which the *development* had been built up is too important to be missed out in the recapitulation. The piano, on its own responsibility, states it exactly as we heard it on the strings; then clarinet and bassoon take it up and Mozart treats us to a retrospect of the fairest moment of the day. While the wind start up a four-part counterpoint, the piano again entwines them with its garlands. The game becomes animated and reaches quickly a pitch of excitement like that of ex. 309, but with no sinister intention, in three bars of a dominant pedal where the piano's left hand awakens for the first time and does its best to give body to the whole, if only with an Alberti bass (bars 267–75).[1]

Once this homage paid to the departed and all the forces having been reviewed, the solo concludes with a few bravura bars and reaches its trill. The tutti announce the cadenza and after the execution of this latter, concerning which we will confine ourselves to repeating Beethoven's recommendation in his G major concerto "*La cadenza sia corta*",[2] the orchestra restates the conclusion of the first tutti and adds a short codetta.

II. There is generally more contrast than likeness between the first allegro and the andante of a work in several movements. In this concerto it is not so. The andante maintains the same mood as the allegro, but deepens and clarifies it. The melancholy which shimmered through the smiles in the allegro and shared our attention

---

[1] This original recapitulation calls for some comparisons. The sonata for two pianos also brings in a new theme in the *development* and works it out, but less fully; at the close of the recapitulation the theme reappears. (There is a well-known instance of an important thematic element introduced at half-time in the first movement of the *Eroica*.) Bars 261–75 are a kind of premature coda and hint at the great coda of the quintet in C, also followed by a conventional conclusion which closes the movement by repeating the end of the exposition after the coda. Regarding the dynamic marks, we make the same recommendation as for bars 169–78. Some pianists make a slight rallentando in bar 261; this is right provided they remember that the wind restate the theme, so that, once their exposition is over, they must not hurry on again with their semi-quavers, otherwise the balance between them and the wind will be destroyed; the pace must be steady throughout the section (bars 261–75).

[2] Mozart's cadenza for this concerto has one merit—that of being short. It is often played but might be omitted with advantage. Its existence shows perhaps that the master taught this concerto to a pupil. It is uninteresting.

with them now takes possession of the stage and draws the whole movement to itself. The work had hitherto remained astride joy and sorrow; its nature was somewhat uncertain; there is no longer any doubt; with the first strains of this *danse triste* in F sharp minor, a key Mozart uses here for the only time in his life, the superficial affability disappears and the sombre *daimon* of ex. 309 reigns unchallenged.

As often happens in lyrical andantes, the piano gives out the cantilena and by so doing appears no longer to represent the musician's emotion but to identify itself with it; the instrument's voice becomes the very voice of Mozart's grief. The rhythm is that of a siciliana and is instinct with that melodious sorrow which so readily expresses itself in that form. The long phrase which opens it is in two parts: the first, of four bars; the second, with an unsymmetrical outline, of seven. Mozart often divides thus the cantabile themes of his andantes; after the square-cut rhythm of the first half the irregularity of the rest is a pleasing surprise. The E sharp of the second bar (ex. 310) belongs to the tune and not to the bass; the leap of three octaves and a third imitates, as Tovey has pointed out, the leaps in arias which enhanced the contrast of timbre between two registers of the voice; it is a vocal effect found also in violin and clarinet music which is in danger of appearing meaningless on a keyboard. The pianist should give the impression of carrying off a difficult feat, as if he were a singer; to that end, it may be found helpful to cross the hands and play the E sharp with the right hand.

The orchestra continues with a still more sorrowful song, heavy with beauty, given out in three-part imitation by first violins, clarinet, bassoon and flute, ex. 311 (bars 12–20). The music passes from *piano* to *forte* and the solo repeats the theme, decorating it; but soon diverges with a new subject which leads for a moment to A major. There is a fresh vocal leap in the right hand in bar 50. Then, for the space of a few bars, it wavers between major and minor and the violins echo its wistful strains;[1] finally the major wins, but unconvincingly (bars 20–34).

A brighter theme is heard in the flute and clarinet; it announces the trio, "*Ah! taci ingiusto core!*" in *Don Giovanni*, but without the latent irony (ex. 312); beginning in the wind, it passes to the solo and is followed by a codetta shared between the three groups of

---

[1] How magical an effect when the strings resume their accompaniment at the precise moment when the major appears for the first time (bar 25)!

Ex. 309

Ex. 310

Ex. 311   Ex. 312

Ex. 313

Ex. 314

strings, wind and piano (ex. 313). Two transitional bars in the wind
are enough to recall the mourning hues of F sharp minor and the first
subject (bars 50-1)—two bars full of the pathetic overlapping
harmonies beloved of Mozart, where the spirit of Chopin seems to
hover near us.

The recapitulation follows regular paths, with a dramatic extension
of the first subject, till the piano re-enters with the variation of ex. 311.
Instead of giving out again the A major section, the melody clouds
itself more deeply in dusky hues and the stress rises to the point of
suffering. In the background, flute and clarinet accompany with a
figure which is a kind of augmentation of ex. 311; in the foreground,
the piano's left hand and the bassoon engage in a dialogue over which
the right hand traces "on the wall" mysterious signs, the emaciated
outline of a theme (ex. 314).[1] The languorous Sicilian grace of the
opening has vanished and there reigns a stark mood, with almost
physical pain. After reaching a climax[2] (bar 83), the pain subsides and, as in the andante of the last concerto, the coda unfolds
wearily, rather than peacefully, in an atmosphere where resignation
turns to quiet hopelessness and where the strings' pizzicato accompaniment, with its serenade associations, is well-nigh uncanny. The
piano tune, unfortunately, is merely sketched out; it is as indispensable
to give it life by decorating it as it is needless to say that no soloist
ever thinks of doing so—an omission which deprives it of all sense and
turns this conclusion into a pompous one-finger progress from
top to bottom of the keyboard.[3] Finally, the sorrow dies away
little by little with a threefold recall of the beginning of ex. 311
in which the piano takes part and then, once the woodwind has
finished echoing the last piano chords, nothing more is heard.

Not only its key but also its beat make this andante unusual in
Mozart's work. From 1778 till his death we do not find more than
a dozen 6-8 andantes and very few of these have a siciliana rhythm.
In fact, the movement which most resembles this one is the F minor

---

[1] Which should not be decorated, for once, we think. The motion is
ensured by the basses; to enliven the treble would be to counteract it.

[2] The likeness of this passage with bars 193-200 of the andante of K.482
will be recognized.

[3] In the *Breitkopf* edition, Reinecke proposes a realization; we suggest
another (ex. 315); but the ideal is that each soloist should extemporize his
own, according to his understanding of the movement. When one plays
this movement in the solo piano arrangement, the bareness of the treble is
less apparent because one's attention is taken up by the liveliness of the bass.

adagio of the piano sonata in F major, K.280, of 1774, composed at eighteen. Across the fourteen years that separate them, the thought is picked up afresh; the concerto extends and deepens the sonata; the emotion of the young man is expressed in it with the fullness of the man of thirty.

This is the last minor andante that Mozart will write for a concerto and, except for a few pieces, either separate or else in a special form,[1] the last minor slow movement in his work. It is perhaps the one where we perceive most clearly the union of passion and formal beauty which gives such a price to his music. Abert has written one of his best pages on this matter.

> The best pianists have always recognized that behind (Mozart's) apparent clarity lies an inner life of the greatest variety and complexity. Others—very mistakenly of course—have complained that it lacks passion, allowing only that it possesses the qualities of symmetry, beauty and euphony. They make the great mistake of equating the free expression of passion with passion itself and thus, at the very start, block their own approach to an art like that of Mozart. For, while he cannot be reckoned as a true son of the Rococo age, eager to sing even his sorrows in graceful strains, yet he was no *Stürmer und Dränger*. With unbridled excitement, the chief thing for the latter, he was concerned only inasmuch as it lent itself to artistic control, that is, to form. His interest was not in Nature but in Culture. That does not mean, however, at all that he renounced the artistic presentation of passion in all its forms in favour of a vague and colourless ideal of beauty. Even had he wanted to do this, it would have been downright impossible, for we are well enough acquainted with the daemonic, nay, volcanic side of his nature and we should be underrating his originality as an artist if we considered him capable of being so false to this essential side of himself as to deny it expression in his art. On the other hand, of course, the Storm and Stress that seethed and rioted in his blood was not, in itself, capable of satisfying him completely. Rather did he feel a constant urge to master this raw material of the spirit by giving it form, adding, incidentally, some things as well as eliminating much that a later age was to value more highly, eager throughout to attain a higher standard of clarity and transparency. The most noble fruits of this urge are these adagio themes. Their importance lies, not in the perfection of their formal finish, and in their sensuous beauty, splendid as these secondary features are, but in the deep feeling from which they spring, the feeling that covers the whole wide field of inner life and that, while very far from concealing the inward glow of passion, yet lends it expression without as much as a trace of unhealthy ferment or pretentious subjectivity. To appreciate this, one needs only to compare his work with that of the later Romantics, say, of the young Schumann. With them, everything is

---

[1] B minor adagio for piano, K.540; C minor adagio for strings, K.546; F minor adagio in the first organ fantasia, K.594.

movement, excitement, unbridled passion, such as may well present itself
to youth as the highest ideal of art.   With Mozart, on the other hand,
form, the completed activity, is the main thing, and not the activity for its
own sake.[1]

The interplay of the three groups, strings, wind and piano, is
particularly delicate and masterly.   The woodwind are used much
less by themselves than in the andante of the last concerto and much
more in collaboration with the other groups.   Thus, in the second
subject, ex. 311, twice given out by the orchestra, the clarinet and
flute do not do much more than double, one after the other, the
first fiddles, while the bassoon provides one of the essential parts.
The little phrase that follows the third subject, ex. 312, is given out
first by the clarinets and bassoons, with a piano echo; but when it is
repeated (ex. 313) it is shared by the piano and strings according to
the usual plan; the theme for the latter, a variation for the former;
the echo is provided by the instruments that had given out the theme
the first time.   These two bars (46-7) are an admirable instance of
Mozart's art of combining his instruments while leaving to each one
almost a soloist's independence, and of the thoroughly concertante
quality of his style.   Some composers are content to write for their
piano as concerto writers and for their orchestra as symphonists;
Mozart realizes that the concerto principle must extend also to the
orchestra.   Spohr called Mozart's concertos symphonies with *piano
principale*; they are rather *sinfonie concertante* where first violins and
first woodwind are soloists, in addition to the piano.   Hence, the only
half unjust criticism that they are concertos for wind instruments with
piano obbligato.

The strings, also, behave less egotistically than in the andante of
K.482, where they expounded alone the long refrain.   They preponderate in ex. 311 and they echo back the piano with originality
in the third subject (bars 29-31); their most personal contribution is
their pizzicato at the end, where they accompany the solo's unquiet
wanderings like tormented spirits.

III.   The contrast we expected between allegro and andante is
found between andante and rondo.   The charm of the first two movements came largely from their drooping airs and their touch of morbidity.   The rondo, on the other hand, is one of the most exhilarating
and the most infectious ever sprung from Mozart, overbrimming with

---

[1] H. Abert, op. cit.: II, 227-8.

life and energy. It is the most successful and strongest finale of the whole series; its only possible equal is that of the concerto in F, K.459. A true *moto perpetuo*, it keeps up the irrepressible go of its opening bars without a break, with subtle changes in the length of its phrases. Tune follows on tune; song is more prominent than rhythm; Mozart uses up an incredible number of melodies; but all the time the race is maintained through the kaleidoscopic series of themes. Beneath this sparkling motley, the flow of thought remains more powerfully homogeneous than in some other rondos, such as that of the D minor, for instance, where the opening torrent of fire is quenched long before the end.

After the dying away of the siciliana, the onslaught of the refrain, bouncing with health, is one of the most brutal awakenings in all Mozart and also one of those that bring most relief.[1] That of K.482, at the same moment, was less abrupt, because the rondo opening was less decided. The theme is given out by the piano (ex. 322) and followed by the long tutti usual in those rondos where the refrain is expounded by the solo.[2] After the refrain has been restated by the orchestra, no fewer than five separate motifs can be counted; none of them comes back before the final grand review. The stream flows with irresistible rush and there is no interruption between these different subjects; each one links on inevitably to the next.

Is this not bad organization, one is tempted to ask? A passage of such length, no element of which plays any part in the body of the movement, is surely just wasteful improvisation? To this we would reply that the initial tutti of a rondo, once the main stanza of the refrain has been given out, is not like the exposition of an allegro and does not aim at introducing the chief characters in the play. In a rondo the only character is the hero, the refrain, whom we know already.

The function of these long tuttis is different. Their justification is found, not in the matter expounded, as in an allegro's initial tutti, but in the expounding instruments; the orchestra, rather than the music, is the important thing. The solo has asserted itself by capturing

---

[1] The *Mozarteum* contains two fragments for piano and orchestra in A which may be sketches for the finale of this concerto (Köchel-Einstein, nos. 488 b and e). The first, resembling the theme of the finale of the A major quartet, K.464, heralds a movement similar in mood to the opening allegro; the other, in 6-8, appears to be a theme for variations; it is rather like a major version of the finale of the D minor quartet, K.421.

[2] K.415, 450, 456, 459, 466, 482.

the refrain first; the orchestra has lost its primacy and has to make up for this loss by the length of its subsequent speech. It failed to put in the first word; at least, once its turn has come, it will speak lengthily. Hence the multiplicity of its themes, thanks to which it impresses us as deeply as its rival. When the instruments open the debate, they feel less keenly the need of counterbalancing the solo and their prelude is nearly always short.[1]

In the present concerto, moreover, the refrain demands a numerous following lest, slight and quick as it is, it be overwhelmed by the many other themes that fill the movement. Its escorting motifs are courtiers whose purpose is to draw our notice to it and enable us to recognize it when it returns—an important point for, characteristic though it appear to us, the other main subjects are no less so.

The impetus of these sixty bars flows a little more calmly in the less seething waters of the subject with which the piano opens the first couplet (ex. 317). It does not dally with this theme. Hardly have its first bars been repeated by horns and clarinets when the piano completes it and resumes full flight with one of those ascending scale themes which return so often in Mozart's prestos.[2] This one carries out the regulation transfer into E major; after which, it vanishes in its turn never to be seen again, and the new key is established by a short bravura passage culminating in a trill.

The race comes to a sudden halt and for three-quarters of a bar complete silence reigns. Three-quarters of a bar is not much, but after so inexhaustible an outpouring of animal spirits, the shortest silence becomes dramatic. The flute and bassoon, with string accompaniment, break it with what may be called the rondo's second subject —the subject which, like a sonata second subject, generally occurs in the key of the dominant. Here, it does indeed occur in E, but in E minor (ex. 318). It is interestingly scored. When Mozart subordinates his strings to his wind, he generally keeps only one or two parts of the former; here, it is the whole quartet of strings which sustains the flute and bassoon playing in octaves. When the piano restates the theme, it breaks away from it towards the end with a short digression to C major; then returns to E minor and concludes abruptly in the major (bars 114–29).

There follows a long solo, playful and high-spirited, in which

---

[1] K.467 is an exception.

[2] Ex. 317 itself is based on a tag of ascending scale. We shall hear another later (ex. 319). See also the finale of the E flat piano quartet, K.493.

now one group, now another participates; like several other solos arising from the second subject, it pretends to stop on a trill and sets off again more spirited than ever (bars 130–75). Its effervescence crystallizes at length in a theme which serves as conclusion, another fragment of an ascending scale, set on a long horn pedal. When the wind reiterate it after the piano (in the whole movement, the strings give out no tunes but those of the refrain, and even so they share most of them with the wind!), the solo muddles it with a witty counterpoint derived from the motif just given out (ex. 319). The game closes with a fragment (ex. 320) which the piano uses to bring back the refrain.

As usual, only the first part of the refrain is repeated. As soon as the tutti intervene, the music diverges abruptly and modulates to F sharp minor, the key of the siciliana. But there is no suggestion of the mood of this movement. The minor passage which opens the second couplet is no return to sadness. At most does the movement gain for an instant in vigour and earnestness. The solo figure is an impersonal one much favoured by Mozart at this time; he had used it already in the allegro of the E flat concerto and returns to it three months later, less felicitously, in the finale of the E flat piano quartet. Here, it is completed by an answer in the woodwind (bars 230–45). After its repeat, the same answer, instead of returning to the dominant chord whence we had started, jumps sharply into D major.

There is nothing unnatural in the appearance of this key in a work in A; what is astonishing is the perfunctoriness with which Mozart does not even modulate from one key to the other, but merely juxtaposes them (ex. 321).

Such a juxtaposition, not only of keys but also of the moods for which they stand, is something of a shock. The unprepared substitution of a waggish tune (ex. 322) for a passionate and earnest one seems to us to savour of frivolity or, if we confine ourselves to considerations of form, of a lack of organization, a faulty architecture where straight jointing replaces bonding. Such abrupt transitions are not uncommon in Mozart; there is one quite as brusque in the finale of another concerto in A, that for clarinet (bars 157–8), and yet another in the finale of the C minor (on the appearance of the A flat variation).

These changes remind us of one of the most pronounced characteristics of later 18th century music: its strophic build. Reduced to its simplest expression, a *galant* work consists of three or four successive themes or strophes, well contrasted, separated rather than connected

Ex. 315

Ex. 316

Ex. 317   Ex. 318

Ex. 319

Piano

Vento

Ex. 320   Ex. 321

Ex. 322

Ex. 323a

Ex. 323b

Ex. 324

Ex. 325

Ex. 326

Ex. 327

Ex. 328   Ex. 329

by less important ornamental passages. First tune; passage; second tune; passage; third tune—and so on: such is, with extreme but not deforming simplification, its outline. Between these different parts there are the same breaks as between the strophes or verses of a poem. We can put the same idea rather differently and say, with Bernard Shaw, that 18th century music is dancing music—a music beneath the progress of which is found a small number of fundamental rhythms, common to all dancing: 2-4, 4-4, 6-8, and the assembling of phrases in symmetrical groups as in the dance.

But comedy, even more than dancing, sheds light on passages like this one. Opera buffa has, indeed, deeply impregnated the orchestral music of the latter part of the century and between it and the concerto the common element of the soloist establishes a close link. Of the instrumental forms of the *galant* period, the quartet is without doubt the furthest from opera, the concerto the nearest. It is true that Mozart, in his soaring flight of the last three years, has left farther and farther below him the dramatic models whence he started, like all his South German contemporaries; yet the proximity of comedy elements—overtures, arias, finales—is still perceptible in his early concertos, whatever their solo instrument. This is also true of certain works of 1784: the D major opens like an opera seria overture; the F major is a sublimation of comedy and certain codettas and closes in both its allegros have stepped straight out of opera buffa; but the E flat and the second B flat of the same year, the D minor, the two first movements of the C major and the andante of the 1785 E flat owe little or nothing to dramatic practice. Nor do the allegro and andante of this concerto. In the finale, the most conservative of the three movements, a return is often made to dramatic origins. The only operatic echoes heard in the D minor are in the rondo; after two serious movements, the C major has a 2-4 finale whose tunes might have come from comedy, and in the finale of the E flat we found an interlude which was to reappear in *Cosi fan tutte*. Here, despite a slighter likeness with opera buffa, the cascade of tunes in the opening tutti recalls on a broader scale the coda of an overture, and the first couplet and especially the second are operatic finales transposed for piano and orchestra.

Looked at in this manner, a change of front like that in bar 260 comes to appear as natural as the abrupt entry of a new character, shedding new light on the situation, would be in a comedy. A moment in the finale of the second act of *Figaro* reminds one of this passage. The countess, Susanna and Figaro have just been singing the moving trio (in C) where they beseech the count to give, without delay, his consent to the marriage of the barber and maid. The hesitations of the nobleman, who is reckoning largely on Marcellina's arrival to get him out of his fix, adds to the fullness of the ensemble;

it is one of the most serious and most poetic moments in the score. Hardly is the trio over when the gardener rushes in to complain that a man has fallen out of the window on to his flower-bed. At one bound, the music jumps into F major and becomes as frivolous and clownish in its bustle as it was meditative and grave a moment earlier. Yet nothing offends us; the appearance of the gardener, stammering with anger, is reason enough for the change.

We have the equivalent of this here. Mozart's public, for whom the language of opera buffa was the musical language *par excellence*, recognized it and behaved in presence of this concerto as it would have done in the theatre. Since then, the parts have been reversed; opera has become the tributary of symphony and we no longer respond to the allusions to dramatic music that we hear in the instrumental works of the 18th century.

Each of the two halves of ex. 322 is given out by the clarinets and flute with piano accompaniment[1] and repeated by the solo, doubled by the violins in a simplified version (bars 262–93). The tune does not evolve into a passage but vanishes as unceremoniously as it had come, like a comrade who is shown out as soon as he is no longer needed. A few bars of dialogue between piano and wind and a solo passage bring us back to the key of A, but the pace of the movement is so swift that its impetus carries it, so to speak, beyond its point of arrival and when we regain a footing we are in ex. 317, the first subject of the recapitulation couplet. The refrain has been skipped altogether.[2]

As usual in the sonata rondo, the third couplet is the recapitulation. It differs from the recapitulation of a first movement in that, not having to collect material which had been scattered over the first tutti and the first solo, it is generally shorter than the exposition, whereas in an opening allegro it tends to be longer. The part which follows the reprise is at once modified and shortened. Ex. 317 itself, given out by the piano, is darkened by the woodwind who restate it in the minor and its last notes are repeated and exchanged two or three times by them and the piano. We pass immediately to the second subject, ex. 311; the previous theme had concluded in the minor and this one is expounded by the wind in the major. When

---

[1] Ex. 302 in the finale of K.482 had been treated likewise.

[2] A similar device had been used in another "irrepressible" rondo, K.459. It occurs more than once, notably in the piano quartets and in K.456. Beethoven uses it in his concerto in G.

the piano gives it out after them, it returns to its original mode. From it evolves the graceful dialoguing passage we noticed earlier.[1] The bravura passages and concluding subject are repeated with no changes except that of the. key, and after a rather more spacious "bridge" the refrain comes back for the last time.

The coda is worthy of the rest. The last return of the refrain is followed by all the motifs we have not heard since the first tutti. Mozart shares them out between orchestra and solo in the order of their first appearance, but he interrupts them once to recall his concluding subject, ex. 319. He brings in the whole of it, developing the dialoguing section, and in the key of D, unexpected so near the end; after which he resumes the catalogue of the material from the first tutti. Then, at the last moment, the piano remembers ex. 320, the continuation of the previous theme, and with this late-comer it whips its cream and sets going the indispensable *strepitoso*. Thanks to this frisking figure, the last bars are among those which produce most vividly in all Mozart the sense of physical strength. All the end is admirable for the manner in which the composer transforms the material of the opening tutti. Now he replaces the orchestra by the piano in the whole of one phrase (bars 464–8; cf. with bars 24–8), adapting the phrase to his new instrument; now he gives the solo the larger share, but leaving a small one to a group of the tutti (bars 468–71; cf. with bars 28–31); now the orchestra keeps the main part and the piano takes over the line of a single instrument (bars 502–5; cf. with bars 46–9); and even in the purely orchestral bars Mozart varies the general effect with imperceptible touches (bars 473–6; cf. with bars 33–6; bars 496–9; cf. with bars 40–3). Never was the accusation of reproducing unchanged whole sections of his movements less deserved than here.

We have already mentioned the importance of A major in Mozart; it is a key he uses seldom during his mature period and only for first-rate works. Those we enumerated at the beginning of this chapter are all related in one or more of their movements to our concerto. Nearly all show that mingling of joy and tears which characterizes the first movement and which is certainly the family sign of the key. The only one in whom this kinship is not apparent, the violin sonata, K.526, comes near our concerto in its rondo which is, both in form and inspiration, a kind of second version of the concerto rondo—a fine one, no doubt, but borne forward with a less

---

[1] Ex. 1.

irresistible spirit than the original.[1]   This mingled feeling, expressed with a caressing sweetness that reminds us how close voluptuousness is to regret, is kindled in Mozart by the dusky, passionate tones of the clarinet; two of his three works for this instrument are in A.   Chromatic themes, a tendency to hover between major and minor are the most recognizable means of expression of this mood.   It is hard to find preferences in this bunch of great works, where deep emotion is never accompanied by violence or murkiness, where the texture is always diaphanous, and if we owned to a greater liking for one than for the other it could be but an irrelevant personal confession.

----

[1] The theme of the refrain comes from a sonata of C. F. Abel, op. V, 5. Abel, whom Mozart, as a child, had met in London, had died in that city on June 22nd, 1787.   Mozart's sonata is dated August 24th of the same year. Saint-Foix (op. cit., V, 319–20) suggests that the use of Abel's theme was a tribute to the memory of the old composer.   A similar tribute to the memory of John Christian Bach may be recognized in the andante of K.414 (see p. 140, note 2).

5. The Twentieth Concerto: K.491 in C Minor

Concerto No. 20 in C minor (K.491)[1]
Finished March 24th, 1786
    (Allegro): 3-4
    Larghetto: C (in E flat)
    (Allegretto): C
Orchestra: String, flute, two hautboys, two clarinets, two bassoons, two
    horns, two trumpets, two kettledrums.

It is customary to wonder at the fruitfulness with which Mozart, during the summer of 1788, composed his three great symphonies in twice as many weeks, and this feat is indeed admirable. But there is as much reason to marvel at this month of March, 1786, during which, at three weeks' distance, he produced two works as fine and as different as the concertos in A and C minor. And our wonder is still greater when we remember that the writing of these concertos was not his only occupation. *Idomeneo*, composed six years earlier, was to be revived on the Vienna stage and he was busy overhauling it and even writing a new aria and duet to replace those which the taste of the Austrian capital was likely to find too simple. These numbers were finished between the completion of the concerto in A and that of the C minor.

Such fruitfulness rivals that of the Lents of 1784 and 1785. Like the latter, the Lent of 1786 presents two great twin works, conceived simultaneously or nearly so, which light up opposite aspects of their composer's soul. The difference between them, however, is less great than between the D minor and C major concertos of the previous year, and it is now the more sorrowful of the two which follows the other.

The C minor concerto is the last but one of the great twelve which spread over these three years. With its companion in C major, K.503, which was to crown the series the following winter, it is the glorious culmination of Mozart's work as a concerto writer. In these two we

---

[1] *Gesamtausgabe*, no. 24.

find united the most admirable of the features which characterize it as a whole but which had hitherto not been found in one single concerto. Lofty thought, breadth of structure, close and well-balanced collaboration between tutti and solo, rich scoring, thematic *developments*, finales rivalling first movements in importance: these characteristics, which had appeared separately in one or other concerto, are all present in the C minor and C major of 1786.

Like the D minor, this concerto is isolated in Mozart's work. But we will not make in its favour the exception we made for the former and call it Beethovenian. Unconnected with any particular composition, it is nevertheless in the main stream of Mozartian inspiration. Tempest-tossed it certainly is, but with less intensity and less obsession than the D minor. It expresses a soul driven hither and thither by the storm; the D minor was itself the storm. For one instant only, in the short *development*, does it attain the stress and compelling force of the elder work; the rest of the time, its predominating mood is elegiac rather than dramatic. It is the rule to speak of both works as if they formed a closely related pair and it is no doubt natural to wish to liken one to the other the two concertos Mozart wrote in the minor mode; but the attempt is idle. The fact that they are so different from the rest of his work is almost all they have in common.

I. The evolution of music at the end of the 18th century and the beginning of the 19th carries it away from the sectional and strophic design of the *galant* style towards a closer structure where the joins between the parts of a movement are less clearly distinguishable. To borrow a metaphor of Ernest Newman's, it is less and less like a table and more and more like a tree. This is, of course, merely the start of an evolution which has gone on to our own day and appears to culminate in the symphonies of Sibelius.

Mozart was too susceptible to the influence of his time for this evolution not to affect him. Beside movements like those of many a sonata,[1] where the quasi-autonomous divisions are marked off one from the other by emphatic cadences, themselves often preceded by noisy bars of tonic and dominant harmony,[2] he has left pieces like most of his quartets and quintets where the sections are joined by

---

[1] The allegro of the duet sonata in C, K.521, is the most successful of these movements in *galant* style, with well-marked-off divisions.

[2] Wagner's "clatter of dishes at princely banquets".

bridge passages almost as significant as the groups of main themes themselves. It is no doubt in his chamber music that he moves farthest away from *galant* conventions, whilst the sonata and the concerto, genres more fashionable because involving the honour of an executant, are those where he remains most faithful to them. But his greatest concertos possess themselves of so vast an extent of his personality, they reflect it so fully, that it was impossible they should not be influenced by this tendency. We recognize it in the works of these three years: first, in exceptional movements like the finale of K.449; then, in the allegro of the G major, the allegro and andante of the C major and, to a lesser degree, in the allegro of the D minor. Beside these more unified movements we continue to find, mixed with them, others built strophically, such as the allegros of K.482 and 488. And, in spite of the progress in unification proved by many works, movements with separate sections continue to occur to the end of his life. His last concerto and his last quintet both let us hear once more the clamorous cadences of *galant* music.

On the whole, however, the twelve concertos of 1784 to 1786 bear witness to progress towards a homogeneity which reaches its highest point in the C minor. The noisy, expressively vigorous cadences of the D minor have gone and the groups of themes link on to one another unbroken. In this the work recalls the C major, K.467, the twin of the D minor, from which it is very different in most other respects.

The opening theme resembles no other first subject of Mozart's; the only one which might recall it a little would be that of K.449, ex. 74. It takes us as far as the D minor did from the marches and flourishes with which most of his concertos begin. The ternary beat, seldom used by them, strengthens the impression of originality (ex. 323 a). It unfolds in unison,[1] without a clear-cut outline at first, unstable and chromatic; with no definite key, it seems to return to the same place and yet in reality moves forward; in the ninth bar it gains a little in concentration; though it ends by coming back to the tonic, one feels it is not compelled to do so and might pursue for a long time its wandering course.

Of the conventional *galant* opening Mozart keeps here nothing but the *piano* to *forte* plan.[2] In the thirteenth bar the orchestra

---

[1] Notice the expressive held note in the hautboys from the eighth bar onward.

[2] See p. 240.

enters *ff*—the largest orchestra in all these concertos, the only one
with both clarinets and hautboys. The theme is repeated and its
instability is now blended with an increasing strength, especially
noticeable in the prolongation and insistence of the last bars. Instead
of concluding with a return to the tonic, without interrupting its
march it is quickened by the "fluttering seconds" of the violins and
when it rests, for a brief moment, on a dominant chord, it is not
replaced by a new, contrasted subject but sets off afresh with heightened
vitality.

The bars that follow appear in their own right and not as heralds,
and yet they turn out to be a bridge to ex. 324. Without a change of
discourse, but softly, as at the opening, the woodwind trio rises one
degree at a time, exchanging and opposing two tags of the first theme
(ex. 323 b); nothing warns us that their climb is near its end when
suddenly there glides down from the sky a new figure, just a scale of
a little over an octave, whose desolate gentleness defines more clearly
the mood of the beginning (ex. 324). It has the shape of a canon at
the octave between flute and bassoon. It is not the second subject
but one of those engaging snares thanks to which Mozart avoids
casting his concertos in the mould of orthodoxy; it will not reappear
till the recapitulation. It lengthens and loses itself in a budding of a
fragment from ex. 323 b. This latter opens out and brings back
the first subject, which rumbles in the bass, where it is confined, and
tries to rise through the repeated notes of the violins and the held notes
of the woodwind, seeming to conclude. But now, at a turning, we
fall suddenly into the beseeching sweetness of the subdominant of
the relative major, a surprise all the greater that Mozart seldom
modulates in his initial tuttis. We stop an instant, whilst violins and
flute call to each other; then resume our march, return to C minor,
and a chain of ascending scales, suspended between flute, clarinet and
bassoon above a fragment of four notes from ex. 323 a which had
already served in the transition, ex. 323 b, leads to a new *forte*, and
the concluding subject, a rhythmical and wrathful phrase in which
we recognize the leaps of the first theme.

This stirring tutti is comparatively one of the shortest[1] and contains but a small part of the movement's material. If we omit the
mock second subject, ex. 324, and the concluding theme, which return
only at the end, it is all an exposition and development of the initial
strain which, in the shape either of a simple statement (bars 1-27,

---

[1] A little more than one half the solo exposition.

63–73), or of a working-out (28–44), or of a passage based on one of
its fragments (74–87), is almost constantly present. No theme of
Mozart's is so rich in possibilities of elaboration for no other is as
fluid, no other leaves the door as wide open behind it. Its transformations throughout the movement are many and diverse (ex. 325),
and through them it permeates the whole allegro. We have met
with passages where one rhythmical feature from the first persisted
throughout,[1] but here it is the melodic outline—the leaps of a sixth
and a seventh, the four descending notes, the chromatic rise at the
end, as well as the characteristic rhythm ♪| ♩♩♩| ♩ ♩ which pene-
trates and unifies the work. Mozart has given up the more primitive
and formal method, inherited from the aria, of using "link themes"—
secondary motifs gathered from the opening tutti which reappeared
like familiar faces to reassure us and act as landmarks. He had indeed
made little use of them since 1784.

This tutti is therefore an introduction and not an argument. It
is like the tutti of the E flat, K.482, in that the solo exposition takes
from it only the opening theme and that more than half of it, given
out by the solo or restated by the orchestra with piano decoration,
reappears in the recapitulation. These concertos are not the first
where Mozart repeats thus passages already heard, with piano ornamentation; in those in D and G of 1784 he had done so at the very
beginning of the first solo; but the postponement of the reunion
between piano and orchestra till the end of the movement is a step
forward, since it heightens the dramatic sense of the work.

These first hundred bars, by insisting on the main theme, have
fixed the bounds to the field on which the movement will open out.
With the piano entry, the action itself is engaged.

The monologue with which the solo introduces itself unfolds in
three strains, like so many Mozartian themes; the third is prolonged
and crumbles away into a succession of sighs, collapsing on the tonic.
The general line of the music, starting from the dominant, rises little
by little, to drop abruptly at the end with a gesture of discouragement
(ex. 326). Like the tutti, this prelude announces an elegy rather than
a drama (bars 100–18).

The orchestra re-expounds the first subject harmonized by the
brass; the woodwind take it from the strings at the fourth bar and
the piano from them at the sixth (ex. 325 a). But the piano takes it

---

[1] For instance, the dotted quaver of K.459, the march of K.467.

over only to deform it, to exaggerate its leaps which, from sevenths, become twelfths and fourteenths; then, enlivening it, transforms it into a scale passage which in a few bars leads to B flat, the dominant through which we approach the key of the relative major (bars 118–47).

A new tune starts (ex. 327); it seems to sing of peace after strife but recalls in its outline the lament of the first tutti, ex. 324. Its serenity is but apparent; the lowering of the leading note at its third repetition and the B natural betray instability and remind us of the proximity of C minor. It occupies the place of the solo subject and the piano gives it out; but instead of continuing with a bravura passage, the solo becomes silent and the woodwind repeat the theme, enriching it with imitations in hautboy and clarinet (bars 148–64). It would therefore be a true second subject, were it not that the presence later on of another subject in E flat prevents us from fitting this movement into the framework set up by the textbooks.

The wind have not done when the mood changes suddenly and the idyll turns to tragedy. Passion speaks out, though still piano, with the entry of the solo instrument which cuts off the last notes of the theme and hovers a moment in the key of F minor (ex. 325 b; ex. 328). The alarm is sudden but short and we soon regain E flat; but the excitement keeps up; it is a far cry from the piano's plaintive note in its first solo to the fiery race on which it has now started. Whilst its right hand keeps a very lively "Alberti bass" going in the treble, its left rises from the deep with wrathful scales which remind us for the briefest of instants of the angry runs in the D minor. The harsh tones are to some extent belied by the graceful interlacings of the flute and hautboy (ex. 325) which round off the rough outlines. After three smoother bars (175–7), uncertainty again envelops us; we oscillate between B flat, A flat and E flat; in each of these keys piano and violins repeat a panting figure (ex. 329) which resolves into a lightning train of arpeggios and scale fragments whose curving line rises and drops and finally carries off the E flat trill in a triumphant onslaught.

Thereupon, hautboys and clarinets give out another subject caressed by a wavy violin figure (ex. 330 a); from third to third, it percolates to the depths of the bassoon whence its second half rises (ex. 330 b). The piano repeats it and decorates the line of descending thirds, whilst the strings repeat them as they were.

The major mode now appears to have set in for good and the first bar (220) of a fresh working out section seems to confirm it. No doubt we are about to hear some of those bravura passages which conclude the solo exposition and are laid entirely in the complementary key. Yet the reviving agitation, marked by repeated notes in the strings, should put us on our guard. Moreover, we should remember how precociously the major had banished the minor on the piano's appearance. Too mild a February heralds frost in the spring. And true enough, the chord of E flat, punctuated by the strings, which concludes ex. 330, turns out in its second bar to be but the beginning of the initial subject, ex. 323 a, which had lorded it over the first tutti and was hibernating since the start of the solo. Enunciated in the upper register of the flute, it is harmonized by the quivering fiddles and violas and whipped along by the piano's arpeggios (ex. 331)—all this in E minor. In the seventh bar it breaks away from its original form and enters the key of F sharp minor, so exceptional in Mozart. Here the storm rages. Again idyll and elegy yield to an atmosphere of strife; the piano part runs tersely up and down the keyboard, escorted by the sketchy arpeggios of the wind and the syncopations of the strings (ex. 332). Then the waves of sound become less ample, shorter phrases appear, and with some of Mozart's beloved subdominant modulations and a last thrust of the minor, the rhythm breaks up and slackens and we return to the peaceful zone of E flat.

This time the calm seems to be final. The restless tutti accompaniment is silent and the piano disports itself alone for a few bars with ingenuous and limpid passage work (bars 241–8). But its energy is not exhausted. It makes sure of its victory in a well-scanned dialogue with the wind in which the strings double it; all three seem to be congratulating each other on having passed unscathed through such redoubtable alarums (bars 249–56).

Except at the beginning of the stormy section, ex. 331, the initial theme has been much less discussed than in the opening tutti. It now falls to it to provide the material for the second tutti, but illumined and glorified by its transposition into E flat major and the inversion of its sinister leaps (ex. 325 d). This short passage of eighteen bars breathes a certain humour for, beginning with ex. 323 a, with its claws drawn, it concludes with the final bars, also transposed, of the first tutti; it is therefore a miniature in bright hues of that dusky opening.

The second solo promises to be similar. It begins, like the first, with ex. 325 a, translated into the major. But at the very first repetition of the fragment the assertion turns into a question, the wind echo dreamily, and the question is put a third time, then a fourth, in the minor. It is perhaps a memory of his other minor concerto which leads Mozart to open his *development* with the first notes of the solo;[1] at any rate, he does not make the same use of this device as in K.466; the hour is not for pathetic questions or sighs but for action, and from elegy the work, with a brusque movement, passes once again to tragedy.

It is the return of ex. 323 a, in F minor, which lets loose the strife. After the orchestra has restated its first bars, the piano takes its leap from the top of the keyboard and swoops down on the strings with its usual weapons of arpeggios and mutilated scales. It rushes to the onslaught in four bar phrases, thrice repeated in different keys: G minor, C minor and E flat, while the instruments defend themselves with a fragment of ex. 323 a (ex. 325 e). The contact with E flat does not bring any relaxation and the scales continue tracing their angry wake against the troubled background of strings and wood-wind. At the moment of greatest struggle, the orchestral defence gives way and the piano comes hurtling down three octaves. With the simplest technical means, Mozart produces a poignant effect; in these few bars, we feel the firmament collapsing better than in the most chord-laden passages of Liszt or Tchaikovsky (ex. 333). The power of the effect is due largely to the skill with which the moment has been prepared.

The section which now opens is one of the few in Mozart where passion seems really unchained. Ex. 334 is an appeal to physical sensation most exceptional with him. There is here an attempt to move us by the sheer force of the attack, to take us by the shoulders and shake us; an attempt which still succeeds, provided the conductor realizes and renders the composer's intention.[2]

To the quivering instruments there answers an upward rush on the piano; it is now the attacked party that takes the offensive. The duel starts four times, each time in a different key;[3] at the fifth, we witness a kind of reconciliation and piano and wind travel together over the registers in great strides full of anger (ex. 325 f, for the bass),

---

[1] They are the only concertos of Mozart's which, like Beethoven's op. 61, behave thus.

[2] Saint-Foix (*Les symphonies de Mozart*, p. 167) points out the likeness between these bars and the climax (also in C minor) of the *development* in the great E flat symphony. Here, nevertheless, the wildness is more aggressive, the physical appeal more direct. In both works, the formal nucleus is nothing but the "fluttering seconds" so common in Mozart at moments of intense emotion, but so transformed by its context and by the passion with which the composer charges it that we do not at once recognize it.

[3] Progression by fourths, once again.

Ex. 330

Ex. 331

Ex 332

Ex. 333

Ex. 334

enlivened by a torrent of breathless arpeggios in the treble. Then, dropping its voice to *piano*, the solo returns to the tonic via the dominant; behind the line of its scales can be perceived an echo of the ever-present first subject, bounding from one wind instrument to the other (ex. 325 g).

This *development*, as short as most of Mozart's, is certainly one of his most eventful. From the moment when, with an impatient gesture, it rid itself of the "elegiac" tune, we have not stood still one instant. Often, Mozart's *developments*, after a few expressive bars, are but a wending back towards the first subject and the recapitulation. Often, too, they toy with a fragment of a theme already heard. And in his concertos, we have noted the preponderance of the fantasia[1] and virtuosity. Thematic *developments*, which appear as early as K.271, become commoner after 1784 and reveal the heart of the drama as in the D minor and A major concertos, and here. Of the three, the C minor's is the most varied. Recall of the first subject in F minor, fierce piano onslaught (bar 309) swooping down on the orchestra like an eagle on its prey, shattering collapse of ex. 333, shock tactics in the tutti in ex. 334, new adventure of the piano and wind (bars 346–53) and finally a gliding back over the light swell of the accompaniment: so many episodes stamped, truly enough, with one same passionate spirit, but diverse in their degrees of stress, in the passing of the initiative from one instrument to the other, in the particular mood—yearning, wrath, aspiration—which is lighted up, and in their constant modulation. None of the keys through which we pass is as remote as F sharp minor in the first solo; we remain in the zone of C minor and its relative major; but the motion is unceasing and Mozart, with limited means, wins as much variety as if he was exploring less closely related keys. In no other concerto is the ceaseless passing to and fro, from one key to another, kept up so long. Hence the impression that this work is not only one of his strongest but also one of his most highly coloured.

Between the tutti and solo expositions there is the same difference as in the concertos in C, K.467, and E flat, K.482. One subject only is common to both; the second exposition, instead of repeating and amplifying the material of the first,[2] introduces entirely fresh elements. The recapitulation's task will be to link up the two and to recall all their themes. It will perform this task as concisely as possible, without allowing any leisure for virtuosity.

---

[4] Cf. K.414, 450, 451, 453, 456, 459, 467, 482.
[5] As do K.451, 466 and 488, for instance.

It is as if, after the passionate outburst of the *development*, everything had been said: great vital energy has been expended and the life of the movement is limited. Certain it is that all this last part expresses profound depression. Its somewhat defeatist spirit consents, it is true, to recall the serene and almost happy themes of the first solo, exs. 327 and 330; but, according to Mozart's invariable practice, it does so in the minor; moreover, it changes their order, so that the more pathetic of the two, ex. 327, follows the other. And, in order to insist with finality on the meaning of the movement, to this latter there links on at once the lament, ex. 324, which we had not heard since the opening tutti. Though there are no more explosions of fury as in ex. 334 or certain angry bars of the *development*, the atmosphere grows ever darker and a sadness, where elegy triumphs again over tragedy, prevails more and more deeply till the magnificent coda.

The first subject is repeated *forte*, as after the solo prelude, and we follow at first the solo's and not the tutti's exposition. We part from it in the codetta added by the piano and come back with the conclusion which had followed in the first tutti (bars 28–33 and 381–6). Without closing, this passage acts now as a bridge to the third subject, ex. 330, given out with no change other than the transposition into C minor. Drastically cutting out all virtuosity, the movement links it up with the second subject, ex. 327, very affecting in its new mourning garb. The piano gives it out as before, but, when the wind restate it, interposes between each repetition a touching ascending phrase; this is one of the loveliest moments in the concerto. The theme is profoundly transformed by these tragic parentheses of the piano's. The fine modulating passage, ex. 328, succeeds it (bars 165–8 and 428–34), quickly modified, and loses itself in a variation of the first subject. The scoring is completed and the line of melody decorated and enlivened by the piano and suddenly there falls from the sky ex. 324. The working-out which prolongs it is also reproduced with piano co-operation and, at the same point as in K.482, exhibits at its highest the art with which Mozart introduces the piano into a passage originally entrusted to the orchestra, without disturbing the instrumentation or upsetting the balance of tone. Compare bars 35–62 with 435–62; to within a few details, the scoring is laid out in the same manner and Mozart no longer relies exclusively on the trick of giving the solo the former flute or hautboy part; he adds it to the wind in ex. 323 b and to wind and strings together in ex. 334, to thicken the bass with its lively arpeggios, to emphasize a

particular bar with some detail, to decorate with one hand the treble
or bass; for four bars, finally, he uses the replacement device already
described.

Again we leave the paths of the first tutti and a bravura passage—
the only one in the recapitulation—short but powerful, concludes
for the nonce the piano's part. A last statement of ex. 323 a ushers
in the cadenza. Mozart has not written one for this concerto but
the return of the tutti shows that it should not close with a trill but
link on to what follows. Then comes a repetition of bars 80-99,
leading up to the conclusion.

Mozart is not content to finish thus, although he had done so
elsewhere, even in his greatest and most personal works; he adds a
coda, the only true one in these concertos.[1] The music drops to *piano*
at the end of the quotation from the opening tutti and, softly, the
solo makes its last entry. It moves swiftly over a tonic pedal in a
mysterious twilight of diminished sevenths, whilst violins and wind
keep going from one to the other a light-footed accompaniment figure,
maintaining the first subject's rebounding semi-quavers which give
such spring and such vigour, despite its quietness, to this superb close
(ex. 335). At the very end, the *nuance* drops to *pianissimo*.

This recapitulation is shorter than most and its absence of virtuosity
is noteworthy. There is no trace of those torrents of notes with which
the soloist seems to try and stamp his image deeply on the minds
of his hearers at the last moment; on the contrary, the piano part
now does honour to the composer rather than to the pianist. Play-
wright prevails over actor; intent upon fulfilling its mission, the
music hastens towards its conclusion. Only at the end, when all has
been said, does Mozart remember he is a *virtuoso* and in his coda
combine both functions.

Beethoven's admiration for this concerto is well known. He
never imitated it but he certainly remembered it in his own concerto
in C minor, composed, like this one, at thirty, and, in his own way,
he felt and expressed the same mood, as far as a mood can be identical
from one man and from one work to another. However Beethovenian this concerto be—of a very young Beethoven—it is not fanciful
to consider it as a homage to Mozart; it is perhaps not by chance that
its major subject is one of the most Mozartish in all Beethoven, and
the general tone of the work is much nearer Mozart than usual with
him. When Beethoven is not just himself, he comes nearer to Haydn

---

[1] But which had a humble forerunner in K.271.

or Clementi than Mozart; but for once we recognize in his third concerto a composition which would perhaps not have seen the light of day without this latter's C minor work.

This is probably the best place to speak of an important problem to which we have already alluded in an earlier chapter.[1] Although it is of a general nature, we have preferred to postpone discussion of it till the diligent reader has neared the end of the greater works of Mozart's Viennese period and is familiar through them with the character of his concerto form. As this problem is solved with most consummate art in the C minor, the time appears ripe for dealing with it.

It is this.

The tutti exposition, the solo exposition that follows it, and the recapitulation are three parts of a first allegro into which enter identical elements. Hence the danger of some monotony, especially in the recapitulation which runs the risk of merely reiterating the solo exposition. Does Mozart avoid this danger, and how does he avoid it?

The question is really twofold. What difference does a concerto make between the tutti and solo expositions? How does a recapitulation differ from these and especially from the solo exposition? Though they are distinct, the success with which a classical composer solves the second of these questions depends on the way in which he has already solved the first.

Some concertos distinguish the first tutti from the solo that follows it only by the inevitable introduction of passage work. They repeat tutti elements in the solo, in the same order, modulating to the dominant, and adding the piano part to that of the orchestra, or more often substituting it for the latter. The majority, however, bring in a subject reserved for the solo and this is usually the chief difference between the two expositions. The majority, also, omit a few less important fragments which they usually, but not always, reinstate in the recapitulation; the concluding subject is often among these. Such differences are trifling—far less noteworthy than those resulting from the presence of the piano and the reshuffling in the orchestration which it necessitates.

But in a few concertos the differences, though no greater, are more significant. The number of secondary motifs which appear in the first tutti to be left out in the solo exposition may be increased and the presence of the mock second subject in one and its replacement in the

---

[1] I, 2; pp. 33, 34.

other by the true second subject emphasizes the difference all the more in that its apparent importance makes its future absence more noticeable.

Finally, in a few others, most of them works of the great period,[1] the first subject, present on both occasions,[2] and the conclusion are the only elements common to the two expositions, and even the latter is sometimes new in the solo. In the concerto to which this chapter is devoted and in the C major, K.467, the importance of the first subject, both before and after the piano entry, connects tutti and solo, in spite of the small number of details common to both. Such a procedure is obviously the most interesting because it is the richest in possible new combinations in the last part of the movement.

As the *developments* of Mozart's concertos generally take none of their material from both expositions, the novelty of the recapitulation will depend on the use it makes of the material drawn from either of them. When there is little difference between them, the recapitulation will tend to be largely a repetition of both. When the difference is great, the recapitulation has the chance of holding surprises in store for us. There are exceptions, but this is true of three-quarters of the concertos.

In the early and late works, and even in a few belonging to the great period, the recapitulation is content with repeating the first solo with the necessary transpositions. It is then with changes in the order of the material, in the solos, harmonization, scoring, distribution of themes between solo and tutti, and at least once with a heightening of the passion, that Mozart prevents it from merely reiterating the solo exposition. The concerto in A, K.488, renews its last part by introducing a theme from its *development*; this felicitous device does not occur elsewhere.

When the difference between the expositions is perceptible without being great, the recapitulation can bring together all the important elements of both, and the order in which it reviews them offers chances of variety of which several concertos have availed themselves.

Finally, when the difference between them is very wide, it would entail too great a length in the recapitulation to include in it all their elements. A choice is therefore needed. Here, five concertos act in a particularly interesting manner and their devices are not repeated.

-----

[1] K.365, 415, 459, 467, 482, 491, 503.

[2] One of the horn concertos, K.417, even introduces a new first subject in its solo exposition.

That for two pianos drops its mock second subject which had re-appeared in the *development*, and a part of the solo subject, but calls up again a secondary theme and a codetta from the first tutti. The F major, K.459, leaves out the whole of the solo subject, modifies the solos and repeats several secondary motifs from the initial tutti. The C major, K.467, acts likewise and, moreover, recalls its mock second subject. The E flat, K.482, at first sets out as if to bring back every-thing; actually, it omits half its second subject and the whole of the solo one; moreover, its bravura passages are modified and cut down and all the part of the first tutti that the solo exposition had left out is put back into the movement at this stage. Finally, the C minor brings together all the important themes of both expositions, but the solos are so much reduced that in reality only a small part of the solo exposition is repeated, and here, as in K.482, the recapitulation is a kind of *revanche* of the first exposition over the second.

In this respect, the 1784-6 concertos are the most interesting to study, although two earlier ones, K.271 and 365, had managed to vary greatly these three sections and although several works com-posed during these years had been content with repeating the second exposition as it was or had sought to renew their recapitulations in some other way. In the two concertos of 1788 and 1791, the problem ceases to interest Mozart; one of them dwells especially on virtuosity; the other pours out its originality in its *development*. The three chief formal problems of a concerto are those of the relations between expositions and recapitulation, and between orchestra and piano (inter-play), and that of the *development* (this last one common, of course, to all subdivisions of sonata form). If there is any concerto of Mozart's which has faced and solved them all in an equally masterly manner, it is certainly the C minor. And, if we remember that the very essence of a work of art, its inspiration, is here of the loftiest, it will be granted that the first movement of this concerto is the high-water mark of Mozart's concerto art.

II. The plan of the larghetto is as simple as the allegro's was com-plex. A refrain—aba—a couplet in the relative minor; the return of the first part of the refrain—a; a couplet in the subdominant; a third return of the refrain, entire—aba—a short coda. The plan of each couplet is similar: two four-bar phrases, given out by the orchestra, repeated and varied by the solo; moreover, the second couplet links on to the refrain with a bridge of four tutti bars.

The feeling appears as simple as the design but its simplicity is

that of a complex soul at rest and not of an artless one. All melodic
beauty defies analysis in the last resort but that of this refrain laughs
at it even more contemptuously than most; all that one can say is
that the wavy accompaniment adds to the magic of the canto, especially when the tutti take it up. The theme is at first sight implacably
symmetrical; in reality, its fourth bar contains an element of surprise;
the first two bars had accustomed us to the familiar opposition of a
rhythmical motif and a melodic and expressive one; in the last bar,
instead of the expected singing phrase, a purely rhythmical bar is
followed by another no less so (ex. 336).[1] But that is not all its
secret and we make no claim to disclose it. Out of the well-worn
progression: tonic—dominant—tonic—dominant seventh—tonic—
never had there been struck such loveliness.

The second part of the refrain, reserved for the solo, is but a sketch
which the pianist must at all costs fill in; to play it as it is printed is
to betray the memory of Mozart. As it returns at the end of the
movement the soloist will have to draw on his imagination to adorn
it a second time.

The refrain once given out, we pass without transition into C
minor. The first movement finished such a short while ago that this
feels like a return; we rediscover the principal key of the work rather
than enter a new one. Like a great part of the allegro, this couplet
has an elegiac tone, and the rising arpeggios in the flute and piano
remind us of the piano echo in the recapitulation of ex. 327. It is a
fragment of a woodwind serenade; hautboy and flute share the tune
or co-operate in enriching it, and the lively bassoon part borrows its
best features from the treble instruments (ex. 337). The strings are
confined to sustaining the piano when it follows the wind's lead and
varies their exposition. Once again we observe how skilfully Mozart
gives expressive beauty to an apparently quite formal decoration and
renders deep feeling through the medium of ornament.

After the four bars of refrain, we again leave E flat, which clearly
is but the official key of the movement, and plunge into the warm,
relaxing atmosphere of the subdominant as abruptly as we plunged
just now into the relative minor. To elegy and lamentation succeeds
a soft, voluptuous melody (ex. 338). But, though the feeling changes,
the wind remain none the less masters of the field; the strings join in
only to add their warmth to the piano by doubling it at the lower

---

[1] The alteration of A flat to A natural the second time the piano gives out
the tune (bar 17), and on all later occasions, will be noticed.

Ex. 335

Ex. 336

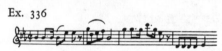

Ex. 337

Ex. 338

Ex. 339

Ex. 340

octave.[1]   At the beginning of the second half, we touch on the minor;
then voluptuousness reaches an almost painful pitch of intensity (bars
50–4).   The feeling survives a while in the strings which lead to a
pedal over which float airy thirds and sixths in bassoons, hautboys

and flutes, the last echoes of the figure 🎵🎵 which is the
motto of the passage.[2]

---

[1] Bar 48 is but a sketch (ex. 339).
[2] The reader will remember at this point the transition pedal, so close in
feeling to this passage, in the A flat larghetto of the E flat piano quartet,
K.493, a contemporary of this concerto.

One word of advice. Some conductors and pianists tend to slow down in this second couplet and to decrease the speed even further in the passage which leads back to the refrain (bars 59–62). When the soloist repeats this latter, he returns to *tempo primo* and a rough unseating of the rhythm is the result. To avoid it, the couplet should not have a rallentando and the refrain should not be speeded up. The secret is to keep an equal tempo in the different sections of the larghetto and above all not to drag in bars 59–62 or hurry in ex. 336.

When the whole refrain has been restated,[1] the woodwind build up the coda on two figures: one, descending, in clarinets and bassoons; the other, ascending, in the piano, crossed by a scale in the hautboy. The strings are still confined to accompanying and the last bars belong to the piano, seconded by a very active bassoon and adorned by the comments of hautboys and flute.

III. The commonest form for a concerto finale is the rondo. But Mozart dislikes completely minor rondos. He has left only three, all in sonatas;[2] a fourth rondo which begins in the minor, that of the concerto K.466, concludes in the major. Elsewhere, in minor works, he uses either the fugue,[3] the sonata form[4] or, as here, variations.[5]

The theme of this finale is certainly one of the most personal of those he has "varied". Measured but not slow, spare but not dry, it reminds us both of a march and a hymn. It is composed of two halves of eight bars each, with repeats, and modulates from tonic to dominant and not, like so many minor pieces, to the relative major. It remains throughout in the shadow of grief and is only distantly connected in feeling with the two earlier movements; less melodious and more reserved than the allegro, it has nothing of the serenity and voluptuousness of the larghetto (ex. 340).

However austere be this theme and its harmonization, the scoring is exquisitely subtle. The tune is given out from end to end by the first violins, *piano*, with an accompaniment in the other strings which

---

[1] Including the sketch passage!

[2] K.304 for violin in E minor; K.310 for piano in A minor; K.457 for piano in C minor.

[3] K.173, string quartet in D minor.

[4] K.183 and 550, symphonies in G minor.

[5] K.388, serenade in C minor; K.421, string quartet in D minor; K.491, this concerto. The G minor piano quartet and string quintet, K.478 and 516, have finales in the major.

shows independence only in the last bar of each half. The rhythm, on the other hand, is as full of contrasts as the outline of the tune is smooth. Marked at first with crotchets (a), it broadens into minims and semibreves (b); then follows the line of the tune with crotchets, *legato* (c).

All the wind help to mark (a); in (b), the flute doubles the fiddles at the octave; in (c) (bars 5–6), the bassoon doubles the horns; in bars 7–8, all four woodwind double or complete the string harmonies. Comparable but not identical behaviour occurs in the second half, with the result that, in a theme almost bleak with austerity, there prevails a glistening colour to which every instrument in the orchestra, even the kettledrums, contributes something at one moment or another.

This theme is followed by eight variations.[1] The first has double bars; nos. II, III, IV, V and VI are "double" variations; VII is a single one, without repeats; VIII is in different time and is followed by a coda.

As in other variations in these concertos, the piano takes no part in the theme. The first variation belongs to it exclusively; the strings provide a reticent accompaniment to the *melismas* with which it decorates the tune. The woodwind expound the second variation, a literal repetition of the theme with new harmonies and rhythm but without the original contrasts; despite its smoothness, the bassoon quavers betray a slight rise in emotion. The piano repeats each half in semi-quavers, using scales the first time and arpeggios the second; the strings sustain it with a simplified reading of the tune.

A greater intensity of feeling corresponds to the third variation. The mark rises to *forte*. The piano attacks alone. With the right hand it repeats the substance of the theme, but lashes every second and fourth beat with a dotted quaver; with the left hand, it climbs up the lower register in triplets, falling back and starting up again after each ascent. This is the first appearance of a rhythmical element in the tune itself. The dotted quaver persists in the tutti repeat in which the whole orchestra plays, and the place of the triplets is taken by the second fiddles which keep up a rapid, undulating accompaniment on their lower strings. The impression produced by strings, woodwind, brass and drums, emphasizing repeatedly the ♫♩ ♫♩

---

[1] Not numbered in the text. Here are the bars at which each one begins: I, 16; II, 32; III, 64; IV, 96 (A flat); V, 128; VI, 164 (C major); VII, 200; VIII (in 6–8), 221.

rhythm which now invades the whole theme, is powerful and warlike, not in the manner of some popular rondo militaire, but like Beethoven's C minor violin sonata.   Such purely physical effects, we said in speaking of the allegro, are not common in Mozart and all the more impressive when they occur.

This fanfare stops suddenly and in its stead clarinets and bassoons sing out a gentle tune in A flat, full of subdominant softness, a variation which retains neither the outline nor the rhythm nor the harmonies nor the spirit of the original, and is more an interlude (ex. 341).   The rhythm is still military, but neither warlike nor fierce. The piano repeats it almost exactly, doubled by the strings in their lower registers.   Only in the second half does it allow itself a few runs in scales and broken chords.

The fifth variation which, like the earlier ones, links on to its predecessor is one of the most moving.   It returns all at once to the elegiac inspiration we recognized so often in the other movements and which had been missing hitherto in this one.   It belongs wholly to the piano; the only intervention of the orchestra consists in the held notes of the strings towards the end of each section.   The first part begins with a true variation, and no longer an interlude, in free four-part counterpoint, melodious and very Mozartian in its diaphanous texture (ex. 342).   Somewhat unexpected here, it is the kind of writing one meets in the *minore* of a series of major variations.   Its second part recalls the pugnacious dotted quaver rhythm in the treble, whilst from the bass surges up wave after wave of scales rising one degree at a time with occasionally modal resonances (ex. 343).   The other half is similar, except that the counterpoint is mostly in two parts.

Again the mood becomes serene, and this time the transparent key of C major announces a heavenly peace, very different from the warm caresses of the A flat interlude (ex. 344).   It is a conversation between hautboy, flute and bassoon that reminds us, both in its inspiration and its writing, of the C major episode in the andante of the E flat concerto, K.482.   The violins take possession of the tune when the piano relinquishes it to soar upwards; right at the end, the wind take their place and the conclusion is a dialogue between the solo and them.

This is the last genial moment in the concerto.   Henceforward, attempts at pacification having failed, the work gives itself up to suffering.   The seventh variation opens like the theme, but an interruption by the piano and woodwind between fragments (a) and (b) (cf. ex. 340) brings us at once close to passion, whose realm we enter when at (c) the solo adds a quivering two-handed accompaniment of arpeggios and Alberti bass. This variation where piano, strings and woodwind interplay constantly has no repeats; it seems to hasten onward towards the issue. Instead of letting it finish, the piano adds three bars of flourishes like those of ex. 335 which lead to a dominant chord and the cadenza.

As in the allegro, the cadenza does not end in a trill but links on to the next variation without intervention of the tutti. This last variation is in 6-8 time like the conclusions of many rondos and arias, but the mode remains obstinately minor. The piano speaks alone (ex. 345). Not only its dancing rhythm but also the preponderance of the treble for both hands gives it a light-footedness which contrasts with the gravity of its thought and heightens the feeling of grief and almost of tragedy. We often find these deliberate contrasts between matter and manner in the 18th century, and in Mozart in particular. They are the musical equivalent of the use of a short, skipping verse for the utterance of sorrow. Programme notes usually draw attention to the haunting presence of the so-called Neapolitan sixth[1] in this variation and the coda which flows from it (bars 225-6, 233-4, etc.; ex. 345 a). The emotion is now that of the first movement with a return of that physical appeal which we heard in its *development*; and yet something raises it above the ordinary world of passion and bears it far away into planetary space. One feels this more strongly still when, dwelling on a motif derived from the variation, the piano rushes up to the higher octave and, doubled lower down by the strings (a favourite scoring device in this concerto), attacks furiously a chromatic succession of sixths, grating enough to set one's teeth on edge (ex. 346).

To mark that this passage is the climax of the movement and the concerto's final message, Mozart repeats it (bars 240-56, 257-73); then, having sounded for the last time the fragment (a) of ex. 345, he throws himself with the orchestra into the concluding fanfare which proclaims with desperation the triumph of the minor mode.

This concerto is in all respects one of his greatest; we would fain say: *the* greatest, were it not impossible to choose between four or five of them. We have tried to analyse the chief elements of its greatness or at least to draw attention to them; there remains one of which we have not spoken.

---

[1] Chord on the subdominant composed of a minor third and a minor sixth.

It concerns the collaboration of piano and orchestra.

The *interesting* complexity of such collaboration is the element *par excellence* of the concerto. A concerto whence it is absent may be good music but cannot be a good concerto, for it is because of the co-operation of the solo and the orchestral instruments that a work is a concerto and not a symphony. It is a *formal* ideal, but one inseparable from certain possibilities of expression which are the sole property of the genus. A concerto which does not set this ideal before it may be, we repeat, a beautiful work, but does not deserve the title it bears.

Now, this ideal is kept in mind and attained very unequally by Mozart's twenty-three piano concertos. Remote from it in his first nine, he draws nearer to it in 1784, in which year those in D, G and F attain it fully. But their success in this exceeds their emotional importance, and when with the D minor he expresses in concerto form a greater depth of passion than he had expressed hitherto in any instrumental composition, he moves away from the ideal of co-operation to return to that of alternation and opposition between the protagonists. He loses in *concertante* complexity and richness what he gains in earnestness of thought.

We saw that he won back a good deal in the concertos in E flat (recapitulation) and A (*development* of the allegro and andante). In the C minor, all the lost ground is regained; about to withdraw from the concerto stage, he excels here equally in greatness of inspiration and richness and variety of interplay between piano and tutti.

Let us say at once that the piano scarcely ever plays alone in the allegro and larghetto. The prelude which marks its entry (ex. 326) is the only entirely solo passage of any length;[1] at other times the orchestra is sometimes silent for three or four bars, either to allow it to sing more clearly the temporary serenity of the end of the exposition (bars 241–4), or so that its isolation may make the outburst of passion at the climax of the movement, ex. 333 (bars 325–9), more dramatic because more personal. In the larghetto, the first and third expositions of the refrain (bars 1–4, 63–6) are given by the unaccompanied piano. For the rest of the time in both movements, representatives of the orchestra play with it.

Yet the constant presence of the tutti by the solo's side does not constitute in itself the merit of a concerto. The resulting complexity must be *interesting*. Now, the C minor concerto surpasses

---

[1] Eighteen bars.

all its predecessors and two out of the three that come after it by the large number of original and expressive accompaniments and the abundance of moments of masterly collaboration. There is no need to enumerate them.[1] Well-worn formulas, held or repeated notes, are uncommon and, when present, are in situations which restore all their forcefulness to them.[2] Mozart prefers here expressive and melodious figures: the woodwind "question and answer" over the restless piano runs (ex. 325 c; bars 170–4), the breathless violin echoes in ex. 329. But, above all, the instruments are no longer content with accompanying in the strict sense; they complete the tones or line of the solo: its tones, by doubling it and adding the warmth, sharpness or softness of their *timbres*; its line, by sustaining it with one or other of the fragments from the first subject with which the movement is shot through. Here, examples are obvious at almost every page of the score and we must refer the reader to passages from which we have quoted a few bars such as exs. 328 and 335.[3] Strings or wind sustain the piano semi-quavers constantly and at moments of stress their diverse figures and rhythms raise the whole to a fine degree of power.[4] We mention only as a reminder the device of a tutti passage enriched at its repetition by the piano's presence, of which bars 435–62 in the recapitulation are an impressive example. Here, and in several of the passages we have instanced, one protagonist is no longer subordinated to the other, but co-operates on equal terms; piano and orchestra both subdue their egotism to the common ideal of the work, without obscuring their personality or turning the concerto into a "symphony with piano".

The piano writing itself retrieves something which had vanished and unites two features hitherto separate. It combines the D minor's varied line and quick use of different registers with the massive virtuosity of the C major, almost entirely missing from K.482 and 488. Blending the wiry strength and the fire of the one with the weight and mass of the other of the two great concertos of the previous winter, this one, with the three other piano works in C minor, marks the limits of the emotional power Mozart ever drew from his favourite instrument.

Spohr's oft-quoted expression is no juster here than elsewhere, but the semi-humorous description: concerto for woodwind and

---

[1] We have tried to classify Mozart's *interesting* accompaniments in I, 3.

[2] Held notes in the strings in ex. 325 a (bars 125–33, 369–80); repeated notes, especially in ex. 331 (bars 220–7).

[3] Also, bars 239–40, 252–6, 310–24, 388–90, 463–8.

[4] Ex. 332; bars 346–54, 355–61, coda.

piano, is perhaps more suitable. This concerto, already so many-hued in its harmonies and keys, so fruitful in constant and sometimes daring modulations, is also one of the richest in *timbre* colour, thanks to the number of its woodwind and their importance. In no other concerto has Mozart treated his woodwind so generously. Not only is it the only one with seven woodwind instruments, but they have frequently true *concertante* parts. On several occasions they play alone; in the larghetto they do it to such an extent that we called some parts of it "woodwind serenades". Both times the strings are excluded from participating in the second subject of the allegro, ex. 327; and as for the third subject, ex. 330, whereas the flute and hautboy give it out each time, the strings do but accompany them and are allowed to repeat it after them only together with the piano. The mock second subject, ex. 324, belongs also to the wind; the strings mix with them but keep an inferior position, and when, in the recapitulation, flute, clarinet and bassoon yield up some of their pre-eminence, the piano and not the violins profits thereby. When there is a melody, whether to be given out or to be accompanied, Mozart prefers frankly his hautboys, clarinets and flute.

The allegro and finale of this concerto, the andantino of K.271 and the andante of K.482 are the only movements of his piano concertos for which Mozart used the key of C minor. This key is as uncommon in the rest of his work. This concerto, the wind serenade, K.388, the piano sonata, K.457, are the only sonata-form works which use it; with the first interlude in *King Thamos*, the two piano fantasias, the *Masonic Funeral Music* and the prelude and fugue, K.546, they complete the list of his instrumental compositions in this key.

C minor is clearly exceptional with him. Exceptional because of its infrequency; exceptional, too, in the value of the works that use it. As with all minor keys, Mozart uses it only when he feels deep emotion, and most of the compositions mentioned are among his masterpieces. But for this reason it is hard to generalize about its character in his music, for in many respects each one of his "C minors" is unique. We have already said this in speaking of this concerto and it is as true of his other works in this key. The fiery passion, uttering itself through rhythmical rather than melodic effects, carrying us away rather than overcoming us with the magic of its song, which was a character of the D minor concerto and the finale of the G minor symphony, belongs also to the *King Thamos* interlude, the C minor sonata and some parts of the serenade. One should therefore not argue from the fact of its non-predominance in our concerto that it is foreign to the key. On the other hand, the singing and often elegiac tone which is heard in all three movements prevails also in the D minor quartet which has not the stormy nature of the concerto in the same key and is nearer in feeling to this one. It is therefore perilous to generalize about the characters the key of C minor may, or may not, have in Mozart's music.

Neither sonata nor serenade have the dignified melancholy, yielding only occasionally to violence, of this concerto. Both proceed by violent oppositions, causing a calm, singing phrase to follow an incisive, rhythmical one. If Beethoven remembered our concerto, one wonders whether he did not also remember the serenade, for the first movement of his op. 37 advances by contrasts like that work, and its Mozartish E flat theme bears cousinly, if not brotherly, likeness to its second subject. His concerto comes near to Mozart's, as we have said, in its coda, and here is also the point of contact between Mozart's concerto and sonata, for the last bars of the sonata express more tersely the feeling with which the concerto closes its first movement.

We end, therefore, with a thought that had come to us at the beginning of this chapter: this concerto, like the D minor, is isolated in its author's work. About to forsake the genre which had given him his chief means of expression for three years, Mozart embodied in it the passionate sorrow that dwelt in him, which has left witnesses in many of his works, but had only occasionally permeated a whole composition. Before concluding the series of his twelve masterpieces with a song of triumph in December of this same year, he lets us hear his song of grief. When, eighteen months later, he composes his last symphonies, he will do likewise and pass through the valley of tears with the G minor to reach victory with the C major.

6. The Twenty-first Concerto: K.503 in C

CONCERTO NO. 21 IN C MAJOR (K.503)[1]
Finished December 4th, 1786
    Allegro maestoso: C
    Andante: 3-4 (in F)
    (Allegretto): 2-4
Orchestra: Strings, flute, two hautboys, two bassoons, two horns, two
    trumpets, two kettledrums.

D URING more than two years now, for Mozart the composer
and virtuoso, the piano concerto has been holding the first place
in his musical consciousness. During more than two years, neither
symphony nor chamber music nor even opera has been able to compete with it. The first is quite eclipsed; only at distant intervals does
he return to the second[2]; as for opera, which was so often his favourite,
except for the curtain raiser, *Der Schauspieldirektor*, he leaves it to one
side almost as completely as the symphony. He does not come
back to it till the end of these two years; if Lorenzo da Ponte is right
in saying that the music of *Le Nozze di Figaro* was written in six
weeks, this opera must have been begun a short while before the
completion of the concerto in C minor.

And we too, for a long time, for more than two years perhaps,
have been living with these great works. It is a long time, it seems
to us, since we resumed with fresh zest the study of his concertos
when our progress through his life brought us to the threshold of
those years, 1784, 1785 and 1786, with the E flat, K.449. From one
work to the next, we have followed the young master with an interest,
nay more, with a love easy to imagine; we have watched him growing
ever more clearly conscious of the problems raised by the genre and
which he hardly suspected in his earlier concertos, attacking them
and solving them separately at first, then all together after the great

---

[1] *Gesamtausgabe*, no. 25.

[2] Quintet for piano and wind and B flat string quartet in 1784; quartets in
A and C early in 1785, in G minor during the summer.

step forward of the D minor, triumphing at length over all the difficulties they presented in the very great concerto the pages of which we have just closed.

These two years were a fine day in his short maturity and it is with sadness that we see them draw to their end. Twelve masterpieces in the same genre in thirty-three months should be enough to assuage the most voracious appetite; but every end brings sadness, however long the life, and the splendour of the sunset does not console us.

Splendid, at any rate, this sunset will be, and it is with a work which is not only one of the two or three peaks of the whole series— at once the rival and the complement of the C minor—but also one of the greatest works of his life, that Mozart the concerto writer makes, as the saying goes, "his last appearance".[1] Let us then take courage; night is not yet come; once more we may admire the way in which he faces and solves the problems of the game and makes the game itself an opportunity for expressing, as never hitherto, the "Olympian" nobility of his soul.

Lent having come to an end, the Viennnese concert season is over and Mozart does not appear again on the platform till the winter. Moreover, the composition of *Le Nozze di Figaro* and the various preparations for this opera occupy him fully till May 1st. The creation of this work, the first in date of his great *opere buffe* and the first opera he had written since *Die Entführung*, four years earlier, is a turning point in his life in that the concerto, without disappearing completely, soon ceases to be the genre which expresses him fully and into which he pours what is most precious. Henceforward, opera, then the quintet and the symphony, take its place.

1786 is one of his most fruitful years. Usually, we notice a falling off or a stop in his composing during the months when his patrons leave Vienna and concerts are suspended. But this year the output does not cease. The great effort of *Figaro* is followed in June by the second of the six piano quartets ordered by the editor Hoffmeister, a partly derivative work, full of reminders of other E flat compositions, embodying a unique experience only in its moving larghetto. In spite of its charm, the editor greeted it with the words one knows: "Write more popularly!" and it is not surprising that Mozart preferred to forgo the rest of the order.

---

[1] All virtuosi, as we know, make several "last appearances" and Mozart confirms the rule, since he composed two other concertos a few years later.

To the end of the same month belongs the last of the horn concertos written for Leutgeb. It has the same character as the others; the great piano concertos have passed but have left no mark upon it.[1] In July arrives the first work of a genre that Mozart had scarcely cultivated hitherto: the trio for piano and strings.[2] Its only example in his work had been a divertimento, K.254, an undistinguished bauble composed years ago in Salzburg. The genre will never be one of those into which his genius puts of its best, except for brief instants. Actually, the andante of this trio is one such instant; a profound *Seelenleben*, under the apparent calm, is discovered through the imitative arabesques of its one and only subject. This return to a genre attempted in his youth is followed by another when he turns to the duet sonata, a form in which he had produced two little works thirteen or fourteen years earlier. He goes back to it with enthusiasm and one might think it was to replace the concerto, for he treats his grand F major work, K.497, with a breadth and power of thought and dimensions that are unparalleled in his works for two hands. A great adagio introduction, worthy of his last symphonies, opens the allegro; in the andante, he uses again with a slight alteration in time the theme of the romance in his last horn concerto; it is instinct with that yearning which is so personal to him, which remains on this side of elegiac melancholy and shines through the second movements of the G minor quartet and the concerto in D, K.537. In the rondo, the middle couplet contains passionate rushes of ascending scales, ending in space, which haunt Mozart at this period and occur in the allegros of the G minor quartet and the G major trio.

Early in August there comes a fresh trio, this time for friends, the Jacquin family. It is the first of a family of three—trio, quintet and concerto—which friendship, and also admiration for the clarinet, drew from him. The humblest of the three, it attains nevertheless a sombre grandness in its minuet, with the disquieting and demonic trio. A fortnight later Mozart completes a string quartet in D, K.499, the first since the six dedicated to Haydn. As beautiful as any of them, it is very different; the only work of his which it recalls is the quintet in the same key of 1790; in the adagios, especially, there is close relationship; both belong to the rich line of meditative

---

[1] Not so with the G minor quartet, the beginning of which is "quoted" in the romance (bars 55-6).

[2] K.496 in G major.

slow movements[1] which stretch from the harpsichord concerto of 1773 to the quintet. The minuet, tartly concise, records, like that of the clarinet trio, a step towards those of the quintets, symphonies and quartets still to come, so full of meaning, so far from being mere "diversions."

And still his activity continues! A piano allegro, the first movement of an unfinished sonata,[2] the original conception of which comes perhaps from a sonata of Clementi's, op. 10, III; then, a second attempt at a duet sonata, K.357, consisting of a strange allegro, original rather than beautiful—one of Mozart's few attempts of which this can be said—and a finale where the piano writing announces (or recalls, for the date is not certain), the most original bars in the rondo of K.503, and where he tries to combine in a single movement andante and rondo. This experimental work, like so many others, remained incomplete.

After some variations in B flat for piano two hands, K.500, his infatuation for duets is expressed, less ambitiously, early in November in other variations, K.501. They are followed at a fortnight's distance by another trio, in B flat, K.502, a second cousin of the violin sonata in the same key of two years earlier, K.454, more substantial than that in G and the finest, perhaps, of the series of trios. This is the last work before the C major concerto.

We have dwelt at some length on the output of these few months because of its abundance and diversity. It is mainly concerned with chamber music, which is natural since concerts were in abeyance, but within its limits it deals with five or six different combinations,[3] producing a significant work in each of them. The diversity of material is no doubt responsible for the diversity of content. It is

---

[1] Cf. I, 2; p. 40.

[2] Left unfinished by Mozart, but not by publishers, thanks to an andante which is but a *pasticcio*, or a travesty, of that of K.450, to a magnificent minuet, certainly by Mozart and as certainly conceived for orchestra, and to a rondo which apes that of the same concerto K.450. In this form, it figures in several modern editions. The allegro is no. 498 a in Köchel-Einstein. Dr. Einstein upholds the authenticity of the allegro which has been impugned by Richard S. Hill (*The plate numbers of C. F. Peters' predecessors*, in *American Musicological Society*, 1938, p. 129). Einstein maintains that it is quite foreign to the style of A. E. Müller to whom it is attributed by some editions (and by Hill). See *Music Review*, vol. 2 (1941), p. 330.

[3] And even so, we have not mentioned the group of little duets for bassett horns, K.487, which Mozart dates August 1st but which he had perhaps composed at various times.

absolutely impossible to characterize in a few words the emotional streams of these nine months as we tried to do with those of the previous year. It is a transition epoch in that, among its genres, there are some that Mozart is using for the last time; others to which he is returning after leaving them for a period; others, again, which he had given up so many years ago that on returning to them he could consider them as new. The string quartet alone had figured constantly in his work for four years, and alone, also, with the opera, it is still to provide important works. The others either will be given up in the course of the next year or else, like the trio, will survive awhile but never be employed for great ends. One word only can apply to such a period: that of experimental; we adopt it to characterize the months that separate the twentieth concerto from the twenty-first, on condition, however, that it imply no judgement of inferiority for the three or four finest compositions that fall within its confines.

In the course of November Mozart began at approximately the same time a big piano concerto and a symphony. He completed them at two days' interval, the concerto on December 4th, the symphony on the 6th.

In this concerto his power is raised to its highest pitch; with the C minor, it is the climax of his development during the last three years. Except in the quintets of the next year and in the finale of his C major symphony, he never attained elsewhere such breadth and might. But the might has nothing stiff about it and does not exclude sweetness. Like the quintet in C, to which it is near, this concerto is one of his most melodious works and its many tuneful themes are gentle and caressing as well as strong; spacious and self-assured, with a broader and more pliant rhythm than usual, they are also indulgent. They are the creatures of a great man in the prime of life who, trusting in his vigour, does not disdain to be tender.

The three concertos of this year have been likened by Tovey to the symphonic trilogy of 1788, and the analogy is partly true. Though it may be a rather far cry from the concerto in A to the symphony in E flat, the second works in each group start from more neighbouring planes in Mozart's soul, and as for those in C, they both express that blend of sweetness and "Olympian" power which made an unknown Romantic call the symphony *Jupiter*. Of the two, it is certainly the concerto that deserves the title best; its first movement is permeated throughout by the heroic inspiration we associate with the ruler of Olympus; or, if one prefers, the same idea can be expressed by calling it Mozart's *Eroica*, or his *Emperor* concerto.[1]

Like the C minor, it brings together all the best in the art of concerto writing that its predecessors contained. Its orchestra is one of the largest; the C minor's alone surpasses it by including clarinets.[2] Its first movement—four hundred and thirty-two bars in common time—is the longest in all Mozart[3]; its themes, the broadest and most supple; its developments, the most sustained; its modulations the freest. The collaboration between piano and orchestra is equalled for interest and continuity only by the C minor; its middle section, the so-called *development*, entirely thematic, is close-knit and masterly; other *developments* are more dramatic, but drama is foreign to this serene work. The thought moves constantly in lofty regions and the earnestness of the first movement is found again in the rondo which is one of Mozart's few concerto finales whose scope is that of an initial allegro. Only the finale of the *Jupiter* shows Mozart the symphonist in full possession of his powers better than this work, and the public's ignorance of this king of his concertos hinders it from seeing his full stature and realizing of what calm, sustained might he is capable. To those who look on him as a pretty trifler, if any yet breathe, there is no better answer than this concerto's opening tutti.

I. Few of Mozart's compositions show themselves to the world with as original a frontispiece and none open in such bold tones. Its heroic nature is apparent in its first bars—not the sham heroism of an overture for which a few impersonal formulas suffice, but that which expresses greatness of spirit. The C minor concerto was a conflict which no victory had ended. Here, now, comes the *revanche* —a triumph whence every shadow of strife has vanished, where the display of the might, without which no strife could have been waged, is the only remains of the conflict.

A succession of majestic chords in which the whole orchestra takes

---

[1] But, *au fond*, all such names are best discarded altogether!

[2] The same orchestra (with hautboys instead of clarinets) is used in K.451, 466, 467, and 537.

[3] Beethoven's C minor concerto has the same length (444 bars); that in G, 370; that in E flat, 583. Mozart's longest allegro after this one is the first movement of the quintet in C.

part opens the first movement.[1]   Built upon the triad of C major,
they descend with slow stateliness from realms above, hastening a
little as they draw near us, then rise again to beyond their starting-
point (ex. 347).   After this proud assertion of serene power, the
work reveals at once the other aspect of its greatness: tenderness and
love; the music drops to *piano* and bassoon and hautboy exchange
two touching little complementary phrases (ex. 348).   Then, symmetrical yet quivering with life, as sumptuous as an emperor's suite,
the succession of chords resumes its progress, unfolding now in the
dominant, and again all take part in it.   Once more the movement
turns its gentler face towards us, and hautboys and bassoons again
exchange their confidential phrases.   Then, with a lowered third which
is a *coup de théâtre*, everything changes; the day clouds over, and
the happy, triumphant face shows itself as that of a soul which has
suffered and remembers it.   It is a memory, indeed, rather than the
expression of a present sorrow, but the memory is tenacious, and
we have to sojourn awhile in its shadow before the cloud passes.

As soon as the little phrase ex. 348 which introduced us into this
new landscape is repeated, we hear a rhythmical fragment which
passes all through the movement and is like its signature.   Here it
is, as it comes forward on its first appearance, in its two shapes, at the
foot of a mysterious ascent where only the harsh, disembodied voices
of the flute and hautboy trace a smooth line above the panting mur-
murs of the violins (ex. 349).

This ascent, like the triumphal downward progress at the beginning, comes back to its starting-point on the tonic; after which, the
work rediscovers the broad daylight of the major as simply as it had
lost it.   But the rhythmical fragment does not stop on this account;
it is not the servant of any one mood but of the whole work and is
to be present at every incident of the day.   Confined for the nonce
to basses and bassoons, it resumes the climb, *forte*, against the chords
of woodwind and brass, and on its shifting bass there builds up a proud
train of scales, a display in action of the power pent up in the opening
chords (ex. 350).   Half-way up, treble parts and basses change over;
the latter now take the scales whilst the former hammer out the three
repeated notes whose rhythm is enriched by the flute imitations (ex.
351).   The sense of strength grows when we enter the field of the

---

[1] Which is marked *maestoso* and not *brillante*; the memory of an unfortunate experience obliges us to insist on this point.   The work is majestic,
not festive; if it is taken too fast the majesty vanishes and breadth of line
gives place to something skimped and curtailed.   We suggest $\text{\musnote} = 132$.

dominant and the rhythmical fragment turns into a series of repeated quavers enlivened by octave leaps in the violins and basses (ex. 352).

Reaching the summit of its power, the energy suddenly overflows in a stream of quavers in the second violins, but firsts and basses still maintain the imitative sport of ex. 351. All this is finally summed up in a downward rush of two octaves and three powerful G major chords which carry over into the proclamation of the authentic rhythm: ♩♩♩♩, in unison in the whole orchestra. Thereupon, everything rests awhile.

No other work of Mozart, we said, opens with a grander page. Its only possible rival, which has no close likeness to it, would be the quintet in C with which this concerto has such affinity. Grand this beginning is, but not as immutable as one might at first think. The slow descent of the chords may call up a majestic baroque portal, with all the frigidity such an association implies; but, once the little hautboy phrase is repeated in the minor, the portal opens wide and lets us view, not the circumscribed cella of the god, but a boundless horizon. We were in port, moored in sight of a fine spectacle; now we are at sea, bound for some unknown but certainly heroic adventure, sailing on waters where none has ever preceded us. Everything, to the very rhythm of the movement at the point at which we have stopped—a broad period decomposing into the wavelets of fragment (a)—suggests this comparison.

And now, this great development over, we wait, full of expectancy. The change is complete and of all that has gone before only the persistent rhythm (a) with which the new theme begins, is left. From far away, it seems—so different is what follows—the fiddles fetch one of Mozart's simplest and most moving tunes, a fairy march whose scoring, at first slender, becomes richer as it goes on. The beauty of the melody is most strikingly enhanced by its preparation; the ancient device of contrast has seldom been used more freshly (ex. 353). This theme, given out at first in C minor, is not the second subject but is nevertheless destined to play an important part later on. Hautboys, horns and bassoons restate it, transposed into C major, and thus confirm the main key which we do not leave again till the end of the tutti; the flute crowns the tune with an undulating counter-point, the elements of which enter into the *development* (ex. 354). After a fanfare, one of the three or four appearances which Handel's *Alleluia* makes in Mozart's music, a secondary theme, sinuous and caressing leads the prelude towards its end on a more lyrical note (ex. 355).

We recognize the rhythm of (a) in it, and the same rhythm blossoms out again in the concluding theme, a song rising from the depths of the heart and whose apparent levity disguises thinly its intensity of feeling (ex. 356).[1]   Many are the bars where Mozart has sustained a tune with Alberti basses in his seconds or violas, but there are few in which this well-worn formula is as significant as here, it sets off the gossamer lightness of the dancing tune above it.

The experience of earlier concertos[2] has taught us to await the piano entry with emotion.   This dramatic moment happens some-times quite simply, and even in some of his most personal concertos Mozart brings his piano in straight away with the first subject.[3] But, in most instances, the concertos of the great period, especially in 1785 and 1786, find original shifts for calling the solo on to the stage.   Sometimes it makes itself heard as the spokesman of a more intimate feeling;[4] sometimes, as a new character ready to show off.[5]   In the other C major concerto of these years, K.467, after an imposing prelude, its voice had been lifted up timidly and it was only with hearing itself speak that it gathered courage.   The charm of these varied entries after the long orchestral introduction is a source of beauty of which post-Beethovenian concertos have deprived themselves by bringing their piano in at the very beginning of the movement.

Here, the tutti has been so massive and so sumptuous that the piano cannot hope to equal it at one stroke and, far from imposing itself, it waits to be called in, almost to be fetched, before it dare appear, like a little child acting for the first time in a nursery play who waits in the wings when his turn comes, crying and refusing to advance on to the stage.   His nurse goes to fetch him; here, the strings fulfil this function and invite the solo to appear with a most winsome sighing trill.   Fearfully, the right hand of the piano responds, with a fragment complementary to that of the strings, in the treble, but steps forward no further (ex. 357).   A second invitation follows, similar to the first; a second response is a little bolder, for semi-quavers replace quavers; finally, a third time, the strings, feeling their mission

---

[1] From its third bar on, hautboys and bassoons complicate the motion with an imitative answer, like that of the flute in ex. 351.

[2] Notably of K.271, 450, 466, 467, 482 and 491.

[3] K.451, 453, 488 and others.

[4] K.466, 482, 491.

[5] K.271, 450.

to be at an end, change their sighing motif into a cadence and are silent. After this threefold appeal,[1] the piano seeks its way alone, in short trial runs at first, and repeating its first motif three times; then, quickly, it grows bold and soars up into flight like a butterfly whose wings have expanded and dried; carried up by its scales and broken octaves, it goes and perches triumphantly on the heights of the first subject which looms up in the orchestra (bars 92–112).

Adopting now the plan of several earlier concertos, the movement resumes the whole of its stately opening, enriching it with the piano part. Never had this device been used so sumptuously. The first six bars belong to the tutti and it is at the first *piano*, with the little phrase ex. 348, that the solo is again heard; it decks out the wood-wind confidences with lavish embroidery, typical of this concerto, in a stepped outline (ex. 358). Then, the series of chords having been resumed, we remain at *piano*[2] and only the wind represent the tutti and alternate their chords with the solo's. Thus, with close collaboration, with a touching union of gentleness and mass, we reach ex. 349, around which the piano again embroiders its festooning counter-subject.

The working-out passage in C minor is gone through again for some eight bars, but without the support of the wind. Against the hammering rhythm of (a), the piano rises and falls in scale fragments whose graceful waves recall ex. 351. The opposition and reconciling of the strings' sharp rhythm and the solo's supple caresses is a fresh manifestation of this great work's rich, many-sided nature.

The delicate sport comes to an end and the piano forges ahead alone, climbing up from the bass with an amplification of the wavy figure with which it was accompanying the strings. A cadential figure concludes the passage; wavering between C minor and G major, it chooses the latter key but is uncertain of the mode, and a tutti phrase, on the incisive three quaver rhythm thrown thrice from first violins to the rest of the orchestra and back, remains in the same un-decided frame of mind.

The piano releases us from it by modulating with mischievous simplicity into the key of E flat, the natural and yet unexpected exit from the C minor into which we were involved, and starts upon its own subject. The majestic tenor of the movement is nowise broken

---

[1] May we once again point out Mozart's love for threefold divisions and repetitions?

[2] Soloists and conductors should be careful to obey this mark.

Ex. 357

Ex. 358

Ex. 359

Ex. 360

Ex. 361

Ex. 362

Ex. 363

by this change of direction; indeed, to have got rid of the orchestra appears to have made it freer, for the solo theme opens out with an ease, almost a carelessness, in rhythm most uncommon in Mozart's allegros. The first part, lightly harmonized, spreads itself with a mixture of pride and indolence (ex. 359). But oneness, not contrast, is the hallmark of the movement and into this easy rhythm there intrudes the three quaver figure, first of all as it was, then, enlivened by Mozart's "fluttering seconds". The figure makes the phrase firmer but does not trammel its flight; the progress of the theme is merely a little hastened thereby before it breaks up into a long chromatic scale (ex. 360). The end of the passage is discreetly sustained by strings and wind in turn.

With increasing excitement the movement hurries now towards the second subject into which it opens out a few bars later. This is not the march, ex. 353, but a new theme, as stiff as that of the solo was loose and melodious (ex. 15 c); its rhythmical gait is softened a little by the held notes with which the strings shade off its contour. Most of the orchestra take no part in it; only flute, hautboys and bassoons repeat it to a busy piano accompaniment. It is in G major but its closing bars hesitate between major and minor; it contains a possibility of development which is exploited in the recapitulation. It is the representative of a type we have met with in two earlier C major concertos, K.246 and 415.[1] The end of the solo consists of ascending scales in tenths and a great display of octave passages in both hands, of a technique heavier than anything we have heard since K.467. Twice over the octaves are held up in their race by the quiet but decisive intervention of the wind in the upper registers; the second time, yielding for an instant to this spirit of recollection, the solo gathers towards the middle of the keyboard, then ascends once again and culminates on the final trill with a chromatic phrase of seven quavers which straddles across three bars with complete disregard of bar lines.

This solo exposition, like that of many an earlier concerto, has carried us far away from that of the tutti. After the twenty-four bars of the first subject, it has forsaken entirely the paths trodden by the orchestral prelude. After these bars, too, the piano predominates and the orchestra, satisfied with showing itself the solo's equal on its first appearance, falls back and delegates to the woodwind the task of speaking for it in the second subject. But, though the instrumental

---

[1] See pp. 93 and 152.

centre of gravity has changed, the spirit remains the same; no contrast in mood comes to break the lovely, smooth line of the music, comprehensive enough to hover at times between major and minor and incorporate the key of E flat with those of the tonic, dominant and tonic minor without disrupting the whole, so that this exposition, which modulates further and longer than that of any other concerto of Mozart's, is also one of his most homogeneous.

After the first subject, we said the exposition made no allusion to the material of the opening tutti. To this latter Mozart now turns for his *development*. To introduce this part of the movement, he repeats the transition he has already used; he goes again over bars 26–30 and 41–50, transposing the former into G minor. The latter, on the other hand, being already in G major, he leaves them as they were (cf. ex. 350 and the latter part of ex. 352). And so we arrive at the downward rush of three octaves and the three G major chords prolonged by the proclamation of the ♩♩♩ ♩ rhythm and followed by the same silence.

This close had originally heralded the wistful, roguish "march" in C minor. Now, two bars of minims in the strings, punctuated by the same rhythm on the piano, slip down towards B minor, and ex. 353 is given out by the solo in this key, the relative minor of the "ultra-dominant".

The fifty bars that follow busy themselves exclusively with this theme which they restate and break up, and on whose fragments they end by erecting a complex contrapuntal structure.

Once the piano has given out the march, and after two transition bars where the parts of solo and instruments are reversed, the wind repeat it in A minor. The "authentic" rhythm is again asserted; there is a fresh downward slide, and the piano begins the tune again, in F major. This time a tactful but firm intervention of the woodwind holds it up half-way through and it starts once more, one degree higher up, in G minor. There is a fresh wind interruption, whereupon there opens the game which is the central portion of this *development* and one of the most original moments in all Mozart.

Let us glance at ex. 354. Subject and counter-subject, seemingly so united, are to break up, alternate, superpose, mingle with the solo's arpeggios and scales. We distinguished the three fragments into which the subject was to split up. To piano, hautboys and bassoons devolves (a); to the flute (b) and (c), parts of its original counterpoint. The first three make their entries in canons at the sixth and the octave beneath the flute's garlands; once their fragment over, the piano pours out the overflow of its energy in arpeggios; the first hautboy joins the flute; the others remain silent. Then, the figure starts again with the piano; this time (a) belongs to hautboys and flute; (b) and (c) to bassoons. The round starts in A minor and closes in D minor.

The second round is a repetition of the first in the major. The players go through the same movements, but in G and C. During this time, the strings, kept in the background, mumble in unison or in octaves a modification of (a). All this diversion, so transparent in performance, is really in eight-part counterpoint (ex. 361).

The game now grows freer, and bases itself on imitation: imitation of (b) by hautboys and bassoons, of (a), modified, by violins and lower strings—somewhat disconnected figures held together by the rockets of scales ceaselessly let off by the piano. In a few bars we climb up to the pedal of G which announces the climax of the movement and the approach of the reprise. This latter takes place with an increase of power and a display of piano arpeggios in contrary motion which recall ex. 259 in K.467; then, while the piano's broken octaves descend, a scale in the wind rises to the chord of C, proclaimed *forte* by the whole orchestra, with which the first subject opens (ex. 347).

Our study of Mozart's concertos has shown us that their *development* is generally a kind of fantasia where virtuosity runs freely. As the concerto in his work grew in poetic import, so expression won the day over pure virtuosity, and in the works in D and G of 1784 the middle part witnessed the complete release of the spirit of adventure. Yet, as well as the fantasia, some of Mozart's concertos know also the true *development*, so-called "thematic", of which Philip Emmanuel Bach's concertos afforded several examples. Already the E flat, K.271, was one of these. Yet, with the doubtful exception of K.449, we had to wait till the D minor to find a second. There, almost everything was drawn from the opening bars of the two expositions. The C major, K.467, and the last of the E flats, K.482, had returned to the fantasia. In the A major, the *development* was again thematic; the theme in question had appeared, it is true, only after the first solo, but it was important enough to figure in the recapitulation. That of the C minor, without being actually thematic, was so near to the rest of the allegro in the spirit which infused its runs and the form of its accompaniments that it belonged to both kinds.

Here, finally, the *development* is the strictest we have found since K.271. A *development* based on a theme from the exposition always adds to the formal unity of a movement; here, this result is still more marked. The absence of ex. 353 in the first solo was one of the chief differences between it and the first tutti; by returning to it and giving it so important a part, the *development* reintegrates it into the work and at the same time wipes out the distance between the two expositions.

> In Mozart's great works the repercussion of such *developments* on the rest of the piece is so weighty that, even if the recapitulation is similar to the beginning, its components are transfigured by it; there is a hidden, inexpressible power, a kind of rebounding of the elements stirred up by the powerful, sovereign rudder.[1]

This happens here; the sense of triumph in the first subject is glorified by the *development* which precedes it and by the pedal point, with its powerful virtuosity, which brings it back.

Yet it returns unchanged. The bringing together of tutti and first solo, a task which generally falls to the recapitulation, having been accomplished by the *development*, there is no reason why this last part should differ much from the first solo. So we find that all the beginning (bars 290–322) reproduces faithfully the corresponding part of the exposition (bars 112–54), with a few trifling changes.[2]

Only when the solo subject arrives do we leave the beaten track. Instead of reaching G major through D minor, the theme suddenly rises and, modulating enharmonically, traverses swiftly E flat minor, B major, B minor and G minor, before returning via G major to the tonic—a most poetic excursion which adds to the breadth of the section. The second subject unfolds at first with no change but that of key; then, again, Mozart's instability asserts itself and just as we think it is to close in C the theme ventures forth through unexpected modulations, borne on the wings of its last four notes, while the piano, completing the harmonies, strings out arpeggios full of pitfalls for those unwary pianists who think that Mozart's technique can be summed up in a few formulae.

We regain the tonic, as before, via G minor, and a reminder of ex. 353 links on to the last runs of the second subject. The reminder is more ephemeral than is usual with mock second subjects, for this

---

[1] Saint-Foix: *Les symphonies de Mozart*, 224–5.

[2] Note that bars 298 and foll. are *piano*.

one has already enjoyed a good innings; only its second half is repeated, under a piano trill which breaks before the end into joyful fountains.

The rest reproduces the end of the first solo, with slight modifications; the tutti which concluded the latter is repeated; then we diverge for a few bars for the cadenza, after which the *Alleluia* fanfare and exs. 355 and 356 return rather shortened, and the movement ends, without a coda, like the first tutti, an extra bar being added to show that the end is really come. Should we have preferred something else—the equivalent, in the sunny light of C major, of the coda of the C minor? . . . Mozart has judged otherwise.

Although this concerto belongs on the whole to those which oppose piano to orchestra, mass to mass, the *development* afforded an instance of collaboration unequalled in its complexity. The work unites, therefore, two ways of considering the relations between tutti and solo; one, in its second exposition; the other, in its *development*.

The lack of marked change in the recapitulation expresses its static nature. Several other concertos expressed something dramatic, in varying degrees, even though the drama were a happy one, and the renewal of their last section emphasized this. Here, the world is as abiding, as far removed from crises and catastrophes, as that of the B flat, K. 456; it is the world of fugue and cathedral, not that of tragedy.

Another work in the same key had shared in this nature: K.467, the first in date of those C major compositions we called Olympian and of which the concerto we are considering is the grandest. The kinship between the two is clear; but K.503 surpasses the earlier one not only in its greater size and breadth, in its more sustained inspiration, in the beauty and organic character of its *development*, but also in strains of sweetness and poetic flights which were much rarer in the other. K.467 could be called "marmorean"; the term might suit K.503 too, perhaps; but it is a marble of Attica, with lines as chaste, it is true, as a Greek temple's, but warmed, like the temple, by the rays of the sun. Mozart's passionate temperament is here quite near the surface; it comes constantly to light in the sudden falls (or shall we say "flights"?) into the minor and in the caressing outlines of nearly all its themes. In Mozart's work, this allegro is a giant, but a giant as warm-hearted as he is powerful.

II. We meet again in the andante the same breadth of conception, the same spacious lines, the same sustained motion of the themes, losing themselves one in the other instead of splitting up into separate sections. We find the same calm, lofty inspiration, more tender, however, as is befitting, and without the shadows which the frequent intrusions of the minor cast over the first movement.

Its form is that of a sonata where the *development* has been reduced to a few bars of transition—a form occurring at all periods of Mozart's life but which appears to have attracted him particularly during these months for he has made use of it in three of his most spacious compositions: this concerto and the two string quintets of the following spring. A few examples of it were to be found in his early concertos but the only other one of the great period to use it was K.459.

The andante consists of two halves, the second of which reproduces the first with superficial differences, preceded by a tutti containing the chief themes. It begins with a group of short phrases whose meaning does not become clear for some bars. Repetition and variation play a great part within the group; bars 3 and 4 are a variation of 1 and 2; 7 and 8 repeat 5 and 6, varying the run; 9 and 10 give out the same phrase on different degrees and 11 repeats it, linking it up with the concluding cadence. The whole is made up of two-bar phrases. But the feeling which inspires them is so homogeneous and their outlines, consisting in rises and falls, are so similar, that they make up but one *song*; within it, the subtle variations of rhythm are such that no monotony has yet been felt when the uniformity is broken by a third bar added to the concluding strain (ex. 362). The violins double in the first four bars; elsewhere, the main work falls to the wind instruments from one to another of which, with great care for colour, Mozart passes the different fragments of his theme.

Hardly is the theme complete when a rustling of semi-quavers in the second violins opens a fresh section. With alternations of loud and soft it lasts for four bars. Its outline takes us back to the concerto for three pianos where a very similar motif had occurred in the same place.[1] Against this background there stands out a fragment which begins *piano* with the first violins and closes *forte* with the whole orchestra; like the previous ones, it is repeated, then extended by a long descending scale which leads, *piano*, to the depths of the G string whence, on the lips of flute and hautboys, the tune rises again and concludes almost at once (ex. 363). Whereupon the final strain unrolls its threefold curve in a dialogue where first fiddles, horns and bassoons answer the other strings, and to which the flute, doubled by the bassoon, adds one last touch (ex. 364).

---

[1] Cf. p. 90.

Such is the essence of the movement. The greater part of this tutti reappears in each of the two halves, with rearrangements in the scoring caused by the presence of the piano. In the first subject, only the horns keep their original part almost unchanged; the other instruments are excluded by the solo. The piano inserts its own theme between exs. 362 and 363; its rhythm is as diverse and as supple as the rest but it is more melodious and thus contrasts with the tutti where mass predominated over line. Not content with this solo, the piano takes over ex. 363 and, encouraged by the example of its fellows in the concerto for three pianos, appropriates the rustling accompaniment which suited the strings so well. It wants also to play the bass and, as its right hand is taken up with the trilling theme, the left hand part is rather heavy. The last fragment is extended by one bar and links on to a new subject which replaces ex. 364. This latter is certainly one of the queerest children of Mozart the melodist (ex. 365). It is an outline rather than a theme. Clearly Mozart wished to express something unusual and we experience at first the kind of surprise that we would like to be admiration, which overtakes us on hearing certain passages in Beethoven's late quartets. But the mystery is cleared up when flute and hautboy, then bassoon, repeat it, modifying its skips, and the piano throws over it the graceful streamers of its scales and arpeggios (ex. 366).

The trill and C major close mark the end of this exposition. Between it and the reprise, instead of a *development*, there extends an ample transition which carries us back to F major, as in the andante of the C major quintet—a movement which gives us the feeling of expressing horizontally, in discursive melody, the mood that this andante expresses vertically and in mass. The transition is longer in the concerto and amounts to one seventh of the movement.

Its base is a pedal on C, held at first by the strings, then by the horns reinforced later by the piano. It is an idealized example of those extemporizations on A with which organists enable an orchestra to tune up before a concert. Over this foundation the piano disports itself with happy majesty.[1] The movement's concentrated thought reaches its fullest utterance in the chords that follow this display of nimble energy; here, the effort, once scattered, gathers itself together;

---

[1] The great leaps in the first bars must be filled in by the soloist; Reinecke's edition indicates upward runs between the dotted crotchet and the quaver; it is quite possible, however, to leave the octaves bare and insert the run on the way down, between the crotchet and the dotted crotchet.

Ex. 364

Ex. 365

Ex. 366

Ex. 367

Ex. 368

Ex. 369

the introduction of the chords by the tutti causes their repetition in the solo to sound like a piano transcription of an orchestral passage. The solo instrument—the cantabile piano of 1780—recovers its true personality when it spins out their power in a flexible line of triplets whose wingspread ends by covering all the upper register and whose impetus flows over into the first bar of the reprise (ex. 367).

The recapitulation leaves out the solo subject and remains in the tonic; otherwise, it reproduces faithfully the first half of the solo. But the limits of the keyboard compel Mozart to modify the detail of ex. 365. The movement ends with ex. 364; the woodwind give it out; then the piano and the other instruments repeat it with the original scoring, or nearly; the concluding upward scale in demi-semi-quavers belongs to the piano alone.

We have seen by what qualities this andante shows that it draws upon the same inspiration as the allegro. But certain features are its own and make it one of Mozart's most original slow movements. Despite its broad sweeps, its thought is concentrated; this is visible in the incessant changes of rhythm in the first and solo subjects, in the sometimes epigrammatic brevity of the other themes whose elements are always very short fragments repeated two or three times. We are conscious in it of a deep feeling which has some difficulty in uttering itself, and a good performance, while it should make the movement intelligible, will yet keep this sense of effort.

This andante, whose form is less easy to grasp at first sight than that of most of Mozart's movements, runs the risk of putting off executants, with its changing rhythms and its lack of sharply marked and melodious themes. It is most important not to hurry it; it is nearer adagio than andantino.[1] The expression of its dignity and breadth depends on its pace remaining even. The only place where a slight accelerando is permissible is in the solo subject, but a return must be made to the original speed with the rustling theme, ex. 363. It is especially disastrous to hurry the descending quavers in the first subject, which above all, should be *lasting*. The main difficulty lies in keeping the parts together; this once overcome, the rest will follow easily.

III. The finale is one of Mozart's most serious-minded rondos. Refrain and episodes have nothing of the merry tone of the usual rondo; one feels that the composer wished to end his concerto with a movement in keeping with the other two. We find the same breadth in the themes and their developments as in the allegro and andante, the same monumental conception and, in the mood, the same vacillation between certainty and doubt, expressed by hesitations between major and minor. The chief difference between this movement and the first is the absence of heroic accents; on the other hand, the middle couplet attains a degree of passion which has no counterpart in the allegro.

Mozart has gone five years back, to the ballet music of *Idomeneo*, to find his refrain. Its first eight bars reproduce almost literally the opening of the gavotte, transposed from G to C. By omitting the

---

[1] We suggest $\flat$ = 100.

portamento of demi-semi-quavers which, in the original, connected the first and second notes, he has made his theme less sentimental, but it remains none the less tinted with melancholy, serious, almost brooding, and full of a languishing grace unexpected in a concerto finale. It is only too easy to falsify its character, either by playing it too fast or by not respecting the phrasing which runs across the beat. The mark *piano* confirms the impression of gentle sadness.

The refrain is rather long and its plan irregular. After the gavotte itself, given out by the strings (ex. 368), the wind let us hear a march fragment, then the first violins repeat the last bars of the gavotte which seconds and violas complete with a cadential phrase (ex. 369). The 'cellos then do likewise, but in the minor, whilst firsts and seconds repeat ex. 369. The wind join in and after two bars the same phrase is repeated once more in the major (ex. 370). This passage is comparable to bars 15-18 of the first movement—a restatement several times over of the same motif, in major and in minor, a device more typical of Beethoven than of Mozart, and very characteristic of this concerto. A short ritornello in the whole orchestra concludes this refrain in which the piano plays no part.

The solo instrument comes on with the first couplet and the orchestra at once withdraws to the background. After an introductory theme, it launches out into a long and grand virtuosity passage where we notice the same care for varying the rhythm as in the other movements. It begins hesitatingly, like an unskilful walker picking his way gingerly in the midst of pitfalls (ex. 371). Then it grows more daring; the left hand engages in semi-quaver triplets, a formula which predominates in the piano part of this rondo. The strings mark the strong beats; the right hand punctuates the weak ones with chords, ending by taking possession of the triplets, and the music falls into its final stride, a firm, moderate gallop, whose majestic grace is in no way lessened by its impetus. The figure ex. 372 is prominent in it. Soon the triplets pass back to the left hand; the right hand accompanies them while it converses with the strings and a short pedal on D announces the second subject which the piano gives out alone (ex. 373). As in the allegro, the wind restate it while the piano, still faithful to its triplets, climbs down and up more than three octaves with scales and arpeggios. The theme once enunciated, the solo enters on a magnificent transition passage, the most sustained and perhaps the grandest in all Mozart (twenty-two bars, 91-113). It is based entirely on a dominant pedal adorned by scales and fragments of arpeggios. The triplets remain hard at work; the orchestral accompaniment grows livelier (ex. 374). Towards the end, we enter the minor and the intensity reaches passion. At this point the whole orchestra intervenes and the wind weave a web of colour round the piano's untiring gallop (ex. 375).

The piano gives out the gavotte; the tutti repeat it *forte*, hammering out the last part. Then follow the little march and exs. 369 and 370, but in this latter the 'cellos repeat the figure in the major and only fragment (b) is in the minor.

The piano opens the second couplet—the *development* of the sonata rondo—with an aggressive theme[1] in A minor, the key in which we had stopped. The theme is repeated and is followed by a few bravura bars as a coda. As soon as it is over, three vigorous chords in the whole orchestra settle its fate and that of its key by removing us, without possible protest, into F major.

The piano now gives out one of Mozart's simplest and most personal tunes. At first sight, it seems almost inert, so calm is it. Many other themes of his are simple but usually their simplicity goes with ingenuousness; behind this one's reserve one feels the experience of maturity (ex. 376). It will be noticed that the true bass is given by the double-basses and not by the piano's left hand. Hautboys and flute restate it, decorating it slightly; the piano accompanies them with an "Alberti" figure; both this and the true bass differ from the bass lines of ex. 376.

The second part is more lively and the return of the triplets in the accompaniment betrays some restlessness (ex. 377). This time the 'cellos alone give out the bass. Hautboys and flute repeat the tune over the piano triplets, and here too there is a change. To express the gradually rising emotion, Mozart adds the warm tone of the bassoon to the double-basses. The advance does not stop at the end of the tune and we modulate quickly through a few bars into C minor. Thereupon the strings enter and oppose the wind and the piano accompaniment becomes more excited. We are on the threshold of the most stirring passage in the rondo.

What follows—a transfiguration of the French rondeau's *mineur* —is profoundly dramatic. The pensive grace of the refrain, the calm assurance of the first solo vanish before a sorrowful and passionate conflict which carries us for an instant into the world of the last concerto. And, as so often happens with Mozart, the moment of

---

[1] It is a transposition of the theme with which the piano had opened the first couplet.

the most poignant emotion is also that of the most complex and closely woven technique.

As in the *development* of the allegro, the kernel of the passage is a figure of a few notes derived from a theme already heard, and the working-out takes a contrapuntal form. As in the allegro, too, and

Ex. 370

Ex. 371

Ex. 372

Ex. 373

Ex. 374

Ex. 375

Ex. 376

indeed whenever Mozart combines closely instruments and solo, the woodwind are to the fore; the strings are reduced to sustaining or to keeping silence. Flute, hautboy and bassoon share the exposition of the drama. Once the key of C minor reached, the flute repeats the first four notes of ex. 376 which the bassoon takes up in a canon

at the octave (ex. 378).[1]   The flute starts again and modulates to the
dominant, G minor (bars 202-6).   The hautboy gives out in its turn
the beginning of ex. 376; the augmentation of one degree in the
leap betrays heightened stress.   The flute replies with an imperfect
canon at the fourth (ex. 379; bars 206-10).   Then the bassoon opens
a further episode with a third exposition of the same fragment; the
leap increases to an octave and the figure climbs swiftly from the
bassoon to the hautboy and thence to the flute (ex. 380).   As in the
preceding episodes, the phrase is repeated, but this time, instead of
passing on to the flute, the fragment returns from the hautboy to the
bassoon (bars 210-16) and the flute starts a last episode, the subject of
which is still the beginning of ex. 376, but inverted, and moving
downwards.   The answers follow each other more closely and the
threefold canon at the octave is compressed now into two bars (ex.
381).   This episode, like the preceding, is given out twice, but nothing
more follows; the orchestral part finishes *en echelon* as each one of
the three instruments withdraws in turn (bars 216-20).   The basses
hold on their fundamental G for two bars more; then, the piano
continues alone and, in a long passage of broken sixths in triplets
which drops and rises two octaves, the passion evaporates and the
emotion returns to the level of the refrain.

Like all very dramatic passages in Mozart this one is short, but in
every respect it is the most significant moment in the finale.   Never
had Mozart used the canon to express such passionate feeling.   The
growing intensity is perceptible, not only in the extending to a
fourth, then to an octave, of the leap in the original figure, but also
in the length of the different episodes.   The two first, in two-part
imitation, decompose into periods of two bars each; the third is also in
two-bar periods, but the counterpoint is now in three parts; it forms
a miniature stretto.   The overlapping phrases and episodes, the
increase in length of periods and in number of parts, and the compression of the last episode, is exhilarating.   No passage reveals more
intimately the perfect union in Mozart between form and thought;
in it we grasp admirably the manner in which one is at the service
of the other, without either of them lording it.   No passage
shows better the meaning of the expression: to think, or feel,
musically.

To round off the analysis of this fine *development*, we should say

---

[1] We meet this figure again at the most dramatic moment (end of the
development) of the B flat quartet, K.589, first movement.

that all that follows the G minor modulation is built upon a tonic pedal. In no work of Mozart are pedals as prominent as here.

And the piano, it will be asked? Has Mozart forgotten that he is writing a concerto and is he sacrificing his solo instrument upon the altar of his woodwind? Not at all. The lines of the design belong to them but the task of evoking the atmosphere, the impressionistic function, is the piano's. We have found in several concertos places where it accompanied a theme which was given out by the clarinet or the flute.[1] But here we have more than an accompaniment. The source of these bars is in the bravura passages of the concertos of John Sebastian and Philip Emmanuel Bach and their contemporaries, where the solo runs were punctuated in the strings by figures derived from the main themes. Already with the Bachs the orchestra's contribution was tending to become as important as the piano's; nevertheless, virtuosity remained the *raison d'être* of the passage. Here the centre of gravity has passed from the piano to the three representatives of the tutti.[2] Its presence is nevertheless indispensable. The waves of its triplets, breaking regularly bar by bar, fill out the slender lines traced by the instruments and punctuate each degree in the great ascent. This use of the piano for mass effects during a whole passage is new in Mozart for he is a conservative in this respect and, at a period when Clementi had been using it for some ten years in a manner resembling Beethoven, confined himself to a purely linear technique. We find similar piano writing in two almost contemporary sonatas: that in two movements in F, K.533, at the end of the following year, and that in G, unfinished, for piano duet, whose kinship of style with this finale is such that Saint-Foix and Einstein both date it from this period.

Only the gavotte is repeated at the reprise; however, the orchestra repeats it after the piano and thus gives the refrain a breadth unusual at this stage of the movement where several other rondos leave it out altogether. This breadth is significant; it stresses the exceptional character of the stormy episode which has just closed. It raises in some sort a barrier between it and the rest of the movement which prevents it from contaminating the recapitulation and shows how foreign the normal nature of this finale is to such outbursts.

The third couplet repeats the first, abridging it; the beginning of the solo is omitted and the long bravura passage shortened. Ex.

---

[1] E.g. the finales of K.482 and 488.

[2] Who should play out, and *espressivo*, all through this passage.

373 is given out in the tonic and the great transition which followed it is replaced by a new and briefer passage, which retains, however, the hesitations between major and minor; it also (bars 301–2) contains a foretaste of the C major quintet.[1]

At the refrain's last appearance piano and tutti join forces. The refrain is given out entire; after the little march the woodwind are silent; the piano takes over the first violin part in ex. 369, that of the basses and wind in ex. 370, decorating them with gruppetti. It adds a rather long solo which it repeats; triplets preponderate in it and the writing recalls earlier solos; the orchestra stands quite in the background. After which, the tutti conclude the movement unceremoniously with the ritornello which had ended the first exposition of the refrain.

The problem with which a composer is presented in a concerto first movement occurs also in a finale when the latter's form is the sonata rondo: to wit, how to ensure that the last part of the movement shall be more than the mere repetition of the exposition. We have seen how Mozart solves it in an allegro. In most of his rondos he deals with it as felicitously as in his first movements. But here, the third couplet is really but a shortened version of the first with precisely the best parts left out. The coda consists in a long solo where virtuosity runs to seed and stifles the thought and the last bars repeat unchanged the commonplace ritornello we know already. As a result, the last quarter of the movement is frigid and we listen to it with some impatience. In spite of the general superiority of the sonata rondo, this is a case where the use of the two part rondo would have been more suitable. The dramatic central section does not dispose us to hear a second time what went before it; we would like to skip the recapitulation and pass at one bound from bar 229 to bar 308. Moreover, the coda, all in runs, is worthy neither of the finale nor of the work as a whole. It is clear that, after his superb *development*, Mozart had nothing more to say and grew tired of the work.

This concerto is the last of the four that Mozart composed in C major. We have connected it with its 1785 predecessor and the string quintet which was to follow it a few months later, and, of course, the word Olympian, which we have used of it, evokes inevitably the so-called *Jupiter* symphony, although that work belongs more

---

[1] Allegro, bars 270–2.

to the allegiance of Apollo than of Zeus. The key of C major, with those of F, B flat and D, is the key which Mozart has used most often; he is alike in this to all his contemporaries. Only, whereas the most used keys are not generally those in which he wrote his most distinctive works, some of his C majors do make up a well characterized family.

It is true that he used this key for many pieces about which there is little to say and, sometimes, in which there is not much to enjoy —works which reflect the personality of his period rather than his own. This is especially true of many youthful masses and symphonies, but also of many a sonata for piano, two or four hands, and for piano and violin, of late years.[1] The flute and harp concerto is no doubt the most successful of these drawing-room pieces since, whilst it keeps the impersonal exterior of the well-bred gentleman, it expresses something which is Mozart's own. But our concerto does not enter into this group.

C major is also the festal key, the key of pompous marches and overtures. It is the key with which he likes to begin and end his operas.[2] Used in this way, it often acquires strength and nobility,[3] and thus it becomes, in the last six years of the master's life, the key which expresses what we have called the Olympian quality of his inspiration. It takes by degrees the place of E flat which, at that period and down to Beethoven, is the essentially "heroic" key[4] and was so with Mozart at the time of the *Sinfonia Concertante* and the wind serenade, K.375. His first C major work where we recognize an unmistakable Olympian inspiration is the symphony K.338 which he composed at Salzburg a year or two before his final departure. Later, he turned to this key for some of his noblest contrapuntal pieces: the fantasia and fugue, K.394, the overture and fugue in the suite, K.399, and above all the massive choruses of the C minor mass: *Cum sancto Spiritu*, *Sanctus* and *Hosanna*. We have noticed the same inspiration in the grand tutti with which the concerto K.415 opened. We find it especially after 1785, spaciously expressed, in the family of works to which our concerto belongs: in the quartet K.465, the two concertos, the quintet and the symphony. After this last work, he gives it up and returns to it only in opera; the

---

[1] K.296, 303, 309, 330, 521.

[2] *Die Entführung, Der Schauspieldirektor, Cosi fan tute, Titus.*

[3] Strength in the *Schauspieldirektor* overture, nobility in that of *Titus*.

[4] Cf. p. 366.

overture of *Titus* is undoubtedly connected with the same stream of emotion as the concertos and quintet.

In spite of our strictures on the end of the rondo, this concerto is a very great work, one of the master's greatest. It is regrettable that, in the Mozart revival of recent years, the composer's trifling works should have received as much attention as his important ones, and even more. No one can maintain that his best violin concertos are not heard as often as they should be, but who will dare say as much of the great piano concertos, far superior to those for violin, which count among the most valuable part of his creation? We know only too well the piano sonatas; those for violin are not neglected; but performances of the string quintets, the peaks of his chamber music, and of the three wind serenades,[1] are still exceptional, whereas one station or another broadcasts every day the tiresome *Kleine Nachtmusik*.

With the concerto in C we reach the end of the period in Mozart's life when the concerto was his favourite means of expression. Two days after finishing it, the guard is changed and the symphony, in the person of the so-called Prague, K.504, takes over duty. This taking over may even date from before the completion of the rondo; it is perhaps because the symphony he was composing had drawn all his vitality to itself that the conclusion of the concerto was so uninspired. However it be, henceforward the master's instrumental personality takes shape in the symphony and the quintet; other genres, including the concerto itself, survive as exceptions and none of them bear fruits as rich as those they have already produced. The period of his piano concertos is over.

SCENA WITH RONDO FOR SOPRANO WITH PIANO OBBLIGATO: "*Ch'io mi scordi di te*"; "*Non temer, amato bene*" (K.505).
Finished December 27th, 1786
Orchestra: Strings, two clarinets, two bassoons, two horns.

A few days before the end of this same year, Mozart completed a curious and beautiful work in which the piano plays with the orchestra, the recitative and aria "*Ch'io mi scordi di te*", written for soprano and piano obbligato, with orchestral accompaniment. The

---

[1] Recently recorded, for the first time, by Les Discophiles Français.

piano part is brilliant and strongly redolent of the neighbourhood of the chamber works with piano and the great concertos.

Earlier in the year he had hoped to have *Idomeneo* produced in Vienna. The hope was never realized but a private concert performance was given at the mansion of Prince Charles von Auersperg in March, and on that occasion he altered the opening of the second act. Originally, it had begun with a scene in recitativo secco between Idomeneo and Arbace. For this was substituted one between Idamante and Ilia, and the latter was given an aria, on words which had not figured in Varesco's libretto (K.490). In December, he again set the text of the solo, but with different words in the recitative that preceded it, for Nancy Storace, the Susanna of *Le Nozze*, who was leaving Vienna and returning to her native city of London. The MS. of this new aria, K.505, bears the remark: "*Composto per la Sigra Storace dal suo servo ed amico W. A. Mozart Vienna il 26 di decbr 786*" (sic) and the entry in his catalogue confirms the dedication: "*Für Mselle Storace und mich.*"

A solo for voice and orchestra with piano obbligato was not in Mozart's time the curiosity it would be to-day. John Christian Bach had composed in 1774 a scena con aria, on words from *Rinaldo ed Armida*, in which there figured obbligato parts for piano and hautboy. At some later date, he played in it with Gainsborough's son-in-law, the hautboist John Christian Fischer and the castrato Tenducci.[1] He and Tenducci were both in Paris in 1778, during Mozart's stay there, and Mozart was asked to write a scena for the singer. He did so, and the work, now lost, had four obbligato parts: piano, hautboy, horn and bassoon;[2] it was probably modelled on Bach's.

In the aria for Nancy Storace, the piano is the only obbligato instrument.[3] The aria proper is preceded by twenty-seven bars of

---

[1] A MS. copy of this scena in the British Museum bears the title: "The Favorite Rondeau sung by Mr. Tenducci accompanied on the Pianoforte by Mr. Bach and on the Hautboy by Mr. Fisher" (C. S. Terry: *John Christian Bach*, p. 250). The piano part is an accompaniment throughout. The scena is published in Landshoff's edition of *Twelve Concert Arias by J. C. Bach* (Peters, 1929).

[2] Köchel-Einstein 315 b. Cf. his letter to his father of August 27th, 1778.

[3] The earlier setting, K.490, had an obbligato violin part, which was played by Mozart's friend, Count August von Hatzfeld. In spite of a certain superficial likeness in the figuration between the solo violin and piano parts, there is little in common between the two settings, and the latter is greatly superior to the earlier one, which is mainly showy virtuosity.

recitative, accompanied only by the strings. The rondo begins with an andante of seventy-three bars, consisting of refrain, couplet, and repetition of the refrain, and an allegretto of a hundred and forty-one bars, with three returns of the refrain, two couplets and a long coda. The refrain in the allegretto, different from that in the andante, may, at a pinch, be considered a free variation of it. In its allegretto form it is very close to the main subject of the finale in the clarinet trio, K.498, composed four and a half months earlier.

The combination of piano and soprano is constant and varied. The writing, we have said, is close in style to the piano parts in both concerto and chamber music, especially in such concertante works as the quintet for piano and wind, K.452, the brilliant B flat violin sonata, K.454, the piano quartets and the clarinet trio. Only twice does the piano give out the theme before the voice, each time in the refrain (bars 4–12 and 73–81).[1] Elsewhere, save for an occasional bar of transition, it never plays alone. Since its presence is our only justification for mentioning this work, we will confine our remarks to the relations between obbligato and solo.

In their intercourse, the piano is either subordinate to the voice or collaborates with it. It is often the solo's equal but never its superior. Twice, in bars 202 and 207,[2] it supports the vocal line a third below. In each of the expositions of the andante refrain, where the voice has a tenuto of a couple of bars (bars 18–19 and 62–63), the piano weaves over it a rococo line of gruppetti, themselves of a coloratura character and not unlike a passage that occurs in the voice part towards the end of the aria (bars 208–9).[3] But as a rule its behaviour to the voice in those passages where it is not collaborating on equal terms consists in harmonizing the vocal line with arpeggios or, once, with an "Alberti-bass" figure in both hands,[4] recalling certain passages in the allegro of K.467[5] or the coda of the first movement of the G minor quartet. The most original instance of such harmonization occurs in a place, which is repeated, where the voice has a slow descending chromatic scale (bars 26–32 and 134–40). On the first occasion the piano superimposes arpeggios over the vocal line; the result is an entrancing chain of diminished sevenths (ex. 381 a). When the text ("*l'alma mia mancando va*") returns in the

---

[1] Our numbering goes from the beginning of the andante.

[2] Bars 205–9 are cut in the *Breitkopf* piano score.

[3] Bars 205–9 are cut in the *Breitkopf* piano score.

[4] Bars 94–5.   [5] Bars 253–8.

allegretto the bass falls to the piano and the harmonization is different; the voice part is now enveloped in the piano arpeggios (ex. 381 b). These are among the most expressive bars in all Mozart's vocal music.[1]

We have classed these bars as accompaniment, but accompaniment of such originality and beauty easily becomes the equal of the solo. In those moments where piano and voice interplay on equal terms we

Ex. 381a

Ex. 381b

Ex. 381c

Ex. 381d

---

[1] Cf. with ex. 181 b, from the allegro of K.456.

Ex. 381e

may distinguish between those when they succeed or answer each other, and those in which they combine.

The most dramatic examples of question and answer occur when a balanced phrase is divided between the partners. There is no more moving strain in the rondo than at the setting of the words: "*Tu sospiri?*" (bars 141-4), where they alternate with a minor two-bar phrase, one of those stylized imitations of sighing beloved of the rococo age (ex. 381 c; the example joins on to ex. 381 b). Sometimes the voice speaks first and the piano replies; it is then, as a rule, in semi-quavers that the instrument rejoins, just as it did in the allegro of the C minor concerto.[1] There is a particularly beautiful example of this treatment in the coda of the rondo (bars 165-70; ex. 381 d).[2]

---

[1] Bars 420-3 of the concerto; it is the return of ex. 327 in the recapitulation.

[2] See also K.452, first movement, bars 8-11 of the allegro moderato.

There are also a few instances of echoes.[1] Such bars are nearer to concerto than to chamber music style.

Another moment when the concertos are close is in the main couplet of the allegretto, the counterpart of the *development* couplet of a concerto rondo. Here, in bars 111–18, the piano right hand comes tumbling down the keyboard in broken chords, while the voice gives out the melodic thread in crotchets, just as, in the finale of K.451 (ex. 146), the wind had toyed with their skeletal theme and the piano had "accompanied" with similar figures. There is an analogy here with other *developments*[2] and with the coda of the first movement of the C minor concerto.

It is, on the other hand, of the chamber works that we think when we hear the piano part rise and fall in runs of semi-quavers—scales or broken scales—under the sustained dotted minims and crotchets of the voice (bars 21–5, 89–93),[3] particularly in the return to the refrain (bars 151–5, ex. 381 e), a most euphonious passage which recalls several rentrées in chamber music rondos.

None of these devices is used for more than a few bars and the incessant shifting of emphasis, the setting off now of piano now of voice must be heard (or seen in the score, alas! since this shapely work never leaves the sheath of the *Gesamtausgabe*) to be appreciated. Mozart has at least a dozen ways of enhancing the soprano tone with the piano's, the piano's with the soprano's, and he passes constantly from one to the other. We, to whom such a combination is foreign, can best realize the effect by imagining an orchestral background added to a lied for voice and piano. The work is very far from being a curiosity or a rhetorical exhibition of instrumental and vocal technique; it is a vital, moving piece, where the music rises generously to the emotional theme: that of the love and fellow-suffering which Ilia feels for Idamante and the assurance she gives him of her fidelity. The few quotations we have given will, we hope, send readers to the score or to the almost unobtainable piano arrangement in the selection of Mozart's concert arias published many years ago by Breitkopf and Härtel.

---

[1] Bars 173, 185 ; cf. ex. 3.

[2] First movements of K.451, 453, 482 and 493; middle couplets of rondos in K.386 and 456 (ex. 200). Note also bar 204, which is almost identical with 92–5 in the first movement of K.365.

[3] Cp., among others, with bars 37–41 in the first movement of the G minor piano quartet and the end of the *development* in the same movement of the E flat piano quartet.

PART V

1. *The Twenty-second Concerto: K.537 in D*

Concerto No. 22 in D major (K.537)[1]
Finished February 24th, 1788
  Allegro: C
  Larghetto: ¢ (in A major)
  (Allegretto): 2-4
Orchestra: Strings, flute, two hautboys, two bassoons, two horns, two
  trumpets, two kettledrums.

"Short-sighted minds, I mean those which are narrow and shut up
in their own little spheres, are unable to understand the universality of
talents that one sometimes observes in one individual; where they see what
is agreeable, they rule out what is substantial; where they think to discover bodily grace, agility, nimbleness, dexterity, they refuse to allow the
gifts of the soul, depth, reflection, wisdom; they erase from the story of
Socrates the fact that he danced."[2]

How well these words of La Bruyère apply to the opinion on
Mozart current in the last century and the beginning of this
one and still surviving here and there! It saw in him above all an
entertainer—a "divine" one, possibly, but an entertainer all the same.
Comparable opinions saw in Beethoven nothing but the "Titan",
in Bach, the "mathematician", in Haydn, the "Papa", in Chopin,
the elegiac author of certain nocturnes. That Bach and Beethoven
should have "danced", that Haydn and Mozart may have wept, that
Chopin should have sung of energy and warlike spirit: this was cut
out of their story.

When one undertakes to study a great figure who is the victim
of such a simplification (and almost every great figure is), one feels
a keen delight on discovering how varied and even how contradictory
his personality may be. Beethoven's minuets and écossaises, Bach's
gavottes, lyrical arias of Handel, mournful adagios of Haydn, martial
polonaises of Chopin come and remind us that these men, like all of
us, knew the most diverse moods, and that posterity's choice, rather

---

[1] *Gesamtausgabe*, no. 26.
[2] La Bruyère: *Les Caractères*, chap. II: *Du mérite personnel*.

than the nature of their work itself, has imposed on us the idea we have of them.

It is impossible to study any of the genres into which Mozart put himself most fully without noticing at every turn how changeful and manifold was his soul. We have recognized it many times while going through our beloved concertos. His variousness is not met with only from one work to another; it strikes us also when we pass from one period of his life to another. Nothing is less true than Lenz's assertion that, though the artist in him had grown, the man had never done so. The study of his Viennese concertos alone, from 1782 to 1786, is enough to prove the contrary, but if their example did not suffice, the works of the two years on the threshold of which we now stand would serve to refute this contention.

The psychological evolution of these years is unmistakable. If we consider the most significant works of 1787 and 1788,[1] among which, alas! his only concerto composed during this period cannot be numbered, we recognize two streams in his inspiration. To one of them correspond powerful, unified works, of the race of the two last concertos: some of them bright and serene (quintet in C, symphonies in E flat and C), others gloomy (quintet and symphony in G minor); but having all of them a frank, straightforward nature, with no other mystery than that which all work of beauty bears in it. To the other stream belong certain movements in which new strains are heard. To find ancestors for these we have to return to the days of Mozart's last stay in Salzburg.[2] The earliest of them is the andante of the Prague Symphony. This work, absolutely contemporary with the great concerto in C, has nothing in common with it. The first movement, less broad and more quivering, has moments of tense strength, of keen feeling, which make one think of the *Don Giovanni* overture. But the andante is the most original piece. Few slow movements of Mozart's are so uneven in progress. We perceive in it a kind of dialogue where the voices, half confused, are those of his daïmon, his divided personality, languishing, caressing, groaning, yielding and striving in turn. The emotional instability of the movement is great; it passes ceaselessly from one mood to

---

[1] Symphony in D, K.504; rondo for piano in A minor, K.511; string quintets in C and G minor, K.515 and 516; violin sonata in A, K.526; piano sonata in F, K.533; adagio for piano in B minor, K.540; adagio for strings in C minor, K.546; the three last symphonies, K.543, 550, 551; divertimento for string trio in E flat, K.563.

[2] Cf. pp. 119-23.

another without ever settling down.[1] More than anywhere else, Mozart is here what a contemporary called him: "Stürmer und Schmeichler" ("stormer and caresser"). The opposition between the tuneful sweetness of the opening strain and the dry, almost mocking tone of the second is typical of the piece.

With its occasional exacerbated chromaticisms, it is the first of those andantes and adagios with discordant passages which now make their appearance and sound a strange, disquieting note in his work. In the B minor adagio—a most unusual key with him—the presence of the voices is clearer; this adagio and the one which he composed as prelude for his arrangement for strings of his fugue for two pianos, K.426, are the movements where the elements of his soul, conversing or struggling, are most dissociated.[2]

In a less acute degree, the same character is found in several other slow movements of this period—in those of the G minor quintet, of the violin sonata in A, whose bleak moorland landscape takes us far away from Mozart to the greyest regions of Brahms, of the F major sonata, where harsh, rasping phrases, laden with chromaticisms, clash with bitter cacophony, and where we again recognize Mozart's power for "thinking musically", since, though so emotional, they are the result of a desire for extreme formal compression. This inspiration appears for the last time in the adagio of the string trio where the very concise *development* has a few bars of almost physical cruelty.

A kindred inspiration flows through the A minor rondo, but is more languishing—we are tempted to say: wilting, if the word be not too strong for Mozart. The feeling which dominates this rondo is on the whole that of all our composer's works in A. Long ago, Reinecke pointed out the likeness between it and some of Chopin's compositions where an exasperated sensibility revels in an orgy of melismas.[3]

As for the quintets, we have already said that they belong to the

---

[1] It is impossible to bring out this basic character of the movement if it is taken, as some conductors take it, as a siciliana or a berceuse, in 2-4; the beat is 6-8 and the speed should not exceed ♪ = 100.

[2] The affecting minuet for piano in D, K.355, of unknown date, comes from the same plane of his consciousness and is perhaps contemporary with this group.

[3] *Zur Wiederbelebung der Mozart'schen Klavierkonzerte*, 1936 edition, p. 40. The andantes of the concertos in D, K.451, and C, K.467, can also be likened to Chopin, for the same reason. It should be added that the breadth of certain periods in the A minor rondo betray the neighbourhood of the concerto K.503 and the C major quintet.

same line of growth as the last two concertos. With the allegro of the F major sonata, they are the works of Mozart where the form spreads itself with greatest breadth. The new stage brings it back to the dimensions of earlier works. Never more does Mozart undertake anything as vast as the allegro of the quintet in C. The likeness of its andante to that of the last concerto has been noted; its finale is a more generous edition of that of the C major quartet, K.465; even the characteristic modulation into A flat of the earlier movement occurs in it. It has less variety than the rondo of the concerto but interest is kept up in it more successfully and it has no dead patches.

The two years 1787 and 1788 are without doubt the most glorious in the story of Mozart's work and every fervent admirer of the master should be able to gaze on them with unmixed joy. But one for whom the concertos have become the favourite children of his genius cannot suppress a feeling of melancholy, for their sole representative at this period, although popular, is one of the poorest and emptiest. We allude to that in D which Mozart composed for the Lent of 1788 and which is dated February 24th. (The fact that the composer played it at Frankfurt in 1790 at the Coronation festivities of Leopold II has earned for it the high-sounding but irrelevant title of Coronation concerto.)

The end of the great concertos corresponds to the end of the period when Mozart was a fashionable pianist and composer. His financial position had never been brilliant; it soon became bad and for the last four years of his life he was often in great want. The stories of his poverty are well known but, to have an immediate impression of it, nothing equals a perusal of the heart-rending notes he sent to his brother mason Puchberg.

When after more than a year he had again the opportunity of coming before the public as a virtuoso composer, it looks as if he made a determined effort to fall in with his listeners' taste and "write popularly". But the gap between the average *galant* taste and his ideal had grown too wide for him to bridge it in so important a work. He could still condescend to what was asked of him for short moments, in trifles like his trios and some of his last sonatas;[1] in a composition of the scope of a concerto, he could do so no longer. The mask stifled him; from time to time he would lift it up to breathe, then put it back more or less correctly; the result was something factitious

---

[1] K.521, 545, 547. K.570 and 576 are not trifles.

which is neither Mozart nor a work quite in the *galant* style of his younger days.

Between the growth in breadth of the C major concerto and the quintets and the growth in concentration of his last symphonies, the concerto in D is, then, a manifestation of the *galant* taste of the time. But it is not a perfect work such as had been in their narrow field the divertimenti and cassationen of Salzburg and the showy concertos of 1784, still near to their public's level. There, the brilliance was the effect of a spontaneous urge of their author, in sympathy with his public and glad to please it. Here, the urge is lacking and this is what saddens us most. In all his other concertos the joy of the maker in the act of creation is present, even in the most insignificant, even in the drooping, resigned work of 1790; only here is it absent.

It is very significant that at the time when Mozart was most ignored, alone among all his piano concertos this one remained on concert programmes, on the Continent at any rate. When in 1891 Reinecke attempted to revive these works and brought out his valuable booklet on how to play them, he drew nearly all his examples from this one. To-day its popularity is not so marked, but it is still more often played than others which are greater.

We shall gain nothing by analysing it with the care we bestowed on the study of its predecessors. We will merely distinguish what belongs in it to the return to *galanterie* and what still bears witness to the ideal that Mozart was unable entirely to forsake.

I. The tutti opens with a mysterious phrase over a repeated bass, portending grave and sombre things (ex. 382). This, however, is bluff; nothing in the movement recalls it and it is in as striking contrast with what follows as the minor adagios which Haydn prefixed to his most joyous symphonies. The *piano* is followed by a *forte*, according to the usual plan of openings in *galant* concertos, and we enter on a chain of subjects and motifs which leads after eighty bars to the piano's entry. One is at once struck by the square, rigid outline of the phrases, subdivided into periods of two and four bars. The only passage which breaks this uniformity is the first violin solo which precedes the second subject. The scoring is much less resourceful than in the previous concertos; the strings preponderate and the woodwind does no more than double them from time to time. The extent to which Mozart seems to have unlearnt his woodwind craft, here and in the solos, is astounding; the work has to be known for so entire a renunciation of his riches to be believed.

Except for the solo subject the prelude contains all the elements of the movement. Their emotional significance is slight; they are amiable, impersonal words; their step is quick, but skipping, not winged.

The piano makes its bow with ex. 382 but the Alberti bass which replaces the repeated notes deprives the subject of its former gravity. As if to emphasize that he renounces all that he had adored in his earlier works, Mozart has recourse to a device borrowed from the aria and found only in his first concertos; he repeats a part of the tutti conclusion after the first solo run—a device which appears quite archaic here.

The impertinent and irrelevant virtuosity which at once overruns the movement in great force makes it mark time instead of carrying us on towards weightier matter. It has not even formal originality in its favour; pianistically, it is more archaic than the piano writing of the concertos in C major. It consists in scales, now in one hand, now in the other, seldom in both together. The lack of all interplay (except in ex. 384) is particularly distressing; no concerto since 1782 had been so devoid of it. Of the ambitions of past years there remains only the movement's great size, for after K.503 it is the longest of Mozart's allegros. But, though the outside be spacious, the inside remains empty.[1]

The solo subject brings us nearer to the true Mozart (ex. 383). its chromaticisms, especially the unexpected flattening in its third bar, and its modulation from A major to D minor, are echoes of the A minor rondo, K.511. The bravura passage which evolves out of it resounds with vigorous strains at first, but the energy soon expends itself in a few bars of scales. When repeating the second subject, strings and solo collaborate an instant (ex. 384) and the little contrapuntal working-out of the piano which follows it (bars 176–87) is Mozart at his best; it recalls the *development* in the two pianos sonata and the fifth variation in the finale of the C minor concerto.

The tutti which concludes the exposition repeats without any marked change some twenty bars of the first tutti[2]; we are far from

---

[1] "The autograph shows the piano part incomplete; thus, the larghetto gives only the tune; the left hand stave is blank. In the finale, the solo is often only sketched out; it is most complete in the first movement" (Köchel-Einstein, p. 687). The first edition was published by André in 1794; it is not known what source he used to complete the solo. "He may even have completed it himself" (id.).

[2] Bars 13–23 and 71–8.

Ex. 382

Ex. 383

Ex. 384

Ex. 385

Ex. 386

Ex. 387

Ex. 388

the grand exposition closes where piano and orchestra co-operated in preparing the *development*.

The *development* here is thematic, but on what a theme! With an utter lack of seriousness Mozart catches hold of the last fragment of the ritornello and gives it first to the piano, then to the strings, then once again to the piano, after the fashion of the E flat concerto, K.482. Then, the piano having launched out into runs, sundry members of the strings accompany it with the same figure (ex. 385) and now we think of the D minor concerto, where in the *development* a thematic fragment had likewise followed the piano in its excursions. But, though the device be the same, what a difference in the artistic import of the figures and the use made of them! Here, it is all a joke, without the slightest dramatic content; what is needed is to kill time and fill in the framework of sonata form.

Yet one cannot go on for ever doing the same thing, so after a few bars the orchestra stops its commentary and the piano forges ahead almost alone. The section (bars 261-9) which begins in B minor is one of the best in the movement. It modulates freely and resembles a recitative—one of those "voices" of which we spoke just now—but it finishes poorly and the stream of its emotion becomes sanded up in passage work.

The recapitulation is scarcely different from the first solo; only towards the end do the strings, and then the piano, recall a part of the concluding subject which had been omitted (bars 381-92). It is in D major, like the rest of this third solo, but just as it is about to conclude, a *fp* chord on the piano, followed by a torrent of scales and arpeggios, breaks out in G minor like a bolt from the blue. Two more claps follow, each one a degree higher; after which the solo ends in D major as if nothing had happened (bars 393-9). These few bars are the most truly Mozartish moment in the whole movement. Letting loose demonic passion, they show that the lion was only slumbering in its court dress and are a revenge of Mozart's genius for the restraint put upon it by its master. But nothing further reveals its existence and the allegro closes with the same bars as the first tutti. The brevity and triteness of the seven bars that follow the cadenza[1] are depressing in a movement of such size; they fully deserve to be covered by the applause of a public carried away by the soloist's performance in the cadenza.

II.   Within the restricted limits of the larghetto, the composer has known how to reconcile *galant* taste and individual expression. It is the best movement of the three, neither great nor deep, but true Mozart, and it deserves the popularity it has always enjoyed and to which many separate editions bear witness.

We find again in it the soft voluptuousness of certain A major arias. Very near to vocal music, it mirrors the same mood as Bel-

---

[1] Mozart has left no cadenza for this concerto; the cadenza sometimes printed with it belongs to K.451.

mont's "O wie ängstlich, o wie feurig!", the duets "S'io no moro" in *Idomeneo*, "Un' aura amorosa" in *Così fan tutte*, and "Ah! perdona!" in *Titus*, and, in instrumental works, the andantes of the D major violin concerto, K.218, and string quartet, K.575. In some pieces in this key, mockery mingles with sensuousness, as in "La ci darem la mano" and "Ah! taci, ingiusto core!" in *Don Giovanni*, but here there is no trace of it. It breathes the gentle voluptuousness, tinted with melancholy, so typical of the end of the Old Regime.

The refrain is a winding tune where theme and accompaniment entwine (ex. 386). Given out by the piano, it is restated by the whole orchestra. The second period belongs to the piano solo, then the first is repeated and the tutti add a coda instinct with true Mozartish yearning; it is the most deeply felt part of the movement (ex. 387). The middle section is a cantilena for piano solo whose general outline and rhythm make us think of the same section in the romance of the D minor and the larghetto of K.595. Some of its bars are sketchy and gain by being filled out (49–53, 63–7), but it is less grievous here than elsewhere to play them as they are written. The last part recapitulates the whole refrain, without repetition, and in ex. 387 the piano adds a few runs to the orchestral song.

III. The finale is a rondo with a plan we have not yet met. This plan is, indeed, its most interesting peculiarity, for its musical content is even slighter than that of the first movement.

In several sonata rondos Mozart, and after him Beethoven, leaves out the refrain between the *development* and recapitulation couplets.[1] The result is to reduce to two the sections of the movement included between the returns of the refrain. This is one simplification. In more than one of the rondos of 1787, notably those of the quintets, the simplification is carried still further and the development itself is reduced to a few modulatory bars or a passing theme and the recapitulation begins almost at once after the second return of the refrain. The finale is then in reality a two-couplet rondo, comparable to the binary sonata andantes.[2] In the Coronation concerto, the second couplet begins with the same subject as the first, but modulates, and these modulations are all that is left of the development. Such a movement may be called a binary sonata rondo.[3]

---

[1] K.456, 459, 488; 478, 493; Beethoven's op. 58.

[2] K.503; 515, 516.

[3] Other binary rondos occur in K.428, 575, 576.

The theme of the refrain in this finale is neither more nor less interesting than those of many other rondos of the time (ex. 388). It comprises a second section and a longish orchestral ritornello; it spreads itself widely and indeed the whole movement is on as spacious a scale as the allegro.

We will not follow it in detail. The same ineffective virtuosity occurs as in the first movement, the same almost complete absence of interplay between piano and orchestra, the same lack of independence in the wind parts. Occasionally, however, the true Mozart reveals himself. The second theme of the couplet brings us a surprise by starting in the minor (ex. 389); it enters the major only when the piano takes it up. On the whole, the movement modulates more freely than the allegro; at the beginning of the second couplet, in particular, we pass swiftly through the keys of B minor, F sharp minor, B flat (an expressive enharmonic modulation), B flat minor, A minor and B minor to land in G minor, whence by slow stages we wend back to the tonic. This inroad of fancy into a prosaic piece lasts unhappily but twenty-five bars.

There comes another most poetic moment, worthy of the master's best works. Twice, at the end of each couplet (bars 136-43 and 287-94), the virtuoso withdraws and the musician lifts his mask. There unfolds then one of those exquisite passages where strings, wind and piano work together, without surrendering their individualities, in a melodious, ethereal counterpoint (ex. 390). The little rising figure with which the string and flute tune ends is a favourite of Mozart's; it occurs again in the E flat symphony,[1] in the finale of the D major quartet, K.575, and elsewhere. And, since beauties are scarce in this concerto, we will draw the reader's attention to the bassoon part in bars 361-2—an unexpected counter-subject which is lost in the piano solo arrangement.

The key of D major, much used at all times by Mozart, is the favourite key for overtures and occasional pieces—divertimentos and serenades—in *galant* music. Its superficial majesty has not the martial strains heard in many a C major composition, capable in certain chosen works of attaining to the expression of heroism, and it easily passes over to showiness and virtuosity. It is the concerto key *par excellence* and in those which Mozart has written in D virtuosity plays a great part. In his violin concertos, the most difficult are in

---

[1] First movement, second subject.

Ex. 389

Ex. 390

Ex. 391

Ex. 392

this key;[1] his D major flute concerto is more *virtuoso* than that in G; it is in D that he writes that one of his three flute quartets which most resembles a concerto; his four piano sonatas in D,[2] especially the first two, are works of technical display, and this is true also of his only violin sonata in this key. Finally, two out of his three piano concertos in D are those where the display of technique enters most deeply into the personality of the work.

Yet all Mozart's music in this key has not this character. Though the pomp of D major never rises to heroism, it sometimes gives us glimpses of sombre depths, as towards the end of the overture of

---

[1] K.218 and Köchel-Einstein, 271 i.

[2] Including that for two pianos, the most brilliant of all.

Idomeneo. A feeling akin to this, less tragic but quite as serious, runs through the joyous vigour of the Prague symphony and the overture of *Don Giovanni.* His finales in D are bursting with physical energy and sometimes make use of close counterpoint.[1] Finally, a few very individual pieces like the opening allegros of the quartets K.499 and 575 and the *Ave verum* cannot be brought under any classification. On the whole, the key shows so many different features in his work that the only general judgement one can pass on it is the rather commonplace one that it contains some of his finest movements.[4]

---

[1] Prague symphony; quartet K.499; quintet K.593.

[2] Overtures of *Idomeneo, Figaro, Don Giovanni*; piano concerto K.451; quartets K.499 and 575; quintet K.593; Prague symphony; *Ave verum.*

2. The Twenty-third Concerto: K.595 in B flat

CONCERTO NO. 23 IN B FLAT (K.595)[1]
Finished January 5th, 1791
  Allegro: C
  Larghetto: C (in E flat)
  Allegro: 6-8
Orchestra: Strings, flute, two hautboys, two bassoons, two horns.

JUST as the period of the concertos had come to a glorious close with the magnificent work in C, so that which followed and was summed up in the quintets and symphonies of 1787 and 1788 culminated in a masterpiece in this same key of C major in which Mozart had so often expressed the "heroic" and "Olympian" sides of his inspiration.   The finale of his last symphony, the only movement of the four to which the name of Jupiter is really suited, crowns gloriously his orchestral work, as the concerto in C had crowned his achievements as piano composer and virtuoso.

The symphony was finished on August 10th; in September, Mozart wrote his one string trio, the divertimento in E flat, K.563, the inspiration of which links it with the period just closed.   Then comes the great silence of the two saddest years of his life.   It is not complete, since now and again it is broken by a chamber work and, once, by an opera, but it is a silence nevertheless when one compares these months with the fruitful periods which had preceded them since he had come to Vienna.

It is good to dwell on this paucity of important works in order to gainsay once more the legend of his miraculous productivity. According to this legend, the young musician was ceaselessly pouring out compositions of all sorts, with the utmost facility and often with a deplorable lack of self-criticism.   When one lives at all continuously with his work, one realizes that, during his maturity, instead of being spread over the eleven years of his life in Vienna, his moments of great productiveness are compressed within a few periods.   Within these,

---

[1] *Gesamtausgabe*, no. 27.

it is true, his fruitfulness is prodigious, but between-whiles he does not write much. The earliest of them comes in February, March and April, 1784, when there appear the first four of his great concertos, a violin sonata and a quintet: six major works in two and a half months. The second is at the end of the same year and the beginning of the next, when in a little under six months he gives forth four important concertos, three quartets and the finest of his piano sonatas: eight major works. Then, in the middle of the year, 1788, which we are about to leave, come the celebrated seven weeks in which he inserts trios and sonatinas between his three great symphonies after the fashion of light interludes between the acts of a drama. Finally, in the last year of his life, from December, 1790, to March, 1791, two string quintets, a piano concerto and two fantasias for mechanical organ follow quickly one upon the other: five works of which three were composed in one month; and this, incidentally, destroys another legend, according to which, at the time of his death, he was spiritually as well as physically exhausted. Surely this is enough to arouse our admiration, without our making him live at constant high pressure![1]

In the spring of 1789, Mozart started on the first large-scale journey he had undertaken since his return from Paris eleven years earlier. Invited by Prince Lichnowsky to accompany him to Berlin, he set out almost without warning on April 8th, yet not without having written a line to a friend, Franz Hofdemel, to borrow the necessary money. The prince and his suite stopped on the way at Prague, Dresden and Leipzig and reached Potsdam at the end of the month. The visit which Mozart made to the aged Doles, a pupil of Bach's and one of his successors at St. Thomas's, Leipzig, has often been told; he extemporized so beautifully on the church organ that Doles exclaimed: "It is my old master come back to earth!" To reward his visitor, he made his choir sing the motet: "Singet dem Herrn ein neues Lied". According to Rochlitz, Mozart listened to it with rapture and declared: "That is something one can learn from!" He had the parts of Bach's other motets brought out, set them on the floor all round him, studied them with enthusiasm and asked for copies.

If this visit to Northern Germany had ever raised hopes in his breast, they were soon dispelled. King Frederick-William II of

---

[1] The basic state of emotional natures is indolence, according to Bain. Mozart's is an "emotional nature" which works only under the stimulus of an occasion, "an irritation, a shock, acting upon a Nirvanic basis", as Julien Benda says in speaking of himself.

Prussia was a keen musician and a good 'cellist, but all the places round him were occupied. Among his court musicians was a certain French 'cellist Duport whom Mozart disliked and whom, it is said, he blamed in insulting terms for "being settled in Germany and eating the bread of Germans" without troubling to learn the language of the country. The king did not even allow him to give a concert of his works. Yet he presented him with a purse of a hundred gold fredericks and ordered six string quartets and six easy sonatas for his daughter, the Princess Frederika.

Mozart tried to hide his disappointment from his wife by writing witty and affectionate letters. It was in joking terms that he informed her of the unprofitable outcome of his journey. "My dear little wife, you must rejoice at my return for love of me rather than for the money." His only earnings were the king's purse and a hundred ducats which a concert in Dresden had brought him, and even so he lent a part of this sum to a friend. Six weeks after his return we find him again writing to the faithful Puchberg: "I am in a state in which I would not wish my worst enemy to be! If you, my excellent friend and brother, abandon me, I am lost, as unhappy as I am innocent, with my poor sick wife and my child!" And as Puchberg did not answer at once, he repeated his request five days later.

This journey and its resulting disappointments separate the period of the quintets and symphonies from that which opens at this point and at the end of which comes his last piano concerto. His financial situation had not been improved by his absence from Vienna. In the fall of 1787 he had succeeded Gluck as court composer, but the remuneration was slender and the duties uninteresting. He had merely to provide dances for the court balls and on a receipt for his salary he wrote: "Too much for what I do, too little for what I would like to do!" His wife's health was bad and cures at Baden, near Vienna, added to the household's expenses.

A second journey in the autumn of the next year was no more remunerative than the Berlin one had been. Early in 1790, Leopold II had succeeded his brother Joseph on the Imperial throne and he went to Frankfurt to be crowned in October of the same year. He took with him a suite which included some fifteen musicians, Salieri, his Kapellmeister, being among them, but Mozart was left behind. The composer determined thereupon to go to Frankfurt at his own expense and set out with his brother-in-law, the fiddler Joseph Hofer. They were absent six weeks and Mozart visited not only Frankfurt but also Munich and Mannheim. He gave only one concert in the

Imperial capital; the programme consisted entirely of his own works and he appears to have played the concertos in F, K.459, and D, K.537; the latter owes its name of Coronation Concerto to this performance.   He met old friends in both places, the Wendlings at Frankfurt, the Ramms and Cannabichs at Munich, renewing acquaintances which went back to the great journey he had made to Mannheim and Paris thirteen years earlier.   His letters give proof of the joy he felt in coming again into touch with these witnesses of a bygone period, yet such an experience must have brought home more vividly and more sorrowfully to him the difference between past and present.   The man of thirty-four, undermined by cares, beginning to suffer in body and spirit from the privations and disappointments of recent years, must have compared himself with bitterness with the stripling of twenty-one, sallying forth from Salzburg full of hope, on the threshold of his independent life.

This journey was as unsuccessful as the Prussian one.   However, on his way back, the Elector of Bavaria asked him to take part in the concert given in honour of the King of Naples, and the musician triumphed at this, for the king had recently passed through Vienna without Mozart having been asked to play before him.   "A great honour," he wrote to his wife, "for the Vienna court, that the king should have to go to foreign parts to hear me!"

His material poverty ended by telling on the very nature of his work.   We find no more the fullness and spaciousness of the compositions of 1787 and 1788 and his inspiration reflects the cares which oppress him.   It is not inferior to that of earlier years, but joy, strength and passion no longer preponderate in it.

If we omit *Cosi fan tutte*, which perforce reveals his mood less than purely instrumental works, the important compositions of these two years are six in number.   Soon after returning from Berlin, he set about fulfilling the orders he had received; he composed his last sonata, in D, K.576, the only one of the series for the Princess Frederika which was ever written and which is far from being "easy",[1] and the first of the quartets for the king her father, also in D, K.575.   At the end of the summer, his friendship with Stadler called forth the quintet for clarinet and strings; then, in the following spring, after the months devoted to *Cosi fan tutte*, he completed two more quartets, the last he was ever to write, in B flat and F, K.589 and 590.   Finally, after

---

[1] The writing in its finale recalls that of the finale of K.503.

more than six months' silence, an order from an Hungarian music lover made him return to the string quintet with the work in D, K.593. This year, 1790, is the most barren in his life.

Through these six works runs a somewhat diverse but characteristic inspiration, proving how thoroughly the master's genius had been affected by the wretched conditions of his existence. We can distinguish in it three elements which sometimes alternate in a single work but never mingle in the same movement.

Of the three, we will put first that which lies closest to the circumstances of his life. It is a spirit of weariness and exhaustion, instinct with a melancholy resignation which saddens us when we remember the superb self-assurance of earlier times. It predominates in the allegros of the B flat sonata, K.570, and the D major and B flat quartets, and in the larghettos which open and close the first movement of the D major quintet. The word "wilting" is hardly too strong to characterize the spirit of the allegro and especially of the larghetto of the B flat quartet ; in the latter movement, the long winding semi-quavers unfold like bands of mourning crape.

The sonata in D, the quartet in F and the allegro of the first movement of the quintet in D reveal another strain of his inspiration, seen most clearly in the quartet. This work has a whimsical character which has put off certain commentators but was well grasped by Abert. It is a sport of the intellect, almost a witticism, in that key of F which is Mozart's joking key. No deep feeling should be sought in it,[1] not even that of discouragement; Mozart has solved the problem set him by the clash between his ideal and reality by turning his back on it. As a result, this quartet leaves an impression of renunciation and detachment, evident also in the preponderance of rhythm over tune in its minuet and in the skeletal outline of the themes in the first movements of sonata and quintet. We think of certain movements in Beethoven's last manner which also seem to be pure sports of the intellect.

These two strains exclude each other and the second may be a defence against the painfulness of the first. The third, on the contrary, combines with melancholy and renunciation. We cannot depict it better than by calling it a thirst, a yearning for beauty. Yearning, indeed, a part of Mozart's music always has been, but the longing of 1789 and 1790 fills whole movements with a more poignant aspiration than anything heard hitherto. It is the "wilting" mood raised

---

[1] We refer, of course, to the allegro, not to the meditative andante.

to a positive plane, and the movements infused by it leave us deeply satisfied. The loveliest of them and at the same time one of the loveliest in all Mozart is the allegro of the clarinet quintet. Here, the longing has been allayed by utterance and the movement bears the mark of triumphant serenity. Nevertheless, the sorrowful feeling at the heart of it is still recognizable, and makes this music, however serene, different from the equally tranquil music of the following year. The andante of the quartet in D belongs to the same climate.

These three strains do not exhaust the emotional content of this group of works. The quartets, languishing or dry in their first movements, awaken in their finales with a nervous, energetic life, prone to find an outlet in counterpoint. The minuets of the B flat and the F and the finales of all three[1] have a breadth and diversity which take us back to the happy days of the "great" concertos; the minuets in particular are as unique in their way as those of the quintets of 1787. This contrapuntal inspiration is present also in the little jig for piano, K.574,[2] a masterpiece of condensation, in the finale of the D major quintet and the allegro of the first organ fantasia, K.594.

Finally, twice over, right at the end of 1790, the yearning grows deeper and evolves into a more contemplative mood, producing two surprisingly introspective adagios: those of the quintet in D and of the first organ fantasia. In the first, the minor episodes, with their threatening repeated triplets, are like a return of the "voices" of earlier times and seem to arise from a conflict, but the serene gravity of the rest calls up rather the andantes and adagios of Beethoven's third manner, which this penultimate year of Mozart's life recalls, therefore, in more ways than one. In the adagio of the fantasia K.594, with its rasping chromaticisms, anguish and serenity are blended as never hitherto, as if Mozart were reaping the harvest of his suffering. And, if it be not fanciful to seek the presence of kindred inspirations in artists separated in time, we would say that through the andante variations of the other fantasia, K.608, there passes a breath of César Franck—the Franck of the larghetto of the string quartet.

Weariness, resignation, detachment, yearning, vigour, introspection: all these are found in the moods of these strange works, whose beauty is somewhat forbidding and un-Mozartish in the ordinary sense. Of this group, the concerto in B flat is one of the last representatives.

·   ·   ·   ·   ·

---

[1] The monothematic nature of the finales of K.589 and 590 and of the first and last movements of K.614 is another aspect of this spirit of renunciation.

[2] Written probably as a pastiche of Bach after Mozart's visit to Doles.

It is because some of these streams flow through his last concerto that we have dwelt so long on the compositions that precede it. This concerto is the finest and fullest of those works to which we applied the perhaps unjust term "wilting". Its form is simple; it shows neither the complexity nor the curious details of its great predecessors, but its inspiration is unique among its kind.

Its immediate foregoer was the most showy and superficial of the series, whilst it, on the other hand, is the most reserved. The intimate nature of its feeling makes almost chamber music of it and renders it unsuitable for performance in a large concert hall; its proper environment is a circle of lovers of music . . . and of Mozart, gathered in the house of one of them. We do not know for what occasion it was written. It is generally agreed that Mozart composed it for his own use, but there is no proof of this and the existence of cadenzas and its introspective character would lead us to think that it had been produced for a pupil.[1] If Mozart had had to play it himself, it seems to us that he would have written a more brilliant work, like the concertos composed for his own use in 1784, 1785 and 1786, and the Coronation.[2] But all this is supposition.

The resignation and nostalgia which infuse the works of these two years are present in all three movements, even in the 6-8 rondo. It spreads not only a veil of sadness over the whole concerto; it also casts on it at times as it were an evening light, announcing the end of a life; the larghetto in particular has the quality of a farewell. Needless to say, we do not look upon this as a forewarning of Mozart's own death; even if he had not been destined to pass away eleven months later, his mood at the close of 1790 would have inspired him with these strains; moreover, most of his works written after this concerto and therefore nearer his death have not this character; nothing, for instance, is further from it than the E flat quintet. This resignation is not present all the time; now and again, his soul remembers its rebelliousness of former years and more passionate notes are sounded, but they do not last and weariness soon reigns supreme again, and is responsible for the noteworthy drops into the minor mode that occur in the allegro and rondo.

I. The allegro begins with a bar of accompaniment—an apparently

---

[1] It will be remembered that the most intimate concertos of 1784 were those he wrote for others.

[2] It is true that he played it himself at the concert given by the clarinettist Beer, but that was two months later, on March 4th.

insignificant detail; but the fact is that, with the allegro of the G minor symphony, this is the only movement of Mozart's that starts thus. It is as if the composer had wished to prepare the ground and induce in his hearers a placid mood before bringing in his first subject.

This latter, as in most classical concertos, expresses the sentiment that predominates in the movement. It unfolds in three strains of unequal length separated by two interruptions of one bar each. The ease and freedom of its rhythm make it one of the most personal and expressive of all Mozart's concerto openings. The three strains, given out by the strings, with their rise and fall, betray the resignation born of weariness which fills the whole movement. Under their heavy yet supple line, the accompaniment keeps up a rocking motion. Twice over, the wind break into the progress of the theme with a warlike unison call; on its third appearance, the call is taken up by the strings and extends into a run which reproduces a figure from the finale of the Jupiter (ex. 391).

Then strings and wind separate again and discuss a motif whose charm lies in its contrast of tone (ex. 392). It leads to a formal close on the dominant and three soft bars usher in the second subject. This expresses much the same feeling as ex. 391, but the way it hovers between major and minor when it is repeated makes it more tearful. It recalls the beautiful demi-semi-quaver passages in the andante of the G minor quartet and, nearer to us, certain bars in the larghetto of the B flat quartet, K.589; but here the motion gives a little more vitality to the long trailing scales (ex. 393).[1]

A very simple decorative figure, based on an ascending scale, which is to return unchanged in the piano, follows the second subject; it rises from *pp* to *forte*. Its semi-quavers introduce some excitement, but we soon fall back to the mood of the beginning with a sudden drop into the minor, all the more unexpected as it links on to a little, innocent-looking cadential figure, ex. 394, on which the tutti exposition appears to be about to close. This excursion into the minor is but momentary; when it is over, the strings expound a long, winding tune on which falls the slanting light of evening; both in outline and feeling it is akin to ex. 391. Then comes the usual noisy close and on it, no doubt, the tutti of a normal concerto would end. But this one adds a very Mozartish wistful phrase which reminds us of the end of the andante in the E flat serenade, K.375.

---

[1] This figure occurs also in the allegro of the B flat symphony, K.319, but in 3-4 time and with a different accompaniment and context.

The twilight atmosphere in which this beginning is veiled takes us far from the concertos of 1784-6, whilst its construction goes back to an earlier stage than they. It is true that its mood is as homogeneous and as sustained as in the most single-minded concertos of that period, but its form is more strophic, more articulated, and its progress is broken by closes. In spite of the personal nature of the feeling, this gives it an archaic appearance beside its predecessors; a cursory glance might lead one to think it earlier than they.

The first solo confirms the hints of the tutti: Mozart is no longer interested in structural problems as in the days when the concerto was his principal means of expression. The solo exposition does not rejuvenate that of the tutti; it follows the same lines and is content with introducing an important piano passage between the first and second subjects, and with modifying and shortening the end to join it on to the *development*. No doubt some earlier concertos had not been more enterprising, but in 1784 to 1786 they were exceptions.

The piano entry has nothing of the dramatic character of more passionate works; it does not in any way disturb the mood. The solo instrument gives out the first subject with a few discreet additions of scales and gruppetti; in the "calls", the strings replace the wind. The subject completed, we hear the *Jupiter* figure sounded by the whole orchestra. The piano repeats it and at once adds a bravura passage—a very simple one, only a few bars long; the orchestra then intervenes with the formal close which had preceded the second subject in the tutti.

The piano advances alone with a touching strain in F minor, more dramatic than what has gone before, where the trailing scales again appear (ex. 395); it becomes almost poignant when the piano rises high into the treble and reiterates thrice a pathetic phrase against which the flute[1] and later the hautboy outline a restrained but expressive counterpoint (ex. 396). Never had Mozart's moderation and reserve betrayed so heart-rending an emotion.

After another formal close in the tutti, asserting for an instant the key of F minor, the emotion gradually quietens down in a characteristic passage. Elsewhere, such a passage would be virtuosity, but here the technique is so simple and the feeling so intimate that the term is out of place. A single hand in the piano, now the right, now the left, sketches delicate filigree patterns beneath which we discern

---

[1] Surely one of the most poignant strains in all flute music! Flautists, play it out!

at first the design of the beginning of ex. 395, and then the rising and falling line which is the movement's signature. Now the fiddles, now the violas and 'cello accompany pizzicato, picking out the line of which the piano part is a decoration; the tone of the combination is very personal in its wistful haziness.

F major ousts F minor and the last piano filigree loses itself in ex. 392, given out in dialogue by piano and wind. We now follow the tracks of the first tutti but in F major. The second subject, ex. 393, is expounded by the strings; in the modulating section the piano doubles the first violins with broken octaves and completes the theme. Devoid of all personal ambition, it does not undertake a bravura passage as in nearly all the other concertos; it confines itself to reproducing the unpretentious decorative passage which the strings had given out in the tutti; alone at first, it is escorted by the wind and then by the strings when it reiterates the section; the last part is livelier and leads to a dramatic interruption to which the pianist should give emphasis by animating and quickening slightly the bars that precede the break. One bar's silence follows; then the wind give out a figure in semibreves twice repeated. To their harsh, hollow voices the piano adds a series of G's, the last of which is held for nearly two bars and is followed by a B natural two octaves higher up; the soloist should trill the first of them and fill up the interval with a scale in the second;[1] played as it is written, the passage is meaningless (ex. 397). In these bars the movement as it were holds its breath and we welcome like a deliverance the few very simple runs which lead us to the customary trill.

As the *development* draws near, Mozart takes interest again in the concerto form. Instead of repeating the conclusion of the tutti and starting the *development* after its last notes, as in the Coronation concerto (where his interest in form was no greater and its absence was not compensated by a personal inspiration), he brings in his orchestra with a new passage. Commonplace to begin with, it soon makes for ex. 394, the figure which, in the tutti, with its innocent air, had called forth the surprise modulation into B flat minor. Its nature is to behave unexpectedly and now, cut down to its first notes and starting from F major, it modulates swiftly and puts us down at the gates of B minor, which the piano unlocks (ex. 398).

The *development* is not only the most noteworthy part of the movement; it is also one of the three or four most masterly developments

---

[1] Or fill up both bars with a chromatic scale, as in the Steingräber edition.

in all Mozart's concertos.   This is saying a lot, especially of a work so unambitious and unrenowned.   Before accusing us of exaggeration, let the reader cast a glance with us at the score.

The orchestra is silent and the piano unfolds ex. 391 in B minor. Thus transposed, this theme, once so resigned, becomes elegiac. The unison call, thrown out by the strings, points to E minor, but a bar of modulation in hautboys and bassoons ushers in C major where the piano repeats its exposition.   This time the call is in the same key the first time, but drops at once into C minor, and when the piano repeats it after the strings, it does so in E flat.   It has not finished when the hautboy steals its theme from it, reduced to the first two bars and modified (ex. 399), and the bassoon replies.   This hints at what is coming.

The piano regains the upper hand and gives out ex. 399 in E flat minor.   After these searchings, this is the beginning of the *development* proper.   For a little more than thirty bars, wind and strings keep up a conversation on the subject of this fragment and the unison call of ex. 391, modulating constantly but generally in the minor, whilst the piano is almost always excluded from taking part in the discourse and wreathes round the orchestral parts an unbroken line of arabesques, now close to the line of the melody, now far from it (ex. 400).   Save for one moment, the instruments remain to the fore, but their number is never great enough to veil the slender piano filigree.   The solo technique is as simple and transparent as elsewhere; there is no trace of the mass effects and two-handed passages of the last two C major concertos; the piano style has become as archaic as the structure and the novelty of the emotion and of the collaboration is all the more obvious.

These thirty bars are among the most interesting in all the concertos.   The dialogue which unfolds, at first between the woodwind, then between the violins, on the score of ex. 399, is in counterpoint and takes the shape of two-part imitation.   The unison call stands out now against the piano's broken chords and loses its combativeness; it is shared impartially between wind and strings.   When it is the violins' turn to lead the game, they alter ex. 391 a second time and give it out in a canon at the fifth (ex. 401).

We said that the music modulated unceasingly.   Without ever stopping for more than two bars in the same key it travels through E flat minor, F sharp minor, A flat, F minor, G minor, C minor, F minor, B flat, E flat (ex. 400), F minor, C minor and G minor.   Here the piano breathes awhile and gives out a third alteration of the first subject (ex. 402), accompanied by a single held note in the bassoon. Once again the emotion is sorrowful and it reaches for a moment an acute pitch in what is the climax of the movement. The reprise is negotiated via D minor and a series of imitations between hautboys and bassoons; the piano's arpeggios unroll in triplets over a space of two octaves (ex. 403); we drop gently back to B flat major, and the first subject, which had never really left us, is again in our midst.[1]

There is no need to insist on the originality of this passage. There had been other thematic *developments* in Mozart's concertos,[2] and very grand ones, but in none of them did the orchestra keep up a continuous discourse over which the piano glided carelessly with independent passages. Its closest predecessor would be in K.503, but the sequences on which this latter was founded do not occur here; the music keeps an elasticity which does not tolerate any regular form. It is true that it seems to advance mainly in canon, but, except in ex. 401, none of these canons is regular and ex. 391, which makes up nearly all the substance of the discourse, is really modified several times, so that we feel a slight relief when we meet it in its original state at the reprise.

This movement is one of those which do not seek to vary their recapitulations. We may deplore it, but we must recognize that no work could be further than this one from the world of catastrophes. Nothing is more static than its climate. The variations in its emotional pitch are slight; it recalls in this its B flat predecessor of 1784, K.456. We do not deny that a renewal of the last part enriches any concerto allegro, whatever its substance, but it is certain that dramatic movements require it most urgently. Here, the tenor is so even that only on analysis does one perceive the identity of the two expositions, and no monotony is felt on that account. Moreover, after so original a *development* it would be ungracious to complain.

The first important change in the recapitulation occurs after the reappearance of ex. 397 (now in B flat). After the piano trill, the orchestra continues with ex. 394; the piano completes it, then reinserts the C minor parenthesis which had vanished from the first solo and

---

[1] We would urge conductors to make their violins, flute, hautboys and bassoons play out all through this development. It is absolutely necessary, not only that they should be heard, but that one should feel them to be what matters most and the piano to be but subordinate. For lack of this, the passage loses most of its point. The weakness of the H.M.V. recording lies in that one has to have the score in hand to hear the orchestral parts.

[2] K.271, 466, 491, 503.

the winding theme with its evening light.[1] Then comes the cadence
which followed this passage in the first tutti, and the cadenza. This
return of material which had not been heard since the first tutti just
before the cadenza is another archaic device which Mozart had
scarcely ever used in his "great" concertos.[2]

The movement closes with the cadence of the solo exposition and
the last bars of the opening tutti which let it die, *piano*, on the note of
depression and renunciation on which it had begun.

We have referred to the simple technique of this movement. We
would go further and say that virtuosity is almost entirely absent.
No other concerto is so devoid of it, not even the A major of 1786, to
such an extent that Mozart appears to renounce his very conception
of the genre and bring his piano down to the level of an orchestral
instrument. Not a breath of opposition separates the protagonists;
on the other hand, the closest unity reigns between them. In other
concertos, too, it is true, K.451 and K.466, piano and orchestra collaborated to the same end, but the solo's intervention always increased the
intensity of the emotion and modified the affective tone of the movement. There is nothing like this here. The piano's entry alters in
nowise the intensity of the gentle melancholy of which this allegro
is the expression. All that belongs exclusively to the solo is the
theme exs. 395 and 396, and the eight bars that follow it, with their
pizzicato accompaniment. At the end of the first exposition and of
the movement, when one expects the concluding solo which was not
missing in any other concerto, it repeats an orchestral passage. In
the *development*, finally, it finds a new function for itself which
brings this concerto still nearer to the "symphony with piano" and
looks forward, not to Beethoven's concertos, as Abert says, for in
them no such *development* occurs, but to those of Liszt and Brahms.
This concerto, so simple in plan and at times so archaic, opens surprising views towards the future.

Its chief interest, however, is in its inspiration. Before all, it is
a *Tondichtung*, where the nature of the emotion is more important
than the relations between protagonists. Its sorrow does not break
forth with the rebellious passion of the D minor nor collapse with
the despair of the G minor quintet or the adagio in B minor, K.540;
no less deep than formerly, it is more reserved and more dreamy;
it is so strongly tempered by the spirit of resignation that one might

---

[1] A single bassoon acts as a funeral escort to it.

[2] We have already mentioned that Mozart has left cadenzas for this concerto.

take it at times for mere tearfulness. But its classical restraint hides a sorrow as sincere as that of more vehement music. And above all, this sentiment, which might have been so selfish, is fragrant with that spirit of kindness and love breathed by so much of Mozart's art and for the utterance of which B flat is his favourite key. As we listen to this allegro where there is so little *allegrezza* and which we quit, nevertheless, with a light heart, we are reminded of what one of his forgotten contemporaries wrote of his work, as he heard it in his exile:

> "This music, so harmonious and so lofty in inspiration, so pure, both soft and sorrowful . . . made me forget as I listened to it my past woes and those that the future held perhaps in store for me . . ."[1]

II.   The E flat larghetto[2] dwells in the same mood as the first movement.   The emotion is no more intense; on the contrary, the few passionate strains heard in the allegro have no counterpart here; the music keeps within the limits of an elegy and the light that illumines it is constantly that of the evening.   We insist on this feature, for it gives this concerto, so unambitious in size, its unique place in the series of the twenty-three; in this, too, the work belongs to its period and represents a stage in its author's life.

The refrain which opens the larghetto, a kind of romance, is like a farewell.   It sings of an irrevocable parting.   When a musician has not spoken it is always rash to attribute a precise meaning to any passage in his work; we naturally do not assert that Mozart felt himself, as he composed this refrain, in the mood which accompanies a painful separation; yet the likeness in melody and harmony between this theme and the beginning of Beethoven's *Farewell* sonata may allow us to think that our impression is not wholly unfounded.

The piano gives it out alone (ex. 404); the tutti repeat it, harmonizing it richly and alternating *fortes* and *pianos*.   Between its version and that of the solo there is a trifling difference which persists throughout the movement.   Whereas the ascending motif in

---

[1] Abbe Martinant de Préneuf, 1797; quoted by Baldensperger: *La sensibilité musicale et le romantisme*, p. 44.

[2] Mozart, towards the end of his life, was fond of this mark which was uncommon before 1786 (but see K.413, 447 and 452); in 1786, cf. K.491, 493, 502; in 1788, K.537; in 1789, K.581; in 1790, K.589 and 593; in 1791, this concerto—the Breitkopf edition for piano solo—has andante by mistake. In the H.M.V. recording the soloist has made the worst possible mistake by taking this larghetto as if it were an adagio molto; the movement is completely deformed thereby.

the second bar is in semi-quavers in the piano, it is in demi-semi-quavers in the orchestra. The second part of the refrain belongs to the piano only and is clearly but a sketch. The outline returns four times in all; it is permissible to give it out as it is the first time, but on the three other appearances it must be decorated; the decoration should of course be in keeping with the spirit of the movement.[1] This larghetto has no cadenza and it is within the limits of these few bars that the soloist's extemporizing talent should be displayed.

The piano repeats the first part; as it finishes, the horns sound reiterated B flats, a tonic pedal with which the coda begins. Climbing up the degrees of the chord of the seventh and passing from *piano* to *forte*, the melody rises with some power and eventually comes to rest on the tonic. A trilling figure in the second violins animates pleasantly its ascent. Then, over a wavy motif in the seconds, the firsts outline the fragments of a new theme; on its repetition, the violas join the seconds and the woodwind add held notes (ex. 406). A third figure, a succession of winged sighs in violins and flute (ex. 407), leads the refrain to its conclusion.

The only couplet in this rondo consists in a piano cantilena sustained by a somewhat varied tutti accompaniment. It decomposes into a series of short phrases, each one of which is repeated, usually with slight changes in the tune or the scoring. This part modulates less than certain *developments* of Mozart's; we start from the tonic and pass into B flat and G flat, where we remain for eight bars. The last part unfolds in the minor and the end brings us back to the tonic.

For the first half, the accompaniment consists in repeated notes; when we reach G flat these give way to a marching bass that punctuates each beat with a quaver; the space between the basses and the piano (both hands of which play in the treble clef) is filled by a held note in the first bassoon, a sober but expressive detail of scoring (ex. 408). Towards the end the first violin part becomes so important melodically that it predominates over the piano; we hear an undulating theme whose chromaticisms recall the andante of the D major concerto, K.451; the piano imitates it freely a third above (ex. 409). The weary, "wilting" mood is obvious here. We make our way back to the refrain with a poetic phrase, thrice repeated, ascending in semi-tones from B flat to the tonic; the piano enlivens it with trills.

The first two parts of the refrain are restated almost unaltered, but in the last appearance of ex. 404 the piano's right hand is doubled

---

[1] In ex. 405 we suggest a realization of this passage.

by the flute and first fiddles. Each instrument sticks to its own version of the little figure we have mentioned, which provokes a piquant
contrast in the rhythm. Moreover, as fiddles and flute are playing,
the latter in unison with the piano, the others an octave lower,
sensitive ears will perceive here a succession of octaves and fifths!
But the chief interest of the passage lies in the tone which is the
product of this collaboration of percussion, wind and strings—an
unusual mixture which gives a weird, hollow sound, very un-
Mozartish, caused not only by the blending of the timbres but also
by the lack of bass, since the violins play below the piano's left hand.[1]
We have here a further instance of the renewal, in Mozart the composer of concertos, of the innovating, adventurous spirit which was
lacking in the Coronation concerto.[2]

The coda returns without much change in the melody and harmonization, but the presence of the piano brings about one of those
re-scorings we meet in certain allegro recapitulations[3] which afford
Mozart an opportunity for displaying much ingenuity. In ex. 406,
the line of the seconds and violas is doubled and distributed between
the two hands of the piano; the tune falls to the hautboys; the bassoons
receive a new part and the flute sketches a counter-subject, also new,
whilst the strings are out of the picture. Their substitution by the
wind, in collaboration with the piano, is quite in order, since the
more distinctive wind instruments are the essentially concertante
members of the band.

Finally, after a four-bar insertion for the benefit of the solo, ex.
407 shows us how piano and wind rejuvenate the original part with
two new lines. In these last five bars the flute and first violins seem,
gracefully but firmly, to be leading the piano off the stage.

III. The refrain of the finale takes us back to the "hunts" of former
times[4] by its form, but its spirit is no longer the same as theirs. It
certainly sings of joy, but not the carefree joy of the Salzburg days,
nor the sturdy love of life and success which filled the Viennese

---

[1] A somewhat similar effect occurs in the opening bars of Vaughan
Williams's *Flos Campi*, where flute and first viola play in octaves.

[2] In the finale of K.450 (bars 82–6 and 262–6), flute, piano and violins
also combine in giving out a theme, but the effect is less weird because the
left hand of the piano and the rest of the orchestra accompany them.

[3] Among others, K.482 and 491.

[4] K.450, 456, 482.

Ex. 413

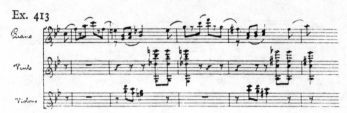

Ex. 414

Ex. 415

Ex. 416

Ex. 417

concertos of the three "great" years. Its joy is more ethereal; it is a foretaste of the disembodied bliss of the E flat quintet.

It begins like a Lied written a few days later:[1] "Komm, lieber Mai, und mache die Baüme wieder grün" (Come, sweet May, and make the trees green again), and it is significant that the title of this Lied contains the word "Sehnsucht". Yearning: this has been one of the chief sentiments in Mozart's music for the last two years, and, in spite of the freshness of its refrain, it inspires parts of this rondo.

The piano gives out the first stanza (ex. 410) and the orchestra repeats it. If the opening reproduces a Lied, the fragment (a) recalls an aria: "E l'amore un ladroncello", from *Cosi fan tutte* (at the words: "Come gli piace al cor," after the pause); the whole refrain is indeed very close to this air both in feeling and form. This fragment is the only chromatic part in a diatonic tune and later on it turns out to be an important element of the movement. The piano gives out the second stanza (ex. 411) and returns to the first, to which the tutti add a conclusion incorporating a reminder of (a) and ending with the habitual clamorous close.

As usual the first couplet is opened by the piano; it starts with a familiar Mozartian figure (ex. 412)[2] and leads to a dominant close. Another concerto would at once admit us into F major where we are in any case destined to arrive some day; this one, in its rondo as in its first movement, takes us along the byways of several minor keys. Using for this purpose a fragment of the refrain, modified, ex. 413, the piano flits from F major to F minor and G minor, urged on by light repeated woodwind chords which continue even when the piano part has spread out into arpeggios and broken scales whose ripples detain us for awhile in the realms of G minor. At length, via F minor and D flat major, we enter F major through its dominant, C, and even so the bit of the refrain which brings in this key hovers between major and minor with a see-saw motion typical of this concerto (ex. 414). A short imitative dialogue between piano and flute precedes the main theme of the couplet, brother to the refrain, equally light-footed and quite as ignorant of the lower registers of the piano. The butterfly flittings of its second bar, one of the last appearances of Mozart's beloved "fluttering seconds", occur several times, in diverse

---

[1] "Sehnsucht nach dem Frühlinge" (Yearning after spring), itself based on a folk-song. Cf. Köchel-Einstein, no 596. This indicates the speed of the rondo which should not be played faster than the voice can sing the song.

[2] See the finales of the Linz symphony, K.425, the horn concerto K.447 and the clarinet concerto.

shapes, in the course of the movement. The wind restate it and the piano accompanies with delicate gestures (ex. 415). An arpeggio passage, an ascending scale on a tonic pedal, leads to a pause where the soloist is expected to improvise a short cadenza; it is followed by the return of the refrain.

The first part only is repeated, first by the solo, then by the tutti, but when we reach fragment (a) (ex. 410), it breaks off; hautboys, bassoons and horns continue alone and, repeating the fragment softly, echo shyly what went before. It is as if the whole orchestra discovered suddenly that it had committed a blunder and stopped, horror-struck, still muttering unconsciously the unfortunate words it had just spoken.

The piano is braver; nevertheless, it is in the minor that it repeats the figure upon which all had stopped, and the executant will do well to introduce a momentary hesitancy into his playing.[1] Then, the solo becomes bolder and finally launches forth into a run. The *development* couplet begins in B flat minor and its starting-point is the fragment (a) of the refrain. This heralds a thematic *development*, and indeed the first part of the refrain is present, in one shape or another, almost all the time.

A bravura passage follows (a); urged on by a restless, wandering impulse, the solo explores the various zones of the upper register with a bold, sweeping flight, brushing past several keys without settling in any. The orchestra at first lets it play alone; then, as if to fix its thoughts, the fiddles recall softly the beginning of the refrain; flute and hautboy likewise (ex. 416). Beneath the solo arpeggios which have replaced the undulations and climb rapidly up and down the two registers of the keyboard, a conversation in an undertone between violins and woodwind keeps the first notes of the refrain[2] constantly before us; this dialogue, which begins in F minor, carried away by the piano's modulations, starts each time in a fresh key: C minor, G minor, D minor, stopping without closing, together with the piano runs, on a chord of the seventh whose resolution is delayed by a pause, then by three questioning chords sounded by the representatives of the orchestra. The piano breaks in roughly upon our expectancy; the harmonies pivot on their bass in an enharmonic modulation and we come out into the clear daylight of E flat major (ex. 417).

---

[1] The Steingräber edition rightly marks: quasi cadenza.

[2] And which reminds us of the dialogue between 'cello and violin at the same point in the finale of the string trio in E flat, K.563.

In this key the refrain makes its third appearance. This return to the first subject or its equivalent in the key of the subdominant is an archaism uncommon in Mozart; an earlier example is found in the allegro of the little sonata in C, K.545. It is not only the key which is irregular here, but also the very form of this return. At the end of the sixth bar (end of [a]), the piano breaks off suddenly, as the orchestra had done earlier, and delegates its authority to the wind who continue, but in the minor. Thereupon opens a little development in the course of which we work up a scale fragment and at each step piano and fiddles recall (a), which clearly has become the chief figure in the movement. Thus, we pass by D flat minor and E flat minor and reach the tonic after a sojourn in the key of the dominant where we again notice the hesitation between major and minor so characteristic of these years (cf. ex. 414). All this passage may be looked on as a continuation of the *development* couplet as well as a new version of the refrain; we have here a cross between the regular sonata rondo where the refrain recurs between the second and third couplets and the other kind where it is omitted;[1] at the end of his life, Mozart rejuvenates once again this rondo form which is the realm of musical architecture where he experimented most freely.[2]

The third couplet begins with ex. 412; when it has been given out piano and woodwind discuss ex. 413 with the usual transpositions. The violins join in wittily. (We quoted their answers in ex. 413; these should now be read a fifth lower.) As in the first couplet, the minor extends nearly to ex. 415. After this latter subject and the short passage which prolongs it, a few tutti bars usher in the cadenza, the last of the collection left by Mozart and one of his prettiest.

The piano restates the whole of the refrain and the tutti add their ritornello. We then enter the coda, consisting in a bravura passage very brilliant for this work and in one last echo of the beginning of the refrain, thrown from fiddles to wind, with piano arpeggios, as in ex. 416. The last bars cast off all morbidity and resound with a joyful unison fanfare in the orchestra, based on the first bar of the movement.

There is not quite the same unity of feeling in this rondo as in the first movement. The inspiration of the refrain corresponds only

---

[1] See also the rondos of the G minor quartet and the clarinet concerto where the refrain is left out but where nevertheless we hear a hint of it before the beginning of the third couplet.

[2] This part of the finale is treated in a similar manner in the adagio and rondo for flute, hautboy, viola, 'cello and harmonica, K.617, composed a few months later.

partly to that of the rest. If we knew nothing more of the finale, we would think it sang of joy—the joy we sought to define a few pages back. The two other themes, exs. 412 and 415, would confirm us in this idea, and so would the witty flute and piano dialogue and the virtuosity passage that precedes and follows it, and the coda. But other passages express a different mood: the minor digressions which separate the two main subjects exs. 413 and 414, the short working-out of ex. 410 which follows the refrain's return in E flat and, above all, the middle couplet which begins with the dramatic interruption of the refrain and unfolds entirely in the minor. On the whole, if the refrain and the two bright spots, exs. 412 and 415, sing of happy thoughts, four times over the music turns from joy and, leaving sun-lit avenues, passes into the shade of doubt. At such moments we encounter something like the sadness experienced in the allegro and larghetto. And even in the brighter bars of the refrain, those which, with the opening, attract Mozart's attention most are just the only ones where chromaticism enters, the fragments (a) which we have heard him work out several times. The note of weariness, however, is absent; at no stage does the rondo belie the vigour of its beginning and as a result its minor passages are more dramatic than those of the first movement.

The constant reappearance of fragments of the refrain (exs. 413, 414, 416) and the fact that the whole *development* couplet, except in the bravura bars, is built on its first notes and fragment (a) gives this rondo a thematic unity uncommon, if not unique, in the finales of these concertos.[1] It is akin in this respect, not to its predecessors in the same genre, but to contemporary chamber works, to the two last quartets and especially the E flat quintet, the most unified of all Mozart's compositions.

The piano style is more brilliant than in the allegro; in the coda virtuosity is for a moment an end in itself, but elsewhere it is always at the service of the emotion and is less prominent than in other concerto finales. The writing is constantly linear and never returns to the mass effects that Mozart renounced in his concertos after K.503. It is also very homogeneous. The runs, which are always short, belong to a small number of types, of which the principal are the wide spread arpeggio (exs. 415 and 416), the broken descending scale and, especially, the broad, wavy line; this latter, which is predominant, is typical of this rondo. The unimportance of the virtuosity and

---

[1] No, not unique, for we remember that of K.449.

its subordination to feeling, which is as noteworthy here as in the two other movements, separates the work from the other concertos and brings it nearer to the symphonies and chamber music.

Mozart has taken more interest in structural problems in this finale than in the other movements. Rondo form always stimulated most strongly his taste for innovations and the plan of this one is among his most distinctive. Piano and orchestra, moreover, collaborate more continuously than in the allegro. Ex. 415 is shared between them when it is repeated; there are many moments when both discuss a fragment of the refrain and when the tutti quicken the piano with an original accompaniment: for instance, the woodwind interruptions in ex. 413, the conversation between wind, strings and solo in ex. 416, the intervention of the wind and the violins in ex. 417. After the listless scoring of the D major concerto, it is consoling to rediscover here the Mozart of the great concertos, eleven months before his death. The discourse is constantly shared by both wind and strings, and the interest kept up by numberless details in the instrumental parts.[1] From whatever angle it is examined, except that of piano technique, this concerto, till recently so neglected, is in every point the equal of the finest and deserves fully to be added to the twelve great works of 1784–6 as one of its author's most personal compositions.

B flat is a favourite key with Mozart. In his mature period, besides the four piano concertos, he used it for two quartets, one trio, two piano sonatas, two violin sonatas, a wind serenade, a duet for violin and viola and a symphony—only one, and that not important. It is in the concerto, the sonata and chamber music that the mood he generally associates with this key should be sought. If we leave aside the three B flat works of 1789 and 1790, and especially if we bring in the ten or twelve slow movements in this key, we recognize that it expresses before all a state of serenity, as absolute a calm as Mozart's restless soul can experience. It calls up a benedictory spirit; applying to it what has been written of an andante of Beethoven, we would say that its mildness is like "grace falling on the soul of a saint". A typical B flat work of Mozart's leaves behind it a feeling of moral well-being the expression of which is accompanied by playfulness in the first movements and gaiety in the finales. We

---

[1] There is not room to say everything! Let us point out only the place where the wind, in the first enunciation of the refrain, give up their function as accompanists and join in the tune when fragment (a) is reached.

perceive it at its clearest in the concerto K.450, the Hunt quartet and the Strinasacchi sonata K.454, but it is as obvious in lesser compositions like the Paris sonata K.333 and the trio K.502. Mozart's most significant B flat andantes are those of the D minor concerto, the G minor quartet,[1] the F major duet sonata and the E flat string quintet; in the latter, the joy has that unearthly quality that permeates so large a part of the master's music in his last year. In 1789 and 1790, mildness persists, but serenity gives way for a while to weariness and disheartenment.

The B flat concerto comes at the end of a period in Mozart's musical development. We shall not meet again the inspiration which gives it life and which had predominated in him for the last two years, save perhaps in the andante of the second organ fantasia, K.608, completed in the following March. The years 1789 and 1790 spoke of sadness and renunciation; 1791, his last, on the other hand, witnesses the surging up in his music of a new growth of spring, the herald of a summer that was never to mature.

This growth is already apparent in the second of the two fantasias that he wrote, against his will, for the mechanical organ—"ein Orgelwerk in einer Uhr"—which a certain Müller, calling himself Count Deym, had set up in an exhibition of curiosities. We know nothing of this instrument but it must have been a sorry tinkle, for Mozart groaned: "Oh! if only it were a big clock, if the mechanism were to produce an organ tone, it would interest me; but the instrument is just a little reed and its tone is shrill and too childish for my liking." [2]

But he could not prevent his imagination hearing the instrument he would have liked and it is indeed for a cathedral organ that these fantasias were conceived. At distant intervals one hears them performed by organists; one would really prefer to hear them in an orchestral arrangement; several such exist but none has been published.

The first of these fantasias dates from the preceding autumn and is still tributary of the inspiration of that period; in the partly fugal allegro of the second, the strength and fullness of the quintets and great concertos are again apparent in the master's art. In the short but distinguished list of his polyphonic movements this allegro takes one of the highest places; in the humbler family of his variations the andante does likewise.

---

[1] Very typical, with its voluptuous and nostalgic figure of trailing scales.
[2] Letter to his wife, October 3rd, 1790.

But it is with the E flat string quintet that the spring proclaims itself fully.

This quintet, his last instrumental work,[1] is indeed a culmination. It is complete and self-sufficient. In it an ideal is attained, and whilst we do not claim that Mozart would have remained at this point if he had lived, we acknowledge a perfection in it which befits the closing act of a fruitful life. The spirit that inspires it and blossoms forth in it so sumptuously is the same which will inspire the "mystical" parts of the *Magic Flute*, that is, precisely the most original parts of that opera.[2] This quintet has been almost completely neglected by performers and even by critics; only in recent years has any appreciation worthy of it been written.[3]

The first impression it makes is one of a pure *jeu d'esprit*. Beethoven's last quartet makes the same impression. Both owe it to their detachment, to the fact that no breath of passion or even of emotion appears to touch them, except in the andantes; they are like intercourse between disembodied spirits. In the chronological study of Mozart's compositions we are tempted at first to class the E flat quintet with works of the last years like the quartet in F where we thought we recognized traces of spiritual dryness. And we do indeed feel that there is an evolutional link between them and it. Its mood does indeed grow out of theirs, but it is not the same. We might express the same idea by saying that the quartet in F had sought, but failed, to embody the ideal embodied by the quintet.

Its true spirit, despite its apparent simplicity, is even less easy to grasp at a glance than that of more normal Mozartian music. Its basic ideas are simple, even mean, if we compare them with other themes of its composers; neither the first subject of the allegro nor the refrain, which is really the only subject in all the finale, are distinctive tunes; one of them is not much more than a rhythmic figure, the other,

---

[1] With the little quintet K.617. The clarinet concerto, which figures as a completed work at a later date in Mozart's catalogue, had been composed in part earlier.

[2] We mean the Temple scenes; Papageno and the Queen of Night derive from other inspirations, already often met with in his work.

[3] Adolphe Boschot, Henry Ghéon, Eric Blom. The Pro Arte quartet recorded it before the war in America, but the recording has never been on sale in Britain.

almost a jingle. It is true that the way in which they are set forth compensates to some extent for their poverty; this quintet is much more a conversation than its predecessors and the substance is divided equally between the different parts. A contrast in colour is thus provided which strikes us in the very first bars where the shrill note of the fiddles answers the husky tone of the violas. In no other quartet or quintet of Mozart does anything similar exist.

It is none the less true that its thematic material is meagre. But its spiritual abundance is in inverse proportion to its material poverty. Its nudity and lack of passion are neither dessiccation nor hyper-intellectuality; our first impression is rectified as we become more familiar with it. It is the soaring flight of a strong personality rising through sheer fortitude above daily cares and finding the appease-ment, but not the forgetfulness, of its sorrow in itself and its art. Serene, this quintet certainly is, but with the rich sereneness of a spirit that has suffered and not the passiveness of a being apathetic or incapable of strong feelings. It is the sanctuary into which Tamino and Pamina enter after the trial by fire and water. As Boschot expresses it, a "Franciscan blitheness" ("une allégresse franciscaine") reigns in it; we hear "the song of a heart living beyond visible things . . . an ethereal, luminous murmur, like the rustling of a grove full of twittering birds conversing with the Poverello of Assisi".[1]

This is particularly true of the allegro and finale. The trio of the minuet, a Viennese waltz, brings a more earthly joy. As for the andante, in it lies a more physical feeling, grace, love, even a touch of longing. If the allegro makes us think of Giotto's frescoes, the andante is redolent with the spirit of Botticelli; it is haunted by the three Graces from the *Primavera*, and the gruppetti which accompany the refrain on its last appearance and persist to the end, call up the flowers that flutter round the goddess in the *Birth of Venus*.

This quintet lives in the same climate as the *Magic Flute* but its kinship with other E flat works is more distant. Very few features recall the symphony of 1788. The finales of both works, it is true, arise in part from the same vein and there is a formal likeness in the "stiff" violin passages which occur in both. But the first move-ment of the symphony has more warmth and passion; its atmosphere is less rarefied and its majestic introduction has no counterpart in the quintet. There is more likeness in the contrast, in both andantes, between the rather prim rhythms and the fullness of the emotion, and

[1] Ad. Boschot: *Chez les Musiciens* (2me série, pp. 22 and 38).

the minuets, both of them haughty with different shades of arrogance, both of them having waltzes for trios, recall one another.

Do we find more relationship between this quintet and its great predecessors, the "Heavenly Twins" of 1787? The two quintets of Mozart's last year are indeed less imposing than those in C and G minor. But they have none the less their own place which nothing else fills. His last quintet in particular is duplicated by no other work. The C major and G minor quintets affect and stir a larger surface of our being, but the corner which the E flat has marked as its own belongs to none other and it is a corner which Mozart alone has explored with success. The 1787 quintets belong to a much more numerous category of works; their ideal is in reality that of most of the great 19th century composers; their climate is nearer that of Beethoven or Brahms than that of the quintet of 1791. With the important reservation that every genius is unique, we would say that in the musical literature of the 19th century there are more compositions of the same character as the quintets in C and G minor than of that of the E flat. Some tastes may prefer the sumptuous, spacious beauty of the former, but there is no doubt that the beauty of the latter is more rare.

We therefore end with this quintet the journey we have undertaken through Mozart's work, a journey in which we chose his piano concertos as our chief landmarks. It is indeed his last instrumental composition. His catalogue, it is true, enters the clarinet concerto after a cantata the date of which is September 28th, but the conception and partial realization of its first movement, at any rate, go back several years, when Mozart had intended it for a bassett horn, so that it does not represent the inspiration of his last months.[1]

What of the *Requiem*? Does it not belong authentically, in its completed portions, to Mozart's last days? Certainly; but its history is so special, as much on account of the feeling imposed by the very words of the Mass for the Dead as of the disturbing circumstances in which it was ordered, that we must consider it as a parenthesis in his life. Fate ordained that the parenthesis should never be closed; it is the *Magic Flute* and not the *Requiem* which concludes the year and which explains and crowns the growth of Mozart's thought since 1787. And the *Magic Flute*, as we have said, in the most personal part of its content, mingles its waters with the stream which, a few months earlier, had flowed through the quintet in E flat.

---

[1] See Köchel-Einstein, nos. 584 b and 622.

Conclusion

THE increasing enthusiasm of our time for Mozart s concertos is far from being accompanied by performances which bring out all their beauty. In the course of many hearings, certain traps have come to appear to us as particularly dangerous and we would like to point them out at the risk of repeating what has been said elsewhere.

There are two common forms of bad Mozart playing. One consists in making him graceful, elegant and gentle; the other, lively and dashing.

These two kinds of style are not always out of place, but they are insufficient. There are indeed passages which should be rendered with elegance and grace and others which should be dashing, but none of Mozart's works demands a performance where both styles, or one of them, preponderate. To interpret him as he deserves other qualities than elegance and brio are needed.

As a matter of fact, the graceful, delicate style is seldom desirable and there are few torments for a keen Mozart lover equal to that of hearing a whole concerto played in this way. Some of his least arresting sonatas may be suited by it, but it should be excluded from his greater works. It has the power of belittling a piece and making a bauble of it; those who favour such a way of playing should therefore confine themselves to the few genuine baubles that he has left.

The dashing style is more often opportune. It is excellent, for instance, in certain concerto rondos, energetic, witty, superficial, eminently suited to a performance con brio. But it is as disastrous to be "smart" in his initial allegros as it is to be "graceful" in them. We have insisted on the witless sacrilege of turning into a *brillante* the *maestoso* with which he sometimes heads his opening movements.

By the light of sudden flashes we get glimpses of depths which open for a moment and close up again at once; the "dashing" performer leaps over them like a mountaineer over a crevasse, without looking into its glinting darkness, and a rich, manifold work becomes sparkling and commonplace.

One of the mannerisms of those who cultivate this style consists in giving rising scales a kind of push by putting down the loud pedal at the beginning and emphasizing the last note with a sforzando, thanks to which the scale goes off like the uncorking of a bottle. Mozart's line, treated thus, loses all breadth and serenity and the composer is turned into a species of anæmic Liszt. One longs for more of those linear, warm-hearted and sensitive performances which Gieseking and Wanda Landowska give us, where we feel the beautiful runs quiver, clean and full of life, under the pianist's fingers.

In reality, no single style is peculiar to Mozart. His music should be played as it is and the pianist should be like it, vigorous, graceful, delicate, merry, witty, sombre, sparkling, deep in turn, and always clear. Clarity is the one quality which is always in season. There is no special technique to adopt; it is the very sensibility of the composer that the executant must assimilate. Which is true of every great musician whose works we play! All this, then, boils down to saying that there is no peculiar Mozart style of playing; the advice given for the performance of any good music applies to his, and that is all!

We have already dwelt on the need for completing those bars which are merely sketched out. The 18th century soloist was a creator; he was associated with the composer and in concertos he had limited scope for extemporization. There is nothing like this in sonatas, for the sonata was not the preserve of the soloist; the amateur who played it was not a creator but a mere executant; he only reproduced the composer's thought and this thought was given him in its perfect state. But certain bars in sonatas give us useful hints how to complete sketchy passages in concertos. For instance, the andante of Mozart's C minor shows how the refrain of a slow rondo should be varied at each return. Reinecke's valuable pamphlet, *Zur Wiederbelebung der Mozart'schen Klavierkonzerte*, was reprinted some ten years ago and we refer the reader to it; every pianist who plays a concerto of Mozart's period should take its advice to heart.[1]

One last piece of advice. Mozart's piano writing is generally linear. From time to time, however, we meet with mass effects. We repeat once again that their exceptional character should compel the pianist to give them their full value. An exaggeration in the direction of heaviness is better than the opposite and is truer to the composer's intention.

---

[1] Let him take as a model the way in which Wanda Landowska plays the larghetto of the *Coronation* concerto in the H.M.V. recording.

Many hearings of these concertos and a few performances in an orchestra have convinced us that a good execution depends still more on the conductor than on the soloist. An intelligent conductor and a good orchestra with a mediocre pianist will give a better result than a first class soloist with a conductor and a band which are not his equals. For each instrument in turn is treated as a soloist and should be conducted accordingly. These concertos make more demands upon the instrumentalists' qualities than many symphonic works: they exact a personal understanding, sensitiveness, a good tone— more, that is to say, than can be obtained by merely adequate conducting. All the parts, when they are not accompanying, should be played with as much care and in the same spirit as solos.

The woodwind, especially, should stand out. In our modern orchestras, where the strings preponderate, the balance between them and the woodwind runs the risk of being broken if the conductor is not aware of the danger. It is principally in those numerous passages where one or other of the wind gives out a theme whilst the solo adorns or accompanies it that the instrument to which the band has momentarily handed over its powers should be heard. Some conductors are so impressed by the difference in strength between the modern orchestra and the piano as Mozart wrote for it that they never allow their players to rise above *mp*; the result is that parts which ought to be heard are unnoticed, whereas one hears only too well everything the piano has to say, even when its discourse is less important than the orchestra's. Many a performance and a recording have been spoilt in this way.

We have at length reached the end of the pilgrimage that we have been making through Mozart's life from the date when his piano concertos first appeared to act as landmarks. The fruit of this pilgrimage is the first book ever wholly devoted to these concertos. We do not in anywise claim that it is definitive, even in the very un-absolute sense in which one can apply this term to sublunary works of learning. For the glory of the master to whom it is dedicated, we ask for nothing more than that further studies, worthier of him, should succeed and displace it. For many a year the twenty-three works with which we have been living will not be exhausted, and we realize that, however bulky our book may be, there are aspects of them we have not touched upon and others, at which we have glanced, that deserve more thorough treatment.

Into the conclusions drawn by a study where a subject as impalpable as the nature of an inspiration plays a large part, an element of arbitrariness is bound to enter. We do not expect that all the different appreciations we have given will be approved by everyone; we do not even hope it, for the diversity of the impressions which a work of art produces on those who contemplate it is a sign of its greatness. There is less disagreement over second and third rate artists than over the great masters. In their presence, our reactions are as different from one man to the next as in presence of the beauties of Nature. Admiration is sometimes their only common element.

One indisputable fact, nevertheless, we believe, results from our study: in Mozart's artistic existence there was not only development of technique; there was also growth in thought. We are far from thinking that no one before us had noticed the organic quality of his work, considered in time; no one who has soaked himself in the composer's music has failed to recognize it. But the opinion that Mozart never grew up and merely repeated himself, with an unconsciousness that some profess to find charming, all through his life, is so slow in dying that we are glad to carry yet another slab to its grave.

Following him through his fifteen most fruitful years has shown us once again to what extent his musical being gained in depth and power from stage to stage, to what extent it discovered new realms for itself and transformed its inspiration from the period of the *galant* concertos with which we began, to the E flat quintet, the *Magic Flute* and the *Requiem*. We saw that, if at certain moments there was a kind of withdrawal and apparent retrogression, under the influence of new surroundings when he settled in Vienna, under that of material worry in 1789 and 1790, there was never decadence nor lack of renewal; to each year of his maturity correspond fresh shades of inspiration and this is true to the very end. Even if this study of his work in his great concertos has only served to make this once more evident, our task will not have been in vain.

The greatness of the concertos themselves no longer needs demonstrating; neither does the pre-eminence of their place in Mozart's output. In them are seen aspects of his genius unperceived elsewhere or more visible here than elsewhere. The constructive power, the architectural side of this musician who was looked on so long as a pure melodist, reveals itself as it does nowhere else except in the two 1787 quintets. No allegro of his symphonies reaches such vast dimensions nor shows so complex a structure as his concertos of the three great years; in no other genre did he carry so far the development of rondo form—the form in which he experimented most, and most successfully. Only a few exceptions like the quartet in A and the Jupiter symphony possess finales whose masterly construction equals that of his best concerto rondos.

And nowhere else, not even in his operas, did he work out contrast of tone with so much skill. His concertos display most clearly his ability to handle the woodwind, to contrast them one with the other, with the strings and with the solo. The presence of a foreign body, the piano, stimulated him and showed him combinations of tone of which he never thought in his symphonies and overtures. It appears paradoxical; but in order to see his absolute mastery of the orchestra, we must turn to his concertos rather than to his works for orchestra alone.

As for his thought, it will be enough to recall what we have already written: it is in the concertos that the Olympian and tragic strains in his inspiration are manifested with greatest power and depth.

Starting from the divertimento conception of the genre, he ended by putting as much of himself into it as into his chamber music and symphonies. Of almost all his concertos composed after he had settled in Vienna it is true to say that each one corresponds to a mood. With many of them it is possible to live continuously. The choice of these is, of course, a matter of taste; yet it seems to us that everyone will grant that the two works in A major, and those in G, D minor, C minor, C major K.503 and B flat K.595 allow us to frequent them intimately without exhausting them, without wearying of them, and that is the test of greatest art.

What is precious in Mozart is the perception he affords us of beautiful and powerful motion, at once delicate and sure-footed, seeing whither it goes and following its aim unflinchingly, with the effort-saving spareness of a tiger bounding towards its prey. This motion is all the more precious for being at the service of a nature belonging to the little band of those artists or thinkers "who seem rather to have come down into the flesh from above than to be straining upwards to free themselves from its limitations."[1]

The revival of Mozart since the opening of the century is one form of the reaction against Romanticism. Yet he is not the "pure" musician, untainted by emotion, whom some thought they saw in him twenty years ago; our study of the concertos has, on the contrary,

---

[1] Lawrence Hyde: *The prospects of humanism*, p. 162. It is we who apply his words to Mozart.

striven towards setting forth the fullness of the affective life in
his music. We have come to love in him one of the healthiest
and most imaginative natures in all art. He is discreet, not because
he has nothing to say, but because he speaks with a moderation and
a sense of form that few artists have so consistently exhibited. Let
us no longer judge him from his minor works, sonatas or trios. His
true face is shown in his best quartets and quintets, his last symphonies
and his Viennese concertos, his operas, his C minor and *Requiem*
masses. There, he throbs with as intense a life as Bach or Beethoven,
and if we compare his last fifteen years with any fifteen years of theirs,
we shall have to admit that he is as manifold and as profound as they.
His inner life is of the richest and most communicative; his work, a
personal revelation which never falls into a series of self-centred con-
fessions. It is as much a testament as that of the greatest masters,
capable of affording unfailing comfort and support.

When we first laid the foundations of this study, a few years after
the 1914–18 war, the rediscovery of Mozart had begun but had
not reached his concertos. Since then, many of them too have re-
entered the field of concerts, especially that of broadcasts and amateur
performances. Our study is itself but a sign among many of his
value for the inter-war generations. A few great concertos are
still absent from our programmes; their revival is surely only a question
of time. Between the years in which we set out on our labours and
that in which we complete them, executants and public have discovered for themselves the greatness of these works; our book does
not come forward as the herald of a new thesis but simply as an
attempt to explain a few points and to co-ordinate thoughts and
sentiments common to all Mozart lovers which it may be convenient
to find assembled in the same volume. In all humility, it offers itself
as a homage of devotion to him of whom it treats.

Appendix I

CADENZAS TO K.365

I

2

3

4

Appendix II

CADENZAS TO K.413

I

2

LIST OF COMPOSERS MENTIONED IN THIS WORK

Schumann, 14, 48, 57, 61, 74, 378.
Sibelius, 390.
Spohr, 213, 412.
Steibelt, 53.

TCHAIKOVSKY, 229, 396.

VIVALDI, 219.

WAGENSEIL, 20, 109.
Wagner, 34, 73.
Weber, 165.
Williams, R. Vaughan, 482.

LIST OF WORKS BY MOZART, OTHER THAN PIANO CONCERTOS, MENTIONED IN THIS WORK

MASSES, MOTETS.

K.317 in C, 105.
K.337 in C, 105, 148.
K.427 in C minor, 119, 123, 126, 148, 160, 168, 308, 324, 330, 360, 443.
K.626: Requiem, 17-19, 123, 176, 301, 308, 330, 331, 350, 493, 497.
K.341: Kyrie in D minor, 105, 119, 122, 123, 330, 331.
K.618: Ave verum, 464.

CANTATAS.

K.429: Dir, Seele des Weltalls, 366.
K.469: Davidde penitente, 360.
K.471: Die Maurerfreude, 366.

OPERAS AND BALLETS.

La Finta Semplice, 75.
Mitridate, 75, 123.
Ascanio in Alba, 75.
Lucio Silla, 75, 123, 167.
La Finta Giardiniera, 82.
Il Rè pastore, 82.
King Thamos, 330, 331, 413
Les Petits Riens, 103.
Idomeneo, 17, 123, 125, 167, 175, 210, 227, 330, 331, 389, 435, 436, 445, 461, 464.
Die Entführung aus dem Serail, 126, 160, 167, 416, 443.
L'Oca del Cairo, 160, 167, 168.
Lo Sposo deluso, 160, 167.
Der Schauspieldirektor, 174, 415, 443.
Le Nozze di Figaro, 167, 174, 353, 385, 415, 416, 445.
Don Giovanni, 167, 330, 331, 375, 454, 455, 461, 464.

Cosi fan tutte, 167, 240, 254, 315, 364, 385, 443, 461, 468, 485.
The Magic Flute, 17-19, 101, 115, 122, 176, 188, 310, 333, 335, 350, 366, 491-493, 497.
La Clemenza di Tito, 443, 444, 461.

ARIAS, DUETS, LIEDER.

K.294: Non so d'onde viene, 106.
K.369: Misero, dove son! 167.
K.416: Mia speranza adorata, 167.
K.489: Spiegarti non poss'io, 389.
K.490: Non più, tanto ascoltai, 389, 445.
K.505: Ch'io mi scordi di te, 444-449.
K.528: Bella mia fiamma, 247.
K.596: Sehnsucht nach dem Frühlinge, 485.

PIANO SOLO.

Sonatas:

K.279 in C, 83.
K.280 in F, 83, 378.
K.281 in B flat, 83.
K.282 in E flat, 83.
K.283 in G, 83.
K.284 in D, 83, 463.
K.309 in C, 109, 114, 443.
K.310 in A minor, 111, 323, 407.
K.311 in D, 463.
K.330 in C, 127, 250, 443.
K.331 in A, 44, 127.
K.332 in F, 127, 290.
K.333 in B flat, 127, 490.
K.457 in C minor, 34, 43, 239, 278, 280, 323, 328, 332, 407, 412-14, 495.

K.533 in F, 31, 300, 301, 441, 454-6.
K.545 in C, 37, 352, 456, 487.
K.570 in B flat, 52, 456, 468, 469.
K.576 in D, 456, 461, 463, 468, 469.

Fantasias:

K.394 in C (with fugue), 127, 148,
212, 443.
K.396 in C minor, 412, 413.
K.397 in D minor, 330.
K.475 in C minor, 316, 350, 412, 413.

Variations:

K.398: *Salve tu, Domine*, in F, 167.
K.455: *Unser dummer Pöbel meint*, in
G, 167, 268.
K.500 in B flat, 418.

Rondos:

K.485 in D, 173.
K.494 in F, 301.
K.511 in A minor, 345, 454, 455, 458.

Various:

K.399: Suite in the style of Handel,
148, 443.
K.E.453a: Funeral March, 178.
K.E.498a: Allegro and minuet in B
flat, 418.
K.540: Adagio in B minor, 42, 318,
327, 328, 378, 454, 455, 478.
K.574: Jig in G, 470.
K.355: Minuet in D, 455.

PIANO DUETS.

For One Piano:

Sonatas:

K.497 in F, 173, 300, 417, 490.
K.357 in G, 55, 418, 441.
K.521 in C, 390, 456.

Variations:

K.501 in G, 418.

For Two Pianos:

Sonata:

K.448 in D, 52, 126, 127, 277, 374,
463.

Fugue:

K.426 in C minor, 148, 413.

VIOLIN SONATAS.

K.296 in C, 37, 443.
K.302 in E flat, 134, 349.
K.303 in C, 443.
K.304 in E minor, 126, 323, 407.
K.306, in D, 89, 463.
K.378 in B flat, 37, 261.
K.376 in F, 126.
K.377 in F, 41, 42, 46, 123, 126, 160,
268, 300, 301, 330.
K.379 in G, 43, 126, 160, 256.
K.380 in E flat, 32, 41, 42, 43, 126,
160, 366.
K.402 in A, 148, 369.
K.454 in B flat, 211, 257, 258, 279,
303, 418, 446, 490.
K.481 in E flat, 351.
K.526 in A, 369, 387, 454, 455.
K.547 in F, 37, 352, 456.

TRIOS.

Strings:

K.E.404a: Preludes, 42.
K.563: Divertimento in E flat, 31, 32,
52, 239, 268, 277, 366, 454, 455, 465,
486.

Piano and Strings:

K.254 in B flat, 417.
K.496 in G, 417.
K.498 in E flat (with clarinet), 417,
446.
K.502 in B flat, 211, 418, 480, 490.
K.542 in E, 352.
K.548 in C, 52, 352.
K.564 in G, 352.

DUETS.

Violin and Viola:

K.423 in G, 256.
K.424 in B flat, 489.

Bassett Horns:

K.487 in C, 418.

QUARTETS.

Strings:

K.155 in D, 75.
K.156 in G, 75.
K.157 in C, 38, 75, 97, 360.
K.158 in F, 43, 75.
K.159 in B flat, 75.
K.160 in (E) Flat, 75.
K.E.Anh.210-213 in B flat, C, A and
 E flat, 75.
K.171 in E flat, 349.
K.173 in D minor, 44, 330, 331, 407.
K.387 in G, 43, 48, 80, 147, 160, 161,
 169, 256, 289, 290, 292, 293.
K.421 in D minor, 34, 45, 46, 123,
 161, 169, 278, 328, 330, 331, 380,
 407, 414.
K.428 in E flat, 169, 278, 341, 349,
 461.
K.458 in B flat, 34, 113, 211, 264, 279,
 280, 289, 303, 415, 490.
K.464 in A, 46, 48, 268, 269, 278, 280,
 302, 350, 369, 380, 415, 498.
K.E.464a in A, 369.
K.465 in C, 40, 48, 278, 289, 302, 350,
 415, 443, 456.
K.499 in D, 40, 91, 417, 418, 464.
K.575 in D, 137, 146, 264, 461, 462,
 464, 468, 469, 470.
K.589 in B flat, 45, 52, 191, 278, 289,
 440, 468-470, 472, 480, 488.
K.590 in F, 34, 278, 301, 468-70, 488,
 491.
K.546 in C minor (prelude and
 fugue), 41, 42, 148, 378, 413, 454,
 455.

Strings and Wind:

K.285 in D (flute), 96, 234, 463.
K.298 in A (flute), 44.
K.370 in F (hautboy), 330.

Piano and Strings:

K.478 in G minor, 34, 54, 218, 256,
 264, 277, 289, 327, 351, 386, 407,
 415, 417, 446, 449, 472, 487, 490.
K.493 in E flat, 52, 277, 366, 381, 382,
 386, 406, 446, 449, 480.

QUINTETS.

Strings:

K.174 in B flat, 81.
K.515 in C, 31, 32, 34, 40, 45, 48, 227,
 237, 278, 289, 302, 332, 347, 374,
 419, 420, 432, 442-44, 455-57, 493.
K.516 in G minor, 31, 33, 34, 40, 43,
 45, 48, 96, 270, 274, 278, 289, 302,
 319, 327, 328, 332, 407, 419, 432,
 444, 454, 455, 457, 478, 493.
K.593 in D, 31, 34, 40, 48, 417, 444,
 464, 469, 470, 480, 493.
K.E.613a in E flat, 273.
K.614 in E flat, 31, 34, 38, 45, 48, 52,
 191, 208, 293, 366, 444, 471, 488,
 490-93, 497.

Strings and Horn:

K.407 in E flat, 169, 365.

Strings and Clarinet:

K.581 in A, 32, 137, 188, 198, 369,
 417, 468, 470, 480.

Piano and Wind:

K.452 in E flat, 199, 238, 257, 277,
 365, 415, 446, 448, 480.

Harmonica, flute, violin, hautboy,
 and 'cello:

K.617 in C, 42, 487, 491.

SYMPHONIES:

K.16 in E flat, 349, 352, 356.
K.96 in C, 360.
K.132 in E flat, 349.
K.183 in G minor, 83, 85, 407.
K.184 in E flat, 38, 97, 349, 360.
K.297 in D, 103.
K.319 in B flat, 472, 489.
K.338 in C, 109, 119, 123, 168, 341,
 366, 443.

K.385 in D, 147, 161, 167.
K.425 in C, 119, 161, 168, 213, 485.
K.504 in D, 31, 40, 48, 174, 227, 278, 289, 419, 444, 454, 464.
K.543 in E flat, 31, 45, 48, 96, 184, 308, 366, 396, 419, 454, 457, 462, 492.
K.550 in G minor, 31, 34, 43, 48, 74, 278, 308, 324, 328, 332, 336, 407, 413, 419, 454, 457, 472.
K.551 in C, 31, 34, 43, 48, 80, 148, 278, 293, 302, 308, 332, 347, 419, 420, 423, 442, 443, 454, 457, 465, 472, 498.

DIVERTIMENTI
FOR ORCHESTRA.

K.252 in E flat, 113.
K.334 in D, 46, 119, 122, 123, 268, 330.

SERENADES
FOR ORCHESTRA.

K.250 in D, 37, 94, 137.
K.320 in D, 119, 122, 167, 330.
K.525 in G (Kleine Nachtmusik), 52, 444.

SERENADES
FOR WIND.

K.361 in B flat, 38, 46, 49, 119, 122, 126, 161, 210, 321, 444, 489.
K.375 in E flat, 31, 49, 119, 120, 122, 123, 126, 160, 210, 349, 365, 366, 443, 444, 472.
K.388 in C minor, 43, 119, 122, 123, 126, 127, 160, 161, 210, 268, 327, 329, 407, 413, 414, 444.

OTHER WORKS
FOR ORCHESTRA.

K.477: Masonic Funeral Music, 122, 174, 350, 351, 412, 413.
K.522: Musical Joke, 45.

WORKS
FOR MECHANICAL ORGAN.

K.594: Fantasia in F minor, 41, 42, 301, 328, 378, 466, 470.

K.608: Fantasia in F minor, 46, 466, 470, 490.

CONCERTOS.
Violin:
K.216 in G, 40, 83, 119, 256, 341.
K.218, in D, 83, 89, 461, 463.
K.219 in A, 27, 83.
K.E.271 in D, 463.
K.268 in E flat, 169.

Two Violins:
K.190 in C (Concertone), 77.

Violin and Viola:
K.364 in E flat (Sinfonia concertante), 27, 41-3, 97, 98, 104, 109, 117, 119-123, 156, 175, 251, 268, 341, 349, 360, 366, 443.

Bassoon:
K.191 in B flat, 77, 83.

Flute:
K.313 in G, 463.
K.314 in D, 78, 463.

Flute and Harp:
K.299 in C, 38, 103, 443.

Horn:
K.412 in D, 169-71.
K.417 in E flat, 38, 169-74, 365, 402.
K.447 in E flat, 169-74, 365, 480, 485.
K.495 in E flat, 169-74, 277, 365, 417.

Bassett Horn:
K.E.584a in G, 493.

Clarinet:
K.622 in A, 54, 293, 369, 382, 417, 487, 491, 493.

Piano and Violin:
K.E.315f in D, 118.

Four Wind Instruments:
K.E.297b in E flat (Sinfonia concertante), 103, 349.

BIBLE
HISTORY

BIBLE HISTORY

A TEXTBOOK OF
THE OLD AND NEW TESTAMENTS
FOR CATHOLIC SCHOOLS

By

Fr. George Johnson, Ph.D.

DEPARTMENT OF EDUCATION, CATHOLIC UNIVERSITY OF AMERICA,
WASHINGTON, D.C.

Fr. Jerome D. Hannan, D.D.

DEPARTMENT OF RELIGION, MOUNT MERCY COLLEGE,
PITTSBURGH, PENNSYLVANIA

and Sister M. Dominica, O.S.U., Ph.D.

FORMER PRINCIPAL OF MODEL SCHOOL, SACRED HEART JUNIOR COLLEGE, AND
NORMAL SCHOOL, LOUISVILLE, KENTUCKY

TAN BOOKS AND PUBLISHERS, INC.
Rockford, Illinois 61105

Nihil Obstat: Arthur J. Scanlan, S.T.D.
                  Censor Librorum

Imprimatur: ✛Patrick Cardinal Hayes
                  Archbishop of New York
                  New York
                  July 1, 1931

Rights purchased from Benziger Publishing Company by TAN Books and Publishers, Inc. in 2000. Reprinted by TAN Books and Publishers, Inc. in 2000.

ISBN 0-89555-692-8

Library of Congress Control No.: 00-136368

Cover illustration: "Christ and the Doctors in the Temple," by Heinrich Hofmann. (Original at Riverside Church, New York.)

Printed and bound in the United States of America.

TAN BOOKS AND PUBLISHERS, INC.
P.O. Box 424
Rockford, Illinois 61105
2000

TO OUR BOYS AND GIRLS

You have learned something of the wonderful story which the Holy Bible tells us, but there is still much more to know. In this book you will study the history of God's Chosen People from the day when He called Abraham to found the Jewish nation until the time when the "Scepter passed from Juda" to the hands of strangers. You will follow God's Chosen People through the history of its exile, its wanderings in the desert, and its return home to the Promised Land. You will learn how God directed Moses to build a sanctuary where He could dwell among His people; how Moses, at God's command, consecrated the first High Priest and instituted the feasts of the Lord. You will see how the Israelites, for so the Jews were called, conquered their enemies; how they grew in wealth and power; how they pleased God and how they displeased Him. Finally, you will see how the nation reached the climax of ingratitude and wickedness in the crucifixion of the Redeemer of the world, of Him Whom God promised to their fathers, to Abraham, to Isaac, to Jacob, and to Joseph. Your *Bible History* will tell you how the Redeemer came unto His own, and His own received Him not.

The New Testament will show you the Redeemer of men as He lived among men. Jesus Himself will speak to you as He spoke to the Jews in the synagogues. He is the Great Teacher of mankind Who teaches the

v

wonderful truths which you must believe. He is the much beloved Friend of the poor and the sick Whom you must console. He is the Savior of the world Who saved you from your sins, redeemed you from hell, and opened Heaven for you. He suffered and died and ascended into Heaven where He is waiting for you to come and enjoy eternal happiness with Him and His blessed Mother and all the saints.

Before Jesus left this world, He established His Church, which is His Kingdom on earth. The *Bible History* tells you how Jesus established His Church. This Church must explain to you all the truths which Jesus taught. It must guide you in life and prepare you for a happy passage to eternity.

We have prepared this book for you, dear boys and girls, that you may learn the truth about your Savior, and in knowing the truth, may love Him who died that you may have abundant life in this world and eternal life in the world to come.

THE AUTHORS

PREFACE TO TEACHER

This book has been written with the aim of providing boys and girls in Catholic Schools with a knowledge of the more important historical facts that are contained in the Sacred Scriptures. The story of the Old Testament is told chronologically, with emphasis on such social, economic, and political details as are within the grasp of pupils of these grades. The New Testament has been organized around the salient features of our Savior's redeeming mission, though at the same time such continuity is maintained as will enable the pupils to appreciate the fact that in Jesus Christ is the culmination of all the events that preceded His coming and the fulfillment of all the promises God had made since the fall of man.

The subject matter of the textbook is presented in the form of eight large units, corresponding to the great epochs in the history of the Redemption. Under each unit such details have been included as were considered essential to an understanding of the whole.

Previews to each Unit have been introduced to serve a double purpose. They prepare the pupil for the central idea in the Unit that follows and at the same time link this idea with the main thought of the preceding Unit. A comprehensive Teachers' Manual accompanies this textbook.

THE AUTHORS

CONTENTS

𝕿𝕳𝖊 𝕺𝖑𝖉 𝕿𝖊𝖘𝖙𝖆𝖒𝖊𝖓𝖙

Unit One
HOW GOD CAME TO PROMISE MAN A REDEEMER

Unit Two
HOW GOD FOUNDED THE NATION FROM WHICH THE REDEEMER OF THE WORLD CAME

Unit Three

HOW GOD PROTECTED HIS CHOSEN PEOPLE AND
LED THEM INTO THE PROMISED LAND

Unit Four

HOW GOD'S CHOSEN PEOPLE LIVED UNDER THEIR KINGS

The New Testament

Unit Six

HOW CHRIST PREPARED TO REDEEM THE WORLD

I. PREPARATION OF THE WORLD FOR THE MESSIAS

PAGE

LIST OF MAPS

PAGE

INTRODUCTION

WHY GOD GAVE US THE BIBLE

God created us to know Him, to love Him, to serve Him in this world and to be happy with Him forever in the next. The better we know Him, the more we will love Him; and the more we love Him, the more eager we will be to do His holy will. Therefore, the most important lessons we must learn are those which help us to know more and more about God.

We can learn many things about God from the world in which we live. The shining stars, the silver moon, the glowing sun, the lovely flowers, the rippling streams and the green fields were made by God. They are *beautiful* and they tell us that God is beautiful. The mighty rivers, the strong winds, the great waterfalls were made by God. They are *powerful* and they tell us that God is *powerful*. Our parents and friends who are kind and good to us and watch over us with loving care tell us that God *loves* and *cares* for us. Thus, the world is like a great book, in which we can read many things about God. Sometimes we call it the Book of Nature. *[margin: The Book of Nature]*

But men are not always able to read correctly the wonderful lessons that are found in the book of nature. The things that God made are so beautiful and powerful and good that we are liable to think more of them than we do of the God Who made them, and give them the honor which is due to God alone. Besides this, *[margin: The Bible]* there are many things which are not written in the book of nature. Some truths are above nature, or supernatural. God knows them, because He is all-wise and knows all things. God wanted us to know these truths because, knowing them, we should have a better idea of Him and know how to love Him and serve Him in a nobler way, and thus be happier than we could ever be if we had to depend on what we were able to learn from the book of nature.

Therefore God gave us another book, which we call The Bible. It helps us to understand better the lessons which are written in the book of nature, but it also tells us many things that otherwise we could never know, and some that we can never fully understand. Children cannot understand everything that grown-ups understand, but even the wisest man in the world could never understand some things that are in the mind of God. God tells us that a thing is true. We cannot understand it, but we know that it is true, because God has told us so. Truths that we cannot understand, even after God has told them to us, we call mysteries.

Divine Inspiration

The Bible was written by men whom God chose specially for that purpose. These men wrote down what God wanted them to write, and nothing else. God guided them so that they could not make a mistake. He recalled to their memories truths which they had learned and put thoughts into their minds which would never have come to them if God were not prompting them. This help which God gave to the sacred writers, we call Divine Inspiration.

After Christ had ascended into Heaven, God in- spired some of His apostles and disciples to write down many of the things which He had said and done. God watched over them and guided them so that they would write all that He wished them to write. After the last apostle died, no one ever had the gift of inspiration again, for by that time God had left us all the truths that are necessary for us to know in order to enter into the Kingdom of Heaven.

Christ founded His Church to guard the truths which He had revealed, and to explain them and preach them to the people. He promised to be with her until the end of time. Because Christ is with His Church, she cannot make a mistake when she tells us what we must believe and do if we wish to become holy and pleasing in the sight of God. Because she cannot make a mistake in these matters, we say she is Infallible.

The Bible is divided into two parts—the Old Testa- ment and the New Testament. The word testament means an agreement, or a contract. Thus, we speak of someone making his last will and testament. The Bible is a contract or an agreement between man and God. God promises to reward man if man does what God commands. Sometimes in the Bible the word covenant is used instead of testament, because the Bible is like a covenant or a treaty of peace between God and man.

The Old Testament is made up of forty-six books. These books tell how God promised man a Redeemer Who would save him from his sins, and how He chose a certain nation, the Jews, to prepare the world for His coming. The New Testament contains twenty-seven books, and tells how God's promise was fulfilled in our Lord and Savior, Jesus Christ, and in the Church which He founded. The Bible, then, is one large book, made up of seventy-three smaller ones.

The books in the Bible are not all alike. Some tell the story of things that happened in the past, and they are called historical books. Others contain rules of conduct and right living, and are called moral books. Others foretell things that will happen in the future, and are called prophetical books. Most of the books are written in prose, but some of them are written in poetry.

Tradition

Not all the lessons which our Lord taught while He was here upon earth are found in the New Testament. St. John says, "There are also many other things which Jesus said and did; which, if they were written every one, the world itself, I think, would not be able to contain the books that should be written." The apostles remembered many of these things, and told them to the people to whom they preached. These in turn told them to others. We call this handing down of the truths of faith by word of mouth, Tradition.

THE BOOKS OF THE OLD TESTAMENT

THE PENTATEUCH

Genesis
Exodus
Leviticus
Numbers
Deuteronomy

THE HISTORICAL BOOKS

Josue
Judges
Ruth
Kings (4 books)
Paralipomenon (2 books)
Esdras (2 books)
Tobias
Judith
Esther
Machabees (2 books)

THE POETICAL BOOKS

Job
Psalms
Proverbs
Ecclesiastes
Canticle of Canticles
Wisdom
Ecclesiasticus

THE PROPHETICAL BOOKS (18)

Major Prophets

Isaias
Jeremias
  Lamentations
Baruch
Ezechiel
Daniel

Minor Prophets

Osee
Joel
Amos
Abdias
Jonas
Micheas
Nahum
Habacuc
Sophonias
Aggeus
Zacharias
Malachias

THE BOOKS OF THE NEW TESTAMENT

THE HOLY GOSPELS

St. Matthew
St. Mark
St. Luke
St. John

THE ACTS OF THE APOSTLES

THE EPISTLES

To the Romans
To the Corinthians (2)
To the Galatians
To the Ephesians

THE EPISTLES (*cont'd*)

To the Philippians
To the Colossians
To the Thessalonians (2)
To Timothy (2)
To Titus
To Philemon
To the Hebrews
St. James
St. Peter (2)
St. John (3)
St. Jude

THE APOCALYPSE

THINGS TO KNOW AND TO DO

1. Why did God give us the Bible?
2. What is meant by Divine Inspiration?
3. What is Tradition?
4. Why are the truths handed down by Tradition as true as the Bible?
5. Why did Christ found His Church?

BIBLE
HISTORY

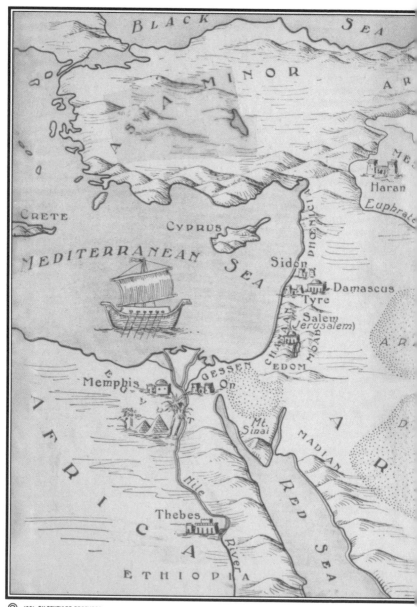

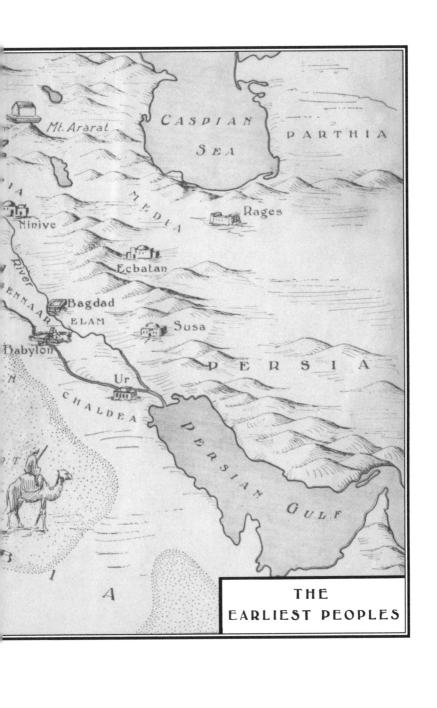

Mt. Ararat

CASPIAN SEA

PARTHIA

MEDIA

Rages

Ninive

Ecbatan

River

SENNAAR

Bagdad

ELAM

Susa

PERSIA

Babylon

Ur

CHALDEA

PERSIAN GULF

A

**THE
EARLIEST PEOPLES**

PREVIEW

Unit One

HOW GOD CAME TO PROMISE MAN A REDEEMER

In this Unit we shall see how God, in order to show forth His glory and to permit all creatures to have a share in His happiness, created the world.

We shall see how some of the angels proved to be ungrateful and were cast into hell because they rebelled against their Creator.

The story of the life of Adam and Eve, the first man and woman, in the Garden of Eden, will be told. We shall learn how in spite of the fact that they were wonderfully happy and had everything their hearts could desire, they listened to the voice of the tempter and ate of the forbidden fruit. For their sin, they were cast out of Paradise and doomed to death.

So great was their sin that they could not make reparation for it. Only God could redeem them. We shall see how God in His mercy promised to send a Savior Who would crush the power of sin and win back for man the happiness that he had lost by his sin.

Yet in spite of the Divine promise, the children of the first man and woman did not remain faithful to God. After a time their sins became so great that God determined to destroy them. Only one man and his family were saved. We shall see how God preserved them in a marvelous way while all the others were allowed to perish.

The Old Testament

Unit One

HOW GOD CAME TO PROMISE MAN A REDEEMER

The Old Testament

Unit One

HOW GOD CAME TO PROMISE MAN A REDEEMER

I. THE STORY OF THE CREATION

1. God Creates the Angels, and Some of Them Sin

From all eternity God existed. He always was, and never had a beginning, just as He will never have an end.

God is infinitely perfect. Nothing is wanting to Him in any way. The Three Divine Persons, the Father, the Son, and the Holy Ghost, are One God, equal to each other in all things, and They possess in Themselves everything that is necessary to make Them happy. All that is true, all that is beautiful, all that is powerful, all that is good, is found in God. God does not have to look to anyone outside Himself for anything whatsoever. There is no truth that He does not know, no power that He does not possess, no happiness that He does not enjoy. He does not need anything or anyone besides Himself.

But God is good, and because He is good, He wanted others to share in His happiness. That is why He created heaven and earth. He brought them forth out

Before the Creation

3

of nothing, not because He needed them, but so that creatures could share in His happiness and in His glory.

The creation of the angels

The highest of God's creatures are the angels. They are most like unto God, because, like God, they are spirits and have no body.

Not all of the angels are alike. It was God's will that some of them should be closer to Him than others. Those that are closest to God are most like unto God.

The Bible tells us that there are nine different kinds, or choirs, of angels. They are: Angels, Archangels, Principalities, Virtues, Powers, Dominations, Thrones, Cherubim, and Seraphim. The most wonderful of all these are the Cherubim and Seraphim. The lowest classes are the Angels and the Archangels. The Angels watch over human beings and protect them. Each one of us has a Guardian Angel.

When God created the angels, He gave them a test. Before they could enjoy the happiness of Heaven, they had to prove that they loved Him more than they loved themselves. God did not force the angels to love Him. Their wills were free, and they could do whatever they chose to do.

The fall of the angels

Some of the angels failed in the test. They were proud and refused to obey God. Their leader was Lucifer, one of the highest angels that God had created.

God did not spare the angels who had sinned. He gave to the angels who obeyed His will the power to cast Lucifer and his followers into hell. The leader of the good angels was Michael. The Bible tells us of

St. Michael and His Angels Overcome Lucifer and the Bad Angels

a great battle in Heaven, in which Michael and his angels fought with the bad angels, and cast them down into hell. Henceforth, Lucifer was known as **Satan,** or the devil.

The good angels were taken into the presence of God, and for all eternity they will see Him face to face, and will love Him and praise Him and be happy with Him. But the fallen angels will never see God. All hope of ever entering the Kingdom of Heaven has been taken away from them.

2. GOD CREATES THE WORLD

The Book of Genesis

The first book of the Bible is called Genesis, and it tells us how God made the world in which we live. It divides up the whole work of creation into six days. The word day, as used in the Bible, does not necessarily mean a period of twenty-four hours. Each of the days of creation may have been a long, long time, just as we sometimes speak of something as having happened in Washington's day or in the day of the stage-coach, or say that the day of the street car is past, when we mean the time that Washington lived, or the time when people traveled in stagecoaches or in street cars. We must bear in mind that God did not inspire the author of the Book of Genesis to tell us exactly how the world was made. His purpose was that all men, everywhere and until the end of time—the most ignorant as well as the greatest scholars—might know "that all things were made by Him, and without Him was made nothing that was made."

The creation of heaven and earth

This is how the story of creation is told in the Book of Genesis: "In the beginning God created heaven and earth. And the earth was void and empty, and darkness was upon the face of the deep; and the spirit of God moved over the waters. And God said, 'Be light made.' And light was made. And God saw the light that it was good, and He divided the light from the darkness. And He called the light Day, and the darkness Night; and there was evening and morning one day.

"And God said, 'Let there be a firmament made

amidst the waters; and let it divide the waters from the waters.' And God made a firmament, and divided the waters that were under the firmament from those that were above the firmament, and it was so. And God called the firmament Heaven; and the evening and the morning were the second day.

"God also said, 'Let the waters that are under the heaven be gathered together into one place; and let the dry land appear.' And it was so done. And God called the dry land Earth; and the gathering together of the waters He called Seas. And God saw that it was good. And He said, 'Let the earth bring forth the green herb, and such as may seed, and the fruit tree yielding fruit after its kind, which may have seed in itself upon the earth.' And it was so done. And the earth brought forth the green herb, and such as yieldeth seed according to its kind, and the tree that beareth fruit, having seed each one according to its kind. And God saw that it was good. And the evening and the morning were the third day.

"And God said, 'Let there be lights made in the firmament of heaven to divide the day and the night, and let them be for signs, and for seasons, and for days and years: to shine in the firmament of heaven, and to give light upon the earth.' And it was so done. And God made two great lights: a greater light to rule the day, and a lesser light to rule the night; and the stars. And He set them in the firmament of heaven to shine upon the earth. And to rule the day and the night, and to divide the light and the darkness. And

God saw that it was good. And the evening and the morning were the fourth day.

"God also said, 'Let the waters bring forth the creeping creature having life, and the fowl that may fly over the earth under the firmament of heaven.' And God created the great whales, and every living and moving creature which the waters bring forth, according to their kinds, and every winged fowl according to its kind. And God saw that it was good. And He blessed them, saying, 'Increase and multiply, and fill the waters of the sea; and let the birds be multiplied upon the earth. And the evening and the morning were the fifth day.

"And God said, 'Let the earth bring forth the living creature in its kind, cattle and creeping things, and beasts of the earth, according to their kinds.' And it was so done. And God made the beasts of the earth according to their kinds, and cattle, and everything that creepeth on the earth after its kind. And God saw that it was good.

"And He said, 'Let Us make man to Our image and likeness; and let him have dominion over the fishes of the sea, and the fowls of the air, and the beasts, and the whole earth, and every creeping creature that moveth upon the earth.' And God created man to His own image: to the image of God He created him; male and female He created them. And God blessed them, saying, 'Increase and multiply, and fill the earth, and subdue it, and rule over the fishes of the sea, and the fowls of the air, and all living creatures that move upon the earth.' And God said, 'Behold, I have given you every herb bearing seed upon the earth, and all trees that have in themselves seed of their own kind, to be your meat. And to all beasts of the earth, and to every fowl of the air, and to all that move upon the earth, and wherein there is life, that they may have to feed upon.' And it was so done. And God saw all the things that He had made, and they were very good. And the evening and the morning were the sixth day.

"So the heavens and the earth were finished, and all the furniture of them. And on the seventh day God ended His work which He had made; and He rested on the seventh day from all His work which He had done. And He blessed the seventh day, and sanctified it, because in it He had rested from all His work which God created and made." **The day of rest**

3. The Happiness of Adam and Eve in Paradise

God created man according to His own image and likeness. He made him of the slime of the earth, and breathed into his face the breath of life. And man became a living being. God called the first man Adam, which means Earthborn.

God made a wonderful garden called Paradise, or the Garden of Eden, and gave it to Adam as his home. In this garden there were all kinds of trees, beautiful to look at, and the fruit that grew upon them was delicious to eat. The Tree of Life stood in the midst of Paradise, and also the tree of Knowledge of Good and Evil. God said to Adam, "Of every tree of Paradise thou shalt eat, but of the tree of Knowledge of **The Garden of Paradise**

Good and Evil thou shalt not eat, for on the day that thou shalt eat of it, thou shalt die the death.''

Then God brought to Adam all the beasts of the earth and the fowls of the air to have him give them a name. And Adam called all the beasts by their names, and all the fowls of the air and all the cattle of the field. But of all the animals of the earth, not one was worthy to be a companion to Adam. He needed some-one like himself. Therefore, God said, ''It is not good for man to be alone; let Us make him a helpmeet like unto himself.''

The creation of Eve

Then God cast a deep sleep upon Adam, and while he was fast asleep, He took one of his ribs and made of it a woman. When Adam awoke, God brought her to him. Adam said, ''This is bone of my bones and flesh of my flesh. Therefore, a man shall leave father and mother and shall cleave to his wife, and they shall be two in one flesh.'' Adam called the woman Eve, which means Mother of All the Living.

When God created Adam and Eve, He did some-thing very wonderful to their souls. He gave them divine gifts of mind and heart which made them like unto Him. He clothed their souls with sanctifying grace, and they became holy and pleasing in His sight and received the right to be happy with Him for all eternity.

Adam and Eve were very happy together in Para-dise. Everything around them was beautiful. There was plenty of food of every kind. The climate was neither too hot nor too cold. A beautiful river flowed through the midst of the garden, and Adam and Eve loved to walk by its side and talk with God. God told Adam and Eve that they and their children would always be happy if they would love Him with all their hearts and obey Him. They would never die, but would finally be taken up into Heaven.

4. ADAM AND EVE SIN AND ARE PUNISHED

Satan envied Adam and Eve. He saw how happy **The Fall** they were in Paradise and how much God loved them. He made up his mind to try to lead them away from God.

One day he appeared to Eve in the form of a serpent, which at that time was one of the most beautiful animals in Paradise.

He spoke to Eve and asked her, "Why hath God commanded thee not to eat of every tree in Paradise?"

"We do eat of the fruit of all the trees in Paradise," Eve answered, "except the one tree in the midst of the garden. God told us that if we touch it, we shall die."

"No, you shall not die," said the serpent; "but God knows that if you eat of the fruit of that tree, your eyes shall be opened and you shall be as gods."

When Eve heard these words, she forgot how happy she had been in Paradise and how good God had been to her. The fruit was beautiful to look at, and she could not forget what the serpent had told her. She took some fruit from the tree, ate of it and brought some to Adam. She told him the strange story of the serpent, and he, too, ate of the fruit.

They had no sooner eaten of this forbidden fruit than they knew they had done a very wicked thing.

They were ashamed and frightened, and they tried to hide themselves from the sight of God. But nothing can be hidden from God.

"Why hast thou eaten of the fruit whereof I commanded that thou shouldst not eat?" God asked Adam.

Adam answered, "The woman whom Thou gavest me to be my companion gave me of the tree, and I did eat."

Then God said to Eve, "Why hast thou done this?"

Eve answered, "The serpent deceived me and I did eat."

5. God Promises a Redeemer

The promise   Then God said to the serpent: "Because thou hast done this thing, thou art cursed among all the beasts of the earth. Thou shalt go upon thy breast and thou shalt eat earth all the days of thy life. I will put enmities between thee and the woman, and between thy seed and her seed; she shall crush thy head."

To Adam, God said, "Because thou hast listened to the voice of the woman and hast eaten of the tree whereof I commanded thee that thou shouldst not eat, cursed is the earth in thy work. Thorns and thistles shall it bring forth to thee, and in the sweat of thy face thou shalt earn thy bread till thou return to the earth out of which thou wast taken; for dust thou art and into dust thou shalt return."

The punishment   God clothed Adam and Eve with garments of skins and cast them out of the Garden of Paradise, and stationed Cherubim and a flaming sword to guard it, so that they could never return.

ADAM AND EVE ARE EXPELLED FROM PARADISE

Adam and Eve had believed the devil when he told them that if they ate of the forbidden fruit, they would become as gods. They had trusted Lucifer and disobeyed God. They had committed a great sin.

God punished them and closed Heaven against them. They were no longer happy. Their minds were disturbed, and their wills were weakened. It became hard for them to know what was true and to do what was right. Their children, too, and their children's children, until the end of the world, would have to suffer for their sin. We call their sin Original Sin. Every child comes into the world with this sin on its soul. The Blessed Virgin Mary is the only human being who was preserved from this sin.

THINGS TO KNOW AND TO DO

1. God Creates the Angels and Some of Them Sin

1. In what ways are men like the angels?
2. Why did God give the angels a trial before He took them into Heaven?
3. Why were Lucifer and his followers cast into hell?
4. Why does the Church pray to St. Michael the Archangel?
5. On what day does the Church celebrate the Feast of St. Michael? *Sept 29th*
6. What should we do to honor our Guardian Angel? *Oct 2nd*
7. After Mass the priest says a prayer in which these words are found: "Cast into hell Satan and all other evil spirits who roam through the world seeking the ruin of souls." How does Satan seek the ruin of souls?

2. God Creates the World

1. Why did God create the beautiful world in which we live?
2. Why is man greater than all the creatures of God on earth?
3. Why are the angels more like God than man is?
4. What do the things that God made tell us about the Creator?
5. Why do we keep one day of the week holy? *Because God is good & deserves this time*

3. The Happiness of Adam and Eve in Paradise

1. Why did God create Eve?
2. Name some of the wonderful gifts God gave to Adam and Eve.
3. What command did God give to Adam and Eve?
4. Why was this command easy to obey?
5. Write a short theme on "The Joys of Paradise."

4. Adam and Eve Sin and Are Punished
5. God Promises a Redeemer

1. Why do you suppose Eve listened to the serpent when he tempted her to sin?
2. How did God punish our first parents for their sin?
3. Why should the whole human race suffer because of the sin of Adam and Eve?
4. Quote the words in which God first promised the Redeemer to man.
5. Why was the Blessed Virgin preserved from all sin?
6. What are the words which the priest uses when he puts ashes on the people's foreheads on Ash Wednesday?

II. THE DESCENDANTS OF ADAM AND EVE

1. Cain and Abel

When God expelled Adam from Paradise, He said to him, "In the sweat of thy face thou shalt eat thy bread." That meant that he would have to work very hard to make a living. Adam and Eve told their children the story of their happiness in Paradise and how they had lost it through sin. They were very sorry that they had disobeyed God. Yet they did not lose courage. God had cursed the serpent. He had promised that a woman would crush his head. They told their children that some day God would save them from the effects of their sin. After the fall of man

Adam and Eve had many children. The eldest were Cain and Abel. Cain made his living from the fruits of the fields, the trees, and the vines. Abel was a shepherd. He led his sheep over the plains, seeking for pasture. Cain and Abel

Adam and Eve taught their children how to adore God. They adored Him by giving back to Him some of His gifts. These gifts they burned up so that they could never be given to anyone except to God. Such an offering we call a sacrifice. It tells God that we wish to honor Him as our Creator, and that we know that we belong to Him and depend upon Him for all things. The sacrifices of Cain and Abel

One day Cain and Abel offered sacrifices to God. Cain offered the fruits of the fields, while Abel placed upon his altar a young lamb from his flocks. God was pleased with Abel's sacrifice, but with Cain's He was displeased because Cain did not give his gift with a good heart. When God rebuked him and pointed out to him the evil of his conduct, Cain became angry. He was jealous of Abel, and too proud to realize that God was displeased with his sinful heart.

2. The Slaying of Abel

The first murder

Cain went off by himself and began to brood. Gloomy thoughts filled his mind. The more he thought about what had happened, the more he hated Abel. Finally, he made up his mind to kill his brother, and invited him to take a walk with him. Abel was glad to go, because he felt sorry for Cain and hoped to comfort him. When they were far away and no one could see them, Cain killed Abel.

As he gazed down at Abel, lying dead before him, Cain heard the voice of God saying, "Cain, where is thy brother Abel?"

Cain answered, "I know not. Am I my brother's keeper?"

The curse of God

God said to him, "The voice of thy brother's blood crieth to Me from the earth. Cursed shalt thou be upon the earth, which hath opened her mouth and received the blood of thy brother at thy hand. When thou shalt till it, it shall not yield its fruits. A fugitive and a vagabond shalt thou be upon the earth."

Filled with great sorrow and remorse, Cain cried out, "My sin is so great that I can never be pardoned. Anyone that findeth me shall kill me."

GOD REBUKES CAIN FOR HIS SIN

But God said, "No, it shall not be so. But whosoever shall kill Cain, shall be punished sevenfold."

Then God put a mark upon Cain so that whoever found Him should not kill him.

3. OTHER DESCENDANTS OF ADAM AND EVE

Among the sons of Cain were Jabel, "the father of such as dwell in tents, and of herdsmen"; Jubal, "the father of them that play upon the harp and the organs"; Tubalcain, "a hammerer and artificer in every work of brass and iron"; and Lamech, the most vengeful man of his time. In place of Abel, God gave Adam another son named Seth, who was pleasing to God.

From Seth was descended Henoch, of whom the Scripture says, "he walked with God and was seen no more, because God took him."

THINGS TO KNOW AND TO DO

1. What is a sacrifice? Compare the sacrifices of Cain and Abel. What great sacrifice can you offer to God daily? Mention some little sacrifices you can offer to God. *not to sin*

2. Show by Cain's conduct that he forgot that God sees and knows all things.

3. What happened to Cain after he killed Abel? *he was shunned*

4. Show by Cain's conduct that jealousy leads to greater sins.

5. Abel is considered a type of Christ. Point out the ways in which Abel prefigured the Savior.

6. In what did Cain's punishment consist?

to wonder the earth

III. THE GREAT FLOOD

1. God Orders Noe to Build an Ark

Adam and Eve had many children, grandchildren, and great-grandchildren, and soon the human family became very large. Many of the descendants of Adam and Eve were disobedient, selfish, and wicked. The good people married the wicked people, and they too became sinful. They no longer served God and soon forgot Him.

Before the Flood

Still, there were a few who believed in God and tried to serve Him. Among these was a good and holy man called Noe. God sent him three sons, Sem, Cham, and Japheth, who grew up to be good men like their father. They were obedient, and loved and served God.

Noe and his sons

When God saw how wicked the people had become, He said to Noe, "I will send a flood to destroy them and the earth." Because Noe and his family were faithful and pleasing to God, He determined to spare them. He told Noe to make a large ark, or houseboat, which should be four hundred and fifty feet long, seventy-five feet wide, and forty-five feet high. A boat of such dimensions would be as long as two city blocks, as wide as four houses, and as high as a five-story building. The ark had three stories, and each story had many rooms. There was a door and a window to let in air and light. When everything was finished, the ark

The Ark

19

NOE BRINGS HIS FAMILY AND THE ANIMALS INTO THE ARK

was covered with pitch to keep out the water. Then Noe took into the ark his family and some of every kind of animal.

2. NOE IS SAVED FROM THE FLOOD

The Flood, or Deluge

The wicked people laughed at Noe for building a boat far away from the sea. They thought he was mad. While they were ridiculing him, it began to rain. For forty days and forty nights it rained as it had never rained before. Soon the rivers and seas overflowed their boundaries. Human beings and animals ran to the hills. Soon the hills were covered with water, and they ran to the mountains. The water rose higher and higher until it stood twenty feet above the highest mountain. Every living thing was drowned. But Noe and those who were with him in the ark were saved.

For five months the ark floated about on the water. One day it came to rest on a mountain. At first, Noe could see nothing from the window but water. After a time, he saw the tops of some mountains, and then he knew that the water was going down. He waited forty days longer and then sent out a raven and a dove. The dove returned because it could not find a place to rest. A week later he sent forth a second dove. This time the dove returned carrying in its beak an olive branch with green leaves. A week later, he sent it forth again, and this time, it did not return. Noe knew then that the flood was over. After seven weeks God spoke to Noe again. He said, "Go out of the ark with thy wife and thy sons and their wives and all the animals that are with thee in the ark."

The water disappears

Noe left the ark, grateful to God for having saved him and his family from the flood. He built an altar to God and offered upon it many fowl and cattle. God was pleased with the sacrifice of Noe, and promised him never more to destroy the earth by the waters of a flood. God set the rainbow in the sky as a sign of the promise He had made to reward the faithfulness of Noe.

Noe's sacrifice

God blessed Noe and his sons and told them that the earth, with all that it contained, was theirs. They began to till the soil, and to plant vineyards, and to live as they had lived before they entered the ark.

Noe and his children made wine from the grapes of

NOE OFFERS A SACRIFICE TO GOD IN THANKSGIVING

Cham's sin his vineyard. One day, not knowing how strong the wine was, Noe drank too much of it. He became drunk and fell asleep on the ground. When Cham saw his father overcome by wine and sleeping on the ground, he called his brothers and made sport of him. But they were grieved at Cham's conduct, and covered their father with a cloak, for they loved him.

When Noe awoke and heard what had happened, he was angry and cursed Cham, saying that he would always be the servant of his brothers. He gave his blessing to Sem and Japheth for the love and respect they had shown him. Noe lived many years after the flood and he was a very old man when he died.

3. THE NATIONS GROW AFTER THE FLOOD

After many years the human race grew larger and **The Tower of Babel** larger, and the descendants of the sons of Noe were in need of richer fields and larger pasture lands. They moved to the fields of Sennaar and dwelt there. Then they said to one another, "Let us make a city and a tower the top whereof may reach to heaven; and let us make our name famous before we be scattered abroad into all lands."

So they began to build the city and the tower. They baked the bricks, and hauled them higher and higher as the tower grew from day to day. But God saw what was in the hearts of the people. He knew that they were proud, and He decided to punish them.

One day while they were working on the tower, they noticed they could not understand one another very well. Little by little the language spoken by one family became entirely different from that of another. They could work together no longer, so they ceased to build the city and the tower.

The Lord scattered them from that place into all **The Dispersion** lands. The city and tower were called Babel, which means confusion, because there the one language which the families of the earth had used up to this time was changed into many different languages. Because of this, the families separated. The five sons of Sem settled in Persia, Syria, Assyria, Chaldea, Asia Minor, and Mesopotamia. Japheth had seven sons, and these became the Scythians, Medes, Greeks, Thracians, etc.

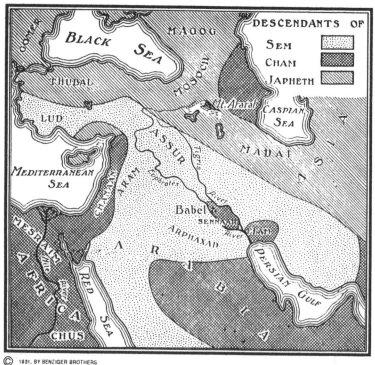

THE LANDS SETTLED BY THE SONS AND GRANDSONS OF NOE

Cham's four sons occupied the land of Chanaan, Ethiopia, and Egypt.

How Egypt was settled One group of people crossed the Isthmus of Suez and settled along the banks of the river Nile in northeastern Africa. The valley of the Nile was very fertile and promised to give them food in abundance. These people began to build cities, and after a time three large cities grew up: On, or Heliopolis, and Memphis in the north, and Thebes in the south. Each one of these cities controlled all the small villages and the country around it. Finally two kingdoms were formed: one in the north, with Memphis as its capital;

and the other in the south, whose capital was Thebes. By and by, these two kingdoms were united under one king, called a pharao. Thus was formed the Kingdom of Egypt.

Not all of the people left the Land of Sennaar when the nations were scattered. Large groups of them remained and in time built cities. Each city was a state with its own king. The people who lived in the southern part of the country were known as Sumerians, and were the descendants of Cham. The people who lived in the northern cities were the descendants of Sem. Little by little the people began to move from one city to another. After a while they became half Sumerian and half Semite.

How the Land of Sennaar was settled

Two great rivers, the Tigris and the Euphrates, flowed through this land, which came to be known as Babylon. The valleys of these rivers were fertile. The people of the land lived by farming. However, they did not dwell on their farms as the farmers of today, because they were afraid of their enemies. They had their homes in the cities, which were strongly fortified, and went out from them to work in the fields.

There were also workers in wood and metal and brick, as well as soldiers. A leisure class, made up of thinkers and writers, developed the art of writing upon clay tablets. They used a wedge-shaped pencil which they pressed into soft clay, after which they baked the clay to make it hard. This method of writing is called cuneiform. It was used by all the people who lived in this region.

It was under Sargon the First that all the cities of

HAMMURABI AND PART OF HIS CODE IN CUNEIFORM

Sargon, the first emperor the land were united to form one empire. Sargon was the first great emperor of history. He conquered the nations to the east of his territory and brought under his rule Syria and the land along the coast of the Mediterranean Sea, which was inhabited by the Chanaanites, the descendants of Cham.

After the death of Sargon, the land of Babylon was conquered by the descendants of Sem, who overran it from the east. They in turn were driven out by the Chanaanites from the west, whose greatest king was Hammurabi. He built canals to supply his kingdom with water and was the author of the famous "Code of Hammurabi." This is the oldest code of laws in the world and contains, in an orderly manner, all the laws that he himself had made, as well as the laws made by the kings who had lived before him.

The Assyrians Some of the Semites who lived in the northern cities did not intermarry with the Sumerians, but kept

A SPECIMEN OF ASSYRIAN RELIEF SCULPTURE

strictly to themselves. Their principal cities were Ninive, Assur and Haran. In later days, they were known as Assyrians.

The Chanaanites, who conquered the cities of Babylonia, belonged to that large group of people that settled in the land between Babylonia and Egypt. They were the descendants of Cham, and are also known as the Hethites, or Hittites. They were a hardy race of mountaineers and were very warlike. In the records of the Egyptians, they are described as men with large noses and receding foreheads and chins, having clean-shaven faces and wearing pigtails.

The Hittites

Their empire consisted of a number of small states, each with its own head and its own capital. But they would unite with one another for the purpose of waging war. We have seen how they conquered the Babylonians on their east, but they were never able to conquer the Egyptians on their west. Their power

A HITTITE WARRIOR

The Chanaanites

was finally broken when, together with a number of other nations, they tried to invade Egypt. They were defeated, and only a remnant of them survived, to be swallowed up by the other peoples.

The Hittites sent colonies into Palestine, and it is to them that the name Chanaanite is usually given. There they built cities and produced metal weapons, ornaments and very fine pottery. Those who lived on the coast became traders, while those who lived in the mountains were herdsmen. They were all idolaters, and worshiped the gods Baal and Astarte. Their territory extended from the Mediterranean Sea to the Jordan River, and from Gaza in the south to the Leontes River in the north.

THINGS TO KNOW AND TO DO

1. God Orders Noe to Build an Ark

1. Why did God send the Flood to destroy the people?
2. Why was Noe chosen by God to build the Ark?
3. Why was such a large Ark necessary?
4. Why did the people ridicule Noe for building the Ark?
5. Write a composition showing how the Ark is a figure of the Church.

2. Noe Is Saved from the Flood

1. What does the Great Flood teach us about sin?
2. Describe the Flood as you imagine it happened.

3. How did Noe show God that he was grateful for saving him from the Flood?

4. List some acts of thanksgiving found in the Ordinary of the Mass.

5. Of what does the rainbow remind us?

3. The Nations Grow after the Flood

1. Locate Sennaar on the map. Find the meaning of Babel in the dictionary.

2. How did God make it impossible for the people to continue the building of the tower?

3. In the Psalms of David we read: "God resists the proud." Show that we can apply these words to the builders of the tower.

4. What must you do to obtain God's blessing on your work every day?

5. Locate on the map the places settled by the people when they left Sennaar.

SELF-TEST

Before leaving Unit One, test yourself with the following exercises. Check your work.

I. Be able to tell the story contained in each section of Unit One.

II. Relate the important facts about the chief characters found in this Unit.

III. Prepare for your notebook:
(a) What this Unit teaches about God.
   1. *The Trinity.* Give the quotations that prove the Trinity of God.
   2. *The Attributes of God.* List the incidents that prove His Holiness, His Omnipotence, His Omniscience, His Wisdom, His Justice, His Mercy.
(b) What this Unit teaches about the world. Give quotations that show:
   1. How the world came to be.
   2. How the world was when it was first created.
   3. What sin brought into the world.
(c) What this Unit teaches about man. Show:
   1. That man consists of soul and body.
   2. That he is the most excellent of God's creatures on earth.
   3. That he is the master of God's creation.
   4. His sin and punishment.
   5. The effects of Adam's sin.
(d) What this Unit teaches about the Redeemer.
   1. What prophecy of the Redeemer is given in this Unit?
   2. What is meant by a type? a figure?
   3. In what way were Adam, Abel, and Noe types of the Redeemer; Eve a type of the Blessed Virgin; the Tree of Life a type of the Blessed Sacrament.
(e) What this Unit teaches concerning the duties of man.
   1. What do the incidents of the Unit teach concerning our duties: (i) towards God; (ii) towards our neighbors; (iii) towards self.

IV. Tell the story of Adam's happy life in Paradise as he probably told it to his children.

V. Collect pictures which tell the stories contained in Unit One.

VI. Prepare for your notebook an explanation of the following:
   1. How people came to be heathens.
   2. Why their great sin was called idolatry.
   3. What the sin of Adam and Eve brought upon the human race.

PREVIEW

Unit Two

HOW GOD FOUNDED THE NATION FROM
WHICH THE REDEEMER OF THE
WORLD CAME

The human race has now begun to spread over
the face of the earth. We shall now see how God
chose one nation to belong to Him in a very special manner. Abraham was called to be the father
of the Chosen People. We shall see how God tested
Abraham and how Abraham proved himself to be
a man of great faith. God's promises to Abraham
are fulfilled when Isaac is born. We shall see how
Isaac's son, Jacob, obtained his father's blessing
and went with his family into the land of Egypt,
where Joseph, his son, had become a great ruler.

Unit Two

HOW GOD FOUNDED THE NATION FROM WHICH THE REDEEMER OF THE WORLD CAME

Unit Two

HOW GOD FOUNDED THE NATION FROM WHICH THE REDEEMER OF THE WORLD CAME

I. ABRAHAM, THE FATHER OF THE CHOSEN PEOPLE

1. God Calls Abraham to Chanaan

Many, many years after the human race had been scattered from Babel, there lived in Ur, a city of Chaldea, a herdsman named Thare. Thare had three sons, Abram, Aran, and Nachor. Aran had a son named Lot, who was left in Thare's care when his father died. Abram's wife was named Sarai. *Abram's relatives*

Thare moved with his family from Ur to Haran. After Thare's death, God told Abram to leave his native land and go into the land which He would point out. He promised to make Abram the father of a great nation, and told him that in him all the kindred of the earth should be blessed. In obedience to God's command, Abram took Sarai, Lot, and all their servants and flocks, and journeyed southwest toward the Land of Chanaan.

Abram lived the life of a nomad chief. His dress was much like that of the modern Bedouin. His home was a tent with a peaked roof, and was divided by a partition of skins into a living room and a sleeping room. His servants, several hundred herdsmen with *Abram's home life*

33

ABRAHAM DEPARTING FROM HARAN

their wives and children, lived in similar tents near to their master's. Their food consisted of butter, milk, herbs, bread, the meat of their flocks, and the fruits of the trees.

Abram builds altars to God
In his wanderings Abram came to a city in Chanaan called Sichem. Here God said to Abram, "To thy children I will give this land." Abram built an altar to God at Sichem. Next he pitched his tent at Bethel, where he also built an altar.

Abram in Egypt
Some time after this, there came a great famine in the Land of Chanaan and, in order to escape it, Abram took his family and went into Egypt. When the famine was over, he returned and dwelt near Bethel.

Abram and Lot now had many sheep, cattle, and

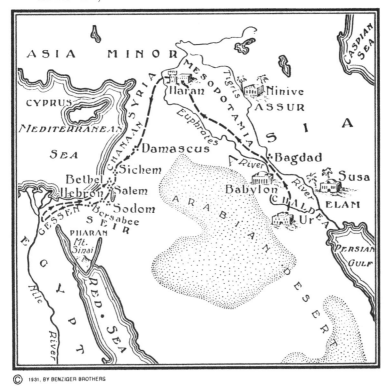

THE JOURNEYS OF ABRAHAM

camels, and there was not enough pasture land to provide fodder for them all.   Quarrels arose among the
herdsmen of Abram and the herdsmen of Lot.   Each
one wanted the best pasture land for his flocks.   Then
Abram said, "Let there be no quarrel between us, for
we are brethren.   Behold, the whole land is before
thee.   If thou wilt go to the left hand, I will take the
right.   If thou choose the right hand, I will pass to
the left."

Lot chose the country about the Jordan near to

*Abram
and
Lot
part
company*

the cities of Sodom and Gomorrha, and he dwelt in
Sodom.

2. GOD MAKES GREAT PROMISES TO ABRAHAM

God's promise

After Lot had departed, God said to Abram, "Lift
up thy eyes and look from the place wherein thou now
art, to the north and to the south, to the east and to
the west. All the land which thou seest, I will give to
thee and to thy children forever. And thy children
shall be as many as the bits of dust on the earth. Arise
and walk through the land, for I will give it to thee."
Abram moved his tent and came to the valley of Mambre and lived there in the hill country. There he also
built an altar to God.

Abram's war

Chodorlahomor, King of Babylonia, came with his
allies to plunder the Chanaanites. He took many cities,
and finally captured Sodom, where Lot lived. He took
the people of Sodom away to make them slaves. Lot
and all his household were among the captives.

When Abram heard of Lot's misfortune, he gathered
together his own men, who numbered three hundred
and eighteen, and formed a league with his neighbors.
Overtaking the Babylonian army at Damascus, he attacked Chodorlahomor and rescued Lot and all his
people.

The Sacrifice of Melchise- dech

When Abram was returning from the battle, Melchisedech, King of Salem, came forth to meet him, bringing bread and wine. Salem was an important town in
the Land of Chanaan, which later on was to become
the great city of Jerusalem. As was often the case in

MELCHISEDECH MEETS ABRAM

those days, the king of this small city-state was at the same time a priest.

Melchisedech blessed Abram and said, "Blessed be Abram, by the most high God, Who created heaven and earth. And blessed be the most high God, by Whose protection the enemies are in thy hands." And Abram offered him a tenth part of all his possessions as a token of gratitude.

Because he offered a sacrifice of bread and wine, Melchisedech is an image of our Lord and Savior. The One Hundred and Ninth Psalm foretells how the Messias would be at the same time a great priest and a great king. It says:

"The Lord said to my Lord; Sit Thou at My right hand:
"Until I make Thy enemies Thy footstool.

"The Lord will send forth the scepter of Thy power out of
Sion: rule Thou in the midst of Thy enemies.

"With Thee is the principality in the day of Thy strength,
in the brightness of the saints: from the womb before the
day-star I begot Thee.

"The Lord hath sworn, and He will not repent: Thou art
a priest forever according to the order of Melchisedech.

"The Lord at Thy right hand hath broken kings in the day
of His wrath.

"He shall judge among nations, He shall fill ruins: He
shall crush the heads in the land of many.

"He shall drink of the torrent in the way: therefore shall
He lift up the head."

God
promises
Abram a
son

God appeared to Abram in a vision and said, "Fear
not, Abram. I am thy protector, and thy reward exceeding great. Look up to heaven and count the stars
if thou canst. So shall thy descendants be." Abram
believed God, and his faith was pleasing in the sight
of the Lord.

But Abram and Sarai were growing old and they
had no children. Sarai had an Egyptian servant maid
named Agar. Sarai advised Abram to take Agar as
his wife, hoping that through her God would give him
a son. In those days, a man was permitted to have
more than one wife, so Abram followed Sarai's advice.

God sent an angel to Agar, who said to her, "Behold, thou shalt bring forth a son, and thou shalt call
his name Ismael. He shall be a wild man. His hand
will be raised against all men, and all men's hands
against him; and he shall pitch his tents over against
all his brethren."

When Ismael was born, God said to Abram, "I am the Almighty God; walk before me and be perfect. My covenant is with thee, and thou shalt be a father of many nations. Neither shall thy name be called any more Abram, but thou shalt be called Abraham (which means Father of Many Nations). And Sarai, thy wife, thou shall not call Sarai, but Sara (which means Princess). And I will bless her, and of her I will give thee a son, whom I will bless. Thou shalt call his name Isaac. And nations and kings of people shall spring from him."

God also told Abram that his descendants would live for a time in a land of strangers, who would make slaves of them and afflict them for many years. But in the end, they would come back to the Land of Chanaan.

3. THREE STRANGERS VISIT ABRAHAM

One day when Abraham was sitting at the door of his tent, he saw three strangers walking towards him. He knew at once that these were not ordinary men, and he went forth to meet them. Bowing low, he greeted them, saying, "Lord, do not pass by my tent. Rest here under the trees, and I shall bring water to wash your feet and food to strengthen you on your way."

The Three Guests

The strangers accepted the invitation, and Abraham hurried to have food prepared for them. Sara baked cakes of meal, and Abraham selected the best calf of his flock and gave it to a herdsman to prepare for cooking. When the meal was ready, it was set before the guests, and Abraham stayed with them while they ate.

One of them told him that Sara would have a son. Abraham knew then that this was God Himself and that the others were angels. When the strangers were ready to leave, Abraham walked a part of the way with them. They went toward the city of Sodom.

Abraham pleads for Sodom As they walked along, God told Abraham that Sodom and Gomorrha would be destroyed because of the sins of their inhabitants. Abraham thought of Lot and the other good men of the city and he prayed to God, saying, "Wilt Thou destroy the just with the wicked? If there be fifty just men in the city, shall they perish? And wilt Thou not spare that place for the sake of fifty just, if they be found therein? Far be it from Thee to do this thing, and to slay the just with the wicked. This is not like Thee, Thou Who judgest all the earth."

The Lord said to Abraham, "If I find in Sodom fifty just men, I will spare the whole place for their sake." Abraham answered, "Seeing I have once begun, I will speak to my Lord, whereas I am dust and ashes. What if there be five less than fifty just persons? Wilt Thou for five and forty destroy the whole city?" And God said, "I will not destroy it if I find five and forty."

Again Abraham prayed, "But if forty be found there, what wilt Thou do?" God answered, "I will not destroy it for the sake of forty."

Once more Abraham prayed. "Lord," he said, "be not angry, I beseech Thee, if I speak. What if thirty shall be found there?'' God answered, ''I will not do it if I find thirty there.''

Still Abraham persevered in his prayer. ''Seeing I have begun,'' he said, ''I will speak to my Lord. What if twenty be found there?'' God said, ''I will not destroy it for the sake of twenty.''

''I beseech Thee,'' said Abraham, ''be not angry, Lord, if I speak yet once more. What if ten should be found there?'' And He said, ''I will not destroy it for the sake of ten.'' Then the Lord departed, and Abraham returned home.

But there were not even ten just men in the cities of Sodom and Gomorrha.

That same evening, two of the strangers came to Sodom and saw Lot sitting at the gate of the city. Lot, not knowing they were angels, invited them to come with him and be his guests. He made a feast for them, and baked unleavened bread, and they ate. While they were eating, a crowd of wicked men of the city came to the house to do harm to Lot's guests. But the angels struck them blind.

Then the angels said to Lot, ''If thou hast anyone that is dear to thee, son-in-law, or sons, or daughters, take them out of this city. For the Lord hath sent us to destroy this place.''

Lot had two daughters whom he had promised in marriage to two young men of the city. Going to these young men, he said, ''Arise, get you out of this place, because the Lord will destroy this city.'' But they thought he was speaking in jest, and refused to go.

In the morning, the angels said to Lot, ''Arise, take

THE DESTRUCTION OF SODOM

thy wife and thy two daughters, lest they perish in the wickedness of the city.'' When Lot lingered, they took his hand, and the hand of his wife and of his two daughters and led them out of the city. Then the angels said to them, ''Save thy life; look not back, neither stay thou in all the country about; but save thyself in the mountain, lest thou also be burnt up.''

The Destruction of Sodom and Gomorrha

Then the Lord rained down brimstone and fire upon Sodom and Gomorrha, and the cities were destroyed, and all the country around them, and all the people who lived in the cities, and all the trees and everything that grew on the earth.

Lot's wife was curious to see what was happening. In spite of the angels' warning, she looked back. Her disobedience was punished immediately.   She was turned into a statue of salt.

When Abraham was one hundred years old and Sara ninety, God's promise was fulfilled.   Isaac was born, and in him Abraham's faith was rewarded. Under the watchful eyes of his parents, the boy grew strong and holy.   He was the joy of his father's heart.

The birth of Isaac

As a little boy, Isaac played around his father's tent with Ismael, the son of Agar, the Egyptian servant maid.   Sara did not like this, and she said to Abraham, "Cast out this bondwoman and her son, for the son of the bondwoman shall not be an heir with my son Isaac."

Ismael is cast forth

Hearing this, Abraham became very sad, and he did not know what to do.   For, after all, Ismael was his son and he loved him.

God told him to heed what Sara said and not to worry about Ismael and Agar.   He said, "I will make the son also of the bondwoman the father of a great nation, because he is thy son."

So Abraham rose up in the morning and, taking bread and a bottle of water, he put it upon the shoulder of Agar and sent her and her boy away.   Heartbroken, she went forth and wandered in the wilderness for days.   At last, the water in the bottle was all gone. She saw Ismael becoming weaker and weaker, and she was sure that he was dying of thirst and weariness. Tenderly she laid him down under a tree.   "I will not see my boy die," she said and, going a short distance away, she sat down on the ground and wept.

The voice of an angel of God called to her from

Heaven, saying, "What art thou doing, Agar? Fear not. Arise, take up the boy and hold him by the hand. For God will make him the father of a great nation."

Agar opened her eyes, and there before her she saw a well of water. Going to it, she filled the bottle and gave it to the boy to drink.

God was with Ismael. He grew up and dwelt in the wilderness of Pharan. He became highly skilled in the use of the bow and arrow and was known in the country all round about as a great archer. His mother chose for him a wife from out of the land of Egypt.

Ismael had twelve sons. He had also a daughter, who afterwards married Esau, the son of Isaac. The Arab tribes who to this day roam the Arabian desert are the descendants of Ismael. When we read of their wild and warlike life, we think of the prophecy that the angel made to Agar before the birth of Ismael: "He shall be a wild man. His hand will be raised against all men, and all men's hands against him."

4. GOD TESTS THE OBEDIENCE OF ABRAHAM

Abraham's faith and obedience

One night, Abraham heard the voice of the Lord calling, "Abraham, Abraham." He answered, "Here I am." Then the Lord said to him, "Take thy only-begotten son, Isaac, whom thou lovest, to a mountain which I will show thee, and there offer him to Me in sacrifice."

Abraham rose up immediately and saddled his ass. He awakened two of his servants and Isaac. They cut wood for the sacrifice and, loading it upon the ass, set out upon their journey.

They had traveled three days when Abraham saw the mountain in the distance. Then he said to his servants, "Stay you here with the ass. I and the boy shall go yonder and, after we have offered sacrifice, we shall return to you."

He took the wood for the sacrifice and laid it upon Isaac. He himself carried in his hands fire and a sword. Together they started out for the mountain.

After a while Isaac asked, "My father, we have fire and wood, but where is the victim for the sacrifice?" "God will provide it, my son," Abraham replied.

When they reached the place which God had shown him, Abraham built an altar and laid the wood in order upon it. He then bound Isaac and placed him upon the pile of wood. As he was raising his sword to sacrifice his son, an angel of the Lord called to him from Heaven, "Abraham, Abraham." He answered, "Here I am." The angel said, "Lay not thy hand on the boy, neither do thou anything to him. Now I know that thou fearest God and hast not spared thy only-begotten son for His sake."

Abraham looked up and saw a ram caught by the horns in the bushes nearby. He took Isaac off the altar and offered the ram as a sacrifice to God instead of his son.

Then the angel repeated the promise to Abraham, **The promise is repeated** "Thy children shall be as numerous as the stars in the heavens and as grains of sand on the seashore, and in your children shall all nations of the earth be blessed, because thou hast obeyed My voice."

Soon after this, Sara died in Hebron. Abraham

AN ANGEL PREVENTS ABRAHAM FROM SACRIFICING ISAAC

bought a field with a double cave facing Mambre and buried her in it.

5. ISAAC MARRIES REBECCA

Rebecca

Before Abraham died, he sent Eliezer, his servant, to Haran to seek a bride for Isaac. The servant took camels and many gifts with him. When he arrived at Haran, he waited at a well outside the city where the maidens came to draw water. He called upon God to help him, saying, "O Lord, the God of my master Abraham, show kindness to him. Grant that the maiden whom Thou hast chosen for Isaac shall reply to my request for a drink, 'Drink, and I will give thy camels drink also.'" Soon Rebecca, the sister of

ELIEZER SPEAKS TO REBECCA AT THE WELL

Laban, came to the well. She was the grandchild of
Nachor, who was Abraham's brother. She filled her
pitcher and was going back, when the servant ran to
meet her and asked her for a drink of water. She
replied, "Drink, my lord, and I will draw water for thy
camels also."

Eliezer was filled with joy. He gave her golden
earrings and bracelets and asked her who she was and
whether he could stay at her father's house. She told
him that she was the daughter of Bathuel, and that
they had ample accommodations for himself and his
camels. She then ran home to tell the family about
him and to prepare for his coming. When Laban

heard her story, he went forth to meet Abraham's servant and conducted him to his home.

After they had welcomed Eliezer, they sat down to eat. But Eliezer would not eat until he had explained his errand. When he told them how his meeting with Rebecca was an answer to his prayer, they consented to let her go with him to Chanaan.

Eliezer gave presents to Rebecca, to her brothers, and to her mother. The next morning they set out for Chanaan. Isaac was the first person to greet them when they arrived home, and, with the blessing of Abraham, his father, he married Rebecca.

Death of Abraham Thirty-eight years after Sara's death, Abraham died and left all his wealth to his son Isaac, who was the child through whom God's promise was to be fulfilled. Isaac and Ismael, his sons, buried him in the cave beside his wife.

THINGS TO KNOW AND TO DO
1. GOD CALLS ABRAHAM TO CHANAAN

1. What were the three commands which God gave to Abram?
2. What were the rewards Abram received for his obedience?
3. Why was Abram's journey from Haran to Chanaan very difficult?
4. How did Abram give an example of great faith in God.
5. Contrast the characters of Abram and Lot. If you had been present at the division of the land, what would you have said to each of them?
6. Point out on the map the places where Abram built altars to God.

2. GOD MAKES GREAT PROMISES TO ABRAHAM

1. How is our Savior "a priest according to the order of Melchisedech"?
2. Memorize Psalm 109.
3. List the promises God made to Abram.
4. Why is Abram praised for his faith?
5. What opportunities have we to imitate the faith of Abram in our daily lives?

3. Three Strangers Visit Abraham

1. What do we learn from Abram's hospitality towards the strangers?
2. What lesson concerning prayer does Abram's example teach us?
3. Describe the destruction of the cities of Sodom and Gomorrha as you imagine it looked.
4. Why did God punish Lot's wife for looking back? What does this incident teach us?
5. Why did God destroy the cities?
6. The Dead Sea is said to mark the spot where Sodom and Gomorrha were located. Find out how it differs from other bodies of water.

4. God Tests the Obedience of Abraham

1. Why was God pleased with Abraham?
2. Describe the greatest test which God gave to Abraham.
3. How was Isaac a type of our Savior?
4. Read the Offertory Prayer in the Mass for the Dead and tell what it says about God's promise to Abraham.
5. Give a floor talk on "Abraham, the Obedient Man."

5. Isaac Marries Rebecca

1. How did God show that it was His will that Rebecca should be the wife of Isaac?
2. Discuss the character of Eliezer. Consider how he did his duty towards God; towards his master.
3. Name the virtues of Eliezer you should imitate.

II. GOD'S GREAT FAVORS TO JACOB

1. Jacob Obtains the Birthright

Esau and Jacob

Many years passed before Isaac and Rebecca had any children. Then twins were born to them, two sons, whom they named Esau and Jacob. Esau, who was born first, grew up to be a large man, rough and hairy. He was a hunter and farmer. Jacob, the younger son, was more like his mother, gentle and quiet. He became a herdsman. Isaac loved Esau, and Rebecca loved Jacob. She had been told by God that the younger son would be greater than the older, and that the older son would serve the younger.

In those days, the oldest son always received what was called the birthright. He was given a larger portion of his father's wealth than the other children, and became the head and priest of the family. He also obtained a special blessing from his father before he died.

Esau sells his birth-right

Esau did not care much about the birthright, but Jacob did. One day, Esau came home hungry from the hunt. Jacob was cooking a pottage, or stew, of lentils. Esau said to him, "Give me of this pottage, for I am exceeding faint." Jacob said, "Sell me first thy birthright." Esau said, "Lo, I die. What good will a birthright do me?" Jacob said, "Swear to me that the birthright is mine." Esau swore to him and, taking bread and the pottage of lentils, he ate and

50

drank and went his way, and made little account of the fact that he had sold his birthright.

The years went by and Isaac grew old. His eyes were dim and he could not see. One day he called Esau and said to him, "Thou seest that I am old and know not the day of my death. Take thy arms, thy quiver and bow, and go abroad, and when thou hast taken something in the hunt, prepare for me a meal thereof as thou knowest I like it. Bring it, that I may eat and my soul may bless thee before I die."

Jacob receives Isaac's blessing

Rebecca overheard this conversation and, after Esau had gone, she called Jacob and said to him, "I heard thy father talking with Esau, thy brother, telling him to bring game from the hunt and make a meal for him, that he might bless him before he dies. Now, therefore, my son, follow my counsel. Bring me two of the best kids from thy flock, that I may make of them a meal for thy father such as he gladly eateth. Thou shalt bring it in to him, so that when he hath eaten, he may bless thee before he dies."

Jacob answered her, "Thou knowest that Esau my brother is a hairy man and I am smooth. If my father shall touch me, I fear that he will think that I am making fun of him and will call down upon me a curse instead of a blessing."

Rebecca said, "Upon me be this curse, my son. Only hear thou my voice and go fetch me the things which I have said."

Jacob brought the kids to his mother, and she cooked a meal of them that she knew would please Isaac. She brought out Esau's best clothes and put them on Jacob.

She covered his bare neck and hands with the little skins of the kids. Then she gave him the meat which she had cooked and some bread which she had baked, and told him to take them in to his father.

When Jacob came into the room in which his father was lying, he said, "My father." Isaac answered, "Who art thou, my son." He said, "I am Esau, thy first-born. I have done as thou didst command me. Arise, sit and eat of my hunt, that thy soul may bless me."

Isaac said, "How couldst thou find it so quickly, my son?" He answered, "It was the will of God that what I sought came quickly in my way." Then Isaac said, "Come hither that I may feel thee, my son, and may prove whether thou be my son Esau or not."

Jacob came near and his father felt of him. Then Isaac said, "The voice indeed is the voice of Jacob, but the hands are the hands of Esau." He did not know that it was Jacob, because his hairy hands made him like his older brother.

Once more Isaac said, "Art thou my son Esau?" Jacob answered, "I am." Then Isaac said, "Bring me the meats of thy hunting, my son, that my soul may bless thee."

After Isaac had eaten the meat and drunk the wine which Jacob offered him, he said, "Come near me and give me a kiss, my son." Jacob came near and kissed him, and immediately, as he smelled the fragrant smell of his garments, he blessed him and said, "Behold the smell of my son is as the smell of a plentiful field which the Lord hath blessed. God give thee the dew of heaven

JACOB RECEIVES THE BLESSING INTENDED FOR ESAU

and of the fatness of earth, abundance of corn and wine. And let people serve thee and tribes worship thee. Be thou lord of thy brethren and let thy mother's children bow down before thee. Cursed be he that curseth thee, and let him that blesseth thee be filled with blessings.''

Jacob had scarcely gone when Esau came in, bring- Esau ing with him the meat which he had taken in hunting. blessed He said, ''Arise, my father, and eat of thy son's venison, that thy soul may bless me.'' But Isaac said to him, ''Why, who art thou?'' He answered, ''I am thy first-born son, Esau.''

Isaac was struck with fear and was very much

astonished. "Who is he, then, that even now brought me venison, and I ate of all before thou camest?" he asked. "And I have blessed him and he shall be blessed."

Hearing his father's words, Esau cried out with a great cry and, falling down on his knees, said, "Bless me also, my father." But Isaac said, "Thy brother came and deceived me and got thy blessing." "But, my father," pleaded Esau, "hast thou not reserved for me also a blessing?" Isaac answered, "I have appointed him thy lord, and have made all his brethren his servants. I have established him with corn and wine, and after this, what can I do for thee, my son?" Esau broke down and wept as though his heart would break. He said, "I beseech thee, bless me also." Isaac's heart was touched with pity for Esau and he said to him, "In the fat of the earth and in the dew of the heaven from above shall thy blessing be. Thou shalt live by the sword and shalt serve thy brother. And the time shall come when thou shalt shake off and loose his yoke from thy neck."

From that moment, Esau hated Jacob for having taken away from him the blessing of his father, and he said in his heart, "The day will come when my father shall die, and then I will kill my brother Jacob."

Jacob goes to Haran

When Rebecca heard that Esau had threatened to kill Jacob, she sent for her son and said, "Behold, Esau thy brother threateneth to kill thee. Now, therefore, hear my voice. Arise, and flee to Laban, my brother, in Haran. Remain with him until the anger of thy brother hath passed. When he hath forgotten the things that thou hast done to him, I will send for thee.'' Rebecca told Isaac that Jacob was going away to find a wife among her own people. She told him that she was afraid that her son would marry some Hittite woman and that, if he did, she would not care to live.

Isaac sent for Jacob and, blessing him, said, ''Take not a wife of the stock of Chanaan. But go to the house of Bathuel, thy mother's father, and take thee a wife of the daughters of Laban, thy uncle. And God almighty bless thee, and make thee to increase, and multiply, that thou mayest be the father of a great people! And may He give unto thee the blessings of Abraham, that thou mayest possess the land which he promised to thy grandfather!''

It is not easy to understand why God allowed Rebecca and Jacob to take the birthright away from Esau by deceit. We do know that God told Rebecca before Jacob was born that he would rule over his brother. Then, too, Esau had grieved his parents greatly by marrying two women of whom they did not approve. One of them was a Hittite by the name of Judith; the other was Basemath, the daughter of Ismael. However, both Jacob and Rebecca were made to suffer for the lie they had told. Rebecca lost both her sons that day, for Esau refused from that time forward to have anything more to do with her, and when Jacob went away, she was never again to set eyes upon him. Jacob was to spend long years in hard labor far from his father's home, and when he would finally return, his mother would be dead.

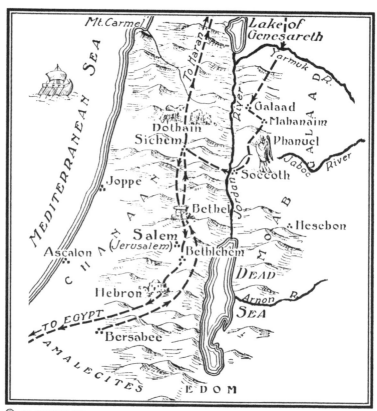

THE JOURNEYS OF JACOB

Jacob's dream
Jacob traveled alone on the way to Haran. One night, a strange thing happened. He was asleep on the ground, with a stone for a pillow, when he saw in a dream a ladder reaching from earth to Heaven. Angels were moving up and down the ladder, and God was leaning on the top of it. God spoke to Jacob and said, "I am the Lord God of Abraham thy father, and the God of Isaac. The land on which thou sleepest I will give to thee and to thy descendants. And they

shall be as the dust of the earth, and in thee and them all the tribes of the earth shall be blessed.'' When Jacob awoke, he exclaimed, ''Indeed the Lord is in this place and I knew it not. How holy is this place! This is no other but the house of God, and the gate of Heaven.''

In memory of his dream, Jacob poured oil on the stone on which he had slept. He called the place Bethel, meaning House of God.

2. The Marriage of Jacob and Rachel

When Jacob arrived at Haran, he met some shepherds near a well outside the city, and inquired of them whether they knew a certain Laban. While he was talking to them, Rachel, the daughter of Laban, came to the well to give water to her father's sheep. The shepherds told Jacob who she was. He helped her to water her sheep and informed her that he was her cousin. Rachel hastened to her father and told him the news of Jacob's coming.

Jacob meets Rachel

Laban went at once to meet Jacob and to welcome him to his house. For a month Jacob was Laban's guest. After that, he began to work for Laban, taking care of his sheep. Laban promised him that if he worked for him seven years, he could have Rachel for his wife. Jacob agreed to these terms, but at the end of seven years, Laban did not keep his word. He forced Jacob to take his elder daughter Lia instead. Jacob reproached Laban for his deceit. He was greatly in love with Rachel and pleaded to be allowed to marry her. Laban finally promised to give him

JACOB MEETS RACHEL

Rachel in marriage within a week if he agreed to work for seven more years. After the seven days had passed, Jacob married Rachel also.

Jacob returns to Chanaan

After more than fourteen years of absence, Jacob was eager to return home, but Laban wished him to stay at Haran. Jacob remained six years longer, in return for a certain share of the flocks. He had become rich in Laban's service and owned many sheep and goats. This caused Laban and his sons to become jealous of him.

Then God spoke to Jacob and told him to return to the home of his fathers. Jacob had now eleven sons and one daughter. The sons were: Ruben, Simeon, Levi, Juda, Dan, Nephtali, Gad, Aser, Issachar, Zabulon and Joseph. His daughter's name was Dina. One day while Laban was away from home shearing his sheep, Jacob took his family, his flocks and his goods and set out for Chanaan. Laban did not learn of Jacob's departure until three days later and at once he set out in pursuit of him. He overtook Jacob in the mountains south of the Yarmuk River, and rebuked him, saying he would have accompanied him gladly had he not stolen away so secretly.

Before Laban and Jacob separated this time, they set up a heap of stones. They prepared a meal and ate upon the heap and made a solemn agreement never to pass this spot to injure each other's possessions. Laban called the heap Galaad, or The Witness Heap.

3. Esau and Jacob Are Reconciled

When Jacob drew near to his native land, he sent messengers to his brother Esau, with droves of camels and cattle and sheep as gifts to gain his favor. Jacob hoped to make peace with him, but when the messengers brought back word that Esau was coming with four hundred men, Jacob was very much afraid. He divided his company into two groups, thinking that if one company were destroyed, the other might escape. Then Jacob asked the Lord to protect him.

The brothers meet

During the night a stranger appeared to him and wrestled with him until morning. Jacob could not be overcome, so the stranger said to Jacob, "Let me go, for it is break of day." Jacob answered, "I will not let thee go unless thou bless me." Then the angel, for such it was, blessed him and said, "Thy name

A VIEW OF BETHEL TODAY

shall not be called Jacob, but Israel, which means Strong against God. Then he disappeared, and Jacob called the place Phanuel, saying, "I have seen God face to face and my soul hath been saved."

The next day Jacob saw Esau coming in the distance. He ran forward and bowed down before him. But Esau was no longer angry, and, raising up his brother, he kissed him. Jacob offered him as gifts great numbers of sheep and other animals. At first Esau was unwilling to accept them, but finally, to please Jacob, he took them.

After Esau had departed, Jacob crossed the Jordan and passed on to Salem, a city of the Sichemites. Here he bought land, for which he paid the price of one hundred lambs. At God's command he stayed for a time at Bethel, where he had seen the vision of the ladder. He built an altar and offered sacrifice to God. Then he went to Bethlehem, where his youngest son, Benjamin, was born, and Rachel his wife died. Jacob mourned for her deeply and built a monument over her grave.

From Bethlehem Jacob returned to his father, who **Isaac's** lived near Hebron, and remained with him until Isaac **death** died. Esau and Jacob buried their father in the cave at Mambre, in which Sara, Abraham, and Rebecca were buried.

At the death of Isaac, Jacob inherited the share of the first-born son and became the patriarch, or father, of a great nation.

THINGS TO KNOW AND TO DO

1. Discuss Esau's conduct in selling his birthright.
2. In what way is a mortal sin like the selling of the birthright?
3. Read the blessing which Isaac gave Jacob. What did Isaac foretell in this blessing? What did he promise?
4. Trace Jacob's journey on the map.
5. How was Jacob punished for deceiving his father?
6. Why did the angel change Jacob's name?
7. Describe the reunion of Jacob and Esau. What lesson does it teach us?

III. THE CHILDREN OF ISRAEL IN EGYPT

The sons of Jacob

1. JOSEPH, THE SON OF JACOB, BECOMES A GREAT RULER

Jacob's sons were herdsmen, and spent their lives tending their sheep and goats. Their work often took them far away from home. One day Joseph saw his brothers commit a wicked deed. He reported it to his father, and from that time they hated him.

There were other reasons why Joseph's brothers did not like him. They knew that their father loved Joseph very dearly, and when he gave him a coat of many colors, they became very jealous. Besides, Joseph dreamed dreams which he told to his brothers. These dreams foretold his future greatness and the power he would one day have over them.

Joseph's dreams

The first time Joseph had a strange dream, he said to his brothers, "Hear my dream which I dreamed. I thought we were binding sheaves in the field, and my sheaf arose, as it were, and stood, and your sheaves, standing about, bowed down before my sheaf."

He dreamed also another dream, which he told to his brothers, saying, "I saw in a dream, as it were, the sun, and the moon, and eleven stars worshiping me."

These dreams made the brothers very angry, and they asked him, "Will you be our king?"

Joseph is sold into Egypt

Some time after this, the brothers had to go great distances from home to find grass for their flocks.

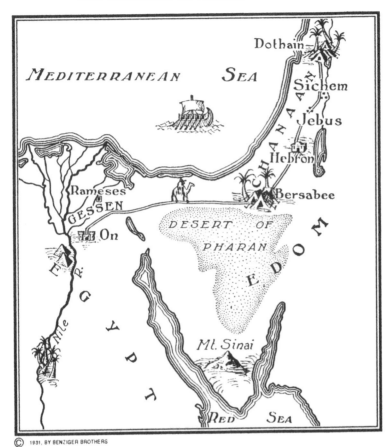

THE JOURNEYS OF JOSEPH AND HIS BROTHERS

While they were at Sichem, a place fifty miles away
from their home, Jacob sent Joseph to find out if all
were well with them. When Joseph reached Sichem,
he learned that his brothers had driven their flocks ten
miles farther north and he went in search of them.

When the brothers saw Joseph coming, they planned
to kill him. Ruben, the oldest, wished to save Joseph
from death and he persuaded the others to throw him

JOSEPH IS SOLD BY HIS BROTHERS

into a pit. He hoped that he might thus later have an opportunity of helping Joseph to escape.

It happened that some merchants, who were on their way to Egypt, passed through the fields. The brothers stopped them, offered to sell Joseph to them, and asked them how much they were willing to pay. The merchants offered them twenty pieces of silver. This sum satisfied the brothers, and Joseph was led away to Egypt.

While this was going on, Ruben was far away in another part of the field. When he learned what had happened, he was much troubled. He knew that his father would place all the blame for the evil deed on him.

In order to save Ruben from Jacob's anger, the brothers then planned to deceive their father. They dipped Joseph's brightly colored coat into the blood of a kid and, sending it to their father, told him that they had found it. Jacob believed that Joseph had been killed by a wild beast. He was filled with grief, and could not be comforted by his other sons.

When the merchants brought Joseph to Egypt, they sold him to the chief captain of Pharao's army. The captain's name was Putiphar. It was not long before Putiphar saw that Joseph was the best of his servants, and he placed him in charge of his house. God blessed Joseph and Putiphar. Under Joseph's management, Putiphar's fortune grew and he became wealthier day by day. *Joseph's success in Egypt*

Putiphar's wife was a wicked woman. Because Joseph would not do wrong to please her, she falsely accused him of sin to her husband. Putiphar was angry. He did not try to find out the truth, but believed the word of his wife, and cast Joseph into prison. *Joseph in prison*

The keeper of the prison was moved by God to look with favor on Joseph, and he placed him in charge of the rest of the prisoners.

After some time Pharao's butler and baker were cast into the prison where Joseph was in charge. One day, Joseph saw that they were troubled. He asked them why they were sad. "We have dreamed a dream," they answered, "and there is no one to explain it to us." Joseph said to them, "Does not the explanation belong to God? Tell me what you have dreamed."

The chief butler told his dream: "I saw before me a vine, on which there were three branches which, by little and little, sent out buds, and then the blossoms brought forth ripe grapes. The cup of Pharao was in my hand. I took the grapes, and pressed them into the cup which I held, and I gave the cup to Pharao."

God was with Joseph and helped him to explain the dream to the butler. "The three branches," he said, "are three days which will pass before Pharao will take you back into his palace. Then you will offer your cup of wine to Pharao as you have done before."

The baker said, "I also had a dream, that I had three baskets upon my head. In the uppermost basket, I had the different kinds of bread which bakers make. The birds of the air ate from this basket."

"The three baskets," explained Joseph, "are three days, after which Pharao will cut off your head and hang you on a cross, where birds of the air will tear your flesh."

Three days after Joseph had explained these dreams, Pharao's birthday occurred and he prepared a great feast. At the banquet he remembered the chief butler and restored him to his charge. But the baker he hung upon a gibbet.

When the butler was leaving the prison, Joseph said to him, "Put Pharao in mind to take me out of this prison, where, though innocent, I am kept." After the butler was released from prison, however, he forgot all about Joseph and what he had done for him.

About two years later, Pharao had a dream. He **Pharao's dreams** dreamed that he stood by the river, out of which seven cows came, very beautiful and fat. Seven other cows followed them, very lean and sickly looking. The fat cows fed in places where there was not much grass. The lean cows fed where the grass was plentiful. After a time the lean cows ate the fat cows.

Pharao had a second dream. He thought he saw seven ears of wheat come up from one stalk, full and fair. Seven others then sprang up on the same stalk, thin and blasted. The seven thin ears ate all the sap of the stalk, and the fat and full ears died away.

Pharao could find no one in his kingdom who could explain these dreams to him. It was then that the butler remembered Joseph in prison. He told Pharao how Joseph had explained his own dream and that of the baker.

Pharao at once commanded that Joseph be brought **Joseph interprets Pharao's dreams** before him to explain the dreams which no one else could explain. Before Joseph began to interpret Pharao's dreams, however, he told him that the power to interpret dreams comes from God. Then he said, "The two dreams mean the same thing. The seven beautiful cows and the seven full ears represent years of plenty. The seven lean cows and the seven thin ears stand for seven years of famine. So great will be the famine that it will consume all the food stored up in the time of plenty."

Joseph advised Pharao to appoint a wise man to prepare for the famine. His duty should be to store away

JOSEPH EXPLAINS THE DREAMS OF PHARAO

in public granaries one fifth of all the grain raised during the seven fruitful years.

Joseph becomes governor Pharao was very grateful to Joseph and much pleased with him. He said, "Seeing God has shown thee all that thou hast said, how can I find one wiser than thou? Thou shalt be over my house, and at the commandment of thy mouth all the people shall obey. Only I on my throne shall be above thee. Behold, I have appointed thee governor over the whole land of Egypt."

Then he took his own ring and put it on Joseph's finger and clothed him in a rich robe and put a chain of gold around his neck. He called for the second finest chariot in the kingdom and ordered Joseph to be

THE INUNDATION OF THE NILE RIVER

driven in it through the streets of the city. A crier Where Joseph ruled was sent ahead of him to proclaim to all the people that he was made governor over the whole land of Egypt and that they should bow their knee before him.

The country over which Joseph was made the ruler occupied the northeastern angle of Africa. It included the delta and the valley of the Nile River. The valley is about five hundred miles long and from ten to thirty miles wide. The Red Sea and Arabia are on the east of this fertile strip. The Mediterranean Sea is on the north.

The fertility of Egypt depended upon the overflow of the Nile. The flood had to reach the height of twenty-five feet to insure good crops for the season. If the flood were lower than eighteen feet, the crops failed and famine followed.

Joseph married Aseneth, the daughter of Putiphare, a priest of Heliopolis. This marriage gave Joseph a high social standing, because the priests belonged to one of the highest classes among the Egyptians. Two sons were born to him. The older, he called Manasses; the younger, Ephraim.

2. Joseph Returns Good for Evil

Preparation for the famine

The seven years of plenty came, and Joseph traveled through every part of the country, directing the building of great granaries, in which he stored up one-fifth of all the grain that was produced. Then began the seven years of famine. Nothing grew throughout the land. Soon the people began to ask Pharao for food. But he said to them, ''Go to Joseph, and do all that he shall say to you.''

The famine increased daily and spread throughout the world. Joseph opened up the granaries and began to sell grain to the Egyptians. They had no money. They gave their land, and in this way Pharao became the owner of almost all the land in Egypt during the years of famine.

Joseph's brothers in Egypt

The famine spread to the Land of Chanaan, and Jacob and his family were among those who suffered. Hearing that there was grain in Egypt, Jacob sent ten of his sons to buy enough to care for their needs. Benjamin, his youngest son, he kept at home.

When the sons of Jacob came to Egypt, they were sent to Joseph the governor. Joseph had changed much since his brothers had sold him to the merchants of Egypt, and they did not know him. But Joseph knew his brothers. He spoke roughly to them and charged them with being spies. They tried to convince him that they were innocent, and told him of their

JOSEPH CHARGES HIS BROTHERS WITH BEING SPIES

father and their youngest brother whom they had left
at home. They told him about Joseph, another
brother, who was dead. They said that they had come
to Egypt to buy grain because of the famine in
Chanaan.

But Joseph pretended not to believe them. He cast
them all into prison and kept them there for three
days, and then released all but one. Simeon, he said,
would have to remain in prison until the others
brought to him, as a proof of their good intentions, the
brother whom they had left at home.

The brothers spoke among themselves. They admitted that they deserved to be treated in this manner
in punishment for their sin against their brother Jo-

Repent-
ance of
Joseph's
brothers

seph. Joseph understood what they were saying, but his brothers did not know it. Secretly he wept for joy to see that his brothers had repented of their sin.

Simeon was chosen by Joseph to remain in prison. He was bound in the presence of his brothers. Then Joseph commanded his servants to fill the sacks of the others with grain. Privately, he told the servants to put in the mouths of their sacks the money which they had paid. In addition to the supplies of grain, he gave them provisions for their journey.

The brothers in Chanaan When the brothers arrived in Chanaan, they told their father all that had happened. Every one, upon spreading his grain on the floor, found tied in the mouth of his sack the money that he had paid for it.

When they asked Jacob to let Benjamin go to Egypt with them in order to set Simeon free, Jacob refused. He had lost one son, and the second was in prison. He would not risk losing a third.

Benjamin goes to Egypt However, it was not long before the family of Jacob again needed grain, and he asked his sons to go to Egypt and buy it. Juda told his father that it would be useless to go without Benjamin. He was certain that the ruler of Egypt would not receive them unless they had Benjamin with them. When Juda promised his father that no harm would come to Benjamin, Jacob consented to let him go.

At their father's command, they took back with them the money they had found tied in the mouths of their sacks. They also were ready to give Joseph gifts for himself and double the amount which they needed to buy more grain. They wished to make certain of the return of Benjamin and Simeon.

When Joseph saw his brothers returning and Benjamin with them, he ordered his servants to prepare a feast. Then Simeon was brought out to them. Joseph asked his brothers if their father was in good health. He was so happy to see his young brother, Benjamin, that he went into his room and wept for joy. Still his brothers did not know him. *Benjamin in Egypt*

After the feast, Joseph told his servants to fill his brothers' sacks with grain. Again he commanded them to put in their sacks the money they had paid. He told them to put his own silver cup in the mouth of Benjamin's sack. The brothers did not know that all this had been done, and the next morning, they placed the sacks upon their beasts of burden and set out for Chanaan.

After his brothers had gone some distance, Joseph sent his chief servant after them. When the servant overtook them, he asked them why they had returned evil for good, and accused them of stealing his master's silver cup. They knew nothing about the silver cup of which he spoke. They were so certain that the cup was not in their sacks that they were willing that he in whose sack it should be found should be put to death. They were ready to become Joseph's slaves if the servant found the cup in any of their sacks. *The silver cup*

They took down the sacks from the beasts and opened them without fear. What a great shock it was to them to see the silver cup in the mouth of Benjamin's sack!

JOSEPH REVEALS HIMSELF TO HIS BROTHERS

The servant ordered them to return to Joseph. When they entered the house, Joseph asked them why they had tried to steal his silver cup. They did not know what to answer. All fell on their knees, bowing low before Joseph, and offered themselves to be his slaves.

Juda pleads for Benjamin Joseph said that he wanted only that man for his slave who had stolen his cup. Juda pleaded with the governor. He told him the story of Joseph's loss. He said that the loss of Benjamin would be too great a sorrow for his father to bear and would certainly cause his death. He offered himself as a slave to Joseph in Benjamin's place.

Joseph could no longer conceal himself from his

JOSEPH MEETS JACOB

brothers. He asked all the Egyptians to leave the room. When he was alone with his brothers, he told them in their own language, amidst tears of joy, that he was Joseph. He told them that it was by God's will that he had been sent to Egypt to save his father and brothers from famine. Then he sent his brothers back to Jacob to tell him of his success in Egypt, and to invite his father to come with all his family to live in the land of Gessen.

Pharao, to show that he was pleased with Joseph's invitation to his father and his brothers, sent wagons to Hebron to move their possessions to Egypt. He gave presents to all the brothers, but he was especially generous to Benjamin. To Jacob he sent cloth-

Joseph reveals himself

THE LAND OF GESSEN

ing made of the finest material and three hundred pieces of silver.

Joseph meets his father
When Joseph learned that his father was on the way, he rode in his chariot to Gessen to meet him. The meeting of the father and son after so many years of separation was a great joy to both. When Joseph saw his father, he fell upon his neck and, embracing him, he wept. And Jacob said to Joseph, "Now shall I die with joy, because I have seen thy face and leave thee alive." Joseph took his father and brothers to Pharao, who gave to Jacob the land of Gessen.

Jacob blesses Ma- nasses and Ephraim
Jacob lived in Egypt seventeen years. One day word was brought to Joseph that his father was sick, and he at once set out to go to him, taking with him his two sons, Manasses and Ephraim. When Jacob heard that Joseph was coming, his strength returned to him, and he sat up in his bed to greet him. Seeing Manasses and Ephraim, he asked, "Who are these?" Joseph answered, "They are my sons, whom God hath

JACOB BLESSES MANASSES AND EPHRAIM

given me in this land." Jacob said, "Bring them to me that I may bless them." When they came close to him, he kissed and embraced them and said, "These two sons of thine who were born to thee in the land of Egypt before I came hither shall be mine. They shall take the place of Ruben and Simeon."

Jacob called his sons around him and foretold all that would happen to them and to their descendants.

To Juda he said, "Juda, thee shall thy brethren praise; thy hands shall be on the necks of thy enemies; the sons of thy father shall bow down to thee. The scepter shall not be taken away from Juda, nor a ruler from his thigh, till He come that is to be sent, and He shall be the Expectation of Nations."

The prophecies of Jacob

Concerning Joseph, he prophesied, "Joseph is a growing son, a growing son and beautiful to behold. The God of thy father shall be thy helper, and the Almighty shall bless thee with the blessings of Heaven above, with the blessings of the deep that lieth beneath. The blessings of thy father are strengthened with the blessings of his fathers until the Desire of the Everlasting Hills should come; may they be upon the head of Joseph, and upon the crown of the Nazarite among his brethren."

These beautiful words the Church uses in the Mass of the Feast of St. Joseph, the foster father of our blessed Savior.

Jacob dies and is buried in Chanaan

When he had finished speaking to his sons, Jacob lay back upon the pillow and died. Joseph ordered his body to be embalmed in the manner of the Egyptians, and then asked Pharao's permission to take the body back to Chanaan for burial. He said, "My father made me swear to him before he died that I would bury him in the burying place of his ancestors in the Land of Chanaan."

Pharao said to him, "Go and bury thy father accord ing as he made thee swear."

So the body of Jacob was carried in a great procession to the Land of Chanaan. All the princes of Pharao's court and the leading men of the land of Egypt went with them. They buried him in the double cave with Abraham and Sara, and Isaac and Rebecca. Rachel, the mother of Joseph and Benjamin, was buried at Bethlehem.

Joseph lived fifty-four years after his father's death. Joseph's death and burial He prophesied that Jacob's race would leave the land of Egypt, and left orders for them to carry his bones with them when they would go.

THINGS TO KNOW AND TO DO

1. Joseph, the Son of Jacob, Becomes a Great Ruler

1. Why did Joseph's brothers hate him?
2. Describe the conduct of Ruben.
3. How does the story of Joseph show that God often brings good out of evil?
4. What lesson may we learn from the ingratitude of the chief steward?
5. How does Joseph remind us of our blessed Lord?

2. Joseph Returns Good for Evil

1. Explain why the prosperity of the Egyptians depended upon the Nile River.
2. Show on the map the route which Joseph's brothers took in going to Egypt.
3. How did Joseph's dreams come true?
4. Give a floor talk in which you show that Joseph returned good for evil.
5. How does the later conduct of the brothers show that they were better men than when they had sold Joseph?
6. Write an essay on one of the following subjects: "Home Life in Egypt." "How the Egyptians Buried the Dead." "The Nile River."

SELF-TEST

Before you leave Unit Two, test yourself with the following exercises. Check your results.

I. Be able to tell the class the story of each section of this Unit.

II. Write the names of the important people of whom you have learned in this Unit.

III. Write a short theme about each of these persons. Tell why they are important.

IV. Prepare for your notebook an explanation of the following:
1. To what vocation God called Abram and what promise He made him.
2. The virtues of Abram—his obedience, his faith, his piety, his peaceableness, his charity.
3. How God punished Jacob for his sin.
4. How the history of Joseph proves that God takes care of us.
5. The prophecy which Jacob made on his deathbed.
6. In what ways Joseph was a figure of our Savior.

V. Write a dramatization of the story of Joseph.

VI. Make a picture of the valley of the Nile and the boundaries of Egypt.

VII. Collect pictures which tell the stories of Unit Two. Add them to your collection of Unit One.

PREVIEW

Unit Three

HOW GOD PROTECTED HIS CHOSEN PEOPLE AND LED THEM INTO THE PROMISED LAND

It was only for a while that the descendants of Jacob were happy in the land of Egypt. We shall see in this Unit how they became slaves after the death of Joseph. But God was mindful of His promises and He raised up a great leader to deliver them from the Egyptians. We shall see how Moses was called to lead the Chosen People back to the land of Chanaan. We shall learn of the wonderful thing that happened in the desert at Mount Sinai and how God, out of love for His people, showed them by means of the Ten Commandments how they must live if they wished to be happy. We shall learn why it was that the Israelites were forced to wander in the desert for forty years before they entered the Promised Land. We shall learn about Josue—the great leader whom God raised up after the death of Moses and who finally led the people into the Land of Promise. We shall see how God Himself watched over the people and ruled them by means of holy men who were called Judges. We shall see how the Judges led the Israelites to victory over their enemies and did not allow them to forget the promises that God had made. From the beautiful story of Ruth we shall learn how God in His providence was laying the foundations for the royal family from whom the King of Kings would come.

Unit Three

HOW GOD PROTECTED HIS CHOSEN PEOPLE AND LED THEM INTO THE PROMISED LAND

Unit Three

HOW GOD PROTECTED HIS CHOSEN PEOPLE AND LED THEM INTO THE PROMISED LAND

I. THE DEPARTURE OF THE ISRAELITES FROM EGYPT

1. Moses Is Rescued from the River

For some time after Joseph's death, the Israelites, as the descendants of Jacob were called, continued to enjoy freedom and prosperity in Egypt. While the descendants of Lot and Esau were leading a nomadic life in the immediate neighborhood of Chanaan, Jacob's descendants were living in peace and growing in power and wealth in Egypt. But finally a new Pharao ascended the throne, "who knew not Joseph." Then everything was changed. The lot of the Israelites became a very hard one. They were reduced to slavery, and were forced to make bricks for Pharao. From being a happy people, they became sad and weary in the service of the Egyptians. *Changed conditions in Egypt*

There were several causes which brought about this change in their conditions. The Pharaos were jealous of the power and wealth of the Israelites. They feared that the Israelites might be friendly to the Semitic *Causes of the change*

83

THE HARDSHIPS OF THE ISRAELITES IN EGYPT

nations to the East. Then, too, the Egyptians needed laborers to work on their temples, canals, and cities.

God permitted the change God permitted these great sufferings to affect His Chosen People because in their day of freedom and happiness, many of them had fallen into the idolatry and the vices of the Egyptians. The hard lot to which the Pharaos subjected them made them again turn their thoughts to God. The years of their sojourn in Egypt were coming to an end and, according to the promise made by God to Abraham, the time for their return to Chanaan was at hand.

In spite of all they had to undergo, the Jews in Egypt constantly increased in number. Pharao feared that they might now rise up in revolt against him. To keep down the number of those who could bear arms in battle, Pharao ordered that every Jewish boy should be killed as soon as he was born.

This order of Pharao was not always obeyed. Many little boys were saved, and among them was one called Moses. For three months the mother of Moses concealed him at home, but, fearing that he might be discovered, she made for him a wicker basket, and covered it with tar. She placed the baby in the basket and set it down among the bulrushes that grew close to the banks of the Nile River. Then she stole away, praying God to take care of her little boy. **Moses is saved**

Miriam, the sister of Moses, stood afar off, watching to see what would happen to her little brother. Now, just at that time the daughter of Pharao, with her maids, approached to bathe in the river. When Pharao's daughter saw the basket, she ordered one of her maids to bring it to her. When she uncovered it, she found the poor little crying babe.

"This is one of the babes of the Hebrews," she said. Miriam, at a distance, trembled for the safety of her brother. But when she saw that the princess looked lovingly at the babe, she ran up to her. "Shall I go and call a Hebrew woman to nurse the babe?" she asked. The princess replied, "Go." Miriam brought her mother. The princess, not knowing the woman, placed Moses in his own mother's care, and promised to pay her for her services to the child.

When Moses was older, the princess took him to her palace. There he was educated as a prince. He ate the best kind of food and wore the finest clothing. **Moses is educated as a prince**

EGYPTIAN CAPITAL SHOWING PICTURE WRITING

Under private teachers, he learned to read and write the picture language of the Egyptians. He studied arithmetic and learned how to survey the land. He learned the religious beliefs of the Egyptians, and came to know the different classes of Egyptian society. He saw how the poor were kept poor, while the rich grew even richer. God was training him to be the ruler, not of Egypt, but of his own people.

Moses flees from Egypt

Though Moses lived like a prince, he never forgot his mother and other relatives. He loved his own people, the Israelites, and it pained him to see how harshly they were treated.

One day when Moses had grown to manhood, he was walking in the neighborhood of the palace. A number of Israelites were hard at work under an Egyptian overseer. The overseer became angry at one of the Israelites and began to mistreat him cruelly. When Moses saw this, he was filled with rage and killed the Egyptian. When the news reached Pharao, he ordered that Moses should be put to death. But Moses escaped and fled to a place called Madian, in the region of Mount Sinai.

On his way, he sat down by a well to rest. While he was there, seven daughters of a priest named Jethro came to water their flocks, but some shepherds drove them away. Moses defended the girls, and when they told their father what had happened, he invited Moses to his house. Jethro begged Moses to remain with him and help him with his flocks. Moses agreed and lived with him for forty years, during which time he married one of Jethro's daughters, Sephora. During these forty years God prepared Moses for the great position of leader of His Chosen People. His life in the open air made him healthy and strong.

God prepares Moses for leadership

One day while Moses was tending his flocks near Mount Horeb, he saw a bush in flames. Yet, strangely enough, the bush did not burn up. Moses drew near in order to discover the cause of this wonderful occurrence. Suddenly a voice spoke from the midst of the flames and said, "Moses." He answered, "Here I am." Then the voice said, "Put off the shoes from thy feet, for the place where thou standest is holy ground. I am the God of Abraham, the God of Isaac, and the God of Jacob.

The burning bush

"I know the sorrows of My people in Egypt. I have seen their affliction and have heard their prayers. I have come down to deliver them out of the hands of the Egyptians, and to bring them to a land flowing with milk and honey. I will send thee to Pharao to bring the Children of Israel out of Egypt."

MOSES AT THE BURNING BUSH

But Moses said to God, "Who am I that I should bring the Children of Israel out of Egypt?"

God instructs Moses

"I will be with thee," God answered, "and this thou shalt have for a sign that I have sent thee: When thou shalt have led My children out of Egypt, thou shalt offer sacrifice to God upon this mountain. Tell the people of Israel that the God of Abraham, of Isaac, and of Jacob sent thee to them to lead them into a land flowing with milk and honey."

Moses said to God, "What if the Children of Israel should say to me, when I tell them that the God of their fathers hath sent me to them, 'What is His name?' What shall I tell them?"

God answered, "I am WHO AM. Tell them that HE WHO IS hath sent thee."

Moses said, "The people will not believe me."

Then God gave Moses three signs to use in order to prove to them that he was to be their leader. God said to Moses, "Cast thy rod upon the ground." He did so, and it was turned into a serpent, and Moses fled from it. The Lord said, "Put out thy hand and take the serpent by the tail." He did so, and it was turned back into his rod.

Again the Lord said, "Put thy hand into thy bosom." When Moses did so and drew it out, his hand was covered with leprosy and white as snow. At the word of God, he put it back into his bosom and drew it forth healed. Then God said, "If they will not believe even these two signs, nor hear thy voice, take some water from the river and pour it out on the dry land; whatsoever thou shalt draw out of the river shall be turned to blood."

But Moses still hesitated. He said that he was slow of speech and feared to approach Pharao. Yielding to the weakness of Moses, God appointed Aaron the Levite, his brother, to speak for him, but Moses was to tell him what to say.

Moses returned to Jethro and, taking his wife and two sons, set out for Egypt. On the mountain of the burning bush, he met Aaron, whom God had led there. Moses explained to Aaron all that God had told him. They then both returned to Egypt. **Moses meets Aaron**

2. The Burdens of the Israelites Are Increased

As soon as Moses and Aaron arrived in Egypt, they began to carry out God's instructions. They gathered

THE PHARAO OF THE EXODUS

the Israelites around them and told them how God had appointed them to be their leaders. They told the people of the wonderful things which had happened on Mount Horeb, and showed them the signs which God had given them to prove their mission. The Jews believed Moses and Aaron and accepted them as their leaders. They were ready to follow them out of the land of Egypt into the Promised Land.

Moses and Aaron before Pharao

Then Moses and Aaron went to Pharao. They asked him to give the Israelites a period of rest in the form of three days' journey into the wilderness, that they might offer sacrifice to their God. Pharao would not listen to such a request. Why should slaves be idle three days from their work? Pharao feared the Israelites, and was not anxious to preserve their health and strength. He sent Moses and Aaron away, and told them never to annoy him again.

Burdens made heavier

As a result of this visit, Pharao commanded the overseers to place new burdens upon the shoulders of Israelites. They were now forced to gather the straw which was necessary to hold the clay together in the form of bricks. Much time was lost in gathering the straw, and the Israelites were not able to make so many bricks as when the straw was supplied to them.

Yet the overseers demanded as many bricks as before and cruelly whipped those who failed to produce the same number.

Some of the chief men of the Israelites went to Pharao and begged for relief. But Pharao's heart was hardened. He laughed at them and said, "You are idle, and therefore you ask for a holiday to worship your God. Go and work. Straw shall not be given you, and you shall deliver the accustomed number of bricks." **Moses and Aaron blamed**

When the chief men of the Israelites met Moses and Aaron, they blamed them for making the burdens of the people heavier.

Moses and Aaron were very sad. They prayed to God again, and He told them to be patient. He promised Moses and Aaron that the time of their delivery from bondage was near. But the people were sad and weary and they heeded not their words.

Again God sent Moses and Aaron to Pharao to demand that he let the Children of Israel go out of the land of Egypt. He told Moses to show Pharao the wonderful signs which He had given to him. **Another appeal to Pharao**

When Moses and Aaron appeared before Pharao, Aaron took the rod and threw it on the floor. It was turned into a serpent. Pharao called his magicians, who did the same thing, and all their rods were turned into serpents. But the serpent from Aaron's rod swallowed up the other serpents, and it became a rod again in Aaron's hand.

But Pharao would not listen to the words of Moses and Aaron, and refused to let the Israelites depart.

THE ROD OF AARON TURNS INTO A SERPENT

3. GOD SENDS TEN PLAGUES TO PUNISH THE EGYPTIANS

The first plague God spoke to Moses again and told him to go out to meet Pharao on the river bank, and to say to him, "The Lord God of the Hebrews sent me to thee, saying, 'Let My people go to sacrifice to Me in the desert.' Until now thou wouldst not hear." Then, lifting up his rod, Aaron struck the river, and the water was turned to blood. The river was polluted, the fishes died, and the Egyptians could not drink the water. There was blood in all the land of Egypt. This was the first of the plagues sent by God.

Pharao's magicians also caused water to turn into blood. Pharao's heart was hardened, and he would

not do as the Lord commanded. He would not let the
Children of Israel go out of the land of Egypt.

When this plague had lasted seven days, God commanded Moses and Aaron to go to Pharao again, and
to say to him, "The Lord God of the Hebrews saith,
'Let My people go to sacrifice to Me. But if thou wilt
not let them go, I will fill all thy land with frogs.
Frogs will enter thy house, and thy beds, and thy ovens
and the houses of thy servants.'" But Pharao heeded
not their words.

The second plague

When they went out from Pharao's presence, Aaron
raised his rod over the waters, and at once the land
was overrun with frogs. The magicians also caused
frogs to come forth upon the land.

Pharao sent for Moses, and said to him, "Pray to
thy God to take the frogs away from me and my people, and I will let the Israelites go to sacrifice to their
Lord."

Moses believed Pharao. He begged God to remove
the plague. In answer to the prayer of Moses, all the
frogs died. They were gathered together in heaps, and
the land was filled with their decaying bodies.

When Pharao saw that the plague had ended, he
refused to let the Israelites leave Egypt. Then Aaron
struck the dust of the earth with his rod, and God sent
a plague of fleas which caused great discomfort. The
magicians also attempted to do the same, but could not.
They therefore said to Pharao, "This is the finger of
God," but he would not heed them.

The third and fourth plagues

At the command of God, Moses met Pharao early in
the morning at the river bank and demanded that he

let the people depart. Pharao refused, and a fourth plague, of flies, was sent upon all the land of Egypt, excepting Gessen, where the Israelites lived.

Pharao called Moses and Aaron and said, "Go, and sacrifice to thy God here in this land." "It cannot be so," answered Moses, "for if we kill the animals which the Egyptians worship, they will stone us." Pharao said, "Go out into the wilderness and worship, but go no farther." Moses prayed and the plague of flies was taken from Pharao and his people. Again Pharao had deceived Moses. He would not let the people go.

The fifth plague So Moses came to Pharao again and told him that, unless he would let the Israelites leave Egypt, all the camels, oxen, horses, and sheep in the whole land, except those in Gessen, would be afflicted with disease and death. Pharao was filled with bitterness and he refused again. All the animals of the Egyptians died, but those of the Israelites were unharmed. Yet Pharao would not let the Israelites leave.

The sixth plague Therefore God punished him and his people still more. All the people and all the animals were stricken with boils. The plague spread over all the land, and the suffering was very great. But Pharao would not obey the word of the Lord.

The seventh plague Moses went before Pharao and threatened a plague of hail if he did not yield to God's will. Once more Pharao refused, and a great hailstorm, with thunder and lightning, swept over the land, beating down the crops and destroying the houses. Only the land of Gessen was saved.

Pharao promised to let the Israelites go into the

wilderness if the storm should cease. Moses went outside the city, stretched forth his hands, and the storm ceased. But Pharao was as unfaithful to his promise this time as he had been before.

Moses and Aaron threatened Pharao with a plague of locusts which would destroy whatever crops were left. The servants of Pharao came and begged him to let the Israelites depart, so that no more harm should come to Egypt. Pharao yielded so far as to say that the men might leave, but he would not let the women and children go.

Another plague therefore followed. Great swarms of locusts filled every field. They ate up every blade of grass. Pharao sent for Moses and Aaron. He promised to grant them their wish if they would remove the plague. They prayed. A strong wind came and swept all the locusts into the Red Sea. But after the plague was gone, Pharao's heart was hardened again. *The eighth plague*

Then came a new plague. Darkness covered the land. Pharao called for Moses and Aaron and told them to go with their men, women and children, but to leave their flocks in Egypt. Moses told the Pharao that they needed them as victims for the sacrifice. Pharao would not yield. *The ninth plague*

In obedience to God's command, the Israelites asked their Egyptian neighbors for gifts of gold and silver. These gifts were in reality but just payment for the hard labor the Israelites had performed these many years. The Egyptians had come to respect the Israelites because of the wonderful things which Moses had *Egyptian gifts* done. They were afraid to refuse their request and they gave them all that they asked. Thus, before their departure from Egypt, all of the Israelites possessed gold, silver, and valuable clothing.

The tenth plague The greatest plague was still to come upon the Egyptians. The Lord said to Moses, "Go to Pharao and say, 'At midnight I will enter into Egypt. Every first-born in the land of the Egyptians shall die, from the first-born of Pharao to the first-born of the handmaid. And all the first-born of the beasts shall die. And there shall be a great cry in all the land of Egypt. But the people of Israel shall not be touched.'"

Pharao was angry. His heart was still hard. He would not permit the Jews to go out from Egypt.

The first Paschal Lamb Moses went back to the Israelites and gave them God's message. "You shall prepare a lamb without a blemish in it," he said, "and on the fourteenth day of the month, you shall sacrifice it to God. You shall sprinkle the side posts and the upper posts of the house with its blood. You shall eat the flesh roasted that night with unleavened bread and wild lettuce. You shall be ready for a long journey with shoes on your feet and staves in your hands. You shall eat in haste, for it is the Passing of the Lord."

About midnight the destroying angel of the Lord entered every Egyptian home, from that of Pharao to that of the humblest man of the land. The first-born of every family of Egypt lay dead.

But the Israelites were spared by the angel, because of the blood of the lamb which they had sprinkled on their door posts.

MOSES LEADS THE ISRAELITES OUT OF EGYPT

This great sorrow softened the heart of Pharao. He summoned Moses and Aaron and told them to lead the Israelites out of the land of Egypt without delay. The Israelites left Egypt two hundred and fifteen years after the kind Pharao, the friend of Joseph, had given the land of Gessen to Jacob and his posterity.

4. GOD PROTECTS THE ISRAELITES IN THEIR DEPARTURE

The number of Israelites who set out from Egypt on that night with Moses and Aaron was six hundred thousand, besides the women and children. They took with them all their possessions of clothing, their ornaments, their vessels of gold and silver, their weapons, *The departure* and their tents, as well as small flocks of sheep and herds of cattle.

Before Joseph died, he had prophesied that the Israelites would leave Egypt. He had made them promise to take his remains with them. Moses and the Israelites remembered the promise which their ancestors had made to Joseph, and when they left Egypt, they carried the body of Joseph with them.

The Lord went before the Israelites to show the way in a pillar of cloud by day, and by night in a pillar of fire. He directed them to choose the route crossing the Red Sea.

Pharao's pursuit Pharao soon regretted that he had let the Israelites leave Egypt. He made ready his chariot and took his army with him. With six hundred chosen chariots and all the captains of the army, he pursued the Children of Israel. He found them encamped by the shore of the Red Sea. Lifting up their eyes, the Israelites saw all the Egyptians coming after them. They were very much afraid, and cried out to the Lord. They told Moses that it would have been better to be slaves in Egypt than to die in the wilderness.

Moses said to the people, "Fear not. Stand and see the great wonders of the Lord, which He shall do this day. The Egyptians whom you see now, you shall see no more forever. The Lord will fight for you and you shall hold your peace."

The Pillar of Cloud The cloud that had preceded the Israelites, now moved behind them and hid them so completely that the Egyptians could not see to attack them. Moses prayed to God for help, and God said to him, "Stretch out thy rod over the Red Sea.'' Moses did as he was commanded. The waters of the sea divided, and a burning wind dried a path through the sea. The Israelites crossed this path to the opposite shore. They passed between a wall of water to their right and a wall of water to their left.

While they were crossing, the pillar of cloud was lifted, and the Egyptians followed the Israelites in haste. They drove their chariots into the path. By the power of God their chariots were overthrown, and the Egyptians cried out, ''Let us flee from Israel, for the Lord fights for them against us.'' But it was too late.

As soon as the last Israelite had crossed over to the opposite shore, God said to Moses, ''Stretch forth thy rod over the sea.'' Moses did as God commanded. The waters closed in, and all the chariots and Egyptians were buried in the depths of the sea. In gratitude to God for their deliverance, Moses and the Israelites recited a canticle of thanksgiving.

They were now able to proceed in peace. On their way to the land flowing with milk and honey, the Israelites had to travel through a desert. They had little food and less water, and the country was strange to them. They encamped at a place where they found a spring, but the water of the spring was bitter, hence Moses called the place Mara, which means bitterness. At the command of God, Moses cast a tree into the water and the bitterness was taken away.

After a journey of six weeks, the Israelites reached

MOSES STRETCHES FORTH HIS ROD, AND THE SEA DESTROYS THE
EGYPTIANS

the Wilderness of Sin. Here they were sorely in need
of food. They murmured against Moses and told him
that they had been better off in Egypt than in the
wilderness, for there they had food to eat, whilst in
the desert they were starving.

The quail and manna God heard the complaints of the Children of Israel,
and said to Moses, "Tell the people that in the evening
they shall eat flesh, and in the morning they shall have
their fill of bread, that they may know that I am the
Lord, their God." That evening, God sent quail into
the camp. In the morning, a heavy dew covered the
earth. It appeared like hoarfrost on the ground.

When the Children of Israel saw it, they asked one

THE ISRAELITES GATHER UP THE MANNA

another, "Manhu?" which means, "What is this?" For they did not know what it was.

"This is bread," said Moses, "which the Lord hath given you to eat. Let everyone gather enough to eat for one day."

Everyone gathered in the morning as much as he needed. The rest melted when the sun grew hot.

The Israelites called this food manna. It was white like the seed of a little flower, and it tasted like flour and honey. The Children of Israel ate this manna until they reached the borders of the Land of Chanaan. Every morning they gathered as much as they needed for the day. They were told to gather neither more

THE JOURNEY OF THE ISRAELITES FROM EGYPT TO CHANAAN

nor less. On Friday they gathered sufficient for the
Sabbath Day, for the manna did not fall on that day.

From the Wilderness of Sin the Israelites went to
Raphidim, and camped at the foot of Mount Horeb,
where Moses had seen the burning bush. Again they
murmured against Moses, because they were thirsty
and had no water. God commanded Moses to strike a

RAPHIDIM

rock. The rock was dry, but when Moses struck it, a torrent of water gushed forth and the thirsty people were satisfied.

At Raphidim, the Amalecites attacked the Israelites and tried to rob them of their possessions. Moses appointed Josue to pick out men to form an army to fight against them. When the battle was about to begin, Moses took the rod of God in his hand, and went up into the mountain with Aaron and Hur, another of the chief men, to pray for victory. Moses held the rod up over his head while he prayed. As long as he held up the rod, the Israelites were successful; the moment he lowered it, the Israelites gave way. When Moses grew weary, Aaron and Hur stood on either side of him, and

The Amalecites are overcome

held up his arms. Thus he was able to keep his arms extended until sunset, and the Amalecites were defeated and driven off. Moses built an altar to God in thanksgiving, thus fulfilling God's prophecy.

The Amalecites

The Amalecites were descendants of Esau. They were a nomad people and their home was in the desert around Mount Sinai. The region in which they lived was too dry for farming, but it offered plenty of fine pasture land for their flocks and herds.

They were a warlike people, and when they saw the great multitude of the Israelites coming into their country, bringing along flocks of sheep and herds of cattle, they immediately attacked them. It was only natural for them to fear that the invaders would use up all the pasture land and leave their own flocks to starve.

Though the original home of the Amalecites was in the desert, many of them had wandered north and settled along the borders of the Land of Chanaan. There grew up a great hatred between them and the Israelites, and this first battle in the desert was but the beginning of a long series of wars between the two peoples.

At Raphidim, Jethro, the father-in-law of Moses, came out to meet him. He brought with him the wife of Moses, and their two sons, who had been sent back from Egypt. Moses welcomed them with joy in his heart and led them to his tent. There Moses told Jethro all that had happened since the Israelites had left Egypt. Jethro offered sacrifice to God in thanksgiving for His favors to the Israelites. He ate bread with the chief men of God's Chosen People.

It was at Raphidim, by the advice of Jethro, that Moses appointed judges to settle the disputes and quarrels among the people.

THINGS TO KNOW AND TO DO

1. MOSES IS RESCUED FROM THE RIVER AND PREPARED FOR LEADERSHIP

1. Why were the descendants of Abraham called Israelites?
2. How did the education which Moses received prepare him for his vocation?
3. Of what value for his future work was the life he was forced to live in Madian?
4. Why did God permit the king of Egypt to oppress the Israelites?
5. Locate Madian on the map.
6. Locate Mount Horeb.
7. What message did God give to Moses from the burning bush?
8. Why did God send Aaron to Moses?
9. How did Moses and Aaron prove to the people that they were sent by God?

2. THE BURDENS OF THE ISRAELITES ARE INCREASED

1. Why did Moses fear to return to Egypt?
2. What was the result of his first visit to Pharao?

3. GOD SENDS TEN PLAGUES TO PUNISH THE EGYPTIANS

1. Name the ten plagues.
2. What lessons can we learn from the conduct of Pharao?
3. Describe the killing of the Paschal Lamb.
4. Why is our Lord called the Lamb of God?

4. GOD PROTECTS THE ISRAELITES IN THEIR DEPARTURE

1. Describe the difficulties of the Exodus as you imagine them.
2. Trace the journey of the Israelites on the map.
3. Tell what God did to protect the Israelites during their travels.
4. Write a composition comparing the manna to Holy Communion.

II. THE REVELATION OF GOD'S LAW ON MOUNT SINAI

1. Moses Receives the Commandments of God

The Israelites receive the Commandments When the Israelites left Mount Horeb, they journeyed to the valley at the foot of Mount Sinai. Here they found springs of water and grass for their flocks

THE VALLEY OF MOUNT SINAI

In this valley, they stayed for two years, during which time God did wonderful things for them.

Here God gave them the great law according to which they and all men were to live, but before He gave them this law, He prepared them for it. First, He asked them whether or not they would be obedient to the law, and promised them that if they were obedient He would make them His Chosen People. Secondly, He ordered all of them to prepare themselves for three days.

When God was ready to give His law to the Israelites from Mount Sinai, He told Moses to draw a boundary line at the foot of the mountain. This line the people were forbidden to pass under pain of death. All of this was done that the Israelites might know the importance of the law they were about to receive.

On the third day, Moses led them out of their tents to the boundary line which he had made. The lightning was flashing, the thunder was pealing, and shrill trumpets were sounding. Mount Sinai, which is nearly 8000 feet high, was covered with a very heavy cloud. Thick smoke rose from the mountain as from a furnace. The sounds of the trumpets grew louder and louder. Finally, the people, waiting in fear of what was to happen, heard God's voice proclaiming:

1. "I am the Lord thy God, who brought thee out of the land of Egypt, out of the house of bondage. Thou shalt not have strange gods before Me. Thou shalt not make thyself a graven thing, nor the likeness of any thing that is in heaven above or in the earth beneath, nor of those things that are in the water under the earth. Thou shalt not adore them or serve them.

2. "Thou shalt not take the name of the Lord thy God in vain.

3. "Remember that thou keep holy the Sabbath Day.

4. "Honor thy father and thy mother.

5. "Thou shalt not kill.

6. "Thou shalt not commit adultery.

7. "Thou shalt not steal.

8. "Thou shalt not bear false witness against thy neighbor.

9. "Thou shalt not covet thy neighbor's wife.

10. "Thou shalt not covet thy neighbor's goods."

The people were struck with fear and stood afar off, saying to Moses, "Speak thou to us and we shall hear. Let not the Lord speak to us, or we shall die." Thenceforth God spoke to the people only through Moses.

Then Moses went up into the cloud where God was, and God spoke to him. God promised Moses that an angel would lead the Israelites into the Promised Land. He ordered them to make no treaty with the inhabitants of Chanaan but to drive them out of the country. Moses came down and told the people all the commands that the Lord had given him, and they promised to obey them. He then wrote the words of God and built an altar. He chose young men from every tribe and made them sacrifice calves upon it. Moses then poured half of the blood on the altar and sprinkled the rest upon the people and the book he had written. This he did as a sign of the solemn covenant between God and His people.

A second time Moses was called by God up into the mountain. He took Josue with him. Seven days after he ascended the mountain, God called him into the cloud, and there he remained for forty days and forty nights. It was then that God gave him, written on two tablets of stone, the Commandments which He had spoken to the people amidst thunder and lightning. He also gave him many instructions concerning divine worship.

GOD WRITES THE COMMANDMENTS ON THE TABLETS OF STONE

The Israelites thought that Moses had forsaken them because he was absent so long. They therefore collected their jewels and, bringing them to Aaron, forced him to make for them a golden calf such as they had seen worshiped in Egypt. When the golden calf was ready, the Israelites adored it and made a great feast in its honor.

The idolatry of the Israelites

When Moses came down from the mountain with the two tablets of the Commandments and saw the people worshiping the golden calf and dancing around it, he was terribly angry. He threw the tablets of stone upon the ground at the foot of the mountain and broke them in pieces. He burnt the golden calf and beat it into powder.

The leaders are put to death

As judge of the people, Moses passed sentence of death on those who had led the others into idolatry. He cried out, "If any man be on the Lord's side, let him join with me." Immediately the sons of Levi stood by his side. At the command of Moses they drew their swords and slew the guilty, whoever came in their way. Twenty-three thousand men were killed. The rest of the people did penance, and God forgave them their sin.

God then commanded Moses to make two tablets like the first. These Moses took up to the mountain and again God wrote upon them the Commandments. Moses remained on the mountain for forty days and forty nights. When he came down to the people, rays of light like horns shone out from his face. The people were afraid to come near him, so he covered his face with a veil and told them all that he had learnt while he was with God on the mountain.

2. GOD TELLS THE ISRAELITES HOW TO WORSHIP HIM

God had given Moses very exact instructions concerning the manner in which the Israelites were to carry on divine worship. Moses now called upon the people to make offerings of gold, silver, brass, dyed skins, fine linen, acacia wood and whatever else was necessary for the sacred vessels, the building of a tabernacle, and the vestments of the priests. So great was the response of the people, that Moses had to forbid them to offer more. Then skilled workers in the various trades volunteered their services to construct everything as God had commanded.

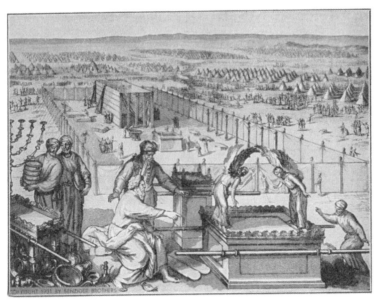

THE ERECTION OF THE TABERNACLE

In the center foreground is Moses, and behind him is Aaron in the vestments of a high priest. Two priests stand at the left, about to place the bread on the Table of Showbreads. To the right of Aaron is the Altar of Incense, and in front of that the Ark of the Covenant.

The Tabernacle The Tabernacle was a portable church before which the Israelites performed their acts of worship. It was made in such a way that taking it apart was an easy matter, for the Tabernacle had to be carried from place to place by the Israelites during their sojourn in the desert.

The Tabernacle was an oblong tent, forty-five feet long, fifteen feet wide and fifteen feet high. The back and sides were made of boards of acacia wood overlaid with gold. They were held together by five poles of the same kind of wood overlaid with gold, which passed through five golden rings on each board. The boards rested in silver sockets.

Four coverings formed the roof. These coverings extended down over the sides. An inside covering of embroidered linen draped the walls. The outer coverings were of goats' hair, and rams' skins dyed red and violet.

At the entrance to the Tabernacle there were five pillars of acacia wood, overlaid with gold, with golden capitals. These pillars were set in sockets of brass. They supported an embroidered linen curtain, which acted as the door of the Tabernacle. Thirty feet beyond this, were four other similar pillars, from which hung another curtain to separate the Holy of Holies, as the room where the Ark rested was called, from the other part of the Tabernacle, called the Sanctuary, or Holy Place.

The Court of the Tabernacle In the Sanctuary were kept the Altar of Incense, the Table of Showbreads and the Seven-branched Candlestick. Here the priests performed their sacred functions.

The Tabernacle was erected at the west end of a long enclosure known as the Court of the Tabernacle, one hundred and fifty feet long by seventy-five feet wide. It was fenced in by embroidered linen curtains supported on brass pillars, with a rich curtain at the entrance. The Altar of Holocausts stood inside the entrance, and between it and the Tabernacle was the Brazen Laver, at which the priests purified themselves.

The Ark of the Covenant was made of acacia wood

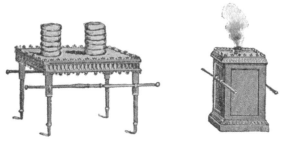

THE TABLE OF SHOWBREADS
THE ALTAR OF INCENSE

and lined inside and outside with gold. It was three **The Ark of the Covenant** and three-fourth feet long, two and one-fourth feet wide, and two and one-fourth feet high. Moses placed the two tablets of the law and a vessel containing some manna in the Ark. Later the rod of Aaron was also placed in it. The cover was of solid gold and on each end were two golden angels whose wings covered the Ark. This cover was called the Propitiatory, or Mercy Seat. Henceforth, when God spoke to Moses, it was from a cloud that rested over the Mercy Seat. The Ark was the only thing placed in the Holy of Holies.

The Table of Showbreads was made of acacia wood **The Table of Showbreads** overlaid with gold. It was three feet long, one and one-half feet wide, and two and one-fourth feet high. On each end of the table were placed six loaves of showbread, or Loaves of Proposition. This showbread was unleavened and was made of the finest flour. The twelve loaves were renewed every Saturday as a constant offering of thanksgiving to God.

The Altar of Incense was made of acacia wood over- **The Altar of Incense** laid with gold. There was a grating in the top surface.

THE ARK OF THE COVENANT
THE SEVEN-BRANCHED CANDLESTICK

It was one and one-half feet long, one and one-half feet wide, and three feet high. It was placed before the veil of the Holy of Holies.

The Seven-branched Candle-stick The Seven-branched Candlestick was hammered out of pure gold. It was made to light the Sanctuary of the Tabernacle, and contained seven lamps, which were to remain lighted continually. Its weight in gold was one hundred and thirty pounds.

The Brazen Laver The Brazen Laver was a bowl of brass used by the priests for washing the hands and feet before they went into the Tabernacle. It stood in the Court, near the entrance of the Tabernacle.

The Altar of Holo-causts The Altar of Holocausts was made of acacia wood overlaid with brass. It was seven and one-half feet long, seven and one-half feet wide, and four and one-half feet high, and had brass horns at each corner. It was hollow, with a grating in the top surface. Beneath the grating there was a hearth for the fire and a pan to catch the ashes from the grating. This altar was placed just inside the entrance to the Court.

3. The Priesthood Is Instituted

God told Moses that Aaron and his sons should be set aside for the worship of the Tabernacle. The first-born son was to be high priest, and the other sons were to be priests. They alone were permitted to offer sacrifice to God.

The high priest wore a long linen robe with sleeves **The High Priest** and reaching to his feet. Over this, he wore a sleeve-less robe of four colors, violet, purple, crimson and white, reaching a little below his knees. It was fringed at the bottom with golden bells and embroidered pome-granates. His outermost garment was called the Ephod. It was something like a cloak of two parts, which was fastened at the shoulders with two onyx stones, each one engraved with the names of six of the tribes of Israel. It was fastened at the waist by a girdle. Over this was worn a breastplate, called the Rational, which was a square of cloth matching the Ephod. On the Rational were set twelve precious stones engraved with the names of the Twelve Tribes. This was fastened by golden chains to the shoulders and by a purple ribbon to the waist.

On his head the high priest wore a white linen miter, or crown-shaped cap, on which was fastened a gold plate engraved with the inscription: Holy to the Lord. The rest of the priests wore only embroidered linen robes with girdles, and the linen miter.

When the Tabernacle was finished, Moses brought **Institution of the Priesthood** Aaron and his sons to its entrance and washed them

THE CONSECRATION OF AARON AS HIGH PRIEST AND OF HIS SONS AS
PRIESTS

Moses is in the act of anointing with the blood of the bullock the
horns of the Altar of Holocausts, which stands before the Tabernacle.
The Brazen Laver is at the left and the victims for the sacrifice are in
the foreground.

with water. He next dressed Aaron and his sons in
priestly robes and anointed with oil the head of Aaron
and consecrated the hands of Aaron's two sons. This
ceremony lasted for seven days. Thus Moses carried
out God's commands, and Aaron and his sons were
ordained priests for the Children of Israel.

The whole Tribe of Levi, because of its fidelity to God at the time of the worship of the Golden Calf, was assigned to help the priests. God provided a ceremony to initiate them into their new position. They were sprinkled with water to purify them, and their hair was shaved from their heads. They were led into the Court of the Tabernacle, where the

A a r o n, t h e F i r s t H i g h P r i e s t

people passed by them, placing their hands on the head of every one of them. This was a sign that the nation was transferring to the Levites the duty of serving God in acts of public worship. Two oxen were then brought before the Levites. Upon the heads of these oxen every Levite placed his hands. The oxen were then sacrificed. One was offered as a sacrifice for sin; the other as a holocaust, in adoration.

4. God Appoints Feast Days and Sacrifices

There were two kinds of sacrifices prescribed by the Law of Moses: the *unbloody*, in which the fruits of the earth, or flour, dried corn, and frankincense, together

Kinds of sacrifices

with oil and wine, were offered; and *bloody*, in which bullocks, lambs, goats, turtledoves or pigeons, all without blemish, were slain. The oblations of flour had to be mixed with salt, oil and frankincense. The priest burnt a portion of these on the altar and retained the rest for his own use. At the same time an offering of wine was poured out at the foot of the altar.

The bloody sacrifices were of four kinds: *holocausts*, in which the entire victim was consumed by fire, an act of adoration to acknowledge God's supreme dominion; *peace offerings*, made as acts of thanksgiving or petition; *sin offerings*, for venial sins; and *expiatory* or *trespass offerings*, to make satisfaction for grievous sins or restitution for injuries done. In these last three, only the fat and entrails of the victim were burnt. The right shoulder and breast, which the priest waved before the Lord, were reserved for himself. The remainder of the animal was restored to the offerer.

Regular
sacrifices

Every morning and evening the priests were obliged to offer a holocaust of a lamb for all the people. Incense also was offered every day on the golden altar of incense. On the *Sabbath*, or day of rest, two victims were offered at the sacrifices. On the monthly feast celebrated at the *New Moon*, many victims were slain, and the feast was announced by the blowing of silver trumpets. The New Moon of the Seventh Month was called the *Feast of Trumpets*, at which a still larger number of victims were sacrificed. Every seventh year was called the *Sabbatical Year*, and during it the

PRIESTS BLOWING THE TRUMPETS AT THE FEAST OF THE NEW MOON

land was to lie fallow, and sowing and reaping were forbidden.

God set aside certain days of the year on which the Israelites were to honor Him with more prayers and more sacrifices than usual. These days were known as feast days. God appointed these feast days because He wanted to remind His Chosen People from time to time in a special manner of the worship which they owed to Him, and to recall to their minds the great events in their history. Thus their hearts would be moved to gratitude for all the favors God had shown them. **Feast days of the Jews**

The *Day of Atonement* was observed on the tenth day of the seventh month. It was the great day of public penance, and no servile work was done, nor was any food eaten. On this day, the high priest **The ceremonies on the Day of Atonement**

A High Priest Offering a Holocaust

officiated. He laid aside his official vestments and clothed himself in a plain white linen garment, similar to that of the other priests, with a girdle and a head covering. This was the one time of the year in which he was permitted to enter the Holy of Holies. When the people were assembled in the morning, he sacrificed a calf. He entered the Holy of Holies, offered incense, and sprinkled the Mercy Seat seven times with the blood of the calf. This sprinkling of blood was to satisfy for his sins and the sins of the priests. When he came back to the Court of the Tabernacle, two goats were brought before him. One of these he chose by lot. He sacrificed it and sprinkled the blood in the same manner as he had sprinkled the blood of the calf. He laid his hands upon the head of the second goat, confessed the sins of the people over it, and then ordered it to be led out into the wilderness. From this, we get the word scapegoat.

After this ceremony, the high priest washed and vested in his usual robes. He then offered two rams to adore God, the Owner of all things. One of these he offered for himself, and the other for the people.

The first of these special days in the calendar of the **The Feast of the Pasch** Israelites was the *Feast of the Pasch*, or Passover, also called Azymes (unleavened bread). It was celebrated on the fourteenth day of the first month, called Nisan (March-April). In the evening of this day the Israelites ate the Paschal lamb in their tents. They roasted the lamb with fixed rites and ceremonies, and ate it with unleavened bread and bitter herbs, standing, dressed in their traveling clothes, with traveling staves in their hands. The celebration lasted for eight days but work was forbidden only on the first and the last day of the ceremonies. This feast was appointed by God to recall to the Israelites the night when He protected them from the destroying angel and led them out of Egypt.

About seven weeks (fifty days) later, the *Feast of* **The Feast of Pentecost** *Pentecost*, or of Weeks, was celebrated. Two loaves of bread made from the new wheat of the harvest, and two spring lambs were offered as sacrifices, because this was a day of thanksgiving for the harvest and the increase of the flocks. It also commemorated the giv-

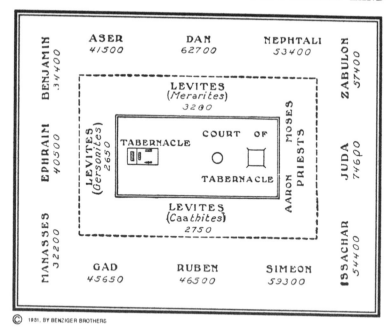

THE ENCAMPMENT OF THE TRIBES OF ISRAEL
AT THE FOOT OF MOUNT SINAI

ing of the Law on Mount Sinai. The people were forbidden to do servile work on this day.

The Feast of Tabernacles

On the fifteenth day of the seventh month began the *Feast of Tabernacles*, which lasted for seven days. It was celebrated in thanksgiving for the fruit harvest, and in memory of their dwelling in tents during their wanderings in the wilderness. During these days more numerous sacrifices were offered than during any other feast. On the first and last day of this feast servile work was forbidden.

THINGS TO KNOW AND TO DO

1. Moses Receives the Commandments of God

1. Locate Mount Sinai on the map.
2. Describe the awful scene in which God gave the Commandments. Why did God make the occasion so solemn?
3. What purpose did God have in giving the Commandments?
4. Who must observe the Commandments?
5. Why do we say that the Commandments make us free and happy?
6. Give a floor talk in which you prove the power of prayer as seen in the example of Moses.
7. Draw a plan of the encampment of the Israelites at the foot of Mount Sinai like the one shown on preceding page.

2. God Tells the Israelites How to Worship Him

1. Why did the Israelites need a house of worship that could be moved?
2. Why did Moses bless all the furniture of the Tabernacle?
3. How did God prove that He was present in the Tabernacle?
4. Have your father help you build a small Tabernacle.
5. Compare the Tabernacle and the Church.
6. Why are frequent visits to the church helpful to boys and girls?
7. What is the connection between the showbread and the Real Presence of our Lord in the church?
8. Read the Litany of the Blessed Virgin and see whether we do not call her by a title mentioned here.

3. The Priesthood Is Instituted

1. Why did God order that there should be priests?
2. Who offered sacrifice to God before Moses appointed priests?
3. Tell if every Israelite could be a Levite and explain the meaning of the name.
4. Compare the duties of the priests of the Old Law and the duties of the priests of the New Law.
5. Make a comparison between the vestments of the Jewish priests and of the priests of the Church today.
6. Why should we honor the priesthood?

4. God Appoints Feast Days and Sacrifices

1. Why were the Israelites obliged to offer sacrifice?
2. Name the victims they usually offered in sacrifice to God.
3. Of what great sacrifice were these only the figure?
4. Compare the fourfold end of Mass with the kinds of sacrifice of the Old Testament.
5. Give a floor talk in which you show why we should try to assist at Mass daily.
6. Why did the Jews have certain solemn feast days?
7. Which are the greatest feast days of the Catholic Church?
8. Explain why the scapegoat was a figure of our Lord.

III. THE WANDERINGS OF THE ISRAELITES IN THE DESERT

1. THE ISRAELITES DEPART FROM MOUNT SINAI

The sign of departure For two years the cloud which guided the Israelites hung over the Tabernacle. Moses took a census of the people at the command of God, and divided them into groups according to their tribes. There were, in all, 603,550, excluding children, the tribe of Levi and, seemingly also, women and strangers. After that time, the cloud lifted into the heavens as a sign that the time of departure had come. It began to move slowly in the direction in which the Israelites were to travel.

The priests blew the silver trumpets as a signal to the people to pack up their tents. Aaron and his sons took down the Tabernacle for the march. They removed the veil that hung before the Ark of the Covenant and covered the Ark with it. The carrying poles were put into the rings on the sides of the Ark, and two violet coverings were placed over the veil. The Table of Showbreads, the Seven-branched Candlestick, the Altar of Incense, and the Altar of Sacrifice were carefully and reverently covered and prepared to be carried on the shoulders of the Levites. Six wagons were needed to carry the hangings, the planks, and the pillars of the Tabernacle.

The marching order When all was ready, the march began. The Levites carried the Ark of the Covenant at the head of the procession. The priests followed. The tribes of Juda, Issachar, and Zabulon were next in line. Next were the wagons carrying the material of the Tabernacle. The tribes of Ruben, Simeon, and Gad followed. Then came the Levites, carrying the sacred furniture of the Tabernacle. The remaining six tribes marched in the following order: Ephraim, Manasses, Benjamin, Dan, Aser, Nephtali.

After a march of about three days, the Israelites were tired and began to murmur against the Lord. God sent down fire which destroyed many of them and caused the rest to repent. At the prayer of Moses the fire was taken away.

Not long afterward, fresh murmurings arose. These were caused by strangers who had accompanied them out of Egypt. The Israelites joined them in rebellion against Moses. They sighed for the fleshpots of Egypt. They had grown tired of the manna with which the Lord fed them daily. Thy complained because they had no fresh meat to eat. The Lord sent a strong wind which carried a great number of quail into the camp and this restored peace for a time. But soon a new revolt occurred. Even his sister, Miriam, and his brother, Aaron, the high priest, rebelled against Moses. God punished Miriam for her sin by striking her with leprosy, which lasted for seven days.

The murmuring of the Israelites

For a while after this, there was peace among the people. The Israelites marched on toward the Promised Land, and at last reached Cades on the border of Chanaan.

ONE OF THE VALLEYS OF CHANAAN

2. The Report of the Scouts Arouses Rebellion

The report of the scouts   Here God commanded Moses to choose twelve men, one from each tribe, and to send them as scouts into the Land of Chanaan. Moses selected the twelve, and among them were Caleb and Josue. He said to them, "Go up by the south side and when you come to the mountain, view the land and see what sort it is; and the people, whether they be strong or weak, few in number or many; and the land itself, whether it be good or bad; what manner of cities there are, walled or without walls; the ground, whether it is rich or barren, woody or without trees. Be of good courage, and bring us the fruits of the land."

The scouts traveled about all the Land of Chanaan for forty days. At Hebron they found a great cluster of grapes. It was so large that, when they cut it off the vine, two men had to carry it upon a pole. They also took pomegranates and figs from that place and brought them to Cades.

All the people gathered together with Moses and Aaron to listen to their report. The scouts said, "We came to the land to which thou didst send us, and in very truth it is a land flowing with milk and honey, as thou mayest see by these fruits which we have brought with us. But the people that live there are very strong, and they have great cities, surrounded by strong walls."

Hearing this, the people began to murmur against Moses, but Caleb, in order to quiet them, said, "Let us go up and possess the land, for we shall be able to conquer it." But the other scouts said, "No, we are not able to go up to this people, because they are stronger than we. The people that we saw are tall; some of them seem to be giants; in comparison with them, we seem like locusts."

When the discontented people heard this report, they refused to go any farther. They told Moses they did not want him as their leader. They decided to elect a captain to lead them back to Egypt. This act was a great sin, because it was rebellion against God. Caleb and Josue tried to calm the people by advising them to go forward and conquer the land, but they could not persuade them. *The rebellion*

Moses and Aaron prayed that God would spare the people in spite of this great sin. God heard their prayer. But the ten scouts, who, by their report, had caused the rebellion, were struck dead. Josue and Caleb had made a favorable report and they were spared. The Israelites, too, were punished for this rebellion. All who were over twenty years of age were condemned to linger in the desert until they died. Only Josue and Caleb were permitted to enter the Promised Land.

But the spirit of revolt continued. Some of the Israelites tried to enter Chanaan against God's command. When they saw that Moses would not lead them, they attempted to enter of their own accord. But God was not with them, and the Amalecites, who dwelt near the border, slew many of them and drove the rest back.

The leaders destroyed After this defeat the Israelites knew that they could not escape the punishment of God, and that they were doomed to wander in the desert until death. But some were still disobedient. Core, Dathan and Abiron, with two hundred and fifty leaders of the people, tried to perform the duties of the priests, but the earth opened up and swallowed them, with all their possessions. Others sought to injure Moses and Aaron, but they fled to the Tabernacle for safety. God then sent a plague to destroy all the rebels.

Now that the leaders of the revolt had been removed, peace was restored. To show the people that this peaceful spirit pleased Him, God caused Aaron's rod to bloom miraculously. This was to be to them a sign that Aaron's priesthood placed him above all leaders except Moses. After this miracle, the rod of Aaron was placed in the Ark of the Covenant.

3. THE ISRAELITES ARE CONDEMNED TO WANDER FORTY YEARS IN THE DESERT

The Israelites wandered about Cades, not far from the southern border of the Promised Land. During these wanderings, Miriam, the sister of Moses, died and was buried at Cades.

The Israelites at Cades

About this time the people complained because they were without water. Moses and Aaron went into the Tabernacle and fell flat on the ground and prayed for the people. God said to Moses, "Take the rod, and assemble the people together, thou and Aaron thy brother, and speak to the rock before them and it shall yield waters."

Moses felt that the people had tried God's patience too far. He doubted the mercy of God for just a moment, and struck the rock twice instead of speaking to it as God had commanded.

God was displeased with this lack of faith and because of it Moses was not permitted to enter the Promised Land.

Thirty-eight years had passed, and Moses knew that the time of exile was nearly over. God told him to move away from Cades and the desert of Seir, but not to engage in battle with the people of Edom, Moab, or Ammon. This was glad news for Moses. He asked the king of Edom to be allowed to pass through his territory, and promised to pay for everything the Israelites might use on their way. The king of Edom refused. So Moses marched around Edom and came to Mount Hor.

The end of the exile

WATER FLOWED AFTER MOSES STRUCK THE ROCK

The plague of serpents

When they reached Mount Hor the Lord commanded Moses to take Aaron and his son Eleazar up into the mountain and to strip Aaron of his priestly robes and clothe Eleazar with them. There Aaron died and the people mourned for thirty days.

The Israelites could not enter the Promised Land through the territory of the Edomites. For this reason they had to pass through the scorching Wilderness of Sin and the desert steppes east and north of it. The heat there was very great, and the people again complained against Moses for having brought them out of Egypt. They were sullen and impatient, but not rebellious. God punished them for this complaint by sending fiery serpents into their midst. The bite of the serpents was very painful and caused the death of many. Moses prayed to God for the afflicted people and God heard his prayer. He said to Moses, "Make a brazen serpent and set it up for a sign. Whoever, being struck, shall look on it shall live." Moses obeyed, and when those who were bitten looked upon the serpent of brass, their wounds were healed.

After this punishment the Israelites were more obedient. They traveled two hundred miles through the desert and steppes and entered the territory of the Amorrhites. Moses sent messengers to the king of the Amorrhites, asking permission to pass through his territory. Like the king of Edom, he refused, and sent his army to meet the Israelites. A battle was fought and the Israelites put them to flight. *The victories of the Israelites*

Next the Israelites marched forward through the land of the Amorrhites, taking possession of their capital and many of their towns. They then marched north and conquered the king of Basan.

Moses divided the territory east of the Jordan, which the Israelites had conquered, among the tribes of Gad and Ruben and the half tribe of Manasses. These three tribes had pleaded for this land, but had promised to cross the Jordan with the other Israelites to help conquer the land west of the river.

Moses knew that the time of his leadership had passed. He appointed Josue, who was of the tribe of Ephraim, to lead the people. Josue had been the faithful lieutenant of Moses. He had gone with him into the mountain when he received the first tablets of stone. He was also one of the twelve scouts sent *Moses appoints Josue his successor*

JOSUE IS APPOINTED LEADER BY MOSES

to explore the Promised Land. In the presence of Eleazar, the high priest, Moses placed his hands upon Josue, to show that from that time he was the civil and military leader of the Israelites. By God's command Eleazar was the high priest and leader in religious matters.

Death of Moses God foretold to Moses the time when he was to die. After blessing the Israelites, Moses went up alone to the top of Mount Nebo. From this mountain God showed him the Promised Land. When Moses saw it, he rejoiced. Here at the ripe old age of one hundred and twenty years, full of gratitude to God, he died. God's angels buried him, but the spot no one knows. God hid the grave of Moses from the Israelites for fear

MOUNT NEBO

they might take his body and adore it, for they were easily tempted to idolatry. The Israelites mourned for Moses for thirty days.

Before the Israelites crossed the Jordan, Balac, king of the Moabites, sent presents to a prophet named Balaam, who lived far away in Mesopotamia, and begged him to come and curse the Children of Israel. God spoke to Balaam and said, "Thou shalt not go with these men and thou shalt not curse this people, because it is blessed." So Balaam refused to go to the land of Moab with the messengers of King Balac.

The story of Balaam

But Balac was not discouraged. Again he sent messengers to Balaam begging him to come and curse the Israelites. This time God told Balaam to go with them and to do what He commanded him.

So Balaam saddled his ass and, with two of his servants, accompanied the messengers to the land of

Moab. As they went along, an angel with a drawn sword stood in their path. Balaam did not see him, but the ass did and ran into a field to get away from him. Balaam beat the ass and forced her to return to the road.

They went on a little farther and came to a place where the road ran between two huge rocks. The angel again stood in the way with sword drawn. The ass refused to go forward and, when Balaam beat her, she went to one side and crushed his foot against the rock. Balaam became very angry and started to beat the ass cruelly. The poor beast fell to the ground, and then a wonderful thing happened. The ass began to speak. She said to Balaam, "Why dost thou strike me? What have I done to thee?" "Because thou hast deserved it," answered Balaam. "If I had a sword, I would kill thee." The ass answered, "Am I not the beast upon which thou hast always ridden until now? Have I ever done anything like this to thee before?"

Then it was that Balaam saw the angel standing ready to kill him with the sword. He fell down on his face, and the angel said to him, "Why dost thou beat the ass? If she had not turned out of the way, I would have slain thee and she would have lived." Balaam replied, "I have sinned, not knowing that thou didst stand against me. And now if it please thee, I will return to my home." But the angel said, "Go with these men and see thou speak no other thing than I command thee."

The king came out to meet Balaam and brought him to a high place where there was a temple of Baal.

Down below they could see the camp of the Israelites. Sacrifices were offered to Baal and then Balaam stood up to curse the Israelites. He said, "Balac, king of the Moabites, hath brought me here to curse Israel, but how shall I curse him whom God hath not cursed?"

Balac was very angry at Balaam for not cursing the Israelites, but Balaam said, "Can I speak anything else except what the Lord commandeth?"

Three times did Balaam try to curse the Israelites, and each time the curse was turned into a blessing. He said, "How beautiful are thy tabernacles, O Jacob, and thy tents, O Israel. As woody valleys, as watered gardens near rivers, as tabernacles which the Lord hath pitched, as cedars by the waterside. He that blesseth thee shall also be blessed; he that curseth thee, shall be cursed."

Then Balac ordered Balaam to leave the land of Moab and to return to his own country. But Balaam prophesied before he left and said, "A Star shall rise out of Jacob and a scepter shall spring up from Israel. . . . Out of Jacob shall He come that shall rule."

THINGS TO KNOW AND TO DO

1. The Israelites Depart from Mount Sinai

1. What signal was given Moses when the march was to begin again?
2. Describe the preparation for the march.
3. Imagine you are trying to make the rebels remember God and tell what you would say.
4. What does this rebellion teach about bad company?

2. The Report of the Scouts Arouses Rebellion

1. Why did Moses send scouts into the Promised Land?
2. On what previous occasion did Moses choose Josue for an important task?
3. Repeat the report made by the scouts.

4. Why did God punish the scouts with sudden death?

5. How can we prepare for a happy death?

6. Compare the conduct of the scouts with that of Abraham.

7. Why does a liar prepare the way for his own destruction?

8. Why should we often make acts of Faith, Hope and Love?

9. Give a floor talk in which you show that the Israelites were an ungrateful people.

10. Tell of the sign God gave to restore peace.

11. Prove from this lesson that we can aid others by our prayers.

3. The Israelites Are Condemned to Wander Forty Years in the Desert

1. Why did the Israelites move from place to place after they reached Cades?

2. Locate Cades and trace the wanderings from this point.

3. Why can we say that the Israelites who entered the Promised Land were a new people?

4. How should Moses have acted when God commanded him to speak to the rock?

5. How did God punish Moses?

6. Make a list of the virtues which Moses practiced.

7. Show why we say the Brazen Serpent is a figure of Christ on the Cross.

8. Give a floor talk in which you explain God's mercy to the Israelites in the desert, describing the many times He forgave them.

9. Memorize the words which Balaam uttered instead of the required curse.

10. Write an essay in which you compare the life of Moses and that of Jesus Christ.

11. Give a floor talk. Prove that Moses was an historian, a priest, and a king.

12. Read "Moses" in "Old Testament Stories," by Rev. C. C. Martindale, S. J.

IV. JOSUE, THE COMMANDER OF THE ISRAELITES

1. THE LAND OF CHANAAN AND ITS PEOPLE

Chanaan, the land of promise, was bounded on the west by Phoenicia and the Mediterranean Sea; on the south, by the Brook of Egypt, the south end of the Dead Sea and the Arnon River. Arabia was on its eastern boundary, and to the north were the Lebanon Mountains and Phoenicia. *Physical character of Chanaan*

It was almost the center of the ancient world and was in the temperate zone. The Bible describes it as "a good land of brooks and of waters and of fountains, in the plains of which and the hills, deep rivers break out—a land of wheat and barley and vineyards, wherein fruit trees and pomegranates and olive yards grow—a land of oil and honey."

From north to south, it was about one hundred and fifty miles long. Its width from east to west was about eighty miles—forty miles on each side of the Jordan River. Altogether, it was about as large as the state of Maryland.

The land east of the Jordan is a great plateau two thousand feet above sea level. Three rivers, the Arnon, the Jaboc, and the Yarmuk, run at right angles to the Jordan and divide the country into three sections. The northern section, between the Yarmuk and the Lebanon Mountains, is a great plain, about fifty miles long and twenty miles wide. In the middle section there are forest-clad hills rich in pasturage. The southern section is bleak, with very little vegetation. *Rivers and plains*

THE JORDAN RIVER

The region east of the Jordan was better suited than that to the west for the raising of flocks and herds.

Along the coast of the Mediterranean runs an unbroken plain from Gaza to Mount Carmel. This plain is about eighty miles long. In the south it is twenty miles wide, but grows narrower to the north. It is very fertile country, though in some places the streams which run through it create marshes.

Fertility and vegetation Between this plain and the Jordan River is a plateau about twenty-five miles wide. Like the plateau on the east of the Jordan, it is more fertile in the north than in the south, where it is bleak and almost barren. However, olives grow here in abundance, and the pine and the laurel are to be found. There is a wilderness just west of the Jordan. Going north, the land becomes more fertile. Here, oranges are grown and forests cover the hills. Still farther north, the vegetation becomes even more plentiful. The hills are clothed with forests of oak, maple, and poplar, and wild flowers grow abundantly. Here we find the Plain of Esdrelon and Mount Thabor, and four miles to the south-west is a mountain called Little Hermon.

The Jordan valley extends from the foot of Mount Hermon to the southern shore of

THE INHABITANTS OF THE LAND OF CHANAAN

the Dead Sea. At the base of Mount Hermon this valley is a thousand feet above sea level, but by the time it reaches the Dead Sea, it has fallen to a thousand, two hundred and ninety-two feet below sea level.

Chains of mountains run practically the whole length of the country—one to the west of the Jordan, the other to the east. West of each mountain chain is a valley, one valley being on the coast of the Mediterranean, the other along the Jordan River.

Mountains

Mount Carmel is the only mountain of importance

A VIEW OF MOUNT HERMON

along the coast. At its highest point, it is one thousand, seven hundred and fifty feet above sea level. West of the Jordan are Mount Hebron, three thousand feet above sea level; Mount Olivet, two thousand, six hundred feet; Mount Hebal and Mount Garizim, each three thousand feet; and Little Hermon and Mount Thabor, each one thousand nine hundred feet.

The Jordan is the most important river in the land. At some places it is one hundred and eighty feet wide and twelve feet deep. It runs from north to south, to the lakes of Merom and Genesareth, and finally empties into the Dead Sea. Its actual course is two hundred and sixty miles long.

Seasons There are two seasons in Chanaan—the rainy season, which lasts from October to May, and the dry season, which extends through the rest of the year.

The rainfall is the greatest during January and February. August is the hottest month of the year, February the coldest. The highest temperature in the dry season is one hundred and ten degrees. Freezing weather is rare, though there is an occasional fall of snow. The flowers begin to bloom and the trees to bud in the middle of April, about six weeks before the end of the rainy season.

Of all the different tribes of people who lived in the Land of Chanaan when Josue led the Jews across the Jordan, none was more powerful than the Philistines. Centuries before, they had lived on the Island of Crete in the Mediterranean Sea. There they had been a great sea power, with large fleets of vessels, by means of which they held sway over the entire Mediterranean and Aegean Seas. Under the mighty King Minos they reached the height of their power. *The inhabitants of Chanaan*

The Philistines

But the time arrived when their enemies became strong enough to defeat them and to destroy their empire. It was then that they set out to find new homes for themselves. They joined with other conquered nations and, landing in Chanaan, they advanced on Egypt with the purpose of conquering that great nation.

The Egyptians defeated them and scattered their forces. Deserted by their allies, the Cretans decided to remain in Chanaan. They settled on the coast in the southern part of the country.

Soon they began to wage war on the tribes to the north and to the east. Their soldiers were well

EXAMPLES OF CRETAN POTTERY

trained, and their weapons were superior to those of their enemies, being made of iron, instead of bronze.

This is the nation that we meet in the Bible under the name of Philistines and from which the Promised Land received the name Palestine. They brought with them into the Land of Chanaan the arts and the crafts which they had learned in Crete. They were a cultured people, but they worshiped idols.

Though the Philistines were to cause God's Chosen People much trouble and suffering, they were also to teach them many useful lessons. From the Philistines the Israelites learned the art of working in iron. It also seems likely that from them they learned how to use the alphabet. The Israelites had brought from Egypt a knowledge of picture writing, but they soon discovered that the script used by the Philistines was better suited for writing down the wonderful story of how God had chosen them and watched over them. Following the example of the Philistines, the Israelites learned to form an alphabet of their own.

A SCULPTURE SHOWING PHILISTINES

The Syrians were a nomad people who had wan- **The Syrians**
dered from Arabia and made settlements throughout
Mesopotamia. They had come as far south as Damascus, where they established a kingdom. They became
very strong and later on caused the Israelites much
trouble.

The Moabites take their name from Moab, a son of **The Moabites**
Lot, who, after the destruction of Sodom and Gomorrha, settled in the country bordering on the east coast
of the Dead Sea. The territory that he chose for
himself and his descendants was at first fifty miles
long and thirty miles wide. It is a plateau which rises
about forty-three hundred feet above the Dead Sea.
Shortly before the Israelites entered the Promised
Land, the Moabites had been driven out of the northern portion of their country by the Amorrhites. The
Moabites were hostile to the Children of Israel, and it

was only after many years that peace was made with them.

The Edomites

The Edomites, also known as the Idumaeans, lived south of the Dead Sea and the land of Moab. They were the descendants of Esau. The enmity between the Israelites and the Edomites was very bitter.

The Edomites were idolaters and worshiped their false gods on the tops of high hills which were called "High Places." They were a source of temptation to the Israelites and led many of them away from the worship of the one true God. The prophets and the holy men often preached against the Edomites and threatened them with destruction. "Thou art exceeding contemptible," said the prophet Abdias to the Edomites. "The pride of thy heart hath lifted thee up, who dwellest in the clefts of the rocks, and settest up thy throne on high, and sayest in thy heart, 'Who shall bring me down to the ground?' 'Though thou be exalted as an eagle, and though thou set thy nest among the stars, thence will I bring thee down,' saith the Lord. 'I shall destroy the wise out of Edom, and understanding out of the mount of Esau. There shall be no remains of the house of Esau, for the Lord hath spoken.'"

The Amorrhites

The Amorrhites were descendants of Chanaan. They first dwelt west of the Jordan, but later crossed to the east and drove the Moabites out of their territory between the Jaboc and the Arnon. Here they formed two kingdoms: the northern, Basan, with Edrai its capital, and Og its king; and the southern, Galaad, with Hesebon its capital, and Sehon its king. The Israelites were commissioned by God to destroy them. God said, "Thou shalt suffer none at all to live, but shalt kill them with the edge of the sword, lest they teach thee to do all the abominations which they have done to their God, and thou shouldst sin against the Lord, thy God."

2. JOSUE CONQUERS THE LAND FOR THE ISRAELITES

Such was the country which was to become the home **Weapons** of the Israelites after forty years of wandering in the desert. They had to conquer the land and drive out the inhabitants. To do so, they used different kinds of weapons. They had the short, pointed sword, the spear, the bow and arrow, and the sling. For armor, the Israelites had shields and helmets made of leather or bronze. To besiege a city, they hammered with large beams against its gates and walls. Sometimes in order to capture a city they dug tunnels under its walls, or they threw torches over the walls, and set the city afire. Sometimes they coaxed the people out into the open, where they engaged them in hand-to-hand battle.

Before Josue crossed the Jordan, he sent two spies **Josue's** to view the city of Jericho and the land in its neighbor- **spies are** **saved** hood. He wished to learn the strength of the city before he attacked it. The spies were recognized and reported to the king. They were living in Jericho at the home of a woman named Rahab. When she heard that the king was sending his soldiers after the men

RAHAB SAVES THE TWO SPIES

to arrest them, she hid them on the roof of her house, under some stalks of flax that were spread out to dry.

The king's soldiers sought them in vain. When the soldiers had gone, Rahab made the spies promise that when the city was taken they would spare her and her relatives. She, in turn, agreed to display a scarlet cord in her window as a sign to Josue that the city was ready to fall. She then let the spies down from the window by means of a rope and they fled to the mountains, where they stayed for three days. Then they crossed the Jordan and rejoined Josue. The spies reported to Josue that there would be no trouble in conquering the city, because the people were overcome by fear even at the thought of the attack.

After three days, at God's command, Josue ordered the priests to carry the Ark of the Covenant into the Jordan. As soon as they had set foot on the water, the course of the river stopped, and a dry path appeared. The priests carried the Ark to the middle of the river and remained standing there until all the Israelites had passed over.

Josue then appointed one man from every tribe to return to the Jordan, and to bring

JEWISH ARMS

back with him a large stone from the river bed. With these stones the Israelites built in the middle of the river a monument to their miraculous passage. Twelve other stones Josue likewise ordered set up in the river where the Ark stood. After the monument was completed, Josue commanded the priests to carry the Ark out of the river bed. As soon as they had done so, the river began once more to take its natural course.

On the western bank of the river, at a place called **The fall of Jericho** Galgal, the Israelites pitched their camp. While in camp they celebrated the Feast of the Passover. The manna which God had provided for the Israelites every day during their long wanderings in the desert now ceased to fall. Their journey was ended.

Jericho was a strong city, but during the night an

THE ARK OF THE COVENANT IS CARRIED THROUGH A DRY PATH IN THE
JORDAN

angel of the Lord with a drawn sword had appeared
to Josue and had given him minute instructions as to
how it was to be taken. Josue sent forty thousand
fighting men to march around the walls of the city
every day for six days. On the seventh day, the
soldiers, the priests carrying the Ark of the Covenant,
and all the Israelites marched around the walls seven
times. At the end of the seventh trip, Josue gave the
command, "Shout, for the Lord hath delivered the city
to you." The seven trumpets used at the jubilee
sounded a continuous blast, the people gave a mighty
shout, and the walls fell. Then the soldiers rushed

THE PRIESTS BLOW THEIR TRUMPETS AND THE WALLS OF JERICHO FALL

into the city from wherever they stood and killed all the inhabitants except Rahab and her family.

Josue next marched against Hai, a city northwest of Jericho. As soon as the people of this town saw his forces, they rushed upon them and put the Israelites to rout. God revealed to Josue that the cause of the defeat was the disobedience of one of his men. They cast lots to discover the guilty man. It was found to be Achan, who had retained some of the plunder of Jericho for himself, after God had commanded that all should be given to the Tabernacle. Achan was punished with death. God then said to Josue, ''Fear not, nor be dismayed; behold I have delivered into thy hand the king of Hai.''

Josue's first campaign

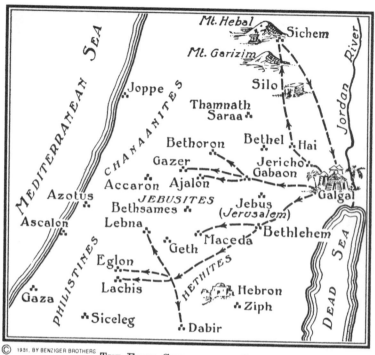

© 1931, BY BENZIGER BROTHERS THE FIRST CAMPAIGNS OF JOSUE

In his second attack, Josue resorted to strategy. He sent five thousand men to lie in ambush back of the city. With another five thousand he approached the gates. As before, the soldiers of Hai rushed forth upon them, and the Israelites, pretending to flee, tricked them into pursuing them far from the city walls. The army in ambush then closed in from the rear, burnt the city, and slew all the people.

Second campaign All the people of Chanaan were now in great fear. Five cities united to attack Josue. The king of Jerusalem was their leader. Because the city of Gabaon would not join their league but made a treaty with

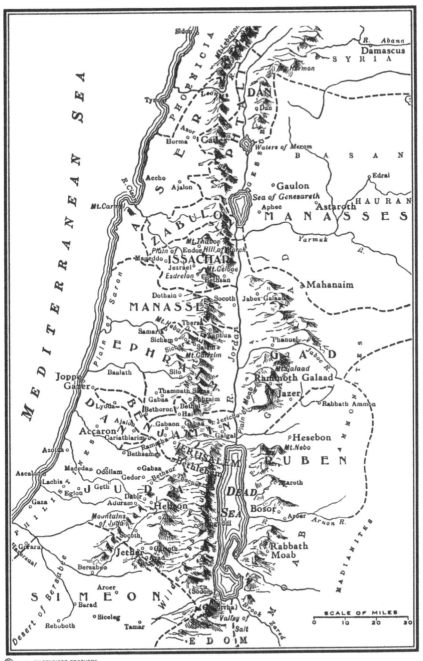

THE ALLOTMENT OF CHANAAN TO THE TWELVE TRIBES OF ISRAEL

151

Josue, they decided to punish it. Josue hastened by night to its assistance, and fell upon the enemy's camp. There was a great slaughter, the Lord also killing many with large hailstones. As Josue feared nightfall would end the battle before complete victory, with great confidence in God, he cried out, "Move not, O sun, toward Gabaon, nor thou, O moon, toward the valley of Ajalon." God answered his prayer and the sun and moon stood still till Josue won the victory. The five kings took refuge in a cave and Josue slew them. By this and other victories he gained control of the southern half of Chanaan.

Third campaign The cities in the north of Chanaan likewise united their forces against Josue. The king of Asor was their leader. But God was with Josue, who marched against their armies and defeated them. He followed the armies until they were nearly all destroyed. Then he returned and took their cities for the Israelites.

The division of the land After the third campaign Josue divided the land west of the Jordan among the tribes. According to the law, certain cities and their suburbs among all the tribes were given to the priests and the Levites. The three tribes whose land was across the river went back to the east shore of the Jordan. They received Josue's blessing before they left. Josue warned the other tribes of the danger of falling into idolatry. The Tabernacle was placed in Silo. Josue set a stone under an oak tree, which stood in the Court of the Tabernacle, to remind them of his parting words.

Josue's last days Josue had ever been God's faithful and obedient servant. He was a great military leader, who led his soldiers to victory in every battle. Now he divided the spoils among them and settled down to a peaceful life at Thamnath Saraa for the rest of his days. He assembled the people at Sichem and exhorted them to observe the law and to avoid idolatry. He died at the age of one hundred and ten years. Eleazar also died shortly afterwards and was succeeded as high priest by his son Phinees. The bones of Joseph which the Israelites had brought from Egypt were buried at Sichem in Jacob's field.

THINGS TO KNOW AND TO DO

1. THE LAND OF CHANAAN AND ITS PEOPLE

1. Why was the new home of the Israelites called Chanaan? Palestine? Holy Land? Promised Land? "Land flowing with milk and honey"?

2. Locate this country on the map.

3. Why were the natural boundaries of the country helpful to the Israelites in the practice of their religion?

4. Suppose you had been a boy or girl who entered the Promised Land with the Israelites. Write a letter to a little friend and tell him about the strange people and the wonderful country.

5. What people would you meet there today?

2. JOSUE CONQUERS THE LAND FOR THE ISRAELITES

1. Relate what you know about Josue.

2. What qualities made him a good leader of the Israelites?

3. Why did God command the Israelites to destroy the people of Palestine?

4. Imagine the feelings of the Israelites as they entered Palestine. Write an essay entitled, "Home at Last."

5. Draw a map of Chanaan and locate the territories of the tribes.

6. How does God's constant watchfulness over the Israelites in the desert teach us always to trust in Him?

7. Write a description of a battle fought by the Israelites.

V. THE ISRAELITES IN THE PROMISED LAND

1. Judges Rule Over the Israelites

The time of the Judges
When the Israelites took possession of their new country, they adopted a very simple manner of life. They did not have one king or ruler over all the people. Each tribe or family was independent and had its own head. The government was patriarchal.

The Israelites now began to enjoy a life of ease and prosperity. They preferred this to the hardships and dangers of war. But too much ease weakened their bodies, and they neglected to train themselves in the art of warfare. Some of the Israelites married their pagan neighbors, and in time many of them became idolaters. The people forgot that God had commanded them to conquer all the territory and to drive out the pagan inhabitants.

God punished the Israelites from time to time by permitting their enemies to make war upon them. The leaders of the Israelites during these wars were men who kept their bodies strong by hard discipline. When some village was threatened, they aroused the people against their enemy and led them in battle. When several tribes had a common enemy, they often chose, under the direction of God, one man to lead their armies. This leader was usually the man who showed the greatest strength and courage, and who could make the other leaders obey him. Such a military leader was called a Judge.

Usually Judges had power to rule only during the time of trouble. When the trouble was over, their power was taken away from them and given back to the heads of the tribes.

The Israelites were ruled by Judges during several centuries. The Bible gives the names of fifteen Judges, the most famous of whom were Debbora, Gedeon, Samson, and Samuel.

God permitted different nations to make war upon the Israelites. Their principal enemies were the Moabites, the unconquered Hittites, or Chanaanites, the Madianites, the Ammonites, and the Philistines.

2. Gedeon Leads His People to Victory

Gedeon first became a hero among the people be- **Gedeon saves the Israelites** cause he had dared to overthrow the altar which his father had built to the false god Baal, and to erect an altar to the true God in its place.

God allowed the Madianites to make war upon the Israelites for seven years. These people laid waste the territory belonging to the tribe of Gad. They also crossed the Jordan River and settled in the valleys which belonged to the tribes of Issachar and Manasses. There they pitched their tents and destroyed the fields of the Israelites. The Israelites were humbled and cried to the Lord for help against the enemy.

God heard their cries and called Gedeon to lead His Chosen People against the invaders. An angel of the Lord appeared to Gedeon and said to him, "The Lord is with thee, O most valiant of men." He told Gedeon that he was to save the Israelites from the hands of the Madianites.

Before Gedeon undertook to lead the army of the Israelites against the enemy, he asked a sign of God. He said to God, "Show me by a sign that Thou wishest to save Israel by my hand. I will put this fleece of wool on the floor. If there be dew on the fleece only, and all the ground beside be dry, I shall know that Thou wilt deliver Israel by my hand."

The Lord granted Gedeon's request. The next morning, Gedeon rose before dawn and, when he picked up the fleece and wrung it, he filled a vessel with the dew. But the ground around it was dry.

Gedeon said again to God, "Be not angry with me if I seek another sign in the fleece. I pray that the fleece only be dry and all the ground wet with dew."

God did that night as Gedeon requested. In the morning, the fleece was dry, while all the ground was wet.

Full of confidence, Gedeon set out to raise an army for the protection of the Israelites. In a short time he gathered about him thirty-two thousand men. But lest the Israelites be tempted to trust too much in their own strength and to forget that God was their Deliverer, the Lord told Gedeon to choose from among them only three hundred men. First, Gedeon persuaded twenty-two thousand to return home. The remaining ten thousand he ordered to drink from the river. At the command of God he watched to see which way they drank the water, and chose those who gathered up water in their hands and drank it from their palms. Only three hundred of them drank in this manner.

With these three hundred men Gedeon descended one night into the Valley of Esdrelon, where the Madianites and their allies were asleep in their tents. He divided his force into three companies and stationed them at different points about the enemy. Every one of Gedeon's soldiers had a trumpet and a pitcher in which he carried a lamp. At midnight Gedeon blew his trumpet as a signal. The three hundred also blew their trumpets, broke their pitchers, showed their lamps and shouted, "The sword of the Lord and of Gedeon!" So great was the din that the Madianites thought they were surrounded by a powerful army and fled away, slaying one another in their panic. Gedeon pursued them until the last of them was slain.

At this time, the Israelites began to say among themselves that it would be better for them if they had a king to rule over them. The nations around them all had kings, and although there was much jealousy among the different tribes, they thought that a king would unite them and make it possible for them to conquer their enemies once for all and bring back peace into the land. They forgot that God was their King and that, if they were faithful to Him, they would be a united people. They tried to make Gedeon their king, but he said to them, "I will not rule over you, neither shall my son rule over you, but the Lord shall rule over you."

Gedeon refuses to be made king

THE SOLDIERS OF GEDEON SURPRISE THE MADIANITES

3. SAMSON BAFFLES THE ENEMIES OF THE ISRAELITES BY HIS DARING EXPLOITS

After the death of Gedeon, the Israelites again fell into idolatry. They neglected to go to Silo on the great feasts and worship at the Tabernacle. God punished them by adding the Philistines to their enemies. For forty years the Philistines waged war upon them. They invaded the territory of the Israelites and took possession of the cities which belonged to the tribes of Juda, Dan, and Benjamin.

Samson's birth Samson was born at Saraa at the time of the Philistine troubles. An angel foretold his birth, and commanded the parents not to cut the hair of their child, nor permit him to drink wine or other strong drink.

Samson was dedicated by his parents to the service of God, Who had destined him to be a scourge to the Philistines. Unlike the other Judges, he had no army, but depended on his own wonderful strength. He was so strong that, once, when he was a small boy and a young lion attacked him, he seized it in both hands and tore it apart.

Samson began his campaign against the Philistines in a strange way. He caught three hundred foxes, tied their tails together and fastened lighted torches to them. Then he set the foxes loose in the fields of the Philistines. All the corn in the fields, all the grapes in the vineyards and all the olives on the trees were burned. The Philistines in revenge burned his father-in-law's house, and Samson's wife perished in the flames. Then Samson went into the city nearby and, after putting to death a large number of the inhabitants, fled into the territory of the tribe of Juda. *He sets fire to the vineyards*

The Philistines sent an army to capture him. The men of Juda, fearing the Philistines, bound Samson and brought him to the enemy. When Samson was brought into the camp of the Philistines, he broke the cords with which he was bound, took the jawbone of an ass which lay on the ground, and with it killed a thousand of the Philistines, while the rest fled in fear. *He slays the Philistines*

One night Samson slept in Gaza, a Philistine city. The Philistine guards surrounded the city and closed the gates so that he could not escape. But he rose up, took the gates of the city with their posts and bolts, put them on his shoulders and carried them to the top of a neighboring hill. *Samson carries away the gates of the city*

SAMSON BREAKS THE PILLARS OF THE BANQUET HALL

Dalila betrays Samson The secret of Samson's great strength was in his long hair. One day he told Dalila, a Philistine woman, that if his hair were cut, his strength would leave him. At night while he was asleep, Dalila cut his hair and called in the soldiers to capture him. The soldiers put out his eyes and cast him into prison, in the city of Gaza.

Samson destroys the banquet hall Some time after this, a great feast was held in the city. Several thousand people were gathered in the banquet hall. Samson was brought from the prison so that the guests might amuse themselves by making sport of him.

By this time, his hair had grown long again, but he

was blind. When he entered the banquet hall, he told
the boy who was leading him to place him near the
pillars that supported the building, that he might lean
against them and rest. Then, calling upon the Lord
to restore to him his former strength, Samson took
both pillars in his hands and shook them. The house
fell, and Samson, the princes of the Philistines, and a
great number of people were killed.

4. Samuel, the Last and Greatest Judge of the Israelites

One day, when Heli, the high priest, was sitting be- The
fore the door of the Tabernacle in Silo, a woman ap- parents
proached and, kneeling down, began to pray fervently of Samuel
to the Lord. Her name was Anna and she was the wife
of Elcana. As she prayed, she began to weep as though
her heart would break. And she made a vow, saying,
"O Lord of Hosts, if Thou wilt look down on the affliction of Thy servant, and wilt be mindful of me and
give me a son, I will give him to the Lord all the days
of his life." Heli thought she was drunk and rebuked
her. She said, "Not so, my lord, I have drunk neither
wine nor strong drink; but I am a very unhappy
woman. For many years I have prayed to the Lord
to send me a son, but He hath not answered me."

Heli said to her, "Go in peace, and the God of Israel
grant thee thy petition."

Anna returned to her home, and it came to pass that The birth
a son was born to her. While he was still an infant, of Samuel
his parents took him to Silo and offered him to Heli,
the high priest. Anna said, "I am that woman who

stood before thee here, praying to the Lord. For this child did I pray, and the Lord hath granted my petition. Therefore I have lent him to the Lord all the days of his life."

Then Elcana and Anna returned to their home, but the child was left behind in the care of the high priest. He was called Samuel, and he grew up in the Tabernacle. He learned all about the divine services and how to minister to Heli.

Among the priests who took part in the divine worship in the Tabernacle were the two sons of Heli, whose names were Ophni and Phinees. They were wicked men. They robbed the people who came to offer sacrifice. They used their holy office to make themselves rich. Heli knew of the wickedness of his sons, but, though he reproved them from time to time, he did not drive them out of the Tabernacle and punish them as they deserved to be punished. For this reason, God was displeased with Heli.

God calls Samuel One night while Heli and Samuel were sleeping in the Tabernacle, the boy heard a voice calling "Samuel, Samuel." The boy rose, ran to Heli, and said, "Here I am, for thou didst call me." But Heli said to Samuel, "I did not call. Go back and sleep." A second time the voice called, and again Samuel ran to Heli, thinking it was the high priest who had called him. Heli said to Samuel, "If the voice calleth again, say: 'Speak, Lord, for Thy servant heareth.'" When Samuel heard the voice calling him the third time, he said, "Speak Lord, for Thy servant heareth." Then the Lord spoke to Samuel and told him of the punish-

THE LORD SPEAKS TO SAMUEL

ment which He was about to inflict upon Heli for his negligence, and upon Heli's sons for their sins.

The next day Heli asked Samuel what the Lord had said to him. Samuel told him all the words of the voice from Heaven and did not hide anything.

When Samuel grew to manhood, the Lord's words **The pun-** to him were fulfilled. The Philistines gained more **ishment** and more of the land of the Israelites. In despair, **and his** the Israelites sent to Silo for the Ark of the Covenant. **sons** They hoped that by carrying the Ark into battle with them they might win the victory. The Ark was brought to them, and the two sons of Heli went with it. The shouts of the soldiers, when they saw the Ark, frightened the Philistines for a time. But they soon

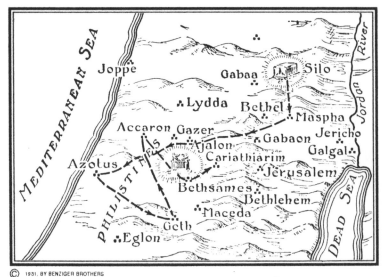

THE JOURNEYS OF THE ARK AMONG THE PHILISTINES

recovered from their fright and, attacking the Israelites, they defeated them again. The two sons of Heli were slain in this battle and the Ark of the Covenant was captured by the Philistines. This news was brought to Heli, now old and blind. When he heard it, he fell from his chair, and died. The two sons were killed for their crimes and the father died in punishment for his failure to correct them.

The Ark of the Covenant among the Philistines   The Philistines took the Ark of the Covenant to Azotus, one of their cities near the sea. They placed it in the temple of Dagon, their god. The next day they found the statue of Dagon on its face before the Ark. They set it up again, but the next morning it was again found on the ground, with the head and hands of the idol broken off. The city was stricken with **a**

plague of mice which caused the death of many of the people.

The chiefs of the Philistines decided to move the Ark from one city to another, but the people of all the cities to which the Ark was taken were afflicted with painful boils. The city of Accaron would not allow the Ark to be placed within its walls. After several months, the Philistines decided to return the Ark to the Israelites. Placing it on a cart, they laid beside it ten vessels of gold as an offering to take away the guilt of their crime. Two oxen which had never been yoked were hitched to the cart. The oxen, without a guide, left the city of Accaron and carried the Ark north to Bethsames, where they stopped in the fields of a priest. The priest broke up the wood of the cart, and, piling it on a stone in his field, offered the oxen as a sacrifice of thanksgiving for the return of the Ark to the Israelites.

Some of the people of the city, prompted by curiosity, raised the coverings which were over the Ark. Fifty thousand died in punishment for their act of irreverence. The rest were frightened and they sent the Ark to Cariathiarim, a city known for its holiness.

After the capture of the Ark, Samuel had lived at Rama. The attacks of Samson and the punishments that followed the capture of the Ark had put fear into the hearts of the Philistines. Samuel thought it was now time to wage war against them. He preached to the people and urged them to return to the worship of God. He gathered an army at Masphath and of-

Samuel attacks the Philistines

fered sacrifice to God to obtain victory. In the midst of the sacrifice the Philistines began battle. God was with Samuel. The Philistines were frightened by an awful storm and were defeated by the Israelites.

THINGS TO KNOW AND TO DO

1. JUDGES RULE OVER THE ISRAELITES

1. Why did God allow the enemies of the Israelites to conquer them from time to time?

2. Give a floor talk in which you show that it is wise to avoid bad company.

3. Why was God always so willing to help the Israelites?

2. GEDEON LEADS HIS PEOPLE TO VICTORY

1. Why could Gedeon hope for victory over the enemy of his people?

2. What does Gedeon's victory over the Madianites teach you?

3. Upon whom could you call in time of need?

3. SAMSON BAFFLES THE ENEMIES OF THE ISRAELITES BY HIS DARING EXPLOITS

1. Mention the things in Samson's life that show he was chosen from childhood to be the friend of God.

2. In what was Samson's manner of defending his people different from that of the other Judges?

4. SAMUEL, THE LAST AND GREATEST JUDGE OF THE ISRAELITES

1. Contrast the characters of Samuel and the sons of Heli.

2. Write an essay, showing how God proved His power against the Philistines as well as to the Jews.

3. "Here I am, for thou didst call me." What do these words of Samuel reveal about his character?

4. Follow on the map the journey of the Ark of the Covenant.

5. Why did evil come to the pagans as long as they kept the Ark of the Covenant?

PREVIEW

Unit Four

HOW GOD'S CHOSEN PEOPLE LIVED UNDER
THEIR KINGS

The people wanted a king to rule over them. In this Unit we shall see how God answered their prayers and sent Samuel to anoint Saul king of Israel. But Saul sinned, and the kingdom was taken away from him and given to David. We shall see how the nation became great under David and Solomon, his son. The Temple is built in Jerusalem and becomes the great means of holding the people together and keeping them mindful of God's promise.

But Solomon was not faithful to God all the days of his life. We shall see how he sinned and how God punished him by allowing his kingdom to decline.

We shall learn how, after the death of Solomon, two kingdoms grew up—the Kingdom of Juda and the Kingdom of Israel. Civil war follows and the people turn away from the worship of the one true God. We shall learn how God in His mercy sent holy men to preach to them and to restore their hope in the Redeemer Who was to come.

Unit Four

HOW GOD'S CHOSEN PEOPLE LIVED UNDER THEIR KINGS

Unit Four

HOW GOD'S CHOSEN PEOPLE LIVED
UNDER THEIR KINGS

I. SAUL, THE FIRST KING OF THE ISRAELITES

1. Saul Is Anointed King by Samuel

The Israelites were not content with the rule of the Judges. They longed to be united under one leader— a king—like the other nations around them. In the time of Samuel, the people became very restless and insisted that he appoint a king to rule over them. In vain did Samuel remind them that God was their King. They would not listen to him. They wanted a human king to lead them to a final victory over the Chanaanites and the Philistines. They thought a human king would prevent civil war and stop them from robbing one another, while he kept the neighboring enemies at a distance. Moreover, though Samuel was a good ruler and governed them well, they were afraid that his sons, who were weak men, would not continue in the footsteps of their father. *Israel cries for a king*

Samuel tried to reason with them. He showed them that they would have to suffer the hardships of taxation for the support of a king—that soldiers must be supplied for a standing army. In order to be a united nation, it was only necessary for them to obey God's *Samuel's advice*

173

command—to worship only at the Tabernacle as the Law of Moses commanded. If their neighbors made war upon them, it was a punishment for their sins and, above all, for their failure to worship at the Tabernacle. Samuel urged them to give up their desire for a king and promised them that the wars would come to an end. By seeking to have a king, they were sinning against the will of God.

God gives the Israelites a king

The people did not heed Samuel. They prayed to God to give them a king, and finally God listened to their prayers and yielded to their desires. In order to bring them back to His worship and to prevent their worshiping false gods, He gave them a human king. He promised them that they would be a great nation under their king as long as they were faithful to Him. The day would come, however, when the Israelites would realize the difference between the cruel tyranny of human kings and the kind and merciful guidance of the divine King.

Samuel anoints Saul

The man whom God chose to be the first king of the Israelites belonged to the tribe of Benjamin. His name was Saul, and he lived in the city of Gabaa. One day Saul was searching for some asses that belonged to his father and that had wandered away. Hearing that Samuel was at Ramatha, he and his servant went into the city to ask Samuel where he might find his father's lost animals. They found Samuel at the gates of the city.

No sooner had Samuel laid his eyes on Saul than the Lord said to him, "Behold the man of whom I spoke to thee. This man shall rule over My people."

captain of Saul's army. He and Jonathan trained the army, and with it Saul drove back his enemies, the Moabites, the Ammonites, and the Syrians.

The Amalecites were annoying the Jews in the south, and Saul was sent by God to make war upon them in their own country and to destroy them and their possessions. Saul won a great victory over the Amalecites, but he did not obey God completely. He took for himself the best of their flocks and their ornaments. He spared their king in spite of God's command.

Samuel reproved Saul for his disobedience, but Saul laid the blame on the people. He was willing to offer the plunder in sacrifice, but God had not asked for sacrifice. He had asked for obedience.

"Doth the Lord desire holocausts and victims," asked Samuel, "and not rather that the voice of the Lord should be obeyed? For obedience is better than sacrifices. . . . Therefore, as thou hast rejected the word of the Lord, the Lord hath also rejected thee from being king." Saul's disobedience was soon punished.

God sent Samuel to Bethlehem to offer sacrifice and to seek out and anoint the man who was to succeed Saul as king. Samuel went to the home of a man called Isai and called him and his sons to the sacrifice. After the sacrifice Samuel asked Isai whether or not all his sons were present. All were there but the youngest, who was in the fields tending the flocks. His name was David. At Samuel's command, David was brought to him.

A new king is anointed

DAVID IS CALLED TO MEET SAMUEL

When David came in, Samuel saw that he was ruddy and beautiful to behold. He had a strong face and was a noble looking boy. The Lord said to Samuel, "Arise and anoint him, for this is he."

Then Samuel took a horn of oil and anointed David in the presence of his family, and the Spirit of the Lord came upon David from that day forward.

David in the palace of the king Saul had now built for himself a royal palace. Four sons and two daughters lived in the palace with him. But neither the palace nor the many victories he had won could make Saul happy. He knew that the kingly office would pass from his family and he became gloomy and sad. One day Saul heard that there was a young man at Bethlehem who played the harp excellently. The young harpist was David. Saul sent for David to entertain him and to cheer him. When Saul saw David and heard the sweet music he played on the harp, he was pleased and made him his armor-bearer. He did not know that David had been anointed to succeed him as king.

3. DAVID SLAYS GOLIATH

Again the Philistines sent their army to attack Saul. The Israelites went forth and met them in the Valley of Terebinth. The Philistines stood on a mountain on one side, and the Israelites stood on a mountain on the other side, and the valley lay between them. A man came out from the camp of the Philistines whose name was Goliath. He was a giant and his height was over nine feet. On his head was a helmet of brass, and he was clothed with a heavy coat of mail. Greaves of brass covered his legs and a buckler of brass covered his shoulders. The staff of his spear was like a weaver's beam.

The
Philis-
tines
again

Goliath came into the valley and his armor-bearer went before him. Standing, he cried out, "I am a Philistine and you are the servants of Saul. Choose out a man of you and let him come down and fight me hand to hand. If he kills me, we will be servants to you; if I kill him, you shall serve us."

When Saul and his army beheld Goliath and heard his challenge, they were filled with despair and were greatly afraid. No soldier was found who was brave enough to fight Goliath, even though Saul had offered

THE VALLEY OF TEREBINTH

his daughter in marriage to anyone who should slay him.

One day David's father sent him to the camp with food for his brothers, who were in the king's army. While he was there, Goliath came out into the valley between the camps and repeated his challenge. David made up his mind to fight Goliath. He told his brothers, and they laughed at him. His oldest brother was angry, because he thought it was pride that led David to think he could kill Goliath.

Saul said to David, "Thou art not able to fight against this Philistine, for thou art but a boy, and he is a warrior from his youth." David answered Saul, "I have killed a lion and a bear, and this Philistine shall be as one of them. I will go and take away the reproach of the people."

Saul said to David, "Go, and the Lord be with thee."

A Shot from David's Sling Hits Goliath

Saul dressed David in his own armor. He put a helmet of brass on his head and armed him with a coat of mail. David said to Saul, "I cannot go dressed this way, for I am not used to it." He laid the **armor** aside, took a sling and five smooth stones, and went forth to meet the Philistine.

When Goliath saw David, he made fun of him and cursed him. He said, "Come to me and I will give thy flesh to the birds of the air."

David answered the Philistine, "Thou comest to me with a sword and with a shield and with a spear. But I come to thee in the name of the God of Israel. This day I will slay thee and take thy head from thee. The Philistine shall know that there is a God in Israel."

David took his sling and whirled a stone at Goliath. The stone struck the giant in the forehead and he fell to the ground stunned. David ran up, took Goliath's sword, and cut off his head. The rest of the Philistines fled. The Israelites pursued them and killed many of them.

When the rest of the soldiers returned from the pursuit of the Philistines, the people sang the praises of David. He was the nation's hero. Everywhere could be heard the cry, "Saul has killed his thousands but David his tens of thousands." This caused Saul to become very jealous of David.

David and Jonathan Jonathan, the son of Saul, was a noble young prince and sought in every way to do the will of God. He was very dear to his father.

David and Jonathan became great friends. Day by day they lived together in the palace and grew to love each other very dearly. The soul of Jonathan was knit with the soul of David, and Jonathan loved David as his very self.

They swore that they would always be loyal to each other. Jonathan took off his coat with which he was clothed and gave it to David, with the rest of his royal garments, even his sword and his bow and his girdle, as a sign of his undying friendship.

4. SAUL PERSECUTES DAVID

Saul plots the murder of David The next day Saul sat in his room in the palace brooding as usual, his mind filled with dark thoughts. David was summoned to play soothing music on his harp, but Saul would not so much as look at him.

Suddenly Saul took a spear and cast it at David, hoping to nail him against the wall. But David stepped aside and escaped.

After this, Saul could not bear to have David in his presence. He feared him because he knew that the Lord was with him. So he gave him a thousand men and sent him on an expedition against the Philistines, hoping that he might be slain. He told him that if he brought back proof that he had killed a hundred men, he would give him his daughter Merob in marriage.

Now, David loved Michol, the younger daughter of Saul, but he accepted the condition of the king. Going forth, he killed two hundred Philistines. Meanwhile the king had given Merob in marriage to another. When David returned, Saul offered him Michol instead. David was much pleased at this, for Michol and he loved each other dearly. They were married amid the rejoicing of the people. Now that David was his son-in-law, Saul's hatred of him grew more and more. He even told Jonathan and his servants of his desire to get rid of David, and Jonathan secretly warned his friend to flee.

Again David went out and fought against the Philistines and again he was victorious. He defeated them with great slaughter and they fled from his army. He returned to Saul and once more the king tried to kill him with a spear. But David escaped in the darkness of the night, and went to his own house.

Saul sent soldiers to watch David's house and to kill him when he came out in the morning. When Michol learned of this, she said to David, "Unless thou

Michol saves the life of David

save thyself this night, tomorrow thou shalt die.''
So she let him down from a window and he fled away.

Then Michol took a statue and laid it on the bed
and put a hairy goat skin at the head of it and covered it with clothes. In the morning the officers of the
king came to arrest David, but she told them that her
husband was sick.

When they reported this to Saul, he sent them back
with orders to bring David to him so that he could kill
him. When the soldiers came into the room, they discovered the trick Michol had played on them. Instead
of David, they found the statue in bed, with the goat
skin at its head. After this, David became a fugitive and wandered from place to place with a band of
four hundred men. Sometimes he hid in the forests.
Whenever he heard that the Philistines were about to
attack the Israelites, he left his hiding place to help
his people. God was with David and he was generally
victorious. But each new victory that David won increased Saul's envy and he was determined that David
must die.

David spares Saul Saul pursued David into the desert of Engaddi, on
the shore of the Dead Sea. David and his men saw
him coming and they hid in a cave. Night came and
Saul, not knowing that David and his men were there,
went into the cave to sleep. While the king slept,
David stole up and with his sword cut off a piece of
the hem of his garment.

The next morning, Saul awoke and, rising up, left
the cave. When he had gone a short distance, he heard
a voice calling, ''My lord, the king.'' He turned about

THE DESERT OF ENGADDI

and saw David standing at the mouth of the cave, holding up the piece which he had cut from his garment.

Seeing this, Saul's heart was troubled. He knew that David could have killed him had he wished and for a while he ceased to hate him. But David did not trust the king. He continued to lead a wandering life, accompanied by his faithful band of soldiers.

Saul soon forgot how David had spared his life and set out once more to pursue him. This time he sought him in the desert of Ziph. One night David and his men came into the camp of Saul when all were asleep. No sentry was on guard to challenge them and David took Saul's spear and a cup of water which was at the king's side. Going off some distance from the camp, David called to Abner, Saul's general, and said, "Why hast thou not guarded the lord, thy king?

David spares Saul a second time

DAVID FINDS SAUL IN THE CAVE AND SPARES HIS LIFE

Thou hast not protected thy master. Where is the king's spear and the cup of water which was at his head?"

When Saul heard David's voice, he said, "Is this thy voice, my son David?" "It is my voice, my lord, the king," answered David. "Why doth my lord persecute his servant? What have I done or what evil is in my hand?"

When Saul realized that David had again spared his life, he was filled with shame and said, "I have sinned. Return, my son David, for I will no more do thee harm, for thou hast spared my life this day."

But David knew how easy it was for Saul to change

his mind. So he sent back the king's spear and went his way. Saul returned to his palace.

It was about this time that the prophet Samuel died. He was mourned by all the people and was buried in Ramatha.

5. Saul Dies and Is Buried

The Philistines gathered together their armies to wage a new war on the Israelites. They camped in Sunam, and Saul assembled his force at Gelboe. When Saul saw how great were the forces of the Philistines, he became afraid and asked the Lord to tell him what to do. But God did not answer him, either by dreams, or by priests, or by prophets. *Saul's last battle*

After the death of Samuel, Saul had driven all the magicians and fortune tellers out of the land. But now he said to his servants, "Seek me out a woman who is a fortune teller that I may go and consult her." They said to him, "There is a witch at Endor." *The Witch of Endor*

Saul disguised himself and, taking two men with him, went to consult the witch of Endor. It was night when he came to her and he said, "Call up the spirit of him whom I shall tell thee."

At first the woman refused. She told them that Saul had driven all witches out of the land. She accused them of being agents of the king who had come to entrap her. But Saul told her that nothing would happen to her. "Whom shall I bring up to you?" she asked. He answered, "Bring me up Samuel."

Hearing this, the woman cried out with a loud voice, saying, "Why hast thou deceived me, for thou art

Saul." But Saul said to her, "Fear not, but tell me what thou hast seen." The woman answered, "An old man cometh up and he is covered with a mantle." Saul knew that it was Samuel, and he bowed his face to the ground.

Then Saul heard the voice of Samuel speaking to him. "Why hast thou disturbed my rest?" he asked. Saul answered, "I am in great distress, for the Philistines fight against me, and God hath departed from me and will not hear my prayers. Therefore have I called thee that thou mayest show me what to do."

Then Samuel said, "The Lord hath departed from thee and gone over to thy rival. He will rend thy kingdom out of thy hand and give it to David, because thou didst not obey the voice of the Lord. The Lord will deliver Israel with thee into the hands of the Philistines. Tomorrow thou and thy sons shall be with me."

Saul fainted and fell to the ground. The words of Samuel filled him with terror and, besides, he had had nothing to eat since the day before. The witch prepared a meal for him, and his servants forced him to eat it. When he had eaten, his strength returned to him, and he journeyed back to his army.

Saul's death

The next day, the trumpets sounded for battle. The Philistines were successful from the start. Thousands of the Israelites were slain and the rest took to flight. Jonathan and his brothers were slain and Saul was wounded by arrows. He begged his armor-bearer to slay him, but the servant was struck with a great fear and refused. Then Saul took his own sword and fell

MOUNT GELBOE

upon it. When the armor-bearer saw that Saul was dead, he too fell upon his sword and died.

When the battle was over, the Philistines found the bodies of Saul and his sons lying on Mount Gelboe. They cut off Saul's head and stripped him of his armor, and sent word to all the people that Saul had been slain. They put the armor of the king in the temple of Astarte and hung his body and the bodies of his sons on the wall of Bethsan.

When the Israelites who lived at Jabes Galaad heard what the Philistines had done to Saul, they chose a band of brave men, who came by night and took the body of Saul and the bodies of his sons from the wall of Bethsan and buried them in the woods near Jabes. Then they fasted for seven days.

David mourns for Saul

When news of the death of Saul was brought to David, he mourned and wept and fasted until evening for Saul and Jonathan and the people of the Lord who had fallen in battle. He said:

"How are the valiant fallen? Tell it not in Geth, publish it not in the streets of Ascalon, lest the daughters of the Philistines rejoice, lest the daughters of the Gentiles triumph. Ye mountains of Gelboe, let neither dew nor rain come upon you, neither be they fields of first fruits, for there was cast away the shield of the valiant, the shield of Saul as though he had not been anointed with oil. Saul and Jonathan, lovely and comely in their life, even in death they were not divided. They were swifter than eagles, stronger than lions. Ye daughters of Israel, weep over Saul, who clothed you with scarlet and gave ornaments of gold for your attire. How are the valiant fallen in battle, Jonathan slain in the high places? I grieve for thee, my brother Jonathan, exceedingly beautiful and amiable to me above the love of women. As a mother loveth her only son, so did I love thee."

THINGS TO KNOW AND TO DO

1. Saul Is Anointed King by Samuel

1. Find four reasons why the Israelites wanted a king. Discuss these reasons.
2. Discuss the arguments against these reasons which Samuel presented.
3. What was the principal reason that the Israelites should have been content with the government as God ordained it?
4. Tell the story of Saul's anointing.

2. Saul Leads His People to Victory, but Is Rejected by God

1. How did Saul force the Israelites to take him as their king? Why did he do so?
2. Why was the kingship taken from Saul's family?
3. Apply to Saul the words "God does not ask sacrifice, but obedience."
4. What do these words teach about the importance of obedience?

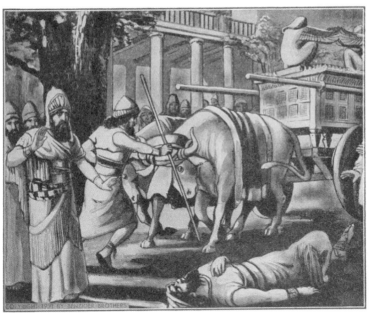

OZA IS STRUCK DEAD FOR TOUCHING THE ARK

the sacrifice. Laying aside his royal robes, he danced before the Ark and played on his harp. The Levites carried the Ark all the way to Jerusalem and placed it in the tabernacle which David had built for it.

3. DAVID EXTENDS HIS KINGDOM AND PUTS DOWN THE REVOLT OF ABSALOM

David extended his empire by overcoming the enemies that surrounded the Chosen People on all sides. Three times he defeated the Philistines and fought successfully against the other nations and forced them to pay tribute to him. David's conquests

David had a son named Absalom, who was very ambitious and jealous of his father's position. He Absalom's revolt

© 1931. BY BENZIGER BROTHERS

THE EXTENT OF ISRAEL UNDER
DAVID AND ABSALOM

made up his mind to become king in David's place. He surrounded himself with a bodyguard of fifty men and fitted them out with horses and chariots. When discontented people came to Jerusalem to plead their cases before the king and obtain his judgment, Absalom pretended that he was their friend. If the king decided against them, it was Absalom who took their part and told them that, if he were king, their wrongs would be righted.

Meanwhile, Absalom was very busy preparing to lead a revolt against David. He obtained his father's permission to go to Hebron, a city a few miles south of Jerusalem, where he had been born. There, likewise, David had first been proclaimed king.

The reason that Absalom gave for wanting to go

to Hebron was that he wished to fulfill a vow and offer sacrifice in that city, but his real object was to have himself made king. He expected an army to join him in the south. With this army he hoped to capture Jerusalem and compel his father to surrender.

When David heard that Absalom had risen up against him, he fled from Jerusalem, for he wished to spare the people of the city the misery of a siege. He commanded two priests to remain in Jerusalem with the Ark, and instructed them to keep him informed of Absalom's intentions.

Absalom and his army entered the city of Jerusalem and took possession of David's palace. He made every effort to win the people over to his side, and when he thought that he had accomplished this purpose and that they trusted him, he set out in pursuit of his father. *Absalom enters Jerusalem*

One of David's followers, a man named Chusai, had remained in Jerusalem to keep the king informed of all that was going on in the capital. Chusai now sent messengers to David, urging him to leave the Jordan, where he was hiding. The king obeyed the instructions of the messengers and fled to the land of Galaad, where he was received with all kindness.

Absalom pursued his father to the land of Galaad. David prepared to meet the attack of his son. He divided his army into three companies, intending to lead one of them himself, but the people of the city persuaded him to remain behind with them.

David's army met the men of Absalom in a wooded valley, where a fierce battle was fought. The army of Absalom was defeated and their leader was put to flight. While galloping away on a mule, Absalom's long hair was caught in the branch of a tree. He was jerked from the mule's back and left hanging in the air. Joab, the captain of David's army, found him there and thrust three lances into his heart. Then he took him down and buried him in a pit and piled stones upon his grave.

David restored to his kingdom It was Chusai who brought the news of the death of Absalom to David. When the king heard that his son was dead, he mourned greatly and cried out, "My son Absalom, Absalom my son, would to God that I might die for thee, Absalom my son, my son Absalom!"

The tribe of Juda determined to restore David to his kingdom and they sent a great escort to meet the king. When David had crossed the river Jordan at Galgal, a quarrel arose. The other tribes were angry with the tribe of Juda because they had not been consulted about bringing David back to the kingdom. After some fighting, David put down the revolt.

4. David Sins and Is Punished

David's punishment for sin David committed a very grievous sin. He desired to have for himself the wife of one of his soldiers. Her name was Bethsabee, and her husband's name was Urias. He gave orders that Urias was to be placed in the front line of battle and that the soldiers were to fall back and leave him there alone to be slain. All happened as he had planned, and David was thus free to marry Bethsabee.

Then God sent Nathan, the prophet, to David.

Nathan said to the king, "There were two men in a city—the one rich, the other poor. The rich man had very many sheep and oxen, but the poor man had nothing at all but one little lamb which he had brought up and fed and which had grown up in his house together with his children, eating of his bread and drinking of his cup and sleeping near him. One day a stranger came to the rich man. The rich man made a feast for him, but he did not kill any of his own sheep and oxen, but took the poor man's lamb and prepared it for the man who came to eat with him."

When David heard this, he was very angry and said to Nathan, "As the Lord liveth, the man who hath done this thing shall be put to death."

Then Nathan said to David, "Thou art the man, and God hath sent me to thee with this message, 'I anointed thee king over Israel, and delivered thee from the hand of Saul. I have placed thee over all the people, and given thee a kingdom to rule. Why, therefore, didst thou kill Urias and take his wife to be thy wife? Therefore, the sword shall never depart from thy house, and I will raise up evil against thee in thy own family.'" David said to Nathan, "I have sinned against the Lord."

When Nathan saw that David was sorry for his sins and asked God to forgive him, he said to him, "The Lord hath taken away thy sin. Thou shalt not die, but the child that is born to thee shall surely die." Nathan returned to his house. Some time later a son was born to David and Bethsabee. The child fell sick and his

THE PROPHET NATHAN REBUKES KING DAVID FOR HIS SINS

life was despaired of. David prayed very hard and fasted, but on the seventh day the baby died.

A second son was born to David and Bethsabee. His name was called Solomon. He was destined to succeed his father on the throne and to rule over the chosen people of God.

David and the Temple At the beginning of his reign, David had dreamed of building a great temple to God. But the prophet Nathan told him that it was God's will that not he, but his son Solomon, should build the temple. Though he was not permitted to build it, David gathered materials that would be used in its construction. He stored up great quantities of copper, iron, timber, stone, and heads of the tribes led a citizens' army in defense of the nation. This army was divided into groups of different sizes, with a commanding officer over each group.

Saul provided a standing army. But all citizens had to answer his call when they were needed. David added to the standing army a bodyguard, composed of skilled warriors who had been loyal to him while he was in exile. David had a council made up of thirty-three wise and brave men.

We see, then, why David was able to defeat his enemies, even the Philistines. He had a large standing army with strong and brave commanders. He and his commanders had acquired great skill in fighting in the days of his exile. They had learned especially how to use mountains, valleys, and rivers to help them in winning battles. **David's military strategy**

David had neither chariots nor cavalry. His enemies had both. David's plan was to draw the enemy into a hilly field, where the chariots could not be used and where the horsemen could not make an attack in a body. Another scheme which David used was to put to flight the bravest men of the army. The rest, seeing these men flee, retreated in great terror. Sometimes he planned to kill the leader upon whom the soldiers depended. After the death of their leader, the rest of the army usually fled.

6. What David Accomplished

The heads of the tribes had much authority of their own, but they accepted David's rule. Six thousand **Local government**

Levites were placed throughout the country to represent David as civil officers and judges. The officers gave their orders to the heads of the tribes in David's name, and the heads of the tribes put them into execution. The judges had duties like those of the judges of today.

David's care for resources David built storehouses for grain, levied as taxes, at convenient places throughout the country. They were looked after by officers. Vineyards, wine cellars, oil cellars, and the valleys where sheep grazed were cared for by an officer of the king. Plowing and planting were directed by skilled farmers, and orchards were cultivated under expert direction.

David's official household In his court David had a civil council, a chief secretary, a chief historian and a chief taxgatherer. Two high priests had charge of the religious ceremonies. David divided the Levites into groups. Some cared for the Ark, others guarded the treasures collected for the Temple, others formed a choir that chanted the sacred music.

David's poetry and music David was a patron of poetry and music. He wrote beautiful poetry and was an excellent musician. Even as a boy he played the harp for Saul. He composed religious hymns for feast days. They are known today as Psalms. Many of these are prophetical, and foretell the sufferings and triumph of the Messias.

One of the most beautiful of these psalms David wrote when Saul was persecuting him. He was thinking of the days when he was a shepherd boy and he

III. THE ISRAELITES UNDER KING SOLOMON

1. SOLOMON SHOWS HIS GREAT WISDOM

Solomon was not yet twenty years old when he became king. Feeling his inexperience, he went to Gabaa, where the Tabernacle stood, to offer sacrifice to God and to ask His blessing upon his reign. One thousand victims were offered to God by Solomon.

Solomon prays for wisdom

That night God spoke to him and asked him to name the gifts that he desired. Solomon asked only one thing—wisdom to govern his people well. God was pleased because Solomon asked for wisdom rather than for wealth or power, and He made him the wisest of all the rulers of his time. Besides wisdom, God gave Solomon wealth and glory and power, and promised him a long life if he would obey the Divine Law.

One day, two women came to Solomon to have him settle a dispute that had arisen between them. Both of them had infants of about the same age. In the middle of the night, the baby that belonged to one of them died. The mother of the dead child took away the living child and left the other in its place. The next morning, when the other woman discovered what had been done, she came to the king and demanded that her child be given back to her.

The wisdom of Solomon

Both women stood before the king and each claimed that the child was her own. Solomon asked for a sword. He ordered an attendant to cut the child in

209

By His Wisdom Solomon Discovers the True Mother

half and to give half of it to each woman. But when the true mother heard this command, she cried out, "Give her the child alive and do not kill it." But the other woman said, "Let the child be neither mine nor thine, but divide it."

Solomon knew at once to whom the child belonged and he said, "Give the living child to this woman and let it not be killed, for she is the mother." And the child was restored to the woman who had pleaded for its life.

The Queen of Saba Many of the wise things that Solomon said are found in the Book of Proverbs. Solomon is also said to have been the author of the Book of Ecclesiastes. Soon his wisdom was known throughout the world, and neigh-

Back of it there was the court with its fountains and gardens.

Solomon's neighbors did not annoy him till close to the end of his life. The empire built up by David extended from the Euphrates to Egypt, and remained intact during the forty years of Solomon's reign. It was this reign of peace that made Solomon's days the golden age of the Kingdom of Israel. The Golden Age of Israel

Solomon protected his kingdom and his traders. He fortified the Temple and palace and built the city of Tadmor to protect his caravans coming from the East. He erected fortresses in Asor to guard the northern frontier; in Mageddo to protect the Plain of Esdrelon; in the two Bethorons and Baalath; and in Gazer, to guard the Plain of Ajalon. Solomon's fortifications

Solomon carried on trade with the neighboring countries. His contact with King Hiram taught him the value of commerce, and now his caravan routes led to the Hittites, the Syrians, and the Babylonians. Egypt sent him horses and chariots. King Hiram built ships for him and he paid sailors from Sidon to sail them. Some Jewish sailors from the tribes of Issachar and Nephtali were also on these ships. Solomon's commercial activity

He sent these ships from Ailath, a port on the Gulf of Akaba, to India for ivory and gold. Every third year he sent his ships with Hiram's to Tharsis in Spain for gold and silver.

4. SOLOMON'S KINGDOM DECLINES

Solomon received great revenues from his caravans and ships. Wealth also came to him in the form of Solomon's revenues rents and taxes. The neighboring states presented him with costly gifts. His income in gold every year was enormous. Besides this, he received cattle and provisions from his own kingdom.

Expenditures The money for the building of the Temple had been saved by David. But Solomon's expenses were heavy. To meet these expenses, the people were taxed in two ways: they were commanded to supply Solomon with meat and grain, and to pay a tax on every article they bought. This tax went to Solomon for the support of the palace. The people became dissatisfied with these heavy taxes.

New divisions Fearing that the Temple would not be sufficient to keep the people attached to the King of Jerusalem, Solomon divided the country into twelve provinces and no longer respected the division into tribes. He thought this new division would destroy the jealousies that had existed among the tribes, and would prevent future civil wars.

But Solomon forgot the one important means for keeping the people united with him. He neglected to worship the true God. His heavy taxes caused the people to hate him, and prepared them to follow the first strong leader who would rise up against him.

Had Solomon remained true to God, he could have pointed to the Temple, and rallied the people around him again. But he did not remain true to God. As he grew older, he became very fond of pleasure, and his great wisdom left him. To please his pagan wives, he built temples to their false gods. This act de·

stroyed the religious unity of the Jews, without which there could be no national unity.

Thus, taxation and idolatry were the two causes that led to the break-up of Jewish unity, the unity which had been the aim of David.

The people were now ready for a rebellion, and the leader of the rebellion was preparing himself. Jeroboam was that leader. He was a brave and talented man, whom Solomon had put in charge of the fortifications of Jerusalem. Later he gave him the office of collecting the tribute from the tribes of Ephraim, Benjamin, and Manasses. *A rebel leader*

One day when Jeroboam was going out of the city of Jerusalem he met the prophet Ahias, who was clad in a new cloak. Ahias walked along with him until they came into the open country. Then, taking off his new cloak, he tore it into twelve pieces and said to Jeroboam, "Take thee ten pieces, for thus saith the Lord God of Israel, 'Behold, I will rend the kingdom out of the hands of Solomon and will give thee ten tribes. But one tribe shall remain to him for the sake of My servant David, because he hath forsaken Me and adored false gods and hath not kept My commandments as did David his father. I will take away the kingdom out of his son's hands and will give thee ten tribes and to his son I will give one tribe. If thou wilt hearken to all I command thee and wilt walk in My ways, keeping My commandments as My servant David did, I will deliver Israel to thee.' "

His work of collecting taxes gave Jeroboam ample opportunity to learn how discontented the people had

THE PROPHET AHIAS TEARS HIS CLOAK

become with Solomon's reign. He encouraged their discontent and tried to make himself popular with them. When Solomon discovered this, he sought to kill Jeroboam, but the latter escaped and fled into Egypt. It was not long, however, before Solomon died, after a reign of forty years, and was buried in Jerusalem.

THINGS TO KNOW AND TO DO

1. SOLOMON SHOWS HIS GREAT WISDOM

1. Describe the first things Solomon did as king.
2. Mention some facts that prove Solomon was very wise.
3. Show that Solomon's reputation for wisdom went farther than his own kingdom.
4. If you read the Book of Ecclesiastes, you will find the following proverbs. Memorize them.

Vanity of vanities, and all is vanity.
Nothing under the sun is new.
Speak not anything rashly.
In many words there shall be found folly.
He that feareth God neglecteth nothing.
Wisdom is better than strength.
Remove anger from thy heart.
Better is wisdom than weapons of war.
Fear God, and keep His commandments.

Give the number of the chapter in which these sayings occur.

5. Read Chapter XV of the Book of Proverbs. Memorize three of the following verses of this chapter: 1, 3, 12, 13, 14, 16, 20, 29, 33.

2. THE TEMPLE IS BUILT

1. Locate the Lebanon Mountains, Tyre, Joppe, and Jerusalem. Show by what way the wood for the Temple was brought to Jerusalem.

2. Why was the preparation for building the Temple unusually hard work?

3. Why were only the finest materials used in building the Temple? Name some of those materials.

4. What promise did God make to Solomon?

5. Read again the description of the Tabernacle and its furnishings and compare them with the Temple.

6. Describe a day spent by the Jews in building the Temple.

7. Write an essay entitled, "Solomon's Reverence for the House of God," describing especially the solemn dedication.

8. Compare the three parts of the Temple with the three parts of your parish church.

3. THE NATION FLOURISHES UNDER SOLOMON

1. Why was Solomon's reign called the Golden Age?

2. Why did he build fortifications?

3. Remind Solomon of the reasons why God made his reign glorious.

4. SOLOMON'S KINGDOM DECLINES

1. What caused the discontent of Solomon's people?

2. Who was the greater king, David or Solomon? Give reasons for your answer.

3. Write an essay in which you show the necessity of perseverance unto the end.

4. Give a floor talk on "Fame and riches were the cause of Solomon's fall."

IV. THE DIVISION OF SOLOMON'S KINGDOM

1. Jeroboam Founds the Kingdom of Israel

Roboam's evil advisers After the death of Solomon, his son Roboam, then forty-one years old, went to Sichem, where he hoped to be anointed king. He was met by representatives of the people, who told him that before they would recognize him as their king they had certain demands to make. They asked that the taxes which his father had imposed upon them be reduced.

Roboam requested that he be allowed three days to consider their petition. He called together his father's counselors and asked them what he should do. They advised him to lighten the burden of the people. Next he called together a number of young men, friends of his and companions of his youth. They advised him to continue to demand the heavy taxes, because he would need the money if he were to continue to live in splendor as his father had lived.

Roboam heeded the counsel of his friends. He sent for the representatives of the people and said to them, "My father made your yoke heavy, but I will add to your yoke; my father beat you with whips, but I will beat you with scorpions."

Ten tribes revolt When the people heard the answer of the king, they rose up in rebellion. The king sent Aduram to calm them, but they stoned him to death. Roboam, realizing that his life was in danger, fled to Jerusalem in his chariot. He intended to raise an army and force the rebels to obey him, but the prophet Semeias forbade him to do so. Roboam obeyed the prophet.

The tribes of Juda and Benjamin remained loyal to Roboam, but the other ten tribes made Jeroboam their king. They fell into idolatry and worshiped false gods, so the Levites left their territory and allied themselves with Roboam. Roboam now fortified the towns of Juda and Benjamin, which were all that was left to him of

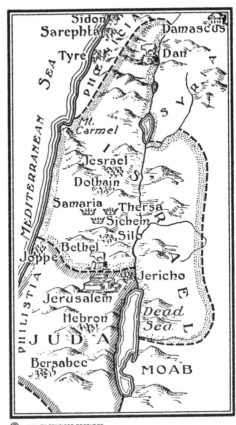

© 1931, BY BENZIGER BROTHERS
THE KINGDOMS OF ISRAEL AND JUDA

the great kingdom of his father. Henceforth it was known as the Kingdom of Juda. The kingdom which Jeroboam set up was known as the Kingdom of Israel.

Jeroboam would not permit the people of the ten tribes to worship in the Temple at Jerusalem. He thought it was necessary to keep them from the Temple in order to keep them attached to himself. To make the division of the tribes lasting, he founded a

Jeroboam sets up idolatry

state religion. He built two temples in which he set up golden calves, one in the northern part of his kingdom, in the city of Dan; the other, in the south, in the city of Bethel. The priests came from the lowest ranks of the people. Any man who could furnish a bullock and seven rams for sacrifice could be made a priest. Jeroboam permitted many altars of sacrifice to be erected throughout his kingdom.

Jeroboam's capital

Jeroboam made Sichem his capital. This city was closely connected with the founders of the Jewish Nation, and appealed to the patriotism of the people. There Abraham had settled when he first came from Ur into the Land of Promise. Jacob too had lived there for some time after his return from the house of Laban. Both Abraham and Jacob had built altars in Sichem and Jacob had dug a well nearby. It was in the fields of Sichem that Joseph looked for his brothers, and there his bones were buried when the Israelites returned from Egypt. Later Jeroboam moved his capital to the city of Thersa.

Josias' war

Shortly after the institution of the state religion, Jeroboam worshiped before the golden calf at Bethel. On this occasion, a prophet from the kingdom of Juda prophesied to him. He foretold that a future king, Josias, would burn the false priests upon an altar. He gave them a sign that the people might know that his prophecy would be fulfilled. He said that the altar of worship was about to be broken and the ashes scattered about on the ground. On hearing these words, Jeroboam pointed to the prophet with his hand, and ordered him to be taken captive. The hand with which

But there was no answer. They cried out and they leaped over the altar which they had made.

When it was noon, Elias jested with them and said, "Cry with a louder voice, for he is a god, and perhaps he is talking, or is on a journey, or is asleep and must be awakened." They cried out louder and cut themselves with their knives till they were covered with blood. But no answer came to their prayers.

Then Elias said to the people, "Come to me now." And the people came near to him. He built an altar to the Lord with stones, and made a trench for water. He placed his bullock upon the wood, and had twelve buckets of water poured over the bullock. The water ran round about the altar and filled the trench.

When it was time to offer the sacrifice, Elias came near and said, "O Lord, God of Abraham, of Isaac, and of Israel, show this day that Thou art the God of Israel, and that I am Thy servant, and that I have done these things according to Thy commands. Hear me, O Lord, hear me, that these people may know that Thou art their God."

Then the fire of the Lord fell and consumed the holocaust, and the wood, and the stones, and dried up the water that was in the trench. And when all the people saw this, they fell on their faces and cried: "The Lord is God! The Lord is God!" *God sends fire on Elias' sacrifice*

Elias commanded the people to take the prophets of Baal to the Brook Cison, which flows at the foot of Mount Carmel. There Elias at God's command put them all to death.

Elias in exile

Jezabel, the wife of Achab, was very angry when she heard what had happened to her prophets. She sent word to Elias that the same death awaited him. Elias fled out of the country. He sat down weary in the desert a short distance from Bersabee. An angel came to him twice and brought him food, saying, "Rise and eat." He arose and looked, and there were a hearth cake and a vessel of water for him. Elias ate and drank, and he walked in the strength of that food for forty days and forty nights to the mount of God, Horeb, where he lived in a cave. Here the Lord appeared to Elias, saying "Go, and return on thy way through the desert to Damascus. There thou shalt anoint Hazael king over Syria. And thou shalt anoint Jehu king over Israel, and Eliseus thou shalt anoint to be prophet in thy place."

As Elias was returning to the northern kingdom, he found Eliseus plowing in a field. Elias came up to him and threw his mantle over his shoulders. Eliseus left his oxen and ran after Elias and said, "Let me, I pray thee, kiss my father and my mother, and I will follow thee." Eliseus followed Elias and ministered to him.

Achab's victories over the Syrians

The relations between the Kingdom of Juda and the Kingdom of Israel were now friendly. But Benadad, the king of Syria, tried to annex Samaria to his kingdom. A prophet had informed Achab that God would grant him victory over the Syrian king. He set out with an army of seven thousand men and drove the enemy back. The second year the same king returned with a powerful army. Achab went out again to meet

him with a small army and badly defeated him. But
Achab spared the life of the king and his counselors,
and made a treaty with him. The prophet told Achab
that because he had spared the life of the king of
Syria, who was worthy of death for his blasphemy, he
would lose his own by a violent death.

Now there was a man named Naboth who owned a
vineyard near the palace of Achab. The king wanted
this vineyard and offered Naboth another vineyard or
the price of it in money. But because the vineyard
was his inheritance from his father, Naboth refused to
sell it. This refusal angered Achab and his wife,
Jezabel. Jezabel paid two men to swear falsely
against Naboth. These two men said to the people,
"Naboth hath blasphemed God and the king." Then
they took Naboth outside the city and stoned him to
death.

Naboth is stoned to death

When Achab heard that Naboth was dead, he went
to take possession of the vineyard. On his way he met
the prophet Elias, who was sent to him by God. The
prophet said to Achab, "In this place where the dogs
licked the blood of Naboth, they shall lick thy blood
also." He also foretold that the dogs would eat the
flesh of Jezabel, and that the Kingdom of Israel would
pass from the House of Achab because he had caused
Israel to sin and to offend God.

When Achab had heard these words, he tore his garments, put on haircloth, fasted and slept in sackcloth.
God was pleased with the penance and the humility of
Achab, and He said to Elias, "Because Achab hath
humbled himself before Me, I will not bring the evil

upon his kingdom in his day; but in his son's day, I will bring the evil upon his house.''

Achab and Josaphat, the king of Juda, undertook another campaign against the king of Syria. Four hundred false prophets said the campaign would be a victory for Achab. Micheas, the prophet of the true God, foretold a defeat for Achab and Josaphat, for which prophecy he was cast into prison. The campaign was undertaken. Achab disguised himself before going into battle, but he was shot by a chance arrow. When Achab's chariot was being washed in the pool of Samaria, dogs licked up his blood as they had licked the blood of Naboth in that spot, and the prophet's word was fulfilled.

Joram, the son of Achab and Jezabel, became king after the death of his father. But his reign was short. He was slain in battle by an arrow from the bow of Jehu, who then became king of Israel.

Jehu was entering the city of Jezrahel on his return from battle, when Jezabel, having painted her face and adorned her hair, looked out the window and called to him, ''Can there be peace for the murderer of the king?''

Jehu said, ''Who is this?'' When they told him it was Jezabel, he commanded them to throw her out of the window. They did so, and the hoofs of the horses trod upon her.

Later on, Jehu said, ''Go and bury that cursed woman. After all, she is the king's daughter.''

But when they went to get the body and bury it, they found that the dogs had eaten her up. When Jehu

heard this, he said, "It is the word of the Lord which
He spoke by Elias the Thesbite, saying, 'In the field
of Jezrahel the dogs shall eat the flesh of Jezabel.'"

2. THE MIRACLES OF ELISEUS IN THE KINGDOM OF JUDA

While Achab was ruling over the Kingdom of Israel, Juda's
Josaphat was king of Juda. He was a wise and peace- peaceful
loving king. He remained true to God all the days of king
his life.

While Josaphat was king, there was peace in his
country. The people turned their attention to the
trades. They cared for the farms and the pastures of
the country, so that the crops and herds were large
and good. Josaphat appointed judges in all the chief
cities.

The kings of Juda who succeeded Josaphat were
weak and sinful. The kings of Israel who succeeded
Achab were also evil men. They worshiped idols and
forced the people to follow their example. War, disease, and death followed as the punishment of the
sinful lives of these kings.

During the reign of Josaphat, Elias and Eliseus Elias
were leaving Galgal, when Elias said to Eliseus, borne to
"Stay thou here, for I am going to Bethel." But Heaven
Eliseus said, "I will not leave thee!" They went to in a
Bethel and Jericho and came to the Jordan. As they chariot
stood by the Jordan, Elias took his mantle, folded it
together and struck the water with it. The water was
divided, and they both passed over on dry ground.
When they had crossed the Jordan, Elias said to
Eliseus, "Ask what thou wouldst have me do for thee

ELIAS IS BORNE TO HEAVEN IN A FIERY CHARIOT

before I shall be taken from thee." Eliseus begged for the spirit of Elias. Elias promised it in these words, "If thou seest me when I am taken away, thou wilt receive what thou askest."

As they were walking along and talking to each other, a fiery chariot and fiery horses parted them, and Elias went up by a whirlwind into Heaven. Eliseus saw him and cried, "My father, my father," and he saw him no more. He took up the mantle of Elias which had fallen upon him, and with it he divided the waters as Elias had done.

The curse of Eliseus One day when Eliseus was on his way to Bethel, some little boys came out of the city. They saw

THE BOYS RIDICULE THE PROPHET ELISEUS

Eliseus and mocked him, saying, ''Go up, thou bald head.'' Eliseus turned back and cursed them in the name of the Lord, and two bears came out of the forest and tore the forty-two boys to pieces.

Naaman was the general of the Syrian army. He was brave and rich. He was great and honorable, but contracted leprosy.

Eliseus cures leprosy

A little girl whom Syrian robbers brought out of the land of Israel was maid to Naaman's wife. One day she said to her mistress, ''I wish my master had been with the prophet that is in Samaria. He would certainly have healed him of the leprosy which he hath.'' When the king of Syria heard of the wonderful prophet in Israel, he sent Naaman with a letter and costly gifts to the king of Israel. He begged him to heal Naaman, his servant, of the leprosy. The king sent Naaman to Eliseus, the prophet of Israel.

Naaman came with his horses and chariots and stood at the door of the house of Eliseus. The prophet sent a messenger to Naaman, saying, "Go and bathe seven times in the Jordan, and thy flesh shall recover health and thou shalt be clean."

Naaman was angry because of this message, and he turned to go away. But his servants showed him that obedience to the prophet's command was a small price to pay for his health. "Wash," he had said, "and thou shalt be healed." Then Naaman went down and washed seven times in the Jordan. His flesh was restored like the flesh of a little child, and he was cleansed from his leprosy.

Naaman returned to the man of God with all his retinue to thank him and to offer him gifts as a sign of gratitude. But Eliseus refused the gifts. Naaman promised from that day never to adore any other god but the God of Israel.

Giezi, the servant of Eliseus, went secretly after Naaman to ask a gift of him in his master's name. When he returned, Eliseus asked, "Where hast thou been, Giezi?" "Thy servant hath been nowhere," untruthfully answered Giezi. But Eliseus saw what had happened, and he said to the servant, "The leprosy of Naaman shall stick to thee and to thy children forever." And the servant went from him, a leper white as the snow.

The power to work miracles remained with Eliseus

even after his death. One day a funeral procession was passing near the tomb of Eliseus, when the funeral party met a band of robbers. In their fright they laid the body of the dead man in the grave of Eliseus and fled. As soon as the corpse touched the body of Eliseus, it was restored to life.

3. Job Gives Glory to God among the Edomites

The Edomites were descendants of Esau. Their country bordered on the southern shore of the Dead Sea. There lived in their midst a holy man named Job.

Job, a wealty Edomite

Job was very wealthy. He lived in a house built of stone. He had seven sons and three daughters, and many servants to wait upon him. He owned seven thousand sheep, three thousand camels, five hundred yoke of oxen and five hundred asses.

On a certain day when the angels came to stand before God, Satan was present among them.

The Lord said to Satan, "Hast thou considered My servant Job? There is none like him in the earth. He is a simple and upright man. He feareth God and avoideth evil."

Satan, answering God, said, "It is easy for Job to fear God. Thou hast given him abundance of everything. Thou hast blessed the work of his hands. Thou hast increased his possessions on earth. But touch all that he has, and he will not bless Thee."

Then the Lord said to Satan, "Behold, I give thee power over all that he has. Do as thou likest with it. But do not touch his person."

JOB DOES NOT COMPLAIN IN SPITE OF ALL HIS TRIALS

Job's afflictions Satan went forth from the presence of the Lord, and began to annoy Job. Great misfortunes came upon Job.

On a certain day, when his sons and daughters were feasting, a messenger came to Job and said, "The Sabeans, our neighbors, rushed into the fields where the oxen were plowing and took them all away. They killed the servants with a sword. I alone escaped to tell thee."

While this servant was speaking, another came and said, "Lightning from heaven hath killed all thy sheep and the servants who were tending them. I alone escaped to tell thee."

While he was yet speaking, another came and said,

"The Chaldeans have fallen upon the camels and taken them. They have killed the servants with the sword. I alone escaped to tell thee."

While he was yet speaking, still another came in and said, "A violent wind shook the house in which thy sons and daughters were feasting. The house fell upon thy children, and behold, they are all dead. I alone escaped to tell thee."

Job rose and, as a sign of sorrow, rent his garments. He fell upon the ground and worshiped God, and said, "The Lord gave, and the Lord hath taken away. Blessed be the name of the Lord."

The patience of Job

On another day Satan stood before God. God said to Satan, "Hast thou considered My servant Job? He hath kept his innocence in spite of his suffering."

Satan answered and said, "All that a man hath he will give for his life. Put forth Thy hand and touch his flesh and bone, and he will not bless Thee."

The Lord said to Satan, "I give thee power over his person, but save his life."

Satan went forth from the presence of the Lord. He struck Job with an ulcer which covered him from the sole of his foot to the top of his head. Job sat on a dunghill and scraped the corruption from his sores. But he spoke not a word against God.

His wife ridiculed him because he blessed God in his suffering. Job answered her, "We have received good things from the Lord. Why should we not receive evil things also?"

Job's friends came to him. Instead of consoling him in his suffering, they added new sorrow. They told him that these sufferings were sent to him in punishment of his wicked life.

But Job knew that he was innocent. His answer to his friends was this, "If I shall be judged, I know that I shall be found just. Even if God should kill me, I will trust in Him. I know that my Redeemer liveth and in the last day I shall rise out of the earth, and I shall be clothed again with my skin, and my flesh shall see my God."

Job's reward Job pleased God by his patience in suffering. God showed that He was pleased with him by rewarding him even in this life. He restored his health. He doubled his wealth, and gave him seven sons and three daughters to take the place of those who were killed.

4. Jonas Preaches in Ninive

Jonas flees from God Ninive was the great city of the Assyrians. Its inhabitants were Gentiles, and they were very wicked. One day the Lord spoke to Jonas, the prophet, saying, "Arise, and go to Ninive, the great city, and preach in it." But Jonas was afraid, and tried to flee from the face of the Lord. He entered a ship which was bound for another city. But the Lord sent a great wind into the sea, and the ship was in danger of being destroyed. The men cried to their gods for help. The ship-master found Jonas fast asleep and said to Him, "Arise, and call upon thy God that we may not perish." But the storm continued. Then they cast lots to find out who was the cause of the evil that had come upon them. The lot fell upon Jonas. Jonas said, "Cast me into the sea and the water will become calm for you, for I

JONAS PREACHES REPENTANCE TO THE JEWS IN NINIVE

know that it is for my sake that this great tempest is upon you." They cast Jonas into the sea, and the sea became calm.

The Lord prepared a great fish to swallow Jonas. So when the sailors cast him overboard, the fish swallowed him up, and Jonas remained in the belly of the fish for three days and three nights. He prayed to the Lord, and God caused the fish to cast him up on the shore.

A second time God spoke to Jonas and said to him, "Arise, and go to Ninive, the great city, and preach in it." Jonas arose and went to Ninive, according to the word of the Lord. He entered the city and cried out, "Yet forty days and Ninive shall be destroyed."

Jonas in Ninive

The men of Ninive believed that Jonas was a messenger from God and began a great fast. All the people, from the greatest to the least, put on sackcloth and did penance. When God saw their humble hearts and their works of penance, He had mercy and spared them.

Our blessed Savior used the story of Jonas when He foretold His Resurrection. He said, "As Jonas was in the whale's belly for three days and three nights, so shall the Son of Man be in the heart of the earth three days and three nights."

THINGS TO KNOW AND TO DO

1. ELIAS CONFOUNDS THE FALSE PROPHETS

1. Give a floor talk on the courage of Elias. Read "Elijah" in "Old Testament Stories" by Rev. C. C. Martindale.
2. Read the Holy Bible, III Kings, Chapters XII-XXII.
3. Imagine you are Elias, and reprove King Achab for his many sins.
4. Find on the map the new capital of the Kingdom of Israel.
5. Name the ways in which God took care of Elias.
6. On the Feast of Corpus Christi every priest must read about Elias walking forty days in the strength of the Heavenly Food. Why does the Church order this?
7. Use Achab as an example to show that we should all be contented with what God gives us.
8. If you had been present, what would you have been doing while the priests of Baal were begging for fire from their god.

2. THE MIRACLES OF ELISEUS IN THE KINGDOM OF JUDA

1. Why did God give Eliseus the power to work miracles?
2. Show from the story of Eliseus that God wants children to respect old people?
3. What story in the life of Eliseus shows how hateful a thing a lie is.
4. Write an essay entitled, "Health Is Better Than Riches."

3. JOB GIVES GLORY TO GOD AMONG THE EDOMITES

1. Locate the territory of the Edomites.
2. Show in a floor talk that Job was a man of heroic patience.
3. What was the reward of his patience?
4. Describe the many ways in which everybody can practice patience.

4. JONAS PREACHES IN NINIVE

1. What lesson does the story of Jonas teach?
2. Of whom was Jonas a figure?
3. Prove that God is still merciful, patient, and ready to forgive.
4. Compare God's command to Jonas with the vocation of the missionary today.
5. How can school children help the missions?

SELF-TEST

I. Be able to tell the story of every section of Unit Four.

II. Write a list of the important people of this Unit.

III. Describe the character of each of these people.

IV. Write a discussion of the following questions:
1. Why God gave the Israelites a king.
2. How the first king ruled the Chosen People.
3. Why the peace of Solomon's reign was disturbed.
4. The cause and results of the division of Solomon's kingdom.
5. What the prophets did for the Chosen People.
6. The Israelites as an ungrateful people under their kings.

V. Make a list of instances in the story of David which show that David was a king of strong faith and confidence in God.

VI. Add to your scrapbook pictures which tell the story of Unit Four.

PREVIEW

Unit Five

HOW GOD'S CHOSEN PEOPLE WERE LED INTO CAPTIVITY AND THEIR KINGDOM WAS DESTROYED

Divided among themselves, the Chosen People were becoming weaker and weaker. Meanwhile the nations that surrounded them were growing in power. We shall see in this Unit how God, in order to punish the people for their sins and to lead them to repentance, allowed their enemies to overcome them and to lead them away in captivity.

We shall see the great prophets rising up to rebuke the people for their disobedience to God and to announce to them that the coming of the Redeemer was near at hand. We shall see how God raised up great men and women to defend His people from their enemies. We shall learn how the Machabees fought bravely to free their nation, only to go down in defeat. The scepter passes from Juda and the prophecies are about to be fulfilled.

Unit Five

HOW GOD'S CHOSEN PEOPLE WERE LED INTO CAPTIVITY AND THEIR KINGDOM WAS DESTROYED

Unit Five

HOW GOD'S CHOSEN PEOPLE WERE LED INTO CAPTIVITY AND THEIR KINGDOM WAS DESTROYED

I. THE ASSYRIAN INVASIONS

1. THE PEOPLE OF ISRAEL ARE TAKEN CAPTIVE

For a while the kingdoms of Juda and of Israel were prosperous. They continued to regain the territory which their enemies had taken from them. They rebuilt their cities and built forts even in the deserts and the open countries to protect themselves from invasions. *Prosperity among the Jews*

The two kingdoms became wealthy. The prophets tell of their jewelry, their houses of stone and their couches of ivory. They had harps and psalteries and songs. They had an abundance of all good things, wine, meats, corn, oil, and flax.

But we also learn from the prophets, and especially from Amos and Osee, that the poor were oppressed in favor of the rich. They were treated cruelly and forced to labor very hard for little pay. The prophets rebuked the people for this and also for idolatry, cursing, dishonesty, murder, and adultery. They foretold that both kingdoms would be punished for all this wickedness.

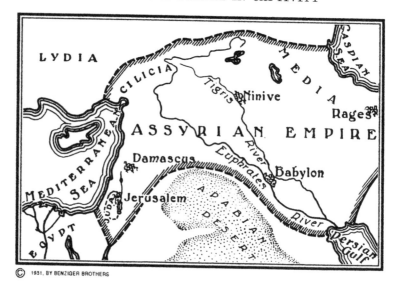

THE ASSYRIAN EMPIRE

The punishment soon came. First, there was rebellion on the part of the poor and downtrodden, and then the Assyrians invaded the land and all prosperity was at an end.

The Assyrians attack the Kingdom of Israel

Assyria was the growing nation. The king of Israel tried to gain the friendship of the king of Assyria by offering gifts of great value. He even promised to pay tribute and to be his faithful ally in order to be free from invasion. But the sins and idolatry of Israel had to be punished, and the king of Assyria came down upon the Kingdom of Israel, laid waste the country, and besieged Samaria. The city was cap-

The Fall of Samaria

tured, the king was cast into prison, and the Samaritans were taken captives. They were brought into

Assyria and made to settle in Media, in the eastern part of the country.

2. TOBIAS REMAINS FAITHFUL TO GOD IN THE CAPTIVITY

Tobias belonged to the tribe of Nephtali. He was one of the Samaritans who were taken captive to Media after the invasion of the Assyrians. Tobias never adored the golden calves set up in his country, and remained obedient to the law which commanded the Jews to worship in Jerusalem. Even while he was a captive in Media, he obeyed the law of Moses which forbade the use of certain meats. *Tobias in Media*

The king of Assyria was very cruel to the captives in Media. Many were put to death, and their bodies were left to rot in the streets. Tobias buried the dead and gave help to their needy relatives. The king heard of this kindness and charity of Tobias. He ordered him to be put to death and his property seized. Tobias fled and hid himself until after the death of the king. *Tobias buries the dead*

Under the new king, the Jews enjoyed more liberty. Tobias returned and his property was restored to him. He continued his works of charity. One day, after much labor, he lay on the ground to rest. While he was lying there, dirt from a swallow's nest fell into his eyes and blinded him. Poverty followed blindness, and he was supported only by the weaving of his wife. *Blindness of Tobias*

Tobias thought that he was about to die and he called his son, the young Tobias, to him and said, "When God shall take my soul, bury my body. Honor thy mother all the days of her life. When she shall have ended her days, bury her beside me. All the days *The advice of Tobias to his son* of thy life have God in thy mind, and take heed never to consent to sin. Give alms. Do not turn away thy face from any poor person. If thou have much, give much. If thou have little, give the little cheerfully, for alms deliver from sin and from death. Never allow pride to reign in thy mind or in thy words. Never do to another what thou wouldst not have done to thee. Seek counsel always of a wise man. Bless God at all times and desire Him to direct thy ways.''

The Angel Raphael as guide to Tobias

In his poverty, the old Tobias thought of some money which he had loaned to his friend Gabelus in Rages in the days when he was rich. He told his son to seek out a faithful man as a companion and to go and collect the debt.

Young Tobias found a strange young man in the city and asked him to go along with him as his guide. The young man consented and they set out on the journey.

Tobias catches a fish

On the way they came to a river. Tobias went to wash his feet, and a large fish came up to devour him. His companion told him to catch the fish by the gills and draw it ashore. He then ordered him to cut out the heart, the gall, and the liver, and to save them for medicine. When Tobias asked his guide what they were good for, the guide told him that the gall was good for anointing and curing eyes.

Tobias marries Sara

Tobias was led by his guide to a kinsman, whose daughter, Sara, he married. Sara's father gave her, as a wedding present, one-half of his property, with the promise of the rest after his death. The wedding feast lasted two weeks. During the feast Tobias'

THE ARCHANGEL RAPHAEL ORDERS TOBIAS TO DRAW OUT THE FISH

guide went alone to collect the debt. He brought Gabelus with him to join in the feast.

After two weeks, Tobias, his wife, and his guide set out for home. When he reached home, he remembered the remedy he had for blindness, and he placed the gall upon his father's eyes. Tobias immediately recovered his sight. *Tobias recovers his sight*

When the old Tobias and his son wished to pay the guide for his great services, the guide said, "The Lord sent me to you, for I am the Angel Raphael, one of the seven who stand before the Lord." In fear they fell upon their faces, but the angel said, "Peace be to you. Fear not, for when I was with you, I was there by the will of God. Bless Him and sing praises to *The Angel makes himself known*

Him.'' When he had finished speaking, he was taken from their sight and they could see him no more.

The death of Tobias After prophesying the fall of Ninive and the re-building of Jerusalem after the Babylonian Captivity, the older Tobias died at a good old age.

3. ISAIAS THE PROPHET IS SENT TO KING EZECHIAS

Ezechias, King of Juda At the time that the Samaritans were taken captive by the Assyrian king, Ezechias ruled over the King-dom of Juda. He was a holy man and listened to the prophets of God. When he was only twenty-four years old he had been made king. He destroyed all the shrines where idols were worshiped and tore down all the altars which had been built outside Jerusalem in defiance of the Law. At his command the priests and Levites cleansed the Temple and removed an altar that had been placed there in honor of the false gods. Seven days were spent in purifying the Temple.

Religious worship reorganized Ezechias also restored the order of the services as they had existed in the time of David. He provided the victims for the sacrifices of the morning and the evening of each day, and for the feast days prescribed by the Law of Moses. He urged the people to pay the priests the first fruits and the tithes as it was ordered in the Law of Moses, and the people obeyed him.

God hears the prayer of Ezechias One time Ezechias became sick unto death. Isaias came to him and said, ''Thus saith the Lord God, 'Get all things in order for thou shalt die and not live!' ''

When Ezechias heard this, he turned his face to the wall and prayed to the Lord, saying, ''I beseech Thee, O Lord, remember how I have walked before Thee in truth and with a perfect heart and have done that which is pleasing to Thee.'' Then Ezechias wept very bitterly.

Isaias was leaving the palace, when God spoke to him and said, ''Go back and tell Ezechias, the king of my people, Thus saith the Lord God of David thy father: 'I have heard thy prayer and I have seen thy tears and, behold, I have healed thee. On the third day thou shalt go to the Temple of the Lord and I will add to thy days fifteen years and I will deliver thee and this city out of the hands of the Assyrians.' ''

Ezechias at first followed the advice of the prophet Isaias, and put his trust in the power of God. Later, contrary to the advice of Isaias, he formed an alliance with Egypt and defied the Assyrians, whose king, named Sennacherib, was a cruel and proud ruler. This king marched westward and forced the Phoenicians, the Ammonites, the Moabites, and the Edomites to accept him as their king. He captured two cities of the Philistines and forty-six cities of the Kingdom of Juda. He was besieging the city of Lachis, when Ezechias offered him an enormous tribute if he would leave the country. *The Assyrians besiege Jerusalem*

Sennacherib withdrew, but he returned in a short time. Twice he sent legates to demand the surrender of Jerusalem. Isaias the prophet encouraged the people to stand firm against the enemy, and Ezechias prayed God to deliver him from Sennacherib. His trust in God saved him.

That night an angel entered the camp of the Assyrians and killed one hundred and eighty-five thousand *Sennacherib's army annihilated* men. Sennacherib was so frightened by the slaughter that he returned to Assyria without tribute from Ezechias. He did not annoy the Kingdom of Juda again.

Ezechias recaptured the cities which had been taken from his father by the Philistines. He strengthened the fortifications of his kingdom and improved the defenses of Jerusalem. He provided a water supply for the city, which would make it safe in time of siege.

4. Judith Saves the Kingdom

Assyria's second attack After the death of Ezechias, when the wicked Manasses was king of Juda, the Assyrians made a second attack upon that kingdom. Jerusalem was captured and Manasses led as a captive to Babylon.

Holofernes, an Assyrian general, with an army of one hundred and twenty thousand footmen and twenty thousand horsemen, laid siege to the city of Bethulia. The people defended the city bravely, but when the Assyrians cut off their water supply, they begged their leader to surrender. They held a council of war and decided that, if no help came within five days, they would give up the city.

Judith volunteers Judith was a rich, beautiful, and virtuous widow of the city of Bethulia. She rebuked the chief men of the city for setting a time limit to the power of God, and promised to put an end to the siege. She prayed for success and then set out for the Assyrian camp. She was brought before Holofernes. She told him that she fled from the city to escape the cruelty of his soldiers

JUDITH PREPARES TO SLAY HOLOFERNES

when the city should fall. Holofernes was pleased with her and gave her and her maids a tent.

On the fourth day after her arrival at the tent of the general, he made a great feast for his officers. Judith was invited. At the feast, Holofernes made himself drunk with wine, and he fell into a deep sleep. The officers left him alone in his tent. Judith then took the sword of Holofernes, cut off his head, hid it in a pouch and hurried to Bethulia. The people welcomed her with great joy. At daybreak the soldiers of the town attacked the Assyrians. They were panic-stricken when they found their general dead. The Jews followed them, killed great numbers of them, and collected the plunder which they had left behind.

Holofernes is slain

Later Manasses was released, and so ended this campaign against Juda.

THINGS TO KNOW AND TO DO

1. THE PEOPLE OF ISRAEL ARE TAKEN CAPTIVE

1. Explain the chief cause of the fall of Samaria.
2. Imagine and describe the conditions in Samaria at the time of the Assyrian Captivity.
3. Sin was the cause of the misery of the Samaritans. Discuss.
4. Why did the Assyrians aim to capture Samaria?
5. From Unit One discuss the early history of the Assyrians and Babylonians.

2. TOBIAS REMAINS FAITHFUL TO GOD IN THE CAPTIVITY

1. Give two reasons why Tobias was pleasing to God.
2. Give a floor talk in which you show that Tobias obeyed the Commandments of God.
3. Write a short theme in which you show that Tobias practiced the corporal and spiritual works of mercy.
4. How did God reward the patience and charity of Tobias?
5. Was God good to Tobias in allowing him to suffer? Discuss
6. Memorize the advice of Tobias to his son.
7. Give a floor talk in which you show how the young Tobias obeyed the Fourth Commandment.

3. ISAIAS THE PROPHET IS SENT TO KING EZECHIAS

1. Name four ways in which Ezechias proved himself a true servant of God.
2. How did God reward the confidence which Ezechias placed in Him?
3. Read in Unit Three how the Jews celebrated the Feast of the Pasch. Describe the celebration.
4. God never disappoints those who trust in Him. How does the story of Ezechias prove this statement?
5. God punishes the proud. Find an example of such punishment in this lesson.

4. JUDITH SAVES THE KINGDOM

1. Show how Judith prefigures our blessed Mother.
2. Make a list of the virtues which make Judith such a great character in history.

II. THE BABYLONIAN CAPTIVITY

1. King Joakim Disregards the Warnings of the Prophet Jeremias

Egypt and Babylonia were now at war with each other. In Juda there were two divisions of the Jews. One favored Egypt, the other favored Babylonia. Joakim was king, and Jeremias, the priest and prophet, warned him to obey God and to trust in Him rather than in an alliance with the king of Egypt. He prophesied the evils that would come to the Jews who relied upon Egypt. Joakim favored the Egyptians, and ordered his arrest, but Jeremias escaped. King Joakim and Jeremias the Prophet

The words of Jeremias were soon fulfilled. Nabuchodonosor, son of the king of Babylon, laid siege to Jerusalem, now allied with Egypt, and captured the city. He carried off the sacred vessels of the Temple. He put the king in prison and took many of the men of the city captives. After a short time in prison, Joakim was released and restored to his throne as a subject of the king of Babylon. The first capture of Jerusalem

Three years later, Joakim rebelled against the Babylonians. An army was sent against Jerusalem. It entered the city and the king and the principal men of his faction were killed. The city was conquered and the son of Joakim placed on the throne. The second capture of Jerusalem

In three months Nabuchodonosor himself came to Jerusalem. He burnt the Temple and carried off the The third capture of Jerusalem

THE PROPHET JEREMIAS WEEPS OVER JERUSALEM

king and his family. He took with him seven thousand Jewish soldiers and every skilled workman. He placed on the throne of Juda as his vassal the uncle of the king, whom he named Sedecias.

Sedecias respects Jeremias Sedecias listened to Jeremias. He asked for his counsel and even for the prayers of the man of God. Jeremias enjoyed liberty under Sedecias. He walked the streets of the city with a yoke upon his neck as a warning of what was in store for the people if they continued their wicked lives and their trust in Egypt rather than in God. He wrote letters to those already taken captive and urged them to be patient and to await the time when they would be free.

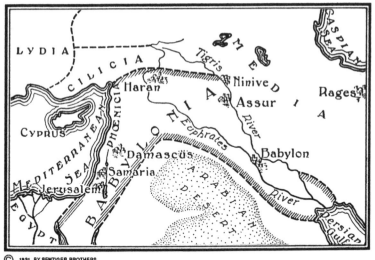

THE BABYLONIAN EMPIRE

When Sedecias joined the Egyptians against the Babylonians, Nabuchodonosor laid siege to Jerusalem the fourth time. During the siege, Jeremias preached in the city and told the people that all who should join the Babylonians would be saved. He was cast into prison.

The fourth capture of Jerusalem

The siege continued for two years. Finally a breach was made in the walls and the city was taken. Sedecias fled, but the enemy pursued and captured him. He and his children were brought to Nabuchodonosor. His children were put to death before his eyes. After his own eyes had been put out, he was taken captive to Babylon.

Everything of value was taken from the houses of

Jerusalem. The important buildings were destroyed. The beautiful Temple of Solomon was in ruins. The very walls of the city were leveled to the ground. Jeremias was spared and he was permitted to remain in Jerusalem.

The Ark of the Covenant saved While the Babylonians were plundering the city and before they reached the Temple, Jeremias and some Levites secretly removed the Ark of the Covenant and the Altar of Incense. They carried them across the Jordan and hid them in a cave in Mount Nebo. The place where they hid them was not marked. It was the sad sight of Jerusalem in ruins that inspired Jeremias to write the Lamentations.

2. The Prophet Daniel Preserves the Faith of the Captives

The Jewish captives were sent to Babylon and the neighboring country. Babylon had been sacked many times and had to be entirely rebuilt. **Nabuchodonosor rebuilds Babylon** Nabuchodonosor used the artisans and the laborers among the Jewish and other captives to carry out his plans. He forced them to work very hard. They repaired the old city wall of Babylon, and built a second outer wall. They dug a canal connecting the Tigris and the Euphrates Rivers a short distance north of Babylon. They restored nearly all the Babylonian cities. They built the elevated terraces known as the Hanging Gardens.

The Jews who belonged to the higher classes were treated more kindly. Among these were a man named Daniel and his three friends, Ananias, Misael and Azarias. They were cared for and educated as mem-

THE HANGING GARDENS OF BABYLON

bers of the king's own family. The prophet Ezechiel was given great freedom. He went about and encouraged the Jewish people to trust in God to deliver them from captivity.

While the Jews were in captivity, they were governed by elders of their own race. These elders often came to the house of a man named Joakim and his wife, Susanna, to judge the cases brought to them by the people.

Daniel saves Susanna

One day when the people had left the house, Susanna walked in her husband's orchard. Some of the elders were hiding in the orchard. When they saw her alone, they tempted her to sin. Susanna turned her back upon them. The elders then threatened to accuse her of sin and to condemn her to death. Susanna sighed and said, "If I do this thing, it is death to me. If I do it not, I shall not escape your hands. But it is better for me to fall into your hands without doing it, than to sin in the sight of the Lord." Susanna cried out with a loud voice. When the servants heard her cry, they ran to her. The elders cried out against Susanna. They accused the innocent Susanna of sin.

The next day the council of elders met in judgment and condemned her to death in the presence of her parents, her husband, and all her friends and acquaintances, who believed that she was guilty.

Susanna wept and looked up to Heaven, for her heart had confidence in the Lord. She prayed, "O eternal God, Thou knowest hidden things. Thou knowest things before they come to pass. Thou knowest that I am innocent, and yet I must die."

The Lord heard her voice. When she was led out to be put to death, the Lord spoke to the spirit of Daniel, who cried out to the people, "Are you so foolish that without examination of the truth you condemn a daughter of Israel? Return to judgment, for they have borne false witness against her."

When all had returned to judgment, Daniel examined each elder separately. Their answer to one question proved their guilt. Daniel asked each one under what tree he saw Susanna. The first elder answered that he saw her under a mastic; the second elder said that he saw her under a holm. Daniel said to both, "You have lied against your own heads. An angel of God waiteth to destroy you."

When the assembly had heard Daniel's judgment, they praised God for saving those who trust in Him. They rose up against the elders and put them to death. Daniel became great in the sight of the people from that day.

One day Nabuchodonosor had a dream which frightened him. But the dream escaped his memory. He called together all the wise-men and the magicians to find among them one who could tell him his dream and explain it to him. No one could be found to do such a difficult thing. In his fury, the king ordered all the wise-men in Babylon to be put to death.

Daniel describes the king's dream

Daniel begged God to reveal the secret to him. The secret was revealed to him in a vision that night.

Daniel went before the king. He told the king that the power which he had to tell the dream came from God, Who reveals deep and hidden things and knows what is in darkness. Then he described the dream which the king had forgotten.

When the king had heard Daniel's explanation of the dream, he cried out, "Truly, thy God is the God of gods, the Lord of kings, and the revealer of hidden things." He made Daniel governor over all the provinces of Babylon and chief of all the wise-men in his kingdom. He placed the companions of Daniel in charge of its buildings and works.

The burdens of the Jewish workers were lightened by their new governor. Gradually they received pay

Living conditions improved

for their labor and were then able to buy their freedom. They settled in colonies, and began to engage in farming and other business pursuits of the country. They were kept from idolatry by the courage of Daniel and other strong leaders among them. The priests and Levites instructed the Jews in the law and counseled them. They could not offer sacrifices as they had done in Jerusalem, but they offered prayers, morning, noon, and evening. They built synagogues where they listened to reading from the sacred writings. Babylon became a great center of Jewish learning.

The three young men in the fiery furnace Some of the leading men of Babylon were jealous of Daniel and his young friends because they were foreigners and the king had placed them in high positions. They pretended, however, that it was because of their religion that they wished the king to persecute them.

Nabuchodonosor erected a statue to the god Bel. He commanded all the chief men of the provinces to come to Babylon and to offer sacrifice to the statue at a given signal. Ananias, Misael, and Azarias, the three companions of Daniel, did not come, and their absence was reported to the king. The king was angry and he commanded the three young men to be cast into a furnace of burning fire. God sent an angel to save them from the fire. They walked through the flames unharmed, and they came from the furnace glorifying God.

Daniel in the lions' den Under the successor of Nabuchodonosor, Evil-Merodach, the people became enraged against Daniel because he had exposed the fraud of the priests of Bel.

They formed a mob and proceeded to the palace. They demanded the life of Daniel, and accused the king of being a Jew. The king was afraid and delivered Daniel up to the people, who cast him into a den of hungry lions. For six days the lions received no food. Daniel was in the midst of them, but they did not harm him.

Now there was in the land of Juda a prophet called Habacuc. He had boiled pottage and broken bread in a bowl and was going into the field to carry it to the reapers. An angel appeared to him and said, "Carry the dinner which thou hast into Babylon to Daniel, who is in the lions' den."

But Habacuc said, "Lord, I never saw Babylon, nor do I know the den."

Then the angel, taking him by the hair of the head, carried him to Babylon and set him down before Daniel. Habacuc said, "O Daniel, thou servant of God, take the dinner that God hath sent thee." Daniel said, "Thou hast remembered me, O God; Thou hast not forsaken them that love Thee." Daniel rose and ate, and the angel took Habacuc back to Juda to his home.

When the king learned that Daniel had not been harmed by the lions, he commanded him to be released, and then ordered his persecutors to be cast into the den. The lions devoured them immediately.

After the reign of Evil-Merodach, the kings of Babylon were usurpers, who had no right to the throne. Daniel's influence with them was not great, though he was not entirely forgotten.

Baltassar, one of these kings, made a great feast

and invited a thousand of his nobles. They feasted throughout the night and the king commanded his servants to bring the vessels of gold and silver which Nabuchodonosor had stolen from the Temple in Jerusalem, in order that all might drink from them.

The sacred vessels were brought into the banquet hall and filled with wine. Then the king and all his guests drank from them in honor of their false gods.

Suddenly a hand appeared on the wall and began to write. When the king saw this, he became terribly frightened. In vain did he try to read the words that were written; he could not make them out. He sent for his wise-men and his soothsayers, and promised that whoever would read the writing and interpret it for him should be clothed with purple and have a golden chain on his neck, and should be made the third man in the kingdom. But the wise-men and the soothsayers could not read the writing nor tell what it meant.

The king became more and more frightened. His guests, too, were greatly troubled. Then the queen advised Baltassar to send for Daniel.

Daniel was brought to the banquet room, and the king said to him, "I have heard of thee and that thou canst interpret obscure things and solve difficult problems. Now, if thou art able to read the writing and show me the meaning of it, thou shalt be clothed with purple and have a chain of gold about thy neck and be the third prince of my kingdom." To this Daniel made answer, "I do not want thy rewards, and

THE PROPHET DANIEL INTERPRETS THE HANDWRITING ON THE WALL

the gifts of thy house thou mayest give to another, but I will read the writing to thee, O king, and show thee the meaning thereof. Thou hast lifted thyself up against the Lord of Heaven, and the vessels of His house have been brought before thee. Thou and thy nobles and thy wives have drunk wine in them and have praised thy false gods. But the God Who hath thy breath in His hands, Who hath charge of all thy ways, thou hast not glorified. Therefore, He hath sent the hand which hath written this that is set down. And this is the writing that is written: MANE, THECEL, PHARES. This is the meaning of the word MANE: God hath numbered thy kingdom and hath finished it. THECEL: Thou art weighed in the balance and art found wanting. PHARES: Thy kingdom is divided, and is given to the Medes and the Persians.''

Then, by the king's command, Daniel was clothed with purple, and a chain of gold was put about his neck, and the king announced that he had power as the third man in the kingdom.

Daniel's prophecy was fulfilled that very night. The Persians turned the course of the Euphrates River and entered the city by way of the river bed. Baltassar was put to death. After a short battle, the Babylonian army surrendered, and Cyrus became king.

3. THE WORK OF THE PROPHETS

Their life We usually think of a prophet as a man who fore-tells some future event. We think of the prophets whose writings are found in the Bible as the holy men who foretold the coming of Jesus. Yet, foretelling the future was only a part of the work of a prophet among the Jews. The prophet was looked upon as the mes-senger of God, who spoke for God in the midst of men. He not only foretold the future, but he also told the people what they must do to please God at the present time.

The prophets lived apart from the people, very much like the members of religious orders today. If anyone wished to become a prophet, he had to go through a special course of training. There were schools of prophets, where most of these holy men studied, though not all of them were prepared to preach the word of God. Then they went forth as missionaries among the people.

The Bible contains the writings of only a few of the **Their writings** prophets. There were many others who had great influence with the people, like Samuel in the days of Saul, Nathan in the days of David, Elias in the reign of Achab, and Eliseus, his disciple. From the very beginning, God sent these holy guides to reveal to His Chosen People His holy will.

The prophets whose writings have been preserved **The Major Prophets** are divided into two classes: the major prophets and the minor prophets. The major prophets are those whose works take up a large part of the Bible. The writings of the minor prophets cover but a few pages each. The major prophets are: *Isaias*, who prophesied between 750 and 700 B.C., at the time that the Jews were conquered by the Assyrians; *Jeremias*, who prophesied between 630 and 580 B.C., when Jerusalem was destroyed by the Babylonians; *Ezechiel*, who prophesied from 600 to 570 B.C., to the Jews in captivity; and *Daniel*, who prophesied between 600 and 540 B.C., also to the Jews in their captivity.

Very little is known about the prophet Isaias. Ac- **The Prophet Isaias** cording to the tradition of the Jews, he belonged to the royal family, and his writings show that he was a very highly educated man. There is also a tradition according to which he suffered martyrdom at the hands of a wicked king.

He lived in the days before the Jews were taken away into captivity. The mighty nation of the Assyrians was threatening them on one side and the Egyptians on the other. The Kingdoms of Israel and of Juda had fallen away from God and no longer

ISAIAS AND HIS PROPHECIES ABOUT OUR SAVIOR

looked to Him for protection. They sought safety in their own strength or in treaties with earthly powers.

Isaias prophesied to the people and told them not to fear their enemies, but to fear themselves. He told them to put their trust in God, Who had saved them in the past and would save them in the future. But he knew the people would not listen to him. They would follow their own ways and one day they would be carried away into captivity and death.

But even if they are taken captive, God will deliver them. First, an earthly king will set them free. This is Cyrus, the king of the Persians. Then later on will come the Great Deliverer Who will save the whole world. "There shall come forth a rod out of the root of Jesse and a flower shall rise up out of his root. And the spirit of the Lord shall rest upon him, the spirit of wisdom and of understanding, the spirit of counsel and of fortitude, the spirit of knowledge and of godliness, and he shall be filled with the spirit of the fear of the Lord. . . . The wolf shall dwell with the lamb, and the leopard shall lie down with the kid. The calf and the lamb and the sheep will abide together, and a little child shall lead them.''

The Bible calls Isaias the Great Prophet because of **The Great Prophet** the wonderful things that he foretold. He clearly foretold the coming of Christ, the bitter Passion and death of our Savior, and the establishment of the Church of Jesus Christ.

Many, many years before the birth of Christ, Isaias said:

''Behold, a virgin shall conceive and bring forth a Son, and His name shall be called Emmanuel.

''A Child is born to us and a Son is given to us, and the government is upon His shoulders. His name shall be called Wonderful, Counselor, God the Mighty, the Father of the World to Come, the Prince of Peace. His empire shall be multiplied, and there shall be no end of peace. He shall sit upon the throne of David and upon his kingdom.''

In his prophecy concerning the sufferings of the Savior, he said:

''I have given My body to the strikers, and My cheeks to them that plucked them. I have not turned away My face from them that rebuked Me and spit upon Me.

''Despised and the most abject of men, a man of sorrows, and acquainted with infirmity.

''He was wounded for our iniquities, He was bruised for

our sins. The chastisement of our peace was upon Him, and by His bruises we are healed.

"He was offered because it was His own will, and He opened not His mouth. He shall be led as a sheep to the slaughter, and shall be dumb as a lamb before His shearers, and He shall not open His mouth."

Isaias foretold that the Church of Christ would draw the people to herself, that all nations would flow to His Church and that the Gentiles would be converted to God. He wrote:

"My spirit is in thee and My words that I have put in thy mouth shall not depart from out thy mouth . . . from henceforth and forever.

"And I will set a sign among them and I will send those who shall be saved to the Gentiles, into Africa . . . into Italy and Greece, to the islands afar off, to them that have not heard Me and have not seen My glory. And they shall declare My glory unto the Gentiles."

The Prophet Jeremias It was in 588 B.C. that the Jews were carried off into captivity by the Babylonians. For forty years the prophet Jeremias had been warning them that this terrible punishment would come upon them unless they repented of their sins and remained true to God. But they would not listen to him. The terrible day came, and we have seen how the king of Juda, all the nobility, the people and the vessels of the Temple were carried off by the king of Babylon.

Jeremias was left behind in the midst of the ruins of the Temple to mourn for his people. It was then that he wrote the Lamentations. This is one of the most beautiful books in the Bible. It describes the

THE VISION OF THE PROPHET EZECHIEL

destruction of Jerusalem and the great suffering of the people. The heart of Jeremias is bowed down with grief and loneliness, yet he does not lose his hope in God. He knows that the day will come when God will deliver His people from bondage. The Church makes use of the Lamentations of Jeremias in the Tenebrae of Holy Week, to picture for us the terrible sufferings of our blessed Savior.

Ezechiel was among those who had been carried away from Jerusalem by the Babylonians. He prophesied for many years after the death of Jeremias. He addresses his message not only to the Jews who were left behind in Jerusalem, but also to those who were in captivity. His message is one of hope and of

The Prophet Ezechiel

victory.   God will be true to His promises and deliver His people from the hand of the enemy.

Ezechiel prophesied in parables, which are very difficult to understand.   It is from the prophecy of Ezechiel that we get the symbols of the four Evangelists—St. John represented as an eagle, St. Matthew as a man, St. Mark as a lion and St. Luke as an ox.   It was in a vision that Ezechiel saw these figures.   He beheld a great whirlwind and a great cloud surrounded by fire.   In the midst of it he saw the likeness of four living creatures.

"And as for the likeness of their faces, there was the face of a man and the face of a lion on the right side of all the four, and the face of an ox on the left side of all the four, and the face of an eagle over all the four."

The Prophet Daniel   We have seen how Daniel lived in Babylon during the captivity, how he received from God the gift of wisdom, which made him a favorite with the king, who treated him as though he were a prince, and how even after the fall of Babylon, when the Medes and Persians came into power, Daniel remained in authority.

Daniel told the people constantly that in spite of the fact that they were captives in the hands of a mighty nation, they should not lose hope.   God had not forgotten His promises and was watching over them. He even foretold to the day, the time of their deliverance and the coming of the Savior.

THINGS TO KNOW AND TO DO

1. KING JOAKIM DISREGARDS THE WARNINGS OF THE PROPHET JEREMIAS

    1. What great lesson did the prophet Jeremias teach the Jews?
    2. Why did Jeremias hide the Ark of the Covenant outside of

Jerusalem? Does this action suggest what a priest would do if his church was on fire? Read the story of St. Tarcisius in "American Cardinal Readers," Book III, and tell it to the class.

2. THE PROPHET DANIEL PRESERVES THE FAITH OF THE CAPTIVES

1. Describe the life of the Jews in Babylon.
2. Point out four incidents in this lesson which show that God takes care of those who put their trust in Him.
3. Give a floor talk in which you prove that Daniel was a fearless prophet.
4. Compare Eve and Susanna in their temptations.
5. Write a short story entitled "Heroes of Faith."
6. "A Catholic I will live and die." Tell when these words ought to be on our lips and in our heart.

3. THE WORK OF THE PROPHETS

1. What were some of the great things which the prophet Isaias foretold?
2. Memorize the prophecy which says that Christ's Mother would be a virgin.
3. Memorize the prophecy which foretold Christ's sufferings.
4. How did the prophets help the kings?
5. Find the writings of the prophets in the Bible.
6. What is a prophecy?

III. THE JEWS IN BABYLON AND PERSIA UNDER CYRUS

1. Cyrus Permits the Jews to Return to Juda

The decree of Cyrus The empire of Cyrus reached from Persia to the Mediterranean Sea, but did not include Egypt. Cyrus saw that it would be to his advantage to have a friendly nation between himself and Egypt. Therefore, he issued a decree which permitted all the Jews to return to Juda. He gave back to them the sacred vessels which had been taken from the Temple by King Nabuchodonosor, and he ordered the Temple to be rebuilt.

The condition of the land of Juda The Jews were captives in Babylon for seventy years. During these years the Assyrians and the Babylonians had ruled over the land of Juda through a governor whom they appointed from a neighboring province.

The exiles return Only forty-two thousand, three hundred and sixty Jews returned to their own country. The majority of these were men of great faith, but there were also some idlers and some who were looking for adventure. Most of the Jews, however, managed to support themselves very well in Babylon and had established homes there. They were afraid to risk the dangers of a journey to Juda, and decided to remain in Babylon.

The people who had been taken captive from Samaria did not return to their country. They had been

THE PERSIAN EMPIRE

in captivity more than two hundred years. They had no religious leadership, and had forgotten their native land.

The leader of the returning exiles was Zorobabel. He belonged to the family of the kings of Juda, but had never seen Jerusalem. He came as the representative of the Persian king and as governor of the province. Josue, the high priest, accompanied him.

The journey from Babylon to Jerusalem took seven months. As soon as the Jews reached the city, they built an altar for the morning and the evening sacrifice. The sacrifices for the great feasts of the Jews were also offered on this altar. Preparations for rebuilding the Temple were made in the second year after their return to Jerusalem. Laying the foundation stone was a solemn occasion. The priests, vested

Preparations for rebuilding the Temple

THE TOMB OF CYRUS

in their robes, played on their trumpets, and the people sang songs of joy.

Rebuilding stopped   Some of the neighboring people, idolaters, offered to help in the building of the Temple. They said that they adored the God of Israel together with other gods. But the Jews would not allow these idolaters to take part in building the Temple to the true God, and this made them angry. They sent word to the king of Persia that the Jews were building the Temple as a fortress to resist him. The king believed this report, and he ordered the governor of Samaria to prevent the completion of the Temple.

Darius permits the rebuilding   The prophets Aggeus and Zacharias urged the people to continue the building of the Temple. At last Darius I, who was now king of Persia, listened to the prayers of the Jews. He permitted them to finish the building, and gave large sums in money and herds of cattle to promote the worship of the Jews. In the year 515 B.C., twenty years after the corner stone had been laid, the Temple was completed.

2. ESTHER SAVES HER CAPTIVE PEOPLE IN PERSIA

After the death of Darius, his son, Assuerus, became king of Persia. Wishing to choose a queen, he sent messengers into all the provinces to bring to the palace the most beautiful women in his empire. **Esther chosen queen**

Among those brought to the king was a Jewish orphan maiden whose name was Esther. She was accompanied by her uncle, a devout Jew, whose name was Mardochai. He thought that if Esther were made queen, she would be in a position to help her people. The moment Assuerus saw her, he chose her for his queen, not knowing that she was a Jew. Mardochai was given a position in the palace. His duty was to stand at the gates and to see that only those entered who had permission from the king.

The king's chief adviser, a proud and haughty man named Aman, entered into a conspiracy with two officers in the king's army, for the purpose of dethroning Assuerus. Mardochai discovered the plot, though he did not know that Aman had part in it. He reported the matter to the king, and the two officers were put to death. Aman was not suspected. But Aman hated Mardochai for defeating his plans. When Mardochai refused to bend his knee to him in reverence, he hated him all the more. **A plot against the king**

In order to revenge himself upon Mardochai, Aman went to the king and told him that the Jews of his

A decree
for the
massacre
of the
Jews

kingdom were preparing to revolt. He advised the king to send out a decree ordering all the Jews to be put to death. Assuerus believed the word of Aman and sent messengers into every part of his kingdom with orders for a general massacre of the Jews.

When Mardochai heard this terrible news, he commanded Esther to go before the king and plead for her people. Now, it meant death for a subject to go before the king without having been called, but Esther was not afraid, for the lives of her people were at stake.

Esther
before
the king

Esther told her uncle to call their friends together and have them fast with her for three days and three nights. On the fourth day she entered the throne room and stood before the king. Far from being angered at her boldness, he was pleased with her. He asked her what she wished and promised to give her even half of his kingdom. Esther told him that she had come to invite him and Aman to a banquet which she had prepared for them that day.

The king came to the banquet, and Aman with him, but Esther did not have the courage to tell her wish. She invited them to come again on the following day.

Aman's
plot

Aman was very proud of the fact that he had been invited to eat with the king and the queen. He told his wife and his friends that now only one thing was wanting to make him perfectly happy. That one thing was to see Mardochai hanging dead upon a gibbet. They advised him to build a gibbet and then to ask the king to hang Mardochai on it. So on the very day of the banquet Aman built a gibbet and made up

QUEEN ESTHER APPEARS BEFORE KING ASSUERUS

his mind to ask the king to condemn Mardochai to death.

That night the king was restless and could not sleep. **Mardochai's reward** He called in the historians of his empire and commanded them to read to him the history of his reign. As he listened to the reading, he heard again the story of how Mardochai had discovered the plot against his life. He asked if Mardochai had ever been rewarded for that loyal deed, and he was told that he had not.

In the middle of the night the king sent for Aman and asked him what kind of reward should be given to the man whom the king wished to honor. Aman thought that the king wished to honor him, so he answered. "The man whom the king wishes to honor

AMAN IS OBLIGED TO LEAD MARDOCHAI IN TRIUMPH

should be dressed in the king's robes, with the king's crown upon his head, and set upon the king's horse. Thus dressed, he should be led through the streets of the capital by the first prince of the land, who should cry out, 'Thus shall be he honored whom the king has a mind to honor'."

The king said to Aman, "Make haste and do as thou hast spoken to Mardochai the Jew, who sits before the gates of the palace."

Esther's petition The next day the king and Aman came to the second banquet which Esther had prepared for them. Again the king asked her to tell him what she wished and again promised that if she desired it, she could have half of his kingdom. Then Esther said, "If I have found favor in thy sight, O king, and if it please thee, give me my life, for which I ask, and the life of my people, for we are given up to be destroyed. We have an enemy whose cruelty influences the king." The king was surprised to hear these words and asked her what enemy had power to do such things. Esther answered, "Aman is our wicked enemy."

Then the king ordered Aman to be hanged on the very gibbet which he had prepared for Mardochai. The Jews were delivered from death and Mardochai was given the position which Aman had held.

3. Esdras and Nehemias Restore Religious Worship in Jerusalem

During the reign of Artaxerxes I, there lived in Babylon a priest whose name was Esdras. He asked permission of the king to gather together as many pilgrims as he could persuade to join him and to go back to Jerusalem. The king granted this permission and at the same time allowed him to take up a collection among the Jews of Babylon. In addition, he promised to give him a large sum of money, as well as much oil and wheat out of the revenues that he himself had received from the land of Juda.

Esdras returns to Jerusalem

The donation that Esdras received from the king was to be used for the restoration of the rites and ceremonies of the Temple. The king likewise gave Esdras full authority to correct any abuses which had crept in among the people. Esdras left Babylon at the head of six thousand Jews. They traveled four months before they reached Jerusalem.

When Esdras reached the Holy City, he found that even the devout Jews had gradually grown lukewarm in the practice of their religion. They had taken wives from among the pagan nations that surrounded them and were in danger of falling into idolatry.

Esdras appointed two priests and two Levites to find out which of the Jews had married idolatrous women. These were ordered to cast the pagan women and their children out of their homes. If they refused to do so, they were not allowed to associate with the faithful Jews.

Esdras saw immediately that the people needed instruction in their religion; hence he set about building synagogues, or meeting houses, in the different cities where the Jews lived. He gave orders that the people were to meet in these synagogues and listen to the reading of the Sacred Books by the Levites. The manuscripts which contained the sacred writings were large and difficult to handle. Therefore, Esdras had small copies made that were convenient to carry about. In this way he brought the Sacred Scriptures back to the people. He also prepared a list of the books that were inspired by God.

Esdras worked hard and zealously. He spared himself no effort and, when he saw that his labors were successful and that religious worship had once more been established in Palestine, he returned to Babylon.

Some time later, the king gave permission to Nehemias, his cupbearer, to return to Jerusalem and rebuild the walls of the city. Esdras made the journey to Jerusalem with Nehemias.

As soon as Nehemias reached Jerusalem, he assigned certain sections of the walls of the city to every family of the Jews. In spite of attacks from enemies, he succeeded in rebuilding the walls in fifty-two days. Nehemias appointed Hanani and Hananias, assistant governors of Jerusalem. Tobias, the Ammonite, was using one of the rooms of the Temple as a warehouse for his goods. Nehemias cast out all the goods of Tobias, and put in their place the vessels of the Lord that belonged there. *Nehemias rebuilds the walls of Jerusalem*

Tobias was angry at this action of Nehemias. He and his friends sent word to Artaxerxes that Nehemias was planning a revolt, and Nehemias was recalled by the king.

The king found Nehemias loyal, and after some years permitted him to return to Jerusalem.

Nehemias continued the work of reform and labored more diligently than ever. He urged the rich to forgive the debts of the poor, and advised them not to demand the rents that were due. He gave them an example by not accepting the gifts from the poor which were due him as governor. He made arrangements for the support of the priests and Levites, and ordered that the sacrifices be offered regularly. He insisted on the proper observance of the Sabbath. Because Manasses, grandson of the high priest, had married a pagan woman, Nehemias banished him from the city. Manasses, however, obtained an appointment as chief priest from the king and built a temple on Mount Garizim in Samaria. Thus began the schismatical worship of the Samaritans. *The schism*

THINGS TO KNOW AND TO DO

1. CYRUS PERMITS THE JEWS TO RETURN TO JUDA

1. Make a map of the Persian Empire and Egypt. Use colored crayon to show each country.

2. Why did the Jews from Samaria not return to Palestine?

3. Describe the people who were in the band which returned to Juda.

4. What sort of people were living in the land of Juda when the Jews returned?

5. Why did the Jews think first and above all of building the Temple again? What does this teach about supporting your church?

6. How did the Jews keep the knowledge of the true God during the time of their exile in Babylon? Imagine yourself one of the Jews returned home, and tell the class your feelings.

7. Write a short essay entitled, "Home Again."

2. ESTHER SAVES HER CAPTIVE PEOPLE IN PERSIA

1. Write a dramatization of the story of Esther and act it in assembly.

2. In a floor talk compare Judith and Esther as to courage and trust in God.

3. Esther is a figure of the Blessed Virgin. Discuss.

4. Write an essay based on the story of Esther in which you show that God is our Helper in need.

3. ESDRAS AND NEHEMIAS RESTORE RELIGIOUS WORSHIP IN JERUSALEM

1. Explain the difference between the synagogues and the Temple.

2. Describe the chief work done by Esdras in Jerusalem.

3. Make a list of the good works which Nehemias did in the city.

4. Why was it necessary to rebuild the walls of Jerusalem?

5. Write a paragraph in which you discuss the faithfulness of Nehemias.

IV. THE LAST DAYS OF THE KINGDOM OF JUDA

1. The Jews Are Ruled by the Greeks

For years after the time of Nehemias, eastern Asia was ruled by the Persians. In vain did Egypt, Cyprus, Phoenicia and the Greek cities of Asia Minor strive for independence. *Conditions in Juda*

In the land of Juda, trouble arose between those Jews who were faithful to the law and to the observances of their fathers, and those who were careless. The former kept the commandments and worshiped God according to the Law of Moses. The latter cared nothing about the law. They married pagan women and went to Samaria to worship on Mount Garizim. The high priest represented the Persian governor, and his authority was respected by the Jews who practiced the true religion.

The Greeks under Alexander finally defeated the Persian army in battle, and made Asia Greek instead of Persian. The Jews refused to pay tribute to Alexander, and he marched against Jerusalem. The high priest went out of the city with all his priests to meet the conqueror. Alexander recognized in the high priest the man whom he had seen in a dream, and who prophesied the success of his army. He greeted the high priest and went into the city and offered sacrifice. Alexander allowed the Jews to live under their own laws and to worship God according to their conscience. *Alexander conquers the Persian Empire*

2. The Jews Are Ruled by the Syrians

When Alexander died, his empire was divided into four parts, each part being given to one of his generals to rule. At first Palestine was under the same king who ruled Egypt, but later on, Jerusalem came under the power of Antiochus the Great, the Greek king of Syria. It was under one of his successors, Seleucus IV, that the following incident took place.

Heliodorus seeks the treasures of the Temple

Onias, the high priest, was a holy man and hated sin and evil. While he was in office, there was peace in Jerusalem and the laws were very well kept.

Seleucus admired Onias and sought to co-operate with him in keeping the Temple holy and in preserving the beauty of the divine worship. He defrayed the cost of all the Jewish sacrifices out of his own revenue.

A man named Simon, who belonged to the tribe of Benjamin and who had been appointed an overseer in the Temple, was jealous of Onias and tried to undermine his influence. He approached Apollonius, the son of the governor of the province, and informed him that there were immense sums of money in the treasury at Jerusalem. He told him that this money was not necessary for the sacrifices, and that it might be possible to turn it all over to the king.

The governor immediately notified the king. The greed of Seleucus was aroused, and he sent Heliodorus, one of his officers, to bring the treasure to him.

Pretending that he was about to visit the cities of the provinces, Heliodorus set out for Jerusalem. The high priest received him with great courtesy and it was only then that he discovered the true purpose of his mission. Onias told him that it was true indeed that there were great treasures of gold and silver laid up in the Temple, but that these either belonged to private individuals, who had left them there for safe-keeping, or they had been set aside to take care of the widows and the orphans.

But Heliodorus insisted that the treasure be handed over to him. He said that he had been ordered by the king to seize the money, and he went to the Temple to find it.

No sooner had Heliodorus entered the Temple, than a heavenly soldier, clad in golden armor and seated upon a horse, appeared to him, accompanied by two other young men, beautiful and strong and glorious in appearance. The horse rushed upon Heliodorus and, striking him with its forefeet, dashed him to the ground. Then the two young men stood on either side of the fallen man and scourged him without mercy.

Heliodorus was carried from the Temple half dead with pain and fright. His companions thought he was dying and begged Onias to offer sacrifice for his recovery. Fearing that the king might suspect that the Jews were responsible for what had happened to Heliodorus, Onias offered a sacrifice for his health and recovery.

While Onias was yet praying, the heavenly messengers again stood before Heliodorus and said, "Give thanks to Onias, the priest, because for his sake the Lord hath granted thee life. And thou, having been

HELIODORUS IS OVERTHROWN AND SCOURGED BY THE ANGELS

scourged by God, declare unto all men the great works and power of God.''

Heliodorus recovered and offered sacrifice to God. He thanked Onias for his prayers and, taking his troops with him, returned to the king.

Antiochus storms Jerusalem   Years passed and Antiochus Epiphanes became king of Syria. While waging war against Egypt, he stormed Jerusalem. He took many of the inhabitants captive or sold them as slaves. Many more he killed. Antiochus entered the Temple and removed the sacred vessels, plundered the treasury, and offered unclean animals upon the altar.

Antiochus was determined to break down the loyalty of the Jews to their nation and to their religion. Two years after his first attack upon the city, he returned and took possession of it. He destroyed the houses and the walls. He made a fort of Mount Sion for the Syrian troops.

Antiochus forbade the Jews to offer sacrifices to their God. He tried to force them to worship the gods of the Greeks. The Temple of the true God was made the temple of the pagan god. Pagans went to the Temple to adore their idols and they offered unclean animals upon the altar. In all the cities of Juda, pagan altars were set up and pagan worship commanded. All who practiced circumcision or who observed the Sabbath were punished by death. Once a month a search was made for copies of the law, and those who had them in their possession were put to death. Great numbers of the Jews fled from the cities. Others were sold into slavery. Strangers from other countries were brought into Jerusalem to take the place of the scattered Jews. **Religious persecution of the Jews**

These persecutions made the Jews strong. They became more devoted to the customs of Israel and to the worship of the true God. Their heroism was so great that many suffered martyrdom. They persevered in their loyalty even unto death. **Jewish martyrs**

Eleazar, a man ninety years old, one of the important men of the nation, was brought before the governor. He was accused of keeping the commandments of the old faith of the Jews. The governor commanded him to eat the flesh of swine, which was forbidden to the Jews. Eleazar bravely refused to do so. The great aged man aroused the pity of the people who were **The martyrdom of Eleazar** standing by. His friends told him to obey the king and save his life. He refused to follow their advice. Then they urged him to pretend that he was eating the swine's flesh, but to eat the meat which he could lawfully eat. But Eleazar would not deceive the king even to save his life. Besides, he told the people that men can deceive their kings, but they cannot deceive God. He thought, too, of the good example which it was his duty to give to the youth of his nation.

For his faith and obedience to God, he was led to the pillar of scourging and beaten to death.

3. The Seven Machabees Are Martyred

Their sublime courage It came to pass that seven brothers, together with their mother, were brought before King Antiochus and accused of disobedience to his law. They were ordered to eat the flesh of swine, and they refused. The king commanded that they be beaten with whips and scourges, but the oldest of them said, "We are ready to die rather than to disobey the laws of God which were received from our fathers."

When the king heard this, he became very angry and ordered huge pans and brazen kettles to be made hot. Meanwhile, the tongue of the oldest brother was cut out and his scalp was torn off. They also chopped off his hands and his feet. His mother and his brothers were forced to watch this cruel scene.

Finally, while he was still alive, he was brought to the fire to be fried in the pan. His sufferings were terrible, but all the while his mother and brothers begged him to keep up his courage and to die like a man.

After the first brother was dead, they took the second and, having torn off his scalp, they asked him if he would eat the flesh of the swine before he was made to suffer like his brother. But he answered, "I will not do it." Then they forced him to bear the same torments that his brother had borne, but with his dying breath he said to the king, "Thou indeed, O most wicked man, canst take away our present life, but the King of the world will raise us up in the resurrection of eternal life, for we die for His law."

The third brother followed him to death, as did the fourth and the fifth and the sixth. Their noble mother stood by and watched them in their sufferings, encouraging them to be brave and not to give in to the king's demands. At last, only the youngest boy was left.

The king, seeing that all his cruelty was having no effect, attempted to win the boy away from God by kind words. He promised him on his oath that he would make him a rich and happy man, that he would take him for his friend and give him everything that he wanted in this life, if he would only turn away from the laws of his fathers.

When the boy refused to listen to him, the king called his mother and told her to advise her son not to be stubborn, but to obey the commands of the king. But she scoffed at the cruel tyrant and, turning to her boy, she said, "My son, have pity upon me who took care of thee as a baby, watched over thee during thy boy-

Even a boy was unafraid

THE BRAVE MOTHER OF THE MACHABEES ENCOURAGES HER SONS TO BE
LOYAL TO GOD

hood and brought thee up unto this age. If thou turn
away from God, I shall lose thee now. So be not afraid
of this monster. Be a worthy partner of thy brothers.
Go bravely to thy death, in order that I may receive
thee again with them.''

While she was yet speaking, the brave boy said, ''I
will not obey the commandment of the king, but the
commandment of the law, which was given us by
Moses.'' Then, turning to the king, he said, ''Thou
hast not yet escaped the judgment of God, Who seeth
all things. My brothers, having undergone a short
pain, are now in eternal life. I, like my brothers, offer
up my life and my body for the laws of our fathers.

Calling upon God to be merciful to our nation, I am taking upon myself the punishment that my people deserve for their sins.''

When the king heard this, he became terribly angry, and ordered the youngest son and the mother to be tortured even more cruelly than the others.

Both died bravely, giving glory to God and refusing to sin against His law.

4. MATHATHIAS AND HIS SONS RESIST ANTIOCHUS

Among the families that fled from Jerusalem during the days of the persecution of Antiochus was that of Mathathias. He had five sons, John, Simon, Judas Machabeus, Eleazar, and Jonathan. They fled to the mountain Modin and lived there.

The flight of Mathathias

Antiochus sent his army in search of the fugitives. When the troops found them, they tried to force the Jews to submit to the commands of the king. Many of them yielded and offered sacrifice to the idols. But Mathathias and his sons refused to offer sacrifice to any but the true God.

Mathathias and his sons escaped and fled again to the mountain. A large group of fighting men, zealous of their religion, gathered about them. With the help of these men, Mathathias attacked various towns and drove out the forces of Antiochus. He punished the Jews who had surrendered to the king. After a year of this kind of warfare, Mathathias died. He gave the command of his army to his son, Judas Machabeus.

Judas Machabeus continued the warfare begun by his father. Though his army was small, he conquered

The victories of Judas Macha- beus

the generals of Antiochus in four battles. After the fourth victory the Jews enjoyed peace for a while. They began at once to purify the Temple, which had been used for the sacrifices of the heathen. They consecrated a new altar of sacrifice by offering victims upon it for eight days. This was afterwards annually commemorated.

A number of the Jews had fled to the territory of neighboring nations for protection, but they were not welcome, and these nations began to persecute them. Judas came to their rescue. He defeated the Edomites, the Ammonites, and the Philistines, and brought the refugees back to Jerusalem.

Sacrifices for the dead After one of the battles with the Edomites, Judas discovered that some of his soldiers who had been killed in battle had carried under their coats votive offerings which they had stolen from one of the heathen temples. They had been forbidden to touch any of these things, and Judas felt that they had been slain for their disobedience. Yet he knew that they had been good and brave soldiers and that they had sinned through human weakness. Therefore, he ordered that a large sum of money be sent to Jerusalem in order that sacrifice might be offered for the sins of the dead, for "It is a holy and wholesome thought to pray for the dead, that they may be loosed from sin."

Punishment of Antiochus Antiochus was in Persia when he heard that his army had been defeated by Judas Machabeus. He himself had just been defeated in a battle with an enemy king. He determined to take revenge on the Jews and started for Jerusalem.

On the way he was struck with a terrible disease. He was in great pain, yet he tried to go on. He continued on the journey until one day he fell from his chariot and could go no farther. The flesh fell from his bones, and the stench from his body was so great that no one could stand to be near him. He cried out to God for mercy and promised to give independence to the Jews, but his repentance was not sincere and God did not hear his prayer. He died a miserable death in a strange country among the mountains.

5. Judas Machabeus Is Slain and the Scepter Passes from Juda

The Syrians still held the fortress on Mount Sion, and Machabeus besieged it. During the siege some Syrian soldiers escaped from the fortress. With traitors from the Jewish army, they went to Antiochus Eupator, who was then king of Syria, to ask for help. The king marched on Jerusalem with a large army. Judas left the siege of Mount Sion and marched to meet him. He placed his army near a mountain pass where he could meet the companies of the enemy's army one at a time. A fierce battle followed. Judas saw that the king's army was too powerful for him. He retreated to Jerusalem, and Antiochus Eupator marched against the Temple. The army of Judas Machabeus had but little food. He would have been compelled to surrender had not quarrels in the Syrian

Macha-
beus
besieges
the
citadel

JUDAS MACHABEUS BEFORE THE ARMY OF NICANOR

state made it necessary for Antiochus to return to Antioch.

Another Syrian invasion
Antiochus Eupator later sent two armies to Palestine. His object was to force Judas Machabeus to allow Alcimus to perform the duties of the high priest. The second of these armies was under Nicanor.

Nicanor slain
Judas tried to drive Nicanor out of the country. He met his troops at Bethoron. Judas had only three thousand men in his army. Before the battle, Onias the high priest and Jeremias the prophet appeared in a vision to Judas and promised him victory. Thirty-five thousand Syrian soldiers were killed and Nicanor was slain.

JUDAS MACHABEUS ENTERING JERUSALEM AFTER HIS VICTORY

At this time Judas Machabeus thought of making an **Macha-beus'** alliance with Rome. Rome had become a very power- **alliance** ful nation and was opposed to the Greeks and Syrians. **with Rome** He sent ambassadors to Rome, where they were received very graciously. In the agreement that was made between Rome and Judas, the Jews promised to help the Romans in war, and the Romans promised to protect the Jews. As a result of this alliance, the Romans sent word to Demetrius, the Syrian, warning him not to molest the Jews any longer or he would have the Roman legions to contend with.

While the ambassadors were still in Rome, a third **Macha-beus** army marched from Syria against Judas. He was **is slain** encamped at Laisa with only three thousand men, most of whom fled when they saw the great numbers of their enemy. Judas commenced battle with only eight hundred men. He was slain and his army was scattered.

Jonathan leads the army

For some time after the death of Judas, the Jews were without a leader. Finally, they asked Jonathan to take his brother's place at the head of the army. The Syrians had become weary of trying to conquer the Jews, and when the warning came from Rome they recalled their army.

Shortly after this, Jonathan was murdered. He was succeeded by Simon, during a great part of whose reign the land was in peace.

The successors of the Machabees

Of all the nations of the world at this time, the Jews alone knew the true God and worshiped Him. The rest of the world was buried in idolatry and sin. After the time of the Machabees, the rulers of the Jewish people were for about five years engaged in civil war. Brother rose up against brother. At last, the Roman emperor appointed a foreigner, an Edomite whose name was Herod, to be king of Juda. The time had come which had been foretold by Jacob on his deathbed. The scepter had passed from Juda and now He Who was sent was about to come, the Expectation of the Nations. The world was waiting for the Savior.

THINGS TO KNOW AND TO DO

1. THE JEWS ARE RULED BY THE GREEKS
2. THE JEWS ARE RULED BY THE SYRIANS

1. What sin did King Antiochus commit when he took the sacred vessels from the Temple?
2. Why were the Jews persecuted by Antiochus?
3. How did the persecutions affect the Jews?
4. Why is Eleazar specially admirable?

The New Testament

Unit Six

HOW CHRIST PREPARED TO REDEEM THE WORLD

I. PREPARATION OF THE WORLD FOR THE MESSIAS

1. The Land Where Christ Was Born

At the time that our Lord was born, Palestine, the **Palestine** Promised Land of the Jews, was about the size of the State of Maryland. West of the River Jordan, which flows through the middle of the country from north to south, were three provinces: Galilee, Samaria, and Judea. The principal towns of Galilee were Capharnaum, Tiberias, Corozain, Cana, and Nazareth. In Samaria were Sichem, the first capital of the rebel kings; Sebaste, the name which Herod had given to the city of Samaria, the last capital of the kings of the Ten Tribes, after he had rebuilt it; and Caesarea Palaestina. Jerusalem, Bethlehem, Jericho, and Arimathea were the principal cities of Judea. On the other side of the Jordan, to the southeast, was the country known as Perea, whose principal city was Pella. Not many Jews lived in this part of Palestine during the time of our Lord. The northeastern part of the country was divided into several provinces.

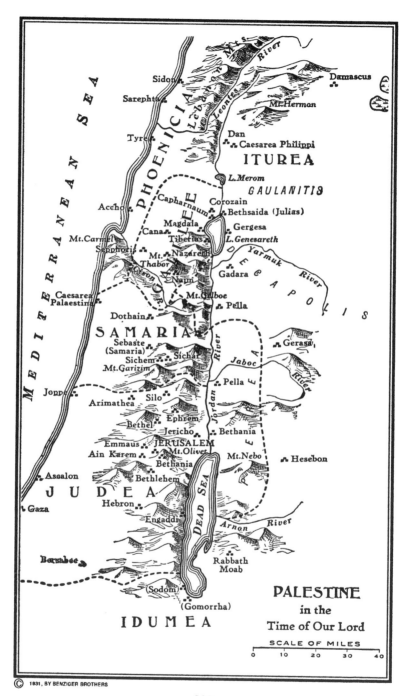

PALESTINE
in the
Time of Our Lord

SCALE OF MILES

Shortly after they had gained control of Palestine, the Romans built ten cities in this region. The neighborhood of these ten cities was known as Decapolis.

Palestine was now a Roman province. The Romans did not govern it directly, but through rulers whom they approved. When our Savior was born, Herod the Great, an Edomite, was king of Palestine. He had been appointed by the Roman ruler, Julius Caesar. The people hated him because he was not a Jew, and also because of his great cruelty. *The government of Palestine*

After the death of Herod, his kingdom was divided among his three sons, Archelaus, Herod Antipas, and Herod Philip. Archelaus governed Judea and Samaria; Herod Antipas was ruler of Galilee and Perea; and Herod Philip governed the northeastern part of the land.

Ten years after the death of Herod the Great, about the time that our Lord was lost in the Temple, the Romans took the government of Samaria and Judea away from Archelaus because he had shown himself incapable of ruling wisely. In his place they put a procurator, or governor. This procurator was a Roman and had his headquarters at Caesarea Palaestina. He went to Jerusalem only on the occasion of the great Jewish festivals.

The Romans kept a garrison of soldiers on guard in the city of Jerusalem. They were stationed in the Antonia, a fortified building northwest of the Temple. Whenever the procurator was in Jerusalem, he lived in a palace which had been built by Herod the Great on Mount Sion, across the valley from the Temple. *The Antonia and Gabbatha*

Between the Antonia and the Temple was a large square or court called Gabbatha. It was in this square that the **procurator** met the people on certain occasions.

The Publicans The Jews were compelled to pay taxes to Rome. The Romans sold the privilege of collecting these taxes to certain men who were called publicans. The publicans tried to enrich themselves at the expense of the Jews. They oppressed the people and forced them to pay as large a tax as possible. The people hated the publicans, not only because they oppressed them but also because they were a constant reminder of the fact that the Jews were no longer an independent nation, but were under the domination of a foreign power. Most of all, they despised those publicans who were Jews, for they considered them traitors to their nation.

Money Roman money was generally used in Palestine. The smallest Roman coin was the quadrans, worth one-half a cent; the next was the as, worth two cents; the sesterce, worth five cents; the denarius worth twenty cents. This is the coin that is called a penny in the Gospel. It took four Roman denarii to make one Jewish shekel. Greek coins were also in use in Palestine. A Greek stater was worth eighty cents, the same amount as the Jewish shekel. The Greek drachma was equal to the denarius. The didrachma was worth forty cents. These are the coins which were entrusted to Judas for the support of the Apostles. The talent mentioned in the Gospel was equivalent to three thousand shekels, or about twenty-four hundred dollars.

COINS USED IN PALESTINE IN THE TIME OF OUR LORD

Only Jewish money was permitted to be offered in the Temple, and this accounts for the presence of the money changers.

2. THE PEOPLE OF JUDEA

Dress of the Jews

The Jews had changed their manner of life very little from the time of Josue to the time of our Lord. They followed the customs that they had found among their neighbors. They wore a cotton or linen sleeveless garment reaching to the knees. Over this was worn a long-sleeved loose garment open at the front and bound at the waist with a girdle. The outermost garment consisted of a long loose robe with or without wide sleeves, and striped with various colors. The most popular colors were white, purple, red, and violet. Around their heads the men wore a piece of wool wrapped in the style of a turban, and the women wore a veil. On their feet they wore sandals.

Houses of the Jews

The houses of the Jews were built mostly of stones piled one upon another. Hardened clay served the purpose of mortar. The house usually had one room and was one story high with a flat roof, round which there was a balustrade. The floors were either unpaved earth or roughly polished stones.

A STREET OF JERUSALEM TODAY

The wealthy people had chairs and couches made of fine cedar wood and beautifully carved. The common people had rough benches and tables made of pine. For beds the Jews used a thin mattress with one or two coverings, which was laid on the floor. They also had little clay lamps in which olive oil was burned, kitchen utensils, bottles made of skins, pitchers and a hand mill for grinding corn.

The rich Jews had plates, knives, bowls, and cups made of gold; the poor had stone and clay vessels. The meals of the rich consisted of the foods brought by merchants from all parts of the Roman Empire. The poor ate mutton, fish, bread, and such fruits and vegetables as Palestine produced.

It was the custom of the time for the people to re-

JEWS RECLINING AT TABLE

cline on cushions while they ate, and all ate with their fingers from the common dish.

The Jews bathed very often, on account of the hot climate and the dust of the roads. They also anointed their skin with oil. Before coming into the house or sitting down at table or going to bed, they washed their feet.

Among the Jews were tradesmen of every kind, carpenters, masons, jewelers, tailors, and shoemakers. There were also shop-keepers who sold food, clothing, and furniture. But most of the people in Judea made their living by herding sheep and cattle or tilling the soil. In Galilee the people lived by fishing and farming. In Samaria they lived chiefly by farming.

Occupations of the Jews

They had no threshing machines in those days, but after the wheat was cut down, the sheaves were brought to a threshing floor. There oxen trampled upon them and loosened the grain from the stock. Usually there was a breeze in the evening. Then the farmer used the threshing fan, which looked like a wide wooden shovel and had a short handle. With this he tossed the wheat into the air. The grain, being heavier, fell to the ground, while the chaff was blown away.

The Day A day with the Jews lasted from sunrise to sunset. The first hour was six A.M.; the third hour, nine A.M.; the sixth hour, noon; the ninth hour, three P.M.; and the twelfth hour, six P.M.

Sacrifices Every morning and evening a lamb was sacrificed to acknowledge God's ownership of all things. Special sacrifices were offered on the great feasts. The Feast of the Pasch and the Feast of Weeks were observed in spring. The Day of Atonement and the Feast of Tabernacles were observed in September. Two feasts had been added to the Jewish calendar after the time of Moses. These were the Feast of Purim, celebrated in February in memory of the occasion when Queen Esther saved her people in Persia, and the Feast of the Dedication, observed in November in honor of the dedicating of the Altar and the Temple by Judas Machabeus. On the first day of every month special religious ceremonies were conducted for the people.

The San-hedrin Though the Jews were under the power of the Roman emperor, they were allowed to govern themselves in many things. For this purpose, they had the Sanhedrin, which was a body made up of seventy-one members, to which belonged the chief priests, as the

THE SANHEDRIN IN SESSION

former high priests were called, the elders, who were the leading men of the people, and the scribes. It was presided over by the high priest, who was usually appointed by the ruler of the country.

The Sanhedrin met in one of the halls of the Temple. It had authority over all religious matters. It controlled the public worship, saw that the Law of Moses was carried out properly, and decided which were true and which were false prophets. It was a kind of supreme court and could pass sentence on those who were found guilty of disobeying the law. However, it had no right to condemn anyone to death. This power was reserved to the Roman procurator.

Sacrifices were offered only in the Temple in Jerusalem, but the Jews met in other buildings, called synagogues, for religious instruction and for the reading of the Books of Scripture. These served also as

Synagogues

schools and court houses. Every synagogue had its ruler, who had the power to excommunicate unworthy members, and associated with him were elders. When the Bible uses the words "cast out of the synagogue," it means that the person in question was excommunicated from the religious society of the Jews. Synagogues were found throughout Palestine and in other parts of the world.

The Scribes The duty of instructing the people in the Law of Moses and of translating and explaining the Scriptures to them had become a special profession in the time of our Lord. The men who performed this duty were known as Scribes. They belonged to the various parties, though most of them were Pharisees, who desired the glory of Judea and the expulsion of the Romans. In the Bible they are also called "lawyers" or "doctors of the law."

The Pharisees The Pharisees were a sect that had been formed after the Jews returned from captivity. Their purpose was to preserve the Sacred Scriptures and to keep them free from error. They were deeply patriotic and tried to keep alive the ancient traditions of the people. In the beginning, they had done splendid work and had brought about a great reform in the conduct of the Jews, but as time went on, they became more interested in the letter of the law than in its spirit. They had a very high opinion of themselves and made a great show of their carefulness in observing every detail of the Law of Moses. They despised others who did not observe the law as they did. At the hours of prayer they recited long prayers in public and wore on their foreheads or arms larger phylacteries than the other Jews. These phylacteries were bands of parchment containing sacred texts. In many cases they were wicked men who kept the law only because

A PHARISEE WEARING PHYLACTERIES

it made them appear holy in the eyes of the people.

The Sadducees

Opposed to the Pharisees were the Sadducees. They denied many of the teachings of the Scriptures. They did not believe in the resurrection of the body or in the life in the world to come. The Sadducees ridiculed the Pharisees for their strictness in keeping the law. Most of them belonged to the wealthy classes and imitated the fashions of Greece and Rome. Some of them were courtiers of Herod the Great and, in contempt, were called Herodians.

The high priest sometimes belonged to the party of the Sadducees, as did most of the members of the Sanhedrin. They were worldly men and followed the external observances of the law only because they feared the people.

The Essenes

The Essenes were another sect that had grown up after the Jews returned from captivity. They lived apart from the people in communities very much like certain monks of the present day. However, they carried their religious zeal to excess. Because they considered all matter to be evil, they denied the resurrection of the body. They taught many other false doctrines.

The Nazarites The Nazarites were a class of men who took a vow to serve God by a life of great penance and mortification. They had existed among the Jews at all times since the days of Moses. During the time that he was bound by his vow, the Nazarite was not allowed to drink intoxicating liquor or to cut his hair. He was not permitted to approach dead bodies.

The Galileans Though the people of Galilee lived according to the Law of Moses, they were not held in very high esteem by the people of Judea. Some of them were fishermen, but most of them were farmers with small farms. They were not as highly cultured as the people of Judea and spoke a dialect.

The Samaritans The people of Samaria had a religion of their own which differed from that of the rest of the Jews. Their Bible consisted of the five books of Moses only. They had their own temple on Mount Garizim, which they insisted was the only temple of the true God. The people of Judea and Galilee avoided them. They would not pass through their territory unless it were absolutely necessary, and would not so much as ask them for a drink of water if they were thirsty.

The languages of Palestine At the time of Christ, four languages were spoken in Palestine. The Sacred Books were written in the ancient Hebrew, which few of the Jews understood. The language used in every-day life was Aramaic.

Usually the men in high positions and many of the Galileans knew Greek, and a few also knew Latin. Public signs and notices were generally written in Hebrew, Greek, and Latin, so that all might be able to read them.

AN ARAMAIC INSCRIPTION

In the time of our Lord, the great Temple at Jerusalem was spoken of as Herod's Temple. This was because Herod the Great rebuilt it after it had been partially destroyed by fire during a siege of Jerusalem. It had the same usual three main divisions—the Porch, the Holy Place, and the Holy of Holies. The Porch was on the east side. It was one hundred and fifty feet high and was like a great hall with three rows of beautiful columns running its whole length. The entrance to the Porch was through beautifully decorated gates.

Herod's Temple

The Temple itself was thirty feet wide. It was made up of the Holy Place, sixty feet long, and the Holy of Holies, thirty feet long. Surrounding the Temple and on a lower level was the large Court of the Priests, which only priests and Levites were permitted to enter. In it was the altar of sacrifice. On the north, south, and west of this was the Court of the Israelites, which all Jewish men might enter. East of this was the Court of the Women, which only the Jewish women were allowed to enter.

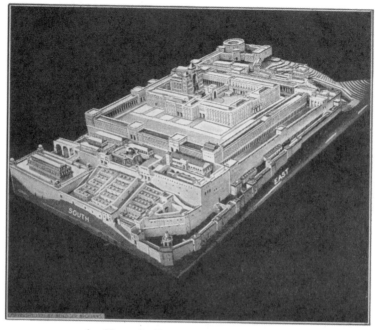

As Herod's Temple Probably Looked

Surrounding the Courts of the Israelites and of the Women was the Court of the Gentiles. It was separated from the other Courts by a wall four and one-half feet high. There were openings in this wall to allow the Jews to enter or leave the other courts. Near these openings were signs in Latin and in Greek warning all those that were not Jews that they would be punished by death if they entered within the enclosure. This Court of the Gentiles through an abuse was used as a market place, where animals for the sacrifices were bought and sold and where the money changers had their booths. It was from this Court that Christ drove the buyers and the sellers. On the outside of this Court there was a large open space, flanked on all sides by a high wall containing porches and halls. At its southeast corner was a high tower known as the Pinnacle of the Temple.

THINGS TO KNOW AND TO DO

1. THE LAND WHERE CHRIST WAS BORN

1. Prepare a class talk on the land where Christ was born and lived. Read "Jesus of Nazareth" by Mother Loyola, Chapter 14, and "The Story of Jesus," by Rosa Mulholland, Introduction. Both will help you to make an interesting talk.

2. Make a map of Palestine as it was in the time of our Lord. Show each province in a different colored crayon. Place in each province the important cities.

3. The following mountains are often referred to in the Old and the New Testament: Locate them on the map in your book. Mt. Olivet, Mt. Carmel, Mt. Garizim, Mt. Thabor.

4. Locate also the Jordan and Cison Rivers. Locate the Dead Sea, Lake Merom and Lake Genesareth.

5. Try to learn more about the people who governed Palestine at the time when Christ lived. Read "Old-World Foundations," by W. H. J. Kenedy—Sister Mary Joseph, Chapter VII.

2. THE PEOPLE OF JUDEA

1. Read "Lessons of the Savior," by a Religious of the Holy Child Jesus, Chapters I-IV.

2. Imagine that you are spending a month in Palestine in the time of our Lord with a companion of your age. Write a letter to your mother telling her about the country and the people whom you met.

3. Read again the description of Solomon's Temple. Was there any difference between the Temple of Herod and the Temple of Solomon?

4. Why was this Temple called Herod's Temple? Who actually rebuilt the Temple?

5. The Samaritans believed in the five Books of Moses. The true Jew believed in all the Books of the Old Testament. The Old Testament consisted of many more books. Look in the introductory chapter of this book to find the number and the names of the books of the Old Testament.

II. THE REDEEMER AMONG MEN

1. THE CHILDHOOD AND YOUTH OF JESUS

The
vision of
ZacharyAbout six miles west of Jerusalem in the little town
of Ain-Karem, lived a priest whose name was Zachary
and his wife, Elizabeth. They belonged to the tribe
of Levi, and the Bible says that they were just in the
sight of God and walked without reproach in the commandments and laws of the Lord. They lived a quiet
and secluded life in this little town in the hill country
of Judea. From time to time, when it was his turn,
Zachary left his home and went up to Jerusalem to
take part in the services of the Temple.

There was one great disappointment in the lives of
Zachary and Elizabeth. For many years they had
been praying to God to send them a son, but they had
given up hope that God would hear them.

One day towards the end of the reign of Herod the
Great, when it was Zachary's turn to serve in the Temple, he went to place incense on the Altar of Incense
that stood in the Holy Place, just outside of the veil
of the Holy of Holies. He was standing before the
Altar when suddenly he beheld an angel near him. He
was frightened, but the angel said, "Fear not, Zachary.
Thy wife, Elizabeth, shall have a son and thou shalt
call his name John. He shall be great before the Lord
and shall be filled with the Holy Ghost. He shall con-
vert many of the Children of Israel to the Lord their

A VIEW OF AIN-KAREM

God." But Zachary doubted the word of the angel. He said, "How shall I know this, for I am an old man and my wife is advanced in years?" The angel, answering, said to him, "I am Gabriel, who stand before God, and am sent to speak to thee and to bring thee these good tidings. And, behold, thou shalt be dumb and shalt not be able to speak until the day wherein these things shall come to pass, because thou hast not believed my word."

Outside, the people were waiting for Zachary and they wondered why he stayed so long in the Temple. When he came out, he could not speak to them. He made signs to them and remained dumb. Then they understood that he had seen a vision in the Temple.

Six months later, the angel Gabriel was sent from The God into a city of Galilee called Nazareth, to a virgin Annunciation espoused to a man whose name was Joseph, of the house of David, and the virgin's name was Mary. Mary was the daughter of Joachim and Anne and was a relative of Elizabeth. In spite of the fact that they were descendants from the royal line of David, Joachim and Anne were poor. Not having a son, they had been forced to espouse their daughter to a young man of their own tribe in order that their property might be kept in their own tribe, as the Law of Moses commanded. Although Mary had promised God to remain a virgin, she obeyed her parents and accepted Joseph as her husband.

The angel, being come in, said to Mary, "Hail, full of grace, the Lord is with thee; blessed art thou among women." When Mary heard these words, she was troubled, and wondered what manner of salutation this could be. But the angel said to her, "Fear not, Mary, for thou hast found grace with God. Behold, thou shalt conceive in thy womb, and shalt bring forth a Son; and thou shalt call His name Jesus. He shall be great, and shall be called the Son of the Most High; and the Lord God shall give unto Him the throne of David His father; and He shall reign in the house of Jacob forever. And of His kingdom there shall be no end." Mary said to the angel, "How shall this be done, because I know not man?" The angel said to her, "The Holy Ghost shall come upon thee, and the power of the Most High shall overshadow thee. And therefore also the Holy One which shall be born of thee shall be called the Son of God. And, behold, thy cousin Elizabeth, she also hath conceived a son in her

THE ANNUNCIATION

old age, because nothing is impossible with God."
Then Mary said, "Behold the handmaid of the Lord;
be it done to me according to thy word." And the
angel departed from her.

The knowledge that she was to be the mother of
God filled the heart of Mary with happiness, but she
did not forget the great joy that had come to Elizabeth. She set out with haste on the long journey from
Nazareth to Ain-Karem to visit her cousin. It was a
journey of four or five days and it is probable that
she made it on foot.

Entering the house of Zachary, she greeted Elizabeth affectionately. In that moment the Holy Ghost

The
Visitation

THE VISITATION

revealed to Elizabeth that Mary was the Mother of
God, and she cried out with a loud voice, saying,
"Blessed art thou among women, and blessed is the
fruit of thy womb. And whence is this to me, that the
mother of my Lord should come to me? Blessed art
thou that hast believed, because those things shall be
accomplished that were spoken to thee by the Lord."

When Mary heard these words, the joy in her heart
knew no bounds, and there burst from her lips the
Canticle the *Magnificat*, a prayer of praise and thanksgiving to the Lord. She said:

"My soul doth magnify the Lord. And my spirit hath
rejoiced in God my Savior. Because He hath regarded the

humility of His handmaid; for, behold, from henceforth all generations shall call me blessed. Because He that is mighty hath done great things in me; and holy is His name. And His mercy is from generation unto generations to them that fear Him. He hath showed might in His arm; He hath scattered the proud in the conceit of their heart. He hath put down the mighty from their seat, and hath exalted the humble. He hath filled the hungry with good things; and the rich He hath sent empty away. He hath received Israel His servant, being mindful of His mercy. As He spoke to our fathers, to Abraham and to his seed forever.''

Mary stayed with Elizabeth about three months and then she returned to her home in Nazareth.

When Elizabeth's son was born, her neighbors and relatives gathered in her house to congratulate her and to praise God, Who had shown His great mercy toward her. On the eighth day the child was circumcised according to the custom of the Jews, as a sign that he belonged to the religion of his fathers and was entitled to all its privileges. *The birth of John the Baptist*

It was at this ceremony that the Jewish child received his name, just as Christian children receive their names in Baptism. The relatives wanted him to be called Zachary after his father, but Elizabeth said, ''Not so; but he shall be called John.'' ''But,'' they said to her, ''there is none of thy kindred that is called by this name.'' Then they made signs to Zachary, asking him how the child should be named. Zachary asked for a writing tablet. He wrote on it, ''John is his name.'' No sooner had he written these words than his tongue was loosed and he spoke, blessing God. Fear came upon all those who were present, and soon the news spread all over the hill country of Judea. All who heard it, said, "What sort of person, think ye, shall this child be? For the hand of the Lord is with him."

Filled with the Holy Ghost, Zachary prophesied, saying:

"Blessed be the Lord God of Israel; because He hath visited and wrought the redemption of His people. And He hath raised up a horn of salvation to us, in the house of David His servant. As He spoke by the mouth of His holy prophets, who are from the beginning; Salvation from our enemies, and from the hand of all that hate us. To perform mercy to our fathers, and to remember His holy testament. The oath, which He swore to Abraham our father, that He would grant to us, that being delivered from the hand of our enemies, we may serve Him without fear, in holiness and justice before Him all our days. And thou, child, shalt be called the prophet of the Most High; for thou shalt go before the face of the Lord to prepare His ways; to give knowledge of salvation to His people, unto the remission of their sins; through the abundance of the mercy of our God, in which the Orient from on high hath visited us; to enlighten them that sit in darkness, and in the shadow of death; to direct our feet into the way of peace." This is the canticle *Benedictus*.

The child of Zachary and Elizabeth grew up strong in body and holy in spirit. When he was still a young boy, he left the home of his parents and went to live in the desert. There he remained for many years until God called him to come forth and preach to the people.

An angel speaks to Joseph After Mary had returned to her home in Nazareth, Joseph learned that she was to become the mother of the Savior. An angel appeared to him in his sleep and said, "Joseph, son of David, Mary, thy wife is to become a mother through the Holy Ghost. She shall bring forth a Son, and thou shalt call His name Jesus. For He shall save His people from their sins." Thus was fulfilled the prophecy of Isaias, "Behold, a virgin shall be with child, and bring forth a son, and they shall call His name Emmanuel, which means, God with us."

In those days it happened that a decree went forth **The birth of Christ** from Augustus, the Roman emperor, ordering that a census be taken of his whole empire. Rome had reached the height of her power, and the emperor wished to know exactly the extent of his rule. The census would likewise reveal to him the resources of the various provinces and he could then put a valuation on them for the purpose of taxation.

Now, whenever the Jews took up a census, they left their place of residence and went to the city from which their ancestors came. Joseph and Mary were descendants of David. Therefore, they went up from Galilee, out of the city of Nazareth, into Judea to the City of David, which is called Bethlehem.

When they reached the little town of Bethlehem, they found it crowded with visitors, and there was no room for them in the inn. They sought in vain for a place to stay, but the best shelter that they could find was a cave in the side of a hill on the outskirts of the town. This cave was used as a kind of stable for animals in bad weather.

Entering the cave, Mary and Joseph prepared to remain there for the night. It was during that night, and in that humble stable, that the Son of God was

BETHLEHEM TODAY

born into the world. Mary wrapped the Divine Infant in swaddling clothes and laid Him in a manger.

The adoration of the shepherds Not far away a group of shepherds were keeping the night-watches over their flocks to protect them from wolves or robbers. Suddenly an angel of the Lord appeared to them, and the brightness of heaven shone about them. The shepherds feared with a great fear, but the angel said to them, "Fear not; for, behold, I bring you good tidings of great joy, that shall be to all the people. For this day is born to you a Savior, Who is Christ the Lord, in the City of David. And this shall be a sign unto you: You shall find the Infant wrapped in swaddling clothes, and laid in a manger."

He had no sooner spoken than the shepherds saw with him a great multitude of angels, and heard them praising God and saying, "Glory to God in the highest; and on earth peace to men of good will." Then the angels disappeared.

The hearts of the shepherds were filled with wonder,

THE SHEPHERDS VISIT THE INFANT JESUS

and they said one to another, "Let us go over to Bethlehem, and let us see this word that is come to pass, which the Lord hath showed to us."

They hastened to Bethlehem, and there they found Mary and Joseph, and the Infant lying in a manger. Kneeling down, they adored their Savior.

The shepherds returned to their flocks, glorifying and praising God for all the things they had heard and seen.

According to the law, eight days later the Child was **The Circumcision** circumcised and His name was called Jesus, which was the name given to Him by the angel Gabriel when he had appeared to Mary. The name Jesus means Savior.

THE PRESENTATION OF THE CHILD JESUS IN THE TEMPLE

The Child Jesus is presented in the Temple   When the Infant Jesus was forty days old, Mary and Joseph carried Him to Jerusalem, where, according to the Law of Moses, He was to be presented to the Lord. While they were offering the sacrifice which the law required of the poor—a pair of turtledoves or two young pigeons—the Holy Spirit led a man named Simeon into the Temple.

Simeon lived in Jerusalem. He was an old man, holy and devout, who throughout his long life had prayed and waited for the Savior. The Holy Ghost had answered his prayer and promised him that he should not see death before he had seen Christ the Lord.

When he saw the Infant Jesus, he took Him in his arms, blessed God and said, "Now, O Lord, dost Thou dismiss Thy servant, according to Thy word, in peace. Because my eyes have seen Thy salvation, which Thou hast prepared before the face of all peoples; a light to the revelation of the Gentiles, and the glory of Thy people Israel." This is the Canticle *Nunc Dimittis*.

Then turning to Mary and Joseph, Simeon blessed them. To Mary he said, "Behold, this Child is set for the fall, and for the resurrection of many in Israel, and for a sign which shall be contradicted. And thy own soul a sword shall pierce, that out of many hearts thoughts may be revealed."

There was also in the Temple a prophetess, named Anna. She was a widow and she was very old, but she stayed in the Temple night and day, praying and fasting. When she saw the Infant Jesus, she knew at once that He was the Savior of the world, and she announced his coming to all that looked for the redemption of Israel.

Soon after this, wise-men came from the East to Jerusalem, seeking the King of the Jews. They said that they had seen His star in the East and had come to adore Him. When Herod heard this, he was troubled. He assembled all the chief priests and the scribes of the people and inquired of them where Christ should be born. They replied, "In Bethlehem of Juda. For so it is written by the prophet [Micheas]: 'And thou, Bethlehem, the land of Juda, art not the least among the princes of Juda, for out of thee shall come forth the Captain that shall rule

The adoration of the Magi

My people Israel.' '' When he learned from them that the King of the Jews should be born at Bethlehem, he called the wise-men privately to learn from them when the star of the new King had appeared to them. Herod sent them into Bethlehem and asked them to return to Jerusalem when they found the Child, that he, too, might go to adore Him.

When the wise-men had learnt from Herod where to look for the Child, they set out for Bethlehem. As they left Jerusalem, the star which had guided them in the East went before them again, until it stood over the place where the Child was.

The wise-men entered the house and found the Child and His Mother and, falling down, they adored Him. They opened their treasures and offered Him gifts of gold, frankincense, and myrrh.

They were afterwards warned in their sleep not to go back to Herod, so they returned home by another way.

The Flight into Egypt

When the wise-men had gone, an angel of the Lord appeared to Joseph in his sleep, and told him to arise, take the Child and His Mother, and flee into Egypt. ''For it will come to pass,'' he said, ''that Herod will seek the Child to destroy Him.''

Joseph arose, took the Child and His Mother, and in the middle of the night started out on the journey into Egypt. Herod waited in vain for the wise-men to return to him. When at last he realized that they were not coming, he became very angry. He sent soldiers into Bethlehem and to all the country around it, with orders to kill every little boy who was two years

THE ADORATION OF THE MAGI

old or younger. It was thus that he hoped to destroy the newborn King of the Jews.

The soldiers entered Bethlehem, tore the babies from their mothers' arms, and murdered them. Thus was fulfilled the prophecy of Jeremias, who said, "A voice in Rama was heard, lamentation and great mourning; Rachel bewailing her children, and would not be comforted, because they are not."

Soon after this, Herod died, and again the angel appeared to Joseph, saying, "Arise, and take the Child and His Mother, and go into the land of Israel. For they are dead that sought the life of the Child."

At the word of the angel, Joseph returned to the

land of Israel. Thus were fulfilled the words which were spoken by the prophet Osee, "Out of Egypt have I called My Son." Hearing that Archelaus, Herod's son, was reigning in Judea in the place of his father, Joseph was afraid to return to Bethlehem, for Archelaus was following in his father's footsteps and treating the Jews with great cruelty. In obedience to a warning that came to him in his sleep, Joseph took Jesus and Mary and went back to their home at Nazareth, in Galilee. Thus again was fulfilled the word of the prophet, "that He shall be called a Nazarene."

The Finding of Jesus in the Temple

Every year in the springtime, Mary and Joseph went up to Jerusalem to celebrate the great Feast of the Pasch. When Jesus was twelve years old, He went along with them. The celebration of this feast lasted seven days. When it was over, Mary and Joseph began their homeward journey, but the Child Jesus remained in Jerusalem, though His parents did not know it. They thought He was with some friend or with one of their relatives.

Great crowds of pilgrims were in the city of Jerusalem for the celebration of the Pasch, and it is easy to understand why there would be much confusion when they were setting out on their homeward journey. Usually the men traveled in one company, and the women in another. Children might be with their fathers or with their mothers. It was only after they had gone quite a distance from the city that the families would be united.

At the end of the first day's journey, Mary and

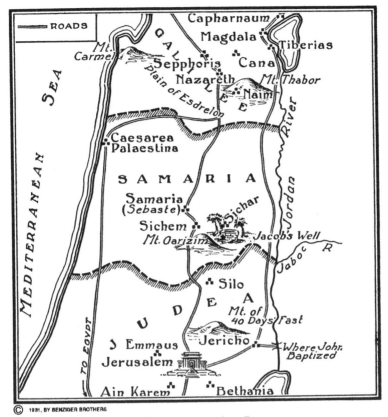

THE JOURNEYS OF OUR LORD

Joseph looked for Jesus among their kinsfolk and acquaintances, but He was not to be found. Fearing that something had happened to Him, and filled with sorrow, they hastened back to Jerusalem.

They wandered about the city and the Temple looking for Him, but in vain. But at last on the third day after His disappearance, when they had about given up hope, they found Him in the Temple, sitting in the midst of the doctors of the law, listening to them and

A PRESENT-DAY VIEW OF NAZARETH

asking them questions. All that heard Him were astonished at His wisdom and His answers.

Mary and Joseph were surprised when they saw Jesus in the midst of all these learned men. Going up to Him, Mary said, "Son, why hast Thou done so to us? Behold, Thy father and I have sought Thee, sorrowing." But Jesus said to her, "How is it that you sought Me? Did you not know that I must be about My Father's business?"

Then Jesus, Mary, and Joseph left Jerusalem and started on their journey to Nazareth. Nazareth was a town of about fifteen thousand people, located in the southern part of Galilee. From the surrounding hills could be seen the Plain of Esdrelon, and in the distance the Mediterranean Sea and Mount Carmel. To the north were the snowcapped peaks of Lebanon and Hermon, on the east Mount Thabor, the low bed of the Jordan and the table-land of Galaad. The country around Nazareth was very fertile. Flowers grew everywhere and the mild climate helped in the raising of pomegranates, oranges, figs, and olives.

Here it was that Jesus lived for thirty years. He was kind and obedient to Mary and Joseph, and the Bible says He advanced in wisdom and age and grace with God and men. Some time during these years Joseph died. The Bible does not speak of his death, but we can imagine how lovingly Jesus and Mary watched over him and took care of him in his last illness, and how happy he was to die in their arms.

2. John the Baptist Prepares the Way for the Redeemer

John prepares for his Mission

Out in the desert, John, the son of Zachary, was getting ready for the great work to which God had called him. He lived the life of a Nazarite, wearing a rough garment made of camel's hair, with a leather girdle around his waist. The only food which he ate was locusts and the wild honey which the bees deposited in the crevices of rocks or in hollow trees. When God revealed to him that the time had come for him to begin his work, he came out of the desert into the country along the River Jordan and began to preach to the people.

John's preaching

There was a ford in the River Jordan, and all day long people were crossing it on their travels to or from Jerusalem. John stood near this ford, and as the people were passing by, he called out to them, saying, "Do penance; for the Kingdom of Heaven is at hand." Hearing these strange words, the people

THE TERRITORY AROUND THE NORTH OF THE DEAD SEA

would stop and ask him what he meant. He would begin to preach to them and to tell them to be sorry for their sins. The very sight of him was enough to move their hearts to repentance. They remembered the words of the prophet Isaias, "A voice of one crying in the wilderness: Prepare ye the way of the Lord; make straight His paths. Every valley shall be filled, and every mountain and hill shall be brought low. And the crooked shall be made straight, and the rough ways plain, and all flesh shall see the salvation of God."

In the beginning, John's audiences were small, but soon the story of this strange preacher was told throughout the land, and great crowds of people came to the Jordan to hear him. Many were converted by his words, and went out and stood in the river, where he baptized them as a sign of their repentance and their resolution to live a better life. This baptism did not wash away their sins, but only prepared their hearts for the coming of the Savior.

The people regarded John, whom they called the

Baptist, as a great prophet. Not since the days of the prophets of old had anyone spoken with such authority.

Many of the Pharisees and Sadducees went to hear him. To them, John said, "Ye brood of vipers, who hath showed you how to flee from the wrath to come? Bring forth fruits worthy of penance. Every tree that bringeth not forth good fruit shall be cut down and cast into the fire."

Some publicans came to him to be baptized, and said, "Master, what shall we do?" He answered, "Do nothing more than that which is appointed you," that is, take only the tax which is just. To the soldiers who came and asked him what they should do, he said, "Do violence to no man, neither calumniate any man. And be content with your pay." To the ordinary people who feared God and tried to do their duty, he said, "He that hath two coats, let him give to him that hath none. And he that hath meat, let him do in like manner."

Many of the people began to wonder in their hearts if John were not perhaps the Savior of the world. But John said to them, "I baptize you with water. But there shall come One mightier than I, the latchet of Whose shoes I am not worthy to loose. He shall baptize you with the Holy Ghost and with fire. His threshing fan is in His hand, and He will purge His floor and will gather the wheat into His barn. But the chaff He will burn with unquenchable fire."

When Jesus was thirty years old, He left Nazareth and came to the Jordan where John was preaching, and asked to be baptized. Knowing that Jesus was

The Baptism of Jesus

THE BAPTISM OF JESUS

the Messias, John said to Him, "I ought to be baptized by Thee, and dost Thou come to me?" Jesus explained to John that He must be baptized because it was part of God's plan for redeeming the human race. Humbly John obeyed, and baptized the Savior of the world.

When Jesus came out of the water, the heavens were opened and the Holy Spirit came down upon Him in the form of a dove. A voice from Heaven was heard, saying, "This is My beloved Son, in Whom I am well pleased. Hear ye Him."

Jesus in the desert After His baptism, Jesus was led by the Spirit of God into the northern part of the desert of Judea, one

JESUS REPULSES THE TEMPTER

of the roughest of all the deserts in Palestine. Here the Savior hid himself away for forty days, praying and fasting in preparation for the great work for which He had come into the world. He had no companions save the wild beasts of the desert. For forty days and forty nights, He took neither food nor drink.

After the long fast, Jesus was hungry. Satan appeared to Him in the desert and said, "If Thou be the Son of God, command that these stones be made bread." But Jesus answered: "Not in bread alone doth man live, but in every word that proceedeth from the mouth of God."

The first temptation of Jesus

Then the devil took Him up into the Holy City, and

The second temptation

set Him upon the pinnacle of the Temple and said to Him, "If Thou be the Son of God, cast Thyself down, for it is written that He hath given His angels charge over Thee, and in their hands they shall bear Thee up, lest perhaps Thou dash Thy foot against a stone." But Jesus answered, "Thou shalt not tempt the Lord thy God."

The third temptation

The devil took Jesus up into a very high mountain and showed Him all the kingdoms of the world and the glory of them, and said to Him, "All these will I give Thee if, falling down, Thou wilt adore me." Then Jesus said to Satan, "Begone, Satan, for it is written: 'The Lord thy God shalt thou adore, and Him only shalt thou serve.'" Then the devil left Him, and angels came and took care of Him.

3. Jesus Calls His First Disciples

Jesus, the Son of God

When Jesus left the desert after His fast of forty days, he went back to the Jordan, where John was still baptizing. When John saw Jesus coming toward Him, he cried out, "Behold the Lamb of God, behold Him Who taketh away the sin of the world."

John and Andrew

The next day John was standing on the banks of the river with two of his disciples, or followers, and again Jesus passed by. Pointing to Him, John said, "Behold the Lamb of God." The two disciples left John and started to follow after Jesus. Jesus turned and said to them, "Whom seek ye?" They answered, "Master, where dwellest Thou?" Jesus replied, "Come and see." They went along and stayed with

Him all that day. Their names were John and Andrew.

Now, Andrew had a brother named Simon. He went **Peter** to look for him, and when he found him, he said, "We have found the Messias." And he took him to Jesus. When Jesus saw Simon, He said, "Thou art Simon; thou shalt be called Cephas." Cephas is the Aramaic word for Peter, a rock.

On the following day, Jesus went into Galilee and **Philip and Nathanael** there met a young man named Philip. He said to him, "Follow Me." Shortly after this, Philip met his friend, Nathanael, and told him that he had found the Messias, Who was Jesus of Nazareth. Nathanael asked, "Can anything good come from Nazareth?" for that city was held in contempt by the rest of the provinces. Philip answered, "Come and see." When Jesus saw Nathanael coming to Him, He said, "Behold an Israelite indeed in whom there is no guile." Nathanael said to Him, "How dost Thou know me?" Jesus answered, "Before Philip called thee, when thou wast under the fig tree, I saw thee." Nathanael answered Him and said, "Master, Thou art the Son of God; Thou art the King of Israel."

From that time, Jesus began to preach to the people **James** and to say, "Do penance, for the Kingdom of Heaven is at hand." Soon great crowds were following Him wherever He went. Many of the people believed in Him and tried to live according to His teachings. One day, when He was walking by the Sea of Galilee, He saw the two brothers, Simon and Andrew, casting a net into the sea, for they were fishermen. He said to them,

JESUS CHOOSES HIS FIRST DISCIPLES

"Come after Me, and I will make you fishers of men."
Immediately they left their nets and followed Him.
Going a little farther on, He saw John in a ship with
his brother, James, and his father, who was called
Zebedee. They were mending their nets. He called
them, and immediately James and John left their nets
and their father, and followed after Him.

Matthew   Another day, as Jesus was passing by a custom-
house, He saw a publican by the name of Matthew,
sitting there and collecting the taxes. He said to him,
"Follow Me." Immediately Matthew rose up and followed after Him.

Some time after this, when they were in Galilee,

Jesus went up to the top of a mountain, alone, to pray. **The Twelve Apostles** He spent the whole night in prayer, and at dawn came down to where His disciples were waiting for Him. Then it was that He chose twelve of them to be His apostles. These twelve were to remain with Him always. They were: Simon, to whom He gave the name Peter; James and John, the sons of Zebedee, whom he called the Sons of Thunder; Andrew, Philip, Bartholomew, commonly considered to be Nathanael, Matthew, Thomas, James, the son of Alpheus, Thaddeus, also called Jude, Simon the Cananean, and Judas Iscariot. All except Judas, who came from Kerioth, a town in Judea, were Galileans. From this time forward the twelve apostles gave all their time to the service of the Savior and followed Him wherever He went.

For nine months, Jesus instructed the apostles and prepared them for their mission. Then He sent them out to preach and to work miracles in Palestine. He gave them power to heal the sick, to raise the dead to life, to cure lepers, and to cast out devils.

The apostles did not preach to the Gentiles or to the Samaritans, but only to the Jews. They went from city to city, without money, food, or extra clothing. They were to place their trust in God and depend for their living upon the faith and piety of the people to whom they preached the gospel of Jesus.

4. John the Baptist Is Beheaded

Herod Antipas, the ruler of Galilee and Perea, had **John the Baptist in prison** unlawfully married Herodias, the wife of Philip, his

brother. John the Baptist rebuked him for this publicly, and Herod ordered him thrown into prison.

At this time, Jesus had entered upon His public life.
He had preached to the people and worked a number
of miracles. From his prison, John sent two of his
disciples to Jesus to ask Him whether or not He were
the Messias. This he did, not because he himself
doubted, but to prove to his disciples that Christ was
the Savior for Whom they had been waiting.

Jesus, making answer, said to them, "Go, and relate
to John what you have heard and seen. The blind see,
the lame walk, the lepers are cleansed. The deaf hear,
the dead rise again, and the poor have the gospel
preached to them."

When the disciples had gone their way, Jesus spoke
about John to the multitude. He said to them, "What
went ye out into the desert to see—a reed shaken by
the wind? But what went ye out to see—a man clothed
in soft garments? Behold, they that are clothed in soft
garments are in the houses of kings. But what went
ye out to see—a prophet? Yea, I tell you, and more
than a prophet. For this is he of whom it is written,
'Behold, I send My angel before Thy face, who shall
prepare Thy way before Thee.' Amongst those that
are born of women, there is not a greater prophet than
John the Baptist."

John is
beheaded

John the Baptist had been in prison about a year,
when Herod Antipas held a great celebration on the
occasion of his birthday. All the public officials and
military officers of Galilee were invited. While the
guests were seated around the banquet table, Salome,

the daughter of Herodias, danced before them. Herod was greatly pleased with her and promised on his oath to give her whatever she should ask of him, even if it were half of his kingdom.

Salome asked permission to consult with her mother. Now Herodias hated John the Baptist, because he had publicly condemned her, so she told her daughter to ask for the head of John the Baptist on a dish.

Salome returned to the king, and said to him, "Give me, on a dish, the head of John the Baptist." When Herod heard this, he was very sad. He knew that John was a holy man, for he had frequently visited him in prison. But because of the oath that he had made before all his guests, he ordered that John should be beheaded. The head was brought to him on a dish and he gave it to Salome, who took it to her mother. Thus was Herodias revenged. The disciples of John took the body of their master and buried it.

In the spring of the following year, Herod moved to his residence in Sepphoris, a town just west of Nazareth. All the people in that part of the country were talking about the teachings and the miracles of our Lord. Herod thought that Jesus might be John returned to life. He was afraid of Him, and yet he was anxious to see the great Prophet. But his desire was not to be satisfied until the day on which our Lord died.

Shortly after Jesus began His public life, He went up to Jerusalem to celebrate the Feast of the Pasch. Now, there lived in Jerusalem a wealthy Pharisee called Nicodemus—a member of the Sanhedrin. While in Jerusalem, Jesus preached to the people and per-

Nicodemus seeks instruction from Jesus

JESUS INSTRUCTS NICODEMUS

formed miracles. When the news of this reached
Nicodemus, he made up his mind to go and see Jesus
in order to find out whether or not He were the Messias. Not wishing the other Pharisees and the members
of the Sanhedrin to know of his visit, he came during
the night under cover of darkness. He said to Jesus,
"Master, we know that Thou art a great teacher from
God. For no one could do the things that Thou dost
unless God were with him."

That night, our divine Lord instructed Nicodemus
and answered all his questions. He told him how God
so loved the world that He gave His only-begotten Son,
and that whoever would believe in Him would not

perish, but would have life everlasting. He foretold that the Son of God would one day be lifted up, even as the serpent was lifted up by Moses in the desert, that all who would look upon Him might be saved. He told him of the new life of grace, which is found in the sacrament of Baptism. "Amen, amen, I say to thee," said the Savior, "unless a man be born again of water and the Holy Ghost, he cannot enter into the Kingdom of Heaven."

Nicodemus admired Jesus and His teachings, but at this time he did not have the courage to follow Him openly.

Among the followers of Jesus was Mary Magdalen. She was so called because she lived in the town of Magdala, on the Sea of Galilee. Before she had met our Lord, Mary Magdalen was known throughout the country as a very sinful woman. *Mary Magdalen anoints the feet of Our Lord*

One day, a Pharisee named Simon invited Jesus to dine with him. Mary Magdalen had heard the people speaking of this young Prophet from Nazareth. Perhaps she herself had seen Him and listened to His message. Anyhow, when she heard that Jesus was at dinner with the Pharisee, she came into the room where they were eating and fell on her knees at the feet of the Savior. Filled with sorrow for her sins, she wept bitterly. She bathed His feet with her tears and wiped them with her beautiful long hair. She kissed them and anointed them with some precious ointment which she had brought with her.

When Simon saw this, he said to himself, "If this man were a prophet, He would surely know what manner of woman this is that toucheth Him, and that she is a sinner.''

Jesus, reading his thoughts, said to him, "Simon, I have something to say to thee." He said, "Master, say it." Jesus said, "A certain creditor had two debtors. The one owed him five hundred pence; the other, fifty. Neither of them had wherewith to pay, so he forgave them both. Which, thinkest thou, loved him most?" Simon answered, "I suppose the one to whom he forgave the most." Jesus said, "Thou hast judged rightly." Then, turning to the woman, he said to Simon, "Dost thou see this woman? I entered into thy house, and thou gavest Me no water for My feet. But she with her tears hath washed My feet and with her hair hath wiped them. Thou gavest Me no kiss, but she, since she came in, hath not ceased to kiss My feet. My head with oil thou didst not anoint, but she with ointment hath anointed My feet. Wherefore, I say to thee, many sins are forgiven her because she hath loved much." Then He said to Mary, "Thy sins are forgiven thee."

All of those who sat at table began to say within themselves, "Who is this that forgiveth sins also?" But Jesus said to Mary, "Thy faith hath made thee whole. Go in peace."

Mary Magdalen's holy life From that moment, Mary Magdalen began to live a holy life. She joined a group of holy women who followed Jesus as He traveled through Galilee. Every day she listened to His sermons, and saw His miracles. Some time afterwards, she returned to Bethania,

BETHANIA AS IT LOOKS TODAY

where she lived with her sister, Martha, and Lazarus, her brother.

When Jesus was on His way to Jerusalem, He stopped in Bethania at the home of Mary and Martha. They greeted Him joyfully, and Mary sat at His feet and listened to every word that He spoke. Meanwhile, Martha was busy preparing a meal for Jesus. Seeing Mary sitting at the feet of the Savior, she complained to Him and said, "Lord, hast Thou no care that my sister hath left me alone to serve? Speak to her and tell her to help me." Jesus, answering, said to her, "Martha, Martha, thou art careful and art troubled about many things. But one thing is necessary. Mary hath chosen the best part, and it shall not be taken away from her." *Mary and Martha*

Besides the twelve apostles, our Savior chose seventy-two disciples, whom He instructed and sent out to preach. Two by two, they went forth into every *The seventy-two disciples* city and place whither our Lord Himself was to come. Jesus said to them, ''The harvest indeed is great, but the laborers are few. Pray ye, therefore, the Lord of the harvest, that He send laborers into His harvest. Go; behold I send you as lambs among wolves. Carry neither purse, nor money, nor shoes. Heal the sick, and say to them, 'The kingdom of God is come nigh unto you.' He that heareth you, heareth Me, and he that despiseth you, despiseth Me. And he that despiseth Me, despiseth Him that sent Me.''

The first missionary tour of the seventy-two disciples lasted one month. They returned to Jesus filled with delight at the success of their work, and told Him all that had happened. They boasted that even the devils were obedient to them. But Jesus said to them, ''Rejoice not in this, that the devils are subject to you. But rejoice in this, that your names are written in Heaven.''

5. JESUS PREACHES TO THE PEOPLE

Jesus teaches in the synagogue

The Son of God became man in order to take upon Himself the sins of the world and to make satisfaction for them to the divine justice by suffering and dying on the cross. But in order that men might profit by His sacrifice, it was necessary for them to learn how to live a holy life. Otherwise, through ignorance they would fall back into their sins. That is why Jesus spent the three years of His public life preaching to the people and telling them what they would have to do if they wished to enter into the Kingdom of Heaven. The people listened to Him and admired His doctrine, for He taught them as one having power and authority, and not as the scribes and Pharisees.

Soon after His temptation in the desert, Jesus returned to Galilee and came to Nazareth, where He had spent His youth. The people of Nazareth had heard rumors of the wonderful things He had done since He left His home. Therefore, when He came into the synagogue with them on the Sabbath Day, they asked Him to preach to them.

The synagogue consisted of a long hall, at the end of which there was a kind of sanctuary. There was no altar in the sanctuary, because sacrifices were never offered in the synagogue, but only a wooden chest covered with a veil, in which the Sacred Books were kept. Near the center was a raised platform upon which the rabbi stood when he preached to the people. The main body of the synagogue was divided into two parts, one of which was reserved for the men, the other for the women.

The services always began with the singing of the Psalms, after which a prayer was said. Then came the instruction. A passage from the Bible was read by the rabbi, just as our priests today read the Epistle and the Gospel on Sunday. The rabbi then explained the passage to the people, and pointed out to them the lessons it taught them for their daily lives. If some stranger or some prominent man were present, the people would ask him to mount the platform and to speak to them.

At the invitation of the people, Jesus rose up to

THE INTERIOR OF A SYNAGOGUE

Jesus announces Himself as the Messias

read. The Book of Isaias the Prophet was handed to Him. Books at that time were written on long scrolls of specially prepared sheep or goat skin, called parchment. Jesus unrolled the scroll and read the following passage, "The spirit of the Lord is upon Me, wherefore He hath anointed Me to preach the gospel to the poor. He hath sent Me to heal the contrite of heart, to preach deliverance to the captive, and sight to the blind, to set at liberty them that are bruised, to preach the acceptable time of the Lord and the day of reward."

The eyes of all who were in the synagogue were fixed upon Him as He rolled up the scroll and handed it back to the ruler of the synagogue. Then He began to speak. He said, "This day is fulfilled this scripture in your ears," and He went on to show them how these words of Isaias the Prophet referred to Himself, and that

He had come to heal the contrite of heart and to set at liberty those that were bruised.

All were delighted with the words which fell from His lips, and they said, "Is not this the son of Joseph?" But soon their delight was turned to anger. They expected Jesus to work miracles for them, as He had done in other parts of the country.

Jesus said to them, "Doubtless you will say to Me the proverb, 'Physician, heal thyself,' and say, 'The great things done in Capharnaum which we have heard spoken of, do the same in Thy native land.' But, in truth, I say to you, a prophet is not held in honor in his own country. There were many widows in Israel at the time of Elias, when the heavens were closed during three years and six months and there was a great famine over all the earth. And Elias was not sent to any one of them, but only to a widow woman of Sarephta. So, also, there were many lepers in Israel under the prophet Eliseus, and not one among them was purified save only the Syrian, Naaman."

When the people heard this, they became very angry. "Does He compare us, the sons of Abraham, with pagan women and lepers?" they said and, rising up, they took hold of Jesus and dragged Him out of the city to a steep hill. They intended to throw Him over a precipice, but He freed Himself from their hands, and passed through the midst of them without harm. He left Nazareth and went to Capharnaum, another city of Galilee.

The Messias had no fixed pulpit, but He went among the people and spoke to them wherever He found them.

The
Sermon
on the
Mount

He taught in the fields, in the streets of the town, in the courts of the Temple, and even from the boat of Simon Peter. One of His sermons is known as the Sermon on the Mount, because it was preached on the side of a small mountain or hill. We can imagine our Savior seated on a rock, part way up the slope of the hill, and the people gathered together below Him, some of them sitting on the ground, some of them standing up.

It was in this sermon that Jesus gave us the Eight Beatitudes. They contain the laws of the Kingdom of Heaven, which Christ came to establish on earth. Jesus said:

"Blessed are the poor in spirit; for theirs is the Kingdom of Heaven. Blessed are the meek; for they shall possess the land. Blessed are they that mourn; for they shall be comforted. Blessed are they that hunger and thirst after justice; for they shall have their fill. Blessed are the merciful; for they shall obtain mercy. Blessed are the clean of heart; for they shall see God. Blessed are the peacemakers; for they shall be called the children of God. Blessed are they that suffer persecution for justice' sake; for theirs is the Kingdom of Heaven. Blessed are ye when men shall revile you, and persecute you, and speak all that is evil against you, untruly, for My sake. Be glad and rejoice, for your reward is very great in Heaven."

Jesus
teaches
the
people
how to
pray

From time to time, our Savior left the people and went alone to the solitude of some mountain to pray. Very often the Gospel tells us how He spent the whole night in prayer. From His example we learn how necessary it is for human beings to refresh and strengthen their souls by frequent conversations with

THE SERMON ON THE MOUNT

God. Not only every word, but every act of Christ's when He was upon earth, is a lesson for mankind. He said of Himself, "I am the way, the truth, and the life."

Once, after Jesus had spent the night in prayer, some of His disciples came to Him and said, "Lord, teach us how to pray."

Then it was that Jesus gave them the following beautiful instructions: "When you are praying," He said, "speak not much, as the heathens do. Be not you therefore like to them; your Father knoweth what is needful for you before you ask it. Thus therefore shall you pray: Our Father, Who art in heaven, hal-

The Our Father

lowed be Thy name; Thy kingdom come; Thy will be done on earth as it is in heaven; give us this day our daily bread; and forgive us our trespasses, as we forgive those who trespass against us; and lead us not into temptation. But deliver us from evil.''

Then Jesus continued, ''Imagine you had a friend, and you went to him at midnight and said to him, 'Friend, lend me three loaves. Because a friend of mine has come off his journey to me and I have not anything to set before him.' Then you would hear the voice of your friend from inside the house, saying, 'Trouble me not. The door is now shut; my children are in bed. I cannot rise and give anything to thee.'

''Yet, if you continued knocking, I say to you that although he would not rise to give it to you because he was your friend, yet because you would not go away, he would rise and give you as much as you needed.

''Therefore, I say to you, Ask and it shall be given you, seek and you shall find, knock and it shall be opened to you. For everyone that asketh, receiveth, and he that seeketh, findeth. And to him that knocketh, it shall be opened to him. What man is there among you, of whom if his son shall ask bread, will he reach him a stone? Or if he shall ask him a fish, will he reach him a serpent? If you, then, being evil, know how to give good gifts to your children, how much more will your Father Who is in Heaven give good things to them that ask Him?''

The holiness of Jesus Wherever Jesus went, great crowds came out to see Him and to listen to His words. They knew that He was different from other men, and that His teaching

was from God. But they were also attracted by His
meekness and His kindness toward everyone. He
loved the poor, and was eager to instruct the ignorant.
He healed the sick, and was merciful to sinners. He
said, "Come to Me, all ye that labor and are heavily
burdened, and I will refresh you. Take up My yoke
upon you and learn of Me, because I am meek and
humble of heart, and you shall find rest for your souls,
for My yoke is sweet and My burden light."

The great holiness of His life could be seen by
everyone. Even His enemies were never able to prove
that He had committed the slightest sin. Because He
was holy, the pure of heart loved to be near Him, while
sinners were turned from their wickedness and came
to Him for forgiveness. Of course, many people came
to Him because they were curious to see Him perform
miracles, but often they, too, received the grace to love
Him and to follow Him.

Jesus did not hold himself aloof from the people, **The
marriage
at Cana**
but was always ready to take part in their innocent
pleasures. Thus, at the very beginning of His public
life, He was invited to attend a wedding feast at Cana,
in Galilee. Mary, His Mother, was also invited. Taking with Him His first disciples, Jesus left the Jordan
and made the long journey into Galilee, in order to be
present at the feast.

In the midst of the feast, Mary noticed that the servants were greatly worried. She asked them what was
the matter, and they told her that the wine had given
out. Mary came to Jesus and said, "They have no
wine." Jesus answered, "What is that to Me and to

JESUS CHANGES WATER INTO WINE

thee? My hour is not yet come." But Mary knew that Jesus loved these people and that He wanted them to be happy on their wedding day, so she said to the waiters, "Whatsoever He shall say to you, do ye."

There happened to be six large waterpots of stone standing near. Jesus said to the waiters, "Fill the waterpots with water." They filled them with water to the brim. Then He said, "Draw out, now, and carry it to the chief steward of the feast." They did as He commanded. The water had been changed into wine, and when the chief steward tasted it, he found it much better than that which he had been serving. He did not know where it came from, and thought that the

A VIEW OF CANA

bridegroom had made a mistake in serving the best
wine last. So he called him and said, "Every man at
first setteth forth good wine, and when men have well
drunk, then that which is worse. But thou hast kept
the good wine until now." This was the first miracle
that Jesus worked. He performed it at the request of
His blessed Mother, so that these friends of His would
not be deprived of happiness on their wedding day.

Our Lord's gentleness toward those who were de- *Zacheus,*
spised is shown by the way in which He treated *the*
Zacheus, the publican. Zacheus was the chief collec- *Publican*
tor of taxes in Jericho and, naturally, the Jews hated
him. On His last journey to Jerusalem, just before
His Passion and death, Jesus passed through Jericho,
where Zacheus lived. Zacheus wanted to see Jesus,
but being very short of stature, he could not see over

the heads of the people standing around. There happened to be a sycamore tree growing near at hand and, running to it, Zacheus climbed up into its branches, so that he might see Jesus as He passed by.

Coming to the tree, Jesus looked up and saw Zacheus. "Make haste," He said to him, "and come down; for this day I must abide in thy house."

Zacheus made haste, came down from the tree, and received Jesus in his home with great joy. When the crowd saw this, they murmured against Jesus because He chose to be the guest of a man whom they considered a sinner. But Zacheus said, "Behold, Lord, the half of my goods I give to the poor. And if I have wronged any man of anything, I restore it to him fourfold." Jesus said to him, "This day is salvation come to this house, for the Son of Man is come to seek and save that which was lost."

Jesus preaches at Sichar Passing through Samaria, Jesus and His apostles came one day to a city that was called Sichar. Outside the town there was a well which had been dug by the patriarch Jacob. It was late in the afternoon, and that day they had journeyed far. Jesus was weary and He sat on the well to rest while His disciples went into the city to buy food.

The Samaritan woman While Jesus was sitting there, a woman of Samaria came to draw water. Jesus said to her, "Give Me to drink." Hearing this, the woman was very much surprised and said, "How dost Thou, being a Jew, ask of me to drink, who am a Samaritan woman? For the Jews do not mingle with the Samaritans."

Jesus did not take offense at this answer. Instead,

JACOB'S WELL TODAY

He said to her kindly, "If thou didst know the gift of God and Who He is that saith to thee 'Give Me to drink,' thou perhaps wouldst have asked of Him and He would have given thee living water." The woman said, "Sir, Thou hast nothing wherewith to draw and the well is deep. Whence, then, hast Thou living water? Art Thou greater than our father Jacob, who gave us the well, and drank thereof himself, and his children, and his cattle?" Jesus answered, "Whosoever drinketh of this water shall thirst again, but he that shall drink of the water that I will give him shall not thirst forever. But the water that I will give him shall become in him a fountain of waters springing up unto life everlasting."

Jesus promises living water

"Sir," said the woman, "give me this water, that I may not thirst nor have to come hither to draw water."

"Go, call thy husband to come hither," said Jesus to the woman. She said, "I have no husband." Jesus said to her, "Thou hast said well, 'I have no husband,' for thou hast had five husbands, and he whom thou hast now is not thy husband. Thou hast answered truly."

The fact that Jesus seemed to know the hidden secrets of her life startled the woman, and she changed her tone. "Sir," she said, "I can see that thou art a prophet. Now, our fathers adored here on Mount Garizim and Thou, being a Jew, say that Jerusalem is the place where men must adore."

Jesus said to her, "Woman, believe Me, that the hour cometh when you shall neither on this mountain nor in Jerusalem adore the Father. You adore that which you know not. We adore that which we know. For salvation is from the Jews. For the hour cometh and now is when true adorers shall adore the Father in spirit and in truth. God is a spirit, and they that adore Him must adore Him in spirit and in truth."

The woman said, "I know that the Messias will come, and when He is come He will tell us all things." Jesus said to her, "I am He Who am speaking with thee."

The return of the apostles By this time the apostles had made their purchases in the town and, returning to Jesus, were very much surprised to see Him talking to a Samaritan woman. But the woman left her waterpot standing at the well and ran away into the city. She stopped everyone she met and said, "Come, and see a man who has told me all things whatsoever I have done. Is he not the

Christ?" Soon a large crowd of Samaritans were on their way out to the well to see Jesus.

Meanwhile, the apostles had set the food they had purchased on the curb of the well and said to Jesus, "Master, eat." But He answered, "I have meat to eat which you know not." The disciples looked at one another and said, "Has any man brought Him something to eat?" But Jesus said, "My meat is to do the will of Him that sent Me."

In the distance they could see a crowd of Samaritans coming out of the city, their white garments gleaming in the afternoon sun. Pointing to them, Jesus said, "Do not you say there are yet four months before the harvest cometh? Behold, I say to you, lift up your eyes and see the country. It is already white for the harvest."

The Samaritans came to Jesus at the well and He spoke to them concerning the Kingdom of Heaven. They begged Him to tarry with them, and He stayed at Sichar two days. Many of the Samaritans believed in Him because the woman had told them that He knew everything that she had done. But many more believed in Him because of His own word. They said to the woman, "We now believe, not for thy saying, for we ourselves have heard Him and know that this is indeed the Savior of the world."

THINGS TO KNOW AND TO DO

1. THE CHILDHOOD AND YOUTH OF JESUS

1. The following books are interesting and they will help you to understand better the story of Jesus and His blessed Mother. Read one of them.

(a) "The Life of Our Lord," by Rev. Martin Healy, C.C.
(b) "New Testament Stories," by Rev. C. C. Martindale, S.J.
(c) "Mary the Queen," by a Religious of the Holy Child Jesus, pages 1-97.
(d) "The Story of the Divine Child," by Very Rev. Dean A. A. Lings.
(e) "The Life of our Lord," by Mother Mary Salome.

2. In Division II of this Unit we have learned the incidents which make up the five joyful mysteries of the rosary: The Annunciation, The Visitation, The Birth of Our Savior, The Presentation of the Child Jesus in the Temple, The Finding of the Child Jesus in the Temple. Memorize these mysteries.

3. Cut and mount a picture of the Annunciation.

4. Find Ain-Karem and Nazareth on the map. Show how the Blessed Mother had to travel in order to visit her cousin Elizabeth. Tell why it was hard for her to make this journey.

5. Bring to class a picture of the "Birth of Our Savior," the "Presentation of the Child Jesus in the Temple," the "Finding of Jesus in the Temple."

6. Write the story that one of these pictures tells you.

7. Memorize verses 45-56 of the first chapter of St. Luke's Gospel.

8 Memorize verses 68-75 of the same chapter.

9. Memorize verses 29-32 of the second chapter of St. Luke's Gospel.

10. You may use these three prayers in your thanksgiving after Holy Communion and at any other time you wish to thank God for His blessings.

11. Write an essay on the love of the Blessed Virgin Mary for her neighbor.

12. Show the connection between the Angelus and this division.

2. JOHN THE BAPTIST PREPARES THE WAY FOR THE REDEEMER

1. How did John the Baptist prepare the way for our Lord?
2. Compare John's preaching with that of the prophets.
3. Why was the forerunner of Christ called the Baptist?
4. Why did Jesus retire to the desert?
5. Describe the three temptations of Jesus.
6. Memorize the answer given by Jesus to Satan each time that He was tempted.
7. Read "John the Baptist" in "New Testament Stories," by Rev. C. C. Martindale, S.J. "Jesus of Nazareth," by Mother Loyola, Chapter XV. "The Life of Our Lord," by Rev. Martin Healy, C.C., Chapter XIV.
8. Give a floor talk in which you show that John the Baptist was brave in explaining the truth, a hero in doing penance, and humble in his opinion of himself.

3. JESUS CALLS HIS FIRST DISCIPLES
4. JOHN THE BAPTIST IS BEHEADED

1. What was required to become a disciple of Christ?
2. Describe a child who is a true disciple of our Lord.
3. What did Jesus do the night before He chose His apostles?

4. What lesson does Jesus teach us by this act?

5. Why did Jesus spend the night in prayer before making His choice?

6. Name the powers which Jesus gave His apostles? What is a miracle?

7. Write a short theme on one of the following subjects: The Call of the Apostles; The Mission of the Apostles; The Power of the Apostles.

8. Was Nicodemus or Mary Magdalen the more admirable? Give reasons for your answer.

9. Read one of the following chapters: "The Life of Our Lord," by Mother Mary Salome, Chapter XVI; "Jesus of Nazareth," by Mother Mary Loyola, Chapter XVII; "The Story of the Friends of Jesus," by a Religious of the Holy Child Jesus, Chapter IV; "Lessons of the Savior," by a Religious of the Holy Child Jesus, Chapters VII and IX; "New Testament Stories," by Rev. C. C. Martindale, "Nicodemus."

10. Read the Gospel of St. Luke, Chapters I-X.

11. God has called everyone to do something for Him. We say this call is a vocation. How will you know your vocation? What should you do daily to know it?

5. JESUS PREACHES TO THE PEOPLE

1. Discuss the words which Jesus read to the people from the Book of Isaias.

2. Why do we say that these words refer especially to our Savior?

3. Why did Jesus compare Himself with the prophet Elias?

4. Show that the Our Father is the most beautiful of all prayers.

5. Memorize verses 3-10 of Chapter V of St. Matthew's Gospel. These verses are the Eight Beatitudes.

6. Write a dramatization of the marriage feast at Cana. What did Jesus teach by His presence at the marriage feast? What do we learn of Mary's power with God at this feast?

7. Read "The Miracles of Our Lord," by a Religious of the Holy Child Jesus, Chapters II and III; "Lessons of the Savior," by a Religious of the Holy Child Jesus, Chapter X; "Jesus of Nazareth," by Mother Loyola, Chapter XVIII.

8. Recall the event of the Old Testament when the Samaritans were separated from the Jews, and prepare to tell the class about them.

9. Write a short theme with this thought in your mind: "Jesus is the friend of sinners."

10. Explain the meaning of the "living water" of which Jesus spoke to the Samaritan woman.

11. When does God give "living water" to souls?

SELF-TEST

Before leaving this Unit, test yourself with the following exercises: After finishing the exercises, check your work.

I. Prepare for your notebook:

1. A list of the names of the apostles and the dates on which the Church celebrates their feast days.
2. A list of the important events of this Unit, and the days on which the Church commemorates these events.
3. A map showing the journeys of Jesus.
4. A diagram of the Books of the New Testament and their authors.

II. Prepare:

1. To tell the complete story of each part of this Unit.
   (a) How God prepared the world for the Messias.
   (b) How the Redeemer of the world lived among men.
2. To state briefly the meaning of the following mysteries referred to in this Unit: (a) The Immaculate Conception, (b) The Nativity, (c) The Circumcision, (d) The Adoration of the Magi, (e) The Annunciation, (f) The Visitation, (g) The Presentation in the Temple.

III. Give a description of the books that you have read while studying Unit Six.

PREVIEW

Unit Seven

HOW CHRIST TAUGHT, WORKED MIRACLES AND FOUNDED THE CHURCH

For three years Jesus went among the people, doing good. We shall see how He spoke to them of the Kingdom of Heaven, corrected their false ideas and told them how they must live if they would be saved.

We shall see how Jesus loved the poor and the suffering, and how He proved that He was the Son of God by working miracles.

We shall learn how He founded a Church which would last till the end of time. He promises to give us Bread from Heaven wherein is sweetness of every kind—His own Flesh and Blood—for the life of our souls.

Unit Seven

HOW CHRIST TAUGHT, WORKED MIRACLES, AND FOUNDED THE CHURCH

Unit Seven

HOW CHRIST TAUGHT, WORKED MIRA-CLES, AND FOUNDED THE CHURCH

I. CHRIST, THE GREAT TEACHER

1. The Kingdom of Heaven Is Announced

Our divine Savior spoke constantly of the Kingdom of Heaven. He began His public preaching by repeating the message of John the Baptist, "Do penance, for the Kingdom of Heaven is at hand." Many of the people thought that He intended to lead a great revolt against the Romans, drive them out, and to win back for Himself the throne of David, His ancestor. But Jesus was not thinking of an earthly kingdom. He was thinking of the time when all men would know that they belonged to God and that they were put here upon earth to do His holy will. God did not create man for this world, yet Jesus saw how many people were living as though money, or pleasure, or earthly power were the only thing that mattered.

Christ teaches the danger of worldliness

Jesus was a wonderful teacher and knew how to present His doctrine in such a clear manner that His listeners would have no difficulty in understanding it. Frequently He spoke to them in parables; that is to say, He compared the things of God to things of their everyday life. If He saw a farmer sowing seed in his

373

THE MOUNT FROM WHICH JESUS PREACHED THE BEATITUDES

field, or a fisherman pulling his net out of the sea, or
a shepherd watching his sheep, or a father and mother
taking care of their children, He would make use of
the fact to point out some lesson concerning the Kingdom of Heaven. Often, too, the parable was a story
which He made up to help them to understand some
difficult doctrine.

The Kingdom of Heaven   In the sermon that He preached from the mountain
side our Savior said, "Lay not up to yourselves treas-
ures on earth, where the rust and the moth consume,
and where thieves break through and steal. But lay
up to yourselves treasures in Heaven, where neither
the rust nor the moth doth consume, and where thieves
do not break through nor steal. For where thy treasure is, there is thy heart also. Be not solicitous for
your life, what you shall eat, nor for your body, what
you shall put on. Is not the life more than the meat,
and the body more than the raiment? Behold the birds

of the air, for they neither sow nor do they reap, nor gather into barns, and your heavenly Father feedeth them. Are you not of much more value than they? And for clothing, why are you solicitous? Consider the lilies of the field, how they grow. They labor not, neither do they spin, but I say to you that not even Solomon in all his glory was arrayed as one of these. And if the grass of the field, which is today, and to-morrow is cast into the oven, God doth so clothe, how much more you, O ye of little faith. Be not therefore solicitous, saying, 'What shall we eat?' or 'What shall we drink?' or 'Wherewith shall we be clothed?' for after all these things do the heathens seek. For your Father knoweth that you have need of these things. Seek ye, therefore, first the Kingdom of God and His justice, and all these things shall be added unto you.''

A crowd of people were gathered in a house at Capharnaum, and Jesus was teaching them. Mary, His Mother, came to the house to see Him, accompa-nied by some of His relatives. Someone noticed them standing outside the door and said to Jesus, ''Behold Thy Mother and Thy brethren stand without, seeking Thee.''

Jesus said to him, ''Who is My mother, and who are My brethren?'' Then, stretching forth His hand to-ward His disciples, He said, ''Behold My mother and My brethren. For whosoever shall do the will of My Father that is in Heaven, he is My brother and sister and mother.'' **The brethren of Christ**

By these words our divine Savior did not intend any disrespect to His blessed Mother. He wanted the people to understand that God loves us, not because we belong to a certain family or to a certain race, but because we do His holy will. No one ever obeyed the will of the Father in Heaven any more perfectly than Mary. That is why she was chosen to be the Mother of God.

Un-divided loyalty Many of those who listened to Jesus were attracted by His doctrine and felt in their hearts a desire to follow Him. But they also loved the things of this world and did not have the courage to give them up. One day, one of the scribes came to Jesus and said, "Master, I will follow Thee whithersoever Thou shalt go." But Jesus knew that he was not sincere and that he loved the things of this world, so He said to him, "The foxes have holes, and the birds of the air nests. But the Son of Man hath not whereon to lay His head."

One of His disciples said, "I will follow Thee, Lord, but let me first take leave of them that are at home." Jesus said to him, "No man putting his hand to the plow and looking back is fit for the Kingdom of God."

"He that is not with Me, is against Me," said the Savior. "He that gathereth not with Me, scattereth. No man can serve two masters, for either he will hate the one and love the other, or he will bear with the one and despise the other. You cannot serve God and Mammon."

In order to show the people how foolish it is to live for this world and its pleasures, He told them this story:

"There was a certain rich man who was clothed in

LAZARUS AT THE RICH MAN'S HOUSE

purple and fine linen and who feasted sumptuously every day. And there was a certain beggar, named Lazarus, who lay at his gates, his body full of sores, and asked only for the crumbs that fell from the rich man's table. But no one gave them to him. And the dogs came and licked his sores.

The Rich Man and Lazarus

"Now it came to pass that the beggar died, and was carried by angels into Abraham's bosom. And the rich man also died, but he was buried in hell. Lifting up his eyes when he was in torment, he saw Abraham afar off, and Lazarus in his bosom. And he cried out and said, 'Father Abraham, have mercy on me, and send Lazarus, that he may dip the tip of his finger in water to cool my tongue, for I am tormented in this flame.'

"But Abraham said to him, 'Son, remember, thou didst receive good things in thy lifetime, whilst Lazarus received evil things. But now, he is comforted and thou art tormented. Besides, between us and you there is a great chasm, so that no one can pass from us to you nor from you to us.'

"Then the rich man said, 'Father Abraham, I beseech thee to send Lazarus to my father's house, for I have five brothers, that he may warn them lest they also come into this place of torment.' Abraham said to him, 'They have Moses and the prophets. Let them hear them.' But the rich man said, 'No, Father Abraham, but if one went to them from the dead, they will do penance.' But Abraham said to him, 'If they hear not Moses and the prophets, neither will they believe if one rise again from the dead.' "

2. JESUS REBUKES THE PHARISEES

Jesus condemns hypocrisy Jesus loved the poor. He was kind to the publicans, and merciful to sinners. But there was one class of people for whom He had no sympathy. These were the Pharisees. "Woe to you Pharisees," He said, "because you love the first seats in the synagogue and the salutations of the people in the market place. Woe to you, because you are like to whited sepulchers, which outwardly appear to men beautiful, but inside are full of dead men's bones, and of all filthiness. So you also outwardly indeed appear to men just, but inwardly you are full of hypocrisy and iniquity."

What was it that moved the gentle Savior to utter such terrible words as these? It was the kind of lives that the Pharisees lived. They were very careful to perform all the outward actions that the Law of Moses commanded, but in their hearts there was no real love of God. They thought only of themselves, and pretended to be good in order to make an impression on the people. If they fasted, they took care that everyone should know about it. They had no pity upon sinners and oppressed the poor. Jesus said to the people, "When you give alms, do not sound a trumpet before you as the Pharisees do in the synagogues and in the streets, that they may be honored by men. For they have received their reward. When you give alms, let not your left hand know what your right hand doth, that your alms may be in secret. And your heavenly Father, Who seeth in secret, will reward you.

"When you pray, do not pray as the Pharisees do, who love to pray in the synagogues and on the corners of the streets, that they may be seen by men. When you pray, enter into your room and pray to your Father in secret. And your Father, Who seeth in secret, will repay you.

"When you fast, be not as the Pharisees, sad. For they disfigure their faces, that they may appear unto men to fast. And they receive their reward from men. But when you fast, anoint your head and wash your face, that you may not appear to men to fast, but to your Father Who is in secret. Your Father, Who seeth in secret, will repay you."

THE PUBLICAN AND THE PHARISEE

The Pharisee and the Publican To make His teaching clear to those who listened to Him, our Savior told them the following story:

"Two men went up to the Temple to pray. The one was a Pharisee, the other a publican. The Pharisee, standing, prayed, 'O God, I thank Thee that I am not like the rest of men—extortioners, unjust, adulterers —as is also this publican. I fast twice in a week, and I give Thee the tenth part of all that I possess.'

"But the publican stood afar off and would not so much as lift up his eyes to Heaven. He struck his breast, saying, 'O God, be merciful to me, a sinner.' "

Then Jesus said, "I say to you that this publican went down to his house justified rather than the Pharisee. Because everyone that exalteth himself shall be humbled, and he that humbleth himself shall be exalted.''

The Law of Moses commanded the Jews to keep holy the Sabbath Day. The Pharisees were very strict about enforcing this law. They taught the people that anything at all that a man did on the Sabbath Day— even the most innocent enjoyment—was sinful. *Jesus and the Sabbath*

Our Savior condemned this false idea of the Pharisees. He told the people that the Sabbath was made for man—not man for the Sabbath. God wanted them to look upon the Sabbath as a day of rest, on which they could raise their hearts to God and gather strength for the work of the coming week. He did not want the Sabbath to be a day of suffering and torture.

There was in Jerusalem a pool named Bethsaida. It was a miraculous place. An angel of the Lord descended at certain times into the pool, and the water was moved. The first person who went into the pool after the motion of the water was cured of whatever sickness he might have. Around the pool there were five porches, in which lay sick, blind, lame, and crippled people, waiting for the moving of the water. *Jesus heals on the Sabbath*

One Sabbath Day, Jesus came to the Pool of Bethsaida. There He found a man who had been an invalid for thirty-eight years. Jesus saw him lying there and knew that he had been waiting a long time, so He said to him, ''Wilt thou be made whole?'' The sick man answered, ''Sir, I have no one to put me into the pool when the water is moved. By the time that I get there, another goes down before me.'' Jesus said to him,

"Arise, take up thy bed and walk." Immediately the man was cured. He took up his bed and walked away.

As he was going along, some of the Pharisees met him and said, "Dost thou not know that this is the Sabbath Day, and that it is not lawful for thee to carry thy bed?" The man said to them, "He that made me whole said to me, 'Take up thy bed and walk.'" They asked him, "Who is that man who said to thee, 'Take up thy bed and walk?'" But the man did not know who it was, and Jesus had disappeared in the crowd.

Some time afterwards, Jesus saw the man in the Temple and said to him, "Behold, thou art made whole. Sin no more, lest some worse thing happen to thee."

The man went his way and told the Pharisees that it was Jesus Who had made him whole. Thereupon, they persecuted Jesus because He did these things on the Sabbath Day. Jesus said to them, "My Father worketh until now, and I work." Hearing this, the Pharisees only hated Jesus the more and sought for a chance to have Him put to death, because He not only broke the Sabbath, but He also said that God was His Father, and made Himself equal to God.

Jesus cures the withered hand on the Sabbath On another Sabbath Day, Jesus was teaching in one of the synagogues. Among those who were listening to Him was a man whose right hand was withered. Some of the Pharisees were present, and they were watching Jesus to see if He would do something that would give them a chance to accuse Him of breaking the law. They asked Jesus, "Is it lawful to heal on the Sabbath Day?"

Jesus knew what was in their minds, so He said to the man with the withered hand, "Arise, stand forth." The man obeyed. Then Jesus said to the Pharisees, "I ask you if it be lawful on the Sabbath Day to do good, or to do evil, to save life, or to destroy it?" They did not answer Him, so He asked them another question, "What man among you, whose sheep fell into a pit on the Sabbath Day, would not lift it out? How much better is a man than a sheep! Therefore, it is lawful to do a good deed on the Sabbath." Turning to the man, He said, "Stretch forth thy hand." He stretched forth his hand, and immediately it was cured.

Filled with rage, the Pharisees rushed out of the synagogue. They sought out some of the influential men of the place who were courtiers of King Herod and asked them to help them find some way of putting Jesus to death.

The Pharisees were strongly attached to earthly riches and pleasures, and they lived very worldly lives. Jesus often told them that their manner of living would prevent them from entering the Kingdom of Heaven. But they believed that they had a right to a place in the Kingdom because they were the children of Abraham. To correct this false idea, Jesus told them the following story:

The Great Supper

"A certain man made a great supper and invited many guests. At the hour of the supper he sent his servant to them who were invited, bidding them to come, for now all things were ready. They began all at once to make excuses. The first said to him, 'I have bought a field and I must go out and see it. I pray thee, hold me excused.' Another said, 'I have bought five yoke of oxen and I am going to try them. I pray thee, hold me excused.' Another said, 'I have married a wife and therefore I cannot come.'

"The servant returned and told these things to his lord. Then the master of the house, being angry, said to his servant, 'Go out quickly into the streets and lanes of the city, and bring in hither the crippled and the poor and the blind and the lame.' After a while, the servant returned and said, 'Lord, it is done as thou hast commanded; yet there is room.' And the lord said to the servant, 'Go out into the highways and to the hedges, and tell them to come in, that my house may be filled. But I say unto thee that none of those men that were invited shall taste of my supper.' "

Thus did our Lord try to make the Pharisees understand that no one had a right to the Kingdom of Heaven simply because he belonged to a certain nation or a certain tribe. Only those would be allowed to enter who heeded the invitation of God to lead a holy life, and thus proved themselves worthy of His reward.

The Wicked Husbandmen God had been wondrously good to His Chosen People. He had watched over them and protected them for many centuries. But they had been ungrateful. They had mistreated the prophets whom He sent to them, and had even put some of them to death. Yet God was patient with them. When they would not heed the prophets, He sent His only-begotten Son to call them to repentance. Him also they put to death. Because of this fact, they were finally rejected by God and their rights to His Kingdom were given to others. This fact, Jesus foretold in the story of the Wicked Husbandmen.

"A certain man planted a vineyard and let it out to husbandmen, after which he went abroad for a long time. When the harvest season came, he sent a servant to the husbandmen, asking them to give him some of the fruits of the vineyard. But they beat the servant and sent him away empty-handed.

"Again, he sent another servant, but they beat him also and, treating him shamefully, sent him away empty-handed. Then he sent a third servant, but they wounded him also and killed him.

"Then the lord of the vineyard said, 'What shall I do? I will send my beloved son. It may be when they see him, they will reverence him.'

"But when the husbandmen saw him, they said, 'This is the heir; let us kill him, and the inheritance shall be ours.' So, casting him out of the vineyard, they killed him. What, therefore, will the lord of the vineyard do to them? He will come and will destroy these husbandmen, and will give the vineyard to others."

Reverence for the House of God

Although the Pharisees were very exact in observing small details of the Law of Moses that were not very important, they allowed many grave abuses to creep into the religious life of the people. As our Lord said about them, "They would strain at a gnat, and swallow a camel." For example, the people showed a great lack of reverence for the Temple of God. Merchants and money changers had set up their booths in the Court of the Gentiles, and there they carried on their business. The merchants sold the doves, pigeons, and other animals which the people offered to the priests for sacrifice. The money changers gave the people Jewish money in exchange for Roman money, since only Jewish coin could be used for the money offerings in the Temple.

In the first year of His public life, when Jesus went up to Jerùsalem to celebrate the Pasch, He saw these merchants and money changers as He passed through the Court of the Gentiles. They were surrounded by crowds of people who were pushing one another about, and there was much loud talking and confusion. The House of God had been turned into a market place.

Moved by a holy anger, Jesus made a whip of little cords and, pushing His way through the crowd, he beat the merchants and the money changers with the scourge and drove them out of the Temple. He overturned their tables and scattered the money on the ground. The sheep and the oxen He also drove out of the Temple, and to them that sold doves He said, ''Take these things hence; and make not the House of My Father a house of business.''

When the Pharisees saw this, they said to Him, ''What sign of authority dost Thou show unto us for doing these things?'' Jesus answered and said to them, ''Is it not written, 'My house shall be called the house of prayer to all the nations.' But you have made it a den of thieves.'' Then, as a sign of His authority, He said to them, ''Destroy this Temple, and

JESUS DRIVES OUT THE MONEY CHANGERS

in three days I will raise it up.'' The Pharisees said, ''Six and forty years it took to build this Temple, and wilt Thou raise it up in three days?'' But the Temple that He spoke of was not the great building of stone but the Temple of His body. When He rose from the dead, His disciples remembered this prophecy.

In the Book of Deuteronomy, Moses wrote, ''Thou shalt love the Lord, thy God, with thy whole heart, and with thy whole soul, and with thy whole strength.'' In the Book of Leviticus we read, ''Seek not revenge, nor be mindful of the injury of any citizen. Thou shalt love thy friend as thyself.'' The people had forgotten the meaning of these commandments. Many of them

The law of love

loved themselves more than they loved God, and because they loved themselves, they loved only those people who were friendly to them and who did them favors. Now, Jesus did not come to destroy the Law of Moses, but to explain it to the people and show them how to obey it as perfectly as possible. He said, "You have heard that it hath been said, 'Love your neighbors and hate your enemies.' But I say to you, 'Love your enemies, do good to them that hate you, bless them that curse you, pray for them that calumniate you, that you may all be children of your Father Who is in Heaven, Who maketh His sun to rise upon the good and the bad, and sendeth His rain upon the just and the unjust. For if you love them that love you, what reward shall you have? Do not even the publicans do this? And if you salute your brothers only, you are doing no more than the heathens. And if you do good to them who do good to you, what thanks are due to you, for sinners also do this. Be ye, therefore, merciful, as your heavenly Father is merciful."

One day, Simon Peter asked our Savior, "How often must I forgive my brother who offendeth against me, seven times?" Jesus answered, "Not seven times, but seventy times seven times.

The Wicked Servant "For the Kingdom of Heaven is like to a king who wished to take an account of his servants. One was brought to him that owed him ten thousand talents. The servant had no money to pay what he owed, so the king commanded that he should be sold and his wife and his children with him and all that he owned, in order that payment might be made. "But the servant, falling down, begged for mercy. 'Have patience with me,' he said, 'and I will pay thee all.'

"Moved with pity, the king let him go and canceled the debt. But when the servant was gone out, he found one of his fellow servants that owed him a hundred pence. Laying hold of him, he throttled him, saying, 'Pay what thou owest.' His fellow servant, falling down, besought him, saying, 'Have patience with me and I will pay thee all.'

"But he would not and went and cast him into prison.

"Now his fellow servants, seeing what was done, were very much grieved, and they came and told their lord all about it. Then the king called him and said, 'Thou wicked servant. I forgave thee all the debt because thou didst ask me. Shouldst thou not, then, have had mercy on thy fellow servant, even as I had mercy on thee?'

"Then the king delivered him to the torturers until he paid all the debt. So also shall My heavenly Father do to you, if you forgive not every one his brother from your heart."

According to the Law of Moses, a man who was injured might seek to avenge himself in certain cases; but the law of love, which our Savior preached, permitted no revenge. Jesus said to the people, "You have heard it said, 'Take an eye for an eye, and a tooth for a tooth.' But I say to you, Do not resist evil, but if one strike thee on thy right cheek, turn to him also the left. And if a man go to law, and take away thy coat, let him also have thy cloak." *The law of revenge*

The Golden Rule

In the Sermon on the Mount, our blessed Lord said, "Judge not, and you shall not be judged. Condemn not, and you shall not be condemned. Forgive, and you shall be forgiven. Give, and it shall be given to you. Good measure, pressed down and shaken together and running over, shall they give it to your bosom. For with the same measure that you shall mete, it shall be measured to you again. And why seest thou the mote in thy brother's eye, but the beam that is in thy own eye, thou considerest not? How canst thou say to thy brother, 'Brother, let me pull the mote out of thy eye,' when thou thyself seest not the beam in thy own eye? Hypocrite, cast first the beam out of thy own eye, and then shalt thou see clearly to take out the mote from out thy brother's eye."

There is one sentence spoken by our blessed Savior that sums up the whole law of love. We call it the Golden Rule. It reads, "All things, therefore, whatsoever ye would that men should do to you, do you also to them, for this is the law and the prophets."

What Jesus taught about divorce

Home is the place where we first learn how to love one another. Children are happy because their parents love them. They see how happy their parents are because they love each other. Now, Jesus wanted all children to have happy homes, and, therefore, He forbade divorce.

According to the Law of Moses, it was lawful to get a divorce for certain reasons. Knowing that Jesus condemned divorce, the Pharisees came to Him one day and asked, "Is it lawful for a man to put away his wife?" By this question they hoped to entrap Him in His speech, for if Jesus said that it was not lawful, they could say that He was teaching doctrines which were contrary to the Law of Moses.

Knowing what was in their minds, Jesus said, "What did Moses command you?" They answered, "Moses permitted us to write a bill of divorce, so that a man could put his wife away." Jesus answered, "Because of the hardness of your hearts, Moses wrote that commandment. But in the beginning it was not so. Have you not read that when God made man in the beginning, He made him male and female, and that He said to them, 'For this cause shall a man leave father and mother, and shall cleave to his wife, and they shall be two in one flesh'? Therefore, what God hath joined together, let no man put asunder."

Once when Jesus was preaching, a lawyer stood up and interrupted him, "Sir," he said, "what must I do to possess eternal life?" The man was not sincere. He was a Pharisee, and his purpose in asking the question was to confuse Jesus and cause Him to say something which would hurt His reputation with the people. *The Good Samaritan*

Knowing this, Jesus said to him, "What is written in the law; how readest thou?" He answered, "Thou shalt love the Lord thy God with thy whole heart, with thy whole soul, with all thy strength, with all thy mind, and thy neighbor as thyself." "Thou hast answered rightly," said Jesus. "Do this, and thou shalt live."

Feeling that he was getting the worst of the argument the lawyer tried to save his face by asking another question. He said, "And who is my neighbor?"

Jesus, answering, said, "A certain man went down

THE GOOD SAMARITAN

from Jerusalem to Jericho and fell among robbers, who stripped him and, having wounded him, went away, leaving him half dead. Now it chanced that a certain priest went down the same way and, seeing him, passed by. In like manner also a Levite, when he was near the place and saw him, passed by.

"But a certain Samaritan, being on his journey, came near to him and, seeing him, was moved with compassion. Going up to him, he bound up his wounds, pouring in oil and wine and, setting him upon his own beast, brought him to an inn and took care of him.

"The next day he took out two pence and gave it to

the host, saying, 'Take care of him, and whatsoever thou shalt spend over and above, I on my return will repay thee.'

"Which of these three, in thy opinion," Jesus asked the lawyer, "was neighbor to him that fell among robbers?" He said, "He that showed mercy to him." Jesus said to him, "Go, and do thou in like manner."

3. Jesus Instructs His Apostles

The apostles were with our Savior all the time. They traveled with Him on His journeys through the country. They listened to His teaching and saw the miracles that He worked. But they did not fully understand His doctrines. Like the rest of the Jews, they thought that when the Messias came, He would establish once more the kingdom of their fathers and conquer all their enemies. When Jesus spoke of the Kingdom of Heaven, they always thought of an earthly kingdom. They believed in Jesus, but their faith was not perfect. Sometimes they became afraid and doubted His word. *The storm at sea*

One evening, after Jesus had spent the whole day healing the sick and teaching the people, He called His apostles, and together with them got into a little ship on the Lake of Galilee. He said to them, "Let us go over to the other side of the lake." Jesus was tired out from the labors of the day, and the ship had hardly left the shore, before He fell asleep.

They were about halfway across the lake when suddenly a great storm arose. The wind blew, and soon

THE APOSTLES CALL UPON JESUS TO SAVE THEM

great waves were dashing against the sides of the boat, and over the gunwhales. They began to ship a great amount of water and it looked as though the boat would surely sink.

All the while Jesus was sleeping peacefully. The apostles came to Him and waked Him, saying, "Lord, save us, we perish." Jesus said to them, "Why are you fearful, O ye of little faith?" Then, rising up, He rebuked the wind and said to the sea, "Peace, be still." The wind ceased, and it became very calm.

Filled with wonder, the apostles said to one another, "Who is this, for both the winds and the sea obey Him?"

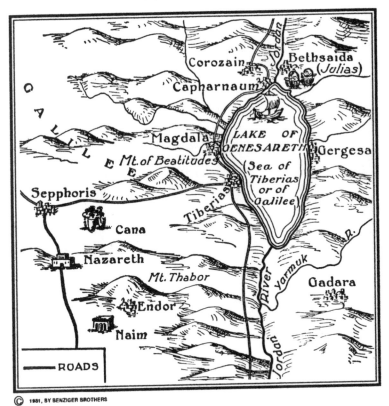

LAKE GENESARETH AND ENVIRONS

A short time after this, Jesus was preaching to the people on the eastern shore of the Lake of Galilee. In the evening, He dismissed the people and told the apostles to get into the boat and row back to Capharnaum. Then He went into a mountain alone to pray.

The sea was rough, and the apostles had a hard time rowing the boat because the wind went against them. **Christ walks on the water** About the fourth watch of the night, they suddenly saw someone coming toward them, walking on the

PETER WALKS TO JESUS ON THE WATER

water. Thinking it was a ghost or a spirit of some
kind, they became frightened and cried out in fear.
But they heard the voice of Jesus saying to them, "Be
of good heart; it is I; fear ye not."

Peter said, "Lord, if it be Thou, bid me come to
Thee upon the waters." And He said, "Come."

Peter immediately got out of the boat and started
to walk toward Jesus upon the water. But the wind
was strong and the waves were rolling high. Peter
began to be afraid and at once he felt himself sinking.
He cried out, saying, "Lord, save me." Immediately
Jesus took hold of his hand and said to him, "O thou
of little faith, why didst thou doubt?" Then they got

into the boat and the wind ceased. Those that were in the boat came and adored Him, saying, ''Indeed Thou art the Son of God.''

Even after these wonderful things had happened, the disciples did not understand what our Savior meant by the Kingdom of Heaven. They remembered what the prophet Isaias had said about the Messias, ''For a Child is born to us, and a Son is given to us, and the government is upon His shoulders, and His name shall be called Wonderful, Counselor, God the Mighty, the Father of the World to Come, the Prince of Peace. His empire shall be multiplied, and there shall be no end of peace. He shall sit down upon the throne of David and upon his kingdom, to establish it, and strengthen it with judgment and with justice from henceforth and forever.''

They were looking for a Messias Whom all the nations of the world would obey, and Who would bring back the Jews who were scattered all over the world and form them into the greatest nation on earth.

This was the great hope of the Jewish people in the time of our Lord. Jesus knew that they were doomed to disappointment, and He tried to make them understand that the Messias was not to be an earthly ruler and that His Kingdom was not of this world.

One day He began to talk to His apostles and disciples about His passion and death. He told them that He would have to go to Jerusalem, where He would suffer many things from the scribes and the chief priests and that He would be put to death, but after three days He would rise again.

Jesus foretells His passion and death

Peter loved our Lord very dearly and he could not bear to hear Him talk about suffering and dying. He began to argue with our Savior, and said, "Lord, be it far from Thee that this should happen unto Thee."

Jesus was disappointed in Peter for being so slow to learn, and He turned round to him and said very sternly, "Go behind Me, Satan; thou art a scandal unto Me, because thou savorest not the things that are of God, but the things that are of men."

Turning to the people, Jesus said, "If any man will come after Me, let him deny himself and take up his cross and follow Me, for he that will save his life shall lose it, and he that shall lose his life for My sake shall find it. For what doth it profit a man if he gain the whole world and suffer the loss of his own soul, or what exchange shall a man give for his soul?"

The mother of the Zebedee
Another day, the mother of James and John, the sons of Zebedee, came to Jesus and told Him that she had a favor to ask of Him. He said to her, "What wilt thou?" She answered, "Say that these, my two sons, may sit, the one on Thy right hand and the other on Thy left in Thy Kingdom."

Knowing that James and John had told their mother to ask this great favor of Him, Jesus turned to them and said, "You know not what you ask. Can you drink the chalice that I shall drink?"

Without a moment's hesitation, they answered, "We can." Jesus said, "My chalice indeed you shall drink, but to sit on My right or left hand is not Mine to give you, but to them for whom it is prepared by My Father."

The other apostles were very indignant at James and John for making a request like this. They accused them of trying to push themselves forward by unfair means, and of using their mother to do something for them that they were afraid to do themselves. A heated argument followed, and angry words were spoken.

But Jesus soon put an end to the dispute. He said, "You know that the princes of the Gentiles lord it over them, that the greater they are, the more power they exercise. It shall not be so among you, but whosoever will be the greater among you, let him wait upon the rest. He that will be the first among you shall be your servant, for the Son of Man is not come to be ministered unto, but to minister; to give His life in redemption for many."

Another time when Jesus was on His way to Jerusalem to celebrate the Feast of Tabernacles, He passed through Samaria. As they neared Sichem, the principal city of the Samaritans, the Savior sent some of his disciples on before Him to find lodgings for the night. But the Samaritans refused them hospitality, because they were Jews on their way to Jerusalem.

A lesson in tolerance for the sons of Zebedee

The messengers came back and told Jesus. James and John, whom our Lord called the Sons of Thunder, became very angry. They said, "Lord, wilt Thou that we command fire to come down from heaven and burn them up."

But Jesus rebuked them, saying, "You know not of what spirit you are; the Son of Man came not to destroy souls but to save,'' and they went into another town.

Another day, John came to Jesus and said, ''Master, we saw a certain man casting out devils in Thy name, and we forbade him, because he followeth not with us.''

But Jesus said, ''Do not forbid him. No man that doth a miracle in My name can soon speak ill of Me. For he that is not against you, is for you.''

The children's Friend One day some mothers brought their little children to Jesus that He might lay his hands upon them and bless them. Knowing that Jesus had been working very hard and was tired out from His labors, the apostles scolded the mothers for not being more thoughtful, and tried to send the children away.

When Jesus saw this, He was very much displeased and said to the apostles, ''Suffer the little children to come unto Me, and forbid them not, for of such is the Kingdom of Heaven. Amen, I say to you, unless you become as little children, you cannot enter the Kingdom of Heaven.'' Taking the children into his arms, He embraced them and, laying His hands upon them, blessed them.

On another occasion our blessed Savior spoke to His disciples about children. ''He that receiveth a little child in My name,'' he said, ''receiveth Me. But he that shall scandalize one of these little ones that believe in Me, it were better for him that a millstone should be hanged about his neck and that he should be drowned in the depths of the sea. See that you despise

JESUS BLESSES THE CHILDREN

not one of these little ones, for I say to you that their angels in Heaven always see the face of My Father, Who is in Heaven.''

Try as they might, the apostles could not bring themselves to believe that Jesus was to suffer and die. Their hearts were filled with sadness. It was a great disappointment to them to know that all their dreams of an earthly kingdom were in vain. Jesus knew what they were thinking. He saw the troubled looks in their faces and He felt a great pity for them. After all, most of them were just simple, hard-working men, and they had been brought up to believe that the Messias would be an earthly king. They could not picture to

The Transfiguration

THE TRANSFIGURATION

themselves a kingdom that was not of this world, so Jesus decided to show them His glory.

They happened to be in the country around Mount Thabor, one of the highest mountains in Palestine. Taking with him Peter, James, and John, Jesus went up to the top of the mountain to pray. While He was praying, a great change came over Him. His face shone like the sun, and His garments became white as snow, whiter than any cloth that was ever seen on earth. He was entirely transfigured.

Suddenly, two men appeared and began to talk with Him. One was Moses; the other was Elias. The apostles listened and heard them speaking about His death that would take place in Jerusalem.

Seeing that Moses and Elias were about to leave, Peter cried out to Jesus, "Master, it is good for us to be here. Let us make here three tabernacles, one for Thee, and one for Moses, and one for Elias." The words were hardly out of his mouth when there came a great cloud, which overshadowed them and covered the top of the mountain. Out of the cloud, they heard a voice, saying, "This is My beloved Son in Whom I am well pleased. Hear ye Him."

Terror filled the hearts of Peter, James, and John and they fell upon their faces. Then someone touched them, and they heard a voice saying, "Arise, fear not." Lifting up their eyes, they saw no one but Jesus. They started down the side of the mountain with Him and, as they went along, Jesus said to them, "Tell the vision to no man till the Son of Man be risen from the dead."

THINGS TO KNOW AND TO DO

1. The Kingdom of Heaven Is Announced

1. What was the Savior's great mission on earth?
2. Why did He speak the parables contained in this lesson?
3. Explain what we mean by a parable.
4. Apply the parable of the Rich Man to people of today.
5. What was the warning which our Lord expressed in this parable?
6. How should rich people use their riches? Name some saints who were very rich and show how they became saints?
7. Why did our Lord preach so often against riches?
8. Write a dramatization of the parable of the Rich Man and Lazarus.
9. Read: "Lessons of the Savior," by a Religious of the Holy Child Jesus, Chapter XVII.

2. Jesus Rebukes the Pharisees

1. Explain the lesson taught by our Lord in the parable of the Pharisee and the Publican?

2. What did our Savior mean when He said: Give alms, pray, and fast in secret?

3. Make a list of the ways in which you can give alms. What must be your intention in giving alms?

4. What do we mean by fasting? When must Catholics fast?

5. Tell the story of the cure of the sick man at Bethsaida.

6. Read again the parable of the Great Supper. Write this parable carefully and tell the lesson which it contains.

7. Recall the history of the Jews in the Old Testament. Prepare a floor talk on Almighty God's patience with the Jews.

8. Memorize a quotation of our Savior on love and forgiveness.

9. Explain the meaning of these words of our Lord: "If a man strike you on the right cheek, turn to him the left also."

10. Read: "The Sermon on the Mount," Gospel of St. Matthew, Chapters V, VI, VII. "Jesus of Nazareth," by Mother M. Loyola, Chapter XXV. "The Divine Story," by Rev. Cornelius J. Holland, Chapter XIII.

3. Jesus Instructs His Apostles

1. Make a picture of your idea of the ship on the stormy sea, or of Christ walking on the waters.

2. What wrong idea of the apostles did Jesus correct by calming the stormy sea? When can you say, "Lord, save me, I perish"?

3. Name the two things that the miracles of the storm at sea and of Christ walking on the water tell about the Savior? What do these two miracles tell about the apostles?

4. Discuss the false idea about the kingdom of Christ that the apostles could not get out of their minds.

5. What did Jesus mean by calling James and John the "Sons of Thunder?" Show this by an example.

6. For what did Jesus wish to prepare the apostles by His Transfiguration?

7. Prove that Jesus had a special love for children. Why does Jesus especially love children?

8. Locate the Sea of Galilee, Capharnaum, Samaria, Sichem, Jerusalem.

9. Read: "The Miracles of our Lord," by a Religious of the Holy Child Jesus, Chapter VII. "The Divine Story," by Rev. Cornelius J. Holland, Chapter XIV. "Jesus of Nazareth," by Mother M. Loyola, Chapters XXVIII-XXXIII. "New Testament Stories," by Rev. C. C. Martindale, S. J., "St. Peter and the Transfiguration."

II. CHRIST, THE FRIEND OF THE POOR AND THE SICK

1. Jesus Lives a Life of Poverty

Our divine Savior was born in a stable, and His first bed was a manger. Mary and Joseph were poor and had to work very hard for a living. His childhood days were spent in an humble little house in Nazareth, a town about which the people used to joke. As a young man Jesus worked with His hands. He was a carpenter like Joseph, His foster father. His food was the food of the poor, his clothing that of a laboring man.

During His public life, Jesus had no home of His own. He and His apostles depended upon the charity of the people for their bodily needs. He ate when and where He was invited, and slept wherever His friends gave Him a bed. Many a night He slept out of doors with only the starry skies overhead for a roof. He would send His disciples into a field to gather the wheat that the owners had left behind for the poor.

Our Lord began His wonderful Sermon on the Mount with the words, "Blessed are the poor in spirit, for theirs is the Kingdom of Heaven." The poor in spirit are those whose hearts are not set on the things of this world. They may be really poor, and have scarcely enough to keep body and soul together, but if they bear their lot patiently, their reward will be

"Blessed are the poor in spirit"

the Kingdom of Heaven. Other people are poor because they have willingly given up all that they own for the love of Jesus; they also shall possess the Kingdom of Heaven. But even those who possess great wealth may be poor in spirit if they use their riches, not merely for their own comfort and enjoyment, but for the glory of God and the good of their fellow man. Theirs also shall be the Kingdom of Heaven.

The rich young man
One day, there came to Jesus a rich young man. He belonged to a noble family and his character was beyond reproach. He kept the Commandments and lived an upright life, but he was not satisfied with himself. His heart was on fire with holy ambitions and he wanted to make better use of his talents and his wealth. He thought that Jesus could advise him what to do.

Coming to the Savior, he asked, "Good Master, what good shall I do that I may have life everlasting?" Jesus answered, "If thou wilt enter into life, keep the Commandments." The young man said to Him, "Which ones?" Jesus answered, "Thou shalt do no murder. Thou shalt not commit adultery. Thou shalt not steal. Thou shalt not bear false witness. Honor thy father and thy mother. And thou shalt love thy neighbor as thyself." "But," said the young man, "all these have I kept from my youth. What is yet wanting to me?"

Jesus looked at him and loved him. He was so different from many others of his age, who were thinking only of pleasure and worldly excess. This boy had in him the making of a great saint. So Jesus called him to the perfect life. "Only one thing is wanting unto thee," He said. "Go, sell whatsoever thou hast and give to the poor, and thou shalt have treasure in Heaven. Then come and follow Me."

When the young man heard these words, he became very sorrowful. Turning around, he went away in silence. He had great possessions, and although he felt a great desire to follow Jesus, he did not have the courage to give them up. After he had gone, Jesus said to His disciples, "How hard it is for those who have riches to enter the Kingdom of God."

Hearing these words, the apostles were astonished. Though they were poor themselves, they had not yet learned to love poverty. Deep down in their hearts they still envied the rich. Jesus repeated what He had said, "How hard it is for those that trust in riches to enter into the Kingdom of Heaven. It is easier for a camel to pass through the eye of a needle than for a rich man to enter the Kingdom of Heaven." **The proper use of riches**

But the apostles were only the more deeply puzzled and they said among themselves, "Who, then, can be saved?"

Looking at them, Jesus said, "With men it is impossible; but not with God. For all things are possible with God." What He meant was that as long as a rich man depends upon himself and puts his faith in what he possesses, he will not be able to gain the happiness of Heaven, even if he can purchase for himself all the finest things of this world. But if God gives him the grace, he may understand the folly of his ways before it is too late and, by giving away his goods to charity, move God to have mercy on him. But our Lord knew that people who have great riches are so taken up with their money and the things that it will buy, that they easily forget that all that they are and all that they have belongs to God. They think that they can live without Him, and pay no attention to the inspirations of His grace.

"We have left all things," Peter said to Jesus. "Behold, we have left all things, and have followed Thee. What, therefore, shall we have?" Jesus answered, "Amen, I say to you, that you who have followed Me, in the day of glory when the Son of Man shall sit on the seat of His majesty, you also shall sit on twelve thrones judging the twelve tribes of Israel. Every one that hath left house, or brethren, or sisters, or father, or mother, or wife, or children, or lands for My sake, shall receive a hundredfold in this life, and shall possess life everlasting."

The widow's mite One day, Jesus was sitting in the Temple, near the treasury, or the place where the people came to make their offerings of money. Many rich people came and cast in large sums. Then there came a widow, who cast in two brass mites, which was a very small amount —less than one cent in value. Calling His disciples to His side, Jesus said to them, "Amen, I say to you, this poor widow hath cast in more than all the rest. For they did cast in of their abundance, but she of her want hath cast in all she had, even her last penny."

How the tax was paid Each year all the Jews, rich and poor alike, whether they lived in Palestine or in foreign lands, were required by the Law of Moses to pay a tax, known as the

CHRIST PRAISES THE WIDOW'S GENEROSITY

Price of the Soul. It was only a didrachma, about forty cents in our money, but with so many people paying it, it brought in a very large sum of money, which was sent to Jerusalem to be used in the service of the Temple.

In the third year of His public life, our blessed Savior came to Capharnaum with His apostles. As they were going through the streets, the taxgatherers stopped Peter and asked him, "Doth not thy Master pay the Temple tax?"

Peter was embarrassed and on the spur of the moment he answered, "Yes." But at once he realized that he had spoken rashly, for he knew that our Savior

A STATER

had no money and that he had no right to promise payment in His name.

While Peter was talking to the taxgatherers, Jesus and the other apostles had gone on and entered a house. When Peter came in, all could see by his face that he was deeply troubled about something. Before he could explain, Jesus said to him, "Simon, how doth this appear to thy mind? Of whom do the kings of the earth exact tribute, of their children or of foreigners?" "Of foreigners," Peter answered. "Then," said Jesus, "the children are free."

Thus did He remind the apostles that He, the Son of God, was not subject to human law, nor bound to pay a "price for His soul."

"But," said Jesus, "that we may not scandalize them, go to the sea and cast in a hook, and that fish which shall first come up, take. And when thou hast opened its mouth, thou shalt find a stater. Take that and give it to them for Me and for thee."

A stater was equal to a shekel, eighty cents, and therefore was sufficient to pay the Temple tax for two persons.

The folly of riches Thus by word and by example did our Lord show how blessed is poverty and how foolish it is to spend one's life in the pursuit of riches. He told the people to beware of covetousness, for a man's happiness does not consist in the abundance of things which he possesses. He spoke a parable to them, saying, "The land of a certain rich man brought forth plenty of fruit, and he thought within himself, saying, 'What shall I do? Because I have no room where to bestow my fruit.' And he said, 'This will I do. I will pull down my barns and I will build greater. And into them I will gather all things that are grown to me and my goods. And I will say to my soul, "Soul, thou hast much goods laid up for many years. Take thy rest, eat, drink, make good cheer."'

"But God said to him, 'Thou fool, this night do they require thy soul of thee, and then who shall own those things which thou hast hoarded up?'

"So is he that layeth up treasure for himself and is not rich toward God."

2. JESUS TEACHES US HOW TO USE THIS WORLD'S GOODS

Our Savior spoke to His disciples the following parable: "There was a certain rich man who had a steward who was accused of wasting his goods. So he called him and said, 'How is it that I hear this of thee? Give an account of thy stewardship, for now thou canst be steward no longer.' The steward was at his wits' end, for, like all people who are dishonest, he never expected that his employer would find him out. Now his position was gone and he had no plans for the future. 'What shall I do?' he said within himself, 'for my lord hath taken away from me the stewardship. To dig I am not able, to beg I am ashamed.'

"All at once, an idea came to his mind. 'I know what I will do,' he said, 'that when I shall be removed

Making friends with the Mammon of iniquity

from the stewardship, they may receive me into their houses.' He sent for each one of his lord's debtors. When the first came, He said, 'How much dost thou owe my lord?' He answered, 'One hundred barrels of oil.' The steward said to him, 'Take thy bill, and sit down quickly and write fifty.' When the second came, he said, 'How much dost thou owe?' He said, 'One hundred quarters of wheat.' The steward said to him, 'Take thy bill and write down eighty.' In like manner he dealt with every one of them.

"When the rich man heard of this, he was, of course, greatly displeased with the steward for having cheated him, but he was forced to admit that it was a very clever scheme and that the steward knew how to make friends for himself."

Our Savior pointed out the moral of the story. He said, "Make unto you friends of the Mammon of iniquity, that when you shall fail, they may receive you into everlasting dwellings."

Our Lord did not mean that we should be dishonest and take money that does not belong to us. He simply teaches us a lesson concerning the proper use of money. He calls it the Mammon of iniquity. Now the word Mammon means riches, the love of which so often hardens the hearts of men toward one another and tempts them to steal and cheat and build up a fortune at the expense of the poor. Thus, iniquity, or sin, is the means that people use to acquire riches, and therefore riches can be called the Mammon of iniquity.

However, it is possible to acquire money by lawful means. But then it must be used, not for selfish purposes, but to help others who are not so fortunate. Rich men are stewards in the house of God, to Whom their wealth really belongs. It is their duty to share it with others by seeing that working men receive better wages, by helping to build schools and colleges, so that more people can receive an education, by providing hospitals and medical care for the sick, and by giving food and clothing and shelter to the poor, the widow and the orphan. All of these, then, become their friends, who will plead for them before the judgment seat of God and win for them the divine love and mercy.

Our divine Savior was constantly reminding those who followed after Him that it was their duty to love their fellow man and to be charitable. "By this shall men know that you are My disciples," He said, "that you love one another." Again and again He warned the Pharisees that love of their neighbor and the relief of God's poor, and not the mere external observance of the letter of the law, would open for them the gates of Heaven. In order to reveal to all how important is charity in the eyes of God, He painted a picture of the Great Judgment that would take place at the end of the world.

How the world will be judged

He told them how the sun would be darkened and the moon would no longer give her light; the stars would fall from heaven; there would be a great roaring of the sea and the waves. All the tribes of the earth would mourn, and men would wither away with fear, waiting for the final destruction of the world.

Then it was that they would see the Son of Man

coming in the clouds of heaven with much power and majesty. "He shall send His angels with a trumpet," said Jesus, "and a great voice, and they shall gather together all the nations, from the four winds, from the farthest parts of the heavens to the utmost bounds of them. And all the nations shall be gathered together before Him, and He shall separate them one from another, as the shepherd separateth the sheep from the goats. And He shall set the sheep on His right hand, but the goats on His left.

The reward of the good

"Then shall He say to those that are on His right hand, 'Come, ye blessed of My Father, possess you the Kingdom prepared for you from the foundation of the world. For I was hungry and you gave Me to eat; I was thirsty and you gave Me to drink; I was a stranger and you took Me in; naked, and you covered Me; sick, and you visited Me; I was in prison and you came to Me.'

"Hearing this, the just, who are on His right hand, shall answer Him, saying, 'Lord, when did we see Thee hungry and thirsty, and gave Thee drink? And when did we see Thee a stranger, and took Thee in? Or naked, and covered Thee? Or when did we see Thee sick or in prison, and came to Thee?'

"But the Lord, answering, shall say to them, 'Amen, I say to you, as long as you did it to one of these, My least brethren, you did it to Me.'

The punishment of the wicked

"Then, turning to those on His left hand, He shall say, 'Depart from Me, ye cursed, into everlasting fire, which was prepared for the devil and his angels. For I was hungry, and you gave Me not to eat; I was thirsty, and you gave Me not to drink; I was a stranger, and you took Me not in; naked, and you covered Me not; sick, and in prison, and you did not visit Me.'

"They also shall answer Him, saying, 'Lord, when did we see Thee hungry, or thirsty, or a stranger, or naked, or sick, or in prison, and did not minister to Thee?'

"But He shall say to them, 'Amen, I say to you, as long as you did it not to one of these least, neither did you do it to Me.' And these shall go into everlasting punishment, but the just into life everlasting."

3. The Sick Are Healed

St. Mark writes in his Gospel, "It was evening, after sunset, and they brought to Him all that were ill and that were possessed with devils. And all the people of the city were gathered together at the door. And He healed many that were troubled with divers diseases, and He cast out many devils. And as the devils went out from their victims, they cried out, saying, 'Thou art the Son of God.'"

An evening in Capharnaum

It is pleasant to picture to ourselves this evening at Capharnaum. We can see the pleading look in the eyes of the poor suffering people as they are brought to Jesus. We can hear their relatives and friends begging Him to cure them. One by one, they are brought to His feet and, looking at them lovingly, He lays His hand upon them. Immediately they are cured. Those who have been lying on stretchers rise up and stand on their feet. The lame throw away their

THE SITE OF CAPHARNAUM

crutches. The blind open their eyes and see Him for the first time. And the poor creatures who have been tortured by devils are now at rest and find in their hearts a great peace.

This is but one picture of what happened wherever Jesus went. The Gospel says, "He went about doing good."

The centurion's servant It was after the Sermon on the Mount and Jesus was returning to Capharnaum, followed by great crowds of people. As they entered the city, the centurion, who was an officer in command of the Roman soldiers quartered in that neighborhood, came out to meet Jesus, and, kneeling at His feet, said, "Lord, my servant lieth at home sick of the palsy and is grievously tormented.''

He was accompanied by the leading citizens of Capharnaum and they joined their prayers with his, saying to Jesus, ''He is worthy that Thou shouldst do this for him. For he loveth our nation and he hath built us a synagogue.''

Jesus said to the centurion, ''I will come and heal him.'' But the centurion, making answer, said, ''Lord, I am not worthy that Thou shouldst enter under my roof. But only say the word and my servant shall be healed. For I also am a man subject to authority, having under me soldiers. And I say to this one, 'Go,' and he goeth, and to another, 'Come,' and he cometh, and to my servant, 'Do this,' and he doth it.''

When Jesus heard this, He marveled, for it was strange indeed that a Gentile, a soldier from pagan Rome, should understand so well the power of the Savior. Turning to the crowds who followed Him, Jesus said, ''Amen, I say to you, I have not found so great faith in Israel.''

Then He said to the centurion, ''Go, and as thou hast believed, so be it done to thee.'' When the centurion returned home, he found that his servant had been healed at that same hour.

The news spread through Capharnaum that Jesus was in the city and was staying at a certain house. Immediately the people stopped whatever they were doing and hastened there to see Him and to listen to His teaching. Soon a great crowd gathered that filled

The man sick of the palsy

the house even to the door. Outside in the street there were many more, who strained their ears to hear the Savior's voice and tried to see Him over the heads of those in front of them.

Four men came along, carrying on a bed a man who was sick with the palsy. In vain did they try to push their way through the crowd and enter the house, but the people would not make way for them. Finally they thought of a plan. They climbed up to the roof of the house and lowered the bed with the sick man on it through an opening that they made by removing some of the tiles.

This act of faith pleased Jesus very much and He said to the man sick of the palsy, "Be of good heart, son. Thy sins are forgiven thee."

Hearing this, some of the scribes who were sitting there were deeply scandalized and thought in their hearts, "Why does this man speak thus? He blasphemeth. Who can forgive sins but God alone?"

Seeing their thoughts, Jesus said, "Why do you think evil in your hearts? Which is easier, to say to the man sick of the palsy, 'Thy sins are forgiven thee,' or to say to him, 'Arise, take up thy bed and walk'? But that you may know that I have the power on earth to forgive sins"—He now turned to the man sick of the palsy—"I say to thee, 'Arise, take up thy bed and go into thy house.' " Immediately he rose up, took up the bed upon which he had been lying, and carried it away into his own house, glorifying God as he walked along.

And the multitude, seeing it, were filled with wonder.

JESUS CURES THE PARALYTIC

They gave praise to God, saying, "We have seen wonderful things today."

There lived in Capharnaum a woman who for twelve years had suffered much with an issue of blood. She had consulted many physicians and had spent all her money trying to be cured. One day, she saw Jesus passing by. A great crowd surrounded Him and she could not get near enough to speak to Him. She said within herself, "If I could but touch the hem of His garment, I should be healed." So she worked her way through the crowd and, when she was near enough, reached out her hand and touched the hem of His garment. Immediately the fountain of her blood was

The woman with an issue of blood

dried up and she felt in her body that she was healed of her sickness.

Jesus said, "Who is it that touched Me?" Peter answered, "Master, the multitudes throng around and press against Thee, and dost Thou say, 'Who touched Me?'" Jesus said, "Somebody hath touched Me, for I know that power is gone out from Me."

Fearing and trembling, the woman came and fell down before Him and told Him what she had done. But He said to her, "Daughter, thy faith hath made thee whole. Go thy way in peace."

Sight to the blind

One day, Jesus was going along the road that leads from Jericho to Jerusalem, and a great crowd of people were following Him. Two blind men sat by the roadside, begging. The name of one of them was Bartimeus. Hearing all the noise and the talking as the multitude passed by, Bartimeus stopped some of the people and asked them what it meant. They told him that Jesus of Nazareth was passing by. No sooner had he heard this than he began to cry out with a loud voice, "Jesus, Son of David, have mercy on us." So much noise did he make that some of the people tried to stop him and told him to hold his peace. But he and his companion cried out all the more, "Son of David, have mercy on us." Hearing their cry, Jesus stopped and commanded the blind men to come to Him. When they came, He said, "What will you that I do for you?" They said, "Lord, that we may see." Jesus had pity on them and touched their eyes with His finger. Immediately they received their sight and joined the crowd that was following after Him.

THE BLIND MEN BEG JESUS TO CURE THEM

Once when Jesus and His apostles were walking **The man born blind** through the narrow streets of Jerusalem, they met a man who was blind from his birth. He sat against the wall, calling out to the people who passed by and begging them for alms. The apostles asked our Lord, "Master, who hath sinned, this man or his parents, that he should be born blind?" They asked this because it was the common belief among the Jews at that time that all sickness and disease were a direct punishment from God for some sin that had been committed.

Jesus answered, "Neither hath this man sinned nor his parents. But he hath been born blind that the power of God may be made visible in him. I must work the works of Him that sent Me whilst it is day. The night cometh when no man can work. As long as I am in the world, I am the Light of the world.''

Then He stooped down and spat on the ground and, making clay of the spittle, He spread the clay upon the eyes of the blind man. Then He said to him, ''Go, wash in the Pool of Siloe.''

So the blind man went to the Pool of Siloe, washed his eyes, and came back with his sight restored.

All this happened on the Sabbath Day. Therefore, the neighbors of the man who had been blind thought that the whole matter should be reported to the authorities. So they brought him to the Pharisees, who asked him how he had received his sight, but he said to them, ''He put clay upon my eyes, and I washed, and I see.'' Hearing this, some of the Pharisees said, ''This man is not of God, who keepeth not the Sabbath.'' Others said, ''How can a man that is a sinner do such miracles?'' And they started to dispute among themselves.

At last they hit upon a scheme. They sent for the man who had been blind and said to him, ''Give glory to God. We know that this man is a sinner.'' He said to them, ''If he be a sinner, I know not. One thing I know, that whereas I was blind, now I see.'' ''What did he do to thee?'' they asked. ''How did he open thy eyes?'' ''I have told you already,'' he answered, ''and you have heard. Why should you hear it again? Do you also want to become His disciples?''

This made the Pharisees very angry. They threatened the man and called him harsh names. And they cast him out.

When Jesus heard what the Pharisees had done to the man whose eyes He had opened, He went out to look for him, and when He found him, He said, "Dost thou believe in the Son of God?" Then the man answered, "Who is He, Lord, that I may believe in Him?" Jesus said to him, "Thou hast both seen Him, and it is He that talketh with thee now." "I believe, Lord," said the man who had been born blind and, falling down, he adored Him.

A man who was deaf and dumb was brought to Jesus **Ephpheta** one day as He was walking along the shores of the Sea of Galilee. His friends begged Jesus to lay His hand upon him and cure him. Taking him apart from the crowd, Jesus put His fingers into his ears and, spitting, He touched his tongue, and looking up to Heaven, He groaned and said to him, "Ephpheta," which is, "Be thou opened." And immediately his ears were opened and the string of his tongue was loosed and he could hear and speak. The people said, "He hath done all things well. He hath made both the deaf to hear and the dumb to speak."

The ceremony used by our Lord when He performed this miracle has been adopted by His Church and she has made it part of the rite of Baptism.

One of the most terrible diseases that can come to **Healing the lepers** a human being is leprosy. It is like a living death, and those who suffer from it in its worst form actually rot away. Nowadays we have hospitals for lepers, where they receive the best that medical skill can give them

But in the time of our Lord the case of the leper was almost hopeless. The disease was looked upon as incurable, and those who suffered from it were driven from their homes and never allowed to set foot in any city or town, or to mingle with the people in any way whatever. They lived out of doors, on the rocky hillsides or in the desert. Their heads were shaven and they were forced to wear torn garments and a veil over their lips, so that those who passed by could see at once that they were lepers. If anyone came too near them, the lepers were commanded by the law to warn them by crying out, "Unclean, unclean!"

From time to time a leper would be cured. Then, according to the Law of Moses, he had to go and show himself to a priest in the Temple. For eight days he would remain in seclusion, washing his body again and again, according to the manner of purification prescribed in the Law of Moses. At the end of this time the priest would proclaim to the people that he had been cured.

One day, our Lord met ten lepers as He was going to Jerusalem. They stood afar off and, lifting up their voices, cried out. They did not say, "Unclean, unclean," but "Jesus, Master, have mercy on us!" Jesus said to them, "Go, show yourselves to the priest." They started out in great haste for Jerusalem and the Temple and as they went along they were suddenly cleansed of their leprosy. One of them, when he saw that he was cleansed, stopped and, going back, fell on his face before Jesus and gave thanks, and this man was a Samaritan. Jesus said, "Were not ten made clean? Where are the other nine? Is there none found to return and give glory to God save this stranger?''

Every human being, from Adam and Eve to the present day, has been forced to do battle with the evil spirits who are constantly trying to lead us into sin. Even our blessed Savior was tempted by the devil. But sometimes the evil spirits go much further than this. They take complete possession of a man, body and soul, so that he is no longer his own master but just a tool of the devil. He does what the devil wants him to do, goes where the devil wants him to go, and says what the devil wants him to say. The devil may torture him, throw him about and hurt him or cause him to suffer some terrible illness. There were many such unfortunate creatures in Palestine when our Lord was on earth.

The driving out of devils

At the very beginning of His public life, Jesus was teaching one day in the synagogue of Capharnaum. Not a sound was heard as the people listened most attentively so as not to miss one word of what He was saying. Suddenly a voice rang out, ''Let us alone, Jesus of Nazareth. We know that Thou art the Holy One of God.'' Immediately all was confusion. The people rose from their seats and looked around the synagogue to see who it was that was speaking. Standing in the doorway, they beheld a man who was possessed by the devil.

Jesus commanded the devil to go out of the man, and the unclean spirit obeyed, crying out with a loud voice.

Amazement and wonder filled the hearts of the people, and soon it was known all over Galilee that Jesus had the power to drive out devils.

The possessed man in the land of the Gerasens The morning after Jesus had calmed the tempest on the Lake of Galilee, He and His disciples landed at Gergesa, which is across the lake from Capharnaum. When they stepped from the ship, they saw waiting for them there on the shore a terrible looking creature. It was a man who for many years had been possessed by the devil. He wore no clothes and lived in a tomb on the hillside. Night and day he roamed about, sending forth horrible screams and yells and cutting himself with sharp stones. Several times the people had tried to capture him and chain him down, but he would break the strongest chain in pieces.

When the possessed man saw Jesus, he fell down on the ground before Him, crying out wildly, "What have I to do with Thee, Jesus, the Son of the most high God? I adjure Thee by God that Thou torment me not." "What is thy name?" Jesus asked him. And he answered, "My name is legion, for we are many."

Jesus knew by this that the man was possessed by not only one, but by a great number of devils. The devils begged Jesus not to drive them away out of the country, but to allow them to enter into a herd of swine that was feeding on the mountain side.

Immediately Jesus gave them leave. He said, "Go." And the unclean spirits, going out, entered into the swine, and the whole herd ran madly down the steep hillside and was drowned in the sea. Altogether it numbered about two thousand swine.

JESUS DRIVES OUT THE DEVIL

When the men who were tending the herd saw this, they were filled with fear and fled away. The news of what had happened spread to the city and to all the villages round about. Crowds of people came down to the seashore, and there they found the man out of whom the devils were driven seated at the feet of Jesus, fully clothed and in his right mind.

The Gerasens did not want Jesus to remain in their country. They were afraid of His power, and the men who owned the swine resented their loss. They begged Him to go away, so He entered the ship and told the apostles to row back to Capharnaum.

The man out of whom He had driven the devils begged to be taken along, but Jesus refused. "Return to thy house," He said to him, "and tell what great things God hath done to thee." So he went his way and told all through Decapolis the story of the great miracle that Jesus had wrought.

The boy who was deaf and dumb When Jesus and the three apostles came down from the mountain after His transfiguration, they found the other apostles surrounded by a great crowd of people. Everyone seemed to be greatly excited and some sort of argument was going on. Jesus asked, "What do you question about among yourselves?" A man pushed through the crowd and said, "Master, I have brought my son to Thee. He has an evil spirit that has made him dumb. The devil takes him and dashes him to the ground. The boy foams at the mouth and gnashes his teeth, and is pining away. I spoke to Thy disciples and asked them to cast out the evil spirit but they could not." Jesus said, "Bring hither thy son."

They brought the boy to Him and at once the devil began to torture him. He threw him upon the ground and the boy rolled about, foaming at the lips. "How long is it since this hath happened to him?" Jesus asked the father. "From his infancy," he answered, "and often-times hath he cast him into the fire and into the water, trying to destroy him. If Thou canst do anything, have pity on us and help us." Jesus said to him, "If thou canst believe, all things are possible." Bursting into tears, the father of the boy cried out, "I do believe; Lord, help my unbelief."

Then Jesus said, "Deaf and dumb spirit, I command thee go out of him. And enter not any more into him."

The devil cried out, and for a moment it looked as though he were going to tear the boy to pieces. But he went out of him, and the boy dropped to the ground. Beholding him lying there, many of the people said, "He is dead." But Jesus, taking him by the hand, lifted him up and restored him to his father.

That evening the disciples came to Jesus secretly and asked Him, "Why could we not cast him out?" Jesus said to them, "Because of your unbelief. For I say to you, if you had faith as a grain of mustard seed, you could say to this mountain, 'Move from here to there,' and it would move. You could say to this mulberry tree, 'Be thou rooted up, be thou transplanted into the sea,' and it would obey you. This kind of evil spirit is not cast out except by prayer and fasting."

In the spring of the third year of His public life, our blessed Savior was teaching in the neighborhood of Tyre and Sidon, when a Gentile woman came to Him and begged Him to cure her daughter, who was possessed by the devil. Jesus paid no attention to her, but she followed after Him, crying out, "Have mercy on me, O Lord, Thou Son of David. My daughter is grievously troubled by a devil." Jesus answered her not a word. His disciples said to Him, "Send her away, for she crieth after us." *The daughter of a Gentile woman*

Finally Jesus said to the woman, "I was not sent but to the sheep that are lost of the house of Israel." By this He meant to let the woman know that His mission was to the Jews, the Chosen People of God. Only later on would His Gospel be preached to the Gentiles.

But the woman threw herself at His feet and said, "Lord, help me." Jesus answered, "It is not good to take the bread of the children and to cast it to the dogs." "Yea, Lord," she said, "but the dogs may eat of the crumbs that fall from the table of their masters."

Jesus, answering, said to her, "O woman, great is thy faith. Be it done to thee as thou wilt."

Rising up, the woman hastened home, and when she entered the house she found her daughter sleeping peacefully in her bed. The devil had left her.

Why our Lord healed the sick and drove out devils Our Lord worked all these miracles to prove that He is God and can do the things that only God can do. But He also worked them because He loved human beings and His heart was touched at the sight of their sufferings. Seeing the miracles of our blessed Savior, the people were reminded of the words of Isaias the prophet, "Say to the faint-hearted, take courage, and fear not. God Himself will come and will save you. Then shall the eyes of the blind be opened and the ears of the deaf shall be unstopped. Then shall the lame man leap as a hart and the tongue of the dumb shall be free."

4. The Dead Are Raised to Life

The son of the widow of Naim Three times did our Lord show that He had power over life and death. One day, as Jesus and His disciples were entering a little town in Galilee called

Naim, they met a funeral procession. The body of a young man was being carried out. He had been the only son of his mother, who was a widow. Many people of the city were accompanying the body to the grave.

Going up to the mother, Jesus said to her, "Weep not." Then turning, He touched the bier upon which the body was being carried, and those who carried it stood still. Jesus said, "Young man, I say to thee, arise." At once the dead man sat up and began to speak and Jesus gave him to his mother. Great fear came upon all those who beheld this miracle. They glorified God, saying, "A great prophet is risen up among us, and God hath visited His people."

The daughter of Jairus, the ruler of the synagogue **The daughter of Jairus** at Capharnaum, was dying. She was only twelve years old, and her heartbroken father came to Jesus, Who was teaching in the city at that time. Falling at His feet, he begged Him to come to his house and cure his daughter.

Jesus started at once for the house of Jairus, but the people crowded around Him and His progress through the streets was very slow. They had scarcely gone halfway when a messenger came to Jairus, saying to him, "Thy daughter is dead. Why dost thou trouble the Master any further?"

But Jesus said to the ruler of the synagogue, "Fear not. Only believe and she shall be safe."

When He came to the house, He would not allow

JESUS RAISES THE DAUGHTER OF JAIRUS TO LIFE

anyone to enter with Him except Peter, James, and John, and the father and mother of the little girl. Inside, many people were standing about, weeping and wailing, but Jesus said to them, "Weep not. The girl is not dead, but sleepeth." But they knew that she was dead and they laughed Him to scorn. He ordered them all to be put out of the house, and, taking the father and the mother and His three apostles, He entered into the room where the girl was lying. Taking her by the hand, He said, "Talitha cumi," which means, "Little girl, I say to thee, arise." Immediately she rose up and walked. Then Jesus told her happy and astonished parents to give her something to eat.

Lazarus of Bethania was sick. His sisters, Mary and Martha, sent a message to Jesus, saying, "Lord, behold, he whom Thou lovest is sick." Now, in spite of the great love that Jesus had for Lazarus, and for Mary and Martha, his sisters, He did not go at once to Bethania; He stayed where He was for two days longer. His apostles wondered why He delayed so long, but finally He said to them, "Lazarus, our friend, sleepeth, but I go that I may awake him out of sleep." The apostles said, "Lord, if he sleep, he shall get well." Then Jesus said to them plainly, "Lazarus is dead. And I am glad for your sakes that I was not there, that you may believe. But let us go to him."

They set out for Bethania, and when they arrived there, they found that Lazarus had been in his grave four days. The house was crowded with friends of Mary and Martha, who had come to comfort them in the loss of their brother. Hearing that Jesus was coming, Martha went out to meet Him, but Mary sat at home. When Martha saw Jesus, she said, "Lord, if Thou hadst been here, my brother would not have died. Now, I know that whatever Thou wilt ask of God, God will give it to me." Jesus said to her, "Thy brother shall rise again." Martha said, "I know that he shall rise again in the resurrection of the last day." Jesus said to her, "I am the resurrection and the life. He that believeth in Me, although he be dead, shall live. And everyone that liveth and believeth in Me shall not die forever. Believest thou this?" "Yea, Lord," answered Martha. "I believe that Thou art the Christ, the Son of the Living God, Who art come into this world.'' Then she hurried back to the house secretly and said to Mary, ''The Master is come, and calleth for thee.''

Jesus had not yet come into the town, but was still in the place where Martha had met Him. Rising up, Mary ran out to meet Him. When she came to where He was, she fell down at His feet and said, ''Lord, if Thou hadst been here, my brother had not died.'' The heart of Jesus was deeply touched by the grief of Mary. The friends of Mary had followed her out of the house, because when she rose up so speedily and went out, they thought she was going to the grave. Now they saw her kneeling at the feet of Jesus and weeping, and they saw that Jesus, too, wept. ''Behold,'' they said, ''how He loved him.''

Jesus asked, ''Where have you laid him?'' And they said to Him, ''Lord, come and see.''

As they were going toward the grave, some of the people said, ''Could not He that opened the eyes of the man born blind have caused that this man should not die?''

Now they had come to the sepulcher. Like all the Jewish tombs of that day, it was a cave hewn out of a rock, and a stone was placed in front of it. Jesus said, ''Take away the stone.''

Martha said, ''But, Lord, by this time he stinketh, for he hath been buried four days.'' Jesus answered, ''Did I not say to thee that if thou believe, thou shalt see the glory of God?''

So they took the stone away and Jesus, lifting up His eyes, prayed, ''Father, I give Thee thanks, for

JESUS RAISES LAZARUS TO LIFE

Thou hast heard Me. And I knew that Thou hearest Me always, but because of the people who stand about have I said it, that they may believe that Thou hast sent Me."

Then, crying out with a loud voice, He said, "Lazarus, come forth." Then Mary and Martha and their friends and the disciples of Jesus who were gathered about beheld a wonderful sight. For, as they looked, Lazarus came out of the tomb, bound hand and foot with the winding band, and his face bound about with a napkin. Jesus gave him back to Mary and Martha, his sisters, saying, "Unbind him, and let him go."

The news of the raising of Lazarus from the dead spread abroad in the land and, hearing it, large numbers of the people were converted to Jesus and confessed that He was the Son of God. Crowds of people went to Bethania, hoping that they might see Lazarus, and others went to the Pharisees and told them the things that Jesus had done.

The Pharisees went to the chief priests and said, "What shall we do? For this man doth many miracles. If we let Him alone, all will believe in Him, and the Romans will come and take away our place and our nation."

Caiphas, the high priest of that year, stood up and said to them, "You know nothing. Neither do you consider that it is expedient for you that one man should die for the people, so that the whole nation may not perish."

He did not realize it, but by these words he stated officially that Jesus was the Savior, for he spoke not as a private individual but as the high priest of that year. In plain words he had prophesied that Jesus should die for the nation. But the Pharisees understood his words as an order to them to secure evidence against Jesus which would be strong enough to have Him put to death. They hoped to find something in His doctrine that sounded like treason against the Law of Moses or against the authority of the Roman emperor. They also sought to have Lazarus put to death, because he was a living proof that Jesus was the Messias and that the power of God was in Him.

THINGS TO KNOW AND TO DO

1. JESUS LIVES A LIFE OF POVERTY

1. Name some of the hardships which our Lord had to endure on account of His poverty.

2. Give two reasons which caused our Lord to choose a life of poverty.

3. Why should the poor be contented in their poverty?

4. What lesson should the rich take from the life and teaching of Jesus?

5. Tell the story of the rich young man.

6. Who besides the apostles leave all things to follow Jesus?

7. Describe the reward promised those who leave all things for Jesus. Can you obtain from God the grace to leave all things for His sake?

8. Why do Sisters promise God never to own anything?

9. Read "The Life of Our Lord," by Rev. Martin Healy, C. C., Chapter XXIV; and "Lessons of the Savior," by a Religious of the Holy Child Jesus, Chapter X.

2. JESUS TEACHES US HOW TO USE THIS WORLD'S GOODS

1. How did our Lord teach most emphatically the necessity of love and charity towards the poor?

2. Think of some of the poor whom you can help. Name some things you can do for them.

3. How do your little mites for the missions satisfy our Lord's command to help the poor? When is your mite worth most?

4. Prepare a talk for the mission meeting. Let your subject be: "Because you did it to one of the least of My children, you did it to Me." Aim to remind the members of your Unit of their duty to help the poor.

5. Write a mission play which will show the hero's great love for the poor.

6. Write a story which will show how your hero or heroine obeyed God's command to help the poor.

7. Memorize the Seven Corporal Works of Mercy. Give a floor talk in which you show that missionaries devote their lives to performing these works.

8. How does the standard by which you will be judged on the Last Day show you what God expects you to do for your neighbor?

3. THE SICK ARE HEALED

1. What is a miracle? Name the kinds of miracles worked by Jesus.

2. Name two reasons that caused Jesus to work miracles to heal the sick.

3. What did our Lord require of those who asked to be healed?

4. What does God still ask of us when we pray to Him?

5. Study the prayer of Bartimeus when he wished to be cured of blindness. How did he pray? When should you use this prayer: "Lord that I may see"?

6. How is the leper when healed like the man who is absolved from mortal sin?

7. Read: "The Miracles of Our Lord," by a Religious of the Holy Child Jesus; "Jesus of Nazareth," by Mother M. Loyola. Chapters XXIII and XXIX.

4. THE DEAD ARE RAISED TO LIFE

1. Why did Jesus raise the dead to life?
2. In what way does death remind us of mortal sin?
3. Why did many of the people of Palestine love Jesus?
4. What reasons have you for loving Him?
5. What is the best way of showing that you love Him?
6. How did the miracles of Jesus affect the Pharisees?
7. Compare the Pharisees with persons who are jealous of others.
8. "To know Jesus is to love Him." Write a short theme about this.
9. Read: "The Miracles of Our Lord," "Jesus of Nazareth," by Mother M. Loyola, Chapters XXIII-XXIX.

III. CHRIST FOUNDS HIS CHURCH

1. THE CHURCH IS THE KINGDOM OF CHRIST ON EARTH

After His death and resurrection, Jesus did not intend to leave us alone, He would remain on earth and continue the work which He had begun. No longer would men be able to see Him in bodily form, but they would see Him and hear Him and feel the comfort of His presence in the Church which He would found. The Church is the Kingdom of God on earth.

Early in the second year of His public life, Jesus was standing on the shore of the Sea of Galilee. A great crowd gathered around Him and asked Him to preach to them. Near at hand was moored a boat belonging to Simon Peter, and, stepping into it, Jesus told Peter to push off a little way from the shore. Sitting down in the boat, He preached to the people who were gathered on the shore. *The founding of the Church*

After He had finished speaking, He said to Simon Peter, "Launch out into the deep, and let down your net." Peter said to Him, "Master, we have labored all night and have caught nothing, but at Thy word I will let down the net."

When this was done, they caught so many fishes that their net began to break. They called to some men who were in another boat to come and help them, and when the net was finally pulled in, it was so heavy with fishes that the boat almost sank. The apostles

439

were overcome with wonder at this miracle and Peter, kneeling at the feet of Jesus, said, "Depart from me, O Lord, for I am a sinful man." But Jesus said, "Fear not; follow Me and I will make you fishers of men." They brought their ships to land and, leaving their nets and all things behind them, they followed Jesus.

One day, toward the end of His public life, Jesus and the apostles were walking through the country to the east of the Jordan. They were near the town of Caesarea Philippi, when Jesus turned to them suddenly and said, "Whom do men say that I am?"

They answered, "Some say Thou art John the Baptist; others, that Thou art Elias; others, Jeremias or one of the prophets." Jesus said to them, "But whom do you say that I am?"

Simon Peter answered in the name of all the rest, "Thou art Christ, the Son of the Living God."

Then Jesus said to him, "Blessed art thou, Simon, son of John, because flesh and blood hath not revealed this to thee, but My Father Who is in Heaven. And I say to thee: thou art Peter, and upon this rock I will build My Church. And the gates of hell shall not prevail against it. And I will give to thee the keys to the Kingdom of Heaven. And whatsoever thou shalt bind upon earth, it shall be bound also in Heaven; and whatsoever thou shalt loose on earth, it shall be loosed also in Heaven."

By these words, our blessed Savior revealed to Simon Peter and to the rest of the apostles the great work that they were to do in the world. Peter would receive the keys to the Kingdom of Heaven. He would be the one to tell men what they must do to please God and to save their souls. Together with the rest of the apostles, he would have the authority to say what was right and what was wrong, what was true and what was false. God would watch over him and protect him from error, and whatever he commanded would be the law of God.

Our blessed Savior sought by means of parables to help the apostles and the people to understand what His Church would be like and what her mission would be. He said, "I am the true vine, and My Father is the husbandman. Every branch in Me that beareth not fruit, He will take away; and every one that beareth fruit, He will purge it, that it may bring forth more fruit. Abide in Me, and I in you. As the branch cannot bear fruit of itself unless it abide in the vine, so neither can you unless you abide in Me. I am the vine. You are the branches. He that abideth in Me and I in him, the same beareth much fruit. For without Me, you can do nothing. If anyone abide not in Me, he shall be cast forth and shall wither, and they shall gather him up and cast him into the fire and he shall burn." *The vine and the branches*

Sheep raising was one of the principal occupations of the people in the days of our Lord, and no figure was more familiar than that of the shepherd watching over his sheep. All day long he would lead them across the countryside in search of good pasture. He would watch over them with loving care, driving them gently with his crooked staff. The sheep would learn to *The Good Shepherd*

SHEPHERDS WATCHING THEIR FLOCKS

know his voice and when he called, they would come scampering to his feet.

At night he would lead them to the sheepfold. This was a kind of yard, surrounded by a stone wall. There was a narrow gate through which the sheep would enter while the shepherd stood and counted them as they went in, in order to be sure that none had been lost. Once they were inside, the shepherd would close the gate and bar it. Then, stretching out on the ground before it, he would go to sleep. But even in slumber he would be watching; and let there be so much as the sound of a strange footstep or the noise of a prowling animal, and at once he would be wide-awake, ready to protect his sheep.

Sometimes the shepherd did not own the sheep, but had hired himself out to take care of them for someone else. In such a case he might not be very careful of his woolly charges. Maybe he would neglect them and in time of danger run away, because the sheep did not belong to him and he had nothing to lose if anything happened to them.

Our Savior compared His Church to a sheepfold and Himself to a shepherd. He said, "Amen, amen, I say to you. He that entereth not by the door into the sheepfold, but climbeth up another way, the same is a thief and a robber. But he that entereth in by the door is the shepherd of the sheep. The sheep hear his voice and he calleth them by name and leadeth them out. He goeth before them and the sheep follow him because they know his voice. But the stranger they follow not, but fly from him because they know not the voice of strangers.

"The thief cometh not but for to steal and to kill and to destroy. I am come that they may have life and may have it more abundantly. I am the good shepherd. The good shepherd giveth his life for his sheep. But the hireling and he that is not the shepherd, whose own the sheep are not, seeth the wolf coming and leaveth the sheep and flieth, and the wolf catcheth and scattereth the sheep. And the hireling flieth because he is a hireling and he hath no care for the sheep. I am the good shepherd. I know Mine and Mine know Me, as the Father knoweth Me and I know the Father, and I lay down My life for My sheep. But other sheep I have that are not of this fold. Them also I must bring, and they shall hear My voice, and there shall be one fold and one shepherd."

Jesus foresaw that not all the members of His Church would be worthy of the great vocation to which they had been called. They would not be true to His

The wheat and the cockle

teaching and would lead sinful lives. He foretold this to the people in the following parable: "The Kingdom of Heaven," He said, "is like a man that sowed good seed in his field. But whilst his servants slept, his enemy came and oversowed cockle among the wheat and went his way. When the blade was sprung up and had brought forth fruit, then appeared also the cockle. The servants of the good man of the house, coming to him, said, 'Sir, didst thou not sow good seed in thy field? Whence, then, hath it cockle?'

"He said to them, 'An enemy hath done this.' The servants said to him, 'Wilt thou that we go and gather it up?' But he said, 'No, lest, perhaps, gathering up the cockle, you root up the wheat also together with it. Allow both to grow until the harvest, and in the time of the harvest I will say to the reapers, "Gather up first the cockle and bind it into bundles to burn, but the wheat gather ye into my barn."

His disciples said to Him, "Explain to us the parable of the cockle of the field." Jesus said, "He that soweth the good seed is the Son of Man. The field is the world, and the good seed are the children of the Kingdom, and the cockle are the children of the wicked one. And the enemy that sowed them is the devil. But the harvest is the end of the world, and the reapers are the angels. Even as cockle, therefore, is gathered up and burnt with fire, so shall it be at the end of the world. The Son of Man shall send His angels, and they shall gather out of His Kingdom all scandals and men that work iniquity and shall cast them into the furnace of fire. There shall be weeping and gnashing of teeth. Then shall the just shine as the sun in the Kingdom of the Father.''

Jesus said His Church was like a net which is cast into the sea and gathers up all kinds of fishes. When the net is full, the fishermen draw it out and, sitting by the shore, pick out the good fishes and cast the bad away. So shall it be at the end of the world when the angels shall separate the wicked from the just. The net

Again Jesus said, "To what shall we liken the Kingdom of God, or to what shall we compare it? It is like a grain of mustard seed, which, when it is sown in the earth, is less than all the seeds that are in the earth. But when it is sown, it groweth up and becometh greater than all the herbs and shooteth out great branches, so that the birds of the air may dwell under the shadow thereof.'' The mustard seed

In order to show the people how important it is to belong to the Church and how we must be ready to make every sacrifice in order to possess the Kingdom of Heaven, the Savior said, ''The Kingdom of Heaven is like to a treasure hidden in a field, which a man having found, for joy thereof goeth and selleth all that he hath and buyeth that field. Again, the Kingdom of Heaven is like to a merchant seeking good pearls, and when he had found one pearl of great price, he went his way and sold all that he had and bought it.'' The treasure hidden in the field

The mere fact that a man belongs to the Church does not make him worthy of the Kingdom of Heaven. It is necessary for him to live a holy life. Our Lord compares our good works to the fruit of a tree. A The barren fig tree good tree produces good fruit. A bad tree produces bad fruit.

Our Lord brought this truth home to His hearers by the parable of the barren fig tree. He said, "A certain man had a fig tree planted in his field. He came seeking fruit on it and found none. Then said he to the caretaker of the orchard, 'For three years I have come seeking fruit on this tree and I found none. Cut it down, therefore. Why doth it take up the ground?' The caretaker said to him, 'Lord, let it alone this year till I dig about it. Perhaps it will then yield fruit. If not, I shall cut it down.'"

The talents

Not all of those who are called to be members of Christ's Church receive the same graces. God, in His providence, gives some more and others less. But whether we have little or much, we are bound to work with what we have and thus prove ourselves worthy in the sight of God of the rewards He has in store for us. In order to teach men this lesson, Jesus spoke this parable: "A certain man about to go into a far country called his servants and gave them charge over his goods. To one he gave five talents, to another, two, and to another, one—to every one according to his proper ability—and immediately he set out on his journey. Now, he that received the five talents went his way and traded with the same and gained another five. And in like manner he that had received the two gained another two. But he that had received the one, going his way, dug a hole in the earth and hid his lord's money.

"After a long time, the lord returned and called his servants for a reckoning. He that had received the five talents, coming, brought other five talents, saying, 'Lord, thou didst deliver to me five talents. Behold, I have gained other five over and above.' His lord said, 'Well done, good and faithful servant. Because thou hast been faithful over a few things, I will place thee over many. Enter thou into the joy of thy lord.'

"He that received the two talents came and said, 'Lord, thou didst deliver two talents to me. Behold, I have gained other two.' His lord said to him, 'Well done, good and faithful servant. Because thou hast been faithful over a few things, I will place thee over many. Enter thou into the joy of thy lord.' But he that had received the one talent came and said, 'Lord, I know that thou art a hard man. Thou reapest where thou hast not sown and gatherest where thou has not strewed. And, being afraid, I went and hid my talent in the earth. Behold here thou hast that which is thine.'

"Then the lord said to him, 'Wicked and slothful servant. Thou knowest that I reap where I sow not and gather where I have not strewed. Thou oughtest, therefore, to have given my money to the bankers, so that at my coming I could have received mine own with interest. Take the talent away from him and give it to him that hath ten talents. For to every one that hath shall be given, that he shall abound. But from him that hath not, that also which he seemeth to have shall be taken away.'"

For three years Jesus preached to the people. Hardly a day passed but that the crowds would gather around Him and He would speak to them of the Kingdom of Heaven. They would listen to Him most attentively. They knew that His doctrine was true and in their hearts they felt a great desire to follow Him. But in the end, very few of them put their desires into practice.

Perhaps the apostles often wondered about this and talked of it among themselves. In order to explain this strange riddle, Jesus spoke the following parable to the people.

It was the day that He preached to them from Peter's boat. On the hillside not far away they could see a farmer sowing seed in his field. He carried the seed in a bag which hung from his shoulders. He would reach into the bag and bring out a handful of seed, and scatter it on the ground as he walked along. Pointing to him, the Savior said to the people, "Behold, the sower went forth to sow. And whilst he was sowing, some of the seed fell by the wayside and the birds of the air came and ate it up; and other some fell upon stony ground, where it had not much earth, and it shot up immediately because it had no depth, and when the sun was risen it was scorched and, having no root, it withered away. Some fell among thorns, and the thorns grew up and choked it and it yielded no fruit. And some fell upon good ground and brought forth fruit that grew up and increased and yielded a hundredfold." Then said He, "He that hath ears to hear, let him hear."

AN EASTERN FARMER SOWING SEED

Later on, when they were alone, His disciples asked Him the meaning of this parable. Jesus said, ''The seed is the word of God, and they by the wayside are they that hear. Then the devil cometh and taketh the word out of their hearts lest, believing, they should be saved. They upon the rock are they who, when they hear, receive the word with joy, but having no roots, they believe a while and in time of temptation they fall away. That which fell among thorns are they who have heard and, going their way, are choked with the cares and riches and pleasures of this life, and yield no fruit. But that which fell on good ground are they who in a good and perfect heart hear the word of God and keep it and bring forth fruit in patience.

The Wise and the Foolish Virgins

Christ expects those whom He has called to His Kingdom to make the best possible use of the grace He has given them and to labor diligently in His service. They must be ready at all times to give an account of themselves to Christ, their Judge. Death may come suddenly like a thief at night. "If a householder knew at what hour the thief would come," said Jesus, "he would not allow his house to be broken into. Be you also ready, for at what hour you know not the Son of Man will come."

"The Kingdom of Heaven," He said, "is like ten virgins who, taking their lamps, went out to meet the bridegroom and the bride. Five of them were foolish and five wise. But the five foolish, having taken their lamps, did not take oil with them. But the wise took oil in their vessels with the lamps. Because the bridegroom was long in coming, they all slumbered and slept.

"At midnight a great cry was made, 'Behold the bridegroom cometh. Go ye forth to meet him.' All the virgins arose and trimmed their lamps. Then the foolish said to the wise, 'Give us some of your oil, for our lamps are gone out.' The wise answered, 'Lest perhaps there be not enough for us and for you, go ye rather to them that sell, and buy for yourselves.'

"Now, whilst they went to buy, the bridegroom came, and they that were ready went in with him to the marriage and the door was shut. After a while, the others came and called out, 'Lord, lord, open to us.'

But he answered, 'Amen, I say to you, I know you not.' ''

Then said Jesus, "Watch ye, therefore, because you know not the day nor the hour."

2. JESUS PROMISES THE BREAD OF LIFE

In the Book of Wisdom there is a sentence which reads, "My delights are to be with the children of men." These words express beautifully the great love of the Son of God for human beings. We want to be near to those we love, and when the Second Person of the Blessed Trinity became Man, it was with the intention of remaining on earth until the end of the world. By showing men how to be good, He could make them happy. By keeping them close to God, He could give them a foretaste of the joys of Heaven. After His ascension into Heaven, they would not be able to see Him face to face, but they could see Him in a different way in His Church. Being members of the Church, they would be united with Him most closely, as the branches are united with the vine, or as the different parts of the body are joined to the head.

But it was not enough for the heart of Jesus to be united with human beings in a general way. He wanted to unite Himself with each and every individual soul. In order to accomplish this, He worked the greatest of all His miracles. He instituted the Blessed Eucharist. But the hearts of men had to be prepared for this wonder of wonders. He could not tell them about it all at once; therefore, He revealed it to them little by little.

The Great Supper

THE SEA OF GALILEE

Jesus feeds the multitude In the beginning of His public life, Jesus was held in great admiration by the people. They were always crowding around Him and they gave Him no chance to rest either day or night. They did not even give Him time to eat. It was no wonder, then, that sometimes Jesus grew very tired.

When the apostles returned from their first missionary journey, they found the Savior worn out. They, too, were weary and footsore, and their hearts were filled with sadness because they had just heard of the death of John the Baptist. Jesus said, "Let us go apart by ourselves into some desert place, and there you may rest yourselves for a little time."

Near at hand was the Sea of Galilee. The apostles found a boat and, accompanied by our blessed Savior, set sail for the northern shore. There they knew they would find a lonely wilderness where, far from the city and the crowds, they could rest their bodies and refresh their souls.

But in spite of all their precautions, someone had seen them sail away. Then, too, the winds were against them and it took them much longer to sail across the lake than they had expected. News of their departure had spread among the people and they followed Jesus, some by boat and some by walking around the lake. Thus when the ship reached the shore, Jesus and the apostles found a great crowd awaiting them.

Passing through the midst of the people, Jesus and His apostles went on into the wilderness. Soon they came to a grass-covered hill and they sat down on the ground to rest.

But there was to be no rest for them that day. The crowds followed after them and soon they were surrounded by about five thousand people.

Jesus had pity on the multitude. He could not send them away, because they were like sheep without a shepherd and they had come to Him to learn the secrets of the love of God. So He forgot His own weariness and spoke to them all day long of the Kingdom of God and healed all their sick.

The day was now far spent and the shadows of the evening began to close in upon them. The apostles came to Jesus and said, "This is a desert place, and the hour is late. Send the people away that, going into the town and villages, they may find food and lodging." Jesus said to them, "They have no need to go. Give you them to eat." They said, "If we had two hundred pence to buy bread, we might be able to

JESUS MULTIPLIES THE LOAVES AND FISHES

give each one of them a morsel to eat." Jesus said to them, "How many loaves have you?" One of the apostles, Andrew, the brother of Simon Peter, said, "There is a boy here that hath five barley loaves and two fishes, but what are these among so many?" Jesus said, "Make them sit down in companies of fifty." The apostles did as Jesus commanded, and soon that great multitude was sitting down upon the green grass.

Then Jesus took the five loaves and the two fishes. Looking up to Heaven, He blessed them, and broke them, and distributed them to His apostles to set before the multitude.

The people were very hungry. Many of them had

left home the night before and all of them had been listening to Jesus all day long. So each one of them ate his fill. Then Jesus said to His apostles, "Gather up the fragments that remain, lest they be lost." They gathered up, therefore, and filled twelve baskets with the fragments of the five barley loaves that were left after all the people had eaten.

When the people saw the great miracle which Jesus had performed, they said, "This is of a truth the prophet that is come into the world." Knowing that they had it in mind to take Him by force and make Him king, Jesus fled into the mountain, Himself alone.

The apostles got into the boat and started back across the lake for Capharnaum. It was that night that Jesus came to them, walking on the water. The people knew that Jesus had not gotten into the boat with His apostles. There was another boat near the shore, and they watched all night to see if Jesus would take it. The next morning they realized that it was useless for them to wait any longer, so they made their way back to Capharnaum, seeking for Jesus. *The promise of the Bread of Life*

There they found Him teaching in the synagogue. They said to Him, "Master, when camest Thou hither?" Jesus answered, "Amen, amen, I say to you. You seek Me, not because you have seen miracles, but because you did eat of the loaves and were filled. Labor not for the meat which perisheth, but for that which endureth unto life everlasting." "What shall we do," asked the people, "that we may work the works of God?" Jesus answered, "This is the work of God, that you believe in Him Whom He hath sent."

They said, therefore, to Him, "What sign therefore dost Thou show, that we may see as it is written, 'He gave them bread from heaven to eat?'"

Then Jesus said to them, "Amen, amen, I say to you. Moses gave you not bread from Heaven, but My Father giveth you the true bread from Heaven. For the bread of God is that which cometh down from Heaven and giveth life to the world." The people said, "Lord, give us always this bread." Jesus answered, "I am the Bread of Life. Your fathers did eat manna in the desert and are dead. This is the bread which cometh down from Heaven, that if any man eat of it, he may not die. I am the Living Bread which came down from Heaven. If any man eat this bread, he shall live forever. And the bread I will give is My flesh for the life of the world." Then the people began to murmur among themselves and to say, "How can this man give us his flesh to eat?" But Jesus said to them, "Amen, amen, I say to you. Except you eat the flesh of the Son of Man and drink His blood, you shall not have life in you. He that eateth My flesh and drinketh My blood, hath life everlasting, and I will raise him on the last day. For My flesh is meat indeed, and My blood is drink indeed. This is the bread that came down from Heaven, not as your fathers did eat manna and are dead. He that eateth this bread shall live forever." Hearing this, the people began to murmur at Jesus and said, "Is not this Jesus, the son of Joseph, whose father and mother we know? How then saith he, 'I came down from Heaven.'"

Even the disciples were troubled at the words which

He spoke, and many of them said, "This saying is hard, and who can hear it?"

Turning to them, Jesus said, "Doth this scandalize you? Remember, it is the spirit that giveth life. The flesh profiteth nothing. The words that I have spoken to you are spirit and life. And there are some of you that believe not."

Jesus knew from the beginning that some of His disciples would not believe in Him and that one of His apostles would betray Him. He said, "Remember, I told you that no man can come to Me unless it be given him by My Father."

After this, many of His disciples went back to their homes and walked no more with Him.

Turning to the twelve apostles, Jesus said, "Will you also go away?" Simon Peter answered Him, "Lord, to whom shall we go? Thou hast the words of eternal life. And we have believed and have known that Thou art the Christ, the Son of God."

THINGS TO KNOW AND TO DO

1. THE CHURCH IS THE KINGDOM OF CHRIST ON EARTH

1. Tell how Jesus founded His Church. Whom did He make head of His Church and what powers did He give him?
2. Why did our Lord compare His Church to a vine and its branches?
3. Whom did He mean by the dead branches?
4. Show that the Church is like a sheepfold.
5. Explain the lesson taught by our Lord when He said that the tree that produced no fruit should be cut down.
6. Explain the meaning of the "oil of the virgins' lamps."
7. Read: "Lessons of the Savior," Chapter III.
8. Make a list of the various things to which our Lord compared the Church.

2. JESUS PROMISES THE BREAD OF LIFE

1. What proof has Jesus left that He loves to be with men?
2. Of what was the miracle of the Multiplication of the Loaves and Fishes a figure?

3. How did Jesus make it very clear during His preaching that He intended to give His Flesh to eat and His Blood to drink?

SELF-TEST

Before leaving Unit Seven test yourself with the following exercises. After you have finished the exercises, check your work.

I. Be able to give a three-minute talk on:
1. How our Lord taught men the way to Heaven.
2. Our Lord hates persons who only pretend to be good.
3. Our Lord loves the poor.
4. Our Lord taught us that we must love the poor.
5. To be a follower of Jesus is to love God's poor.
6. How the rich should use their riches.
7. Our Lord showed by word and example that we must love our neighbor.
8. The virtues which our Lord taught by word and example.

II. Select the parable of this Unit that you like best and tell it in your own words.

III. Show how to think on any one of the parables in this division so as to make it help your soul.

IV. Write in your notebook the answers to the following questions:
1. In what instances did our Lord teach us how to pray?
2. In what parables did He teach us how to put our trust in God?
3. In what parable did He teach that Heaven will be the reward of those who are poor for Christ's sake?
4. What instructions did Jesus give on bestowing alms?
5. In what parables did He teach the importance of love for our neighbor?
6. By what act did He teach reverence for the House of God?
7. When did He teach a lesson on humility?
8. How did Jesus teach us to love and care for the sick?
9. When did Jesus teach that sin is a worse evil than sickness?
10. What prophecies did Jesus make concerning His Church?
11. How did Jesus teach that members of the Church must do good works?
12. How did our Lord promise that He would give us His Flesh to eat and His Blood to drink?

V. Write a theme with this thought in your mind: "Jesus was a tender and patient teacher."

VI. Discuss the books read in studying this Unit.

VII. Make a map of Palestine and show all the places mentioned in this Unit.

PREVIEW

Unit Eight

HOW CHRIST REDEEMED THE WORLD AND RETURNED TO HEAVEN

By His holy life and by His miracles, Christ has proven that He is the Son of God. He has instructed the people concerning the Kingdom of Heaven, then told them what they must do to be saved. Now He performs the final great act by means of which the world is redeemed. In this Unit we shall learn how Jesus suffered and died for our sins. We shall see how He offered Himself up on the altar of the cross and died that we might have life.

We shall behold Him rising gloriously from the tomb and appearing to His apostles and disciples. He remains on earth forty days and then ascends into Heaven. We shall see how He sends the Holy Ghost upon His Church, to remain with her all days, so that she may have the light and strength to carry on the work of redemption unto the end of the world.

Unit Eight

HOW CHRIST REDEEMED THE WORLD AND RETURNED TO HEAVEN

Unit Eight

HOW CHRIST REDEEMED THE WORLD AND RETURNED TO HEAVEN

I. CHRIST, THE SAVIOR OF MANKIND

Christ Has Mercy on Sinners

"Behold the Lamb of God. Behold Him Who taketh away the sins of the world." Thus did John the Baptist introduce our blessed Savior to the people. Like the Paschal lamb which was slain in order that its blood, being sprinkled on the doorposts, would save their first-born from death the night before the Israelites left Egypt, so would the blood of Jesus save from the death of sin those who believed in Him. The sacrifices of the Old Law could not open the gates of Heaven, for only God Himself could take away the sins of the world. By His death on the cross, Christ paid the debt that man owed to God and bought for him the right to enter the Kingdom of Heaven. This is beautifully expressed in the Thirty-ninth Psalm, "Sacrifice and oblation Thou wouldst not, but a body Thou hast fitted to Me. Holocaust for sin did not please Thee. Then said I, behold I come. In the head of the book it is written of Me that I should do Thy will, O God."

It was the will of God that men should be made holy by the sacrifice of the body of Jesus Christ.

The lost sheep

The Pharisees criticized our blessed Savior for associating with sinners. They were scandalized when He permitted Mary Magdalen to kiss His feet. They were shocked when He dined in the house of the publican. Whenever publicans and sinners drew near unto Him to listen to Him, the Pharisees murmured and said, "This man receiveth sinners and eateth with them."

Jesus said to them, "What man of you that hath an hundred sheep, and if he shall lose one of them, doth he not leave the ninety-nine in the desert and go after that which was lost until he find it; and when he hath found it, lay it upon his shoulders rejoicing, and coming home, call together his friends and neighbors, saying to them, 'Rejoice with me because I have found my sheep that was lost'? I say to you that even so there shall be joy in Heaven upon one sinner that doth penance, more than upon ninety-nine just who need not penance. Or what woman, having ten coins, if she lose one coin, doth not light a candle and sweep the house and seek diligently until she find it; and when she hath found it, call together her friends and neighbors, saying, 'Rejoice with me because I have found the coin which I had lost'? So I say to you, there shall be joy before the angels of God, upon one sinner doing penance."

The prodigal son

Then our Savior spoke to them the following beautiful parable: "A certain man had two sons. The younger of them said to his father, 'Father, give me now my share of thy fortune.' So the father divided his fortune and gave to him that portion which he would one day inherit.

"Not many days after, the younger man, gathering up all his possessions, went abroad into a far country, and there he wasted his substance by living a wild and bad life. After he had spent all, there came a mighty famine in that country, and he began to be in want. So he went and hired himself out to one of the citizens of that country, who sent him to his farm to feed the swine. He was so hungry that he would gladly have eaten the husks the swine did eat, but no one would let him have even them.

"At last he came to his senses. He said to himself, 'How many hired servants in my father's house abound with bread, and I here perish with hunger. I will arise and I will go to my father and say to him: Father, I have sinned against Heaven and before thee.'

"Rising up, he made his way homeward to his father. When he was yet a great way off, his father saw him and was moved with pity. Running to meet him, he fell upon his neck and kissed him.

"The son said, 'Father, I have sinned against Heaven and before thee. I am not worthy to be called thy son. Make me as one of thy hired servants.'"

"But the father said to the servants, 'Bring forth quickly the first robe and put it on him, and put a ring on his finger, and shoes on his feet. And bring hither the fatted calf and kill it, so that we can make merry. Because this, my son, was dead and has come to life again; he was lost, and is found.' And they began to be merry.

THE RETURN OF THE PRODIGAL SON

"His elder son was in the field, and when he came and drew nigh to the house and heard music, he called one of the servants and asked what this meant. The servant said to him, 'Thy brother is come and thy father hath killed the fatted calf because he hath received him safe.'

"Hearing this, the elder son became angry and would not go into the house. His father, therefore, came out and began to entreat him to come in; but he, answering, said to his father, 'Behold, for so many years do I serve thee, and I have never transgressed thy commandments, and yet thou hast never given me a kid to make merry with my friends. But as soon as thy son is come, who hast wasted his substance on sinful companions, thou hast killed for him the fatted calf.'

"But his father said to him, 'Son, thou art always with me, and all I have is thine. But it was fit that we should make merry and be glad, for this thy brother was dead, and is come to life again; he was lost, and is found.' "

That sinners might know that God is always ready **The laborers and the vineyard** to welcome them when they repent and that it is never too late to return to Him, our Savior spoke the following parable: "The Kingdom of Heaven is like to a householder who went out early in the morning to hire laborers for his vineyard. And having agreed with the laborers for a penny a day, he sent them into his vineyard.

"Going out about the third hour, he saw others standing in the market place idle and he said to them, 'Go you also into my vineyard and I will give you what shall be just.' They went into the vineyard. Again he went out about the sixth and the ninth hour and did in like manner. But about the eleventh hour he went out and found others standing, and he said to them, 'Why stand you here all the day idle?' They said to him, 'Because no man hath hired us.' He saith to them, 'Go you also into my vineyard.'

"When evening was come, the lord of the vineyard saith to his steward, 'Call the laborers and pay them their hire, beginning from the last even to the first.'

"When, therefore, they were come that came about the eleventh hour, they received every man a penny.

But when the first also came, they thought that they should receive more, and they also received every man a penny. And, receiving it, they murmured against the master of the house, saying, 'These last have worked but one hour, and thou hast made them equal to us that have borne the burden of the day and the heat.'

"But, he, answering, said to one of them, 'Son, I do thee no wrong. Didst thou not agree with me for a penny? Take what is thine and go thy way. I will also give to this last even as to thee.'"

The woman taken in adultery

Early one morning, Jesus came into the Temple. When the people saw Him, they gathered around Him. Jesus then sat down, and He taught them. A number of Pharisees came up to Him, bringing with them a woman who had been taken in adultery. They said to Him, "Master, this woman was even now taken in adultery. Now, Moses and the law commanded us to stone such a one. But what sayest Thou?"

This question was intended to entrap our blessed Savior. If He told them to follow the Law of Moses and put the woman to death, they would say that He did not love sinners. If He set her free, they could accuse Him before the high priest of breaking the law.

Jesus answered them not a word, but, stooping down, He began to write with His finger on the ground.

They watched Him for a moment and then they repeated their question. Rising up, He said to them, "He that is without sin among you, let him cast the first stone at her." Then, stooping down again, He continued to write on the ground.

The Pharisees looked and saw what Jesus had written. Then they began to go away, one by one, beginning with the eldest, and Jesus and the woman alone remained.

Then Jesus, raising Himself up, said to her, "Woman, where are they that accuse thee? Hath no man condemned thee?" She answered, "No man, Lord." Jesus said, "Neither will I condemn thee. Go now, and sin no more."

THINGS TO KNOW AND TO DO

Christ Has Mercy on Sinners

1. Why did the Son of God become Man?
2. Explain the meaning of atonement?
3. What caused Heaven to be closed against man?
4. Why did Jesus use the parable of the shepherd and sheep to show His love for sinners?
5. Write a dramatization of the story of the prodigal son.
6. Bring to class pictures representing the stories contained in this Unit.
7. When ought one specially to think of the lessons given in this division of Unit Eight?

II. THE PASSION AND DEATH OF CHRIST

1. THE ENEMIES OF CHRIST PLOT AGAINST HIM

The Pharisee's hatred   Our divine Savior spent the last six months of His public life in and about Jerusalem. Since the day when by His almighty power He called Lazarus from the grave, the chief priests and the Pharisees had been watching His every movement in the hope that He would do or say something for which they could have Him condemned to death. It is easy to understand why they would hate our blessed Savior. Again and again He had spoken against them in public and said that their piety was only a mask to cover up the sinfulness of their hearts. Because Jesus had criticized the Pharisees, the people were beginning to see them as they really were and to know that they were hypocrites. As a consequence, the chief priests and the Pharisees were beginning to lose their influence with the nation and they were afraid the people would turn against them.

Disloyalty of people   By this time the faith of some of the people, too, had begun to weaken. They had expected that the Messias would be a warlike leader who would free them from the Roman power. They could not bring themselves to accept a Messias Whose Kingdom was not of this world. For three years they had been waiting for the moment when Jesus would claim the throne of David and declare a war of independence against the foreign

JERUSALEM IN THE TIME OF CHRIST

foe that held them in bondage. If He had not fled away after He fed the multitude in the desert, the people would have taken Him by force and made Him king.

When He told them in the synagogue at Capharnaum that He would give them His flesh to eat and His blood to drink, their hopes were at an end. They understood at last that He did not intend to establish an earthly kingdom. Their disappointment was very great. Their love for Him had been selfish. They had followed after Him because they thought He would bring them earthly prosperity. Now their love began to turn into hatred.

No sin that could be committed against the Law of Moses was considered as terrible as blasphemy, for blasphemy is a direct insult to God. Whenever Jesus spoke of God as His Father, or said that He had come down from Heaven, or when He forgave people their sins, the Pharisees would murmur against our blessed Savior and say that He was blaspheming. *Jesus accused of blasphemy*

Yet the Pharisees were afraid to have Jesus arrested and brought before the high priest on a charge of blasphemy. They knew that if they did so, there would be a riot among the faithful followers of Jesus, who, seeing the many miracles that He had wrought, could not believe that He was a sinner. Our Savior Himself had said, "If you do not believe My word, believe My works."

Our Lord said to the Pharisees, "Which of you shall convict Me of sin? If I say the truth to you, why do you not believe Me? He that is of God heareth the words of God. Therefore you hear them not, because you are not of God."

The Pharisees answered, "Do we not say well that Thou art a Samaritan and hast a devil?" Jesus answered, "I have not a devil, but I honor My Father, and you have dishonored Me. But I seek not My own glory. There is One That seeketh and judgeth. Amen, amen, I say to you, if any man keep My word, he shall not see death forever."

Then the Pharisees said, "Now we know that thou hast a devil. Abraham is dead, and the prophets, and Thou sayest, 'If any man keep My word, he shall not taste death forever.' Art Thou greater than our father Abraham, who is dead, and the prophets? What dost Thou make Thyself?"

"If I glorify Myself," Jesus answered, "My glory is nothing. It is My Father that glorifieth Me, of Whom you say that He is your God. And you have not known Him. But I know Him. And if I shall say that I know Him not, I shall be like you, a liar. But I do know Him and do keep His word. Abraham, your father, rejoiced that he might see My day. He saw it and was glad.''

Hearing this, the scribes and the Pharisees became very angry and said to Him, ''Thou art not yet fifty years old, and hast thou seen Abraham?''

Jesus said to them, ''Amen, amen, I say to you, before Abraham was made, I am.''

The enemies of our Savior knew well the meaning of these words. They remembered that when Moses, kneeling before the burning bush, asked God what he should answer to the Israelites in Egypt if they asked him who it was that sent him to deliver them, God answered, ''I am Who am.'' By using these same words, Jesus made Himself equal to God. Therefore they took up stones to cast at Him, but Jesus hid Himself and went out of the Temple.

Herod hated Jesus because he was afraid of Him. **The enmity of Herod** He was a superstitious man and he thought that Jesus might be John the Baptist returned from the dead. Once when Jesus was in Galilee, some of the Pharisees came to Him and said, ''Depart and get Thee hence, for Herod hath a mind to kill Thee.'' But Jesus was not that easily frightened. He said, ''Go and tell that fox, 'Behold, I cast out devils, and do cures today and tomorrow, and the third day My work is done.' Nevertheless, I must work today and tomorrow and the day following, because a prophet cannot perish outside of Jerusalem.''

By these words our Savior showed His great contempt for Herod and let him know that he had no power to harm Him. He also foretold that He should die, not in Galilee, but in Jerusalem.

Nicodemus defends our Lord The agents of the chief priests and Pharisees dogged the footsteps of our blessed Savior, watching for an opportunity to arrest Him. Yet even they were deeply impressed by His teaching and His holy life. The chief priests and Pharisees sent for them and said, "Why have you not brought Him?" They answered, "Never did a man speak like this man." The Pharisees said, "Are you also seduced? Do any of the chief priests believe in Him, or the Pharisees? It is only the common people, who know not the law, that follow after Him." Then it was that Nicodemus, who was a member of the Sanhedrin, spoke up. Ever since the night that he had come to Jesus to ask Him about the Kingdom of Heaven, he had been a disciple of our blessed Savior, but in secret. Now he said, "Doth our law judge any man unless it first hear him and know what he doth?" "Art thou a Galilean?" they answered; "search the Scriptures and see that out of Galilee a prophet riseth not."

Jesus conceals Himself Jesus knew that His enemies in Jerusalem were plotting against Him, but His hour had not yet come. He had work to do before the day on which He should suffer and die. Therefore He remained outside of the city and hid Himself in the little town of Ephrem, which is about sixteen miles northeast of Jerusalem. From Ephrem He went also to other small towns and was a frequent visitor at the home of His friends at Bethania.

MARY MAGDALEN ANOINTS THE HEAD OF JESUS

Six days before the Feast of the Pasch, Jesus and **Palm Sunday** His apostles came to Bethania. There a supper was made for them; and Martha served and Lazarus was among those who sat at table. Mary took a pound of ointment of great price and poured it on the head of Jesus, and anointed His feet and wiped them with her hair. The house was filled with the odor of the ointment.

Seeing this, Judas Iscariot, one of His apostles, became very indignant and said, "To what purpose is this waste? For this might have been sold for more than three hundred pence, and the money given to the poor."

Judas said this, not because he really loved the poor, but because he loved money. Jesus had placed great confidence in him and had given him charge of the offerings which the people made to them from time to time and which they used to purchase for themselves whatever food or clothing was necessary.

Jesus said, "Why do you trouble her? She hath wrought a good work upon Me. For the poor you have always with you; whensoever you will, you may do them good. But Me you have not always. She is come beforehand to anoint My body for the burial. Amen, I say to you, wheresoever this Gospel shall be preached to the whole world, that also which she hath done shall be told for a memory of her."

The entry into Jerusalem

The next day Jesus left Bethania and set out boldly for Jerusalem. Sending two of His apostles ahead to a little town called Bethphage, which is near the Mount of Olives, He said to them, "Go into the town which is over yonder, and when you enter you shall see the colt of an ass tied, which no man hath ever ridden. Loose him and bring him hither. And if any man shall ask you, 'Why do you loose him?' say to him, 'Because the Lord hath need of his service,' and he will immediately let him go."

Now all of this was done that the words of the prophet Isaias might be fulfilled, who said, "Tell ye the daughter of Sion, behold thy King cometh to thee, meek and sitting upon an ass."

The disciples did as Jesus commanded them. The road was crowded with throngs of people on their way to Jerusalem to celebrate the Feast of the Pasch. The

JESUS ENTERING JERUSALEM

colt was brought to Jesus. The apostles threw their garments over it, and Jesus sat upon its back. When the crowds on the road saw Jesus coming, riding upon the ass, they spread their cloaks on the ground before Him and cut down boughs from the trees and strewed them in the way. With branches of palm trees in their hands, they crowded around Him and cried out, "Hosanna to the Son of David! Blessed is He that cometh in the name of the Lord! Hosanna in the highest!"

There were a number of Pharisees in the crowd, and they said among themselves, "Do you not see that we accomplish nothing? Behold, the whole world is running after Him."

Some of them went up to Jesus and said, "Master, rebuke thy disciples." Jesus answered, "I say to you that if these shall hold their peace, the stones will cry out."

The procession had now reached the top of the hill, and across the valley they could see the city of Jerusalem gleaming in the sunlight. High over all the other buildings and houses rose the Temple, its pinnacle pointing heavenward.

Jesus weeps over Jerusalem

Jesus bade them pause. For a while He gazed upon the city silently. Then He began to weep and said, "Jerusalem, Jerusalem, thou that killest the prophets and stonest them that are sent unto thee, how often would I have gathered together thy children as a hen doth gather her chickens under her wing, and thou wouldst not. If thou hadst known, and that in this thy day, the things that are to thy peace; but now they are hidden from thy eyes. For the days shall come upon thee, and thine enemies shall cast a trench about thee, and compass thee around and straiten thee on every side, and beat thee flat to the ground, and thy children who are in thee; and they shall not leave in thee a stone upon a stone, because thou hast not known the time of thy salvation."

Jesus in the Temple

Now they had entered the city and were passing through the narrow streets that led to the Temple. The crowds continued to shout, "Hosanna to the Son of David," and to wave their palm branches in the air. The people ran out of their houses to see what was the matter and they said, "Who is this?" The crowds answered, "This is Jesus, the prophet from Nazareth, of Galilee."

At last they reached the Temple, and the blind and the lame were brought to Him and He healed them. Crowds of children gathered around Jesus, crying, "Hosanna to the Son of David!" Seeing this, the chief priests and the scribes became very angry. They said to Jesus, "Hearest Thou what these children say?" And Jesus said to them, "Yea, have you never read, 'Out of the mouths of infants hath come forth praise'?"

There were a number of Gentiles in Jerusalem at that time. Perhaps they were merchants who, knowing that the Jews gathered in Jerusalem on the feast of the Passover from every part of the country and from many different parts of the world, felt this would be a convenient time to carry on business. Seeing the great excitement that was caused when Jesus entered the city, some of these Gentiles became curious, and, coming to Philip, said, "Sir, we would like to see Jesus." Philip called Andrew aside and told him what they had said, and together they went to Jesus. Jesus said, "The hour is come that the Son of Man should be glorified."

A voice from Heaven

These Gentiles were the first of countless millions who, until the end of time, would come from every part of the world to pay homage to Jesus and accept Him as their Savior. After His death, the apostles would go forth and preach the Gospel to every nation, and all peoples, regardless of race or color, would give glory to Christ the King.

But Jesus knew the price He would have to pay for this great victory. The Son of God would have to die on the cross in order to enter into His Kingdom. Therefore He said, "Amen, amen, I say to you, unless the grain of wheat, falling into the ground, die, it remaineth alone. But if it die, it bringeth forth much fruit. He that loveth his life shall lose it; he that hateth his life in this world, keepeth it unto life eternal. Now is My soul troubled, and what shall I say? Father, save Me from this hour. Yet I know it was for this cause that I came into the world. Father glorify Thy name."

Suddenly, a voice came from Heaven, saying, "I have both glorified it, and I will glorify it again."

The crowds heard the sound of the voice from Heaven, but did not know what it meant. Some of them said, "It thundered." Others said, "An angel spoke to Him." But Jesus said, "This voice came, not because of Me, but for your sake. Now has judgment come upon the world. Now shall the prince of this world be cast out. But I, when I am lifted up from earth, will draw all things to Myself."

Thus did Jesus enter Jerusalem in triumph. All day long there was rejoicing among the people, and in the Temple and in the streets of the city could be heard the cry, "Hosanna to the Son of David. Blessed is He that cometh in the name of the Lord!" When night came, the tumult died down and Jesus with His apostles left the city and went back to Bethania.

The next morning they left Bethania and set out once more for Jerusalem. As they went along, Jesus became hungry. Seeing a fig tree by the wayside, He went up to it. Though it was covered with leaves, there were no figs upon it, and He said, "May no fruit grow on thee henceforward forever."

Entering the city, Jesus went at once to the Temple. In the Court of the Gentiles He came upon the merchants selling the victims for the sacrifices, and the money changers at their tables. As once before, at the beginning of His public life, He began to drive them out and to overthrow their tables and their chairs, and He would not so much as allow anyone to carry anything through the Temple. He said to them, "Is it not written, 'My house shall be called the house of prayer to all nations'? But you have made it a den of thieves." *Jesus purifies the Temple*

And when evening was come, He went forth out of the city back toward Bethania, and spent the night on the Mount of Olives.

On the following morning, which was Tuesday, Jesus and the apostles once more returned to Jerusalem. As they passed the fig tree which Jesus had cursed the day before, they saw that it was dried up from the roots. Peter said, "Master, behold, the fig tree which Thou didst curse is withered away." Jesus answered, "Amen, I say to you, if you shall have faith, and waver not, not only this of the fig tree shall you do, but also if you shall say to this mountain, 'Take up thyself and cast thyself into the sea,' it shall be done."

Entering the Temple, Jesus began to preach to the people. Some of the chief priests and leaders of the people came up to Him and said, "By what authority *The Pharisees question Jesus* dost Thou these things, and who hath given Thee this authority?'' Jesus answered, ''I will also ask you one word, and if you answer Me, I will tell you by what authority I do these things. The baptism of John, was it from Heaven or from men?''

But they said to themselves, ''If we shall say from Heaven, He will say to us, 'Why, then, did you not believe him?' but if we shall say from men, we are afraid of the people, for they held John to be a prophet, and they will stone us.'' So they answered that they knew not whence it was. Then Jesus said to them, ''Neither do I tell you by what authority I do these things.''

The coin of tribute Having tried in vain to prove our Lord guilty of some sin against the Law of Moses, the enemies of our blessed Savior now adopted another course. If they could lead Him to say something against the Roman government, they would be able to go before the Roman governor and accuse Him of treason. They called in some of the members of King Herod's court and, after discussing the matter with them, they sent spies to Jesus to try to ensnare Him in His speech. Pretending that they were sincere Jews and were worried because they did not know whether or not it was sinful to pay tribute to the Roman emperor, they came to Jesus and said, ''Master, we know that Thou art a true speaker, and carest not for any man. For Thou regardest not the person of men, but teachest the way of God in truth. Tell us, therefore, what dost thou think. Is it lawful to give tribute to Caesar or not?''

But Jesus knew what was in their minds and was

THE COIN OF TRIBUTE

not deceived. He said, "Why do you tempt Me, ye hypocrites? Show Me the coin of the tribute." They offered Him a penny. Jesus said, "Whose image and inscription is this?" They said to Him, "Caesar's." Then He said to them, "Render, therefore, to Caesar the things that are Caesar's; and to God, the things that are God's."

Filled with wonder at this answer, they left Him and went their way.

That same day Jesus said to some Pharisees who were gathered around Him, "What think you of Christ; whose son is he?" They say to Him, "David's." He said to them, "How, then, doth David in spirit call him Lord, saying, 'The Lord said to my Lord: Sit on my right hand, until I make thy enemies thy footstool'? If David then call Him Lord, how is He his son?" But no one was able to answer Him, nor did anyone from that day forth dare to question Him. **The Son of David**

So throughout the day He taught in the Temple. But in the evening, going out, He spent the night on the Mount of Olives. The next day the chief priests and the leaders of the people were gathered in the court of the high priest, Caiphas. They were consulting together about Jesus, trying to think of some way in which they could lay hold of Him and put Him to death. The Feast of the Pasch was at hand and Jerusalem was crowded with people, many of whom were followers of our blessed Savior who might rise up and defend Him if anyone laid hands upon Him. So the chief priest said, "Not on the festival day, lest perhaps there should be a tumult among the people."

Judas bargains with the enemy Then it was that Satan entered into the heart of Judas, one of the twelve apostles, who was called Iscariot. Judas had been with our blessed Savior from the beginning and was the only one of the apostles who came from Judea. He knew the ways of the world better than the others, most of whom were poor fishermen, and Jesus seems to have depended upon him to look out for the practical side of His mission. He had charge of the money and no doubt did most of the buying that was necessary.

Judas loved the things of this world. He could not get used to the poverty in which our Savior and His apostles lived. He was happy when he had money in his possession and dreamed of the things that money could buy. In spite of all that our Lord said, he continued to look forward to the day when Jesus would establish His kingdom here on earth.

Perhaps it was that day in Capharnaum, when Jesus told the people that He had come, not to give them bread for their bodies, but food for their souls, that Judas began to hate our blessed Lord. He could have left Jesus at any time and gone back to his home, but his disappointment was so great that he wanted to make Jesus suffer. Angry thoughts filled his mind, and in his heart the desire for revenge grew stronger every day. At last he could stand it no longer and, stealing away from the other apostles, he went to the chief priests and said to them, "What will you give me, if I will deliver Him unto you?" They offered him thirty pieces of silver. Judas agreed to their price and promised to deliver Jesus to them. From that time on, he kept watching for a time when Jesus would be alone and away from the people, so that he might betray Him to His enemies.

2. Christ Institutes the Holy Eucharist

It was Thursday, and the Feast of the Passover was at hand. For seven days the Jews would celebrate the anniversary of their deliverance from the hands of the Egyptians. On the first day, according to the ancient ceremony, they would eat the Paschal lamb.

The Last Supper

Early in the morning, Jesus sent Peter and John into the city to make ready the Paschal supper for Himself and His disciples. When they asked Him where they should prepare the meal, He answered, "Behold, as you go into the city, you shall meet a man carrying a pitcher of water. He will enter a house and you will follow him in and say to the master of the house. 'The Master saith, Where is My supper room, where I may eat the Pasch with My disciples?' He will show you a large dining room, furnished. There prepare ye for us."

Peter and John went their way and came into the city. Everything turned out as Jesus had foretold. They killed a Paschal lamb and roasted it as the Law

THE CENACLE

of Moses commanded. When all things were ready, they waited for the coming of Jesus.

The Last Pasch

At evening, our divine Savior came with the other apostles, and all of them sat down to eat.

We may picture to ourselves this holy scene. Imagine a room fifty feet long and thirty feet wide on the second floor of the house. The walls and ceiling are white and in the center of the floor there stands a low table. Couches are placed along one side of it only. The other side is left free for those who serve the meal and wait on the guests.

Jesus took His place on a couch in the center of the table. John was next to Jesus and Peter and the rest of the apostles were seated on couches at either side of Jesus.

When they were all in their places, Jesus said, "With desire have I desired to eat this Pasch with you before I suffer."

A large cup or chalice of wine was now brought in. According to the ceremony of the Paschal meal, the head of the family was expected to ask a blessing on this cup, and, after taking a sip of it himself, to pass it on to all the others that were at table. All of this Jesus did. When He passed the cup to His apostles. He said, "Take, and divide it among you. But as for Me, I will no more drink of the fruit of the vine until that day when I shall drink it with you in the Kingdom of My Father."

After all had taken a sip from the cup, those who were eating the Paschal meal were supposed to wash their hands. Meanwhile, an argument had started among the apostles as to which of them would be the greater. Jesus rebuked them, saying, "For which is greater, he that sitteth at table or he that serveth? Is it not he that sitteth at table? But I am in the midst of you, as he that serveth." Then it was that Jesus gave to His apostles and to all mankind a beautiful lesson of love and humility. Having loved His own who were in the world, He loved them unto the end. Rising up, He put aside His outer garment and, taking a towel, He girded Himself. Then, putting water in a basin, He knelt down and began to wash the feet of His disciples, and to wipe them with the towel wherewith He was girded.

The washing of the feet

JESUS WASHES PETER'S FEET

It was Peter at whose feet He knelt first. But Peter said, "Lord, dost Thou wash my feet?" Jesus said, "What I do, thou knowest not now. But thou shalt know hereafter." Peter said to Him, "Thou shalt never wash my feet." Jesus answered him, "If I wash thee not, thou shalt have no part with Me." Hearing this, Peter said, "Lord, not only my feet, but also my hands and my head." But Jesus said, "He that is washed needeth not but to wash his feet, but is clean wholly. And you are clean. But not all of you," for He knew who it was that would betray Him.

After He had washed the feet of all His apostles, Jesus put on His garment once more and sat down.

"Know you not what I have done to you?" He said to them. "You call Me Master and Lord, and you say well, for so I am. If then, I, being your Lord and Master, have washed your feet, you also ought to wash one another's feet. For I have given you an example, that as I have done to you, so do you also. The servant is not greater than his lord; neither is the apostle greater than He that sent him."

They now proceeded to eat the Paschal lamb, as the law commanded. Jesus, as the head of the house, explained the different ceremonies as they went along. While they were eating, Jesus became troubled in spirit and a great sadness came over Him. He said, "Amen, amen, I say to you, one of you shall betray Me." Hearing this, the apostles were greatly shocked, and began to be sorrowful and to say to Him one by one, "Is it I, Lord?" He answered, "The hand of him that betrayeth Me is with Me on the table. And the Son of Man indeed goeth, as it is written of Him; but woe to that man by whom the Son of Man shall be betrayed. It were better for him had he never been born." *The traitor*

All this time, Judas had remained silent. Now he leaned forward and said, "Is it I, Rabbi?" Jesus answered him, in a low voice, so that the others could not hear, "Thou hast said it."

John, the disciple whom Jesus loved, leaned over and rested his head upon our Lord's bosom as if to comfort Him. Peter made a sign to him to ask Jesus of whom He was speaking. John whispered, "Lord, who is it?"

In a low voice, Jesus answered, "He it is to whom I shall reach bread dipped."

Now there was an oblong dish on the table filled with a mixture of different kinds of fruit—apples and figs and citron—cooked in vinegar. The cinnamon and other spices used in its preparation gave it a reddish color, and it reminded the Jews of the bricks their forefathers had to make before God delivered them from Egypt. Into this dish Jesus dipped a morsel of bread and handed it to Judas, saying to him, "That which thou dost, do quickly." Only John understood what Jesus meant. The other apostles thought that Jesus meant that Judas should buy the things which they would need for the festival day, or that he should give something to the poor. When Judas had received the morsel from the hands of our blessed Savior he went out immediately, and it was night.

The First Mass

Then it was that Jesus took in His hand a piece of the unleavened bread which was part of the Paschal meal and, giving thanks to God, blessed it, broke it and gave it to His apostles, saying, "TAKE YE AND EAT THIS IS MY BODY." Then once more He took a large cup, or chalice, which was filled with wine, and, giving thanks, He passed it to them, saying, "DRINK YE ALL OF THIS. FOR THIS IS MY BLOOD OF THE NEW TESTAMENT, WHICH SHALL BE SHED FOR MANY, UNTO REMISSION OF SINS."

Now was fulfilled the promise which Jesus had made in the synagogue at Capharnaum. He had given His apostles His flesh to eat and His blood to drink. Then

THE LAST SUPPER

He said, "Do this as often as you shall do it, for the commemoration of Me." By these words He gave to them and to their successors, the priests of the Catholic Church, the power to change bread and wine into His Body and Blood, and to offer up until the end of time the sacrifice of the Mass. Now would be fulfilled the prophecy of Malachias: "From the rising of the sun even to the going down, My name is great among the Gentiles. And in every place there is sacrifice, and there is offered to My name a clean oblation. For My name is great among the Gentiles, saith the Lord of Hosts."

With love in their hearts, the apostles received the

Body and Blood of their Master, and a feeling of peace and happiness came over them.

Jesus then began to talk to His apostles. "Little children," He said, "yet a little while I am with you. You shall seek Me when I am gone. But whither I go, you cannot come. A new commandment I give unto you: That you love one another, as I have loved you, that you also love one another. By this shall all men know that you are My disciples, if you have love one for another.

"This night all of you shall be scandalized in Me, for it is written, 'I will strike the shepherd, and the sheep of the flock shall be dispersed.' But after I shall be risen again, I will go before you into Galilee."

Turning to Simon Peter, Jesus said, "Simon, Simon, behold, Satan hath desired to have thee, that he may sift thee as wheat. But I have prayed for thee, that thy faith fail not; and thou, being once converted, confirm thy brethren."

Peter said to Him, "Lord, whither goest Thou?" Jesus answered, "Whither I go, thou canst not follow Me now. But thou shalt follow hereafter." Peter said, "Why cannot I follow Thee now? I will lay down my life for Thee. I am ready to go with Thee both into prison and to death. Although all shall be scandalized in Thee, I will never be scandalized." Jesus answered him, "Wilt thou lay down thy life for Me? Amen, amen, I say to thee, this night, before the cock shall crow, thou shalt deny Me thrice."

But Peter was sure that this could never be. He said, "Although I should die together with Thee, I will not deny Thee,'' and in like manner said all the apostles.

Seeing how sorrowful they all were, Jesus began to speak to them words of comfort. "Let not your hearts be troubled," He said. "You believe in God, believe also in Me. In My Father's house there are many mansions; I go to prepare a place for you. I will come again, and will take you to Myself, that where I am, you also may be."

Thomas said to Him, "Lord, we know not whither Thou goest; and how can we know the way?" Jesus saith to him, "I am the way, and the truth, and the life. No man cometh to the Father, but by Me."

Philip said, "Lord, show us the Father, and it is enough for us." Jesus answered, "Have I been so long a time with you, and have you not known Me? Philip, he that seeth Me seeth the Father also. Do you not believe that I am in the Father, and the Father in Me? The words that I speak to you, I speak not of Myself. But the Father Who abideth in Me, He doth the works.

"If you love Me, keep My commandments. And I will ask the Father, and He will give you another Comforter, that He may abide with you forever. The Spirit of truth, Whom the world cannot receive, because it seeth Him not, nor knoweth Him; but you shall know Him, because He shall abide with you, and shall be in you. I will not leave you orphans; I will come to you.

"These things have I spoken to you while I have been with you. But the Paraclete, the Holy Ghost,

Whom the Father will send in My name, He will teach you all things, and bring all things to your mind whatsoever I shall have said to you. Peace I leave with you, My peace I give unto you; not as the world giveth peace, do I give unto you. Let not your heart be troubled, nor let it be afraid.''

On the way to the Mount of Olives After they had arisen from the table and had sung a hymn, they left the Cenacle and went out of the city. They walked along the road that led through the valley Cedron. Crossing the bridge which spanned the Brook Cedron, they ascended the Mount of Olives.

As they went along, Jesus continued to speak to them. All around them were vineyards. The vines, in answer to the call of the spring, were beginning to put forth their leaves. Jesus said, ''I am the vine; you the branches. Abide in Me, and I in you. As the branch cannot bear fruit of itself unless it abide in the vine, so neither can you unless you abide in Me. In this is My Father glorified, that you bring forth very much fruit. And this is My commandment, that you love one another as I have loved you. Greater love than this no man hath, that a man lay down his life for his friends. You are my friends if you do the things that I command you. You have not chosen Me, but I have chosen you, and have appointed you, that you should go, and should bring forth fruit, and your fruit should remain. And whatsoever you shall ask of the Father in My name, He will give it to you.''

Jesus prays for the Church Now Jesus paused and, raising up His eyes to Heaven, He prayed: ''Father, the hour is come, glorify Thy Son, that Thy Son may glorify Thee. Thou hast given Him power over all flesh, that He may give eternal life to all whom Thou hast given Him. Now, this is eternal life: That they may know Thee, the only true God, and Jesus Christ, Whom Thou hast sent. I have glorified Thee on earth; I have finished the work which Thou gavest Me to do. And now glorify Thou Me, O Father, with Thyself, with the glory which I had, before the world was, with Thee.''

They had now come to the Garden of Gethsemani, **Geth-semani** which was near the foot of Mount Olivet. Many a night Jesus had spent in this little garden. It was in the midst of a grove of olive trees, and at one time there had been here an olive press, in which the olives were crushed for the purpose of obtaining from them the oil, which was used for so many purposes in those days. The word Gethsemani means olive press. The place was quiet and secluded, and Jesus loved to go there and spend the night in prayer.

At the gate, Jesus invited Peter, James, and John to come with Him farther into the garden, and told the other eight to wait for them. As they went forward, Jesus said to the three apostles, ''My soul is sorrowful even unto death. Stay here, and watch with Me. Pray, lest you enter into temptation.'' Then He went on alone, about a stone's throw, and, falling flat on the ground, He prayed, ''My Father, if it be possible, let this chalice pass from Me. Nevertheless, not as I will, but as Thou wilt.''

Then there appeared to Him an angel from Heaven, to strengthen Him. Being in an agony, He prayed the

THE GARDEN OF GETHSEMANI

longer. And His sweat became as drops of blood, trickling down upon the ground.

After a long while, He rose and went back to His apostles. He found them sound asleep. Waking Peter, He said, "Simon, sleepest thou? Couldst thou not watch one hour with Me? Watch ye, and pray that ye enter not into temptation. The spirit indeed is willing, but the flesh is weak."

Going away again, He prayed, saying: "My Father, if this chalice may not pass away, but I must drink it, Thy will be done."

Coming back to His apostles, again He found them sleeping, for their eyes were heavy. Leaving them, He went again and prayed the third time, saying the selfsame words, "My Father, if this chalice may not pass away, but I must drink it, Thy will be done."

THE AGONY OF OUR LORD IN THE GARDEN

A third time He came to His apostles, but this time He said, "Sleep ye now and take your rest. The hour is at hand. Behold, the Son of Man shall be betrayed into the hands of sinners. Rise up, let us go. Behold, he that will betray Me is at hand."

While He was yet speaking, they heard a great noise in the distance. Voices were calling to one another, and through the trees they could see the glow of torches. It was Judas Iscariot, coming at the head of a band of soldiers and servants whom he had received from the chief priests and the Pharisees. Judas knew that Jesus often came to the Garden of Gethsemani with His apostles. Armed with swords and clubs, with lanterns and torches to light their way, the soldiers

The kiss of Judas

and servants began to search the garden in order to find Jesus. Judas had given them a sign, saying, "Whomsoever I shall kiss, that is He; lay hold on Him, and lead Him away carefully."

Jesus did not try to hide away from the mob, but went forth to meet them. "Whom seek ye?" He asked. They answered, "Jesus of Nazareth." Jesus said to them, "I am He." Then Judas came forward and said, "Hail, Rabbi," and he kissed Him.

Jesus said to him, "Judas, dost thou betray the Son of Man with a Kiss?"

As soon as Jesus had said "I am He," the mob that was with Judas went backward and fell to the ground.

Again Jesus asked them, "Whom seek ye?" They said, "Jesus of Nazareth." Jesus answered, "I have told you that I am He. Then, pointing to His apostles, He said, "If therefore you seek Me, let these go their way."

This time the soldiers came up and laid hands on Jesus and held him.

When the apostles saw their beloved Master in the hands of these ruffians, they cried out, "Lord, shall we strike with the sword?" And Simon Peter, drawing his sword, struck the servant of the high priest and cut off his right ear. The name of the servant was Malchus.

But Jesus said to Peter, "Put up thy sword into the scabbard, for all that take the sword shall perish with the sword. Thinkest thou that I cannot ask My Father, and He will give Me presently more than twelve

JUDAS BETRAYS JESUS WITH A KISS

legions of angels? The chalice which My Father hath given Me, shall I not drink it?"

Then, touching the ear of Malchus, He healed him. Turning to the crowd, He said, "You are come out as it were to a robber, with swords and clubs, to apprehend Me. I sat daily with you, teaching in the Temple, and you laid not hands on Me. But this is your hour and the power of darkness." Then all His apostles, leaving Him, fled away.

3. THE REDEEMER IS CONDEMNED TO DEATH

Now began the journey back from Gethsemani to Jerusalem. Jesus and His captors crossed the Brook Cedron and soon reached the gates of the city. The

Jesus before Annas

soldiers hurried our Savior through the streets and brought Him to the palace of Annas, who was the father-in-law of Caiphas, the high priest of that year.

Formerly, Annas had been high priest himself, but he was deposed by the Roman governor. However, he was still held in great honor by the chief priests and the Pharisees. They felt that the Roman governor, in deposing him, had gone beyond his authority and had unlawfully interfered with their religion, which was no concern of his. Externally, they submitted to his order, but they continued to look upon Annas as the real high priest and to follow whatever advice and counsel he might give them. It was through his influence that Caiphas, his son-in-law, had been raised to the office of high priest.

Word was now sent out to the members of the Sanhedrin, informing them that Jesus had been captured and ordering them to assemble at once in the house of Caiphas, in order to sit in judgment upon Him. Whilst they were waiting, Annas began to question Jesus concerning His doctrine and His disciples. Jesus said to him, "I have spoken openly to the world. I have always taught in the synagogue and in the Temple, whither all the Jews come together; and in secret I have spoken nothing. Why askest thou Me? Ask them who have heard what I have spoken unto them. Behold, they know the things I have said."

One of the servants, who was standing near, struck Jesus a blow upon the mouth, saying, "Answerest thou the high priest so?" Jesus said, "If I have spoken evil, give testimony of the evil; but if well, why strikest

thou Me?'' Then Annas ordered Jesus to be bound
and taken to Caiphas.

The apostles who had told Jesus that they were **Peter's**
ready to go into bondage and death with Him had run **denial**
away at the first sign of danger in the garden. It is
true that Peter did pull out his sword and come to the
defense of our Savior, but when Jesus told him to put
away his sword into the scabbard, he too escaped into
the darkness of the night. The Shepherd had been
struck, and the sheep were scattered.

Peter and John seem to have been the first of the
apostles to realize what cowards they had been. Even
they were not brave enough to take their place openly
at the side of the Savior. They followed after Jesus
when He was taken back to Jerusalem, but they followed Him afar off. John seems to have been known
at the palace of the high priest, and he summoned up
enough courage to enter with the crowd. Peter remained outside in the darkness. It was not long before
John missed him and, going outside, he spoke to the
portress and she allowed Peter to enter.

Inside the gate there was a courtyard, in the center
of which a fire blazed. Around it the servants sat
warming themselves, for the night was cold. Coming
close to the fire, Peter too warmed himself.

Some time later, the portress who had admitted
Peter came to the fire. Seeing him, she looked at him
very closely and said, ''Art thou not a disciple of Jesus
of Nazareth?'' But Peter said, ''Woman, I know Him
not. I know not what thou sayest.''

After a little while, another maidservant, seeing

him, said, "This man also was with Jesus of Nazareth." Again Peter denied this with an oath. He said, "I know not the man." From where Peter was standing, it was possible to look into the room in the palace where the trial of Jesus was being held. He could see our Savior in the midst of His accusers. An hour passed, and Peter began to breathe easier. He felt sure that he had convinced those who were standing around the fire that he was not a disciple of Jesus. He began to talk to the man standing next to him. Looking at him in surprise, the man said, "Certainly thou art one of His disciples, for thy accent betrayeth thee. Thou art a Galilean." Hearing this, another of the servants of the high priest came up and, after looking very intently at Peter, said to him, "Did I not see thee in the garden with Him?" This servant happened to be a relative of Malchus, whose ear Peter had cut off.

Then Peter began to curse and to swear, saying, "I know not this man of whom you speak."

Just then the cock crew, and Jesus, turning, looked at Peter.

Peter remembered the word that Jesus had spoken, "Before the cock crow, thou shalt deny Me thrice." Bursting into tears, he pushed his way through the crowd and, rushing through the gate of the palace, went outside and wept bitterly.

Jesus before Caiphas Assembled in the palace where Caiphas lived, the Sanhedrin was proceeding with the trial of Jesus. From one witness after another they tried to obtain evidence that Jesus had said or done something for which they might condemn Him to death. But their

JESUS BEFORE CAIPHAS

labors were in vain. Many came who bore false witness against Him, but they contradicted themselves, no two of them agreeing in their accusations. Finally, they found two witnesses who said, "We heard Him say, 'I am able to destroy the Temple of God, and after three days to rebuild it.'"

At last, the high priest rose up and said to Jesus, "Answerest Thou nothing to the things which these witnesses say against Thee?" But Jesus held His peace and answered not a word.

Then the high priest said to Him, "I adjure Thee by the living God, that Thou tell us if Thou be the Christ, the Son of God."

Jesus answered, "I am. And you shall see the Son of Man sitting on the right hand of the power of God, and coming in the clouds of heaven."

Pretending to be deeply shocked at these words of our blessed Savior, Caiphas rent his garments and said, "He hath blasphemed. What further need have we of witnesses? You have heard the blasphemy; what do you think?" They cried out in one voice, "He is guilty of death."

Jesus before the San- hedrin Although the Sanhedrin might declare that a man had been guilty of some crime for which he should be put to death, they had no power of ordering his execu- tion. That right belonged to the Roman governor, who at that time was Pontius Pilate. They knew Pilate's reputation. He was very careful to see that the law was carried out as perfectly as possible. He would not condemn a man to death unless he were convinced that he had had a just trial.

By holding a session of the Sanhedrin at night and condemning Jesus to death before the morning sacri- fice, the chief priests had broken the law. Knowing that Pilate would find this out and therefore refuse to condemn Jesus to death, a meeting of the Sanhedrin was called again early the next morning.

All night long, Jesus had been at the mercy of the soldiers and the servants of the high priest. They had heaped insult after insult upon Him, and treated Him like the lowest criminal. They mocked Him, struck Him, and spat upon Him. They blindfolded Him and struck Him in the face with the palms of their hands, saying, "Prophesy unto us, O Christ, who is he that struck Thee?"

Early in the morning Jesus was brought before the Sanhedrin once more. Again they said to Him, "If Thou be the Christ, tell us." Jesus answered, "If I shall tell you, you will not believe Me. And if I shall ask you, you will not answer Me, nor let Me go. But hereafter the Son of Man shall be sitting on the right hand of the power of God." Then they all said, "Art Thou, then, the Son of God?" He said, "You say that I am."

They asked, "What need have we of further testimony? For we ourselves have heard it from His own mouth." Then they rose up, and ordering Jesus to be bound, led Him to Pontius Pilate, the Roman governor.

When Judas heard that our Lord had been con- *The death of Judas* demned to death, he repented of his treason and, taking the thirty pieces of silver, he brought them back to the chief priests and ancients, saying, "I have sinned in betraying innocent blood." They said, "What is that to us? Look thou to it."

Casting the pieces of silver down in the Temple, Judas rushed out and went and hanged himself with a halter.

Gathering up the pieces of silver, the chief priests said, "It is not lawful to put them into the treasury, because it is the price of blood." After discussing the matter among themselves, they finally decided to use the money to buy a potter's field, which would be a burying place for strangers. Thus was fulfilled the prophecy of Jeremias, "And they took the thirty

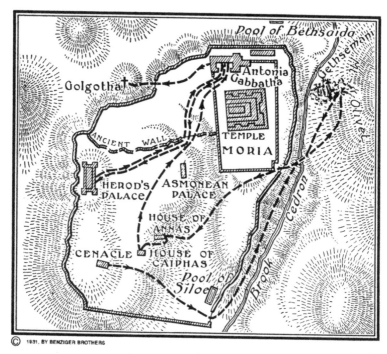

JERUSALEM, SHOWING OUR LORD'S JOURNEYS DURING THE PASSION

pieces of silver, the price of Him upon Whom a price was put, and they gave them unto a potter's field, as the Lord appointed to me.''

Jesus before Pilate
Meanwhile, Jesus had been brought to the Pretorium, the palace of the Roman governor, which was in the Antonia. The members of the Sanhedrin remained outside in the Gabbatha because, according to their law, if they entered the house of a heathen, they would become defiled and would not be allowed to take part in the celebration of the Feast of the Passover. They were not alone in the large square, for by this time the news of the arrest of Jesus had spread

throughout the city, and a great crowd, moved by curiosity or eager for excitement, had flocked to the Pretorium.

Jesus was turned over to the Roman guards and sent alone into the palace to face Pontius Pilate. He was loaded with chains and bore signs on His body of the rough and cruel treatment He had received during the night. When Pilate saw Him, he was moved to pity. He had heard of Jesus and His teaching, and knew that He was not a dangerous rebel. Going outside, he stood on the balcony of the palace and said to the members of the Sanhedrin, "What accusation bring you against this man?" They answered, "If He were not a criminal, we would not have delivered Him up to thee." Pilate said, "Take you Him, and judge Him according to your law." But the Jews said, "It is not lawful for us to put any man to death."

Pilate wished to avoid trouble if it were at all possible. The city was crowded with strangers and it was his duty to preserve order. He did not want a riot to take place. He decided to question Jesus Himself, hoping that he might learn something from Him that he could use as an argument against the members of the Sanhedrin and lead them to change their judgment.

He turned and entered the palace and, going into the large room in which he usually held court, he ordered Jesus to be brought before him. When this was done, he said to our Savior, "Art Thou the King of the Jews?" Jesus answered, "Sayest thou this of thyself, or have others told it thee of Me?" Pilate answered, "Am I a Jew? Thy own nation and the chief priests have delivered Thee up to me; what hast Thou done?" Jesus answered, "My Kingdom is not of this world. If My Kingdom were of this world, My servants would certainly fight that I should not be delivered to the Jews." Pilate therefore said to Him, "Art Thou a King?" Jesus answered, "Thou sayest that I am a king. For this was I born, and for this cause I came into the world, that I should give testimony to the truth. Every one that is of the truth, heareth My voice." Pilate said to Him, "What is the truth?" Then, rising up, he left the room and went out once more to the crowd.

Standing on the balcony overlooking the square, Pilate said to the chief priests, "I find no cause to condemn this man." A roar of anger went up from the crowd. A voice was heard above the din, saying, "He stirreth up the people, teaching throughout all Judea, beginning from Galilee to this place."

Jesus before Herod When Pilate heard them mention Galilee, he asked if Jesus were from Galilee. When he heard that He was, he thought of a plan whereby the whole affair might be settled without any interference on his part. Herod Antipas, who had put John the Baptist to death, was in Jerusalem, and he was the ruler of Galilee. So Pilate sent Jesus to Herod.

When Herod saw Jesus, he was very glad. He had heard the story of the wonderful things Jesus had done in Galilee, and ever since the death of John the Baptist he had been most anxious to see Him, in order to assure himself that Jesus was not John the Baptist risen from the dead. Then, too, his curiosity was aroused and he hoped to see Jesus work a miracle.

He asked Jesus one question after another, but our Savior answered him not a word. All the while, the chief priests and the scribes stood by, repeating their accusations.

The silence of our Savior hurt the vanity of Herod, and he began to make fun of Him and to mock Him. He ordered his soldiers to put upon Him a white garment, as a sign that He was a fool, and then sent Him back to Pilate. And Herod and Pilate, who had been enemies, were made friends that same day.

Once more, Pilate came out and spoke to the people. He said to them, "You have presented me this man as one that perverteth the people; and behold I, having examined Him before you, find no cause in this man in those things wherewith you accuse Him. Nor Herod either. For I sent you to him, and behold, nothing worthy of death is done to Him. I will chastise Him therefore, and release Him." Hearing this, the crowd became very angry and with shouts and cries demanded that Pilate put Jesus to death.

Now there was a custom at that time, whereby on a solemn feast day the governor released to the people one prisoner whom they would choose. There happened to be in prison a man called Barabbas, who, with a number of others, had been arrested for causing a riot in the course of which someone had been murdered. Now, Pilate knew that the chief priests had delivered Jesus up to him out of envy and he thought of a way to free the Savior from their hands. So he said, "Whom will you that I release to you," he asked, "Barabbas, or Jesus that is called Christ?"

For a moment the people did not know what to answer. But soon the chief priests persuaded them to ask for Barabbas, and the whole multitude together cried out, saying, "Away with this man, and release unto us Barabbas! Not this man, but Barabbas!"

Pilate said to them, "What shall I do, then, with Jesus that is called Christ?" And they all cried out again, "Crucify Him, crucify Him!"

Pilate said, "Why, what evil hath He done? I find no cause of death in Him. I will chastise Him and let Him go." But they only cried out the louder, "Crucify Him, crucify Him!"

The scourging at the pillar Then Pilate ordered his soldiers to take Jesus and to scourge Him. They led Him away into the court of the palace and, calling together the whole band, they stripped Him of His garments, bound Him to a pillar, and scourged Him with cruel whips. Then they put upon Him a purple cloak and, making a crown of thorns, they placed it on His head, and put a reed in His right hand, and mocked Him by kneeling before Him and shouting, "Hail, King of the Jews!" They spat upon Him and, taking the reed out of His hand, they struck His thorn-crowned head.

Pilate was sitting in the place of judgment, waiting for Jesus to be brought back to him, when his wife sent a message to him saying, "Have thou nothing to do with that just man; for I have suffered many things this day in a dream because of Him." The governor was deeply moved by this message from his wife, but

THE CROWNING OF OUR LORD WITH THORNS

outside he could hear the shouts of the mob, and he was afraid of what might happen if he released our blessed Savior.

At last, Jesus was brought back before Pilate. When he saw Him clothed in a purple garment, crowned with thorns, and covered with blood and filth, he led Him out to the people and said to them, "Behold the Man." *Ecce Homo*

But the sight of Jesus did not move the people and the chief priests to pity. Instead, they cried out the more, "Crucify Him, crucify Him!" Pilate said, "Take Him you, and crucify Him; for I find no cause in Him." But the Jews said, "We have a law; and

PILATE DECLARES: "BEHOLD THE MAN!"

according to the law He ought to die, because He made Himself the Son of God."

When Pilate heard this, a great fear came upon him and, taking Jesus, he led Him back into the palace again and asked Him, "Whence art Thou?" But Jesus gave him no answer. Pilate said, "Speakest Thou not to me? Knowest Thou not that I have the power to crucify Thee, and I have the power to release Thee?" Jesus answered, "Thou shouldst not have any power against Me unless it were given thee from above. Those that have delivered Me to thee have the greater sin."

Pilate decided to make one more effort to have Jesus

released. He spoke to the chief priests and tried to make them see how unjust they were, and that they were allowing themselves to be carried away by hatred. But they would not listen to him. They said, "If thou release this man, thou art not Caesar's friend. For whosoever maketh himself a king, speaketh against Caesar."

When Pilate heard these words, he surrendered to the will of the chief priests, for he was afraid they would report him to the Roman emperor. He sat down in the judgment seat that was placed in the square of Gabbatha and, taking water, washed his hands before the people, saying, "I am innocent of the blood of this just man; look you to it." A roar went up from the people and they answered, "His blood be upon us and upon our children!"

Pointing to Jesus, Pilate said to the Jews, "Behold your King." But they cried out, "Away with Him; away with Him; crucify Him!" Pilate said, "Shall I crucify your King?" But the chief priests answered, "We have no king but Caesar."

Then Pilate released to them Barabbas and ordered Jesus to be crucified.

4. The Redemption Is Accomplished

Crucifixion was the Roman way of putting criminals to death. Hanging or strangulation, beheading, burning, and stoning were the methods used by the Jews. However, when the Jews came under the power of Rome, the right to inflict capital punishment had been

The way of the Cross

taken away from them. They could try a man, and if they found him guilty of some offense that was worthy of death, the Roman governor would pronounce sentence and see that it was carried out in the Roman way.

At a sign from Pilate, the soldiers led Jesus away. First, they took the purple cloak from His shoulders. His body was bruised and torn and bleeding from the cruel scourging. With rough hands they clothed Him again with His own garments and, setting a cross on His shoulders, led Him away to be crucified.

The sad procession wended its way from the Pretorium, through the crowded streets, toward one of the gates of the city. Once there, it would follow the road that led to a low hill, called Golgotha, or the Skull, so called because its rounded, barren shape gave it the appearance of a human skull. It was on this hill, also known as Calvary, that crucifixions took place.

Two other unfortunate men were to be put to death that day. They were thieves, who had been found guilty of robbery. Four Roman soldiers walked by the side of each prisoner. They carried the nails and the tools that would be used in the crucifixion, and they had orders to stand guard near the cross until the victim was dead and to prevent anyone from trying to rescue him. At the head of the procession, rode a centurion, carrying the boards upon which was written the name of each condemned man and the crime which he had committed. From time to time, as they went along, the centurion would, in a loud voice, proclaim this information to the crowds that lined the streets.

THE WAY OF THE CROSS

It was now about ten o'clock on Friday morning. Jesus had had nothing to eat or drink since the Paschal supper the evening before. He had suffered terribly during His agony in the garden, and after that had followed a night of horror. He had been beaten in the house of the high priest, dragged roughly through the streets to Pilate, and scourged and crowned with thorns. He had suffered intense pain and lost a great quantity of blood. The cross weighed heavier and heavier on His shoulders and several times He stumbled beneath its load. Just as they reached the gates of the city, He staggered and fell to the ground.

Simon of Cyrene

Seeing how weak our blessed Savior had become, the four soldiers who were guarding Him were afraid that He would die before he reached Golgotha. A man was coming into the city from the country. His name was Simon and, though a Jew, he was a stranger in the land, being a native of Cyrene. From his dress and general appearance, he seemed to be a laboring man or a farmer. The soldiers laid hold of him and, though he struggled with them and objected strongly, they forced him to carry the cross after Jesus.

The news that Jesus had been condemned to be crucified spread throughout the city. A mob of people followed the procession, and as it passed through the city, people came out of their houses or gathered in crowds at the street corners. Many in the crowd were friends of Jesus and many others, when they saw Him, were filled with pity.

Many women had gathered at the gate of the city. Whilst the soldiers were forcing Simon to take the cross, Jesus was lying on the ground. Now two of the soldiers raised Him up and, one on either side of Him, they started once more for Golgotha, half carrying Him.

"Weep not for Me"

This sight wrung from the hearts of the women a cry of pity, and they began to weep loudly. Turning His face toward them, Jesus said, "Daughters of Jerusalem, weep not over Me, but weep for yourselves, and for your children. For if in the green wood they do these things, what shall they do in the dry?"

JESUS FALLS BENEATH THE CROSS

According to a tradition that goes back to the early days of the Church, somewhere along this sorrowful journey, Jesus came face to face with Mary, His Mother. Though the Gospel says nothing about this, it seems more than likely that it really happened, for surely Mary would not be far from Jesus at a time like this. Tradition also tells us that a holy woman, named Veronica, came out of her house and offered Jesus a towel with which to wipe the blood and filth from His face. Grateful for this little service, Jesus took the towel from her hands and wiped His face. When He handed it back to her, she beheld on it, outlined in blood, the image of His sacred countenance.

At last they reached Calvary. The crosses were laid on the ground, and Jesus and the two thieves were stripped of their garments. The Jews had a custom of giving to those about to be crucified a cup of wine mixed with myrrh. This was an act of mercy, for when the victim drank the wine mixed with myrrh, he became drowsy and his sense of pain was deadened. A society of noble ladies had been formed in Jerusalem for the purpose of supplying this merciful drink to all of those who were about to be crucified. But when a soldier offered the wine mixed with myrrh to Jesus, He refused to drink it.

Now Jesus was stretched upon the cross, and a spike was driven into each of His hands and His feet. It is quite likely that ropes were tied around His arms, to hold them to the cross. Then they raised the cross and dropped the end of it into one of a number of holes that had been prepared for this purpose. The cross was not very high, the feet of the Crucified being about two feet from the ground.

They placed over the head of Jesus the board which the centurion had been carrying, and on which was written His name and the offense for which He had been condemned. Pilate himself had written the title for the cross of Jesus, in Latin, Greek, and Hebrew. It read: Jesus of Nazareth, King of the Jews.

Meanwhile, the two thieves had been nailed to their crosses; and one of them was placed on the right of Jesus, the other on His left.

No sooner had Jesus been raised on the cross, than

MARY AND THE DISCIPLES WEEP OVER THE CRUCIFIED CHRIST

He opened His mouth in prayer. "Father, forgive them, He said, "for they know not what they do."

Yet, even in His agony, the enemies of our Savior did not spare Him. A number of the chief priests and Pharisees stood at the foot of the cross and mocked Him. "Vah," they said, wagging their heads, "Thou that destroyest the Temple of God, and in three days dost rebuild it, save Thyself; come down from the cross! He saved others," they shouted, "Himself He cannot save. Let Christ, the King of Israel, come down now from the cross that we may see and believe. He trusted in God; let God now deliver Him. For He said, 'I am the Son of God.'" The soldiers also

At the foot of the Cross

THE INSCRIPTION ON THE CROSS

mocked Him, saying, "If Thou be the King of the Jews, save Thyself."

Meanwhile, someone had told Annas and Caiphas what Pilate had written on the title over the cross of Jesus. Immediately, they went to him and said, "Write not, The King of the Jews, but that He said, I am King of the Jews." But Pilate answered, "What I have written, I have written."

The soldiers divide the garments of Jesus It was the custom for the soldiers who guarded a man who was crucified to divide his garments amongst themselves. Without much argument, they disposed of the outer cloak of Jesus, the girdle and the sandals. But when they came to the inner garment, which had been woven in one piece, without a seam, they were puzzled. If they attempted to divide this, they would destroy it. They said, then, one to another, "Let us not cut it, but let us cast lots for it, in order to find out whose it shall be."

Thus were fulfilled the words of the Psalmist, who wrote, "They have parted My garments among them, and upon My vesture they have cast lots."

All the while, the Pharisees and the members of the Sanhedrin continued to heap insults upon our blessed

Savior. When they heard that Pilate had refused to change the title on the cross, they became all the more bitter. They were afraid that the people might think that Jesus had some right to be called the King of the Jews. They therefore sought to prevent this by showing that they, the leaders of the people, who ought to know better than anyone else, were convinced that He was not King of the Jews.

One of the robbers who was hanging by the side of Jesus began to curse and swear at Him, saying, "If Thou be the Christ, save Thyself and us." But the other robber rebuked him. "Hast thou no fear of God?" he said. "We have received the just reward for our deeds; but this man hath done no evil." **The good thief**

Then he said to Jesus, "Lord, remember me when Thou shalt come into Thy Kingdom." "Amen, I say to thee," Jesus answered, "this day thou shalt be with Me in Paradise."

The friends of Jesus had forsaken Him. They did not dare come near the foot of the cross, where the Pharisees and chief priests were gathered, because they were afraid something might happen to them. But four there were who were not afraid. Boldly they pushed their way through the crowd and stood beside the cross. These were Mary, His Mother, and her sister, John, the disciple whom He loved, and Mary Magdalen. Looking down from the cross, Jesus saw His Mother and John, His beloved disciple, gazing up at Him in pity and in love. Tenderly He spoke to Mary. "Woman," He said, "behold thy son." Then He spoke to John, "Behold thy Mother." John under- **"Son, behold thy Mother"**

MOUNT OLIVET, WITH GETHSEMANI IN FOREGROUND

stood what Jesus meant. This was the Savior's death-bed legacy to him and to all men until the end of time. In the hour of death, Jesus gave to us His greatest treasure on earth, His Mother. From that hour, John took her for his own.

The death of Jesus   It was noon when Jesus was nailed to the cross. About that time it grew very dark, as though a great storm were coming, and the darkness continued for three hours. It was almost three o'clock when Jesus cried out with a loud voice, "Eli, Eli, lamma sabacthani!" that is, "My God, my God, why hast Thou forsaken Me?'' When those who were standing about heard this, they said, ''Behold, He calleth Elias.''

A moment later, Jesus said, ''I thirst.'' One of the soldiers took a sponge and, filling it with vinegar, put it on a reed and, running up, he held the sponge to the lips of the dying Savior. Some of the others tried to stop him, saying, ''Let be, let us see whether Elias will come and deliver Him.''

Jesus had refused the wine mixed with myrrh, because He did not want His sufferings to be made easier. Now He drank the vinegar which was offered Him, in order that He might suffer the more and thus drink the last drop from the chalice which His Father had prepared for Him. At last, He said, ''It is finished.'' With a loud voice He cried out, ''Father, into Thy hands I commend My spirit,'' and, bowing His head, He died.

At once, frightful things began to happen. Over in Jerusalem, the veil of the Temple was torn in two, from the top to the bottom. The earth quaked, and great rocks were broken into pieces. The graves opened; the dead came out of their tombs. When the centurion who had charge of the crucifixion saw all of this, he was sore afraid. Striking his breast, he said, ''Indeed this man was the Son of God.'' The crowd, too, was filled with awe, and they hastened back to Jerusalem, striking their breasts.

Evening had come, and the Sabbath Day was at hand. Not wishing the bodies to remain on the cross over the Sabbath Day, the chief priests asked Pilate

The Sacred Heart is pierced

to have their legs broken, that they might be taken down from the cross and buried.

They usually broke the legs of those who were crucified when, for some reason or other, there was not time to allow them to hang upon the cross until they were dead. Breaking their legs would not kill them, but it would cause them to suffer great agony and thus make up for the shortening of the time of their crucifixion. Immediately after the breaking of the bones, the stroke of a sword or a lance would put an end to their life.

The soldiers took clubs and broke the legs of the thieves who were crucified with Jesus. But when they came to Jesus, they saw that He was already dead, and they did not break His legs. One of the soldiers took a spear and pierced His side, and immediately there came out blood and water.

The burial of Jesus There was a man named Joseph, of Arimathea, a city of Judea, who, although a member of the Sanhedrin, was in secret a disciple of Jesus. Heretofore, he had been afraid to profess his faith openly, but now he went boldly to Pilate and asked him for the body of Jesus.

Pilate was surprised to hear that Jesus was dead so soon. He sent for the centurion and when he had found out from him that Jesus was really dead, he gave the body to Joseph.

Joseph took the body of Jesus down from the cross and wrapped it in fine linen which he had brought for that purpose. But this time he had been joined by Nicodemus, he who first came to Jesus by night, who

JESUS IS LAID IN THE SEPULCHER

brought with him a mixture of myrrh and aloes, about a hundred pounds in weight.

Together they brought the body of Jesus to a new tomb which belonged to Joseph. It had been hewn out of a rock not far from Calvary. Placing the body in the tomb, together with the spices, according to the burial custom of the Jews, they rolled a great stone across the door of the tomb and went away.

Mary Magdalen, and a number of other women who had followed Jesus from Galilee, stood by and watched while all this was going on.

The following day, the chief priests and Pharisees went to Pilate and said, "Sir, we have remembered

The guard at the tomb

that that seducer said, while He was yet alive, 'After three days I will rise again.' Command therefore that His sepulcher be guarded until the third day, lest perhaps His disciples come and steal Him away, and say to the people, 'He is risen from the dead,' and the last error shall be worse than the first.''

Pilate said to them, ''You have a guard; go, guard it yourselves.''

Going to the sepulcher of Jesus, the chief priests sealed the stone and set guards to watch it.

THINGS TO KNOW AND TO DO

1. The Enemies of Christ Plot Against Him

1. Name some of the classes of people who were enemies of Jesus. Find the cause of the hatred of each class.

2. Why did Jesus hide Himself before Palm Sunday?

3. Describe the events of Palm Sunday.

4. What was the song of joy which the people sang?

5. In what part of the Mass do we sing the same prayer?

6. What lesson should we learn from the act of Jesus in cleansing the Temple?

7. Read the ceremonies for Palm Sunday in your Missal.

8. Study the prayers which the priest reads when he blesses the palm.

9. Why do we keep palm in our homes?

10. Judas was an apostle. Think of the many good things which Jesus did for him. What do you think of Judas? How will you avoid being ungrateful to God?

11. How will you make sure Jesus will not weep over you?

2. Christ Institutes the Holy Eucharist

1. Of whom was the Paschal Lamb a figure?

2. Describe the important events that took place at this last Pasch.

3. Make a poster. Either cut or print one of the promises made by our divine Lord at the Last Supper.

4. Read the Mass which the priest says on Holy Thursday.

5. Read the prayers of the Mass of Corpus Christi.

6. Memorize the Collect of the Mass of Corpus Christi. Say this beautiful prayer in visiting the Blessed Sacrament.

7. Show that the manna in the desert prefigured the Holy Eucharist. Write your discussion.

8. Make a window picture of Christ in the Garden of Gethsemani.

9. Read one of the following: "Jesus of Nazareth," by Mother M. Loyola, Chapter XXXVIII. "The Life of Our Lord," by Mother Mary Salome, Chapter XXXIV. "New Testament Stories," by Rev. C. C. Martindale, S.J., "The Last Supper."

3. The Redeemer Is Condemned to Death

1. Make a list of the insults which our Lord suffered in the presence of His human judges.

2. What could Peter have done to avoid his sin?

3. Write a description of Jesus before His judges.

4. Tell the reason which caused Caiphas to condemn Jesus. Was the real reason the same as the one on which he based the sentence of death?

5. Why did Pilate condemn Jesus? Show that he did not think Him guilty.

6. Discuss the meekness of Jesus before His judges.

7. Jesus taught you how to bear injuries. Discuss.

8. Read: "Jesus of Nazareth," by Mother M. Loyola, Chapter XXXIX. "A Life of Christ for Children," by Mary Virginia Merrick, Chapters XCVII to CIV. The History of the Passion according to St. John. See your Missal.

4. The Redemption Is Accomplished

1. In divisions three and four of Unit Eight we have the five sorrowful mysteries of the rosary. Name them.

2. Describe the picture which is in your mind when you meditate on the first sorrowful mystery; the second; the third; the fourth; the fifth.

3. Why do we make the Way of the Cross, that is, the Stations?

4. Describe the scene on Calvary.

5. Memorize the Seven Last Words. Explain the meaning of each.

6. Make a colored poster and entitle it, "Behold Thy Mother."

7. Read: "The Life of Our Lord," by Mother M. Salome, Chapter XXXVI.

8. Read in your Missal the ceremonies for Good Friday. Why is the Mass of the Pre-sanctified said on this day?

9. Why do the priests chant the Tenebrae on Wednesday, Thursday and Friday evenings of Holy Week?

10. Connect the law of Friday abstinence with this division.

11. Name five ways in which the Church honors the cross.

III. THE PROOF OF CHRIST'S DIVINITY

1. JESUS RISES GLORIOUSLY FROM THE DEAD

The Resurrection

The Sabbath was over. The first rosy glow of the dawn could be seen in the east, announcing that it was Sunday, the first day of the week. Suddenly, there was a great earthquake, and an angel of the Lord descended from Heaven, and coming, rolled back the stone and sat upon it. And his countenance was as lightning and his garments white as snow. Seeing him, the guards were struck with terror and fell fainting to the ground.

Shortly after sunrise, Mary Magdalen and Mary, the mother of James and Salome, came to the tomb of Jesus, bringing with them sweet spices with which to anoint the body. On the way they said to one another, "Who shall roll us back the stone from the door of the sepulcher." For it was very large, and they knew that they were not strong enough to move it back themselves.

When they came to the sepulcher, they found that the stone had been rolled back, and going in, they found that the body of the Lord Jesus was gone. The guards, too, had disappeared.

By this time the apostles had gathered together in the upper room of the Cenacle, where Jesus had eaten with them the Last Supper. Knowing this, Mary has-

THE RESURRECTION OF JESUS

tened back to the city and, calling Peter and John aside from the others, she said, "They have taken away the Lord out of the sepulcher, and we know not where they have laid Him."

In the meantime, Mary, the mother of James and Salome, had been joined by the other women who had been faithful to our blessed Savior. They decided to look into the sepulcher again and, when they did so, they saw a young man sitting on the right side, clothed in a white robe, and they were astonished. But he said to them, "Be not affrighted; you seek Jesus of Nazareth, Who was crucified. He is risen; He is not here. Behold the place where they laid Him. But go, tell

His disciples and Peter that He goeth before you into Galilee; there you shall see Him, as He told you." Hearing this, the women fled from the sepulcher, trembling with fear and joy. They hastened to Jerusalem to tell the apostles. But the words of the women seemed idle tales to the apostles and they did not believe them.

Peter and John at the sepulcher Peter and John had left the Cenacle when they heard from Mary Magdalen that the body of Jesus had disappeared. They ran to the sepulcher, John outrunning Peter and arriving there first. Stooping down, he looked inside and saw the linen cloths, yet he did not go into the tomb but waited for Peter. A moment later Peter came up, and together they went in and saw the linen cloths, and the napkin that had been tied about the head of Jesus, not lying with the linen cloths, but apart, folded up. When they saw this, both of them believed, for as yet they knew not the Scripture, according to which Christ must rise again from the dead. Then they returned to the other apostles and told them what they had seen.

Jesus appears to Mary Magdalen Some time later, Mary Magdalen returned to the sepulcher and stood at the door waiting. Stooping down, she looked inside and saw two angels in white, sitting there, one at the head and one at the feet, where the body of Jesus had been laid. They said to her, "Woman, why weepest thou?" She said to them, "Because they have taken away my Lord, and I know not where they have laid Him."

Rising up, she turned around and saw Jesus standing there, but she did not recognize Him. He said to her, "Woman, why weepest thou? Whom seekest thou?"

Thinking it was the caretaker, she said to Him, "Sir, if thou hast taken Him hence, tell me where thou hast laid Him, and I will take Him away." Jesus said to her, "Mary." Then she recognized Him and, falling down at His feet, said, "Rabboni, Master." Jesus said, "Do not touch Me, for I am not yet ascended to My Father. But go to My brethren, and say to them: I ascend to My Father and to your Father, to My God and your God."

Then He disappeared from her sight and she rose up and hastened to Jerusalem and said to the apostles, "I have seen the Lord, and these things He said to me."

When the guards who had been sent to watch the sepulcher recovered from the fright that came over them at the sight of the angel, they fled to Jerusalem and told the high priest everything that had happened. The high priest at once called the Sanhedrin together, in order to decide what should be done. They voted to give a great sum of money to the soldiers on condition that they would tell the people that the disciples of Jesus came by night and stole His body whilst they slept. *The report of the guards*

At first the guards hesitated, because they were afraid that Pilate would hear of it and punish them for their negligence in going to sleep. The chief priests told them that they would explain the whole matter to Pilate, so they took the money and, going

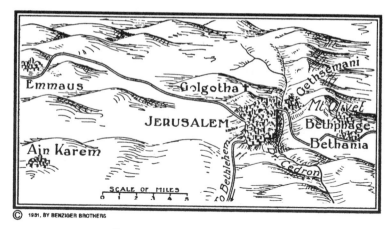

JERUSALEM AND NEARBY TOWNS

out, told the people how they had fallen asleep and the apostles had come and stolen the body of Jesus.

The two disciples on the way to Emmaus Early on Sunday morning, two of the disciples of our Lord left Jerusalem and set out for Emmaus, a town about sixty furlongs away. As they walked along, they talked of all that had happened since Thursday night. Their hearts were sad within them, as they tried in vain to understand why it was that Jesus, in Whom they had believed so sincerely, had come to such a terrible end.

As they were going along, they met a stranger, who asked if he might walk with them. It was Jesus, but they did not recognize Him. "What is this conversation that you hold with one another as you walk," He asked, "and are sad?"

One of them, whose name was Cleophas, answered, "Art thou a stranger in Jerusalem, that thou knowest nothing of what has been done there?" He asked,

"What has been done?" They said, "Concerning Jesus of Nazareth, Who was a prophet, mighty in work and word before God and all the people; and how our chief priests and princes delivered Him to be condemned to death, and crucified Him. But we hoped that it was He that should have redeemed Israel. Now today is the third day since these things were done. It is true that certain women of our company who went to the sepulcher before dark did not find His body, and frightened us by coming back and saying that they had seen a vision of angels who say that He is alive. Some of our people went to the sepulcher and found that what the women said was true. But they did not find Jesus."

Then Jesus said to them, "O foolish and slow of heart to believe in all things which the prophets have spoken. Ought not Christ to have suffered these things, and so to enter into His glory?" And, beginning at Moses and down through all the prophets, He explained all the things that the Scriptures had foretold concerning Him.

At last they drew nigh to the town whither they were going and, bidding them farewell, Jesus started to go on farther. But they begged Him to remain with them, saying, "Stay with us, because it is toward evening, and the day is now far spent." And He went with them into Emmaus.

It came to pass that whilst He was at table with them, He took bread, and blessed and broke it and gave it to them. That moment their eyes were opened and they knew Him; and He vanished out of their

THE DISCIPLES BEG JESUS TO REMAIN AT EMMAUS

sight. Their hearts filled with wonder, and they said one to the other, "Was not our heart burning within us, whilst He spoke in the way, and opened to us the Scriptures?" And, rising up at once, they hastened back to Jerusalem.

There they found the eleven apostles gathered in the Cenacle, together with a number of other disciples of our Savior. Seeing Cleophas and his companion, the apostles greeted them with the words "The Lord is risen indeed, and hath appeared to Simon."

Then the two who had been to Emmaus told them of all that had happened on the way; and how they knew Him in the breaking of the bread.

2. The Sacrament of Penance Is Instituted and Peter's Primacy Is Proclaimed

Late into the night, the apostles and the others re- *The power to forgive sins*
mained in the Cenacle, talking about the wonderful
things that had happened. They had locked the doors,
for fear that some agent of the chief priests and
Pharisees might find them out. Suddenly, Jesus stood
in their midst, and said to them, "Peace be to you."

They became frightened, because they thought that
they were seeing a ghost. But He said, "Why are you
troubled, and why do thoughts arise in your hearts?
See My hands and feet, and know that it is I Myself;
handle, and see, for a spirit hath not flesh and bones,
as you see Me to have." When He said this, He
showed them His hands and feet. But though their
hearts were filled with joy, they were not quite sure
that it was Jesus in truth. So He said, "Have you
here anything to eat?" And they offered Him a piece
of broiled fish and a honeycomb. And when He had
eaten before them, taking the remains, He gave to
them.

Now they were sure that it was Jesus, and not a
spirit. Then said He, "Peace be to you. As the
Father hath sent Me, I also send you." When He
had said this, He breathed on them, and said, "Receive
ye the Holy Ghost. Whose sins you shall forgive, they
are forgiven them; whose sins you shall retain, they
are retained."

Now Thomas, one of the apostles, who was also *The unbeliev- ing Thomas*
called Didymus, or the Twin, was not with them that

THE APOSTLE THOMAS PLACES HIS HAND IN THE WOUND OF OUR LORD

night when Jesus came. When he returned the next day, they told him how they had seen the Lord. But he said, "Except I shall see in His hands the print of the nails, and put my hand into the place of the nails and put my hand into His side, I will not believe."

Eight days later, they were again assembled in the upper room, and Thomas, this time, was with them. The doors were shut, but Jesus came and stood in their midst and said, "Peace be to you." Then, going up to Thomas, He said, "Put in thy finger hither, and see My hands; and bring hither thy hand, and put it into My side; and be not faithless, but believing."

Falling down on his knees, Thomas said, "My Lord

and my God!" But Jesus said to him, "Because thou hast seen Me, Thomas, thou hast believed; blessed are they that have not seen, and have believed."

At the command of our blessed Savior, the apostles left Jerusalem and went back to Galilee. One day a short time later, Simon Peter, and Thomas, and Nathanael, and James and John, and two others, were standing together on the shore of the Sea of Galilee. Peter said to the others, "I go a-fishing." They said, "We also come with thee." And they went forth and entered into a ship. *By the Sea of Galilee*

All night long they labored, but they caught nothing. When morning was come, they rowed for the shore. They were still some distance out when they saw a man standing at the water's edge. He called out to them, "Have you any meat? Have you anything to eat?" They answered, "No." Then He said to them, "Cast the net on the right side of the ship, and you shall find fishes."

They did as He directed, and caught so many fishes that they were not able to draw in the net.

Seeing this, John said to Peter, "It is the Lord." At once, Peter girt his cloak around him and, casting himself into the sea, swam for the shore. The other apostles came in the ship, dragging after them the net with the fishes in it.

They beached the boat, and saw hot coals lying there, and a fish laid on them, and bread. Jesus said to them, "Bring hither some of the fishes which you have caught." Simon Peter went up and drew the net to land, and it was full of great fishes, a hundred and

JESUS APPEARS TO THE APOSTLES ON THE SEASHORE

fifty-three, but the net was not broken. Jesus said to them, "Come and dine." Then they all sat down on the ground with Jesus, and He served them the bread and the fish and ate with them. None of them dared ask Him "Who art thou?" for they knew it was the Lord.

The Primacy conferred on Peter When they had finished eating, Jesus said to Peter, "Simon, son of John, lovest thou Me more than these?" Peter answered, "Yea, Lord, Thou knowest that I love Thee." Then Jesus said, "Feed My lambs." A moment later, He said to him again, "Simon, son of John, lovest thou Me?" Peter said, "Yea, Lord, Thou knowest that I love Thee." Jesus said,

JESUS PLACES PETER IN CHARGE OF HIS CHURCH

"Feed My lambs." A third time, He said, "Simon, son of John, lovest thou Me?" Peter was grieved, because Jesus had asked him this same question a third time, and he said, "Lord, Thou knowest all things; Thou knowest that I love Thee." Then said Jesus, "Feed My sheep. Amen, amen, I say to thee, when thou wast younger, thou didst gird thyself, and didst walk where thou wouldst. But when thou shalt be old, thou shalt stretch forth thy hands, and another shall gird thee, and lead thee whither thou wouldst not."

By these words our blessed Savior prophesied that the words which Peter spoke at the Last Supper would

JESUS COMMANDS THE APOSTLES TO TEACH ALL NATIONS

one day come true. He would go into bondage and death for the Savior, and be crucified for His sake.

Rising up, Jesus said to Peter, "Follow Me." As Peter was going along with Jesus, he turned and saw John, the disciple whom Jesus loved, following in the distance, and he said to Jesus, "Lord, what will this man do?" Jesus said to him, "So I will have him remain till I come. What is it to thee? Follow thou Me."

These words of our Savior gave rise to a rumor among the apostles that John would not die. But Jesus did not mean that John would not die, but rather, that he would not die a martyr's death.

Jesus commanded the eleven apostles to meet Him **"Teach all nations"** on a certain day on a mountain in Galilee. When they arrived there, they saw Jesus waiting for them and, kneeling down, they adored Him. Jesus said to them, "All power is given to Me in Heaven and in earth. Going, therefore, teach ye all nations; baptizing them in the name of the Father, and of the Son, and of the Holy Ghost; teaching them to observe all things whatsoever I have commanded you; and behold I am with you all days, even to the consummation of the world. He that believeth and is baptized, shall be saved; but he that believeth not shall be condemned. And these signs shall follow them that believe: In My name they shall cast out devils; they shall speak with new tongues. They shall take up serpents; and if they shall drink any deadly thing, it shall not hurt them; they shall lay their hands upon the sick, and they shall recover."

3. JESUS ASCENDS TO HIS FATHER

It was now forty days since Jesus had risen from **The Ascension** the dead. Once more the apostles were gathered together in the Cenacle, and Jesus sat at table with them. For the last time they received from His divine hand His Flesh and Blood under the form of bread and wine. Then He commanded them not to leave Jerusalem, but to wait there for the coming of the Holy Ghost, Whom He had promised them. "John indeed baptized with water," He said, "but you shall be baptized with the Holy Ghost, not many days hence."

Even now, the apostles did not fully understand that

JESUS ASCENDS INTO HEAVEN

the Kingdom of Jesus was not of this world. They asked Him, "Lord, wilt Thou at this time restore again the Kingdom of Israel?" But He said to them, "It is not for you to know the times or the moments which the Father hath in His power. But you shall receive the power of the Holy Ghost coming upon you, and you shall be witnesses unto Me in Jerusalem, and in all Judea, and Samaria, and even to the uttermost parts of the earth.

"All things must be fulfilled which are written in the Law of Moses, and in the prophets, and in the psalms, concerning Me. Thus it is written and thus it behooved Christ to suffer, and to rise again from the dead the third day. And that penance and the remission of sins should be preached in His name unto all nations, beginning at Jerusalem. And you are witnesses of these things. And I send the promise of My Father upon you; but stay you in the city, till you receive the power from on high.''

Then He led them out of the city toward Bethania. When they came to the Mount of Olives, He blessed them, and even as they gazed upon Him, He was raised up and a cloud took Him out of their sight.

They stood gazing skyward, hoping to catch one last glimpse of Him, when suddenly they saw two angels standing by them in white garments, who said, ''Ye men of Galilee, why stand ye looking up into Heaven? This Jesus Who was taken up from you into Heaven shall so come to you as you have seen Him going into Heaven.''

Then they went back to Jerusalem with joy in their hearts, praising and blessing God.

4. JESUS SENDS THE HOLY GHOST

The upper room, where Jesus had eaten with them Pentecost the Last Supper, now became the home of the apostles. There the eleven of them were gathered together: Peter and John, James and Andrew, Philip and Thomas, Bartholemew and Matthew, Simon and James, the son of Alpheus, and Jude, his brother. The Blessed Virgin Mary was with them, and Mary Magdalen, and the other faithful women who had ministered to Him during His life here upon earth. Other disciples and followers of our Savior came to the

Cenacle each day, and all together spent the time in prayer.

One day, when about a hundred and twenty persons were present, Peter stood up in the midst of them and told them that the time had come to appoint a succes-sor to Judas Iscariot, so that there would be twelve apostles. He suggested that they choose some disciple who had been with Jesus from the baptism of John un-til the day of His ascension, so that he could be a witness, with the other apostles, of the Resurrection.

Two names were suggested, Joseph Barsabas, who was also called the Just, and Matthias.

Then all knelt down and Peter prayed thus, "Thou, Lord, Who knowest the hearts of all men, show us which of these two Thou hast chosen to take the place from which Judas hath, by his sin, fallen."

Then they cast lots, and the lot fell upon Matthias, and from that time he was numbered among the apostles.

The coming of the Holy Ghost Ten days had passed, and it was the Feast of Pente-cost. The upper room was crowded with the apostles and disciples of our blessed Savior. Suddenly there came a sound from heaven, as of a mighty wind, and it shook the whole house where they were assembled. Tongues of fire appeared to all those in the room and sat upon every one of them, and they were all filled with the Holy Ghost. And they began to speak differ-ent languages, according as the Holy Ghost gave them to speak.

It was a festival day and Jerusalem was crowded with strangers, Jews and devout men from every na-

THE HOLY GHOST DESCENDS UPON THE DISCIPLES

tion under the heavens. The noise of the great wind
was heard all over the city, and crowds came running
together and surrounded the house where the disciples
were staying. There they beheld a wonderful sight.
The twelve apostles were standing on the roof top,
preaching to the multitude. And a great fear came
upon the people, because every man in the crowd heard
them speak in his own tongue. And they said, "Behold, are not all these that speak, Galileans? And how
have we heard, every man our own tongue wherein we
were born? Parthians, and Medes, and Elamites, and
inhabitants of Mesopotamia, Judea, and Cappadocia,
Pontus and Asia, Phrygia, and Pamphylia, Egypt, and

the parts of Libya about Cyrene, and strangers of Rome, Jews also and proselytes, Cretes, and Arabians; we have heard them speak in our own tongues the wonderful works of God.''

In accordance with the command of our blessed Savior, the apostles now went forth into the whole world to preach the Gospel. As our Savior had promised them, they had the power to work miracles. The number of those who believed in their preaching grew constantly. At first they preached to the Jews, but later they went forth to the Gentile nations and they made great numbers of converts. They ordained priests to assist them in their ministry; they consecrated bishops who would be their successors and carry on the work of the Church after their death. Thus it was that the Church of Christ began its mission here upon earth. Like the mustard seed of which our Savior spoke, it grew from small beginnings until it became the great institution which today continues to spread throughout the world, preaching the Gospel to every creature.

THINGS TO KNOW AND TO DO

1. Jesus Rises Gloriously from the Dead

1. Why does the Church honor the Resurrection of Jesus as her greatest feast day?

2. What do we learn about St. Peter from the fact that John did not enter the tomb until Peter arrived there?

3. Show that after His Resurrection Jesus proved that He loves repentant sinners.

4. How did Jesus just after His Resurrection show His sympathy for the sorrowful?

5. Explain how the guards proved the Resurrection of Jesus even by the lie which they told the people.

6. Read the Mass for Easter Sunday. Point out the main thoughts of the Church in Her prayers of this day.

7. Show that the Resurrection is the greatest proof of Christ's Divinity.

2. THE SACRAMENT OF PENANCE IS INSTITUTED AND PETER'S PRIMACY IS PROCLAIMED

1. Why did Jesus greet His disciples with the words: "Peace be to you"?
2. How did Jesus institute the Sacrament of Penance?
3. To what beautiful words of the Apostle St. Thomas has the Church attached an indulgence?
4. When especially ought we to say this prayer?
5. Why did our Lord ask Peter three times about his love for Him?
6. Tell all you can about the powers left by our Lord to the Church through the apostles.
7. Show that the institution of the Sacrament of Penance is a proof of God's love and compassion.

3. JESUS ASCENDS TO HIS FATHER

1. Why did the apostles ask Jesus if He would restore the Kingdom of Israel?
2. Imagine the feelings of the apostles when they saw Jesus ascending into Heaven. Describe them.
3. Why did Jesus ascend into Heaven?
4. On what day does the Church celebrate the Feast of the Ascension?
5. The Feast of the Ascension celebrates the triumph of Jesus. Read in your Missal the Mass for this day and point out the triumphal tone of the Church's prayers.

4. JESUS SENDS THE HOLY GHOST

1. Why is the Feast of Pentecost considered the birthday of the Catholic Church?
2. Describe the first novena to the Holy Ghost made in the Church?
3. Tell about the event by which the apostles began to be "fishers of men" on that first Pentecost day.
4. Name the Seven Gifts of the Holy Ghost.
5. Read the Sequence, "Veni Sancte Spiritus," and the Hymn, 'Veni Creator Spiritus." Compare these two hymns of the Church.
6. Memorize the one which pleases you the more.
7. Read the Mass for Pentecost. Explain the main thought of the Church on this day.
8. Why ought every Catholic practice frequent devotion to the Holy Ghost?

SELF-TEST

Before leaving Unit Eight, test yourself with the following exercises. Check your work.

I. Be able to tell the story contained in each section of Unit Eight.

II. Give a floor talk in which you discuss the enemies of Jesus.

III. Write an essay in which you show the timidity of His friends.

IV. Read the prayers of the Canon of the Mass in your Missal. Find how many times the Church reminds us of the Passion, Resurrection, and Ascension in these prayers.

V. Read the same prayers again and list the instances in them which excite to contrition.

VI. Write a short meditation on each of the mysteries of the Rosary contained in this Unit.

VII. Tell why meditation on the Passion of Jesus will help to make us holy.

VIII. Collect pictures which tell the story of Unit Eight.

IX. Write a review of one of the books which you read in studying this Unit.

INDEX AND PRONOUNCING VOCABULARY [1]

ā as in fate
à as in fare
à as in fat
ä as in far
a as in fall
å as in senate
ch as in church
ē as in me

ĕ as in met
ē as in ever
è as in event
g as in go
ī as in ice
ĭ as in pin
ñ as in cañon (kan'yun)

ō as in old
ô as in orb
ŏ as in not
ò as in obey
oi as in oil
y as in yet
ū as in huge

ŭ as in up
û as in unite
û as in burn
ōō as in noon
ōō as in brook
ou as in sound

*An asterisk next to a number indicates that there is an illustration of the subject on that page.

Aa'ron (âr'ŭn), meets Moses, 89; appeals to Pharao, 89-97; rod of, turns to serpent, 92*; consecrated by Moses, 116*, 117; death of, 130
A'bel (ā'bĕl), 15, 16, 17*
Ab-di'as (ăb-dī'ăs), 144
A-bi'a (ă-bī'ă), 223
A-bi'am (ă-bī'am) †, 225
A-bin'a-dab (ă-bĭn'ă-dăb), 196, 197
A-bi'ron (ă-bī'rŏn), 128
Ab'ner (ăb'nēr), 178
a-bom'i-na'tion (ă-bŏm'ĭ-nā'shŭn), feeling of extreme disgust and hatred; anything very wicked
A'bra-ham (ā'brä-hăm), call of, 33; departs from Haran, 34*; journeys of (map), 35; God's promises to, 36; and Melchisedech, 37*; and the strangers, 39; God tests the obedience of, 44; and the sacrifice of Isaac, 44-46*
A'bram (ā'brăm). See Abraham.
Ab'sa-lom (ăb'să-lŏm), 197-200
a-ca'cia (ă-kā'shä), a tree with light incorruptible wood
Ac'c-aron (ăk'ă-rŏn), 165
A'chab (ă'kăb), 227-235
A'chan (ā'kăn), 149
Ad'am (ăd'ăm), 8-13*
A-du'ram (ă-dū'răm) †, 220
Ae-ge'an (ē-jē'ăn) Sea, 141
A'gar (ā'gär), 38, 43, 44

Ag-ge'us (ă-gē'ŭs) †, 280
Ag'on-y (ăg'ŏn-ĭ), in the Garden, the, 493-495*
A-hi'as (ă-hī'ăs) †, 217, 218*, 223, 224
A-hi'o (ă-hī'ō), 196
A'i-lath (ā'ĭ-lăth) †, 215
Ain-Ka'rem (ān-kä'rĕm), 322, 323*
Aj'a-lon (ăj'ă-lŏn), Plain of, 152, 215
A'ka-ba (ä'kä-bä) †, Gulf of, 215
Al'ci-mus (ăl'sĭ-mŭs), 300
Al'ex-an'der (ăl'ĕg-zăn'dēr), 289
Al-phe'us (ăl-fē'ŭs) †, 347
Altar of Hol'o-causts (hŏl'ō-kôsts) †, 114, 116*, 120*
Altar of In'cense (ĭn'sĕns), 113*, 114, 213, 262
Am'a-lec-ites (ăm'ă-lĕk-īts) †, 103, 128, 179
A'man (ā'măn), 281-284*, 285
Am'mon (ăm'ŏn),129
Am'mon-ites (ăm'ŏn-īts), 155, 177, 179, 255, 298
Am'or-rhites (ăm'ŏ-rīts) †, 131, 144, 145
A'mos (ā'mŭs), 249
Am'ri (ăm'rī) †, 227
An'a-ni'as (ăn'ă-nī'ăs), 262, 265, 266
An'drew (ăn'drōō), follows Jesus, 344
an'gels (ān'jĕlz), 4

---

[1] The spelling of proper names follows the Douai Version throughout. The pronunciation is based on that of the "International Standard Bible Encyclopedia" (with the permission of the publishers, The Howard Severance Co., Chicago), except such words as are indicated by a † which are according to Webster's Unabridged Dictionary, latest edition, or based upon its principles of pronunciation.

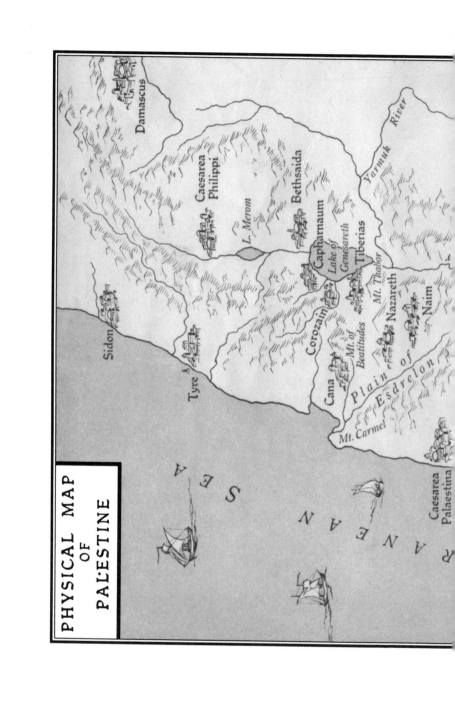

PHYSICAL MAP OF PALESTINE

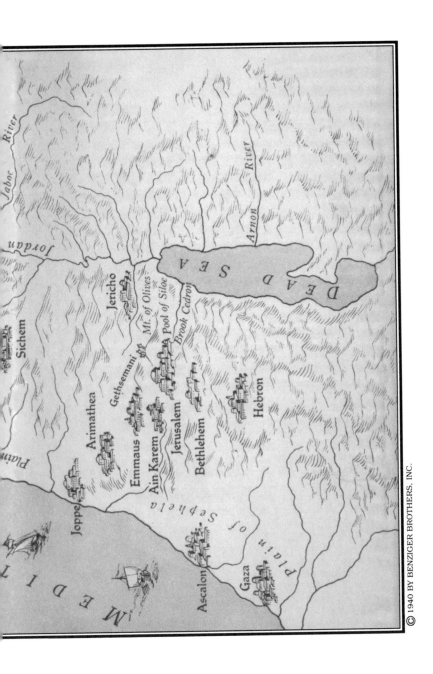

If you have enjoyed this book, consider making your next selection from among the following . . .

Christian Perfection and Contemplation. *Garrigou-Lagrange, O.P.* 21.00
Practical Commentary on Holy Scripture. *Bishop Knecht.* 40.00
The Ways of Mental Prayer. *Dom Vitalis Lehodey* 16.50
The 33 Doctors of the Church. *Fr. Christopher Rengers, O.F.M. Cap.* 33.00
Pope Pius VII. *Prof. Robin Anderson* 16.50
Life Everlasting. *Garrigou-Lagrange, O.P.* 16.50
Mother of the Saviour/Our Int. Life. *Garrigou-Lagrange, O.P.* 16.50
Three Ages/Int. Life. *Garrigou-Lagrange, O.P. 2 vol.* 48.00
Ven. Francisco Marto of Fatima. *Cirrincione*, comp. 2.50
Ven. Jacinta Marto of Fatima. *Cirrincione* 3.00
St. Philomena—The Wonder-Worker. *O'Sullivan* 9.00
The Facts About Luther. *Msgr. Patrick O'Hare* 18.50
Little Catechism of the Curé of Ars. *St. John Vianney.* 8.00
The Curé of Ars—Patron Saint of Parish Priests. *Fr. B. O'Brien* 7.50
Saint Teresa of Avila. *William Thomas Walsh* 24.00
Isabella of Spain: The Last Crusader. *William Thomas Walsh* 24.00
Characters of the Inquisition. *William Thomas Walsh* 16.50
Blood-Drenched Altars—Cath. Comment. on Hist. Mexico. *Kelley* 21.50
The Four Last Things—Death, Judgment, Hell, Heaven. *Fr. von Cochem* . . . 9.00
Confession of a Roman Catholic. *Paul Whitcomb* 2.50
The Catholic Church Has the Answer. *Paul Whitcomb* 2.50
The Sinner's Guide. *Ven. Louis of Granada* 15.00
True Devotion to Mary. *St. Louis De Montfort* 9.00
Life of St. Anthony Mary Claret. *Fanchón Royer* 16.50
Autobiography of St. Anthony Mary Claret. 13.00
I Wait for You. *Sr. Josefa Menendez* 1.50
Words of Love. *Menendez, Betrone, Mary of the Trinity.* 8.00
Little Lives of the Great Saints. *John O'Kane Murray* 20.00
Prayer—The Key to Salvation. *Fr. Michael Müller.* 9.00
Passion of Jesus and Its Hidden Meaning. *Fr. Groenings, S.J.* 15.00
The Victories of the Martyrs. *St. Alphonsus Liguori* 13.50
Canons and Decrees of the Council of Trent. *Transl. Schroeder* 16.50
Sermons of St. Alphonsus Liguori for Every Sunday. 18.50
A Catechism of Modernism. *Fr. J. B. Lemius* 7.50
Alexandrina—The Agony and the Glory. *Johnston.* 7.00
Life of Blessed Margaret of Castello. *Fr. William Bonniwell* 9.00
Catechism of Mental Prayer. *Simler* 3.00
St. Francis of Paola. *Simi and Segreti.* 9.00
St. Martin de Porres. *Giuliana Cavallini.* 15.00
The Story of the Church. *Johnson, Hannan, Dominica.* 22.50
Hell Quizzes. *Radio Replies Press* 2.50
Purgatory Quizzes. *Radio Replies Press* 2.50
Virgin and Statue Worship Quizzes. *Radio Replies Press* 2.50
Meditation Prayer on Mary Immaculate. *Padre Pio* 2.50
Little Book of the Work of Infinite Love. *de la Touche* 3.50
Textual Concordance of The Holy Scriptures. *Williams. pb.* 35.00
Douay-Rheims Bible. *Hardbound* 55.00
The Way of Divine Love. *Sister Josefa Menendez* 21.00
The Way of Divine Love. (pocket, unabr.). *Menendez* 12.50
Mystical City of God—Abridged. *Ven. Mary of Agreda* 21.00

Prices subject to change.

Visits to the Blessed Sacrament. *St. Alphonsus* 5.00
Moments Divine—Before the Blessed Sacrament. *Reuter* 10.00
Miraculous Images of Our Lady. *Cruz* 21.50
Miraculous Images of Our Lord. *Cruz* 16.50
Raised from the Dead. *Fr. Hebert* 18.50
Love and Service of God, Infinite Love. *Mother Louise Margaret* 15.00
Life and Work of Mother Louise Margaret. *Fr. O'Connell* 15.00
Autobiography of St. Margaret Mary. 7.50
Thoughts and Sayings of St. Margaret Mary 6.00
The Voice of the Saints. *Comp. by Francis Johnston* 8.00
The 12 Steps to Holiness and Salvation. *St. Alphonsus* 9.00
The Rosary and the Crisis of Faith. *Cirrincione & Nelson* 2.00
Sin and Its Consequences. *Cardinal Manning* 9.00
St. Francis of Paola. *Simi & Segreti* 9.00
Dialogue of St. Catherine of Siena. *Transl. Algar Thorold* 12.50
Catholic Answer to Jehovah's Witnesses. *D'Angelo* 13.50
Twelve Promises of the Sacred Heart. (100 cards). 5.00
Life of St. Aloysius Gonzaga. *Fr. Meschler* 13.00
The Love of Mary. *D. Roberto* 9.00
Begone Satan. *Fr. Vogl* 4.00
The Prophets and Our Times. *Fr. R. G. Culleton* 15.00
St. Therese, The Little Flower. *John Beevers* 7.50
St. Joseph of Copertino. *Fr. Angelo Pastrovicchi* 8.00
Mary, The Second Eve. *Cardinal Newman* 4.00
Devotion to Infant Jesus of Prague. *Booklet* 1.50
Reign of Christ the King in Public & Private Life. *Davies* 2.00
The Wonder of Guadalupe. *Francis Johnston* 9.00
Apologetics. *Msgr. Paul Glenn*. 12.50
Baltimore Catechism No. 1 . . . . 5.00
Baltimore Catechism No. 2 . . . . 7.00
Baltimore Catechism No. 3 . . . . 11.00
An Explanation of the Baltimore Catechism. *Fr. Kinkead*. 18.00
Bethlehem. *Fr. Faber* 20.00
Bible History. *Schuster* 16.50
Blessed Eucharist. *Fr. Mueller* 10.00
Catholic Catechism. *Fr. Faerber* 9.00
The Devil. *Fr. Delaporte* 8.50
Dogmatic Theology for the Laity. *Fr. Premm* 21.50
Evidence of Satan in the Modern World. *Cristiani* 14.00
Fifteen Promises of Mary. (100 cards). 5.00
Life of Anne Catherine Emmerich. 2 vols. *Schmoeger* 48.00
Life of the Blessed Virgin Mary. *Emmerich* 18.00
Manual of Practical Devotion to St. Joseph. *Patrignani* 17.50
Prayer to St. Michael. (100 leaflets) 5.00
Prayerbook of Favorite Litanies. *Fr. Hebert* 12.50
Preparation for Death. (Abridged). *St. Alphonsus* 12.00
Purgatory Explained. *Schouppe* 16.50
Purgatory Explained. (pocket, unabr.). *Schouppe* 12.00
Fundamentals of Catholic Dogma. *Ludwig Ott*. 27.50
Spiritual Conferences. *Faber* 18.00
Trustful Surrender to Divine Providence. *Bl. Claude* 7.00
Wife, Mother and Mystic. *Bessieres* 10.00
The Agony of Jesus. *Padre Pio* 3.00

Prices subject to change.

Prices subject to change.

At your Bookdealer or direct from the Publisher.

Toll-Free 1-800-437-5876   *Fax 815-226-7770*
Tel. 815-229-7777   *www.tanbooks.com*

Prices subject to change.